BIOMECHANICS

BIOMECHANICS

A QUALITATIVE APPROACH
FOR STUDYING HUMAN MOVEMENT

Second Edition

ELLEN KREIGHBAUM, Ph.D.

Professor of Physical Education
Montana State University
Bozeman, Montana

KATHARINE M. BARTHELS, Ph.D.

Professor of Physical Education
California Polytechnic State University
San Luis Obispo, California

MACMILLAN PUBLISHING COMPANY
New York
COLLIER MACMILLAN PUBLISHERS
London

Macmillan Publishing Company
866 Third Avenue, New York, New York 10022

Collier Macmillan Canada, Inc.

Library of Congress Cataloging in Publication Data

Kreighbaum, Ellen.
    Biomechanics: a qualitative approach for studying human movement.

    Includes bibliographies and index.
    1. Human mechanics.   2. Biomechanics.   I. Barthels, Katharine M.   II. Title
QP303.K72   1985   612'.76   84-28526
ISBN 0-02-366480-0

Printing   7 8   Year   9 0 1

ISBN 0-02-366480-0

The authors dedicate this text to their parents, who guided, influenced, and instilled attitudes necessary to pursue such a task; to professional colleagues, who inspired and encouraged their questioning; and to their students, whose comments and criticisms were an integral part of the text development, and who provided the main reason for its writing.

CONTENTS

CHAPTER 3

BIOMECHANICS OF THE MUSCULOSKELETAL SYSTEM 160

CHAPTER 4

BIOMECHANICAL RELATIONSHIPS IN THE UPPER EXTREMITY 192

CHAPTER 5

BIOMECHANICAL RELATIONSHIPS IN THE LOWER EXTREMITY 216

CHAPTER 8

ANALYSIS OF PROJECTILE-RELATED ACTIVITIES 342

CHAPTER 9

APPLICATIONS OF AERODYNAMICS IN SPORT 380

CHAPTER 10

APPLICATION OF HYDRODYNAMICS IN SWIMMING 420

CHAPTER 13

ANALYSIS OF ACTIVITIES IN WHICH THE BODY ROTATES WHILE SUPPORTED 560

CHAPTER 14

ANALYSIS OF THROW AND PUSH PATTERNS 584

CHAPTER 15

APPLYING THE KINETIC LINK PRINCIPLE IN PERFORMANCE ANALYSIS 618

FOREWORD

In their second edition of *Biomechanics: A Qualitative Approach for Studying Human Movement*, Ellen Kreighbaum and Katharine Barthels have accomplished the difficult task of improving an already excellent product. While retaining their clear, conversational writing style and refreshingly original descriptions and illustrations to convey the anatomical and mechanical principles underlying human movement, they have rewritten and reorganized a major portion of the text.

The introduction of a series of concept modules, situated at strategic intervals among the 15 chapters of this text, is the most striking innovation in the second edition. These concept modules provide the student and instructor with a readily accessible source of fundamental anatomical and mechanical information. The concept modules also serve as prerequisite units to be studied or reviewed prior to assignment of chapters that deal with application of the concepts to activities that have a common mechanical purpose. Organization of the text in this modular format allows an instructor the option of selecting different combinations of concept modules and chapters to arrive at the course content most suitable for the specific needs of the students or program to be served. Kreighbaum and Barthels have skillfully provided the material and organizational framework to permit use of this text in a biomechanics course that has a decidedly anatomical emphasis or in a course that has a predominantly mechanical focus.

A distinctive feature of the first edition was the conceptual, qualitative approach used to present and apply biomechanical principles in human movement and sport activities. This feature has been maintained and even strengthened in the second edition with the conversion of several numerical examples into qualitative descriptions. The authors emphasize qualitative analysis and support it with numerous examples, graphic illustrations, and pertinent learning activities. By so doing, they hope to give students, including those with a limited mathematics or physics background, a firm grasp of basic biomechanical concepts and principles. They also provide a foundation for those who may choose to pursue more advanced study.

If biomechanics instruction is to be meaningful and useful in preparing undergraduate students to become physical education teachers or coaches, some means must be provided by a text or by the instructor to help students bridge the gap between theoretical, scientific material and its application in a practical setting. Indeed, the 1980 AAHPERD[1] Kinesiology Academy Guidelines and Standards state that command of the qualitative method of analysis must be one of the primary goals of all introductory kinesiology courses. The Understanding sections presented after major topic subdivisions within each chapter and concept module include many laboratorylike activities in which students have the opportunity to practice the qualitative method of analysis. These sections should encourage the student to actively demonstrate comprehension of the biome-

---

1. This organization formerly was called the American Alliance for Health, Physical Education and Recreation (AAHPER). In 1980, its name was changed to reflect its growing involvement in dance. The abbreviation AAHPERD will be used for all references to the organization in this text, regardless of its actual name at the time.

chanical concept under consideration and also should enhance the interest and involvement of the student in applying the concept to practical situations.

In this readable text, Ellen Kreighbaum and Katharine Barthels bring mechanics to life. Both authors are recognized and respected by their peers and students for their ability to devise creative teaching aids and learning activities that greatly facilitate biomechanics instruction. Many of these creative ideas are incorporated into this text and still others are included in the instructor's supplement accompanying each instructor's desk copy. Students and instructors are fortunate to have a text that contains such interesting and thorough descriptions of biomechanics concepts and principles and that communicates the authors' enthusiasm for the subject matter and for its meaningful application in a practical setting.

Anne E. (Betty) Atwater
University of Arizona

The revision of the first edition of this text was undertaken for four purposes: (1) to incorporate recent information from research in sport biomechanics that illuminates the material presented, (2) to expand on some of the generalizable principles and concepts proposed in the first edition, (3) to condense portions that require less detailed coverage to be understood, and (4) to modify the division and organization of content to facilitate use in courses with different content emphasis.

In keeping with the AAHPERD Kinesiology Academy Guidelines and Standards, the conceptual, qualitative approach has been maintained to facilitate the student's grasp of the ideas presented. A number of quantitative examples have been replaced with qualitative illustrations in the main text; however, the quantitative relationships, which are used in many courses, are included in an appendix for convenient reference. Quantitative material is expressed in metric units, with the British equivalent inserted parenthetically. The inclusion of the British units with the metric should assist the reader in conceptualizing magnitudes if metric is still unfamiliar.

Presentation of content is still focused on promoting understanding of biomechanical principles that govern the effectiveness of the skills performed. Furthermore, the focus is on presenting appropriate biomechanical principles to be used with skills that have a common mechanical purpose. Chapter 1 introduces the student to the process of skill analysis based on these mechanical purposes. With an awareness from the beginning that skills can be improved through the implementation of biomechanical knowledge, the student should be readily motivated to learn and apply the material presented. The relevance of understanding biomechanics is made evident through examples of its application to improving performance among athletes in popular and contemporary sports.

We created most of the illustrations for the first edition, and the majority of these have been retained. Some of our original figures have been modified to enhance their communicative value, and a number of new illustrations that we prepared from high-speed cinematography have been added.

Fundamental anatomical and biomechanical information has been reorganized and presented in a sequence of concept modules that are interspersed logically among the chapters that utilize that information for applications to skills analysis. At the beginning of each concept module and chapter, prerequisite units are indicated. Also, main content headings are listed for each concept module and chapter. The instructor's task of assigning specific content is thereby facilitated, especially for portions of concept modules or chapters for review prior to beginning a new content area. This division of content also allows a modular approach to course content design for the instructor who wishes a less serially oriented text. For example, an anatomically based course could best use Concept Modules A, B, C, and D and Chapters 1, 2, 3, 4, 5, 6, and 7. A mechanically based course could best use Concept Modules A, B, C, D, E, F, G, and H and Chapters 1, 3, 8, 9, 10, 11, 12, 13, and 14.

Meaningful examples accompany the introduction of new material to help the student conceptualize the information presented. Understanding sections, which present review questions and easy-to-do activities, have been expanded within the concept modules and chapters for the purpose of reinforcing learning and aiding retention of the material. The Instructor's Supplement, which accompanies the instructor's desk copy, provides the expected answers or responses to the questions posed in the Understanding sections. Other sections in the instructor's supplement provide useful information and direction for the instructor whose biomechanics preparation is limited or who is using the text with students whose entrance competencies may vary. The Instructor's Supplement also includes a section on sources of biomechanics information (literature, organizations, and meetings) and supplementary experiences for learning.

The references and recommended readings are retained for each chapter and concept module and have been updated to include the most recent sources. These revisions were made after thoughtful evaluation of the first edition by ourselves, respected colleagues, and students who had used the text. Our hope is that this second edition will continue to provide a meaningful qualitative approach to the study of human movement.

Contributions from several individuals to the production of this text are appreciated, and we wish to thank the following sincerely:

Brigitte Kohler, who did the final inking of the authors' original illustrations in the first edition, most of which are included in this edition
Bob Schwarzkopf and Jeannie Zumwalt, who served as subjects for some of the illustrations
Lori Geremia, who did much of the word processing for this edition and who assisted greatly in taking the manuscript to its final form
Don Jensen, who assisted with several of the illustrations for the second edition

A special note of appreciation is given to Anne E. (Betty) Atwater, who continues to be a source of inspiration and who graciously wrote the foreword to both editions of this text.

Prerequisites

None

Chapter Contents

THE STUDY AND ANALYSIS OF HUMAN MOVEMENT

The primary objective of a course of study in physical education is to understand the nature and function of human movement in sport, dance, physical recreation, and adapted movement activities. The competent professional should be well versed in the body of knowledge or subject matter of this specialized field, which demands an understanding of numerous subdisciplines (Figure 1.1).

SECTION 1

KINESIOLOGY AND BIOMECHANICS: AREAS OF STUDY

Within the broad definition of kinesiology, the physical educator or coach may study human movement from a variety of perspectives—psychological, philosophical, sociological, or physiological. In an undergraduate physical education curriculum, **kinesiology** is the title traditionally given to a course concerning the anatomical and mechanical bases of human movement related specifically to sport, dance, and adaptive activities. The combination of knowledge of the biological and material properties of the skeletal, articular, and neuromuscular systems and of the laws and principles set forth in mechanical physics has provided the foundation for the development of a new name for this subdiscipline—biomechanics. Generally, **biomechanics** is defined as that area of study wherein the knowledge and methods of mechanics are applied to the structure and function of the living human system. Biomechanics is not an area reserved for study by the physical educator or coach, however. Figure 1.2 presents an overview of a variety of movement-related fields and occupations in which biomechanics information is applied.

Biomechanical knowledge is used in several diverse disciplines that include biology, physiology, medicine, and mechanical physics. Many professionals—engineers, designers, physical therapists, oral and orthopedic surgeons, cardiologists,

Figure 1.1.   Biomechanics for the teacher or coach.

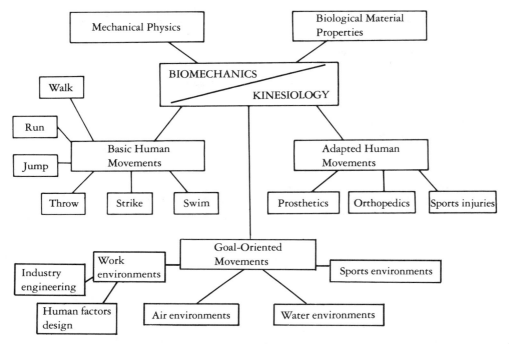

Application of biomechanics to movement-related fields.

Figure 1.2.

and aerospace engineers—make practical applications of biomechanics. A biomedical engineer may study the biological and material properties of the human body and their mechanical aspects to understand the flow of blood within the arteries. The knowledge gained may then be applied to help reduce or solve circulatory problems. A human factors designer may study the physical characteristics of the human body and the mechanical aspects of its movements that are necessary in using a given work space. Such knowledge would then enable the designer to determine an efficient height for a worktable or to provide sufficient space between one work area and another. A teacher or coach studies the physical characteristics of the human body and the principles of mechanical physics so that guidance concerning mechanically effective performances can be given to the learner.

Physical Characteristics of the Body

Knowing and applying knowledge of the physical characteristics of the human body is important when attempting to analyze its movement qualities. Information about the growth and structure of the bones, joints, and muscles can be applied.

The area of study concerned with measures of the body's physical characteristics is **anthropometrics.** Data gathered from research on human anthropometrics are presented in Appendix III (p. 656). These measures of human body size, shape, and composition include measures of height, weight, and volume. Similar measures may be taken on each segment of the body—its length, weight, and volume. Anthropometric studies may be made by classifying the human population into two or more groups (e.g., by gender, age, body shape, or athletic participation) and by collecting and comparing the anthropometric measures of the groups.

Mechanical Characteristics of Human Movement

The area of study concerned with the mechanical aspects of any system is called **mechanics** and may be divided into two categories: **statics,** the study of factors associated with nonmoving systems, and **dynamics,** the study of factors associated with systems in motion. These relationships are shown in Figure 1.3.

One may attempt to remain motionless, but doing so is almost impossible. Even

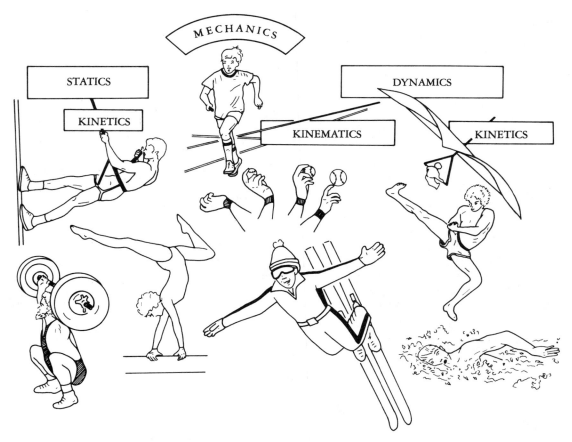

Figure 1.3.   Areas of study in biomechanics.

while standing, the body sways from side to side and forward and backward. Nevertheless, a static analysis may be made of the human body in near-static activities such as while standing, balancing, and doing certain resistance exercises. In most sport situations, however, dynamic analysis is required because total body or segmental movement takes place. The area of dynamics is further divided into *kinematics*, the study of the time and space factors of motion of a system, and *kinetics*, the study of the forces acting on a body that influence its movement.

SECTION 2

APPROACHES FOR STUDYING MOVEMENT

Two approaches are used for studying the biological and mechanical aspects of human movement—a quantitative approach and a qualitative approach. The **quantitative approach** involves describing a movement of the body or its parts in numerical terms. Such quantification of movement characteristics helps eliminate subjective description since it relies only on numerical data obtained from the use of instrumentation. Numbers obtained by measuring or counting can describe the physical situation. The observer then may use this quantification to explain or describe the actual situation. Usually, it is not economical or a wise use of time for a teacher or coach to analyze the movements of each of the performers quantitatively; the instrumentation is expensive and often not readily available, and the techniques of quantitative analysis are, for the most part, quite time consuming. An understanding of the information that may be derived from a quantitative analysis should be within the grasp of most teachers and coaches, however, so that the current scientific literature on a given sport or activity can be used.

The **qualitative approach** attempts to describe movement in nonnumerical terms (i.e., without measuring or counting any part of the performance). The impressions gained from a qualitative analysis may be substantiated with quantitative data, and many hypotheses for research projects are formulated in such a manner. The qualitative evaluations of a performance should be based on the affirmation of the appropriateness of a particular principle, law, or mechanism and its influence on a movement. This affirmation is derived through the use of quantitative research. Subjective conclusions based on qualitative analyses can be rejected or affirmed on the basis of quantitative study.

Both qualitative and quantitative analyses provide valuable information about a performance; however, a qualitative assessment is the predominant method used by the teacher or coach in analyzing the movements of performers.

In most teaching and coaching situations, analysis of movement is based on visual observation. The usual method employed in everyday situations is a qualitative analysis based on observation and memory of a performance so that subsequent evaluation can be made. Videotapes and motion pictures are also used, and they are the preferred methods since they provide visual records that may be viewed and reviewed to identify more variables than can be recognized by observation and memory alone.

Although films can provide records from which measurements may be taken for a detailed quantitative analysis, great care must be taken to prepare and conduct the filming so that valid measurements may be obtained. Often this is not possible unless special arrangements are made. Therefore, mechanical analyses based on films and videotapes are usually qualitative rather than quantitative.

Videotapes and films enhance the learning process because they provide valuable visual feedback to the performer. The teacher or coach should be able to perform a visual analysis if film or videotape is being used, so that an immediate comment can be given the performer while the movement experience is still fresh. The observer's knowledge of biomechanics becomes increasingly important as the refinements become more minute. Without videotape or film or some other form of analytic tool, minute refinements could not be observed at all owing to the limitations of human perceptual abilities.

UNDERSTANDING THE STUDY OF HUMAN MOVEMENT

1. Determine whether each of the following activities require a static or dynamic analysis: (a) a cartwheel, (b) a handstand, (c) a sprint starting position, (d) a hammer throw, (e) the en garde position in fencing, (f) a football line stance, (g) a chip shot in golf, (h) a basketball free throw.

2. A list of hypothetical articles related to movement follows. Which articles examine the kinematics of a movement, and which concern the kinetics of a movement?

 a. "The Timing of the Segments During a Golf Swing"
 b. "The Strength of the Erector Spinae Group During the Lifting Action in Man"
 c. "The Flight of the Discus"
 d. "Accuracy in the Tennis Forehand Drive"
 e. "Muscular Force Involved in Baseball Batting"
 f. "The Effects of Variation of Speed and Direction of Object Flight on Catching Tasks"
 g. "Ground Reaction Forces in the Golf Swing"
 h. "Force Production in the Clean and Jerk"
 i. "Mechanical Analysis of the Initial Velocity in the Standing Broad Jump"
 j. "Comparisons of the Force Production of Good and Poor Long Jumpers"
 k. "Effects of Stride Length and Stride Frequency on Running Velocity"

3. The following statements are from analyses of movement activities. Indicate which are qualitative and which are quantitative.

    a. The greater the angle of takeoff, the greater the vertical velocity component.
    b. The angle of takeoff was found to be 23 degrees.
    c. The style of high jump was more effective for jumper A than for jumper B.
    d. Jumper A jumped 30 cm higher than jumper B.
    e. Raising the arms over the head will raise the center of gravity within the body.
    f. An object swung in an arc and released from its circular path will travel in a new path tangent to the arc at the point of release.

4. Browse through recent issues of a sport-specific magazine such as *Ski, Golf, Tennis, Runner's World, The Runner, The International Gymnast,* or *Track and Field Quarterly.* Find and list ten phrases or statements that concern the biomechanical, anatomical, or mechanical bases of a movement or a piece of sport equipment.

SECTION 3

THE NATURE OF SKILLS

Constraints to Movement

A **movement pattern** is a general series of anatomical movements that have common elements of spatial configuration, such as segmental movements occurring in the same plane of motion. Examples of movement patterns are walking, running, jumping, throwing, striking, and kicking. These general movement patterns are not limited by any external influence, assuming that the performer has the ability to do them and is not impaired. When a general movement pattern is adapted to the constraints of a particular activity or sport, it is called a **skill.** For example, a high jump is a skill within the general movement pattern of jumping; a racquetball shot is a skill within the general movement pattern of striking. When a particular type of the same skill is performed, it is called a **technique.** The straddle and the flop are two techniques of the skill of high jumping. Different segmental movements are used to perform the two high-jumping techniques, and each technique may be recognized by the series of segmental movements used to perform it. Within each technique, a performer may use individual modifications such as unique timing or movements. These individual adaptations of a technique are defined as the **style** of performance. The curved run-up and the straight run-up to the high bar are two styles of approach used in the flop technique of high jumping.

Skills, techniques, and styles develop because of the **constraints** or limitations of an event or a performer. Event constraints are the three-dimensional physical boundaries of the playing area, the rules governing an event, costume requirements for participants in the event, the equipment specifications, and the environment in which the event is held (e.g., weather, noise, visibility).

Human constraints are the size, muscular strength, power, endurance, flexibility, and skill level of the performer and of the opponents; the position or movement of the performer immediately preceding execution of the skill; and the movements to be executed immediately after performance of the skill.

Both human and event constraints may require a performer to alter the movements of a skill from a mechanically ideal performance to a less than ideal performance. Some constraints may be incorporated into practice sessions. For example, basketball players *know* the height of the hoop, and divers *know* if they are diving off a 3-m or a 1-m board. Some constraints are difficult or impossible to introduce into practice sessions, such as the speed of an opposing basketball team's guards or the limited visibility on a ski hill.

The experienced teacher or coach incorporates as many constraints as possible into practice situations. How these constraints to performance alter the mechanically ideal execution of the skills is the focus of much of this text.

Efficiency and Effectiveness of Performance

The meaning of **efficiency** involves the concepts of work and energy. An efficient movement or skill performance is one in which a given amount of work (the skill) is done with a minimum of energy expenditure. Efficient movement is a definite advantage to performers who want to do as much work as possible before their energy runs out, such as marathon runners or swimmers. A more efficient mover lasts longer given the same pace, or performs at a faster pace with less energy expended than does a less efficient mover. For most sport activities, however, the primary concern is not with teaching how to save energy to keep going. Biomechanists are concerned more with the **effectiveness** of a performance, that is, with determining the most appropriate movements to help the performer successfully accomplish the mechanical purpose of the skill. The degree of work effort required by the skill or the amount of energy expended in performing it are not as important. For example, a 100-m run can be performed more *efficiently* by a runner who runs at half the speed of a more *effective* runner who better accomplishes the purpose of the race.

Maximize, Minimize, or Optimize?

In the 100-m run, the performer's purpose is to run with maximum speed for a short distance. Therefore, the effort put forth (energy output) in the running movements should be **maximized.** If the race were 5 km, however, a maximal rate of energy expenditure would be too great physiologically to maintain for the entire distance, and the runner probably would turn into a walker to finish. Nor would the athlete be effective (successful) in the mile race if the running speed were **minimized** to conserve energy. Instead, the runner would need to **optimize** the running speed (and rate of energy expenditure) to accomplish the purpose of the 5-km run. The optimal speed would be the specific race pace that is the fastest the runner could maintain for 5 km. The runner would learn this pace through practice. Running speed is but one example of mechanical factors or quantities that frequently are *optimized* rather than *maximized* or *minimized*.

Lafortune and Cavanagh (1983) have shown that for cycling, a low correlation exists between efficiency measures and the mechanical effectiveness of the movements used to pedal. This work is a good example of *optimizing the efficiency* to *maximize the effectiveness.*

Classification of Skills

OPEN AND CLOSED SKILLS

All movement is performed in some environment, whether it is a racquetball court, an open field, or with or without other people or equipment. The simplest skill, in terms of the environmental constraints imposed on the performer, is a closed skill. A **closed skill** is one that is done in a *predictable* environment, or one in which the performer is free to execute a skill without having to make quick decisions that would be required if unexpected changes occurred (Schmidt 1982). Examples of closed skills include a tennis serve, a javelin throw, a softball pitch, a high jump, a basketball free throw, a 100-m backstroke, a synchronized swimming routine, springboard diving, and weight lifting. In these activities, the environment is predictable and no quick decision must be made in response to some unexpected variable.

A mover must often perform in response to changes in the environment, as when executing a backhand rather than a forehand return of a tennis serve. When a skill is performed in response to an unpredictable, changing environment, it is called an **open skill.** Examples of open skills include those done in response to the unpredictable action of an opponent or situation as encountered in wrestling or in responding to a serve or a fastball pitch (Schmidt 1982). In situations such as these, the perception and quick decision-making abilities of the performer may well be more important for success than the isolated biomechanical features of the skill performance. Therefore, evaluation of skill performance within an actual game situation should take into account the *perceptual* components of the performance. Variance from using the "ideal" biomechanics of an open skill should be expected in a game because the skill usually must be initiated within a severe time constraint. The time available for actually performing the movements of the skill is only the time that remains *after* the decision to do the skill has been made.

By the time a performer is expected to move in response to environmental demands, the *skills* that are used as tools in the game should already have been drilled for basic mechanical effectiveness. Drills or practice sessions can be constructed for learning the movements that will be used as open skills in games. Practice of these skills in an out-of-game situation frees the learner from the unexpected and allows attention to be given to the biomechanics of performance.

DISCRETE AND CONTINUOUS SKILLS

From a kinematic point of view, skills can be labeled by how they appear. A movement performance can be classified according to whether it has a definite beginning and end—a **discrete skill**—or whether it appears to have no specific beginning and end—a **continuous skill.**

Examples of discrete skills include a tennis serve, a vertical jump, a handstand, a forward roll, a basketball free throw, throwing, kicking, batting, and catching. The high jump, the pole vault, the long jump, diving, gymnastic stunts, the soccer kick, the javelin throw, pass receptions, and the flip turn in swimming are also discrete skills, but they usually are initiated from a running or moving approach, which is an important part of the total performance.

Running is a skill that is of a continuous nature; that is, it is composed of repeated cycles of the same movement pattern. Swimming, the eggbeater kick in water polo, walking, skipping, bicycling, speed skating, and rowing are also examples of continuous skills.

OBSERVING SKILL PERFORMANCES

For ease in observation, a discrete skill may be divided into major phases that comprise the total act. These phases are the **preparation phase, execution phase, and recovery, or follow-through, phase.** The movements in one phase influence the movements in the next phase; therefore, the purpose of each phase is evaluated in terms of its contribution to the effectiveness of the total skill. In the overarm throw in Figure 1.4a, for instance, the preparation phase includes the backswing

Preparation   Execution   Recovery

a   b   c

Figure 1.4.   The three phases of an overarm throw: (a) preparation, (b) execution, and (c) recovery, or follow-through.

movements of the body parts, or the windup. The backswing is a preparation for executing the actual movements that result in the projection of the ball (Figure 1.4b). The recovery or conclusion phase of a discrete skill is the continuation of segmental or body movements following the completion of the execution phase. After the ball has been released from the hand of the thrower, the rotating segments continue forward and around in the same direction they were moving prior to ball release (Figure 1.4c).

The recovery phase of one skill may blend into the preparatory phase of a subsequent skill. This occurs in activities in which a readiness position is assumed between skill executions, as in tennis, racquetball, volleyball, fencing, wrestling, gymnastics, and the martial arts. In games of strategy, the next skill often cannot be predetermined, and the performer must use the recovery movement of the previous skill to move into a general position of readiness that best permits the execution of the next skill. The use of shoulder rolls and backward rolls in volleyball allows the player rapid recovery to a position of readiness. A choreographer for dance, synchronized swimming, skating, or gymnastic routines must consider that recovery movements from one skill serve to prepare the performer for a subsequent skill.

When one examines continuous skills such as running and swimming, one usually assumes that each *cycle* of the pattern is performed in the same way; that is, the one cycle selected for analysis is representative of all the cycles in the total performance. This is not an unreasonable assumption if the performer is highly skilled, since a skilled mover exhibits less variation among repetitions of a movement pattern than does a less-skilled mover. Usually, the observer can more easily analyze a continuous skill because the cycles are repeated continuously for observation. Discrete skills also must be repeated over and over again for observation, but the variability among the performances is usually greater than in continuous skills. The time elapsed between each observed performance is also greater, and the observer lacks the benefit of the instant replay provided by the performance of a continuous skill. Each cycle of a continuous skill may be divided into phases, as discrete skills are, but divisions are arbitrary and vary from skill to skill.

UNDERSTANDING THE NATURE OF SKILLS

1. Consider a runner who is free from all but the minimum constraints; that is, she has the ability to run, an open space in which to run, and an even surface on which to run.

   a. List general categories of constraints that may be imposed on the runner to alter her running technique by placing her in different sport or recreational activities or both. (For example, a general category of constraint that would force her to run differently would be boundaries.)

   b. For each category of constraint listed in part *a*, provide three examples. (An example of a specific boundary constraint would be the lane lines in a 200-m run.)

2. Select a general movement pattern. List five different sport skills that use that movement pattern. For each skill, list as many different techniques of performance as you can. Describe two or three specific and unique stylizations of the techniques listed.

3. Describe three activities in which efficiency should be reduced in favor of effectiveness.

4. Describe an activity in which force is optimized, but not maximized, for the most effective performance.

5. Identify five skills that should be classified as open skills. For each skill, describe how the mechanics of the skill could be practiced for skill improvement.

6. Select three *discrete* closed motor skills. For each, identify the following phases: preparation, execution, and recovery.

SECTION 4

THE PRIMARY MECHANICAL PURPOSE OF A SKILL

To facilitate a biomechanical analysis and to focus our attention on improvements to enhance the effectiveness of a movement performance, we must know the purpose of the movement. Each sport event, sport skill, or movement may be classified according to its **primary mechanical purpose.** The primary purpose is usually expressed in mechanical terms; for instance, the purpose of spiking a volleyball is to project the ball downward into the opponent's court (accuracy of projection). Such an objective is primary, for if the ball does not land in the opponent's court, it is out of play. Secondary purposes of the spiking movement are to project the ball with maximum speed and to send the ball to a particular location within the court (accuracy in which speed enhances its effectiveness).

With a multipurpose movement, an order, or priority, of importance should be established. Is the speed of the ball more important than its placement (direction)? If not, then the secondary purpose (speed) may have to be compromised to allow for the necessary control of ball direction. Such speed-accuracy trade-offs, or compromises, are frequently encountered in sport situations in which the speed of the projectile means little if the target is not hit. Table 1.1 suggests a list of primary mechanical purposes that serve as the basis for the analysis of movement skills.

Some examples in Table 1.1 are single skills that are entire events in themselves, such as the javelin throw, pole vault, dart throw, and diving. Other examples are skills that are part of a larger event but that have primary mechanical purposes in themselves. Each skill has its own primary mechanical purpose, which may or may

MECHANICAL PURPOSES OF HUMAN MOVEMENT ACTIVITIES Table 1.1.

Primary Mechanical Objective or Purpose	Examples
1. To project an object or the body for maximum horizontal distance	Discus, javelin, long jump, triple jump
2. To project an object or the body for maximum vertical distance	High jump, pole vault, vertical jump
3. To project an object for maximum accuracy	Horseshoes, darts, archery, slow-pitch softball
4. To project an object for maximum accuracy when the speed of the projectile enhances its effectiveness	Baseball pitch, volleyball serve, tennis serve, badminton smash
5. To manipulate a resistance	Weight lifting, wrestling, judo, football block, catching
6. To move the body over a prescribed distance with or without a time constraint	Cross-country running and skiing, kayaking, swimming, bobsledding, orienteering
7. To move or position the body or its segments or both in a prescribed pattern with the intent of achieving an ideal or model performance	Gymnastics, diving, trampoline tumbling, body building, dancing
8. To move the body with the intent of interacting with the natural environment	Scuba diving, hang gliding, surfing, mountain climbing

not be the general purpose of an entire event, such as a basketball free throw, a single tumbling stunt in gymnastics, and a football block. One may say that the general purpose of competing in a game of basketball is to score more points than the opponent. One cannot analyze biomechanically how many points were scored, however; one can analyze only the effectiveness of the shots taken. Thus, a basketball shot is a skill with a primary *mechanical* purpose, but the entire game of basketball is not.

On the other hand, many entire events have unique mechanical purposes, and each component of the event contributes to its primary mechanical purpose. For instance, a timed freestyle event in swimming is composed of several skills with the primary mechanical purpose of moving the body as quickly as possible over a prescribed distance. One may argue that the primary purpose of the start is to begin to swim as soon as possible; however, one must keep in mind that the primary mechanical purpose of the start is to reduce the time necessary to move over the prescribed distance.

Generally, one attempts to improve by accomplishing the primary mechanical purpose better than one accomplished it in the past or better than another performer or both. The approach to the process of biomechanical analysis in this text is based on common principles applicable to groups of skills that have a common primary mechanical purpose. Skills that have the same mechanical purpose have the same mechanical principles governing their effectiveness. Knowledge of these principles allows one to develop a system of analysis that may be used for many different skills without having to learn the specifics of each.

SECTION 5

THE ANALYSIS PROCESS

The process of analyzing a performance involves these steps:

1. Identify the primary mechanical purpose of the skill to be analyzed.
2. Identify the biomechanical principles on which the effectiveness of the performance is based. These principles are developed from biological laws related to the neuromuscular and musculoskeletal systems and from mechanical laws based on Newton's laws of motion. (These laws, or principles, are covered thoroughly in subsequent sections.) Thus, information about how the human body functions is merged with mechanical concepts to provide biomechanical principles that govern performance effectiveness. Knowledge in both areas is prerequisite to a proper analysis.
3. Identify constraints to the free performance of each skill. Among these are:
   a. The physical environment in which the skill is performed. Features of the physical environment include the surface of play (grass or wood), wind direction and speed, the height or size of the opponent, and the performer's location relative to the playing area (spiking a volleyball from the 3-m line compared with spiking next to the net).
   b. The size and strength of the performer. For example, one coaches a tall javelin thrower or basketball free-throw shooter differently than a short performer in either of these skills, and one coaches a 12-year-old tennis player differently than a 20-year-old player.
   c. The movements immediately preceding or immediately following the skill being analyzed. For example, movements in performing a back handspring from a standing position differ from movements in performing a back handspring from a roundoff.

Because of the wide variations in structure and movement capabilities of human beings, no two individuals perform the same skill in exactly the same way. No two individuals possess the same structural proportions, joint ranges of motion, musculoskeletal qualities, neuromuscular pathways developed, or motivation. Each performer may exhibit some unique, personalized movements that may be of limited importance in the mechanical execution of the skill or that may limit improvement of the performance. Therefore, one should not assume that *all* the stylized movements of a single-skilled performer, even a performer of national caliber, contribute to a biomechanically ideal performance. The analyst should be familiar with the movement characteristics that are common among *several* successful performers of the skill and should incorporate these common components into an ideal or model performance. What may be of benefit to one may not be of benefit to all.

One should always question the mechanical effectiveness of any new style that emerges on the scene, for the new style may be merely a psychological boost for the user and may serve no mechanical advantage to anyone else. A model performance must be fairly general and should exhibit effective mechanical components.

On the other hand, an analyst should be flexible enough in his or her thinking so as not to feel limited to only those techniques that are prevalent in national competition. One should always be alert to the possibility of making modifications based on sound mechanical principles to improve the model performance or of creating a unique or novel approach for accomplishing the mechanical purpose of the skill.

UNDERSTANDING THE ANALYSIS PROCESS

1. For the following list of activities, state the primary mechanical purpose from Table 1.1.

   a. Pole vault
   b. Baseball batting
   c. Fielding a line drive
   d. 50-m dash
   e. Bobsledding
   f. Mountain climbing
   g. Body building
   h. Shot put
   i. Long jump
   j. Basketball jump ball
   k. Free throw
   l. Softball pitch (fast pitch)

2. List three national caliber athletes in different sports whose performance includes some stylization. State the primary mechanical purpose of the skill. How does the stylization influence the effectiveness of the performance?

3. List three examples of relatively new techniques for performing a skill. Are these new techniques mechanically more effective than the traditional techniques?

4. List three instances in which rules or rule changes prevented or outlawed a new technique for the performance of some skill. Were these new techniques more effective than the accepted techniques in achieving mechanical purpose of the skill?

REFERENCES
SUGGESTED READINGS

Arnold, R. K. "Optimizing Skill Learning: Moving to Match the Environment." *JOPER* 49 (9) (1978): 84–86.

Asmussen, E. "Movement of Man and Study of Man in Motion: A Scanning Review of the Development of Biomechanics." In *Biomechanics V-A: Proceedings of the Fifth International Symposium on Biomechanics*, ed. P. V. Komi, 23–40. Baltimore: University Park Press, 1976.

Atwater, A. E. "Kinesiology/Biomechanics: Perspectives and Trends." *Research Quarterly for Exercise and Sport* 51 (1) (1980): 193–218.

Barham, J. *Mechanical Kinesiology.* St. Louis: C. V. Mosby Co., 1978, pp. 3–19.

Bates, B. T. "Scientific Basis of Human Movement." *JOPER* 48 (8) (1977): 68–74.

Dyson, G. "Coaching Philosophy." *Swimming Technique* 13 (2) (1976): 44–49.

———. *The Mechanics of Athletics.* New York: Holmes & Meier, Publishers, 1977, pp. 11–13.

Faculty of Education, University of Tokyo. "Factors Governing Competitive Swimming Records." *Swimming Technique* 14 (2) (1977): 40–42.

Hatze, H. "The Meaning of the Term 'Biomechanics.'" *Journal of Biomechanics* 7 (2) (1974): 189–90.

Hays, J. "Back to Basics in Physical Education and Dance." *JOPER* 50 (5) (1979): 33–35.

Hebbelinck, M., and Ross, W. D. "Kinanthropometry and Biomechanics." In *Biomechanics IV: Proceedings of the Fourth International Seminar on Biomechanics*, ed. R. C. Nelson and C. A. Morehouse, 537–52. Baltimore: University Park Press, 1974.

Hensley, L. D. "Biomechanical Analysis." *JOPERD* 54 (8) (1983): 21–23.

Hochmuth, G., and Marhold, G. "The Further Development of Biomechanical Principles." In *Biomechanics VI-B: Proceedings of the Sixth International Symposium on Biomechanics*, ed. E. Asmussen and K. Jorgensen, 93–108. Baltimore: University Park Press, 1978.

Hoffman, S. "Toward a Pedagogical Kinesiology." *Quest*, NAPECW-NCPEAM Monograph 28 (1977).

Kelley, D. L. "Supporting Biomechanics Subject Matter in the Undergraduate Curriculum." In *Kinesiology IV*, ed. J. G. Hay, 1–11. Reston, Va.: AAHPERD, 1974.

Lafortune, M. A., and Cavanagh, P. R. "Effectiveness and Efficiency During Bicycle Riding." In *Biomechanics VIII-B: Proceedings of the Eighth International Congress of Biomechanics*, ed. H. Matsui and K. Kobayashi, 928–36. Champaign, Ill.: Human Kinetics Publishers, 1983.

Malina, R. M. "Anthropometric Correlates of Strength and Motor Performances." In *Exercise and Sports Science Reviews*, vol. 3, ed. J. H. Wilmore and J. F. Keogh, 249–72. New York: Academic Press, 1975.

McKinney, W. C., and Northrip, J. W. "The Undergraduate Kinesiology Project: Relating Theory to Practice." In *Kinesiology: [Proceedings of] A National Conference on Teaching*, ed. C. Dillman and R. Sears, 183–90. Champaign-Urbana: University of Illinois, 1977.

Miller, D. I. "Body Segment Contributions to Sport Skill Performance: Two Contrasting Approaches." *Research Quarterly for Exercise and Sport* 49 (1) (1978): 219–33.

Norman, R. W. "Biomechanics for the Community Coach." *JOPER* 46 (3) (1975): 49–52.

———. "An Approach to Teaching the Mechanics of Motion at the Undergraduate Level."

In *Kinesiology:* [Proceedings of] *A National Conference on Teaching,* ed. C. Dillman and R. Sears, 113–24. Champaign-Urbana: University of Illinois, 1977.

Sapega, A., et al. "Sport Specific Performance Factor Profiling, Fencing As a Prototype." *American Journal of Sports Medicine* 6 (5) (1978): 232.

Schmidt, R. A. *Motor Control and Learning.* Champaign, Ill.: Human Kinetics Publishers, 1982.

Singer, R. N. *The Learning of Motor Skills.* New York: Macmillan, 1982.

Tichonov, V. N. "Distribution of Body Masses of a Sportsman." In *Biomechanics V-B: Proceedings of the Fifth International Congress on Biomechanics,* ed. P. V. Komi, 103–08. Baltimore: University Park Press, 1976.

THE SKELETAL SYSTEM AND ITS MOVEMENTS

Prerequisites

None

Concept Module Contents

Four anatomical disciplines directly relate to human body movement. They are (1) osteology, the study of the skeletal system, (2) arthrology, the study of the articulations, (3) myology, the study of the muscles, and (4) neurology, the study of the nervous system. Not all the information relating to these systems is directly applicable to the biomechanics of movement; however, those characteristics and properties of the skeletal and articular systems that do concern human movement are presented in the following section.

SECTION 1

THE SKELETAL SYSTEM

Structurally, the human skeleton is divided into two parts, the **axial skeleton,** which includes the skull, thorax, pelvis, and vertebral column, and the **appendicular skeleton,** which includes the upper and lower extremities. Figures A.1a and b illustrate the anterior and posterior views of the human skeleton.

The axial skeleton consists of the skull (29 bones), the thorax (25 bones), and the vertebral column (26 separate bones). In addition to the 12 pairs of ribs, the sternum is the only other bone in the thorax. The sternum is a fused unit of three parts: the manubrium, the body, and the xyphoid process. Although the three separate sections of the sternum are fused, knowing their locations is important for understanding muscle attachments and the mechanics of muscle pull. The vertebral column (Figure A.1c) consists of five regions: the cervical spine (7 bones), the thoracic spine (12 bones), the lumbar spine (5 bones), the sacrum (5 bones fused into a single unit), and the coccyx (4 bones).

The appendicular skeleton consists of two basic divisions, the upper right and left extremities (32 bones each) and the lower right and left extremities (31 bones each). The upper extremity begins with the shoulder girdle complex and ends with the fingertips. The lower extremity begins with the pelvic girdle and ends with the toes. The individual carpals (bones in the hand) and tarsals (bones in the foot) are not of primary functional significance in the biomechanics of sport, although two tarsals do play an important function in weight bearing and should be identified: the talus (directly below the tibia) and the calcaneus (the great bone of the heel, directly below the talus).

The skeleton has several important functions: (1) to protect vital organs within the body, (2) to support soft tissues, (3) to serve as the factory for making red blood cells, (4) to serve as a reservoir for minerals (calcium and phosphate), (5) to provide the attachments for skeletal muscles, and (6) to act as a system of machines to receive muscle torques and to make movement possible. Of these services, the last two are of particular concern to biomechanists and kinesiologists.

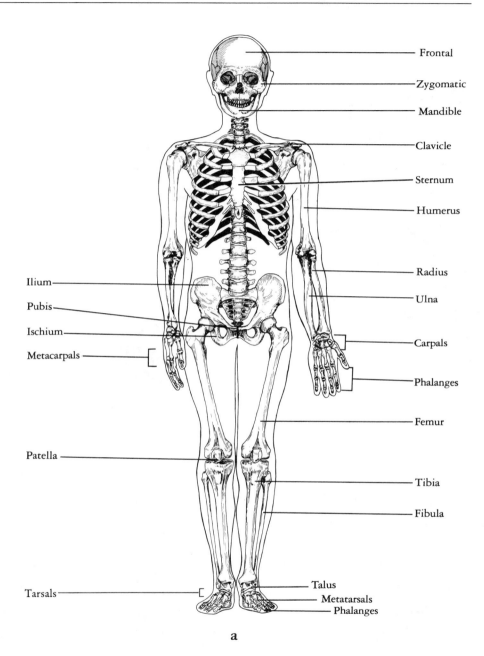

Frontal
Zygomatic
Mandible
Clavicle
Sternum
Humerus
Radius
Ulna
Carpals
Phalanges
Femur
Tibia
Fibula

Ilium
Pubis
Ischium
Metacarpals
Patella
Tarsals

Talus
Metatarsals
Phalanges

a

(a) Anterior (front or ventral) aspect of the human skeleton. (b) Posterior (back or dorsal) aspect of the human skeleton. (c) Side view of the vertebral column.

Figure A.1.

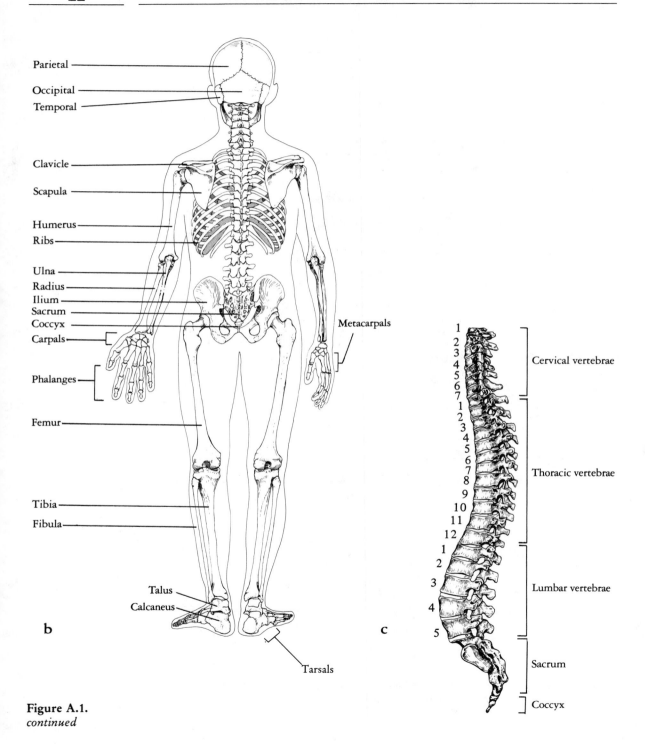

Parietal

Occipital
Temporal

Clavicle

Scapula

Humerus
Ribs

Ulna
Radius
Ilium
Sacrum
Coccyx
Carpals

Phalanges

Femur

Tibia
Fibula

Talus
Calcaneus

b

Tarsals

Metacarpals

1
2
3
4
5
6
7 } Cervical vertebrae
1
2
3
4
5
6
7
8
9
10
11
12 } Thoracic vertebrae
1
2
3
4
5 } Lumbar vertebrae

Sacrum

Coccyx

c

Figure A.1.
continued

Classification of Bones

One method of classifying bones is by shape. The shape of a bone to some extent determines its main function, and conversely, the function may alter the shape slightly. Long bones are the predominant bones in the extremities and serve a particular function in providing levers for movement. The long bones in the lower extremities are generally larger and stronger than those in the upper extremities, for they must repeatedly bear the weight of the body during locomotion, and therefore, are subjected to repeated stress. The long bones in the upper extremities are generally smaller and lighter since they are used mainly in reaching, grasping, and throwing rather than weight bearing. Some smaller bones may be subjected to repeated stress, such as the humerus of a baseball pitcher or the metatarsals of runners. Although the forces on these bones are large, they are not severe enough or repetitious enough to require bones as heavy or large as those in the leg.

The short bones generally appear as chunks of bone and are found predominantly in the hands and feet. They are compact and serve collectively to provide elasticity, range of motion, and shock absorption. The flat bones, such as those in the skull and scapula, usually provide a protective covering for structures lying below them and also serve as locations for muscular attachments. Irregular bones, such as the vertebrae, protect the spinal cord and branching nerves. The spinous and transverse processes of the vertebrae serve as "handles" for muscular attachments and as levers for muscle pull, and the bodies of the vertebrae partially absorb the shock of landing in walking, running, or jumping.

Gross Structure of Bone

The microscopic anatomy of a bone is of little importance to sport biomechanists; however, knowledge of some basic structural properties is useful for understanding structural functional relationships. Figure A.2 illustrates the important parts of a typical long bone, flat bone, and irregular bone.

If a long bone is in the extremities, the end of the bone closest to the trunk is the **proximal** end, and the end farthest away from the trunk is the **distal** end. The **lateral** side of the bone is that side away from the midline of the body, while that side closest to the midline is the **medial** side.[1] If a bone is part of the axial skeleton, the border closest to the head is the **superior** border of the bone; that closest to the feet is the **inferior** border. Although some bones do not possess all of these characteristics, knowledge of the following landmarks is useful in identifying parts of the skeleton (Langley and Christensen 1978):

Condyle (Figure A.2a)   A rounded process of a bone for articulation.

---

1. When anatomical position is assumed with palms facing forward, as in the left upper extremity in Figure A.1.

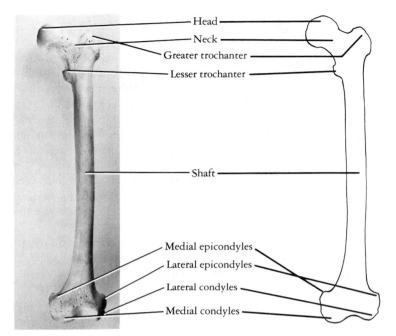

Head
Neck
Greater trochanter
Lesser trochanter

Shaft

Medial epicondyles
Lateral epicondyles
Lateral condyles
Medial condyles

a

Olecranon process
Olecranon fossa
Radial head
Coronoid process
Radial neck
Radial tuberosity

Ulna

Radius

Styloid processes

b

Figure A.2.   Important parts of a long bone: (a) femur, (b) radius and ulna. (c) Parts of a flat bone (scapula). (d and e) Parts of an irregular bone (vertebrae).

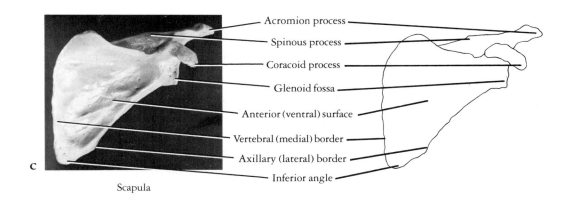

Acromion process

Spinous process

Coracoid process

Glenoid fossa

Anterior (ventral) surface

Vertebral (medial) border

Axillary (lateral) border

Inferior angle

c

Scapula

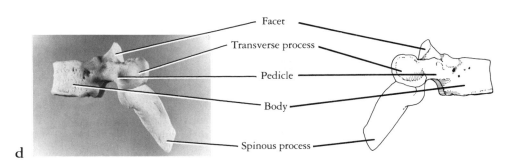

Facet

Transverse process

Pedicle

Body

Spinous process

d

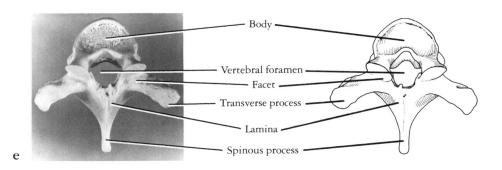

Body

Vertebral foramen

Facet

Transverse process

Lamina

Spinous process

e

Epicondyle (Figure A.2a)	A small condyle.
Facet (Figure A.2d, e)	A "little face." Any small, fairly flat, smooth surface of a bone, generally an articular surface.
Foramen (Figure A.2e)	A "hole." Generally refers to a hole in a bone through which nerves or vessels pass.
Fossa (Figure A.2b, c)	A shallow, dish-shaped section of a bone that provides a space for an articulation with another bone or a muscle attachment.
Process (Figure A.2b, c, d, e)	A bony prominence.
Tuberosity (Figure A.2b)	A raised section of bone to which a ligament muscle attaches; usually created or enlarged by the stress of the muscle's pull on that bone during growth.

Development of Long Bone

The articular surfaces of long bones, those parts that form joints with adjacent bones, are located at the distal and proximal ends of the bones. Just inside the articular surface is a section of bone called the **epiphysis,** which appears as a prominence on either end of the bone. The growth of a long bone takes place along discs of cartilage called epiphyseal plates that are located on the inner side of the epiphysis (Figure A.3a).

The **metaphysis** is on the center side of the epiphyseal plate and is the location of new bone growth. The center, or shaft, of the bone is called the **diaphysis** and is the primary center of ossification. Thus, as the bone develops and grows, the new bone cells (osteoblasts) are placed along the epiphyseal plates at the metaphysis. In this manner, the bone continues to get longer until internal maturational or nutritional signals indicate a stopping time. The **apophysis** and its apophyseal plate are located on the shaft of the bone and usually comprise a portion of the bone that serves as the attachment of a predominant muscle. They serve a function similar to that of the epiphysis and epiphyseal plate. The bone growth occurring along an apophyseal plate contributes to configurational aspects of bone growth but not to length. The completion or closure time of these plates varies with different bones and also varies for the same bones between the sexes.

Of special interest to developmental kinesiologists is the role of forces in changing the composition, size, and structure of bones. The primary determinant of the size and shape of bones is genetic; however, small adaptations may take place due to the amount and kind of stresses to which the bone is subjected, nutrition, injury, or disease. Injury and the amounts and types of stress on bones, including training effects, have important implications for the development and application of exercise programs for children and adults.

Bone tissue is composed of an outer shell of compact bone, an internal structure of spongy or cancellous (porous) bone, and the medullary cavity (as illustrated in Figure A.3b). The cancellous bone is made up of a network of bony tissues called

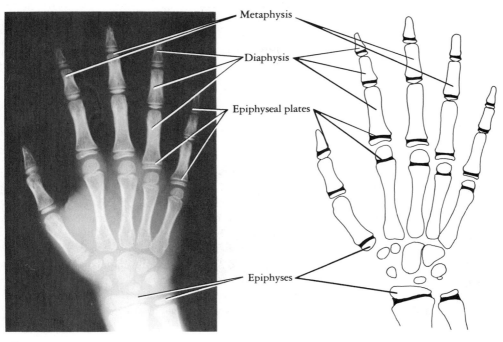

Metaphysis

Diaphysis

Epiphyseal plates

Epiphyses

a

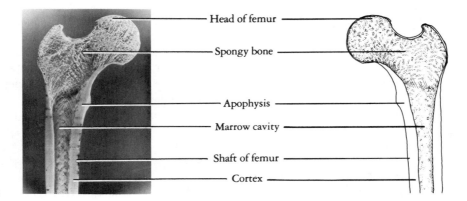

Head of femur

Spongy bone

Apophysis

Marrow cavity

Shaft of femur

Cortex

b

Long bone growth and structural characteristics.

Figure A.3.

trabeculae, which are formed during bone growth partially in response to the forces and stresses to which the bone is subjected. Trabeculae direct themselves to best support those forces.

Body tissues are adaptable. This adaptation is particularly evident during the time before closure of the epiphyseal plate. Thus, if a child is active in a wide variety of activities, the child's bones grow and strengthen to accommodate stresses related to those activities. Similarly, if a child is subjected to a single activity repeatedly, such as throwing a baseball or playing tennis, the utilized bones grow and develop in a slightly different configuration than the less-stressed bones on the opposite side. A muscle's pull on a bone stimulates bone growth at the apophyseal plate, and the shape and strength of the bone-muscle junction accommodate that type of activity. This adaptation provides a physiological reason (aside from the philosophical argument) for starting children early in activities that require specialized body movements, such as gymnastics and ballet. The inherent disadvantage to this type of program is that repeated stresses of isolated body parts that are integral to a sport may prove injurious to young musculoskeletal structures. For example, the impact of a tennis ball on a racket provides a sometimes overwhelming stress on an immature arm, and practicing baseball pitches repeatedly or pitching an entire game may be more than an immature arm can handle safely. When subjected to stress in this way, the bone may show signs of wear: small portions of the joint cartilage may chip off, the epiphysis may pull off the bone entirely, or the epiphyseal plate may close at an early age and thus arrest growth in the bone. From the standpoint of developmental kinesiology, these factors have serious implications for intensive youth sport programs. Although impact and repeated stress do not always result in permanent injury, their effects may be severe in children prior to closure of the epiphyseal plates in the bone. Researchers have found that separation "of the medial epicondyle of the humerus is not uncommon prior to epiphyseal closure" in Little League pitchers (Woods, Tullos, and King 1973). Torg (1973) describes the specific effects of **compression** (pressing together), **tension** (pulling apart), and **shear** stresses (tearing across) on bone growth and development. Compression of either the epiphyseal or apophyseal plates prior to closure retards bone growth. Tension on the bone, such as that produced by muscle pull, activates bone cell growth, and shearing forces tend to separate the plate from the newly calcified bone. In addition, epiphyseal injuries have been reported in adolescent weight lifters (Ryan and Salciccioli 1976). Jackson (1976) reports a four-times-higher incidence of low back pathologies in young female gymnasts than in the rest of the population.

The large size of a child is not an indicator of bone maturation; in fact, many times the opposite is true. The child who is overweight or excessively large may be among the latest to mature physically. Considerable evidence confirms that exercise and nontraumatic stress on the bones of children and adults enhance the size and strength of the bones. In growing animals, a low-intensity training either does not affect or stimulates bone growth in length and girth, but high-intensity training inhibits length and girth development. Bone density, on the other hand, is increased by high-intensity training, but is not influenced by low-intensity training (Booth and Gould 1975).

Other factors that alter the relative structure of bones are age, nutrition, and hormonal changes. Little research is available on how exercise either prevents or slows the effects of these factors on bone deterioration.

SECTION 2

ARTICULATIONS

The human skeleton is a system consisting of bones joined together to form segments or links. These links are movable and provide for the attachment of muscles to produce movement. The junction of two bones is called an **articulation.**

Classification of Articulations

Articulations are divided into three basic classifications according to the amount of movement possible. Figure A.4 illustrates the types of articulations.

A **synarthrodial** articulation is the juncture between two bones that do not display any particular movement and thus are considered immovable but that do have the ability to absorb shock. The sutures between the bones of the skull are examples of synarthrodial articulations. **Amphiarthrodial** articulations are slightly movable since a fibrocartilagenous disc (between the vertebrae) or a ligament or membrane links the two bones (scapula to the thorax). Because of the connective tissue, the two bones may shift slightly in their relative positions. These types of joints also absorb shock by providing some "give" to the forces that tend to separate or force together the two bones.

Synarthrodial
(sutures)

a

Amphiarthrodial
(intervertebral)

b

Diarthrodial
(hip)

c

Examples of the three types of articulations: (a) synarthrodial (skull), (b) amphiarthrodial (vertebrae), and (c) diarthrodial (hip).

Figure A.4.

The most common type of articulation encountered in the study of human movement is the freely movable joint named the **diarthrodial** articulation. There are several types of diarthrodial articulations, but understanding only their general structure and the types of movements they make possible is important for our purposes.

Hyaline cartilage covers the adjoining ends of the bones. Such cartilage is the smooth, elastic substance found on the ends of chicken bones. Its main functions are to absorb shock and provide a relatively frictionless surface over which the bones may move. When degeneration of articulations occurs, as is sometimes seen in **overuse syndromes**[2] such as pitcher's elbow, the hyaline cartilage cracks, chips, or wears away from the end of the bone, resulting in painful movement due to uncovered bone endings or from chips or spurs of cartilage becoming lodged within the joint.

The joint cavity provides a space for the movement of the two bones and houses the synovial fluid, a fairly viscous (thick) material that lubricates the hyaline cartilage. There is some indication that the viscosity of the fluid may change with activity; this has been implicated as being part of the "warm-up" effects that occur during the initial stages of movement. The synovial membrane surrounds the joint cavity but does not cover the hyaline cartilage. It is filled with nerve endings and is quite sensitive to changes within the capsule or pressure from foreign objects such as bone spurs. On the outside of the synovial membrane is the articular capsule. The capsule surrounds the articulation like a collar and helps hold the bones together. Ligaments are the connective tissue structures connecting the two bones and are on the outside of the capsule. Tendons, which are also on the outside of the capsule, are connective tissues that attach the muscles to the bone. Not all muscles have tendinous attachments. Some muscle fibers attach directly to the periosteum (covering) of the bone itself. A tendinous attachment serves two functions: (1) it concentrates the force of the muscle's pull into a small area on the bone, and (2) it allows a greater freedom in changing the angle at which the muscle pulls on the bone. The importance of this second factor will become more evident in the discussion on muscle mechanics. The fibrous attachments of the muscles are generally found on the origin (the least movable end) of the bone and are associated with large muscles, which may develop great force and pull on relatively large bones such as the pelvis or the scapula.

Material Properties of Articular Connective Tissue

Evidence indicates that the tensile strength of connective tissue (tendons and ligaments) improves with exercise, thus decreasing the possibility of tearing or rupture (Booth and Gould 1975). In addition, both have **elastic** properties; that is, they return to their original shapes and lengths after being stretched. There is a limit to the stretching, however, after which the tissue becomes somewhat **plastic**; that is, the tissue maintains the stretched shape. Generally, a tissue stretched beyond its **elastic limit** does not return to its original shape with time, and thus surgery becomes

---

2. The pathological symptoms created by repeated use of a body part under physically stressful conditions are commonly called overuse syndromes.

the only method by which integrity may be reinstated. This is why a bone fracture can be much less serious than a severe **sprain**, since a bone normally heals to a state that is stronger than the original whereas a ligament does not. The local injection of steroids into tendons to reduce inflammation also can alter the material properties of the tissue, reduce the strength of tendons, and predispose them to complete rupture (Unverferth and Olix 1973).

Stability of Articulations

The **stability** of an articulation is defined as the ability of the skeletal framework to absorb shock and withstand motion without injury to the joints and their surrounding tissues, such as dislocation of the joint, sprain of the ligaments, or **strain** of the muscle tissue.[3] Three sources of stability for an articulation are: (1) a strong bony arrangement at the joint, whereby one bone "fits into" or around another, as at the elbow or hip, (2) a strong ligamentous arrangement, whereby the ligaments surrounding the joint are of sufficient quantity and quality to be able to resist dislocating forces, as is provided in the ligaments of the hip joint, and (3) strong muscular arrangements, whereby the muscles surrounding the joint and their lines of force during tension tend to pull the two bones together, as at the shoulder joint.

Two factors determine the possibility of a strong articulation: first, whether the articulation has the structures to provide the stability, and, second, how strong the available structures are. For instance, an articulation may have few ligaments on the anterior side; thus, the anterior side has a weak ligamentous arrangement. If there are ligaments on the anterior side, however, these ligaments may be strong or weak, depending on their condition. The stability of any articulation depends on the strength of the bony, ligamentous, and muscular factors. If one of these is weak, the entire articulation is somewhat weak. A person cannot do much to change the stability of the bony structure of an articulation, but evidence suggests that one can increase the strength of the ligaments through exercise, to help them resist any dislocating forces, and one can undergo strength training programs for the muscles so that they may better maintain the integrity of the joint. Particularly in the case of articulations such as the knee and the shoulder, where the bony arrangements provide minimal stability, the muscles surrounding these joints must be strong to stabilize joints against dislocating forces and to help hold the two bones together.

Mobility of Articulations

The **mobility** of an articulation is defined as the degree to which an articulation is allowed to move before being restricted by surrounding tissues. Mobility is determined by the articulation's **range of motion** (ROM), which is the total amount

---

3. In mechanics, the word **stress** denotes a force, whereas strain denotes the deformation of a material under stress. In this text, the anatomical definition will be used. That is, **strain** refers to deformation or the tearing of muscular tissue, whereas **sprain** refers to the deformation or tearing of ligamentous tissue.

of movement (usually measured in degrees) through which the articulation's segments may pass. This quality is commonly called **flexibility.** The ROM of an articulation depends on the shape of the articulated parts of the bone and the tightness of the ligaments and muscles surrounding it. Figure A.5 illustrates how each of these three structures limits the ROM at the elbow.

Figure A.5a shows an elbow hyperextended to a point where the olecranon process has contacted the olecranon fossa and hence has stopped its motion. If movement is forced beyond this point, bruising or breaking of the bone will occur. Usually, an articulation is prevented from reaching the point of bony contact by the ligaments or muscle tendons that cross the joint and become taut before bone contact is made. Figure A.5b illustrates the end of the elbow extension due to ligamentous and

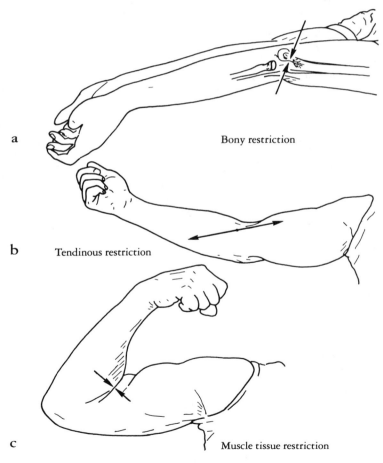

a   Bony restriction

b   Tendinous restriction

c   Muscle tissue restriction

Figure A.5.   The elbow joint is restricted in its range of motion by (a) bony tissue, (b) tendinous tissue, and (c) muscle tissue.

tendinous tightness. Flexibility exercises are designed to increase the ROM of joints by increasing the "stretchability" of the ligaments and tendons. Finally, an articulation is inhibited in its ROM by the compressing of two adjacent tissue structures, as shown in Figure A.5c. In this case, the elbow is flexed to the point where the tissues of the forearm make contact with the biceps muscle on the anterior side of the humerus. The larger the tissue bulk, or the more adipose (fat), the sooner the tissues contact each other and limit motion.

Thus, an articulation's ROM is the total range through which the segments can move before being stopped by bony, ligamentous, or muscular structures. Note that the stability and mobility of a joint are not mutually exclusive; that is, an articulation may have good stability and still maintain its mobility. (Consider a strong but flexible gymnast.) The term *muscle-bound* is used commonly to describe a person with large muscular tissue development that limits ROM because the adjacent tissues touch. A certain amount of muscle bulk develops when a person continually engages in intensive muscle-strengthening exercises through a relatively small ROM and does not bother to stretch the muscles sufficiently. The articulation becomes bound to a relatively limited ROM because of ligamentous, tendinous, and tissue bulk limitations. The concept that weight training causes a muscle-bound condition is a myth, for muscle bulk develops only with a high-resistance, low-repetition exercise program that does not incorporate any stretching following the workout. Females generally do not develop the muscle bulk that males do with similar training programs. This is due primarily to hormone differences (President's Council on Physical Fitness and Sports 1975).

No evidence suggests that a flexible joint (one with a large ROM) is less strong than an inflexible one. The added ROM merely allows a flexible articulation to move safely into positions that an inflexible one cannot assume. Flexibility, then, is an important factor in the prevention of injuries and in efficient skill performance, but to satisfy these purposes, flexibility must be accompanied by ligamentous and muscular stability surrounding an articulation. The gymnast who is strong enough to perform on the rings also must have flexibility in the shoulder joints to allow the body to swing down to a long hang from a handstand. The movement requires not only strength to guide and control it but also enough flexibility in the surrounding tissues to prevent muscle strains and ligament sprains when the articulation is brought forcefully to the end of its range.

Most of us have met or heard about a person who is described as double-jointed and is able to move the body parts in ways not normally possible to others. Excluding some pathological deformity, the term is a misnomer, for no double joints exist. The condition is seen in articulations that are weak ligamentously and muscularly and thus allow excessive ROMs. An extended elbow that allows the joint angle to move beyond 180 degrees and knees that hyperextend beyond the normal straightening are typical examples of the lack of ligamentous and muscular stability in those joints. Although double-jointedness is used by some as an excuse for not being able to perform certain exercises, it is not the condition of exaggerated ROM that inhibits performance; it is the lack of muscular strength and tissue support in the joint that increases the required amount of force necessary to execute the exercise. The hyperextended position is not an efficient position from which to move because of the muscles' angles of pull. A discussion of this concept is in Chapter 3, Biomechanics of the Musculoskeletal System.

UNDERSTANDING THE SKELETAL-ARTICULAR STRUCTURES

1. Using the skeleton shown in Figure A.6, identify by name the bones important to human movement in physical education and athletics. (Exclude individual bones of the skull, the hand, and the bones distal to the calcaneus in the foot.)

2. Study all the articulations of the bones in Figure A.6. Label these by name on

Figure A.6.   The human skeleton.

the drawing. There are 13 articulations, counting the vertical column as one. List which bones articulate together to make each articulation.

3. Using a manual goniometer or a protractor, roughly measure the ROM of elbow flexion, knee flexion, and hip flexion with the knee straight and with the knee flexed. Measure two females and two males. What are the differences between the ROMs of the males and females? Can you explain the differences among individuals within the group?

4. Measure and list the general ROMs for the following movements:

   a. *Hip:* flexion-extension, hyperextension, mediolateral rotation
   b. *Ankle:* dorsiflexion and plantar flexion
   c. *Elbow:* flexion-extension
   d. *Radioulnar joint:* pronation-supination
   e. *Shoulder joint:* mediolateral rotation

5. Are there differences between individuals in any of the above movements? Why?

6. Locate a person who can hyperextend the knees. Measure the ROM of the knee flexion and extension motion. What stops the flexion motion? What stops the extension motion? Locate a person who cannot hyperextend the knees. Answer the same questions as above and compare and discuss the differences.

SECTION 3

THE LINK SYSTEM AND ITS MOVEMENTS

As we have seen from studying the skeleton and its articulations, the body is composed of segments linked together at their articulations. Thus, we say that the body is basically a system consisting of movable segments or links. The skeleton may be divided into minute divisions for precise description in which each bone, no matter how small, is considered a separate unit; or it may be divided into the largest possible units for simplicity (e.g., the head, neck, and trunk; the upper extremity; and the lower extremity). The more numerous the identified links, the more precise the description of what the body is doing; however, the description may become too intricate for practical purposes. The fewer the links, the simpler the description. If too few are included, however, identification of many important movements is impossible. Thus we must compromise. For our purposes, the body is divided into 11 functional segments, or links: head and neck, thorax and thoracic vertebrae, lumbar vertebrae, pelvis, thigh, leg, foot, shoulder girdle, arm, forearm, and hand. Technically, some of these segments are made up of more than one link (e.g., the shoulder girdle, the vertebral column, the hand, and the foot). The links are shown in Figure A.7.

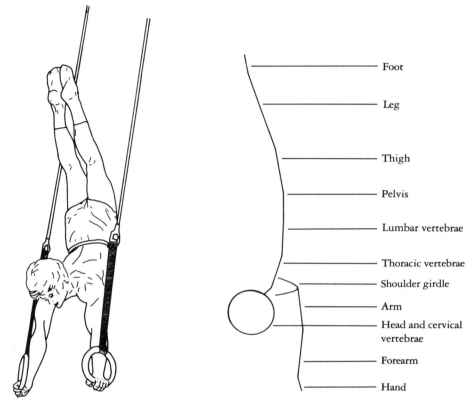

Figure A.7.   The segmental links, used in describing human movement, identified for a body on the rings.

Anatomical Position

The upright position, in which all joints are extended and the palms are facing forward, is called the anatomical position of the body. The skeleton in Figure A.1a illustrates the anatomical position.

Although this position is a convenient one to begin movement description, it is not a practical position to use when studying human movement because most movements of the body in sport or daily activities are not initiated from the anatomical position. Starting positions in sport activities begin from an infinite number of positions, and the movement patterns proceeding from these positions also involve complicated combinations. By using the anatomical position as a frame of reference, however, it is easy to describe and define the movements and positions of muscles, bones, and ligaments.

Body and Segmental Planes and Axes

A concept that is useful in defining segmental and body movements is the concept of the **plane of motion** created by a movement and an **axis of rotation** around which the movement occurs. If one were to punch a hole in the center of a piece of cardboard and insert a pencil through the hole, one would have a representation of a plane (cardboard) and an axis (pencil). If a dot were drawn on the cardboard, it would circle around the pencil when the cardboard was rotated around the pencil.

The pencil represents an axis *around* which movement occurs. The cardboard represents a plane of movement *along* which movement occurs. Thus, the dot on the cardboard moves *around* the axis (pencil) and *along* the plane (cardboard). If the pencil axis were inserted through a human body from the right side to the left side, the body could turn around the axis and move along the plane. Note that the axis and the plane are always perpendicular to each other; that is, they form a 90-degree angle.

When an axis runs in a side-to-side direction relative to the body, as in this example, it is called a **mediolateral** (ML) **axis.** (The ML axis is sometimes referred to as the frontal axis or the transverse axis.) The rotation of the body or any segment around an ML axis is along an invisible plane that is perpendicular to the axis. This plane, which divides the body into right and left sections, is called a **sagittal plane.** Movement of the total body around an ML axis and along a sagittal plane is shown in Figure A.8a.

When the axis and plane are used to describe total body movement, as in the previous example, they are designated as the **body's axis** or **plane.** In cases where the body rotates free of support, the body's plane and axis of movement pass through its center of gravity (CG). The planes and axes that pass through the body's CG

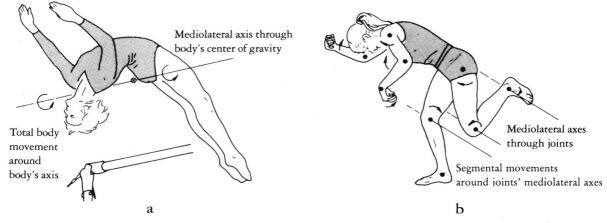

Mediolateral axis through body's center of gravity

Total body movement around body's axis

Mediolateral axes through joints

Segmental movements around joints' mediolateral axes

a

b

(a) Movements of the total body around the body's mediolateral axis and along a sagittal plane.
(b) Segmental movements around a mediolateral axis and along a sagittal plane.

Figure A.8.

divide the body into equally distributed mass halves (right and left, top and bottom, front and back), and they are called **principal** or **cardinal** planes and axes. In the example in Figure A.8a, the body is moving along a principal sagittal plane and around a principal ML axis. When the body is supported by the ground or another surface, the planes and axes of total body movement are not necessarily through the body's CG. For example, a gymnast swinging around the high bar moves along a sagittal plane and around an ML axis located at the bar, not through the body's CG. The axis in this illustration is not a principal axis.

A body segment that moves along a sagittal plane and around an ML axis is a **segmental plane** and **axis.** The plane and axis have the same orientation as the body's plane and axis of movement, but are located through the joint in which the movement occurs. Example movements are lifting the arm or the leg forward from the anatomical position. Shown in Figure A.8b are segmental movements occurring around ML axes and along sagittal planes. The location of these segmental axes is through the respective joints that are represented by dots.

Other examples of segmental movements around an ML axis and along a sagittal plane include pulling the foot up toward the leg, flexing the elbow joint, and bending over to touch the floor.

If the total body is turning in the air as in an aerial cartwheel as shown in Figure A.9, the body is turning around an axis that runs through the body from front to back, and the body is moving along a plane that passes from side to side (Figure A.9a).

In this case, the plane is called a **frontal plane** because it divides the body into front and back parts. The axis around which the body turns is passing from front to back and is called the body's **anteroposterior** (AP) **axis** or sagittal axis. A segmental movement also may be around a joint's AP axis and along the joint's frontal plane. Figure A.9b illustrates the motion of the arm and leg when moving around an AP axis and along a frontal plane of the shoulder and hip, respectively.

Other examples of moving segments around the AP axis and along a frontal plane include flexing the trunk or the head to the side and moving the hand toward the thumb side or little-finger side of the forearm.

The third possibility for movements is represented in Figure A.10. The total body is performing a twisting movement around an axis running from the head end to the foot end of the body. The motion of the body is along a plane that is perpendicular to the axis and that divides the body into upper and lower parts. The axis is called the body's **longitudinal axis,** and the plane, the body's **transverse plane** (Figure A.10a).

The segmental movements shown in Figure A.10b are around a longitudinal axis and along a transverse plane. The segmental longitudinal axes are longitudinal relative to the bones and segments that are moving and not necessarily longitudinal relative to the total body. The plane and axis are mutually perpendicular and pass through the joint centers where the movements are taking place, in this case, the respective hip and shoulder joints. Other movements of the body segments around longitudinal axes and along transverse planes include rotating the head to the side and rotating the forearms in order to turn the hands.

Total body movement around anteroposterior axis

a

Segmental movements around joints' anteroposterior axes

b

Motions of the body (a) and of the arm and leg (b) when moving around the anteroposterior axis and along the frontal plane.

Figure A.9.

Segmental movements around longitudinal axis of shoulder and hip joints

Total body movement around body's longitudinal axis

a

b

(a) Total body movement around the body's longitudinal axis and along the body's transverse plane.
(b) Segmental movements around a segmental longitudinal axis and along a segmental transverse plane.

Figure A.10.

In daily activities, sports, and games, the human body rarely uses the anatomical position, and movement occurs infrequently along only one of the three principal planes. Most movement occurs diagonally among all the principal planes. Aside from isolated movements such as a forearm curl, movements of the body begin and end from positions that require rather complicated descriptions. Nevertheless, all movements of the body segments take place around axes and along the planes perpendicular to the axes.

Since all possible axes and planes do not have individual names, those other than the ones described previously are called **diagonal** or oblique. The diagonal axis and the diagonal plane can be imagined in space, and the plane along which a movement occurs is always perpendicular to the axis around which it occurs. Figure A.11a shows the diagonal plane of motion and axis of rotation of a golfer in the midst of a swing.

To locate the axis and plane for the golfer's upper extremity movement, we can start by demonstrating the plane of that movement, or the plane along which the arm and club travel during the swing. The plane is diagonal; that is, it does not correspond to any single one of the three body planes just described. The plane is diagonal to the ground, and the axis is perpendicular to the plane.

A second example of a diagonal movement is the leg motion in a football punt (Figure A.11b). As the leg is brought up and forward, it moves across the front of the body slightly, thus producing a diagonal movement. The axis for the motion of the thigh is through the hip joint, and the plane of motion follows along the motion of the thigh and is diagonal to the three body planes previously described.

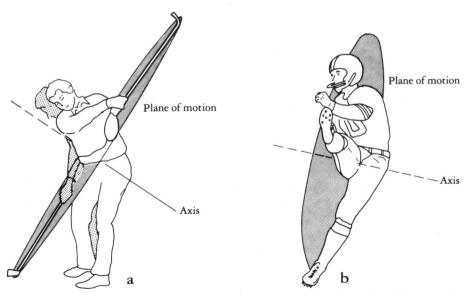

Figure A.11.   (a) A golfer during the swing of the club, showing the plane and axis of rotation of the left arm. (b) A football punt, showing plane and axis of motion of the lower extremity.

Terminology for Describing Segmental Movements

As we have seen, any skeletal link (segment) moves around an axis that passes through a joint and along a plane. Movements are named according to the articulation where the movement occurs and not for the segment doing the moving (e.g., elbow flexion rather than forearm flexion). Most movements of the segments occurring at the articulation can be categorized according to the plane of movement and the joint's axis of rotation. The unique movements of some joints are designated by special terms. Although the movement terms are somewhat the same from joint to joint, they usually must be memorized. As an aid to memorization, Tables A.1 through A.3 list the joint movements occurring around similar axes and along similar planes. With the exception of the transverse motions at the shoulder and hip joints, the movements may be initiated from the anatomical position.

Table A.1.

SEGMENTAL MOVEMENTS OCCURRING AROUND A MEDIOLATERAL AXIS AND ALONG A SAGITTAL PLANE

Movement Names	Articulations
Flexion, extension, and hyperextension	Hip, knee, shoulder, elbow, wrist, phalangeal joints, and vertebral column
Dorsiflexion and plantar flexion	Ankle joint
Transverse abduction (extension) and transverse adduction (flexion)[a]	Shoulder and hip joints

[a]Transverse abduction (extension) and adduction (flexion) movements occur around the ML axis and along the sagittal plane of the humerus and femur if moved into the transverse *body* plane by abduction of the shoulder or hip joints.

Table A.2

SEGMENTAL MOVEMENTS OCCURRING AROUND AN ANTEROPOSTERIOR AXIS AND ALONG A FRONTAL PLANE

Movement Names	Articulations
Lateral flexion	Vertebral column
Abduction and adduction	Shoulder, hip, and metatarsophalangeal joints
Radial and ulnar flexion (deviation)	Wrist joint
Elevation and depression	Sternoclavicular joint
Upward and downward rotation	Acromioclavicular joint
Transverse abduction (flexion) and adduction (extension)[a]	Shoulder and hip joints

[a]Transverse abduction and adduction movements occur around the AP axis and along the frontal plane of the humerus and femur if moved into the transverse *body* plane by flexion of the shoulder or hip joints.

Table A.3.   **SEGMENTAL MOVEMENTS OCCURRING AROUND A LONGITUDINAL AXIS AND ALONG A TRANSVERSE PLANE**

Movement Names	Articulations
Medial and lateral rotation	Shoulder and hip joints; knee joint at 90-degree flexion
Pronation and supination	Radioulnar joint
Transverse rotation	Vertebral column
Protraction and retraction[a]	Sternoclavicular joint[b]
Inversion and eversion	Subtalar joint (talocalcaneal)

[a]Protraction and retraction of the shoulder girdle are sometimes called abduction and adduction, respectively, when referring to the movement of the scapula relative to the vertebral column.

[b]Axis and plane are named relative to the sternum, not to the clavicle.

MEDIOLATERAL AXIS–SAGITTAL PLANE MOVEMENTS

Table A.1 lists the articulations and their movements that occur around an ML axis and along a sagittal plane. Movements illustrating these joint motions around an ML axis and along a sagittal plane are shown in Figure A.12a–h.

ANTEROPOSTERIOR AXIS–FRONTAL PLANE MOVEMENTS

Table A.2 lists the articulations and their movements that occur around an AP axis and along a frontal plane. Movements illustrating these joint motions around AP axis and along a frontal plane are shown in Figure A.13a–f.

LONGITUDINAL AXIS–TRANSVERSE PLANE MOVEMENTS

Table A.3 lists the articulations and their movements that occur around a longitudinal axis and along a transverse plane. Movements illustrating these joint motions around a longitudinal axis and along a transverse plane are shown in Figure A.14a–f.

In free space, the entire body may move around an axis and along a plane. The body's axis and plane associated with a given total body movement remains the same no matter what orientation the body segments assume. For instance, Figure A.15 shows a body turning around its ML axis in tuck, pike, layout, and back-arch positions. Similarly, with segmental motion, the joint's axis and plane remain the same no matter what orientation the body part assumes or what position the body is in. For instance, the flexion of the elbow occurs around the elbow's ML axis whether it is flexed from anatomical position or flexed when the arm is abducted at the shoulder joint.

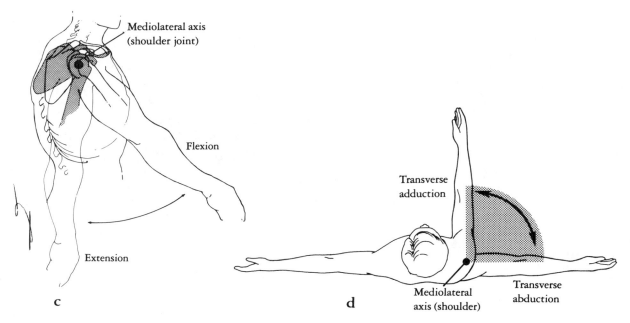

Segmental movements illustrating joint motion around a mediolateral axis and along a sagittal plane.   **Figure A.12.**

Figure A.12
continued

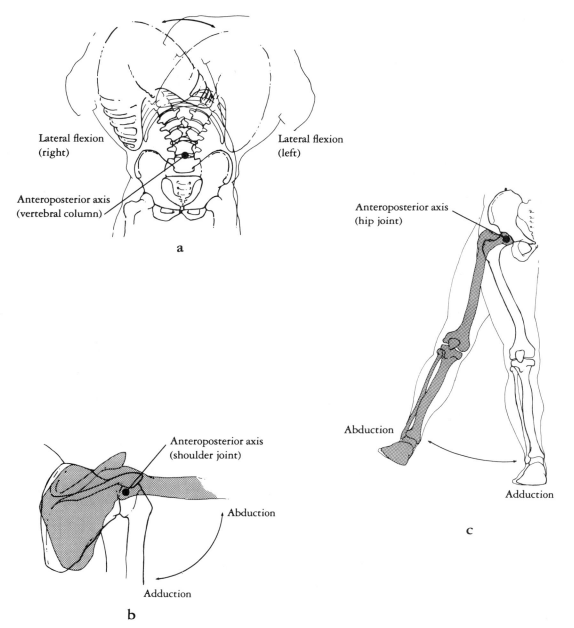

Segmental movements illustrating joint motion around an anteroposterior axis and along a frontal plane.   **Figure A.13.**

Figure A.13
continued

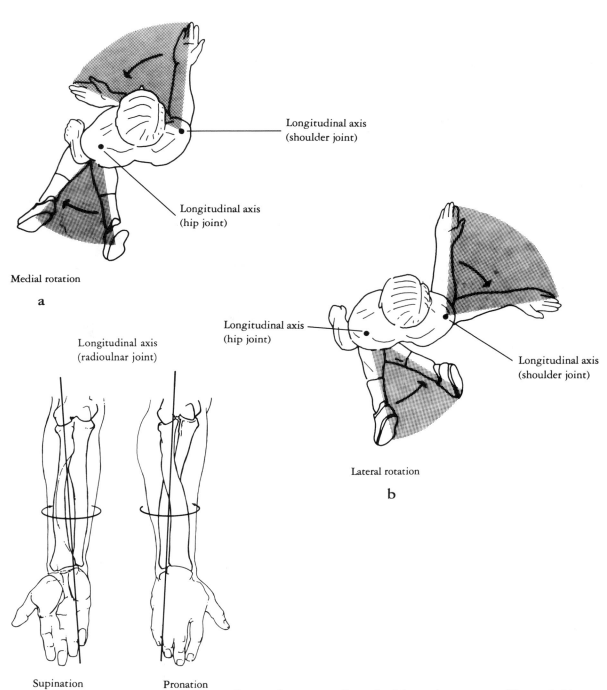

Longitudinal axis
(shoulder joint)

Longitudinal axis
(hip joint)

Medial rotation

a

Longitudinal axis
(radioulnar joint)

Longitudinal axis
(hip joint)

Longitudinal axis
(shoulder joint)

Lateral rotation

b

Supination   Pronation

c

Segmental movements illustrating joint motion
around a longitudinal axis and along a transverse plane.

Figure A.14.

Figure A.14
continued

Tuck

Pike

Layout

Back arch

A body turning in space in four different body positions around similar parallel axes: (a) tuck, (b) pike, (c) layout, and (d) back arch.

Figure A.15.

Spatial Planes and Axes and Orientation of the Moving Body

The planes and axes just described were identified according to their relationship to the human body. That is, if a plane cuts the body or segment into right and left parts, that plane is called sagittal and the axis perpendicular to it is called mediolateral; if a plane cuts the body or segment into front and back parts, it is called frontal and the axis perpendicular to it is called anteroposterior; and if a plane cuts the body or segment into upper or lower parts, it is called transverse and the axis perpendicular to it follows the length of a body or segment and is called longitudinal.

Planes, axes, and directions of movement may also be identified according to their relationship to the ground. They are then called **spatial** planes, axes, and directions. Since there are three dimensions in space, there are three planes and axes so named. The two axes that are perpendicular to each other and horizontal to the ground are designated the x and y axes. The x axis is that axis parallel to the ground and directed to the observer's right and left, right being designated positive and left being designated negative. The y axis is that axis parallel to the ground and directed forward and backward from the observer, the forward direction being positive and the backward, negative. The third axis, which is perpendicular to the other two, is a vertical axis, and is designated the z axis. The upward direction along this axis is positive, and the downward direction is negative. These axes are shown in Figure A.16.

The x, y, and z axes may be used to describe the direction of movement of the body or an object. For instance, the path of the golf ball shown in Figure A.16 may be described in this manner: the ball moves along the fairway in the positive x direction, but may drop in the negative z direction or slice in the positive y direction.

When the body is standing in the anatomical position, the longitudinal body axis corresponds to the z axis, the ML body axis corresponds to the x axis, and the AP body axis corresponds to the y axis.

When the spatial orientations x, y, and z are used, the body may be moving around a single spatial axis (the z axis, for example) while also moving around any one of the body's three principal axes. Figure A.17a, b, and c shows a body moving around the x spatial axes while moving around the body's AP axis (Figure A.17a), the body's longitudinal axis (Figure A.17b), or the body's ML axis (Figure A.17c).

In such cases, designating both the spatial plane and axis and the body's plane and axis is important for visualizing the movement in space as well as the position the body has assumed relative to that plane and axis.

An understanding of the spatial, body, and segmental planes and axes of movement facilitates description of any movement of the body or its segments that occurs during human movement and sport activities.

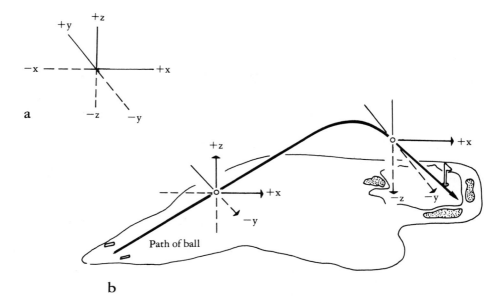

Figure A.16. Spatial axes for the directions of motion of a spinning golf ball during its flight.

A body moving around a single spatial axis while assuming different positions.

Figure A.17.

UNDERSTANDING THE BODY'S LINK SYSTEM AND ITS MOVEMENTS

1. Refer to Figure A.6. For each articulation labeled, list all the anatomical movements possible. Demonstrate each. Name the plane and axis used for each of the movements listed.

2. Demonstrate the anatomical position and movements along each of the three anatomical planes and around each of three axes of the body. Identify and name the plane and axis of the total body movement used in each of the following figures: H.2, 12.5, and 12.8.

3. Experiment with the articulations of the body previously named. Determine the number of axes around which the more distal segment moves. (Since there are only three axes, the number will be zero, one, two, or three: nonaxial, uniaxial, biaxial, or triaxial, respectively.)

4. For the body illustrated in Figure A.6, name the segments in the body's link system most important to the biomechanist.

5. List all the articulations that are triaxial, that are biaxial, and that are uniaxial.

6. For the following movements, list the axis and plane used during the force phase of the movement: (a) the breathing movement for the front crawl (neck), (b) the vertical jump (knee), (c) the elementary backstroke (shoulder joint), (d) the forehand drive in tennis (shoulder joint), (e) the placekick (knee), (f) turning a door handle (radioulnar joint).

7. For each of the following figures, list the articulation through which the axis of rotation is passing, the axis and plane being used, the segment that is moving, and the anatomical movement name: 3.15a and b, 3.20b, 3.21, 5.5, 5.8, 12.6, 12.8, and IV.5.

8. With the help of a partner, perform an easy run, a sit-up, a jumping jack, and a push-up. Describe the articulations being used, the axis and plane of movement of each segment being moved, and the degrees of motion of each segment.

9. With the help of a partner, perform the following movements: (a) flex the knee 90 degrees, (b) abduct the hip 30 degrees, (c) transverse abduct the shoulder 60 degrees, (d) medially rotate the shoulder joint 20 degrees, (e) laterally rotate the hip 30 degrees, (f) pronate the radioulnar joint 180 degrees, (g) medially rotate the knee 10 degrees, (h) laterally rotate the knee 20 degrees, (i) invert the subtalar joint as far as possible, (j) flex the elbow 90 degrees and then flex the fingers as far as possible and move the wrist in radial and ulnar flexion.

10. From the anatomical position, rotate the shoulder. (To be sure the movement is from the shoulder joint, flex the elbow.) How far does it rotate medially? laterally? What is the ROM of the pronation and supination of the radioulnar joint? At what joint do these movements occur? Explain the difference between the rotation of the shoulder joint and the rotation of the radioulnar joint. When the elbow is extended, what is the total ROM of the hand rotation together with the shoulder and forearm rotations? Can you think of any sport examples of using these structures and motions in combination?

11. For the objects rotating around axes in the following figures, name the spatial axis of rotation (x, y, or z): A.8a, A.9a, 8.9, 12.9, and 12.17.

SECTION 4

ANTHROPOMETRIC CHARACTERISTICS OF THE BODY

Many factors contribute to an athlete's success or effectiveness in exercise and sport performance. Among these factors are motivation, nutrition, interest, and opportunity for practice. Moreover, an athlete's size, weight, proportions, or physique also contribute to performance effectiveness in many sports and exercises. For example, a professional basketball player is typically thought of as being larger than average and a female gymnast, as being smaller than average. Size factors are related to **anthropometics**, a subdiscipline concerning the measurement of size, shape, and proportions of the human body and its segments. The area of study concerned with the physical measurements of the human body as they relate to physical development, exercise, and sport performance is **kinanthropometrics** (Hebbelinck and Ross 1974).

Because the gathering of anthropometric data is often time consuming, studies using human measurements do not employ the exact measures of single subjects but rather use data gathered from a population of similar subjects. Subjects are most frequently grouped by gender and by athletic event. The most gross generalizations are those comparing male athletes to female athletes across all events. Many investigations compare anthropometric measures within gender and between sport groups, such as between female high jumpers and female sprinters or between male weight lifters and male wrestlers. Care must be taken, however, when considering *average values* from grouped data because stereotypes of a group's physical characteristics may be developed from averages or norms. One should keep in mind that averages represent nothing more than a general impression of a group of individuals, each of whom actually may be quite different from the average. In fact, wide variations frequently exist among individuals measured.

A comparison between the heights of males and females is an example of the misuse of group means. To believe that all males are taller than all females because the mean height for males is greater than the mean height for females is obviously erroneous. Similar stereotypical descriptions of weight, body fat, muscular endurance, strength, and other physical characteristics also may be misused. Physical characteristics of individuals within a population range from the greatest to the least on a continuum, and the division of a population into two or more groups usually results in considerable overlap of the groups. The heights of males and females are estimated to overlap by 60%; that is, according to heights, the upper 60% of females coincide with the lower 60% of the males.

A second consideration when using anthropometric data is the unclarity of how much of any measure is dependent on genetic factors and how much is dependent on an individual's training activity over several years. Although training does not affect a person's height, it does affect a person's weight. Whenever weight of the total body or of its segments is considered, the data are influenced by the individual's training state. deVries (1980) discusses a heavyweight class U.S. weight lifter who gave up his weight lifting career and took up long-distance running. After three years, he had lost 64 lb of body weight, and his total snatch and clean-and-jerk lift weight had decreased by 196 lb. When his lift was measured per unit of body weight, however, he was stronger after three years of running than when he had been weight lifting competitively. He had lifted 3.23 lb per pound of body weight competitively, but lifted 3.30 lb per pound of body weight as a distance runner. Other measures affected by training are circumferences of segments, lean body weight, and segmental proportions.

A third factor relating to anthropometric data concerns biomechanical advantage an individual may have due to a given anthropomtric measure. Any biomechanical advantage must be considered in light of other characteristics of the athelete, such as physiological capacities. In addition, certain anthropometric measures are more important for success in some events than others. For example, weight is more important to success in wrestling than in throwing events. Within a given event some anthropometric measures contribute more biomechanically to an individual's success than do other anthropometric measures. For example, height is more important than arm length for success in jumping.

Height and Weight

The most commonly encountered anthropometric measures, and those most easily gathered, are the height and weight of the body. The mean height and weight values for male and female athletes who participated in the 1968 Olympics are presented in Figure A.18.

Expected differences occur among heights and weights of athletes in different events. Male basketball players are the tallest, and weight throwers, the heaviest. Female gymnasts and divers are among the shortest and lightest. Hebbelinck and Ross (1974) report that in sports in which greater height has a biomechanical advantage, the mean height of athletes tends to increase over the years. Due to the selection process, the mean height of basketball players, rowers, and weight throwers as a group is increasing, whereas the mean height of athletes in events in which height does not give an advantage, such as gymnastics, is remaining stable. The height-weight relationship is important in wrestling since weight limitations exist within classifications. Although a long-limbed tall wrestler has an advantage in reaching and in increasing the size of his base for increased stability, a short opponent is likely to be a stronger wrestler. The short wrestler's weight consists of more muscle mass than the tall wrestler's weight, which consists of more skeletal weight.

Ponderal Index

The **ponderal index** (PI) is a measure of stature, or stoutness. It is determined by a particular ratio of the height and weight of an individual. One equation used to calculate the PI is the following:

Equation A.1

$$PI = 10^3 \times \sqrt[3]{W}/H$$

where W is body weight and H is body height.

According to the equation, two people of equal weight and height have equal stature, or PI. Given equal weight, a tall person has a smaller stature, or PI, than a short person. On the other hand, if two people are the same height, their PIs vary according to their weight differences. The person weighing the most has the larger

Mexico Olympics 1968

Height and weight anthropometric parameters of 1968 Olympic athletes (adapted from Hebbelinck and Ross 1974).   **Figure A.18.**

PI. The PIs of elite athletes do not vary considerably between most events. Table A.4 presents data on several groups of Olympic athletes from the 1928, 1960, 1964, 1968, and 1972 games (Hebbelinck and Ross 1974).

The distance runners and the basketball players tend to have the smallest PIs, whereas the throwers tend to have the greatest. Surprisingly, the marathon runners have a slightly higher PI than the 5,000-m and 10,000-m runners. As one would expect, the marathoners are lighter, but they are also shorter. Thus, the marathoners are more short than they are light as compared to the distance runners, and consequently their PI is slightly greater.

Before basketball players were encouraged to weight train, they were tall, lean, and had relatively little body mass. Their PI was small because they were relatively light. Since weight training has been incorporated into basketball conditioning programs, players have increased their muscle mass and have become heavier. Although as a group they have also become taller, their PI has increased because their average weight has increased more than their average height. PI does not distinguish between fat weight and muscular weight.

Somatotype

Related to an athlete's measure of stature is the measure of body type, or configuration. Although qualitative assessment of body types was used by the ancient Greeks, the best-known classification system, **somatotyping**, was named and developed by Sheldon in the 1940s. Somatotyping uses three classifications: the endomorph, the mesomorph, and the ectomorph. The **ectomorph** is described as being tall and thin; the **endomorph,** as being short and fat; and the **mesomorph,** as being stout and muscular. The mesomorph is what is commonly termed an "athletic build" (Morehouse and Rasch 1963).

Since Sheldon's work, the somatotyping process has undergone many refinements. Because no definite delineations exist among the types, a person can have a somatotype consisting of differing degrees of all three components. The most commonly used rating method is the Heath-Carter somatotype method. The rating is a quantitative assessment of the amount of all three components. The endomorphic component is the relative fatness of the body; the mesomorpohic component is a musculoskeletal rating per unit of body height; and the ectomorphic component is the "linearity" of the body. In a study using the Heath-Carter method, athletes rated higher on mesomorphy and lower on endomorphy than nonathletes. Athletes from different sports varied in their degrees of endomorphy and ectomorphy, but all the athletes had a high mesomorphy component.

Body Proportions

Absolute measures—the height of the body and the length of its segments—are probably more important than the sizes of the segments relative to each other.

HEIGHT (cm), WEIGHT (kg), AND PONDERAL INDEX FOR OLYMPIC COMPETITORS IN SELECTED OLYMPIC GAMES

Table A.4.

Event	Amsterdam 1928	Rome 1960	Tokyo 1964	Mexico 1968	Munich 1972
100 m, 200 m, 4 × 100 m					
Height	172.7	177.7	176.0	175.4	176.0
Weight	64.7	70.8	70.8	68.4	69.8
Ponderal index	23.25	23.28	23.51	23.32	23.39
800 m and 1,500 m					
Height	174.4	180.5	177.0	177.3	177.2
Weight	66.7	68.9	65.8	65.0	67.2
Ponderal index	23.25	22.71	22.81	22.68	22.94
5,000 m and 10,000 m					
Height	167.7	172.2	173.6	171.9	172.4
Weight	60.3	60.7	60.3	59.8	61.3
Ponderal index	23.11	22.82	22.84	22.75	22.87
Marathon					
Height	166.1	168.3	170.3	168.7	170.0
Weight	59.6	60.2	60.8	56.6	60.2
Ponderal index	23.52	23.29	23.09	22.76	23.05
Jumpers					
Height	178.9	179.9	181.4	182.8	181.6
Weight	69.1	71.9	73.2	73.2	73.8
Ponderal index	22.94	23.06	23.06	22.88	23.10
Throwers					
Height	180.09	191.3	187.3	186.1	187.4
Weight	88.6	101.7	101.4	102.3	107.3
Ponderal index	24.64	24.40	24.90	25.13	25.36
Javelin					
Height	180.9	182.2	183.0	179.5	181.4
Weight	88.6	87.3	83.4	76.5	87.5
Ponderal index	24.64	24.35	23.87	23.65	24.47
Basketball					
Height		189.7	189.4	189.1	192.6
Weight		79.5	84.3	79.7	85.5
Ponderal index		22.67	23.15	22.76	22.87
Rowers					
Height	181.1		186.0	185.1	185.5
Weight	76.9		82.2	82.2	84.5
Ponderal index	23.48		23.38	23.49	23.66
Gymnasts					
Height	169.6		167.2	167.4	168.0
Weight	61.8		63.3	61.6	64.1
Ponderal index	23.31		23.84	23.59	23.82

Adapted from Hebbelinck and Ross 1974.

Basketball, high jumping, throwing events, and volleyball are sports in which the absolute height of the body is important to success; the taller, the better. Given two performers of equal height, however, measurements can reveal quite different **proportions,** or relative lengths, of the segments making up that height. One person may have long lower extremities and a relatively short trunk; the other person may have a long trunk and short lower extremities; yet a third may have equally proportioned extremities and trunk. All would be the same height when standing. When seated, however, the person with the longest trunk would be taller than the person with the shortest trunk. If these same individuals were seated against a wall so that their legs were extended out from that wall, their leg lengths would reflect the opposite difference of their seated heights. Figure A.19 illustrates the average arm, leg, and trunk lengths of athletes in the 1968 Olympics.

ARM LENGHTHS

Long upper extremity segments are advantageous to athletes in sports that include throwing and striking skills because a long lever affords greater ROM than a short lever. A long-armed boxer, wrestler, and martial artist have a distinct advantage in reach over a short-armed opponent. Notice in Figure A.19 that basketball players, weight throwers, and rowers have the greatest arm lengths. The shortest arm lengths are found in gymnasts, divers, canoe paddlers, and weight lifters.

LEG LENGTHS

Proportional differences may give certain athletes a biomechanical advantage in their sport. Athletes with the greatest leg lengths are reported to be basketball players, weight throwers, rowers, and field event athletes. The shortest leg lengths occur in gymnasts, divers, wrestlers and boxers.

The **crural index,** the ratio of the length of the lower leg to that of the thigh, is used to describe the proportions of the leg. A ratio greater than one indicates a leg longer than a thigh; a ratio less than one indicates a leg shorter than a thigh.

A study of the proportions of animals of different species indicates that the fast runners and jumpers are those that have long distal segments, such as the horse, kangaroo, and the cat. The thigh segment of these animals is short, ending before the segment leaves the pelvis or flank area. The leg segment is longer than the thigh; the foot segment is the longest, and the toes are also quite long. The animals described as the best jumpers have a leg considerably longer than the thigh segment and therefore a large crural index.

Burke and Brush (1979) reported that a select group of teenage female distance runners had on the average a longer leg length to thigh length than the teenage female nonathlete. These authors speculated that a short thigh allows the runner to bring her leg through fast and with ease.

Long lower extremities are a disadvantage to the gymnast who must lift, hold, and swing those segments. Long legs offer greater resistance than short legs, and thus are often prohibitive to performing some gymnastic skills effectively. One

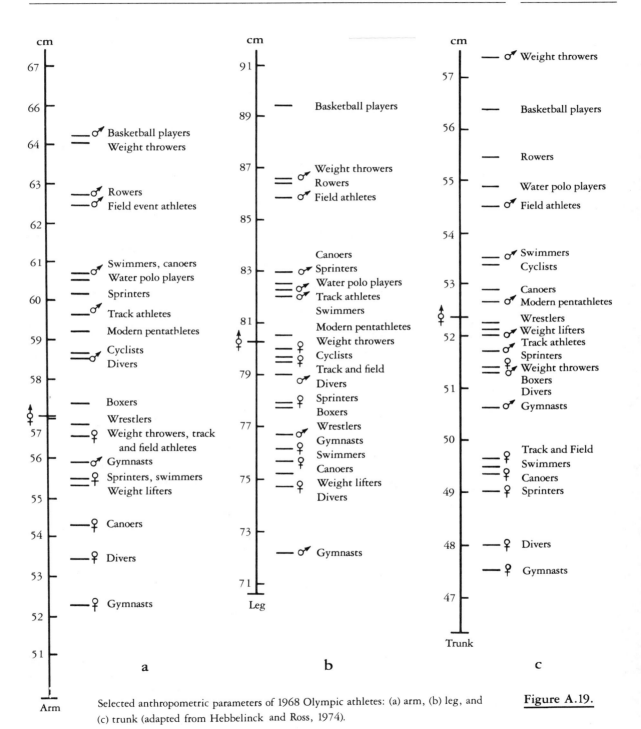

Selected anthropometric parameters of 1968 Olympic athletes: (a) arm, (b) leg, and (c) trunk (adapted from Hebbelinck and Ross, 1974).

Figure A.19.

should always keep this in mind when teaching gymnastics to the nonathletes, for the tall, long-legged person will surely be at a disadvantage.

TRUNK LENGTHS

Truck lengths follow the trends set for arm and leg length measures. Weight throwers have longer trunks than basketball players; however, both of these groups have the greatest trunk length compared to other athletes. Again, gymnasts, divers, and boxers have the shortest trunks.

Implications of Anthropometrics in Teaching and Coaching

The anthropometric characteristics of individuals are often used as a rationale for success or lack of success in a particular activity. Anthropometeric characteristics are certainly considered by coaches in selecting athletes for particular sports. (What basketball coach has not tried to recruit the tallest kid in the class?) Although a person's physical characteristics may provide an advantage, the effectiveness of movement patterns used to perform skills are also determined by these factors: the extent to which mechanical principles are used, motor ability, and motivation. For instance, individuals with long body segments experience more difficulty in performing many gymnastics skills than individuals of short stature; however, the quality (effectiveness) of a gymnastics performance also depends on the use and application of mechanical principles and the performer's motor ability, muscular strength, and endurance characteristics.

Physical characteristics may give a mechanical advantage in the performance of certain skills, especially in those events in which height or weight or both are primary factors for success. Therefore, learners should not be subjected to evaluative tools (skills tests) in which successful performance depends on the physical characteristics of the performer. For example, vertical jumping ability should not be assessed by measuring the height attained from the floor. Rather, it should be assessed by measuring the distance from an initial reach height to jump reach height since this method eliminates the influence of differing physical statures on the score.

UNDERSTANDING ANTHROPOMETRIC MEASURES

1. Record your height, weight, and the segmental lengths of your head and neck, pelvis, upper arm, forearm, hand, thigh, and leg. Calculate each segment's percentage of your total body height by dividing the length of each segment by your total height. Compare your percent lengths with those given for your gender in Appendix III.2. Compare and discuss your findings with others in the class. Make some generalizations for tall, short, and average-height people. Are the percentages the same regardless of height?

2. Calculate your PI using Equation A.1. In Table A.4, find the sport group that you most closely match. Discuss your findings with others in the class. Are the matches between the statures and sport groups plausible?

3. How could a person's PI contribute biomechanically to success in movement activities?

4. Calculate your crural index by dividing your leg length by your thigh length. Of what importance might this be to performance?

5. According to the data reported in Figures A.18 and A.19, to which sport groups do you closely compare in height, weight, arm length, leg length, and trunk length? List these sport groups. Are they different or generally the same? How do you explain the results?

6. Draw a person of average stature. Imagining that the person you drew has a PI of 25, draw a person with a PI of 21 and a person with a PI of 28.

REFERENCES
SUGGESTED READINGS

Acuff, R. V. "Advanced Skill Attainment and Skeletal Development." *Gymnast*, November 1975, 47.

Adams, J. E. "Bone Injuries in Very Young Athletes." *Clinical Orthopedics and Related Research* 58 (1968): 129–40.

American Academy of Pediatrics. "Weight Training and Weight Lifting: Information for the Pediatrician." *The Physician and Sportsmedicine* 11 (3) (1983): 157–61.

Arnold, J. A., Brown, B., Micheli, R. P., and Coker, T. "Anatomic and Physiologic Characteristics to Predict Football Ability." *American Journal of Sports Medicine* 8 (2) (1980): 119–22.

Benton, J. W. "Epiphyseal Fracture in Sports." *The Physician and Sportsmedicine* 10 (11) (1982): 63–71.

Booth, F. W., and Gould, E. W. "Effects of Training and Disuse on Connective Tissue." In *Exercise and Sports Science Reviews*, vol. 3, ed. J. H. Wilmore and J. F. Keogh, 95–103. Santa Barbara, Calif.: Journal Publishing Affiliates, 1975.

Bowers, K. D. "Patellar Tendon Avulsion As a Complication of Osgood-Schlatter's Disease." *American Journal of Sports Medicine* 9 (6) (1981): 356–59.

Burke, E. J., and Brush, F. C. "Physiological and Anthropometric Assessment of Successful Teenage Female Distance Runners." *Research Quarterly* 50 (2) (1979): 180–87.

Cage, J. B. "Intracondylar Fracture of the Femur in an Adolescent Athlete." *The Physician and Sportsmedicine* 11 (6) (1983): 115–18.

Carter, J. E. L. "Somatotypes of Female Athletes." In *The Female Athlete*, ed. J. Barnes, M. Hebbelinck, and A. Venerando, vol. 15, 85–116. Basel: S. Karger, 1981.

Clarke, H. H. "Characteristics of the Young Athlete: A Longitudinal Look." In *Kinesiology Review*, ed. D. H. Clarke, 33–42. Reston, Va.: AAPHERD, 1968.

deVries, H. A. *Physiology of Exercise.* Dubuque, Iowa: William C. Brown Co., 1980, 403–04.

Dominguez, R. H. "Shoulder Pain in Age Group Swimmers." In *Swimming Medicine IV: Proceedings of the Fourth International Congress on Swimming Medicine,* ed. B. Eriksson and B. Furberg, 105–09. Baltimore: University Park Press, 1978.

Fimrite, R. "Stress, Strain, and Pain." *Sports Illustrated,* 14 August 1978, 30–43.

Freedson, P. S., Mikevic, P. M., Loucks, A. B., and Girandolas, R. N. "Physique, Body Composition, and Psychological Characteristics of Competitive Female Body Builders." *The Physician and Sportsmedicine* 11 (6) (1983): 85–90.

Gerber, S. "Are Kids Too Young to Avoid Sports Injuries?" *Science Digest,* October 1975, 44–52.

Goldberg, V., and Aadalen, R. "Distal Tibial Epiphyseal Injuries: The Role of Athletics in 53 Cases." *American Journal of Sports Medicine* 6 (5) (1978): 255–62.

Gugenheim, J. J., et al. "Little League Survey: The Houston Study." *American Journal of Sports Medicine* 4 (5) (1976): 189–200.

Haas, A. D. "Kids' Sports Programs: How Safe." *Family Weekly,* 18 September 1977, 11–13.

Hebbelinck, M., and Ross, W. D. "Kinanthropometry and Biomechanics." In *Biomechanics IV: Proceedings of the Fourth International Seminar on Biomechanics,* ed. R. C. Nelson and C. A. Morehouse, 537–52. Baltimore: University Park Press, 1974.

Howard, M. H., and Piha, R. J. "Fractures of the Apophyses in Adolescent Athletes." *Journal of the American Medical Association* 192 (1965): 842–44.

Hunter, L. Y., and O'Connor, G. A. "Traction Apophysitis of the Olecranon." *American Journal of Sports Medicine* 8 (1) (1980): 51–52.

Jackson, D. "Low Back Pain in the Young Gymnast." *International Gymnast,* December 1976, 50.

James, S. L. "Biomechanical and Neuromuscular Aspects of Running." In *Exercise and Sport Science Reviews,* vol. 1, ed. J. Wilmore, 201–04. New York: Academic Press, 1973.

Jensen, R. K. "The Effect of a 12-Month Growth Period on the Body Moments of Inertia of Children." *Medicine and Science in Sports and Exercise* 13 (4) (1981): 238–42.

Katch, V. L., Katch, F. I., Moffatt, R., and Gittleson, M. "Muscular Development and Lean Body Weight in Body Builders and Weight Lifters." *Medicine and Science in Sports and Exercise* 12 (5) (1980): 340–44.

Kozar, B., and Lord, R. M. "Overuse Injury in the Young Athlete: Reasons for Concern." *The Physician and Sportsmedicine* 11 (1983): 116–22.

Krokenbuhl, G. S., Wells, C. L., Brown, C. H., and Ward, P. E. "Characteristics of National and World Class Female Pentathletes." *Medicine and Science in Sports* 11 (1) (1979): 20–23.

Krokenbuhl, G. S. "Influence of Exercise on Bone Growth and Metabolism." In *Kinesiology Review,* ed. D. H. Clarke, 43–48. Reston, Va.: AAPHERD, 1968.

Langley, L., and Christensen, J. B. *Structure and Function of the Human Body.* Minneapolis: Burgess Publishing, 1978.

Larson, R. L., and McMahan, R. O. "The Epiphyses and the Childhood Athlete." *Journal of the American Medical Association* 196 (1966): 607–12.

Larson, R. L. "Little League Survey: The Eugene Study." *American Journal of Sports Medicine* 4 (5) (1976): 201–09.

Marino, M. "Sports Medicine in Action: A Look at Swimming." *Muscle and Bone* 3 (3) (1983): 3–10.

Merriman, J. S. "Learning Descriptive Movement Terms." *JOPER* 47 (4) (1976): 52.

Micheli, L., and Jupiter, J. "Osteid Osteoma as a Cause of Knee Pain in the Young Athlete: A Case Study." *American Journal of Sports Medicine* 6 (4) (1978): 199–208.

Morehouse, L. E., and Rasch, P. A. *Sports Medicine for Trainers.* 2d ed. Philadelphia: W. B. Saunders, 1963.

Morey, E., and Baylink, D. "Inhibition of Bone Formation During Space Flight." *Science* 201 (22) (1978): 1138–41.

Morrison, W. G., Frank, H. F., and Greg, R. "An Analysis of Anthropometric Data from Female Olympic Rowers." In *Science in Sports: Proceedings of the International Congress of Sport Sciences,* ed. J. Terauds, 185–92. San Diego: Academic Publishers, 1979.

Morrow, J. R., Jackson, A.S., Hosler, W. W., and Kachwick, J. K. "The Importance of Strength, Speed, and Body Size for Team Success in Women's Intercollegiate Volleyball." *Research Quarterly* 50 (3) (1979): 429–37.

Nicholas, J. "Report of the Committee on Research and Education." *American Journal of Sports Medicine* 6 (5) (1978): 295–304.

Nilsson, S., and Roaas, A. "Soccer Injuries in Adolescents." *American Journal of Sports Medicine* 6 (6) (1978): 358–61.

Pappas, A. M. "Epiphyseal Injuries in Sports." *The Physician and Sportsmedicine* 11 (6) (1983): 140–48.

Perrott, J. W. *Structural and Functional Anatomy for Students and Teachers of Physical Education.* 3d ed. Baltimore: Williams & Wilkins, 1977.

Peterson, C. A., and Peterson, H. A. "Analysis of the Incidence of Injuries to the Epiphyseal Growth Plate." *The Journal of Trauma* 12 (1972): 275–81.

Plagenhoef, S., Evans, F. G., and Abdelnour, T. "Anatomical Data for Analyzing Human Motion." *Research Quarterly for Exercise and Sport* 54 (2) (1983): 169–78.

President's Council on Physical Fitness and Sports. "Joint and Body Range of Motion." *Physical Fitness and Research Digest* 5 (4) (1975): 17.

Pruett, D. M., and Lopez, R. "Preventing Injuries in Young Ballet Dancers." *JOPERD* 52 (October 1981): 26–29.

Rarick, G. L. "Motor Development: Its Growing Base." *JOPERD* 51 (September 1980): 26–27, 56–61.

Ryan, J. R., and Salciccioli, G. G. "Fractures of the Distal Radial Epiphysis in Adolescent Weight Lifters." *American Journal of Sports Medicine* 4 (1) (1976): 26–27.

Salter, R. B., and Harris, W. R. "Injuries Involving the Epiphyseal Plate." *Journal of Bone and Joint Surgery* 45A (1963): 587–622.

Schwab, S. A. "Epiphyseal Injuries in the Growing Athlete." *Canadian Medical Association Journal* 117 (1977): 626–30.

Shaffer, T. E. "The Uniqueness of the Young Athlete: Introductory Rewards." *American Journal of Sports Medicine* 8 (5) (1980): 370–71.

Shambes, G. M., and Campbell, S. "Inherent Movement Patterns in Man." In *Kinesiology III,* ed. C. J. Widule, 50–58. Reston, Va.: AAHPERD, 1973.

Slaughter, M. H., and Lobman, T. G. "An Objective Method for Measurement of Musculo-Skeletal Size to Characterize Body Physique with Application to the Athletic Population." *Medicine and Science in Sports and Exercise* 12 (3) (1980): 170–74.

Smith, E. L., Reddan, W., and Smith, P. E. "Physical Activity and Calcium Modalities for Bone Mineral Increase in Aged Women." *Medicine and Science in Sports and Exercise* 13 (1) (1981): 60–64.

Spence, D. W., Dinch, J. G., Fred, H. L., and Coleman, A. E. "Descriptive Profiles of Highly Skilled Women Volleyball Players." *Medicine and Science in Sports and Exercise* 12 (4) (1980): 299–302.

Stanitski, C. L. "Low Back Pain in Young Athletes." *The Physician and Sportsmedicine* 10 (10) (1982): 77–91.

Torg, J. "Little League: The Theft of a Carefree Youth." *The Physician and Sportsmedicine,* June 1973, 72–78.

Unverferth, L., and Olix, M. L. "The Effect of Local Steroid Injections on Tendon." *Journal of Sports Medicine* 1 (4) (1973): 31–37.

Ward, T., and Groppel, J. L. "Sport Implement Selection: Can It Be Based Upon Anthropometric Indicators?" *Motor Skills: Theory Into Practice* 4 (2) (1980): 103–10.

Wilkins, K. E. "The Uniqueness of the Young Athlete: Musculoskeletal Injuries." *American Journal of Sports Medicine* 8 (5) (1980): 377–82.

Wilmore, J. H. "Body Composition in Sport and Exercise: Directions for Future Research." *Medicine and Science in Sports and Exercise* 15 (1) (1983): 21–31.

Woods, G. W., Tullos, H., and King, J. "The Throwing Arm: Elbow Joint Injuries." *Journal of Sports Medicine* 1 (4) (1973): 43–47.

FUNDAMENTAL MECHANICAL CONCEPTS

Prerequisites

None

Concept Module Contents

65

HOW WE LOOK AT MOVEMENT—FRAME OF REFERENCE AND SYSTEM

The concepts related to force and the motion of bodies form the foundation for examining movement. Whether the movement is that of the human body or of some object or group of objects in the environment, its analysis should be based on an understanding of the ways in which things can move and how their movements are affected by different forces. A first step in examining movement is to identify the system. A **system** is a body or group of bodies or objects whose motion is to be examined; it might be an arm, a leg, a whole body, a pair of football players, a tennis ball, or a racket. To analyze the motion of the hand, for example, we would picture the hand as a segment subjected to the force of muscle pull, the contact forces at the wrist joint, gravity, and other environmental forces acting on it. Figure B.1 shows the hand isolated as the system to be examined.

We also need to identify some frame of reference within which a system's movement takes place. The frame of reference within which we view movement can be

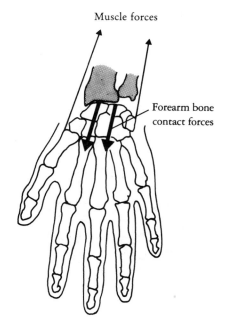

Muscle forces

Forearm bone
contact forces

Figure B.1.   The hand-wrist segment visualized as a system. Muscle forces acting across the wrist joint are external forces. The forearm bone contacting the wrist bones are also external forces acting on the system.

the stationary environment or something that is moving. Using something stationary as a frame of reference is the least complicated. For example, we can describe the motion of a runner in terms of the body's change in location relative to the ground or relative to space. If a body segment is the system being studied, the frame of reference might be an adjacent segment, the midline of the body, a point on the head, or some other reference point on the body or in the environment. In the chin-up shown in Figure B.2a the hand moves relative to the shoulder, but the hand does not move relative to the stationary environment (the bar).

The same arm movement occurs when a chin-up is simulated without a bar. The hand moves relative to the shoulder, but it also moves relative to the stationary environment (Figure B.2b). The body does not move relative to the bar as it did in the actual chin-up, however. Recognizing such relative motion of different parts of the body is important in analyzing movements of the body, its segments, and objects in the environment.

Some basic definitions for quantities related to human movement activities are presented in the sections that follow. Measurements of quantities are made in British or metric units; Appendix I contains British and metric equivalents. The Glossary is a handy source for quickly reviewing definitions of common biomechanical terms.

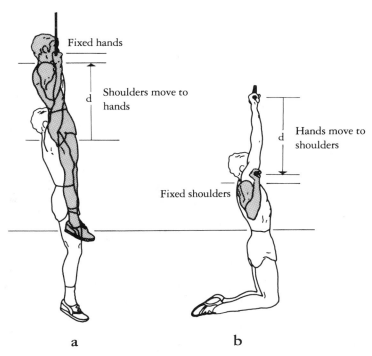

Motion occurs relative to a frame of reference. (a) The shoulders are pulled up to the stationary hands. (b) The hands and movable bar are pulled down to the stationary shoulders with the same elbow and shoulder joint movements.

Figure B.2.

SECTION 2

FORCE

A **force** can be thought of as a push or pull, a blow exerted by actual contact or the pull of the earth's gravitational attraction on a body within its field. In other words, a force is something that causes or tends to cause a change in the motion or shape of an object or body. It is measured in pounds (British units) or in Newtons (metric units). For example, you can push on a door with a force of 22 N (~5 lb) to open it.

SECTION 3

PRESSURE

The definition of **pressure** is the amount of force acting over a given area:

Equation B.1

$$p = F/A$$

where p is pressure, F is force, and A is area.

Pressure is expressed in Newtons per square centimeter or per square meter (N/m^2), or pounds per square inch ($lb/in.^2$ or psi). Pressure is not synonymous with force. For a given force, if the area is halved, the pressure is doubled. For example, a person weighing 400 N standing on both feet (area = 200 cm^2) exerts a pressure of 400 $N/200$ cm^2 = 2 N/cm^2 on the floor. The same person standing on only one foot exerts a pressure of 400 $N/100$ cm^2 = 4 N/cm^2.

SECTION 4

MASS AND WEIGHT

Any body is composed of a certain amount of matter, or **mass.** Mass is common to all material things, whether solid, liquid, or gaseous, and is a measure of a body's resistance to having its state of motion changed. The term given to such a resistance is *inertia.* Inertia is the property of a body or object that resists changes in the body's motion *in any direction.* The inertia of a body is related to how much mass the body possesses; the more mass, the more inertia. The inertia of the arm, for example, is less than the inertia of the leg because of the difference in their masses. The inertia, or sluggishness of a body, is measured by how many slugs (British) or kilograms (metric) of mass the body possesses.

Not to be confused with the mass of a body is the **weight** of the body. A body's weight is a measure of the force with which the earth pulls on the body's mass. Such a weight force always acts in a downward direction, toward the earth's center. A body's mass and weight are directly proportional; that is, the more mass a body has, the greater the earth's force of attraction on it, and therefore, the more it weighs. Mass and weight, however, should not be thought of as the same quantity. Weight is a force; mass is not. A person with a mass of 58 kg would weigh ~569 N. (In British, a mass of 4 slugs would weigh ~128 lb.)

Mass does not have a direction associated with it, nor does the mass of a body alter with changes in the gravitational force. Since the weight force is always directed downward toward the center of the earth, the magnitude of the body's weight will vary slightly according to differences in gravitational attraction. For example, a body will weigh slightly more at the earth's poles than at the equator because the magnitude of gravitational force is slightly greater at the poles.

SECTION 5

VOLUME AND DENSITY

The concept of mass is often confused with that of **volume,** or size. Volume is the space a body occupies; it has length, width, and height. It is not necessarily true that the larger a body, the greater its mass. Consider, for example, the relative mass of a golf ball and of an inflated balloon. The amount of matter in the golf ball is contained in a smaller volume (e.g., 40 cc) than is the matter in a balloon of 1000 cc (1 liter) of air and rubber. A golf ball also may be compared to a Ping-Pong ball. The golf ball has more mass within the same volume because the material inside is denser than the air inside the Ping-Pong ball. The **density** of an object or body is its mass per unit volume, or a measure of how compactly the body's matter is contained in its volume. Weight per unit volume is defined as the **weight-density** of a body.

$$WD = W/V$$

Equation B.2

where W is weight and V is volume.

For example, the weight-density of water is 9.9 N per liter (62.4 lb/cu ft), and the weight-density of air is about 0.01 N per liter (0.075 lb/cu ft). The fact that the weight-density of the human body is approximately the same as that of water is an important consideration in studying the buoyancy of the body in water.

Because the human body is composed of a variety of materials, its density is not uniform; that is, each body segment has a somewhat different density. The large thorax volume is not as massive or heavy as it appears due to the low-density air in the lungs. Bones, muscles, and body fluids are relatively high-density materials in the body, whereas fat and air have lower densities.

SECTION 6

CENTER OF GRAVITY

Recall that the earth exerts a force on each segment of a body in direct proportion to each segment's mass. The total effect of the force of gravity on a whole body, or system, is as if the force of gravity were concentrated at a single point called the **center of gravity** (CG). The center of a system's mass distribution also is called its **center of mass** and may be thought of as that point at which all the body's mass seems to be concentrated. The CG also can be thought of as the balance point of a system, since the system's mass balances out on all sides of this point. In a rigid object of uniform density, the CG is at the center of the object. In a segmental body whose parts can be rearranged, however, the location of the CG is dependent on the arrangement of the segments and their relative masses. Figure B.3 shows the locations of the CG for some familiar masses.

SECTION 7

WORK

Physical **work** is the product of force times the distance through which that force moves a load:

Equation B.3
$$w = F \times d$$

where w is work, F is force, and d is distance force is applied.

If a force of 10 N moved a body 5 m across a floor, the work done on that body would be 10 N × 5 m = 50 Nm. If the object did not move when the 10 N of force were applied, zero work would have been done even though the effort was felt.

SECTION 8

ENERGY

Energy is defined as the ability to do work. Many kinds of energy exist, such as heat, chemical, electrical, and mechanical. Mechanical energy is of primary significance in biomechanics, although in many instances the conversion of mechanical energy into heat occurs.

Center of gravity locations of some common systems.

Figure B.3.

Mechanical energy has three forms that are useful in understanding how the body interacts with the environment: kinetic energy, gravitational potential energy, and elastic potential energy.

Kinetic Energy

Kinetic energy is the energy a body or object has because of its motion. It is expressed by:

$$KE = 1/2 \ mv^2$$

Equation B.4

where KE is kinetic energy, m is mass, and v is speed.

The kinetic energy of a 10-kg medicine ball traveling at 3 m/sec is 1/2 (10 × 3²) = 45 Nm, which does work on the catcher who feels the force of impact during the time the ball's motion is brought to zero. The kinetic energy is transformed to heat energy in the catching process.

Gravitational Potential Energy

Whenever a body or object is in a position from which it can fall or be lowered by gravity, it possesses **potential energy** due to its height above the surface on which it will land. Quantitatively, gravitational potential energy is expressed by:

Equation B.5

$$PE = W \times h$$

where PE is gravitational potential energy, W is weight, and h is height above the surface.

A 400-N diver on a 10-m platform has $400 \times 10 = 4000$ Nm of potential energy before the dive. As the diver descends, the body progressively loses its potential energy because it is being converted into energy of motion, or kinetic energy. By the time the diver hits the water surface, all the body's energy is kinetic, and this kinetic energy performs the work of moving a large mass of water during entry as well as creating heat.

Elastic Potential Energy

Elastic energy, or *strain* energy, is the ability of a body or object to do work while it recoils (or reforms) after being stretched or compressed or twisted. All the implements and balls used in sport have some degree of elasticity, or recoil ability, that provide force. Springboards and trampolines and shoe soles have recoil ability. Human bones, muscles, and connective tissues have some elasticity, fortunately, that contributes significantly to movement efficiency in activities using wind-ups, or sudden stretching during muscle contraction. Kinetic energy is the energy used to deform the body or object, and it is converted into elastic energy and heat.

SECTION 9

POWER

In sport, the term **power** is often misused to describe feats of strength, or force application. Correctly, power is the product of force times the speed with which that force is applied. A strong, fast muscle contraction is more powerful than that same muscle force applied slowly. From another perspective, power is the rate during which physical work is performed. Both expressions use the same quantities for determining power:

Equation B.6

$$P = \frac{F \times d}{t} = F \times \frac{d}{t} = F \times v$$

where P is power, F is force applied, d is distance force is applied, t is time force is applied, and v is speed force is applied.

In biomechanics, looking at power in terms of force times velocity is meaningful. For example, a force of 100 N applied at a speed of 2 m/sec is a power output of 200 Nm/sec, or 200 watts.[1] The greatest power achieved for a particular effort is always a compromise between great force and great speed rather than a maximization of either one at the expense of the other. This is discussed further in the section on power training in Chapter 7.

SECTION 10

TYPES OF MOTION EXHIBITED BY A SYSTEM

A system's movement takes the form of **linear** motion or **rotary** *(angular)* motion or a combination of these types of motion.

Linear Motion

When a system is forced to move in a path that is a line, it exhibits linear motion, that is, a change in location from one place to another within a spatial frame of reference. If the path is a straight line, it is called *rectilinear,* and if the path is curved, it is called *curvilinear.* For example, a dropped ball travels a rectilinear path toward the ground, or a jumper travels a curvilinear path over a high bar. The path of a pencil along a ruler is rectilinear; the path of a thrown discus moving through the air is curvilinear. Using only the word *linear* to mean rectilinear is customary.

The distance (**d**) that a system moves in a straight line is measured in linear *measurement units* such as meters, feet, centimeters, inches, kilometers, or miles, and is called the linear **displacement** of a system.

Regardless of what the system is—the human body, a body segment, two body segments, or some object in the environment—we need to use some point in the system that represents the total system and whose motion we can follow. That point is the CG of the system. For example, to describe the path of a jogger's body, we would track his CG from moment to moment, and it would form a wavy horizontal line as he bounced along his way.

Rotary Motion

If some point within a system is restricted or secured so that the system rotates around this point when it receives a force, that point serves as an **axis of rotation,** and the motion is called rotary or angular motion. In the human body, each segment

---

1. 1 Nm/sec = 1 watt of power.

is connected to one or more adjacent segments to form joints. The joints serve as the location of the axes of rotation for the body segments. For instance, if you hold your elbow in 80 degrees of flexion and receive a weight in your hand, the force of the weight does not cause the entire forearm segment to move linearly downward because it is attached to the rest of the body or restricted from moving at the elbow joint, which provides resistance to downward motion of the elbow end of the forearm; the hand end of the forearm is free to move, however, and consequently rotates about the ML axis of the elbow joint (Figure B.4a).

The change in location of a rotating body is called its **angular displacement** and is designated by the Greek letter theta, θ. The path of a rotating body is measured in angular measurement units such as revolutions, degrees, and radians. (A radian is a proportion of a circle and is equivalent to approximately 57.3 degrees.)[2]

Equation B.7   radians = θ/57.3 degrees

where θ is angular displacement (in degrees).

Examples of angular displacement of a system exhibiting rotary motion include the sweeping of the second hand on a clock through 360 degrees with each revolution, shaking the head "no" as it rotates about a longitudinal axis through the neck, and rotating the forearm through 80 degrees as a weight is lowered (Figure B.4a).

Due to the structure of the body's skeletal system and the articulation of the segments, nearly all segmental movements are rotary. As a segment rotates, each single point on the segment describes its own circular path around the joint axis, as shown in Figure B.4b.

2. For more information about the radian, see Appendix V.

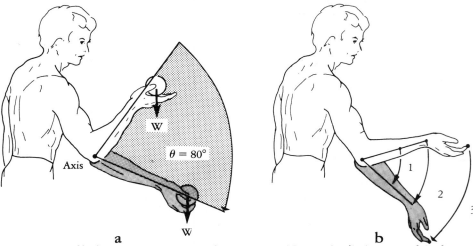

Figure B.4.   Rotary motion of body segments occurs around joint axes. (a) The angular displacement of the forearm/hand is 80 degrees. (b) The greater the radius of rotation of a point, the longer the curvilinear or circular path it forms around the axis.

The distance from any point on the rotating segment to the axis of rotation is called that point's **radius of rotation** and is the radius of the circle formed by that point as the segment rotates. The radius of the point and the length of the circular arc that the point forms are measured in linear measurement units (e.g., feet, meters, inches, centimeters) because they are linear distances. The entire rotating segment sweeps along an imaginary surface or plane, and the segment's movement (displacement) is measured in angular measurement units (degrees or radians).

Linear and Angular Motion

In most human movements the whole body or its segments or both move linearly and rotate at the same time. For example, the diver in Figure B.5 is falling linearly downward while simultaneously rotating around her CG, which serves as the axis of rotation for any rotating object free of support.

A somersaulting diver falling linearly downward exhibits rotary motion around her center of gravity.

Figure B.5.

Other examples in sport include the legs of a runner moving forward as they rotate around the knee joints, the body of a pole vaulter as he rotates around his grip on the pole while being thrust upward in a curvilinear path, and a gymnast performing a somersault dismount from a balance beam.

UNDERSTANDING THE NATURE OF MECHANICAL QUANTITIES

1. If the total human body is the system that you are examining, what is the single point you should follow to describe the body's motion?

2. Rank the following objects in order of most massive to least massive: (a) a basketball, (b) a shot, (c) a baseball, (d) a volleyball, (e) a Frisbee, (f) a medicine ball, and (g) a golf ball.

3. Rank the objects listed in item 2 in order of most weight to least weight. Compare the two rankings of mass and weight. Are they the same, or do differences occur? Explain.

4. Rank the objects listed in item 2 in order of most to least volume. Rank them in order of most to least density. Compare the volume, density, and mass rankings. Are they the same, or do differences occur? Explain how and why.

5. Rank the following body segments in the order of most to least mass, volume, and density: head, trunk, thigh, and forearm. Explain the differences in rankings. (See Appendix III.)

6. By balancing each of the following items on the edge of your hand, find the CG for each: (a) a baseball bat, (b) a tennis racket, (c) a badminton racket, (d) a racquetball racket, (e) a fencing foil, (f) a ruler or meterstick.

7. From a piece of cardboard, cut out a shape similar to that shown in Figure B.6. Using a pencil, nail, pin, or paper clip, punch a hole anywhere in the cardboard. Suspend a string from this pencil and attach a weight to the end. Hold the pencil so that the cardboard shape and the string are free to swing around it. Allow the cardboard and string to come to rest. With a felt-tip pen, draw a line that follows the line of the string across the cardboard. Repeat the previous procedure, using another hole anywhere on the cardboard. Make a distinct mark at the intersection of the two lines. Repeat the procedure again. The third line should intersect at the same point. What is this point called? What is the definition of this point? Explain why this experiment works.

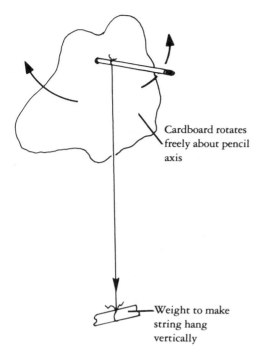

Cardboard rotates freely about pencil axis

Weight to make string hang vertically

If a flat body is suspended from an axis around which it can freely rotate, the center of gravity will come to rest directly under the axis support.

Figure B.6.

8. If you run a distance of 50 m and a buddy runs 60 m alongside you from the same starting point, how far will your buddy have run relative to you?

9. Give an example in sport in which the same force is applied to a body but the pressure is different.

10. Differentiate between a body with kinetic energy and one with gravitational potential energy.

11. What aspect is similar between a body with gravitational potential energy and one with elastic potential energy?

12. Define power in terms of how force is used and in terms of how work is performed.

13. Using an arm and a hand and a foot and a leg, demonstrate linear and rotary motion. Estimate the linear and angular displacements of the parts used.

14. Describe five examples in sport or dance in which something (a) moves linearly (rectilinearly or curvilinearly), (b) rotates about some axis, and (c) moves with both linear and rotary motion.

REFERENCES
SUGGESTED READINGS

Barham, J. *Mechanical Kinesiology.* St. Louis: C. V. Mosby Co., 1978.

Hopper, B. J. "Units and Measurements in the Mechanics of Track." *Track Technique* 29 (1967): 908–12.

Resnick, R., and Halliday, D. *Physics.* Part I. New York: John Wiley & Sons, 1977.

Wheeler, G. F., and Kirkpatrick, L. D. *Physics: Building a World View.* Englewood Cliffs, N.J.: Prentice-Hall, 1983.

FORCE

Prerequisites

Concept Module B

Concept Module Contents

SECTION 1

FORCES ACTING ON A SYSTEM

Forces account for the motion and changes of motion of all things in the environment, including the whole body and the body segments. With this general understanding of the meaning of force, we can examine the nature of forces and the different kinds of forces.

Whenever a body or object moves, it changes its position or location relative to some frame of reference; it does so because some external force has been applied to it. Forces can be identified as **internal** or **external** forces.

Whenever we speak of internal or external forces, we mean internal or external relative to the system we are examining. For example, if we are interested in the motion of a baseball struck by a bat, our system is the ball, and the bat's force on

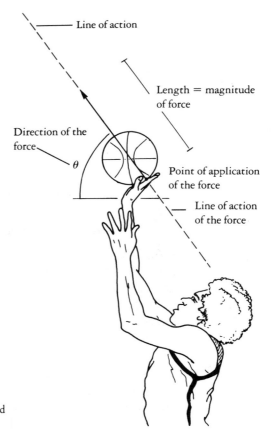

Figure C.1.   The four properties of an external force applied
to a basketball by the player's hand.

it is external relative to the system (the ball). If we are interested in the motion of both the ball and the bat, the system is the ball and the bat, and the force of the bat on the ball is internal relative to the system (the ball and bat). If we consider the entire human body as a system, the external forces are those that originate from some source outside the body itself. Internal forces are those originating from some source within the body, or the system. Muscle forces are internal forces when the whole body is the system. If we choose a single body segment to be the system, however, a muscle's force acting on the bone is an external force relative to the system. The effects of internal and external forces are discussed in a later section.

SECTION 2

THE FOUR PROPERTIES OF A FORCE

All forces have four unique properties (Figure C.1): (1) **magnitude,** how much force is applied (e.g., 44 N, or ~10 lb), (2) **direction,** the way the force is applied (e.g., forward, south, vertically upward, perpendicular to a surface, at an angle of 60 degrees above the horizontal), (3) **point of application,** where the force is applied on the body or system receiving it (e.g., against the heel, on the fingertips, 1 m from the front edge of a table), and (4) **line of action,** the straight line extending through the point of application and extending indefinitely along the direction of the force. The line of action of a force is also called the line of force.

SECTION 3

REACTION FORCES: NEWTON'S THIRD LAW OF MOTION

We now focus on an important source of external forces, which can act to cause movement of the total body. We know that we can move our bodies from place to place by walking, running, jumping, diving, swimming, or rolling without the application of any *apparent* external force to cause this motion. If the body is the system, the muscles are internal forces that in themselves cannot cause movement of the system. Although internally initiated movements of the segments are necessary to move the body, the force responsible for displacement of the whole system (body) must be external to the body, and therefore it must be generated by the environment with which the body interacts. The body segments move to exert a force on something in the environment, and the environment delivers a **reaction force,** or counterforce, to the body. For example, to move the total body upward in a push-up, the arm segments are caused to move by the internal forces created by the arm muscle contractions. The system is shown in Figure C.2a.

The hands placed against the ground are felt to exert a push downward as the joint actions in the arm occur. In response to the downward force of the hands on the ground, the earth exerts an equal and opposite force upward against the hands. This upward reaction force is the external force causing upward motion of the body. Another way to picture the situation is to think of the earth as preventing the hands from moving downward away from the body as the arms straighten so that the body must move upward away from the hands. Note that the earth, a system, experiences an external force applied to it by the hands, but the inertia (mass) of the earth is so great compared with that of the body that the earth's movement is negligible (too

Figure C.2.   External forces responsible for the motion of the body are often the reaction forces generated by the forces applied by the body against another less movable mass.

small to be measured). If this same push-up movement were performed in space where no physical contact with another mass exists, the arms would move away from the body and the body would move away from the arms so that the center of the system's mass would experience no change in position in space. In Figure C.2b the jumper pushes against the ground and generates the resulting ground reaction force that pushes her upward. Similarly, the block reaction force generated by a sprinter's push-off propels her forward (Figure C.2c).

The phenomenon of an equal and opposite reaction force occurring in response to every force applied was first described by Sir Isaac Newton about 300 years ago and is the subject of what is known as Newton's third law of motion: For every force applied by one body on a second, the second body applies an equal and oppositely directed force on the first. Figure C.3 presents examples of oppositely directed applied forces and reaction forces. Visualization of the counterforces, or reaction forces, exerted by the ground in response to forces applied by the body is necessary for understanding movement of the whole body (of its center of gravity [CG]). Also keep in mind that the forces we exert on the ground have their effect, as illustrated by a ballerina who, following a demi-plié, "jumps two feet into the air. The Earth, balancing her momentum, responds with its own sauté and changes orbit by one ten-trillionth of an atom's width." (Lightman 1983)

Every reaction force by one mass on another is equal in magnitude and opposite in direction to the applied force.

Figure C.3.

SECTION 4

FRICTION FORCE

Friction is the force created between two contacting surfaces that tend to rub or slide past each other; it is the force that prevents the foot from slipping on the ground during walking. Friction force does not exist unless some sliding tendency exists or unless actual sliding occurs between two surfaces. When one surface exerts a friction force on a second surface, an equal and opposite friction force is applied by the second on the first. The amount of friction force that resists such a slipping or sliding tendency depends on the textures of both surfaces and on how much force is pressing the surfaces together. Wet or lubricated surfaces offer considerably less frictional resistance to each other than do dry ones. More friction force exists between rough-textured surfaces than between objects with smooth surfaces. When examined microscopically, even an apparently flawless surface has tiny bumps and grooves that "catch" the bumps and grooves of another contacting surface when there is cause for the surfaces to slide past each other.

The greater the force pressing the surfaces together—called the *normal* or *perpendicular force*—the greater the resistance to sliding. Thus the force applied to move the box in Figure C.4 must be greater than the opposing frictional force applied against the box by the floor surface. Note also in Figure C.4 that the **apparent contact area** does not alter the frictional force.

The explanation for the independence of the surface area to the frictional force is based on the fact that the **actual contact area** is the area of contact of the bumps on each surface. The smaller the apparent contact area of a body on a surface, the greater the force per unit area *(pressure)*. Greater pressure will cause greater flattening of the bumps, which creates a larger actual surface contact area, even though the apparent contact area is smaller. The decrease in apparent surface area when the box rests on its small end is compensated for by an increase in actual surface area, and thus the frictional force will remain the same. This occurs even with very hard surfaces (Resnick and Halliday 1977).

The implication of this fact is that changing the apparent area of contact does not change the force of friction if the normal force and the surface qualities are the same. For example, someone wearing size 12 shoes has no more friction force on their feet than someone wearing size 6 shoes. Nor does a car with wide tires have any greater friction force than that same similar car with narrow tires. (Large contact area tires are used not for greater traction but for longer wear owing to less friction per unit area of tread.

A way in which the friction force can be modified by increasing the normal force is explained by this example: When you have a tight grip on a jar lid, the friction between your hand and the lid becomes greater than the friction between the lid and the jar, and the lid turns with your hand.

To quantify the force of friction between two surfaces, two facts must be known: (1) the normal force pressing the surfaces together and (2) a quantity known as the **coefficient of friction** for the two surfaces, which depends on their hardness and

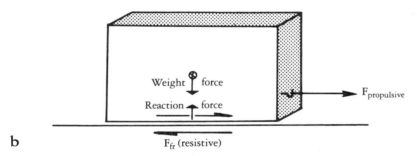

Static friction force is increased if the force pressing the two surfaces together is increased or if the textures of the surfaces are rough or both. If the weight and surface textures are the same, changing the area of contact from that shown in (a) to that shown in (b) does not change the force of friction.

Figure C.4.

surface texture. The coefficient of friction for two surfaces that tend to slide under the influence of some motive force but have not yet begun to move is called the *coefficient of static friction.*

The coefficient of friction between two surfaces is the ratio of friction force to normal force:

$$C_{fr} = \frac{F_{fr}}{F_{\perp}}$$

Equation C.1

where C_{fr} is the coefficient of static friction, F_{fr} is the maximum static friction force, and $F_{\perp}$ is the perpendicular ($\perp$) force pressing the surfaces together.

The coefficient for surfaces that are already sliding on each other is called the *coefficient of kinetic friction,* which is smaller than the coefficient of static friction.

The static friction force between two surfaces that have not started sliding is greater than the kinetic friction force between the same two surfaces during sliding. As a force is applied to cause sliding of one body on another, the magnitude of the static friction force increases until it reaches a maximum value just prior to actual sliding. Any further increase in the force, therefore, would cause the body to slide past the other surface. Once sliding begins, the moving body experiences less frictional resistance to the applied effort because of the lower coefficient of friction. Such a drop in resistance of a moving load that has started to slide partially accounts for the claim that to start something moving is more difficult than to keep something moving.

The friction force acting on a rolling object is much less than the kinetic friction encountered in sliding. The reduced friction on a rolling object is a result of the relative ease with which the rolling surface is peeled away from the contacting surface in contrast to two sliding surfaces that have to resist the "catching" of bumps and grooves. For example, when one brakes a car that is rolling on an icy street, the braking force is applied to the rolling tires, and this force causes a sliding tendency. Thus, the tire-road interface assumes a static friction condition and has a higher frictional limit prior to actual sliding. Once sliding occurs, the situation involves kinetic friction and thus the friction force decreases. The brakes should be released to resume the tires rolling and the brakes applied again.

In cycling, slipping usually occurs in cornering, especially on wet or gravelly surfaces. In wet weather, a thin film of water (and often road oil) exists between the tires and the road surface. This fluid acts as a lubricant to significantly reduce the friction available for turning, and the tires may slip out from under a leaning cyclist. Cyclists learn to slow down and make wide turns under such conditions. In dry weather, a cyclist taking a sharp corner may encounter a patch of gravel or oil that instantly decreases the friction needed for turning, and a mishap may occur.

Maximum static friction is also desirable in sports played on grassy surfaces, such as football, baseball, and golf. Players of these sports wear shoes with cleats since smooth-soled shoes provide little friction on grass and thereby cause slipping. In activities in which hand-implement friction must be increased, as in baseball, golf, or racquetball, the hand or implement or both are provided with a friction-increasing covering such as a glove, wrappings, or tacky resin. In some situations, friction is a disadvantage to performance, as in the case of the skater who wishes to slide across the ice with minimal resistance or the dancer who turns on the ball of the foot in a pirouette.

SECTION 5

CENTRIPETAL AND CENTRIFUGAL FORCES

Whenever a body is restricted to traveling in a circular path around a central axis, such as a whistle on a string swinging in a circle, it experiences a force that is directed along the radius (string) toward the center of the circle (toward the hand holding the string). If the string is released, the center-seeking force disappears and the whistle is cast off in a linear path tangent to the circle. Such a center-directed force is called a **centripetal force** and is responsible for continually forcing the rotating object to follow the circular path. The equal and opposite reaction force is called the **centrifugal force**, and is the force that the rotating body exerts along the radius on the central axis. The hand swinging the string and whistle experiences this outward force as the whistle circles.

The greater the mass of the object or the faster it travels, the greater the centripetal and centrifugal forces. The larger the circle, the smaller these forces. Many activities involve rotary motion in circles or parts of circles: a swing on a rope or rings, a giant swing on a high bar, a hammer throw, a discus throw, a swing of a skating or dancing partner, a swing of a baseball bat, a swing of a bowling ball or softball, and a swing of a lacrosse stick and ball. All these activities require a centripetal force to keep the body or object traveling circularly. A handgrip often provides the connection to the central axis, and it must be strong enough to maintain the connection when the rotation is fast or the body or implement is heavy. Figure C.5 illustrates the pulling-away tendency of a gymnast's rotating body and how she must maintain her grip on the bar so that the bar can exert centripetal force on her.

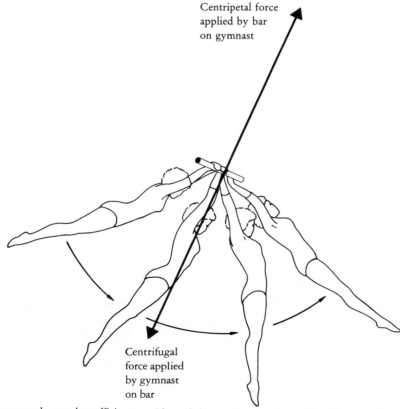

Centripetal force applied by bar on gymnast

Centrifugal force applied by gymnast on bar

The grip strength must be sufficient to withstand the centripetal and centrifugal force tending to extend the fingers.

Figure C.5.

In running around curves on a track or in ball games, a runner must lean inward and press outward on the ground (centrifugal force by runner on ground) to generate the centripetal ground reaction friction force (by ground on runner) to be able to run in a curved path. Cyclists must do the same when rounding curves. If they travel too fast, however, the centrifugal and centripetal friction forces are not great enough, and they slip. This friction problem is alleviated by banked curves that permit runners and cyclist to press into a "wall" when they turn (see Figure 11.17 on page 523).

SECTION 6

THE INFLUENCE OF INTERNAL AND EXTERNAL FORCES ON A SYSTEM'S MOTION

The Effect of Internal Forces

The movements of a system's CG relative to the ground or to some other frame of reference in the environment must be accounted for by forces that are external to the system. For example, the CG location of a golf ball, does not change relative to the ground until an external force is applied to the ball. The only internal forces occurring within the ball (the system) are molecular collisions, and the forces from these collisions cancel each other so that the overall effect is equivalent to no force influencing the motion of the ball's CG.

To further clarify this concept, picture a coiled spring bound tightly with string that is tossed into the air. The spring is isolated from physical contact and is subject to no external force except that of gravity (Figure C.6a). If the string breaks from the tension of the spring (an internal force), the spring expands to its normal, uncompressed length. The coils of wire comprising the spring (the system) change their positions relative to one another, but the location of the CG of the whole spring is not altered by the action of the internal force. Therefore, the only force influencing the motion of the spring's CG is the force of gravity acting downward. The human body behaves in the same manner when free of external forces (other than gravity).

A body free in space and weightless has no external force to act on it; therefore, it does not exhibit any change in the movement of its CG when its body segments move. (Note that gravity is an external force that causes the system to move toward the ground.) When the whole body is the system, its CG location is not affected by any forces generated within the body. For example, muscle forces cannot change the location of the CG of the unsupported body. When the whole body is the system, therefore, muscle forces are internal forces that cannot cause movement or work against the existing movement of the whole body's CG. If a movement is performed while the body is free of support as in the case of the person in a tuck

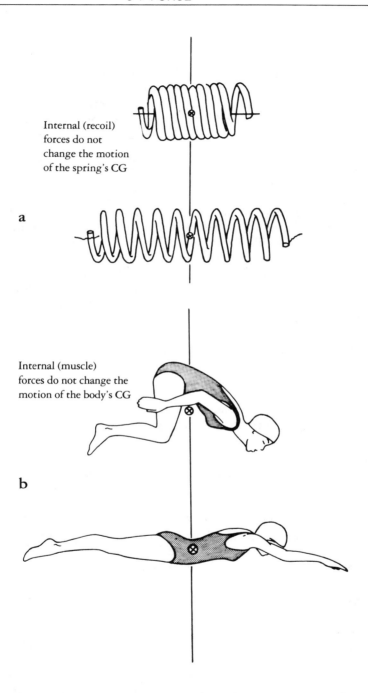

Forces that are internal to a system do not change the location of the center of gravity of that system in space.

Figure C.6.

position (Figure C.6b), her CG location in space does not change when she assumes a layout position. Internal muscle forces serve only to change the shape of her body; they cannot move her CG position relative to the ground.

Such is the plight of an isolated astronaut in a weightless condition, free of any contact with another object or surface. Any segmental movements only change the shape of the body around its CG; no segmental movements can cause the CG to move. The astronaut is stuck until help arrives. Such help must be in the form of an external force. The astronaut can move the body parts, arms and legs, in any way imaginable, but cannot change the body's CG location relative to the environment because the only forces acting upon the system are internal forces.

Returning to earth, recall that the external force of gravity acts on the CG of a system. If we consider the movement of a platform diver changing body positions during a descent, that is, from layout to pike to tuck to layout, we realize that gravity causes the body's CG to move downward no differently than if the diver were not changing shape. The body parts are merely changing their positions around the CG, and the CG is that which is responding to the external force of gravity. This same phenomenon occurs during any activity that includes a flight phase, or period of nonsupport, such as in long jumping, high jumping, rebound tumbling, running, aerial gymnastic stunts, and falling. The effect of the external force of air flow on the human body in many nonsupported aerial activities is so slight as to be insignificant. The effect of air resistance in some endeavors cannot be ignored, however. A sky diver, for example, encounters upward air resistance, which limits the rate of falling.

The Effect of External Forces

When a system is in contact with the ground or another support, it is capable of moving its CG. By changing its shape *against* the support, the system applies a force to the support that generates a reaction force against the system. This reaction force is the external force responsible for moving the system's CG. Consider the coiled spring bound with string (Figure C.7a) that is placed against a wall. When the string breaks, the spring uncoils, and because the wall is in the way, the spring pushes against it. The wall responds with an equal and opposite reaction force that is applied to the spring, causing the spring's CG to move in space. Similarly, the tucked body against the block in Figure C.7b uses internal muscle forces to change her shape to push against the block. The reaction force then serves as the external force propelling the person away from the block.

The difference in the movement of the CG while the body is supported and while it is not supported is an important concept that is used frequently in the analysis of the performance of various sport skills.

Consider now the effects of other external forces on the movement of the whole body as a system. For example, a collision with an opposing player in basketball moves the body's CG in the direction of the force applied. The movement of the body's CG is readily apparent as the struck player moves from one location on the

Reaction force of wall
on expanding spring
moves its center of
gravity

CG motion

Wall
reaction
force

a

Block's reaction force
on body is external
force causing body's
center of gravity to move

CG motion

Block
reaction force

b

Forces that are external to a system do change the location of the center of gravity of that system in space.   **Figure C.7.**

floor to another. Such changes in the location of the CG are not always so easily observed. For example, the force applied by a basketball to the hands and arms of a player catching it causes the arms to move backward, closer to the rest of the body mass, as the elbows flex. When this happens, the player does not change her location on the floor; however, the segmental masses of the body are forced into a new configuration, and the CG of the body shifts backward slightly. Thus, the external force moves the body's CG but not the location of the player's feet on the floor. Such a situation also serves as an example of how an external force can change the shape of a system.

SECTION 7

RESISTIVE AND MOTIVE FORCES

A movement of some system (body, body part, or group of parts) can be examined in terms of the forces that act on that system. To affect the motion of the system, these forces must be external forces relative to the system. An external force that causes an increase in speed or change in direction is called a **motive**, or **propulsive,** force. An external force that acts to resist the motion caused by some other external force or to decrease the speed of a moving system is called a **resistive** force.

Resistive Forces

Resistive forces oppose or resist the movement of a system within a frame of reference, and they must be external relative to the system. If we select a body segment as our system, we can identify several sources of resistive forces that are external to the segment but are found within the human body. These sources are: (1) the tension in muscles acting to resist movement of a segment as it is acted upon by some force that succeeds in moving it or that merely attempts to move it, (2) the resistance of connective tissues to being stretched by some force, (3) the actual contact of forces, such as the touching of two body segments as they approach one another (e.g., the contact of large biceps with the forearm muscles, bone on bone within a joint, or slack ligaments across a joint become taut), and (4) the degree of viscosity (thickness) of the fluids within muscle tissues and joint capsules.

These restrictive forces help provide joint stability since they restrict excessive joint movement that could cause injury to the joint surfaces. Occasionally, however, the tissues are torn when the motive force causing the segmental movement is greater than the resistive force that the internal structures can provide. This happens especially in contact sports.

Normally, before the movement of a segment is restricted or stopped by the structures of an *articulation* (joint), the muscles crossing over the articulation play an important role in gradually slowing the segment's movement. In arm wrestling, the descent of the loser's arm is slowed by the tension of the muscles of the shoulder and elbow. If these muscle groups were to relax instead of maintaining tension while they lengthened, the arm would be taken down much more rapidly. The role of muscle tension as a resistive force during lengthening should not be underestimated.

Resistive tension is as important—and as frequently employed—as the muscle contractions that *cause* bodily movements. Resistive contractions (eccentric, or lengthening, muscular contractions) constantly control the extent and speed of segmental movements. Resistive muscular tensions control the speed of segmental movements that we normally take for granted. They are the braking forces applied near the end of the range motion of body segments so that the movements slow gradually rather than halting abruptly as a result of tissue impact or the sudden stretching of joint structures.

The connective tissues in muscles provide resistance to stretch as a segment is moved toward the end of a joint's range of motion (ROM). In bouncing stretches done in a straight-leg sitting position on the floor, the forward reaching movement of the arms and trunk is brought to a halt as their posterior muscles and associated tendinous tissues become stretched taut. The recoil of this *elastic* tissue subsequently provides the motive force to bounce the upper body segment back again. Stretches of a violent bouncing type are usually discouraged because of the possibility of overstretching by "throwing" the mass of the body parts with too much speed.

Another source of resistance to a system's movement is contact with any mass or force other than those within the system being considered. If the body is the system, such contact may be with the earth, another person or object, air and water resistance, or friction force. Resistive forces are specific as to direction. Recall that the weight of a body is a force that acts only in a downward direction and occurs only because of the earth's gravity. Weight, then, is a force that resists a body's upward movement. An outfielder running to catch a fly ball may encounter the horizontal resistive force of the center-field fence. A runner stealing second base slides to a halt as a result of the resistance provided by the ground friction on his body. Similarly, a rolling ball eventually stops as a result of the friction force of the ground against it. A swimmer moving through the water experiences the resistive force of the water flowing backward, and a skier experiences the resistive force of the air flow during a downhill run.

Tight-fitting clothes, often overlooked as a restrictive force, can be a significant source of resistance for segmental movements of the body. A vivid example of how restrictive such clothing can be is provided by a student wearing tight jeans attempting to climb stairs two at a time.

Motive Forces

Forces that cause a change in the way a body segment is moving can originate from within the human body or from outside the body, as long as the forces are external with respect to the segment (system). Motive forces for the segmental movements include those provided by muscle contractions and the recoil of elastic connective tissues. When a muscle is stretched and then released, the elastic recoil of the stretched connective tissues can cause the initial motion of the body segment. For example, when you sit on the floor with legs extended and reach forward toward your toes, the posterior spine and hip muscles and their connective tissues are stretched; consequently, you experience a rebound movement of your upper body.

Of the forces generated within the human body, contraction of the skeletal muscles yields the major motive force causing segmental movements. If a group of muscles contracts and shortens (concentric contraction), the attached body segment is caused to move by that motive force. For example, with your forearms and hands identified as the system, picture yourself opening a window by pulling upward with your hands. Your elbow flexor muscles would shorten to raise your forearms and hands. The external resistive force acting against the motive force in this situation is the weight (the force of gravity) of the segment and window and the friction force exerted on the window by the frame.

The most significant motive force causing motion of the total body is the pull of gravity. Gravitational force (for activities here on earth) is always present, always acts in a downward direction toward the center of the earth, and exerts its force on the CG of all masses. Gravity is the obvious motive force for the descent of a diver or the sinking of a lean swimmer attempting to float. Gravity is also the motive force for the downward movement of the forearms and barbell in a forearm curl.

Other motive forces occur in conjunction with some external object or another person, with which contact causes or tends to cause movement of the system. The recoil of a depressed diving board provides a motive force for projecting a diver upward (the whole body as the system). The loser in an arm-wrestling contest has his arm put down by the motive force applied by the opponent's hand. Note that from the point of view of the loser, her arm (the loser's system) has been subjected to the motive force of the opponent's push; whereas, from the winner's point of view, the pushing arm (the winner's) was caused to move by the motive force of muscle contraction and was resisted by the loser's applied force.

A strong wind propelling a skateboarder is another example of a motive force acting on a body. Water's force of buoyancy is normally thought of in terms of support; however, it acts as a motive force for the upward movement of a buoyant, submerged swimmer holding his breath.

In addition to being a resistive force, friction can be a motive force. A performer walking or running on an exercise treadmill finds that her leg is moved backward relative to her body by the frictional force applied to her shoe sole by the treadmill belt as it moves backward. If a person were running across the ground instead, the forward friction ground reaction force to the foot's backward friction force applied to the ground would be the external force causing the forward motion of the runner's CG.

SECTION 8

FORCE DIAGRAMS AND VECTORS

When a force is shown in diagrams, each of its four properties may be represented by an arrow whose length is drawn to a scale selected to represent the magnitude of the force—for example, 1 cm = 5 N or 1 in. = 10 lb. The arrow is drawn to point in the direction in which the force is applied, and the tail of the arrow is placed at the force's point of application. The line of action of the force may be imagined as continuing indefinitely in both directions (head and tail end), although the actual arrow, if drawn to scale, must remain a given length. A graphic representation of a force of 100 N acting at a 30-degree angle to a table being pushed is shown in Figure C.8.

Since force has the two properties of magnitude and direction, it is known as a **vector** quantity. Vector quantities are different from **scalar** quantities because vectors always have direction specified and direction is an important characteristic of the quantity. Scalar quantities have only magnitude—a size or amount of a certain quantity—and no direction is associated with them. Mass, volume, and area are examples of scalar quantities.

The Effect of Two or More Forces on a System: Vector Composition

When more than one external force is applied to a system simultaneously, all the external forces must be considered, for it is their **net** effect that determines the motion of the body. The net effect, or **resultant,** of the applied forces, is determined by combining the force vectors. The combining of forces is called **vector addition,** or **vector composition,** and it differs from scalar addition (regular numerical addition) in that the direction of the force is just as important as the magnitude of the force. Vector addition can be accomplished graphically by drawing diagrams to scale and measuring or by using trigonometry.[1]

To demonstrate the concept of a single resultant force, or net force, formed by two different forces we will consider the motion of a ball falling in a side wind, as shown in Figure C.9. Gravity pulls vertically downward on the ball with a force equal to the ball's weight of 3 N (~10 oz). A wind blowing horizontally toward the west exerts a force in that direction equal to 9 N (~30 oz). The motion of the ball is determined by the resultant of these two forces, which act simultaneously (Figure C.9a).

---

1. Trigonometric methods of vector composition are in Appendix V.

F = 100 N

A force vector drawn to show the application of a 100 N force directed 30 degrees below horizontal. Drawing the tail of the arrow at the point of application of a force is customary.

Figure C.8.

The force vectors are drawn to a convenient scale that is similar to a road map scale; for example, in Figure C.9 1 cm represents 3 N of force. The force vector that represents the object's weight, therefore, is drawn 1 cm long in the vertical direction, and the wind-force vector is drawn 3 cm long in the horizontal direction to represent its 9 N of force.

Figure C.9b shows how the two forces are visualized as two sides of a rectangle and how the opposite sides are then drawn to form the whole rectangle. The resultant force, R, is represented by the diagonal that is drawn from the corner of the rectangle formed by the tails of the two force vectors (Figure C.9c). The direction of the resultant force is downward and westward, and the exact angle of the force can be measured with a protractor. The magnitude of the resultant force may be determined by measuring the length of R with a ruler and converting the length to Newtons of force, using the same scale to which the two forces were drawn originally (1 cm = 3 N). Since the length of R measures 3.16 cm, the magnitude of R equals:

$$3.16 \text{ cm} \times \frac{3 \text{ N}}{1 \text{ cm}} = 9.48 \text{ N}$$

The ball's motion, therefore, is in the direction of the resultant force, R, applied to it as shown. This example enables us to see the difference between scalar addition

Figure C.9.   The net effect of two forces—the ball's weight and a sidewind—is found by vector composition. The resultant force, R, will determine the ball's motion.

of quantities and vector addition. Vector addition is influenced greatly by the directions of the component vectors.

If the component force vectors (the two independent forces acting together) are perpendicular components (i.e., if they form a 90-degree angle with one another), the magnitude of the resultant can be calculated by the *Pythagorean theorem*. (See Appendix V.) The Pythagorean theorem specifies that the length of the hypotenuse of a right triangle is equal to the square root of the sum of the square of the two sides:

$$R = \sqrt{3^2 + 9^2} = \sqrt{9 + 81} = \sqrt{90} = 9.48 \text{ N}$$

We can calculate in this manner only when the component force vectors are perpendicular to each other.

Let us look at another example in which a resultant force determines the motion of a body. Suppose a soccer ball is kicked simultaneously by two players. The force diagram of this situation is shown from an overhead view in Figure C.10a. We use the same process of drawing each applied force to a convenient scale. In this case, we will visualize the two force vectors as two sides of a nonrectangular parallelogram (i.e., a four-sided figure whose opposite sides are parallel) (Figure C.10b). A third vector is drawn from the tails of the two force vectors to the opposite corner of the parallelogram. This resultant vector is the net force applied to the soccer ball, and its magnitude is found by measuring the length with the same scale used for drawing the original forces. The ball's motion will be changed in the direction indicated by the resultant force and will be proportional to the magnitude of that force.

Another situation in which the motion of a body is determined by a **net force** acting on it is one in which a weight is lifted. Figure C.11 shows the vector diagram of the forces acting to cause the upward motion of the load. For this situation, the resultant of two opposing forces must be found. Forces that lie along the same line as those in the example are called *colinear forces*. A parallelogram cannot be drawn as before because no corner is formed at the tails of the two force vectors. Therefore, the algebraic sum of the two forces is found by means of vector addition, with the

a

b

The net effect of two nonperpendicular forces applied to a soccer ball, as seen from a top view.

Figure C.10.

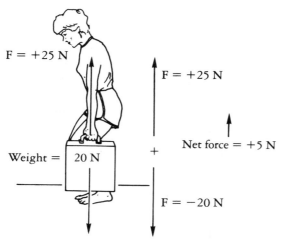

Figure C.11. When two oppositely directed forces act on a system, the net force is the algebraic sum of the two forces. The system's motion is determined by the net (resultant) force.

upward-directed force being termed a positive force and the downward-directed force, a negative one. The algebraic sum of the two is determined as follows:

$$(+25 \text{ N}) + (-20 \text{ N}) = +5 \text{ N}$$

The positive 5 N is the net force experienced by the load, and it is moved upward (in the positive direction). If one were to exert only 20 N of upward force, the positive 20 N would match the negative 20 N of weight; that is, the sum of the forces in the vertical direction would equal zero, and with zero resultant force, no movement would occur.

The Directional Effects of a Force: Vector Resolution

To identify the resultant of two or more external forces on a system, we use a process called *vector addition* or *vector composition*. The multiple forces are then represented by a single net force acting on a system in some resultant direction. Recall that a vector is any quantity that has magnitude and direction associated with it. Three of the most common vector quantities with which we deal are forces, displacements, and velocities. Any single vector quantity may be added or composed with another of like kind.

Often an occasion arises in which the observed movement of a system or a single force acting on a system is to be analyzed in terms of identifying its component directions. In such cases, the single vector quantity given is divided into two components (e.g., a horizontal component and a vertical component). These two components, if composed, represent the single resultant vector. The directions of these components are relative to some reference, such as the ground or a body segment, and are usually perpendicular to each other. Such a procedure may be thought of as the reverse of the process of vector composition. The operation is called **vector resolution,** and is the method for determining two component vectors that form the one vector given initially.[2]

As an example of vector resolution, let us examine the linear path of a baseball projected horizontally. Figure C.12a illustrates the side view of the path of the ball downward and forward. The total displacement of the ball from the release to the ground is represented by the vector R and can be resolved into a forward displacement and a downward displacement. These are the horizontal and vertical components,

2. Trigonometric methods of vector resolution are in Appendix V.

The process of vector resolution. The distance a ball travels from release to the ground is resolved into its horizontal distance component and its vertical distance component.

Figure C.12.

respectively. The operation of resolving the given vector, R, into two mutually perpendicular components is illustrated in Figure C.12b–d.

Resolution consists of these steps: (1) draw the vector given initially to a selected scale (Figure C.12a), (2) from the tail of the vector, draw lines representing the desired directions of the two perpendicular components (Figure C.12b), (3) from the head of the vector, draw lines parallel to each of the two directional lines so that a rectangle is formed (Figure C.12c), and (4) draw an arrow head on each directional line at the point formed by the intersection of each parallel line (Figure C.12d). Each head represents the head of one component vector.

The length of the component vector is measured from the tail to the head, according to the same scale used to draw the initial vector.

Basketball provides another example of the use of vector resolution and vector addition in analyzing motion occurring in sport. Figure C.13 shows a player dribbling the ball. The ball is the system subjected to two external forces, the downward force of gravity (the ball's weight) and a forward and downward push by the player. The push has two directional components: a forward horizontal force component, which makes the ball cover horizontal distance, and a downward vertical force component, which moves the ball to the floor faster than would gravity alone. The first step in the analysis is to draw the hand's forward and downward force components to scale (Figure C.13a). Next, the weight vector is added to the hand's downward component to obtain—to scale—the total downward force acting on the ball (Figure C.13c).

The significance of this kind of force-and-motion analysis also is apparent when

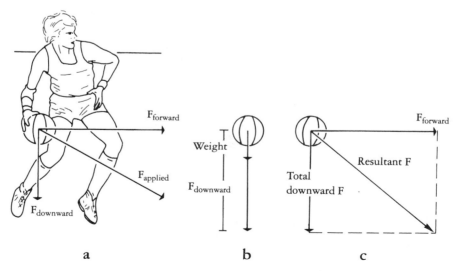

Figure C.13.   (a) The resolution of the force applied by the hand to a basketball into its horizontal and vertical components. (b) The downward component of the hand's force is added to the downward force of the ball's weight. (c) The total downward force on the ball is combined with the hand's horizontal force to obtain the resultant (net) force acting on the ball at the time of contact.

the motion of a fastball pitch is explained. Such a pitch appears to rise near the plate; however, the upward force acting on the ball due to its backspin is not as great as the downward force of the ball's weight. Therefore, the net force is downward, and it accelerates in that direction (Kreighbaum and Hunt 1978). Because the ball does not drop as quickly as would be expected (that is, without backspin), the illusion of the ball rising is created.

In the human body, vector resolution is used extensively to visualize the effects of muscle pull on bone. Figure C.14a shows a force diagram for the biceps muscle pulling on the forearm. The muscle's force is represented by the force vector F, its length is drawn to scale (e.g., 1 cm = 40 N of force), and the angle it forms with the bone is the same as the muscle's line of pull in that position. The two directions of interest in muscle-bone activity are not horizontal and vertical as in the previous examples. A muscle's force is resolved into one component that is perpendicular to the bone and one component that is parallel to the bone (Figure C.14b). Using the

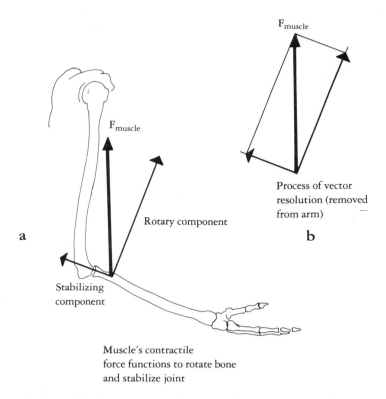

F_{muscle}

Process of vector resolution (removed from arm)

F_{muscle}

Rotary component

a

b

Stabilizing component

Muscle's contractile force functions to rotate bone and stabilize joint

Force vector diagram of the biceps muscle pulling on the forearm. The muscle force is represented by a vector whose length represents the amount of force applied in the direction shown. It is shown resolved into two components, one that is perpendicular to the forearm (it rotates the arm around the elbow axis) and one that is parallel to the forearm (it stabilizes the elbow joint).

Figure C.14.

same scale (1 cm = 40 N) each force component is then measured to determine how much is directed perpendicular to the bone, acting to turn the bone (the **rotary component**), and how much is directed along the bone to force it into the elbow joint (the **stabilizing component**). (Note that horizontal and vertical components in such muscle-bone diagrams would serve no purpose, hence we choose the directions of the components to be those of functional significance.)

UNDERSTANDING FORCES

1. The total body is the system to be examined. Describe an example of (a) a motive force applied to the system, (b) a resistive force applied to the system. In each case, are muscle forces internal or external forces?

2. Which type of force can be a motive force relative to the system—internal or external? Which can be a resistive force?

3. Consider the following forces that act on a system and cite examples in which each serves as a motive force and in which each serves as a resistive force: (a) muscular tension, (b) friction, (c) gravitational forces, (d) air flow, (e) water flow, and (f) contact with an external object.

4. Discuss why the location of the CG does not change relative to the ground due to segmental movements for a person free of support and why the CG location does change relative to the ground due to segmental movements for a person supported.

5. Differentiate among these three "pairs" of forces by giving an example that clarifies each pair: internal and external, action and reaction, motive and resistive.

6. Identify or calculate the four properties of each of the forces shown in Figure C.15. Determine the magnitude, using a scale of 1 cm = 20 N of force. Identify the point of application with a P and the lines of action with dashes.
7. Draw a force diagram showing the force of a bat being applied to a baseball. If the baseball is the system, show the four properties of the bat's force.

8. A runner pushes downward with 300 N of force and backward with 400 N of force against the ground. Using a protractor and ruler, perform this vector analysis: Draw to scale the two force vectors, considering magnitude, direction, and point of application. Find the magnitude and direction of the resultant force applied to the ground by the foot.

9. According to Newton's third law of motion, what is the resultant force being received by the runner in question 8? What is the vertical reaction force received by the runner? What is the horizontal reaction force received?

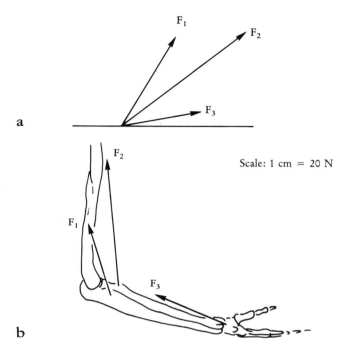

Scale: 1 cm = 20 N

Figure C.15.

10. Using a ruler and protractor, perform the following vector resolutions:

(a). The runner pushes downward and backward with a total force of 200 N at an angle of 40 degrees to the ground. Resolve this force to obtain the magnitude of the vertical and horizontal components. Draw the vertical and horizontal ground reaction forces acting on the runner.

(b). A desk is pulled with a force of 60 N in the following directions: (1) forward and upward at an angle relative to the horizontal of 45 degrees, (2) forward and upward at an angle of 30 degrees, (3) forward at an angle of 0 degrees, and (4) downward at an angle of −10 degrees. Find the vertical and horizontal force components for each situation.

11. Arrange six of these textbooks side by side on a tabletop. Slowly push horizontally on the end book, and note the amount of resistance encountered just before motion begins. Stack the six books vertically on top of one another, push on the bottom book, and note the amount of resistance as before. Compare the resistance encountered in the latter situation with that encountered when the books were aligned horizontally with more of their surface area touching the tabletop. In each case, relate the amount of resistive friction to the total weight of the load and to the surface area of the supportive base.

12. Describe the centripetal forces acting on (a) a rotating bat, (b) a gymnast doing a giant swing on a high bar, and (c) a person swinging on a playground swing. In each case, identify the centrifugal force that is acting.

REFERENCES
SUGGESTED READINGS

Alexander, R. M. *Biomechanics: Outline Studies in Biology.* New York: John Wiley & Sons, 1975.

Barham, J. *Mechanical Kinesiology.* St. Louis: C. V. Mosby Co., 1978.

Cooper, J. M., and Glassow, R. B. *Kinesiology.* 4th ed. St. Louis: C. V. Mosby Co., 1976.

Kreighbaum, E. F., and Hunt, W. "Relative Factors Influencing Pitched Baseballs." In *Biomechanics of Sports and Kinanthropometry,* ed. F. Landry and W. A. R. Orban, 227–36. Miami: Symposia Specialists, 1978.

Lightman, A. "Pas de Deux." *Science* 83, 3 (3) (1983): 33.

Resnick, R., and Halliday, D. *Physics.* Part I. New York: John Wiley & Sons, 1977.

Tricker, R. A. R., and Tricker, B. J. K. *The Science of Human Movement.* New York: American Elsevier Publishing Co., 1967.

Wheeler, G. F., and Kirkpatrick, L. D. *Physics: Building a World View.* Englewood Cliffs, N.J.: Prentice-Hall, 1983.

Prerequisites

Concept Modules A, B, C
Chapter 1

Chapter Contents

NEUROMUSCULAR ASPECTS OF MOVEMENT

GENERAL CHARACTERISTICS OF THE MUSCULAR SYSTEM

Muscle Properties

Among the several types of muscle tissue in the body, the skeletal (striated) muscles are of concern to us because they are the force-producing agents that cause or control the movements of our body segments. Skeletal muscle tissue has four functional properties, described by Gowitzke and Milner (1980) as *irritability, contractibility, distensibility,* and *elasticity.* Because skeletal muscle tissue is irritable, it responds to stimulation by contracting, or producing tension to pull its ends (attached to bones) closer together. The cessation of contraction is *relaxation.* Contraction takes time to develop to maximum value, and relaxation takes time to occur completely as contraction diminishes. Muscle can be distended, or stretched, within limits, to allow for nonrestricted joint movement caused by an antagonist (opposite) muscle or some other force. The fourth property of muscle and its connective tissue network is its elasticity, which gives it the ability to recoil from stretch.

Four aspects of muscle function that are of significance in physical education and athletics are flexibility, strength, power, and muscular endurance. **Flexibility** refers to the state of the muscle's length, which restricts or allows freedom of joint movement. **Strength** is the maximum amount of force that can be exerted by a body segment by means of muscular tension. Muscular **power** refers to the rate at which muscular force is applied to move a load, or the rate at which physical work is done. Normally, if a large muscular force is used to move a load at a fast rate, it is called a powerful movement. Muscular **endurance** is the ability of the muscles to exert force repeatedly or constantly.

These four muscle qualities are specific to each muscle group in the body; that is, each quality exists to some degree in a given muscle group, depending on the routine requirements placed on the muscle group.

Musculoskeletal Relationships

The skeletal muscle system is a voluntary system; that is, it needs an intact nerve supply to contract, and does so mostly as a result of conscious direction from the brain. The location and organization of the skeletal muscle tissue relative to the bones and articulations dictate the skeletal system's movements. All skeletal muscles have at least two attachments, each one being on a different bone so that the muscle crosses at least one articulation. Although labeling the attachments of a muscle is of little value in biomechanics, they may be identified by saying that their origin is usually the more proximal attachment, is usually the more fleshy attachment to the periosteum of the bone, and is usually on the more stable or stationary bone. The insertion of a muscle is normally considered to be the distal attachment, is usually tendinous, and is attached to the more movable bone. These characteristics, however, are only generalizations. If one flexes the hip to punt a soccer ball, the more movable attachment for the muscles acting across the hip is on the thigh and leg. On the other hand, if one performs sit-ups from a supported straight-leg position, then the trunk and pelvis become the more movable attachment for those same muscles.

The important characteristics of a muscle or muscle group are the *location of the attachment* on the bone, the *angle* found at the attachment, and the *number of articulations crossed* by the muscle between attachments.

Functional Muscle Groups

Frequently it is convenient and adequate to refer to the action of *groups* of individual muscles rather than trying to name each one that is or might be acting. The group name is based on the joint movement that the muscles are *able* to cause. For example, the muscles that are able to cause elbow extension belong to the functional muscle group called elbow extensors. Note that the elbow extensors *can* cause elbow extension, but that does not mean every time elbow extension occurs that the elbow extensors necessarily cause it. After flexing your elbow 90 degrees (caused by the elbow flexors), the lowering of your arm is the joint movement of elbow extension, but it is caused by gravity, *not* the elbow extensors.

In summary, a muscle group name reflects the name of the joint movement that the group *can* but not necessarily *does* cause.

Classification of Muscles

Anatomists classify muscles or muscle groups in several ways, and muscles are named for any number of factors.

The names of muscles have been derived from: (a) their situation, as the Brachialis, Pectoralis, Supraspinatus; (b) their direction, as the Rectus, Obliquus and Transversus Abdominis; (c) their action, as Flexors, Extensors; (d) their shape, as the Deltoideus, Trapezius, Rhomboideus; (e) the number of divisions, as the Biceps, Triceps, Quadriceps; (f) their points of attachment, as the Sternocleidomastoideus, Omohyoideus. (*Gray's Anatomy* 1966, p. 381)

From the perspective of the biomechanist, however, more meaningful classifications exist, and they are discussed in the sections that follow.

MUSCLE CLASSIFICATION BY FIBER STRUCTURE

Of interest to some biomechanists is the fiber structure of the muscles. Two basic types of fiber structures exist in skeletal muscle: fusiform and pennate. As shown in Figure 2.1a, **fusiform** muscle fibers run longitudinally to, and somewhat parallel with, the muscle's long axis. Although a single fiber does not run the entire length of the muscle, the many fibers that make up the muscle are aligned parallel with the muscle's long axis. The pennate muscles (Figure 2.1b–d) have tendons that run parallel with the muscle's longitudinal axis, and their fibers run obliquely to this tendon. There are three basic **pennate** structures: the unipennate (Figure 2.1b), in which one set of parallel fibers runs obliquely to a single tendon; the bipennate (Figure 2.1c), in which two sets of parallel fibers run obliquely to a single tendon; and the multipennate (Figure 2.1d), in which there is more than one tendon with associated pennate structures.

Mechanically, there are advantages associated with each type of muscle structure. The relative ranges of motion (ROM) caused by the contraction of the fiber types are represented by the arrows in Figure 2.1. In muscles with longitudinal structure, the fibers are longer and can shorten a greater effective distance. (As shown by the vector arrow, 100% of the muscle's contraction distance contributes to moving the attachment.) These fibers can therefore pull the bones through a greater ROM. Structurally, however, the longitudinal muscle does not allow for a great deal of

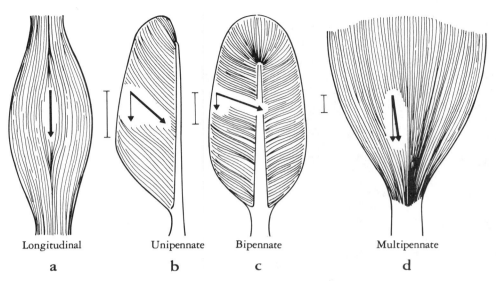

Longitudinal   Unipennate   Bipennate   Multipennate

    a   **b**   **c**   **d**

Figure 2.1.   The various forms of gross muscle fiber structure have different force and range of motion (ROM) advantages.

force production because it has fewer fibers per unit area. The pennate structure allows for a greater number of fibers within a smaller area because the fibers are short and because their oblique placement allows for more short fibers than fewer long ones. The pennate structure produces less ROM than the longitudinal structure for a given shortening distance of the muscle fibers, however. For example, suppose a muscle fiber is aligned 20 degrees from being parallel with the muscle's tendon. Recalling the resolution of a vector presented in Module C, one can determine a shortening component along the long axis of the muscle and an inward component directed perpendicular to the long axis. The greater the angle of the muscle fiber to the long axis of the muscle, the smaller the effective shortening component. In a given muscle, the more sets of oblique fibers, the greater the force available, but the lesser the ROM produced by that muscle. Thus, the multipennate structure allows for greater force but less ROM than the bipennate; the bipennate, more force but less ROM than the unipennate; and the unipennate, more force but less ROM than the longitudinal.

MUSCLE CLASSIFICATION BY RELATIONSHIP TO ARTICULATIONS

An important functional classification of muscles and muscle groups is by the number of articulations crossed by the muscle. A muscle can affect the movement of each articulation that it crosses. The simplest is the **uniarticulate** (one-joint) muscle. Although the muscle may function to produce, help produce, or restrict movements of the articulation it crosses, it can affect and be affected by only that articulation. When the muscle shortens, it can produce motion in that single articulation; similarly, when the uniarticulate muscle is stretched, it is stretched to accommodate only the ROM of that single articulation.

The **biarticulate** or **multiarticulate** muscle crosses two or more articulations. When it shortens, it tends to pull the two bony attachments toward the center of the muscle and therefore tends to produce motion in all the articulations that it crosses. Thus, the two-joint muscle is considered more efficient than the uniarticulate muscle because it can produce motion in more than one joint at the same time. Most of the muscles in the lower extremities that are used for locomotion are two-joint muscles and can efficiently cause motion in two or more of the articulations used for ambulation. Two-joint muscles have an important disadvantage, however. The two-joint muscle fibers cannot exert enough tension to shorten sufficiently to cause full ROM in both joints at the same time. This phenomenon has been called **active insufficiency** (Gardner and O'Connell 1972). Similarly, it is very difficult for a two-joint muscle to be stretched enough to allow for a full ROM in both joints at the same time. This phenomenon has been called **passive insufficiency** (Gardner and O'Connell 1972). Figure 2.2 illustrates the insufficiency concept of two-joint muscles.

An example of a two-joint muscle's insufficiency is that of the hamstring muscle

Active insufficiency
(contracted)

Passive insufficiency
(stretched)

Insufficiency of two-joint muscles to produce or allow total range of motion (ROM) over both joints. Active insufficiency of the hamstrings during simultaneous hip extension and knee flexion. Passive insufficiency of the hamstrings during hip flexion and knee extension.

Figure 2.2.

group on the posterior side of the thigh. The muscles that constitute the hamstring group function to extend the hip and flex the knee. If both of these motions are to occur simultaneously, the hamstring group is not capable of shortening enough to produce full hyperextension in the hip while also producing full flexion at the knee (active insufficiency). The hamstrings can easily flex the knee fully if the hip is flexed. Similarly, the hamstring group is not capable of being stretched enough to allow full hip flexion and full knee extension, as when toe touches are performed from the long sitting position (passive insufficiency). The hamstrings do allow full extension of the knee, however, if the hip is also extended, because the muscles are stretched at the knee end but are not stretched at the hip end.

To summarize, the multijoint muscles are more efficient in that they can produce motion in two or more joints with a single contraction; however, they are insufficient to produce or allow full range of joint motion in both joints at the same time.

A second concept relating muscle positions to the articulations is the **agonist-antagonist** relationship. Those muscles that cause or help cause motion are called the agonists (movers). Those muscles that can perform the movement opposite to the movement being done are called the antagonists. When the agonist muscle group contracts to produce motion at an articulation, the antagonists relax to allow full ROM to occur. This phenomenon is called **reciprocal inhibition.** Because muscles can only pull on bony levers and cannot push, the opposition provided by the agonist-antagonist relationship enables the body to perform the variety of movements of which it is capable.

SECTION 2

TYPES AND FUNCTIONS OF MUSCULAR TENSION

Thus far we have mentioned only a single function of muscles in the body: to produce the force necessary to move a bone. Unfortunately, the movement function is so overemphasized that one tends to forget or to be unaware of the other important roles that muscles play in movement. Single muscles, movements, and functions should not be isolated, since muscles may change functions from one movement to another. Secondly, remember that muscular tension (contraction) is not the only force that produces movements of the body and its parts. Other external forces, produced by objects, other people, and gravity, may affect the function of a muscle as it contracts. One of two situations occurs when tension is produced in a muscle: a segment moves or it does not move. If the segment moves in the direction of applied muscular tension or opposite to the direction of the applied muscular tension, the tension is called **dynamic tension** or **dynamic contraction.**[1] If a muscle produces

---

1. Traditionally, dynamic tension has been called *isotonic.* Isotonic means "same tension," which is not necessarily the case for a muscle that is changing its length. Static tension traditionally has been called *isometric,* which means "same measure"; that is, the muscle does not change its length.

tension or force against an opposing force or resistance, and the segment does not move, the tension is called **static tension** or static contraction.

Generally, there are three functions of muscular contractions: (1) to act as a motive force to move a body part, (2) to act as a resistive force to resist the movement of a body part, and (3) to act to stabilize or fixate a body part. Any other function can easily fit into one of these three categories.

Moving a Body Segment

If a muscle contracts and shortens sufficiently to cause movement in the articulation that it crosses—that is, causes one or both attachments to move closer to the middle of the muscle—then that muscle's function is to move a body part(s), and it is said to be in a **concentric** type of dynamic contraction (*concentric* meaning "moving to the center"). Concentric tension of a muscle is that to which anatomy texts refer when they list the movements caused by that muscle. The hamstrings flex the knee. The elbow flexors function as the movers when the body is *pulled up* to a chinning bar (see Figure B.2a, p. 67). The elbow extensors function as movers during the *upward* phase of a push-up (see Figure C.2a, p. 82).

Resisting the Movement of a Body Segment

Muscle forces are not the only forces that may move a body segment. If another force is doing the moving, the muscles that perform the opposite function to the body movement being performed (antagonists) may be under tension to resist the movement. For instance, if one is lifting a barbell overhead, muscles are required to move body parts and the barbell against gravity to the up position, and thus the muscles function as movers. On the way down, however, gravity moves the body parts and the barbell. To control that downward movement, a certain amount of resistance must be applied *against* gravity. The resistance is applied by tension of the muscles that could produce the *upward* motion. If we consider the muscles that extend the elbow on the upward movement, we can see that they function to extend the elbow to lift the barbell. On the way down, gravity is pulling the barbell, and the elbow is *flexing;* however, the *elbow extensors* control the descent by providing a resistive force. The elbow extensor muscles are being lengthened as the elbow is flexing, but the extensor muscle fibers must exert tension to provide the resistance and, thus, the control for the movement. Since the tensed muscle is also changing its length—in this case, lengthening—it is dynamic tension. This lengthening tension of a muscle group (e.g., the elbow extensors) is called **eccentric tension** (*eccentric* meaning "away from the center"). Muscles that function in this manner control the speed or direction of movement by resisting movement caused by another force (which may include another muscle's force). The segmental motion and muscular tension exhibited by the loser in an arm-wrestling match provides a good example of eccentric tension. The resistive (eccentric) functioning of the elbow flexors against the force of gravity is shown in the downward movement in a pull-up. The elbow extensors function as the resistance during the downward phase of a push-up.

Stabilizing or Fixating a Body Segment

Muscle tension that does not provide enough force to cause a movement and does not give way to another force attempting to cause movement of a body part is termed **static tension,** or more commonly, **isometric contraction.** There is muscular tension, but no discernible movement occurs between body parts. The muscles may attempt to shorten to move the body part, but, because of resistance provided by an external object, person, or another muscle, the body part does not move. Examples of static tension include the muscular tension that develops when you attempt to abduct your arm against a wall, the muscular tension that develops when you arm wrestle with someone of equal strength, and the muscular tension that develops in an antagonistic muscle when a two-joint muscle functions to produce motion in a single joint. In the last case, the antagonistic muscle must counteract the motion in the second joint of the two-joint muscle to allow movement in only the first joint. The stabilization role as described in the last example may be used when a force acts to produce movement of a body part and that movement is not wanted. For example, while performing a push-up, one expects to work the shoulder and arm muscles. Gravity is also pulling on the trunk, however, so that without muscles to counteract the pull of gravity by fixating or stabilizing the trunk, the vertebral column would hyperextend. Figure 2.3 illustrates the fixating or stabilizing function of the trunk flexors during a push-up.

a   **b**

Figure 2.3.   The vertebral column flexors perform a stabilizing function during a pushup. (a) Vertebral column hyperextension. (b) The flexors stabilize the vertebral column in a neutral position.

Sometimes the classification of muscular functions includes a function called **synergy**. *Synergy* means "working together," and is used to describe two muscles working together or helping each other to produce a single movement. For example, if a two-joint muscle is functioning to produce movement at one joint, the second joint must be stabilized by the contraction of an antagonist. This relationship is called true synergy.

The second type of synergy is seen when two muscles have a common mover function. Each muscle also has a second function. The second functions of these two muscles are antagonistic to each other. This relationship is sometimes called helping synergy, because the two muscles help each other perform the common movement while their antagonistic movements are canceled.

Although synergy is an important concept, it is not a real function of a muscle, but rather a description of how muscles work together. Certainly, one must always remember that muscles must work cooperatively to produce any quality of movement—forceful, smooth, or well-timed.

UNDERSTANDING THE CHARACTERISTICS OF THE MUSCULAR SYSTEM AND MUSCULAR TENSION

1. Using illustrations from a muscle anatomy textbook, name the fiber structures of the following muscles: (a) deltoid, (b) trapezius, (c) subscapularis, (d) triceps, (e) semimembranosus, (f) biceps femoris, (g) rectus femoris, (h) adductor magnus, (i) tibialis posterior, (j) gastrocnemius.

2. What is the advantage of a fusiform muscle fiber structure in movement as compared with a pennate structure?

3. What advantage does a pennate fiber structure have over a fusiform structure?

4. Differentiate between active and passive insufficiency in two-joint muscles.

5. With the elbow flexed 90 degrees and the wrist in anatomical position, flex the fingers. With the elbow in the same position but with the wrist flexed 90 degrees, repeat the finger flexion. What is the difference in the ROM that the fingers display in the two situations? What is the name of this phenomenon and the reason for its occurrence?

6. Flex the shoulder joint 90 degrees and then flex the elbow as far as possible. Repeat the elbow flexion with the shoulder joint flexed 180 degrees. Is there any discomfort? Why should one expect the second task to be more difficult? What is the name for this phenomenon?

7. Flex the hip joint with the knee flexed. Flex the hip joint with the knee extended. Note the ROM of each of these movements. Why is there a difference? What is the name for this phenomenon?

8. Stand on one foot and flex the hip and the knee of the free leg as far as possible. Stand on one foot, hyperextend the hip, and flex the knee as far as possible. Is there any difference in the two exercises? What is the difference called, and why would you expect a difference?

9. If the muscle is the motive force for a segment's rotation, what type of muscle contraction is taking place?

10. What type of muscular tension serves to stabilize a body segment to prevent it from moving under the influence of another force?

11. If gravity is the motive force for vertebral flexion, what muscle group contracts to resist or control the speed of this movement, and what type of tension is this?

12. To what muscle *group* does a muscle belong if it can help produce wrist flexion? What is the name of the muscle group that can cause knee extension? hip abduction? shoulder transverse abduction? flexion of the vertebral column? medial rotation of the hip?

13. To what muscle group does a muscle belong if it *resists* knee flexion? if it *resists* knee extension? if it *resists* ankle dorsiflexion? if it *resists* hip abduction? if it *resists* radioulnar supination?

14. Name four pairs of agonist-antagonist muscle *groups* acting across joints you select.

15. In Figure 2.4a–k, a person is performing a series of exercises. Identify for the initial movement and the return movement:

- a. Each articulation where the movement is occurring
- b. Each joint movement occurring
- c. The motive force causing each joint movement
- d. The resistive force acting against each joint movement occurring
- e. The functional muscle group used and the type of contraction used during each joint movement
- f. The body parts or joints needing stabilization during the whole exercise

Exercises used for developing strength or endurance or both in specific muscle groups.

Figure 2.4.

g

j

h

i

k

Figure 2.4
continued

GENERAL CHARACTERISTICS OF THE NEUROMUSCULAR SYSTEM

The musculoskeletal mechanism is set into action and generally controlled by the nervous system. A thorough study of the nervous system is far too complex to be undertaken here; however, several important concepts of neuromuscular functions are examined because they aid understanding of kinesiological and biomechanical factors.

The nervous system consists of the central nervous system, which is composed of the brain and spinal cord, and the peripheral nervous system, which consists of nerve branches from the central nervous system that are arranged in pairs for each side of the body. Twelve pairs of cranial nerves and 31 pairs of spinal nerves are divided as follows: cervical, 8 pairs; thoracic, 12 pairs; lumbar, 5 pairs; sacral, 5 pairs; and coccygeal, 1 pair. These spinal nerves are associated with the vertebral column sections mentioned previously.

The spinal nerves are regrouped into functional sections called plexuses. Further dividing of these nerves takes place peripherally, and thus, the nerves radiate out into areas of the body and its extremities. The names and functions of the plexuses are: the *cervical plexus*, which innervates the muscles of the neck and consists of cervical spinal nerves 1 through 4; the *brachial plexus*, which innervates the shoulder, shoulder joint, and upper limb and consists of cervical spinal nerves 5 through 8 and thoracic spinal nerve 1; the *lumbar plexus*, which innervates the hip and the anterior and medial portions of the thigh and consists of lumbar spinal nerves 1 through 4; and the *sacral plexus*, which innervates the posterior thigh and the entire leg and foot and consists of lumbar spinal nerve 5 and sacral spinal nerves 1 through 3. These plexuses are considered to comprise mainly motor nerve fibers, but sensory nerve fibers also are associated with their pathways. Therefore, the spinal nerve pathways provide the motor nerves necessary for skeletal muscle contraction to produce movements and also the sensory nerves that provide the pathways for sensations back to the central nervous system. The mechanisms for voluntary muscular contractions, the sensory receptors, and the neuromuscular reflexes are important in kinesiological, biomechanical, and physical therapy applications.

The Motor Unit

The spinal nerves continue to subdivide until they come to the end of the nervous pathway and integrate with the muscle. The last single nerve fiber (axon) puts out branches to attach to the skeletal muscle fibers and thus allows the electrical impulses to reach the site where they can stimulate the chemical reaction that initiates muscular contraction.

The last single nerve cell body—nerve fiber (axon) and its branches and their associated muscle fibers—is the smallest functional unit of neuromuscular contraction, and is called a **motor unit.** Generally, motor units can be classified as slow or fast, and possess different characteristics that are discussed in a later section.

Many motor units exist within a single muscle, and the number and type vary among muscles according to muscle size and function. The number of muscle fibers supplied by a motor neuron varies according to the precision required of the particular muscle. For example, those muscles that do small, precise movements, such as those in the fingers, have fewer muscle fibers associated with their many motor units than do the more powerful but less precise muscles of the thigh. Even in the simplest task, many motor units, with each of their respective associated muscle fibers, are required to be active.

The muscle fibers in a given motor unit are dispersed among a number of different bundles rather than being located in one small region. This means that any particular section of a whole muscle consists of fibers from different motor units. When an impulse is transmitted to muscle fibers from their common motor neuron, not all the muscle fibers in that motor unit contract. The stimulus does not reach the thresholds of some "lazy fibers." They can be activated on summation of stimuli, however (Gowitzke and Milner 1980). The motor unit, therefore, does not exhibit an all-or-none response; only those fibers whose threshold is reached can respond together. The total muscle's tension is determined in part by the total number of fibers activated at any given time.

SECTION 4

FACTORS INFLUENCING THE EFFECTIVENESS OF MUSCULAR TENSION

Recruitment

A single motor unit with all its muscle fibers contracts if the stimulus is adequate for each of the fibers. To produce more force, more motor units must be used. An increase in the number of motor units and thus muscle fibers stimulated to produce a stronger contraction is called **recruitment.** Recruitment is the main muscular response used to produce greater muscle tension.

Firing Frequency and Synchronization[2]

Increasing the **frequency** of the nervous stimulus also produces increased muscular tension. Also, if the contractions are synchronized, additional tension results. This **synchronization** of motor unit contractions plays a major role in the level of skill of a performer. A skilled performer has developed the ability to synchronize the

2. For comprehensive coverage of microscopic substructure and biochemical properties of contraction, the reader is referred to Gowitzke and Milner (1980).

motor unit firing to produce a smooth, well-timed, forceful movement, whereas an unskilled performer may have somewhat erratic motor unit activity and thus may lose coordinated movement as well as some tension production by the muscle being used.

Muscle Temperature

Deep muscle temperature affects the speed of muscular contraction and relaxation. Cooler muscles require more relaxation time than warmer muscles, and incomplete relaxation may cause resistance to contracting antagonist muscles (deVries 1980). The value of muscular contraction warm-up exercise prior to demanding activity is significant. Heating the muscles through warm-up muscular contraction (active warm-up) is more effective than externally heating the area for faster contraction and relaxation (passive warm-up).

Muscle Fiber Type

Two fiber types, slow twitch (ST) and fast twitch (FT), were identified in the early stages of fiber type studies. Now, three fiber types (associated with their motor unit types) have been identified and classified according to various characteristics (Burke and Edgerton 1975, deVries 1980). Type I fibers previously called ST are now called slow, oxidative (SO). They have a low strength of contraction, low anaerobic capacity, and are small in size, but they have high capillary density and are highly resistant to fatigue.

The FT fibers are now differentiated into two types. Type IIa fibers are fast, oxidative, and glycolytic (FOG). They are the largest fibers, and they have a large capillary density for good blood supply. Their speed of contraction is fast and their contraction strength is great. They have medium aerobic and anaerobic capacities, but they are more fatigable than SO fibers.

Type IIb fibers, the second type of FT fibers, are fast and glycolytic (FG). These fibers are the most fatigable, having low aerobic capacity and small capillary supply. On the other hand, they are strong and large, and they have a high anaerobic capacity.

All muscle fibers within one motor unit are of the same type, but within any given muscle is a mixture of motor unit (fiber) types. The percentage of fiber types varies among all the muscles in an individual. The fiber-type makeup of any one muscle in an individual is generally believed to be established early in life and to be unchangeable. Metabolic characteristics of fiber types, however, can be changed with training (Gollnick et al. 1972). For example, the aerobic capacity and glycogen content of the muscle can be improved with training.

Wood et al. (1983) indicate that changes in the motor neuron and changes at the neuromuscular junction occur with training. Such neural changes with training may account for the changes seen in FOG and FG fibers. Distance running, for example, seems to produce a shift from FG fibers to FOG fibers, and following weight training, from FOG to FG fibers (deVries 1980).

SELECTIVE RECRUITMENT OF FIBER TYPES

The recruitment of fiber types usually occurs in a preferential manner. SO fibers are recruited during light to moderate ongoing activity. The FOG and then the FG fibers are recruited during exercise demanding greater muscular tension or high power or speed of movement or a combination of these (Campbell et al. 1979).

Gans (1982) reports results of studies on fatiguing activity that show a "standard" order of recruitment of fiber types. First recruited are SO fibers, then FOG, and lastly, FG. This same order of fiber recruitment has been found in fatigued downhill skiers (Eriksson 1976).

The percentage of each fiber type, or the predominance of one type, also varies among individuals, but not between the sexes. Occasionally, muscle biopsies are used to determine the percentage of one fiber type over another in the same muscle of different individuals. An explanation for an athlete's success might be based on a certain fiber predominance in the muscles used in an activity. For example, individuals who have a predominance of one type or another may have an advantage in muscular endurance types of activities (SO fibers) or in quick, forceful activities (FOG, FG fibers).

Because fiber-typing has been related to predictions of success in endurance or in speed events, incentive exists to develop a simple test to predict fiber-type predominance so that individuals can be placed in those activities to which they may be best suited. A muscle biopsy is *not* such a simple test.

In a study of muscle fiber composition in women and their performance capacities, Campbell et al. (1979) found that predominance of one fiber type over another (determined by biopsies) had no relationship to performance before and after training; that is, of the four tests administered—before and after training—none were useful in discriminating between those with high and low percentages of FT fibers. These tests, which were not predictive, included: a maximal oxygen uptake on a cycle ergometer, a high-anaerobic-load power test on a cycle, a low-anaerobic-load power test, and a Sargent jump.

Improvement of all subjects occurred with training, but no significant differences in improvement were noted that would favor a high or low percentage FT group in terms of benefiting more from the training.

The complexity of contraction patterns and fatigue level during exercise may obscure any relationship that may exist between muscle fiber composition and *objective* measures of performance. Studies have not yet found a repeatable correlation. Efforts continue, however, because identification of "success" variables would be rewarding to coaches and athletes.

Elastic Energy: Storage and Recoil

When a muscle is in a tensed state and is then forcibly and quickly stretched immediately before shortening, the elastic recoil provides a significantly large initial force to move the segment in addition to the force provided by the muscle's contractile elements.

The stiffness, or the contracted state, of the muscle is necessary for the storage of elastic energy upon external stretching. The tension developed in individual fibers within a muscle is transmitted to the connective tissue network that envelopes the fibers to form bundles of fibers, which in turn are incorporated into larger and larger bundles. These connective tissues blend with the strong tendon tissues that then attach to the bones. The connective tissue network, which interfaces the contractile muscle fibers with the tendons and bones, has an elastic component that recoils following its stretch. It is stretched by tension applied by internal contraction of muscle fibers and by the resistance of the segments on the ends of the muscle. This *series elastic component* allows the shortening of the muscle fibers to be smoothly transmitted to the bones. It also brings the muscle back to its original length following stretching.

Gowitzke and Milner (1980) report that during the early fast shortening of the fibers, the elastic components are stretched and start to exert passive elastic tension that is initially small. The elastic tension rises rapidly as the fiber shortening continues to maximum intensity and then begins to decline. The fiber contractile tension and elastic tension reach equal intensity just prior to the decline of fiber contractile tension. During the decline of fiber contractile tension, the elastic components recoil to stretch the contractile units back to resting length.

Applications of this contractile-elastic mechanism may be useful in activities in which short, quick stretching of muscle groups occurs simultaneously with innervation of these muscles. The short, quick stretch pulls the elastic elements a bit beyond what the muscle fiber shortening could do. Relieved of the task of shortening to stretch the elastic components, the shortening fibers can exert more tension (Gowitzke and Milner 1980).

Vertical jumps following quick landings from approach steps are noted as being higher than those without the approach and landing. Vertical jumps following landing from a 0.4 m height (depth jump) have been found to be higher than those made from a semisquat with or without a countermovement, or dip (Asmussen and Bonde-Petersen 1976, cited by Cavagna 1977). Jumping from greater heights than 0.4 m, however, does not seem to produce as favorable a result. An explanation for this might be that upon landing, a deeper, slower flexion is required for shock absorption, and therefore the elastic energy may be dissipated during this process, rather than used immediately for leg extension. Generally, it has been found that the smaller the amplitude of joint movement during the stretch and the quicker the stretch, the greater the speed of recoil and the greater the power developed. When movement takes place against a given mass, the effect of stretching is the generation of greater power to accelerate the mass. For example, the mass could be the body itself, as in jumping, or a segment with an implement.

Ikegami et al. (1981) report that a javelin thrower's kinetic energy (energy due to the running approach) appears to be stored as elastic energy in the early part of the throwing motion when the body is arched and the javelin is back. This elastic energy is then released to accelerate the javelin.

Prestretches or windups of segmental movements such as in throwing, striking, and kicking patterns can therefore augment the muscle contractile force that is to come. Shock absorption (stretching at foot plant) in running can contribute to greater force of push-off (Cavagna, Dusman, and Margaria 1968). In sprint running, the power developed at each push-off was found to be increased due to the contribution of the muscle's recoil from the quick stretch applied at contact (0.15 to 0.1 sec).

In addition to the force production capability of the muscle fiber, some evidence suggests that the muscle fiber's contractile portion also has some elasticity (Schmidt 1982). Moreover, indications are that SO and FT fibers have different elastic properties (Komi and Bosco 1978), with the SO fibers being reported to have the greater elasticity (Gowitzke and Milner 1980). If this were so, individuals varying in fiber-type composition in a given muscle group would also tend to vary in their ability to store and use elastic energy in activities utilizing prestretch along with motive muscular contraction force.

Length-Tension Relationship

A factor that influences the force of muscle contraction is its length at the time it is stimulated. The **length-tension relationship** states that the contractile tension the muscle is able to produce increases with the length of the muscle and is maximum when the muscle is at its resting length. The contractile tension produced decreases as the muscle becomes shorter, or as it is stretched beyond resting length. In normal (intact) muscles, greater tension is produced when the muscle is stretched, apparently contradicting the length-tension rule. The increased tension seen with stretch, however, is not contractile muscle tension; it is due to the contribution of the elastic component in the tissues. Figure 2.5 shows a simplified length-tension curve for contractile tension and for the increase in total tension due to the elastic component.

If a muscle is *overly* stretched, that is, forced beyond the length to which it normally can be stretched in the body, the increase in elastic tension cannot make up for the decrease in contractile tension that occurs progressively from resting length. Just how much stretch is optimum depends on the muscle. Gowitzke and Milner (1980) report that parallel-fibered muscles produce maximum total tension near resting length, whereas other fiber arrangements can be stretched farther for more tension. In general, Gowitzke and Milner indicate that the greatest total tension can be produced at between 120% and 130% of resting length.

An example of a muscle group in a fully extended position to gain the maximum effect of the length-tension relationship is the leg and foot relationship at the ankle when the feet are placed in starting blocks (Figure 2.6a). Another example is the thigh, leg, and foot position at the hip, knee, and ankle when the starting position for swimming is assumed (Figure 2.6b). Both of these positions place the ankle plantar flexors at a length that is greater than their resting lengths, thus increasing the possible tension developed upon contraction. The placement of the segment in a position to gain maximum tension due to the length-tension relationship should not be confused with the dynamic situation in which the segment is moved into a position that causes a fast stretch on the muscles crossing a joint, as in a backswing.

Minimum tension at the shortest length usually occurs at the end of the range of motion of the joint across which the muscle has shortened. Gowitzke and Milner

The length-tension relationship in skeletal muscle. The increase in total tension is due to the elastic component.

Figure 2.5.

Placing muscles on stretch prior to contraction enables them to contract more forcefully.

Figure 2.6.

(1980) report that at lengths shorter than 50% of resting length, no contractile tension is able to be generated.

Force-Velocity Relationship

The relationship that exists between the velocity of muscle shortening and the tension it is able to generate may be an important constraint, or limiting factor, in the performance of rapid movements. Laboratory experiments with excised muscles indicate that the tension a muscle is able to exert decreases as the speed of muscle shortening increases. In intact muscles within a given individual, the muscles that move light segments shorten faster than the muscles that move heavier segments (Gans 1982). According to the *force-velocity relationship,* the velocity (speed) at which a muscle shortens is inversely related to the load it must move: that is, if the load is great, the velocity of shortening is slow; if the load is light, the tension required is small, and the shortening velocity is fast. Figure 2.7 shows a force-velocity curve that includes concentric, isometric, and eccentric contractions. Note

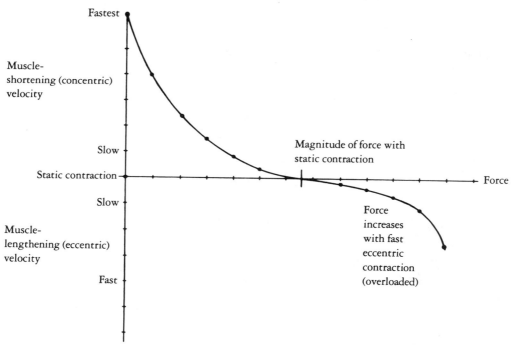

Figure 2.7.   Force-velocity curve for an isolated muscle. The maximum contractile force is least for fast concentric tension and greatest for fast eccentric tension when overloaded.

that the shortening velocity is zero for isometric (static) contraction; this occurs when the load becomes great enough so that the muscle cannot shorten. Such static or isometric loads are used often as measures of a person's maximum strength, since using zero velocity is a convenient way to standardize the tests. As the resistance is lightened, the muscle is able to shorten, and the velocity of muscle contraction increases. The shortening velocity is maximum when the load (tension developed) is zero. The maximum speed with zero load depends on the speed of contraction for the contractile units in the particular muscle examined (SO, FOG, and FG fiber types).

An investigation of this phenomenon noted that although our understanding of this process is incomplete, some type of neural regulatory mechanism may be involved in limiting the maximum voluntary tension levels, possibly as a safety mechanism for preventing anatomical injury (Perrine and Edgerton 1978). The possible limitation set by the force-velocity relationship is noteworthy in performances in which the speed of muscular contractions must cause a segment to keep up with or catch up to an object that is already moving to apply an accelerating force to that object. An example is striking a racquetball in a forward direction as it is moving forward from a rebound off the back wall. If the segments cannot move faster than the ball, there can be no impact force to accelerate the ball, that is, to force the ball to move faster than it is already moving. Another feature of the force-velocity relationship, as can be seen on the curve in Figure 2.7, is that when the muscle is "superloaded," thereby causing eccentric contraction against the moving load, the tension able to be generated increases with lengthening velocity, but to some limiting value. To generate muscle tension that is greater than the maximum isometric tension, the load must be greater than the isometric load that cannot be moved by the muscle; otherwise a decrease in tension is observed by the muscle simply acting with a submaximal, controlling tension to lower the load. Eccentric strength training, using supermaximal loads, has been incorporated into weight programs of athletes, although such work is reported to generate the greatest amount of muscle soreness.

Muscle Power

The force-velocity relationship is an important consideration in the production of muscle power, the ability of a muscle to exert a large amount of force at a fast rate. Because an inverse relationship apparently exists between the amount of force produced and the velocity of application, a trade-off between these two variables must occur. Since power equals force applied times the velocity with which that force is applied, some optimum rate of muscle shortening could be expected to produce the most powerful contraction. Such an optimum rate has been found to be approximately 25% to 30% of the fastest rate of contraction (Astrand and Rodahl 1977). At this rate, the force of contraction is approximately 30% of the maximal isometric force. Muscular power is required in activities in which an object or the body must be forced to a high speed quickly. For example, bursts of muscular power are needed in the shot put, sprint starts, high jump takeoff, segmental movements through water in competitive swimming, and dance leaps. An increase in power production can result from increasing strength or the speed of force application or both. More is said about muscular power and training in Chapter 7. For now, note that the power of muscular contraction varies with different combinations of muscle force and speeds of contraction.

Angle of Muscle Pull

A final consideration in determining the effectiveness of a muscle's tension is the angle at which the muscle pulls on the bone. The angle of pull influences the magnitude of muscle force needed to cause segmental movement. When a muscle's angle of attachment is 90 degrees to the bone on which it pulls, 100% of its force contributes to the bone's movement. Since most muscles are unable to achieve a 90-degree attachment angle, the joint position for which the muscle's attachment angle is closest to 90 degrees provides the greatest rotary force for movement of the segment. A complete discussion of the reasons for force changes with changes in the muscle-bone angle is in Chapter 3.

UNDERSTANDING THE NEUROMUSCULAR SYSTEM AND FACTORS AFFECTING MUSCULAR TENSION

1. List the components of a motor unit.

2. List the ways in which a muscle may increase the total tension it can produce.

3. Identify the functional differences among SO, FOG, and FG muscle fibers.

4. Speculate about the relative proportions of fiber types in the muscles of championship performers: (a) the legs of a marathon runner, (b) the arms of a shot-putter, (c) the arms of a gymnast, (d) the arms of a baseball pitcher, (e) the legs of a downhill skier, (f) the legs of a cross-county skier, and (g) the legs of a mountain climber.

5. Explain how the elastic component in skeletal muscle is useful in movement.

6. List and describe three activities in which the force-velocity relationship of muscular contraction may be influential.

7. Describe three activities in which the length-tension relationship could influence performance.

SECTION 5

GENERAL CHARACTERISTICS OF THE SENSORIMOTOR SYSTEM[3]

The Sensory Unit

The coordination of the muscular system, that is, the initiation of changes in individual muscles (e.g., contractions, relaxations, force adjustments), depends on a continuous supply of information about the immediate state of those muscles. Information on the position, length, tension, and speed of contraction of individual muscles is supplied through an extensive network of **sensory units** that are grossly similar in structure to the motor units. Each sensory unit consists of the following: (a) sensory **receptors,** which are located within various muscles and connective tissues (intrinsic) or cutaneous tissue (extrinsic), (b) an **axon,** and (c) a **nerve cell.** Some of the sensory systems provide the sensations necessary to produce appropriate muscular responses of a reflex nature. Others provide sensations to the brain to be integrated and acted on consciously and voluntarily by the performer depending on the purpose of the movement and the background experience of the performer. The mechanism by which the sensory system orders responses is similar to that of the motor system, but it works in a reverse manner. The variation of the strength or importance of the stimuli or both on the tissues determines the response of the sensory receptor as it transmits different strengths and frequencies of electrical impulses to the central nervous system (the spinal cord). There they either synapse with a motor nerve to produce an immediate movement or continue to travel to the brain where they are integrated and sorted before being sent down the spinal cord to synapse with motor neurons to produce the appropriate movements. The former (immediate) motor responses are reflex in nature; the latter (consciously controlled) movements are voluntary in nature.

The Sensory Receptors

Sensory receptors can be classified and named according to the location of the source of the stimuli (Powers 1976). The **exteroceptors** are located in or around the skin. They respond to changes in the environment that directly influence the exterior of the body. Examples of environmental changes of this sort are temperature and

---

3. The complexity of neuromuscular processes and sensorimotor control mechanisms preclude a detailed treatment of these aspects of movement within this text. Excellent coverage is provided by Schmidt (1982).

pressure. The **teleceptor** is a special type of exteroceptor that includes the receptors that respond to odors, noises, and things seen in the environment. The stimuli affecting these receptors are provided by indirect changes in the outside environment. **Interoceptors** are located inside the body; they receive and respond to information from the internal environment. The functioning of the viscera is controlled by these receptors. The **proprioceptors** are located in and around the joints, muscles, tendons, and the inner ear. They respond to changes in joint position, muscle length, muscle tension, acceleration of segmental movements, and, in general, postural changes.

EXTEROCEPTORS

Cutaneous receptors are sense organs located in the skin. They help a performer respond to pressure of varying intensity by producing various strengths and frequencies of impulses in response to the nature of a stimulus. The performer commonly perceives these sensations as those of touch and pain. Some of the sensations provided by the receptors reach the level of consciousness; that is, sensory impulses are transmitted to the brain so that a feeling or knowing of pain or touch is possible.

An individual's ability to perceive pressure on the body and to know the sensation of different bodily pressures is made possible by the cutaneous receptors. For the individual to make appropriate, conscious motor adjustments to a new sensation, his/her pressure receptors must be provided with information that can be compared or associated with sensations that are stored in his/her brain as a result of previous similar experiences.

Pressure receptors also provide an individual with important information about the position of her body in space. The disorientation that a gymnast feels when leaving the bed of a trampoline is partially due to lack of touch or pressure on body segments (e.g., feet, knees, buttocks). In this situation, the touch of the spotter's hand can provide the gymnast's pressure receptors with information to help orient the body. A performer also may learn to use effectively the sensations that are perceived from the touch of equipment, such as the feel of a spotting belt around the waist. Less common touch orientation such as this must be sensed several times before the perception can be used effectively to provide the performer with information that will be helpful in making appropriate movement responses. After several encounters with stimuli produced by unusual situations, an individual is able to store and use those perceptions as comparators in future situations. A person unfamiliar with the feeling of being without the typical pressure sensations (i.e., being free of support in the air and unfamiliar with the perception provided by a spotting belt around the waist) will feel uneasy until the feeling is established.

The stimuli that one senses on the palm of the hand when attempting to throw objects of various sizes provide the perceptions for positioning and grasping the objects. Consider the act of throwing a football. If the hand is large enough, it can grasp the ball and control its direction until the fingers release it. If the hand is small, however, the fingers may slip off the ball prematurely, resulting in reduced speed of the ball and a projection direction different from that desired. The ball may even slip off the hand entirely during the preparation or execution phase of the throw and land on the ground near the thrower. Because of the cutaneous receptors in the hand, one can feel the onset of lack of control and the possibility of slippage. Thus one can either adjust the placement of the hand to the smaller part of the ball or adjust the pattern of movement in the throw by tipping the nose of the football downward slightly so that the forward movement of the hand pushes against the ball without slipping out from underneath it.

Variations in the stimuli on the pressure receptors in the soles of the feet are provided by running on different surfaces such as sand, gravel, and uneven terrain. Such variations provide an individual with sensations that are stored in the brain and later used to make adjustments in the position of the lower extremities when running or walking on uneven surfaces. Perceptions such as these decrease the probability of ankle sprains or other injuries caused by lack of control.

The reflex nature of some movements initiated by stimulation of the cutaneous receptors include the righting reflexes used in balance activities and the postural reflexes used in balance and upright standing. Reflexes are involuntary sensory motor responses, although an individual is usually aware of such a movement as or after it happens. One of the main reflexes is the extensor thrust reflex, which elicits an extension reaction in the lower extremity when pressure is applied to the sole of the foot. This reflex may help in the extension of the lower extremity that is necessary in activities such as diving, rebound tumbling, running, and jumping. The extensor thrust reflex is one of the important reflexes used in postural alignment in standing, during which a continual sway of the body produces variations in pressure on the soles of the feet and thus results in motor adjustments for balance.

Teleceptors. The teleceptors are specialized sense receptors that respond to non-direct stimuli from the external environment, such as odor, light, and sound (Powers 1976). They are mentioned here because they receive many stimuli that affect movement. The responses to these stimuli may be of a reflex nature, as when one blinks the eyes in response to an approaching object or jumps in response to a loud, unexpected sound. The responses also may be conscious in nature, such as when a basketball guard responds to the observed movement of an opponent or when a dribbler responds to the sound of an opponent's footsteps approaching from behind.

Most of the usefulness of the teleceptors lies in their contribution to the performer's conscious awareness and understanding of the immediate significant environment. For instance, the smell of smoke may elicit a relaxing response if it comes from a campfire, but quite a different response if it comes from a burning building or a junkyard. The stimuli must be associated with the situation, and a period of trial-and-error muscular responses must have been experienced before the performer can utilize the stimuli effectively in judging and making appropriate movements.

Coaching drills and instruction in physical activities frequently emphasize visual perceptions or cues as a means of diagnosing situations and prescribing necessary movements for a given situation. For example, a basketball coach may cue players to keep their eyes on the ball or on the opposing players. As necessary as these visual cues may be, little thought or practice goes into developing another important ability: the perception of auditory signals. Sometimes the visual stimuli must be occluded to enable practice of auditory perceptions.

PROPRIOCEPTORS

Proprioceptors are internal receptors that are located in and around the joints and muscles, in the skin, and in the inner ear. They respond to changes in position and acceleration of body segments. According to Schmidt (1982), the term *proprioception* traditionally has been used to mean the perception of the body's movement and its position in space whether it is still or moving. A term often used synonymously with proprioception is **kinesthesis.** As more is learned about the sensorimotor mechanisms, it appears that all sensory receptors can contribute to kinesthesis and that sense of position and movement is not restricted to only those classified as proprioceptors. Four of the more predominant types of proprioceptors used for movement perception are cutaneous receptors, joint receptors, musculotendinous receptors, and labyrinthine receptors.

Cutaneous Receptors. In addition to specialized cutaneous receptors used for outside information (exteroceptors), those that sense deep pressure or touch and very light touch, including movement of hairs on the skin, serve as important proprioceptors for kinesthetic sense and an awareness of how the body is interacting with its environment.

Joint Receptors. Receptors located in the joint capsules and the surrounding ligaments respond to stimuli that produce sensations relating to positions, velocities, and accelerations occurring at the joints. The receptors are stimulated by pressure changes from within and surrounding the articulation and are sensitive to pressure changes resulting from as little as 2 degrees of change in joint position (Gardner and O'Connell 1972). The receptors provide information about the position of the joint at any given time, velocity of the movement that may be occurring at that joint, and acceleration and deceleration of segmental movements.

Pressure receptors within joints, particularly in the lower extremity and especially in the foot, add to the sensations provided by the cutaneous receptors and are used for postural adjustments. Pressure changes within the intervertebral joints stimulate the muscles that maintain the upright position of the trunk and contribute to the balance of the body's weight. The distribution of the body's weight from one limb to the other has important implications for single-limb weight bearing. The pressure changes within the supporting hip joint when the other limb is lifted off the ground provide sensory information that stimulates the stabilizing muscles surrounding the hip joint. The body responds by pulling the body weight over the supporting limb so that the unbalanced body weight does not pull the body over to the unsupported side. The changes in the hip joint position then stimulate, through sensory pathways, the surrounding muscles to help lift the pelvis so that it does not tilt to the unsupported side.

Velocities and accelerations of body segments also serve to stimulate the joint receptors, and the sensations are frequently used to adjust the speed of these segmental movements. The most obvious example concerns an object that is perceived to be heavier than it actually is. When the object is lifted, too many motor units are activated in anticipation of the perceived weight, and the object is lifted much faster and farther than expected or desired. Sensing the inappropriate speed of the movement, the joint receptors send impulses to the brain to indicate the incorrect response. The brain then sends impulses down through the motor pathways to correct the error.

A similar feedback system is used in producing and correcting sport skill performance. Skilled performers are able to sense, by way of the joint receptors, movements that are too fast, too slow, or in the wrong direction, and consequently, are able to correct their future responses. The skilled free-throw shooter can sense the success of a shot as the ball leaves the hand. The skilled golfer can sense the accuracy of a chip shot as the ball leaves the club face. On the other hand, the beginner has nothing with which to compare the sensations; thus performance becomes a trial-and-error procedure until adequate sensations of a successful performance are established as one passes through the intermediate and advanced stages of learning.

Musculotendinous Receptors. A third type of proprioceptor used in muscular control and coordination is the musculotendinous receptor. There are two such types of receptors—the tendon receptors and the muscle receptors.

Specialized receptors located between the muscle and its tendon are called the **Golgi tendon organs.** These receptors are sensitive to the stretch of the muscle tendon produced by the *contraction* of its associated muscle (active stretch). Their response to this stretch is to inhibit the contraction of the associated muscle (autogenic inhibition) and thus relieve the tension produced at the musculotendinous junctions and to excite the antagonistic muscle group. This inhibition of the contraction of its muscle has important implications for physical activity and conditioning programs. The Golgi receptors in the tendon of a strongly contracted muscle respond by inhibiting the contraction of that muscle. Such a muscle can be stretched fully more easily than a muscle not under the influence of this response. Secondly, since the Golgi organs facilitate the contraction of the antagonists, the contraction of a muscle group to stimulate the Golgi organs enhances the contraction of the opposite muscle group. One use of these receptors may be when an individual attempts to stretch a muscle fully. A strong static (isometric) contraction of the muscle just prior to the stretch may stimulate the Golgi tendon organs and thus inhibit the muscle and enable it to be stretched to a greater degree. If one wants a strong contraction of muscle group A, then one should contract the antagonistic group B just prior to the desired contraction of A to stimulate the Golgi tendon organs in group B; this Golgi stimulation will have an excitatory effect on muscle group A, enhancing its contraction.

Findings of research presented by Schmidt (1982) indicate that the Golgi tendon organs are sensitive detectors of tension in distinct, localized regions of their host muscle. As sensors of degrees of tension within parts of the muscle, they are probably important contributors to fine motor control, as well as protective agents.

The **muscle spindle** is a second type of musculotendinous receptor. Muscle spindles are located throughout the muscle and are situated between and parallel to individual muscle fibers. In this position they are stretched when their adjacent muscle fibers are stretched. When the whole muscle is stretched, the stretch of the muscle spindles causes a reflex contraction of their host muscle. This response is called the *myotatic* or *stretch reflex.* The knee-jerk reflex is an example.

The internal structures and functions of the muscle spindle are highly complex, and are not yet fully understood. By no means should muscle spindles be remembered only for their elicitation of the stretch reflex. On the contrary, their functional substructure provides for constant monitoring and regulation of sensorimotor function that enables appropriate body movement, both reflexively and voluntarily. The role of muscle spindles in motor control is described in detail by Schmidt (1982). Although muscle spindles previously were not thought to contribute to the conscious perception of position or movement, recent work indicates that the spindles can be sources of information that contribute to kinesthesis when combined with other sensory input (Schmidt 1982).

Muscle spindles respond to either active or passive stretch and are sensitive to the speed of the stretch; that is, the faster the stretch, the stronger the response of muscle contraction. The spindles provide information on the length of the muscle as well as the speed of the stretch. Evidence exists also that the acceleration (rate of speed increase or decrease) of spindle stretch and the speed of stretch are directly related to the stretch reflex response (Perot and Goubel 1981). Because the muscle contracts more strongly immediately after it is put on stretch, the spindles also cause the inhibition of the antagonists, which is a process called **reciprocal inhibition.** Both the stretch reflex and the reciprocal inhibition of the antagonistic muscle group are used effectively in activities in which a strong contraction is desired.

A great contribution of the spindle's response to stretch in sport and dance activities is how it prepares the muscle for using its elastic energy. The work of Nichols and Houk (1976), cited by Schmidt (1982), provides evidence that the reflex muscle contraction caused by the stretch reflex (as in a backswing or in shock absorption) causes the contracted state necessary for a subsequent quick short stretch to store elastic energy in the muscle. A degree of stiffness is thereby provided the muscle to be stretched again so that it can recoil to help accelerate the movement.

Examples of use of the stretch reflex together with the recoil of stored elastic energy are found in throwing and striking activities in which a preparatory phase puts on stretch the muscles that are going to do the striking or throwing just prior to their contraction. A slight movement of all segments to the right just prior to a swing of the bat in baseball, a long backswing in golf, or the backswing of a bowler not only gives the muscles more range of motion during the force phase of the movement but also puts the motive muscles on stretch, thus enhancing their contractile force as well as facilitating the recoil of elastic tissue. For example, picture the stretch of the shoulder joint muscles of a baseball pitcher as he takes his windup. During the initial forward phase of the throw, the rotation of the trunk forward and the lagging back of the upper extremity put the anterior shoulder muscles on stretch just prior to the contraction of the muscles to bring the arm forward and consequently stimulate their contraction prior to the final quick stretch. In this manner, the forward speed of the arm is greater when the pitcher throws the ball.

Labyrinthine Receptors.   Receptors located in the inner ear are specialized to respond to changes in the position of the head relative to the downward pull of gravity and to changes in the linear and rotational speeds of the head. The predominance of these reflexes depends on the physical maturation of the individual. Some predominate during the infant stage and are gradually phased out as the infant assumes the upright sitting or standing posture; others are facilitated by the upright postures, but are not observed in the infant.

The tonic labyrinthine responses are evident in infants and are stimulated by the head and body positions. These reflexes excite the joint extensors when the body is in a supine (lying on the back) position and the flexors when the body is in a prone (lying face down) position. Similarly, the extensors are stimulated on the underside of a side-lying body, while the flexors are stimulated on the upper side. Upright postural positions are initiated by the development of labyrinthine righting reflexes, which are associated with head positions relative to the downward pull of gravity. Stimulation of the appropriate muscles in the neck and trunk assists in correctly aligning the body segments with the line of gravity; thus, the child is able to sit and eventually to stand. The labyrinthine receptors are eventually incorporated into a set of righting and equilibrium responses that help maintain posture, balance, and stability.

Integrated Sensorimotor Responses

POSTURE AND EQUILIBRIUM[4]

Body orientation and balance depend on a large combination of sensory units. As a child begins to assume upright posture, the righting reflexes develop to help stimulate the appropriate muscles in the neck and trunk to assist in aligning the body segments correctly with gravity, and thus the child is able to sit and eventually stand. The joint receptors in the neck respond to positional orientations of the head and neck as well as to neck movements. Once the body can be held upright, other reflexes must predominate so that the body can maintain equilibrium. These other equilibrium reflexes are the labyrinthine receptors, which respond to movements of the head about all axes and in all directions. The position of the head is important in maintaining postural equilibrium, and the impulses generated provide the postural adjustments to body sway while standing. A complicated set of rules govern the equilibrium responses; however, let it suffice to say that these responses to movement stimulate the appropriate muscles so as to maintain the balance of the body and prevent it from tipping over.

The equilibrium reflexes are aided by the stretch reflex and other regulatory

---

4. For a more detailed discussion of the postural and equilibrium responses, the reader is referred to Goodwin (1976), and Gowitzke and Milner (1980).

information provided by the muscle spindles of the antigravity muscles, those extensor muscles of the trunk and lower extremity that counteract the force of gravity and prevent the body from collapsing or tipping over. As one sways while standing, the muscles antagonistic to the direction of sway are stretched, thus stimulating the muscle spindles, which cause a reflex contraction of those muscles to bring the body back into alignment. Further help is given by the cutaneous receptors in the soles of the feet, which respond to alterations in pressure from the ground, and by the joint receptors in the foot and ankle. External pressures and intrajoint pressures stimulate these receptors and allow a person to make appropriate adjustments to uneven terrain.

SKILLED MOVEMENT

Much of the awareness of one's own body position and movements is provided by visual feedback. For example, when one moves a body part, one can usually see the movement relative to the environment and thus judge its correctness and accuracy. Because of the reliance on visual feedback of this sort, one tends to neglect the sensations and information provided by the cutaneous, joint, and muscle receptors. *Kinesthetic sense,* or *kinesthesis,* is an important capability that is well developed in athletes and that increases the performance quality of daily activities of the nonathlete.

To develop a frame of reference for kinesthetic sensations, an individual must experience a variety of positions and movements in many environments. The perceptions associated with those situations are then stored in the brain for use as a reference or comparator for future movements. Precise and accurate motor responses are developed from the integration of information from the cutaneous, joint, tendon, muscle, and labyrinthine receptors. Visual cues may reinforce or be a means for correcting a kinesthetic perception; that is, if one stands in front of a mirror and views one's body positions, one can develop an awareness of the sensations produced when a given body position is assumed. The sensations are provided by the joint and musculotendinous receptors and are associated with the visual information provided by the mirrors. Correctness or incorrectness of a prescribed position (e.g., a fencing en garde position) may then be determined.

Auditory and olfactory (smell) stimuli may also affect the motor responses by providing information about the environment. As with the kinesthetic cues and responses, the teleceptor cues and responses must be practiced in an environment designed to reinforce those responses. If too much reliance is placed on visual feedback, auditory responses will contribute minimally to the accuracy of a movement. For instance, the success of a golf shot is typically determined by looking at where the ball goes. A good shot also may be determined in part by the sound of the impact, however. A poor shot sounds like a crack and a good shot sounds like a click.

Unfortunately, many teachers and coaches of movement skills train their athletes to rely heavily on visual perceptions to gauge movement, and they neglect to stress the development of auditory feedback and of the kinesthetic sense.

UNDERSTANDING THE SENSORIMOTOR SYSTEM

1. Select a sports activity in which the exteroceptors and teleceptors play an important part, and describe how they do so.

2. Describe how the Golgi tendon organs facilitate and inhibit muscular contractions. Cite a sport-specific example.

3. Describe how the muscle spindles facilitate and inhibit muscular contractions. Cite a sport-specific example.

4. Describe two sport situations in which a teacher or coach may want to teach the performer to use information provided by kinesthesis.

REFERENCES
SUGGESTED READINGS

Alexander, R. M. *Biomechanics: Outline Studies in Biology.* New York: John Wiley & Sons, 1975.

Asmussen, E., and Bonde-Petersen, F. "Storage of Elastic Energy in Skeletal Muscles in Man." *Acta Physiologica Scandinavica* 91 (1974): 385–92.

Astrand, P., and Rodahl, K. *Textbook of Work Physiology.* New York: McGraw-Hill, 1977.

Basmajian, J. V., and MacConaill, M. A. *Muscles and Movements—A Basis for Human Kinesiology.* Huntington, N.Y.: Robert E. Krieger Publishing Co., 1977.

Burke, R. E., and Edgerton, V. R. "Motor Unit Properties." In *Exercise and Sports Science Reviews*, vol. 3, ed. J. H. Wilmore and J. F. Keogh, 31–81. Santa Barbara, Calif.: Journal Publishing Affiliates, 1975.

Caiozzo, V. J., Perrine, J. J., and Edgerton, V. R. "Alterations in the In Vivo Force-Velocity Relationship." Abstract in *Medicine and Science in Sports and Exercise* 12 (2) (1980): 134.

Campbell, C. J., Bonen, A., Kirby, R. L., and Belcastro, A. N. "Muscle Fiber Composition and Performance Capacities of Women." *Medicine and Science in Sports* 11 (3) (1979): 260–65.

Cavagna, G. A. "Storage and Utilization of Elastic Energy in Skeletal Muscle." In *Exercise and Sports Sciences Reviews*, ed. R. S. Hutton, 82–129. Philadelphia: Franklin Press, 1977.

Cavagna, G. A., Dusman, B., and Margaria, R. "Positive Work Done by a Previously Stretched Muscle." *Journal of Applied Physiology* 24 (1968): 21–32.

Coyle, E., et al. "Skeletal Muscle Fiber Characteristics of World Class Shot Putters." *Research Quarterly* 49 (3) (1978): 278–84.

Coyle, E., Costill, D. L., and Lemes, G. R. "Leg Extension Power and Muscle Fiber Composition." *Medicine and Science in Sports* 11 (1) (1979): 12–15.

Craske, B. "Perception of Impossible Limb Positions Induced by Tendon Vibration." *Science* 196 (1977): 71–73.

deVries, H. A. *Physiology of Exercise.* Dubuque, Iowa: William C. Brown Co., 1980.

Eriksson, E. "Sports Injuries of the Knee Ligaments: Their Diagnosis, Treatment, Rehabilitation, and Prevention." *Medicine and Science in Sports* 8 (1976): 133–44.

Gans, C. "Fiber Architecture and Muscle Function." In *Exercise and Sports Sciences Reviews*, vol. 10, ed. R. L. Terjung, 160–207. Franklin Institute Press, 1982.

Gardner, E. B., and O'Connell, A. *Understanding the Scientific Bases of Human Movement.* Baltimore: Williams & Wilkins, 1972.

Goldfuss, A., Morehouse, C., and LeVeau, B. "Effects of Muscular Tension on Knee Stability." *Medicine and Science in Sports* 5 (4) (1973): 267–71.

Gollnick, P. D., Armstrong, R. B., Saubert, C. W., Piehl, K., and Saltin, B. "Enzyme Activity and Fiber Composition in Skeletal Muscle of Trained and Untrained Men." *Journal of Applied Physiology* 24 (1972): 312–19.

Goodgold, J., and Eberstein, A. *Electrodiagnosis of Neuromuscular Diseases.* 2d ed. Baltimore: Williams & Wilkins, 1977.

Goodwin, G. M. "The Sense of Limb Position and Movement." In *Exercise and Sports Science Reviews*, vol. 4, ed. J. F. Keogh and R. S. Hutton, 87–124. Santa Barbara, Calif.: Journal Publishing Affiliates, 1976.

Goodwin, G. M., McCloskey, D. I., and Mathews, P. B. C. "Proprioceptive Illusions Induced by Muscle Vibration: Contribution by Muscle Spindles to Perception?" *Science* 175 (1982): 1382–85.

Gowitzke, B. A. "Kinesiological and Neurophysiological Principles Applied to Gymnastics." In *Kinesiology Review*, ed. D. H. Clarke, 22–32. Reston, Va.: AAHPERD, 1968.

Gowitzke, B. A., and Milner, M. *Understanding the Scientific Bases of Human Movement.* 2d ed. Baltimore: Williams & Wilkins, 1980.

Gray, H. *Anatomy of the Human Body.* 28th ed. Ed. C. M. Goss. Philadelphia: Lea & Febiger, 1966.

Harris, F. A. "Facilitation Techniques in Therapeutic Exercise." In *Therapeutic Exercise.* 3d ed. Ed. J. V. Basmajian, 93–137. Baltimore: Williams & Wilkins, 1978.

Hof, A. L., Geelen, B. A., and VanDen Berg, J. W. "Calf Muscle Moment, Work and Efficiency in Level Walking; Role of Series Elasticity." *Journal of Biomechanics* 16 (7) (1983): 523–37.

Homma, S. "The Stretch Reflex as Motor Control." In *Biomechanics VIII-A: Proceedings of the Eighth International Congress on Biomechanics*, ed. H. Matsui and K. Kobayashi, 189–205. Champaign, Ill.: Human Kinetics Publishers, 1983.

Ianuzzo, C. D. "The Cellular Composition of Human Skeletal Muscles." In *Neuromuscular Mechanisms for Therapeutic and Conditioning Exercise*, ed. H. G. Knuttgen, 31–53. Baltimore: University Park Press, 1976.

Ikegami, Y., Miura, M., Matsui, H., and Hashimoto, I. "Biomechanical Analysis of the Javelin Throw." In *Biomechanics VII-B: Proceedings of the Seventh International Congress of Biomechanics*, ed. A. Morecki, K. Fidelus, K. Kedzior, and A. Wit, 271–76. Baltimore: University Park Press, 1981.

Ito, A., Komi, P. V., Sjodin, B., Bosco, C., and Karlsson, J. "Mechanical Efficiency of Positive Work in Running at Different Speeds." *Medicine and Science in Sports and Exercise* 15 (1983): 299–308.

Komi, P. V. "Biomechanics and Neuromuscular Performance." *Medicine and Science in Sports and Exercise* 16 (1) (1984): 26–28.

Komi, P. V. "Measurement of the Force-Velocity Relationship in Human Muscle Under Concentric and Eccentric Contractions." In *Biomechanics III: Proceedings of the Third*

International Biomechanics Seminar, ed. S. Cerquiglini, A. Vernerando, and J. Warten-weiler, 224–29. Baltimore: University Park Press, 1973.

Komi, P. V., and Bosco, C. "Utilization of Elastic Energy in Jumping and Its Relation to Skeletal Muscle Fiber Composition in Man." In *Biomechanics VI-A: Proceedings of the Sixth International Congress of Biomechanics*, ed. E. Asmussen and K. Jorgensen, 79–85. Baltimore: University Park Press, 1978.

Lamb, D. R. *Physiology of Exercise.* New York: Macmillan, 1978.

Nichols, T. R., and Houk, J. C. "The Improvement of Linearity and the Regulation of Stiffness That Results From the Actions of the Stretch Reflex." *Journal of Neurophysiology* 39 (1976): 119–42.

Osternig, L. R., et al. "Function of Limb Speed on Torque Patterns of Antagonist Muscles." In *Biomechanics VIII-A: Proceedings of the Eighth International Congress on Biomechanics*, ed. H. Matsui and K. Kobayashi, 251–257. Champaign, Ill.: Human Kinetics Publishers, 1983.

Perot, C., and Goubel, F. "Control Mechanism of Bifunctional Muscles: A Reflex Approach." In *Biomechanics VII-A: Proceedings of the Seventh International Congress of Biomechanics*, ed. A. Morecki, K. Fidelus, K. Kedzior, and A. Wit, 84–88. Baltimore: University Park Press, 1981.

Perrine, J. L., and Edgerton, V. R. "Muscle Force-Velocity and Power-Velocity Relationships Under Isokinetic Loading." *Medicine and Science in Sport* 10 (3) (1978): 159–66.

Polit, A., and Bizzi, E. "Process Controlling Arm Movements in Monkeys." *Science* 201 (1978): 1235–37.

Powers, W. "Nervous System Control of Muscular Activity." In *Neuromuscular Mechanisms for Therapeutic and Conditioning Exercise*, ed. H. G. Knuttgen, 1–30. Baltimore: University Park Press, 1976.

Rasch, P. J., and Burke, R. K. *Kinesiology and Applied Anatomy.* 6th ed. Philadelphia: Lea & Febiger, 1978.

Sapega, A., et al. "Sport Specific Performance Factor Profiling: Fencing as a Prototype." *American Journal of Sports Medicine* 6 (5) (1978): 232.

Schmidt, R. A. *Motor Control and Learning.* Champaign, Ill.: Human Kinetics Publishers, 1982.

Shambes, G. M., and Campbell, S. "Inherent Movement Patterns in Man." In *Kinesiology III*, ed. C. J. Widule, 50–58. Reston, Va.: AAHPERD, 1973.

Sjogaard, G. "Force-Velocity Curve for Bicycle Work." In *Biomechanics VI-A: Proceedings of the Sixth International Congress on Biomechanics*, ed. E. Asmussen and K. Jorgensen, 93–99. Baltimore: University Park Press, 1978.

Tsarouchas, E., and Klissouras, V. "The Force-Velocity Relation of a Kinematic Chain in Man." In *Biomechanics VII-A: Proceedings of the Seventh International Congress of Biomechanics*, ed. A. Morecki, K. Fidelus, K. Kedzior, and A. Wit, 145–51. Baltimore: University Park Press, 1981.

VanLeemputte, M., Spaepen, A. J., Williams, E. J., and Stijnen, V. V. "Influence of Pre-Stretch on Arm Flexion." In *Biomechanics VIII-A: Proceedings of the Eighth International Congress on Biomechanics*, ed. H. Matsui and K. Kobayashi, 264–70. Champaign, Ill.: Human Kinetics Publishers, 1983.

Viitasalo, J. T., and Komi, P. V. "Rate of Force Development, Muscle Structure and Fatigue." In *Biomechanics VII-A: Proceedings of the Seventh International Congress of Biomechanics*, ed. A. Morecki, K. Fidelus, K. Kedzior, and A. Wit, 136–41. Baltimore: University Park Press, 1981.

Wolf, S. "The Morphological and Functional Basis of Therapeutic Exercise." In *Therapeutic Exercise*. 3d ed. Ed. J. V. Basmajian, 43–85. Baltimore: Williams & Wilkins, 1978.

Wood, G. A., Pyke, F. S., LeRossignol, P. F., and Munro, A. R. "Neuromuscular Adaptation to Training." In *Biomechanics VIII-A: Proceedings of the Eighth International Congress on Biomechanics*, ed. H. Matsui and K. Kobayashi, 306–11. Champaign, Ill.: Human Kinetics Publishers, 1983.

TORQUE

Prerequisites

Concept Modules A, B, C

Concept Module Contents

SECTION 1

TORQUE AND ROTARY MOTION

When an external force acts on an unrestrained system, it causes that body's center of gravity (CG) to move in a linear path (e.g., a thrown softball, a pushed opponent, a projected jumper). If the system is restricted to moving around an axis, however, the body rotates when the force is applied, but only if the force does not act directly through the axis of rotation; that is, the point of application of the force must not be at the axis and the line of action of the force must not pass through the axis. For example, to open (rotate) a door, the force is applied at a point far from the hinges, and the direction of the pull is not in toward, or away from the hinge axis. To turn a steering wheel, the hand applies a force at the rim, not the center.

Such an off-axis force is called an **eccentric** (off-center) **force,** and the turning effect it has on the body is called **torque.** The off-axis distance to the force's line of action is called the **force arm** (or sometimes moment arm, lever arm, or torque arm). The greater this distance, the greater the torque produced by the force. The specifications of a force arm must be noted, however. *The force arm is the shortest distance from the axis of rotation to the line of action of the force.* The shortest distance is always the length of the line that is perpendicular (90 degrees) to the force's line of action ($d_\perp$). Recall that *perpendicular* is designated by the symbol $\perp$. This definition of a force arm is essential in determining how much torque is acting on a system.

Properties of Torques

All forces have unique properties that must be considered when dealing with rotating systems. The properties are *magnitude* (how much force), *direction* (the way the force is applied), a *line of action* (the theoretical line represented by the dashes that go forevermore in either direction), and a *point of application* (the point at which the force is being applied to the system). These properties also are associated with torque: *magnitude*, $T = F(d_\perp)$, and *direction*, clockwise ($-$) or counterclockwise ($+$). The *point of application* and *line of action* of a torque are the same as the point of application and line of action as the force producing the torque, and in addition, a torque must include a *force arm* ($d_\perp$).

Torque is produced by muscles when they pull on bones, and the result is rotary motion of the body segments. Figure D.1 illustrates a muscle force on a bone to produce torque. The stronger the contraction of a muscle, the greater the torque on the bone; the longer the force arm, the greater the torque. Although the point of application of a muscle's force on a bone (insertion point) cannot be changed, the line of action of a muscle's pull (in line with the direction of the muscle's shortening) changes relative to the bone (the angle of muscle insertion). As a result of the changing direction of muscle force on the bone as the bone rotates, the force arm changes

A muscle force vector with its four properties identified: magnitude, direction, line of action, and point of application. The muscle force is torque-producing because its line of action does not pass through the axis of rotation.

Figure D.1.

length. Therefore, the torque that a muscle is able to exert on a bony segment changes as the segment position changes. Such changes are examined in detail in Chapter 3.

Calculating Torque

The amount of torque acting to rotate a system is found by multiplying the magnitude of the applied force by the force arm distance from the line of force to the axis of rotation:[1]

$$T = F(d_\perp)$$

Equation D.1

where T is torque (Newton meters or pound-feet), F is force (Newtons or pounds), and $d_\perp$ is the length (meters or feet) of the shortest line drawn from the axis to where it meets the line of action of the applied force at 90 degrees.

---

1. Trigonometric calculations of torque also are used, and the appropriate concepts are included in Appendix V.

Since force is measured in Newtons or pounds[2] and the distances are measured in meters or feet, the appropriate torque unit is Newton meters (Nm) or pound-feet (lb-ft). We could also refer to the units as torque units. For example, if a force of 50 N were applied with a force arm of 2 m, the torque produced by that force would be 100 Nm, or 100 torque units. The larger the force or the longer the force arm or both, the larger the torque. For this reason, with two equal forces applied, the force that has the longer force arm produces the larger torque.

Figure D.2 illustrates a teeter-totter as a system capable of rotation when a torque is applied to the plank. The torque of 100 torque units (Nm) is the product of the 50-N eccentric weight force times the perpendicular distance of 2 m from the line of force to the axis of rotation, and the plank rotates in the direction of the applied torque (Figure D.2a).

Note that if the weight is lighter, it creates less torque (Figure D.2b). Also, if the weight is placed closer to the axis, it creates less torque. In fact, if the line of force of the weight is directed through the axis itself, zero distance ($d_\perp$) results (therefore zero torque) and no rotation is produced (Figure D.2c).

Note that the distance between the axis and line of force is not necessarily the distance between the axis and the point of force application. An example illustrating this concept is shown in Figure D.3. The trapdoor is caused to rotate around its

---

2. Units in British and metric systems are listed in Appendix A.

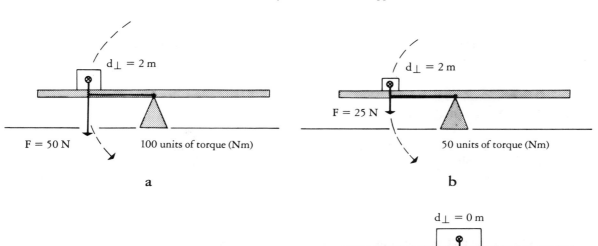

Figure D.2.   (a–b) A plank balanced on a fulcrum is caused to rotate by a torque produced by a weight placed on the plank at some distance from the axis. (c) No torque is produced when the weight is placed over the axis, and the plank does not rotate.

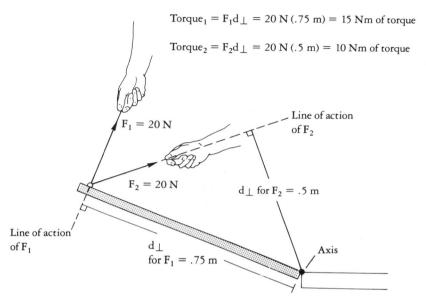

$$\text{Torque}_1 = F_1 d_\perp = 20\,N\,(.75\,m) = 15\,Nm \text{ of torque}$$

$$\text{Torque}_2 = F_2 d_\perp = 20\,N\,(.5\,m) = 10\,Nm \text{ of torque}$$

The force arm is the distance from the axis to the line of action of the applied force, not to the point of application of the force.

Figure D.3.

hinges (a horizontal axis) when a pulling torque ($F_1 d_\perp$) is applied at the door handle. The distance from the axis must be perpendicular to the line of force, which, as shown for F_1, is also perpendicular to the door itself. If the force is applied at some angle other than 90 degrees to the door, as in F_2, the $d_\perp$ is shorter and the torque is reduced.

SECTION 2

THE EFFECT OF TWO OR MORE TORQUES ON A SYSTEM: VECTOR COMPOSITION

When more than one external torque is applied to a system at the same time, all the torques must be considered, for their net effect determines the rotary motion of the body. Using the algebraic method to find the resultant torque on a system that has multiple torques applied to it is the same process as that discussed under net force for linear motion.

Figure D.4 shows a segment with two external forces applied to it and the torques they produce. Diagrams of such situations are drawn to a convenient scale, such as 2 cm on paper equals 40 N (~9 lb) for representing force and 2 cm on paper equals 10 cm for representing distance.

$$\text{Torque}_1 = 60 \text{ N } (1 \text{ m}) = +60 \text{ Nm} \qquad \text{Torque}_2 = 90 \text{ N } (.3 \text{ m}) = -27 \text{ Nm}$$

$$\text{Net torque} = +33 \text{ Nm (counterclockwise)}$$

Figure D.4. Two forces are applied to a lever free to rotate about an axis. The torque produced by each force is $T = F(d_\perp)$.

The two applied torques in Figure D.4 tend to rotate the segment in opposite directions; they oppose one another. Conventionally, a counterclockwise (ccw) direction is called the positive direction of rotation, and a clockwise direction (cw), the negative direction. The rotary-motion response of the segment is determined by the **net torque** applied to it, just as the linear-motion response of a body is determined by the net force. Calculating the net torque is similar to finding the net force on a system and may be found by algebraically adding the two or more applied torques, with plus and minus signs used to indicate the directions of each:

$$(+60 \text{ torque units}) + (-27 \text{ torque units}) = +33 \text{ torque units}$$

The segment thus rotates ccw in response to a torque of $+33$ torque units (Nm).

The graphic method of vector composition of torques on a system is useful for analyzing a system in rotary motion, as is the vector composition of forces on a system in linear motion. Since torques are vector quantities, the direction of the torques on a system may be specified by what is known as the **right-hand thumb rule.** Figure D.5a illustrates this convention. If the fingers of the right hand are curved in the direction of the torque around an axis of rotation, the extended thumb points along the axis and represents the direction of the applied torque. To determine the net torque on the system shown in Figure D.5b, two arrows are drawn to scale to represent the magnitude and direction of each of the torques acting. In this case, the torque produced by Force 1 is $+60$ torque units ccw, and (applying the right-hand thumb rule) is directed parallel to the axis of rotation, which is directed away from the page in Figure D.4. Since the ccw direction is positive, this vector is drawn upward to scale to represent $+60$ torque units. The torque produced by Force 2 is 27 torque units cw, and (applying the right-hand thumb rule) is directed parallel to

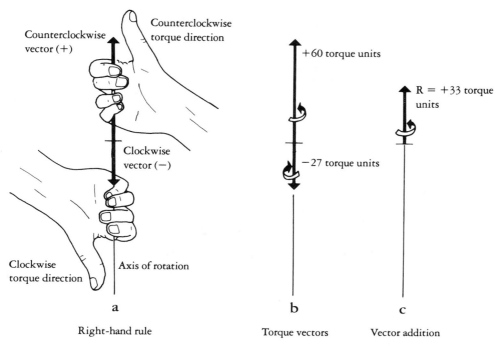

Right-hand rule Torque vectors Vector addition

(a) The right-hand thumb rule for finding the direction of a vector in angular quantities. When the fingers of the right hand are flexed about an axis of rotation in the same direction as the torque, the vector direction is indicated by the direction of the thumb. (b) and (c) show the graphic method for determining the net torque on the lever in Figure D.4.

the axis of rotation in the reader's direction, into the page in Figure D.4. Since the cw direction is negative, this vector is drawn downward to scale to represent -27 torque units. We now have illustrated the torque vectors in magnitude and direction and can now add or compose these vectors into a net torque acting on the system, as shown in Figure D.5c.

As can be seen, the resultant torque on the system as calculated by this method is the same as that calculated by the algebraic method, that is, a net torque of $+33$ torque units acting in the positive direction to cause ccw rotation with the vector directed out from the page.

SECTION 3

SYSTEMS IN LINEAR AND ROTARY MOTION

Purely linear motion of a system's CG is caused by a net external force whose line of action passes through the body's CG. Purely rotary motion of a body occurs when a torque is applied on a body with a fixed axis. Both linear and rotary motion occur for a body not restrained to a fixed axis, that is, when the system is free to travel. Such is the case in many sport events, particularly activities in which a system is projected into the air. Any unsupported rotating system rotates around an axis that passes through its CG. As an example, a volleyball served with spin is shown in Figure D.6a. The ball's CG travels along a curvilinear path. At the same time, the ball rotates around an axis passing through the CG. A force must be applied eccentric to the axis of rotation to produce these linear and rotary motions (Figure D.6b).

During the time that the striking hand is in contact with the ball, the force of the hand acts forward and upward and eccentric to the axis of rotation at the CG. Thus, this force causes initial upward and forward linear motion of the ball's CG. The torque on the ball can be determined by multiplying the magnitude of the applied force produced by the hand and its perpendicular distance from the CG (axis of rotation). If the line of action of the hand's force passes through the axis of rotation, no torque is produced and therefore no spin.

The same principle applies to projecting the human body in aerial somersaults in gymnastics and diving and in twists and spins in dance leaps. In a push-off, the reaction force's line of action must not pass through the body's CG if rotation is desired (see Figure H.1b, p. 487).

UNDERSTANDING TORQUE

1. Define torque and draw a force diagram of torque being applied to an object to cause it to rotate. How could you increase the torque without increasing the magnitude of the applied force?

2. Draw a force diagram of two teachers on a teeter-totter in a balanced position. Insert magnitudes for each person's weight (force) and the distance that each force is from the axis (fulcrum). How much torque is being applied to the teeter-totter by each person? According to the numbers you selected, is the teeter-totter balanced? If not, what could be changed to make it balance?

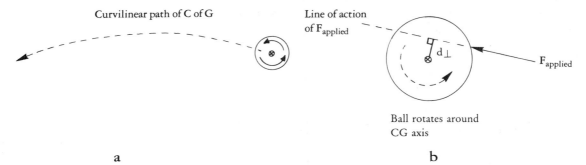

Figure D.6.   (a) A volleyball displaying linear and rotary motion. (b) Application of torque to cause spin.

3. For each of the illustrations shown in Figure D.7, calculate whether the torques shown are motive torques or resistive torques, and calculate the direction of motion of the system.

4. In each of the four systems shown in Figure D.8, use dashes to indicate the lines of action of each force. Draw the force arms for each of the forces in each system. Then answer these questions:

   a. Compare the force arms and directions of Force 1 (F_1) in each of the four systems. What generalization can be made about the relationship between the direction of the forces and the magnitudes of their force arms? (F_1 is equal in magnitude in all systems.)
   b. If all the forces are of equal magnitude in all the systems, compare the torque-producing capabilities of each, and then state a principle about the direction of pull of the force and the magnitudes of the torques that a force can produce.
   c. Using the convention of a plus sign for ccw and a minus sign for cw, indicate for each torque whether it is a ccw- or cw-producing torque by placing a plus or a minus sign by the vector.
   d. Using a scale of 1 cm = 10 N of force, and 1 cm = 1 cm of force-arm distance, calculate each of the torque magnitudes for each of the systems. Place the appropriate sign in front of each torque and sum the torques acting on each system.

5. In Figure D.9, identify the four properties of the muscle force and its force arm.

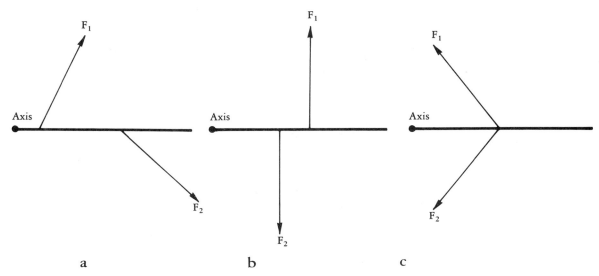

The forces applied to each system in (a), (b), and (c) are all of equal magnitude.

Figure D.7.

Figure D.8.

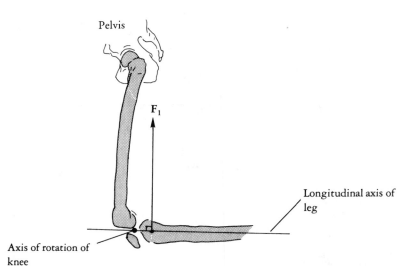

Figure D.9.

SECTION 4

TORQUE AND THE BODY'S CENTER OF GRAVITY LOCATION

Because the CG is frequently the point in a system that is used for motion analysis, the factors that determine its location should be understood. The CG of a body is that point through which the force of gravity acts; all the body's weight seems to be concentrated at this point. The magnitude of the force of gravity acting on the body is called the weight of that body. The point of application of the force of gravity is at the body's CG; its line of action is vertical, toward the center of the earth.

The force of gravity actually pulls on every particle of mass in the body and thus gives each part weight. From a practical standpoint, it is useful to consider the individual movable body segments as the smallest divisions of the total body's mass. Each body segment, or mechanical link, has its own mass, weight, and CG, and gravity exerts a downward force through each CG. Figure D.10 illustrates the approximate locations of the CGs of the body segments, or links.

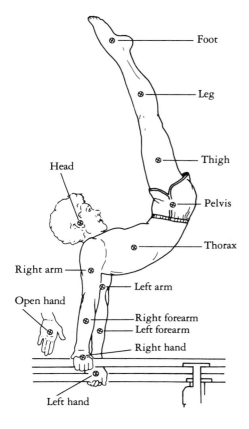

Segmental center of gravity locations.

Figure D.10.

As would be expected, the CG of each segment is situated closer to the more massive end of the segment (usually toward the proximal end). The force of gravity pulling on each segment is equal to the weight of the segment, which may be estimated as being some proportion of the total body weight. Thus, the total body weight may be found by adding all the multiple downward-directed forces (the segmental weights). The estimated proportion of the total body weight given to each segment (for males and females) is listed in Appendix III, Table III.1.

Each segment's weight influences not only the total body *weight* but also the body's CG *location*. One definition of the CG of a system is that the CG is an imaginary point about which the body's weight is equally *distributed*. The key to this definition and to the relationship of the CG to torque is the word *distributed*. According to the definition, the sum of the segmental weight *torques* on all sides of the body's CG point must be equal to zero. The definition does *not* mean, however, that the sum of the *weights* on all sides are equal. When the body is free of external support, the CG serves as the point around which the body balances. The body balances on either side of the CG *without regard to the body's orientation in space*.

To understand the importance of segmental weight torques to CG location, we will examine first the illustration of blocks of various sizes and masses shown in Figure D.11. The weights of the various blocks are analogous to the various weights of the human body segments. For the system to be in balance, the opposing torques on each side of the fulcrum must be equal. That is, the blocks must be *equally distributed* about the axis of rotation or fulcrum, which means that the sum of the torques on one side is equal and opposite to the sum of the opposing torques on the other side. If the opposing torques are equal, the balance point, or fulcrum, is in line with the CG of the system. The condition illustrating that the CG is over the fulcrum is shown in Figure D.11a.

In Figure D.11b, the total weights on each side of the fulcrum are the same; however, the sum of the torques produced by these weights does not equal zero because of the distribution of the weights relative to the axis of rotation. Each weight must be multiplied by its $d_\perp$ to determine its torque. For the arrangement in Figure D.11b, a new balance point for the system has to be located. (Note that the system in Figure D.11a is divided into equal mass [weight] halves, and that the opposing torques are also equal. In Figure D.11b, however, the opposing torques are *not* equal even though the system is divided into equal mass halves.

Similarly, the balance point, or CG, of the human body for any given arrangement of body segments may be found by locating the point around which are equal opposing segmental torques on all sides. The CG point must be located in all three dimensions; that is, it is a representation of the point around which right and left, front and back, and top and bottom segmental torques are equal.

If a transverse plane were inserted somewhere through the pelvic region, depending on the individual's body build, a fairly good estimate would be that the CG is located on that plane. This plane dividing the body into equally distributed masses would pass through the CG point. A body balanced on a board and fulcrum such that its CG is located directly above the fulcrum is shown in Figure D.12a.

Similarly, if a plane were located through the body that equally distributed the masses into right and left portions, these portions would balance on either side of

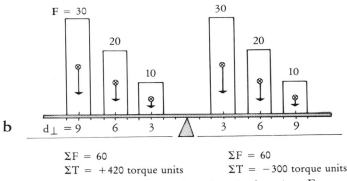

The weight of each mass segment produces a torque about the axis of rotation. (Σ means "sum of.")   **Figure D.11.**

the fulcrum, as shown in Figure D.12b. The plane dividing the body in this manner would pass through the CG point. Another plane that divided the body into equally distributed front and back parts would serve to balance the body in the position shown in Figure D.12c. This plane also would pass through the CG.

To visualize a body's CG location, the body does not need to be in a standing or lying position. The same visualization process is followed for determining the CG location in any body position. Picture three "cuts" through the body, each one being made at right angles to the others so that the segmental masses are equally distributed on either side of each plane. The point at which all three orthogonal (perpendicular) planes intersect is the location of the body's CG. Figure D.13 shows the approximate location of the body's CG for three bodies in different positions.

As with the boxes on the board shown in Figure D.11, the CG location of the human body depends on the arrangement of the body segments at any given time. When an arm or leg is moved, the trunk is flexed, the head is lifted or turned, or if some mass is added to the body, the location of the system's CG is changed according to the direction, distance, and amount of mass that is shifted or added. This is due to the fact that if one or more segments move relative to the others, the torque of that segment also changes; therefore, the position of the CG relative to the rest of

Top and bottom portions balance

a

Right and left portions balance   Front and back portions balance

b   **c**

Figure D.12.   A body will balance on the teeter-totter if the fulcrum is located in vertical alignment with the body's center of gravity. Top and bottom (a), right and left (b), and front and back (c) portions balance.

the body changes accordingly as shown in Figure D.14. If the relative position of the body segments remains the same (the system is in the same posture), but the total body position is changed in space, as shown in Figure D.14b, the CG remains in the same location in space.

The CG location is an important factor in movement analysis, and therefore one must be able to locate the CG of the total body with the body segments in different positions. Since the segmental weights do not change during movement, the positions of the segments relative to one another is the important factor in producing a change in the segmental torques and thus the position of the CG of the body.

Locations of the center of gravity for three different bodies. **Figure D.13.**

a   b

Effects of segmental movements on the total body's center of gravity location.   **Figure D.14.**

For teaching and coaching applications, one need not calculate the CG location but need only understand the concept of balancing the torques on each side of the CG. The two steps in this process are illustrated in Figure D.15. First, one must imagine the location of the CG in anatomical position (usually in the pelvic region, and equidistant from front to back and from right to left sides). For each segment that is moved from this anatomical position, the CG location moves in the same direction. If the leg is moved up and to the right, the CG of the body moves up and to the right *relative to the rest of the body*.

One must also consider the relative weight of the segment being moved. For example, a leg being moved the same distance as an arm has a greater effect on the shift of the CG location.

Once an estimate of the CG location has been made, one may test the acccuracy of the prediction by marking three lines through the estimated CG location and visualizing whether or not the body would balance on a fulrum, or plane, along that line. For example, would the body balance if placed on plane A-B, C-D, or E-F? If the answer is yes, then the estimated CG location is approximately correct. If the answer is no, then the estimated CG location must be changed accordingly so that the body will balance.

The CG location of any system is based on equally distributed weights of the

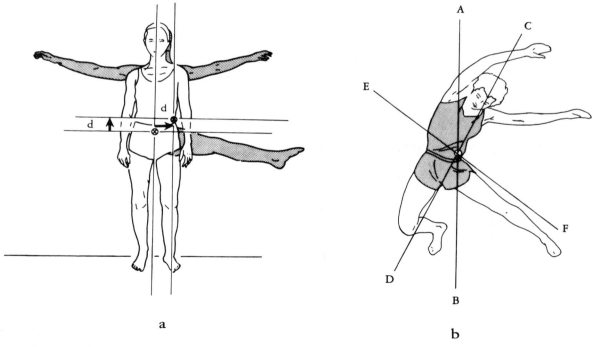

a   b

Figure D.15.   Estimating shifts in the body's center of gravity.

body's segments where distribution incorporates the torque produced by those segments relative to the CG location. The teacher or coach should be able to visualize and track the CG location of performers as they move in space.

If further calculations are necessary, refer to Appendix IV, Methods of Calculating the Center of Gravity.

UNDERSTANDING THE CENTER OF GRAVITY

1. What is the approximate location of your body's CG when you assume an upright (standing) position? How is your body's CG location changed when you assume the following positions: (a) raise both arms out to the side to a horizontal position, (b) raise both arms forward to a horizontal position, (c) raise only one arm as indicated in a and b above. Select other positions and track the changing locations of your body's CG.

2. Figure D.16 shows several blocks of various weights placed on a board supported at each end. A scale is located under the knife edge on the left-hand side of the system. Determine the position of the CG for each of the two block arrangements shown. Discuss why and how the CG changes when the arrangements are changed.

3. When a person moves a body segment or segments, the CG location changes. How far and in what direction the total body CG changes is dependent on two factors. What are these factors?

4. If a person measuring 64 cm and a person measuring 74 cm each has a CG height of 56% of standing height, what does that tell you about their relative body statures?

5. Three people, all the same height, have different CG locations—52%, 55%, and 58%. What can you say about their relative body builds?

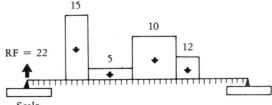

Blocks of various weights.   Figure D.16.

Figure D.17. A gymnast performing an iron cross on the rings.

CG
(left arm)

CG
(head)

Figure D.18.
A runner with segmental centers of gravity identified.

Figure D.19.
A gymnast with segmental centers of gravity identified.

6. Place a dot where the CG is located for the person shown suspended from the rings in Figure D.17. Discuss the change in CG location when the legs are raised to an *L* position.

7. On the following figures place a dot where you would estimate the CG to be: D.18, D.19, 1.3.

REFERENCES
SUGGESTED READINGS

Barham, J. *Mechanical Kinesiology.* St. Louis: C. V. Mosby Co., 1978.

Cooper, J. M., and Glassow, R. B. *Kinesiology.* 4th ed. St. Louis: C. V. Mosby Co., 1976.

Gowitzke, B. A., and Milner, M. *Understanding the Scientific Bases of Human Movement.* 2d ed. Baltimore: Williams & Wilkins, 1980.

Hay, J. G. "The Center of Gravity of the Human Body." In *Kinesiology III*, ed. C. J. Widule, 20–44. Reston, Va.: AAHPERD, 1974.

Resnick, R., and Halliday, D. *Physics.* Part I. New York: John Wiley & Sons, 1977.

Tricker, R. A. R., and Tricker, B. J. K. *The Science of Human Movement.* New York: American Elsevier Publishing Co., 1967.

Wheeler, G. F., and Kirkpatrick, L. D. *Physics: Building a World View.* Englewood Cliffs, N.J.: Prentice-Hall, 1983.

Prerequisites

Concept Modules A, B, C, D
Chapters 1, 2

Chapter Contents

CHAPTER 3

BIOMECHANICS OF THE MUSCULOSKELETAL SYSTEM

The mechanical aspects of bone-muscle arrangements should be used as the basis for developing exercises for musculoskeletal training and conditioning programs. Knowledge of the machinelike mechanisms used in producing segmental movements is necessary to understand the effect of various body positions during exercise, the effects of motive and resistive forces on the body segments, and the resulting movements during exercise and sport activities.

Any machine may be described as having one or more of these four functions: (1) to balance two or more forces, (2) to provide an advantage in force whereby less motive force is required to overcome a greater resistive force, (3) to provide an advantage in range of linear motion and speed of movement (i.e., to move the resistance or load a greater distance or faster than the motive force moves), or (4) to change the effective direction of the applied motive force (i.e., to move the resistance in one direction while the motive force is being applied in another direction). Three types of musculoskeletal arrangements in the human body serve as machines to provide the structure's ability to produce movement. These three machinelike structures are the lever, the wheel-axle, and the pulley.

161

LEVERLIKE ARRANGEMENTS

A lever system consists of an axis of rotation (sometimes called a fulcrum) around which a rigid lever moves and two categories of torques—motive torques, which act to move (rotate) the lever, and resistive torques, which act to resist the rotation of the lever.

The axes of rotation for segmental body levers are the same joint axes that were introduced in Concept Module A: anteroposterior, mediolateral, and longitudinal. Any movement of a segment around a given axis occurs along a segmental plane of motion: frontal, sagittal, and transverse, respectively. The plane of segmental movement is always perpendicular to the axis of rotation.

Forces and Torques Applied to Bones

Recall that all forces have four unique properties: (1) magnitude, (2) direction (relative to the bone), (3) a line of action, and (4) a point of application (the point of attachment to the bone). Figure 3.1 illustrates the four force characteristics of a muscle acting on a bone. Since the bone levers rotate around axes of rotation, the only forces that can affect the *rotation* of these segmental levers are those that are torque producing.[1] To be torque producing, a force must have a force arm (sometimes called a moment arm, lever arm, or torque arm). Since all muscle lines of force are located eccentric to the axis of rotation through the joint, all muscles can affect the rotational motions of the bones to which they are attached. It is important to remember that *each* muscle has its own *unique* force arm.

In the case of a long bone, the direction of muscle pull is measured from the easily seen longitudinal axis of the bone. In the case of a flat or irregular bone as shown in Figure 3.2, the direction of muscle pull is measured from a line connecting the point of application of the muscle force to the axis of rotation. The flat bone shown has two forces acting on it at the same point of application, F_1 being at 90 degrees to the line connecting the point of application and the axis, and F_2 being directed at a larger angle. The difference in the length of the force arms for these two forces should be noted.

Recall from Chapter 2 that muscle *tension* is dependent on the number of fibers (motor units) contracting, the tension developed in those fibers, the length of the muscle during its contraction (length-tension relationship), and the velocity of short-

---

1. A torque, in addition to affecting the rotary motion of a body, also affects the linear motion. For a body segment, linear effects of the torque are counteracted by an equal and opposite reaction force at the joint, thus the sum of the linear forces in all directions is zero.

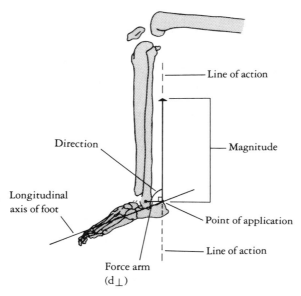

A muscle force vector showing the four properties of forces—magnitude, direction, point of application, and line of action.

Figure 3.1.

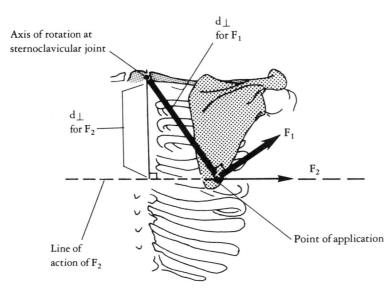

Forces acting at angles to a flat bone. F_1 acts at 90 degrees to a line connecting the point of application of the force to the axis of rotation in each bone. F_2 acts at an angle greater than 90 degrees.

Figure 3.2.

ening. All of these factors influence the magnitude of force that a muscle applies to a bone. The *torque* production of any force is also dependent on the length of the force arm.

Remember that a force's line of action extends forever. Thus, if a force arm drawn from the axis to the muscle force vector cannot be made perpendicular to that vector, then the force's line of action must be extended until such a perpendicular line may be drawn to the line of force. Figure 3.3 illustrates several examples of forces whose lines of action are directed at various angles to the longitudinal axis of the bone.

The effect of changing the direction of a force on the length of its force arm may

Figure 3.3.   Four examples of muscle forces acting on the forearm.

be seen by comparing the force-arm lengths of the forces in Figure 3.3a–c. Note that as the force is directed closer to the axis, the force arm is reduced (Figure 3.3a); conversely, as the force is directed farther away from the axis—up to 90 degrees to the lever—the force arm becomes larger (Figure 3.3b). Beyond 90 degrees, the force arm again becomes smaller (Figure 3.3c). What would be the length of the force arm when the force is directed through the axis of rotation, as is the weight force of the forearm and hand in Figure 3.3d?

This relationship between the length of the force arm and the direction of the force (angle from the lever) holds true for all forces acting on a system, whether they are motive forces or resistive forces, muscle forces or other external forces. Consider the force of gravity, which has a fixed downward direction. As the lever moves through various positions, the angle of the weight force changes with respect to the moving lever, but the force's direction is always toward the center of the earth. When the line of action of the weight force is directed closer to the axis of rotation (i.e., at a smaller angle, less than 90 degrees) or farther away from the axis of rotation (i.e., at an angle greater than 90 degrees), the length of its force arm is reduced; therefore, the torque production of that force is also reduced.

The lever system may be static (motionless) or it may be dynamic (moving). The sources of motive forces must be external to the lever system and may or may not lie within the human body. Any forces that serve to move a body lever are considered external to the lever system itself. Most commonly, muscle forces are thought of as being the only forces that create segmental movement; however, other forces also act to move the body segments, such as gravity, external objects, and other people. A muscle torque acting on a lever not only may create or change movement but also may hold the bony lever in a particular position by resisting other external torques. If the muscles are functioning in this manner, they are in an isometric (static) tension state. If an imbalance of torques is operating on the bone, the lever assumes a dynamic state and begins to rotate in the direction of the greatest torque (net torque). Recall that if the muscle forces are acting on the lever in the direction opposite to its movement, the muscles are contracting eccentrically and are producing resistive torques. Figure 3.4 presents three examples of lever systems in static and dynamic tension states.

A static situation is shown in Figure 3.4a. The two external forces are represented by arrows. The external *torques* are equal in magnitude and opposite in rotary direction; therefore, the segment is not moving. Notice that the muscle-force arrow is directed along the belly of the muscle toward the nonmoving attachment and that the resistive torque produced by the weight of the segment is directed from the center of gravity (CG) of the segment toward the center of the earth.

In Figure 3.4b, the muscle torque provides the motive torque; the muscle contracts concentrically and moves the segment in the direction of the muscle pull. The weight torque is a resistive torque. In Figure 3.4c, the segment moves in the direction of the weight force, and thus gravity serves as the motive torque. The muscle force provides the resistive torque, and the muscle contracts eccentrically.

Sometimes dynamic situations are analyzed as if they were a series of static positions, but such analyses are unrealistic. The inertial or resistive properties of a

Figure 3.4. Lever systems representing static and dynamic states of motion: (a) static, (b) dynamic concentric, and (c) dynamic eccentric.

dynamic rotary system affect the way the body moves. These factors are examined in Concept Module G.

Effect of Net Torque on a Bone-Lever System

In the body's lever system, the torques are divided into motive torques (i.e., those that produce the motion) and resistive torques (i.e., those that resist the motion). If the segment is moving clockwise (cw), then all torques directed cw are motive torques and all those directed counterclockwise (ccw) are resistive torques. Likewise, if the segment is moving ccw, the ccw torques are motive torques, and the cw torques are resistive torques.

To determine whether a segment will move ccw, cw, or remain stationary, one must find which torques are greater by adding all the ccw torques and adding all the cw torques. (Note that the torques and not merely the forces are added.) If the sum of the ccw torques is equal to that of the cw torques, the segment will not accelerate in any direction; it will be in rotational equilibrium. If the opposing sums are not equal, the segment will accelerate in the direction of the larger sum. Figure

3.5 provides two examples. To maintain consistency in calculations, all cw torques are designated as negative ($-$), and all ccw torques are designated as positive ($+$).

To determine the net torque acting on the leg lever in Figure 3.5a, identify each force and multiply its magnitude by the length of its respective force arm. The weight torque of the leg equals the weight of the leg multiplied by its force arm.

$$\text{leg weight torque} = W(d_\perp)$$
$$-6 \text{ metric torque units} = -40 \text{ N} \times .15 \text{ m}$$
$$[-4.42 \text{ British torque units} = -8.98 \text{ lb} \times 0.49 \text{ ft}]$$

The torque produced by the weight of the leg is designated as negative because the weight would make the leg rotate cw if no other torques were acting on it.

The torque produced by the ankle weight equals its weight multiplied by its force arm.

$$\text{ankle weight torque} = W(d_\perp)$$
$$-15 \text{ metric torque units} = -30 \text{ N} \times .5 \text{ m}$$
$$[-11.06 \text{ British torque units} = -6.74 \text{ lb} \times 1.64 \text{ ft}]$$

The torque is negative because it would produce a cw movement of the leg.

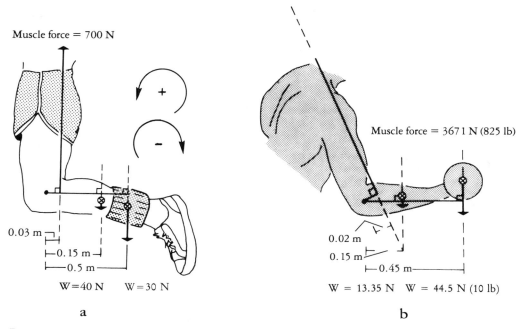

Forces acting on a lever system. (a) The leg holding an ankle weight. (b) The muscles of the forearm attempting to hold a barbell.   **Figure 3.5.**

Finally, the muscle torque equals the muscle force times its force arm if no other torques were acting on it.

$$\text{muscle torque} = F(d_\perp)$$
$$+21 \text{ metric torque units} = 700 \text{ N} \times 0.03 \text{ m}$$
$$[15.48 \text{ British torque units} = 157.30 \text{ lb} \times 0.10 \text{ ft}]$$

The muscle torque is positive, as illustrated in this example, because it would produce a ccw rotation of the leg if no other torques were acting on it.

Since the total cw torque—the sum of the leg weight torque plus the ankle weight torque—is equal to a negative 21 torque units and the total ccw torque—that of the muscle force—is equal to a positive 21 torque units, the leg will be held stationary. To make the comparison clearer, one can set up an equation and merely add the torques:

Equation 3.1

$$\Sigma T = 0$$

where Σ is sum of and T is torque.

$$\text{leg torque} + \text{ankle weight torque} + \text{muscle torque} = 0$$
$$(-6 \text{ metric torque units}) + (-15 \text{ metric torque units}) +$$
$$(+21 \text{ metric torque units}) = 0$$
$$[(-4.42 \text{ British torque units}) + (-11.06 \text{ British torque units}) + (15.48 \text{ British}$$
$$\text{torque units}) = 0]$$

If the net torque (sum of all the torques) is zero, no movement of the system will occur. If the sum is a negative number, the cw torques will be greater, and the segment will move cw. If the sum is a positive number, the ccw torques will be greater, and the segment will move ccw.

Figure 3.5b illustrates a similar case with the forearm. The amount of force necessary to hold the barbell in the position shown is determined by adding the torques acting on the forearm with the elbow serving as the axis of rotation. The magnitude or direction of the applied muscle torque is unknown, however. The solution to the equation will indicate a sign for the muscle torque, and thus a direction.

$$\Sigma T = 0$$
$$(F_m \times d_\perp) + (F_{bb} \times d_\perp) + (F_{fa} \times d_\perp) = 0$$

where F_{bb} is weight of the barbell, F_{fa} is weight of the forearm and hand, and F_m is muscle force required.

$$F_{bb} \times d_\perp = -44.5 \text{ N} \times .45 \text{ m} = -20.03 \text{ metric torque units}$$
$$[-10 \text{ lb} \times 1.5 \text{ ft} = -15 \text{ British torque units}]$$

$$F_{fa} \times d_\perp = -13.35 \text{ N} \times .15 \text{ m} = -2.00 \text{ metric torque units}$$
$$[3 \text{ lb} \times 0.5 \text{ ft} = -1.5 \text{ British torque units}]$$
$$F_m \times d_\perp = F_m \text{ N} \times 0.06 \text{ m} = 0.006 \ F_m \text{ metric torque units}$$
$$[F_m \text{ lb} \times 0.02 \text{ ft} = 0.02 \ F_m \text{ British torque units}]$$

The sum of the torques equals:

$$(-20.03 \text{ metric torque units}) + (-2.00 \text{ metric torque units}) + (0.006 \ F_m$$
$$\text{metric torque units}) = 0$$
$$F_m = 3671 \text{ N}$$
$$[(-15 \text{ British torque units}) + (-1.5 \text{ British torque units}) + 0.02 \ F_m \text{ British}$$
$$\text{torque units} = 0]$$
$$F_m = 825 \text{ lb}$$

Thus, 3671 N (825 lb) of muscle force acting ccw ($+$) is necessary to hold the forearm, hand, and a barbell weighing 44.5 N (10 lb) in a static position. If the muscle applied more torque, the system would move ccw; if the muscle applied less torque, the system would move cw.

UNDERSTANDING TORQUES ON THE MUSCULOSKELETAL SYSTEM

1. For the three diagrams shown in Figures 4.6, 4.8, and 5.2, determine the axis of rotation and the force arm of each muscle force shown.

2. What are the two requirements for producing a torque?

3. Figure 3.6 shows three boxes on a board with an axis (fulcrum) in the middle of it. The weights of the boxes are given as well as the distance that each is located from the axis: B is 1 unit from the axis, C is 2 units from the axis, and D is 3 units from the axis. How far does box A have to be from the axis to make the system balance if A weighs 100 units? if A weighs 40 units?

4. If a bone-muscle system is in static equilibrium, what does that tell you about the torques acting on the system?

5. If the shoulder joint is being abducted, what happens to the resistance torque of the arm's weight force as abduction takes place to the horizontal position? What happens to the resistance from a 90-degree abduction to a position over the head? Explain why.

6. If the person in Figure 3.17 were going to lift the object shown, what could the person do to make the lift easier, and why?

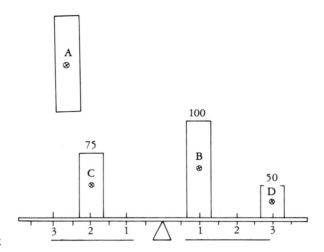

Figure 3.6.

7. Consider the person doing leg levers in Figure 2.4f to answer the following questions:

a. How much force does a hip flexor group have to exert to hold the lower extremity in its position? (The CG of the thigh is 10 units from the hip, the CG of the leg and foot is 28 units from the hip, the thigh weighs 20 units, the leg weighs 9 units, the foot weighs 3 units, and the line of action of the resultant muscle force passes 3 units from the hip joint.)

b. If the person flexes the knee so that the CG of the leg and foot is 15 units from the hip, how much force does each hip flexor group have to expend?

c. Would a short- or long-legged person have more difficulty in doing this type of activity? (Consider gymnastics and calisthenic activities in general.)

Analysis of the Musculoskeletal Lever System

The analysis of leverage in musculoskeletal systems has several applications that are useful for the physical education teacher or coach. The advantages derived from knowing muscle mechanics are emphasized in the sections that follow.

ROTARY AND JOINT-STABILIZING COMPONENTS OF MUSCLE FORCES

The effect of changing a muscle's angle of pull on the magnitude of muscular torques was briefly examined previously. The force of a muscle, or a muscle group, may be represented by an arrow. This arrow is called a resultant force vector and represents the magnitude (amount) and direction (angle of pull) of a muscle or muscle group on a bone. For example, if the arrow representing the magnitude of the muscle's force is drawn 4 cm long based on the scale 1 cm = 20 N (89 lb), the muscle's force will be 80 N (356 lb). The direction will be the angle that the resultant force arrow makes with the longitudinal axis of the bony lever to which it is attached.

Graphically, this force-vector arrow with its magnitude and direction can be resolved into two components that are perpendicular to each other and represent two important directions in which the muscle pulls in a two-dimensional muscle system. Figure 3.7 illustrates how one resolves a muscle force vector. The two components are labeled in this manner: **Ro** for the **rotary component** that is always perpendicular to the bone lever, and **Stabl** or **Disl** for the **stabilizing** or **dislocating component** that is parallel to the bone lever. The rotary component of a muscle's force is that part of the resultant force that acts to rotate the bony lever. The rotary component of a muscle's force is less than the resultant force, unless the resultant force acts at 90 degrees to the bone, in which case, the resultant and rotary forces are the same. The force arm for the rotary component is always directed parallel to the lever and is the distance between the line of force (also the point of application) of the Ro component and the axis of rotation.

The second component is stabilizing if it is directed parallel to the long axis of the bone and *toward* the axis of rotation (i.e., if it tends to pull the two bones together at the joint). (See Figure 3.7a.) The second component is dislocating if it

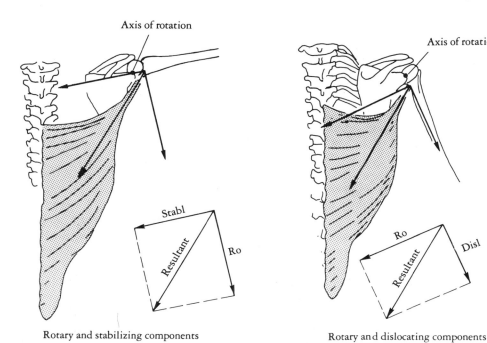

Rotary and stabilizing components

a

Rotary and dislocating components

b

Resolving a muscle's resultant force into two perpendicular components.

Figure 3.7.

is directed parallel to the bone and *away* from the axis of rotation (i.e., if it tends to pull the bones apart at the joint). (See Figure 3.7b.) Because the stabilizing or dislocating components are parallel to the lever and their lines of action run through the axis of rotation, they never have a force arm; therefore, they never provide any torque. (There is no perpendicular distance between the line of action of these components and the axis.) Thus, stabilizing or dislocating components can never influence the rotation of the lever; they can only tend to stabilize or dislocate. Although one might think that a 100% rotary force would be ideal, the stabilizing functions of some muscles are important in maintaining the integrity of joints, particularly the more lax joints such as the shoulder and the knee.

Exact magnitudes of the components can be determined by rather sophisticated techniques, but what is important to understand here are the relative magnitudes of the two components of a muscle's force on a bone. These can be estimated by comparing the sizes of the two component vectors. One should also understand how the muscle attachment angle to the bone affects the sizes of the two components. As the resultant muscular force (R) approaches 90 degrees to a line connecting the point of application of a muscle to the axis of rotation, its rotary component becomes larger, and the stabilizing or dislocating component becomes smaller, until, at 90 degrees, the resultant force is 100% rotary (Figure 3.3b). Thus the greatest torque may be generated by a muscle whose direction of pull is 90 degrees to the shaft of its bone (Figure 3.5a).

EVALUATION OF SEVERAL JOINT POSITIONS IN RELATION TO A MUSCLE'S EFFECTIVENESS

As the joint angle changes in the course of a movement, the muscle-to-bone angle changes as well. The two angles are associated, but they should not be confused. Certain positions of the joints allow for greater rotary muscle torque; these muscle torques are related to the angle of the muscle attachment as well as the length of the muscle at any given instant.

To analyze the most effective joint angle for producing muscle torque, how the angle of attachment changes as the joint angle changes must be understood. For this purpose, the action of the hamstring muscle at the knee will be used as an example. Figure 3.8 illustrates three positions of knee flexion, each with its related hamstring angle of attachment to the leg. The largest force arm that can be achieved by the hamstring muscle at the knee is that produced when the muscle pulls at 90 degrees to the leg bones (position 2). In this position, the knee *angle* is slightly less than 90 degrees. Prior to the 90-degree muscle angle, the muscle has a rotary and stabilizing component of force (position 1). When the muscle pulls at 90 degrees to the bone, the muscle force is 100% rotary. When the muscle angle is greater than 90 degrees (continued flexion of the knee), the rotary component diminishes, and the dislocating component increases (position 3).

The length-tension relationship presented in Chapter 2 is significant here because the muscle is a two-joint muscle. If the hip joint is held in a position of extension, as in a standing position, the *tension* able to be produced in the muscle continues

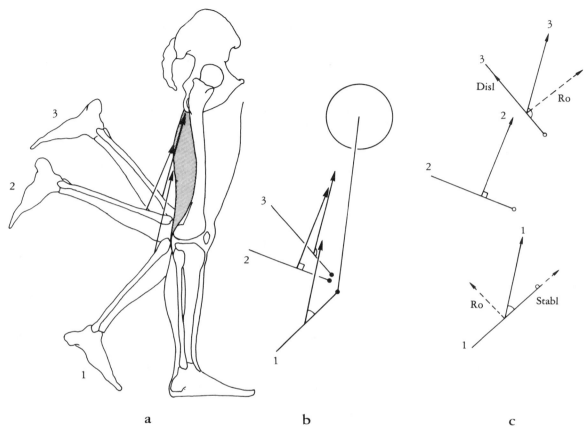

The angle of attachment of the hamstring muscle in three knee positions: (a) on a skeleton (b) on a line drawing, and (c) with the muscle forces resolved into two components.   **Figure 3.8.**

to decrease as the muscle shortens to flex the knee. The muscular tension is less when the muscle is at a 90-degree attachment to the bone than when the knee first started flexion. Assessing the net effect of what is lost due to the length-tension relationship with what is gained due to the changing attachment angle is difficult.

The increased tension at the lesser attachment angles occurs when the muscle has a stabilizing component, not a dislocating component. Because the muscle is a two-joint muscle, certain adjustments to the length of the muscle may be made as the muscle is shortening (i.e., as the knee flexes, the hip may be flexing). Thus, the length of the muscle may be maintained, for it shortens to flex the knee while it lengthens with flexion of the hip. Consequently, if the hip is flexed as the knee is flexed, the muscle does not lose the tension advantage of its resting length as it would if it were merely flexing the knee. This ability to maintain the length of a two-joint muscle during its contraction may allow the muscle greater tension when it begins to generate a dislocating component (i.e., when its attachment is greater than 90 degrees to the bone).

COMPARISON OF SEVERAL MUSCLES PERFORMING A SIMILAR MOVER FUNCTION

Consideration of certain physical activity situations, physical therapy in particular, requires an understanding of the torque production of several different muscles that perform the same motive function. A prime example concerns the torque contributions of the three elbow flexors that act on the forearm segment: the biceps brachii, the brachioradialis, and the brachialis. These muscles are important in terms of their angles of pull, their force arms, and thus their rotary and stabilizing contributions to the working of the elbow joint. Figure 3.9 shows the positions of the three muscles.

Several previously introduced examples emphasized that the larger the force arm of the resistive force, the greater the motive force or force arm or both needed to hold a given resistance in equilibrium. The force arms of the muscles have certain restrictions due to the permanence of the muscles' attachments. The only practical adjustment is to place the resistance close to the joint axis to decrease the resistive torque and thus decrease the motive torque needed. As the angle of the muscle force approaches 90 degrees to a long bone lever, its force arm increases. The closer the joint angle is to the point at which the muscle angle of attachment is 90 degrees, the more effective that muscle force is in producing torque to hold the resistance. When comparing the relative effectiveness of several muscles performing the same function (e.g., elbow flexors), one may start by comparing the relative sizes of their respective force arms. Several points must be considered. First, the brachioradialis can never

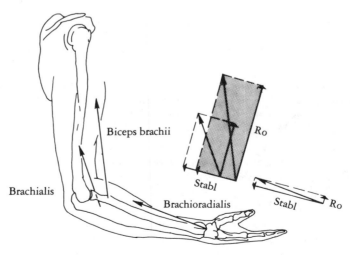

Figure 3.9.   Vector resolution of three elbow flexors.

approach an angle of 90 degrees to the forearm, and, in fact, always has a small angle of pull. Thus, the brachioradialis always has a large stabilizing component in its resultant muscle pull. Furthermore, it can never achieve even a 45-degree angle of pull; therefore, the stabilizing component is always greater than the rotary.

Second, when the attachment angles of the brachialis and the biceps brachii are compared, the attachment angle of the brachialis is always less than that of the biceps. During the range of motion of the forearm, however, both muscle attachments have the possibility of reaching a 90-degree attachment angle. Therefore, either can be put in a position where 100% of its force is rotary. Because the angle of attachment of the brachialis to the ulna is always slightly less than the angle of attachment of the biceps to the radius, the biceps achieves 100% rotary force at a larger elbow angle than does the brachialis. The larger elbow angle means that the biceps muscle is at a greater percent of its length than the brachialis when its 100% rotary position is achieved.

On the basis of the discussion of the length-tension relationship in Chapter 2, the biceps is at a more favorable length than the brachialis when each achieves a 90-degree attachment to the bone. Furthermore, since the biceps is a biarticulate muscle, its proximal attachment can make the muscle more effective due to the length-tension relationship when it is stretched over the shoulder joint (in shoulder joint hyperextension) while attempting to contract. As a one-joint muscle, the brachialis does not have the ability to adjust its length. Thus, the concept of mechanical advantage of one muscle over another in producing torque is not the only relevant consideration. Other factors important to a muscle's force are the relative strength of the muscles involved,[2] the position of the other articulations of a biarticulate muscle (e.g., shoulder joint and radioulnar positions), and the muscle fiber arrangement.

UNDERSTANDING APPLICATIONS
TO MUSCULOSKELETAL STRUCTURES

1. Which of the following angles of muscle pull has the greatest rotary component: 40 degrees, 23 degrees, 35 degrees, 65 degrees, 100 degrees, or 140 degrees?

2. Which of the angles listed in question 1 has the greatest stabilizing component?

3. With the aid of a ruler and protractor, determine what the rotary and stabilizing (or dislocating) components are for a muscle exerting 50 N of force (222.5 lb) at a 30-degree angle to the bone.

---

2. A muscle producing 100 units of force with 20% of it rotary is less effective than a muscle producing 50 units of force with 50% of it rotary.

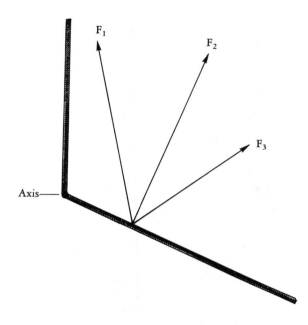

Figure 3.10

4. Construct a diagram of each of the forces in Figure 3.10, using a scale of 1 cm = 20 N (4.50 lb) of force. Draw the rotary and stabilizing components to each force. Measure the force arms for each resultant force and its rotary component. Compare and discuss what you find.

5. The systems in Figure 3.11 are muscle forces on bones. For each system, draw the stabilizing or dislocating force and the rotary components of force. (The force parallel to the bone may be dislocating instead.)

   a. How does the direction of the resultant force change with changing angles of the joint?
   b. How does the direction of the resultant force change the stabilizing, dislocating, and rotary components of the muscle's force?
   c. In what position does one get 100% rotary force out of the muscle's tension?
   d. Complete this sentence: If one were going to lift (resist) a heavy load, one would want to position the body segments doing the lifting so that . . . .
   e. After observing the situation of the stabilizing and rotary components of a muscle's pull, what can you say about the body segment's trade-off between the stability of the articulations (i.e., working against dislocation) and its mobility (i.e., the ability to produce motion)?

6. Figure 3.8 includes a representation of the hamstring muscles holding the leg in three different positions. Redraw the system and perform the following operations for each position:

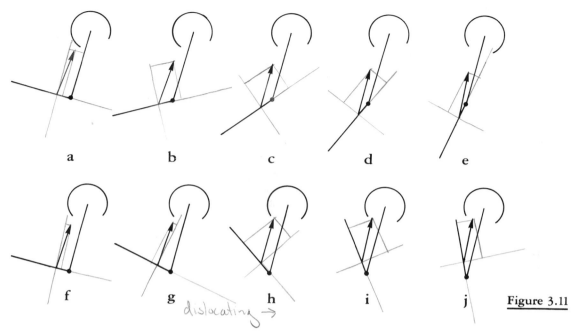

a   b   c   d   e

f   g   *dislocating* →   h   i   j   Figure 3.11

a. Determine the magnitude of the force, using the scale 1 cm = 100 N of force (22.5 lb).
b. Place a dot on the point of application of each force.
c. Determine the direction of the pull of the forces by measuring the angle with a protractor.
d. Draw the lines of action of the forces, using dashes.
e. Draw the force arm for each force and measure it in centimeters.
f. Answer the following questions:
  (i) Which position allows for the greatest magnitude of force?
  (ii) In which position does the greatest muscle torque act on the leg?
  (iii) In which position does the muscle force act at the greatest angle to the bone? the smallest angle to the bone?
  (iv) What is the relationship between the muscle's angle to the bone and the amount of torque that it produces?
  (v) What angle is optimum for torque production of a muscle (or of any other force)?
  (vi) Which factor is more important to the torque production of a muscle, the magnitude of the force or the length of its force arm?

7. In Figure 3.12 are musculoskeletal diagrams and stick diagrams. On the stick diagrams, draw and label the following:

a. Resultant muscle force (R)
b. Motive force arm (MFA)

a

b

Figure 3.12

c. Rotary force component (Ro)
d. Stabilizing or dislocating component (Stabl or Disl)
e. Resistive force (RF)
f. Resistive force arm (RFA)

Calculating Mechanical Advantages in Musculoskeletal Lever Systems

Typically, a considerable amount of muscle force is necessary to rotate or hold static a given resistive force. For the example illustrated in Figure 3.5b, the muscle force necessary to hold static a 44.5-N (10-lb) barbell plus the weight of the forearm and hand was calculated as 700 N (157.30 lb), an astonishingly greater sum. The same is true for all muscles in the body. They are at a mechanical disadvantage in force; that is, they must exert a much greater force than the resistance they are manipulating. The reason for this lies in the fact that muscles' lines of action run very close to the axes of rotation for the joint movements. Consequently, muscles do not have very large force arms, and thus, they have a smaller torque-producing capability than the resistive forces. For the few muscles able to achieve the 90-degree angle of pull, which maximizes their force arms, the points of attachments are still relatively close to the joint axis of rotation, which reduces their force-arm distances.

The ratio that expresses the relationship of the resistive force to the motive force is called the *mechanical advantage* (MA), and is calculated by the following equation:

$$\text{Mechanical advantage (MA)} = \frac{\text{resistive force}}{\text{motive force}}$$

Equation 3.2

If the quotient is greater than one, the resistive force is greater than the motive force; if the two forces are equal, there is no advantage; and if the quotient is less than one, the motive force is greater than the resistive force. If a muscle is the motive force (concentric contraction), the muscle always has a mechanical disadvantage in force. The quotient is less than one because the muscle is exerting more force than the resistance it is moving.

Because of the one-to-one relationship between a force and its force arm and the production of torque, MA also may be defined by the ratio of the respective force arms:

$$\text{MA} = \frac{\text{motive force arm}}{\text{resistive force arm}}$$

Equation 3.3

Notice that the motive and the resistive terms are reversed in the two equations. This makes the MA ratio come out the same, since a motive force arm that is smaller than a resistive force arm produces a quotient less than one. In other words, either equation produces the same ratio.

Although the musculoskeletal lever system is designed for a mechanical disadvantage in force, it does have an MA in range of motion (ROM) and speed of movement. When two points on the rotating lever move the same *angular* distance, the point farthest from the axis of rotation moves the greater *linear* distance. This is shown in Figure 3.13. When the ankle dorsiflexes against a resistance, the dorsiflexors

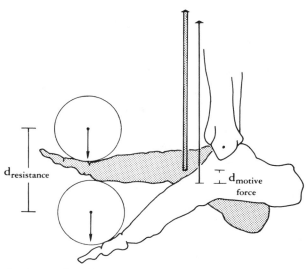

Ankle dorsiflexion showing resulting foot movement, $d_{resistance}$, compared to necessary muscle shortening, $d_{motive\ force}$.

Figure 3.13.

shorten a relatively small distance compared to the movement of the resistance itself, which is located toward the end of the lever. Thus, although muscles have a disadvantage in force, they have an advantage in ROM and speed of movement.

To calculate the MA in ROM and speed of movement, the reciprocal of the previous equations is used. If a muscle has a *disadvantage in force* (e.g., needing 5 motive force units to move 1 resistive force unit), it also has the *advantage in linear distance* of moving 1 unit of linear movement to move the resistance 5 units of linear movement (i.e., it moves the resistance 5 times farther than it moves itself).

Since the muscles in the human body are situated closer to the axis of rotation than are the resistive forces, the muscles always have a disadvantage in force and an advantage in ROM and speed of movement. The speed of movement advantage serves well in activities in which linear speed at the end of a lever is important (e.g., throwing, kicking, and striking activities).

Classes of Levers

Recall that the basic components of a lever system are a rigid lever, an axis, a motive force, and a resistive force and that the musculoskeletal system often functions as a lever system. Three types of levers are classified according to the relative positions of the axis, the motive force, and the resistive force. The function of each class of lever (see p. 161) depends on these relative positions and on the relative sizes of the force arms of all the forces being applied.

FIRST-CLASS LEVER SYSTEMS

Whenever the axis is located between the motive force and the resistive force, the lever is of the first class. Some of these relationships are shown in Figure 3.14.

Common examples include a teeter-totter, a crowbar, a pair of pliers, a pair of scissors, and a hammer removing a nail. The first-class lever is the most versatile of the levers because it can serve any one or more of the four functions of a machine, depending on the arrangement of its parts. In the teeter-totter, the lever is basically used for balancing two equal or unequal forces. When the two forces are unequal in magnitude, however, the torque production of the forces—and thus balance—may be obtained by a slight adjustment in the point of application of the force to give the lighter force a larger force arm (i.e., to position it farther away from the axis). The lesser force then has an advantage in torque (i.e., a lesser force can now exceed or equal the torque of a heavier force), and the greater force has an advantage in ROM (i.e., the heavier force moves the point of application of the lighter force a greater linear distance with equal angular displacements). Furthermore, in the first-class lever systems of the body, the motive and resistive forces act in opposite directions.

Not all first-class levers perform all four machine functions. The versatility of the first-class lever provides the user with the option of employing it in a variety of

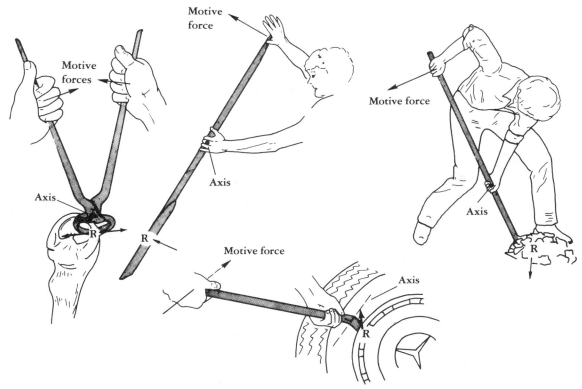

First-class lever systems.

Figure 3.14.

ways, which cannot be done with levers in the other two classes. The hammer removing a nail is an example of a first-class lever that is designed to give a force advantage by putting the motive force (pressure point on the handle) farther away from the axis than the resistive force (the head of the nail acting on the claw). Thus, one can remove the nail with less applied force than the resistance force of a nail, but the applied motive force must move a greater linear distance to do so. This disadvantage in distance is evident to anyone who has ever tried to pull out a long nail with a small hammer. Although the motive-force advantage is enough to pull the nail, the distance that the resistive force is moved during the pull is not enough to pry out the nail. This disadvantage may be overcome by putting a block of wood under the axis and pulling again.

First-class levers are unusual in the musculoskeletal system because the body levers are not generally arranged with the axis of rotation between the muscle attachment and the resistance. Two examples are the triceps acting to extend the elbow overhead and the posterior calf muscles working to plantar flex the ankle against resistance at the ball of the foot, as shown in Figure 3.15. In neither of these examples does the first-class lever arrangement give an advantage in force, since the motive force arms

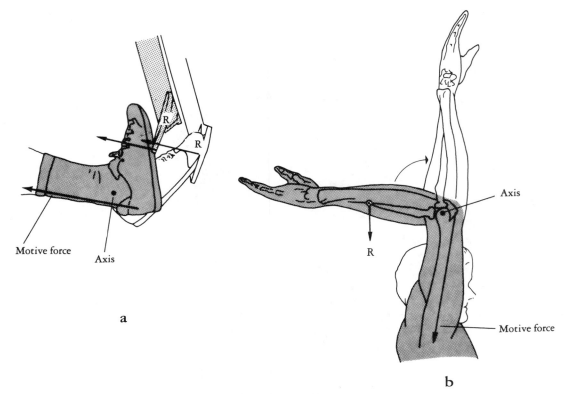

Figure 3.15.   Examples of first-class levers in the musculoskeletal system. (a) Posterior calf muscles working to plantar flex the ankle against resistance at the ball of the foot. (b) The triceps acting to extend the elbow overhead.

are relatively short as compared to the resistive force arms. Rather, these first-class lever arrangements provide an advantage in ROM and speed of movement and change the direction of the movement of the resistance compared to the applied force.

SECOND-CLASS LEVER SYSTEMS

Whenever the rotary component of the resistive force is located between the rotary component of the motive force and the axis, the lever is of the second class. A diagram of this relationship is shown in Figure 3.16.

Common examples of second-class machines include a wheelbarrow, a rowboat, a nutcracker, and a door. The relationship between the rotary components of the motive and resistive forces in the second-class lever system dictates that the force arm for the rotary motive force be larger than the force arm for the rotary resistive force. Therefore, in second-class lever arrangements, a force advantage usually exists for the motive force; that is, less motive force need be applied to move a greater resistance. With a wheelbarrow, one may lift a load of rocks that could not be budged

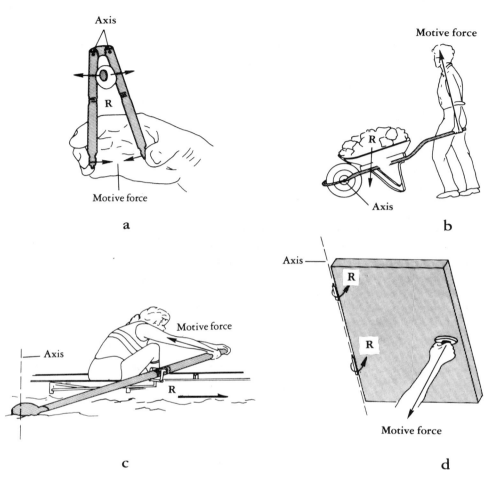

Second-class lever systems.

Figure 3.16.

otherwise. If one needs to lift a load a great distance, however, such as hay bales to a loft, the second-class lever system is not advantageous, since the lifting force has to move a greater linear distance than the hay bales have to be moved.

The second-class lever system is not as versatile as the first-class system because it cannot be used for balance, for gaining advantages in ROM, or for changing the direction of movement of the resistance. It is designed to provide the user with an advantage in force. Second-class lever systems in the body with a muscle as the motive force are unusual. Consequently, the muscles rarely have an advantage in force when moving a body segment. The push-up, however, is an example of the *total body* acting as a second-class lever: the foot is the axis of rotation, the weight of the body at the CG is the external resistive force, and the reaction force of the ground pushing against the hands is the external motive force.

Sometimes, force other than muscle force is the motive force, and the muscles act to resist or control the movement (eccentric contraction). In these cases, the motive force has the force advantage, and the resistive force (muscle force) has the ROM advantage. For example, eccentric tensions in muscles are considered second-class levers, as shown in the lowering of the weight in Figure 3.17.

THIRD-CLASS LEVER SYSTEMS

Whenever the rotary component of the motive force is located between the axis and the rotary component of the resistive force, the lever is of the third class. This relationship is illustrated in Figure 3.18.

Common examples of third-class levers are shovels, deep-sea fishing apparatus, and most implements used in sports events (e.g., rackets, fencing foils, bats). Most musculoskeletal lever arrangements are of the third class when the muscle is the motive force, because the muscle attachments are closer to the joint axis of rotation than are the resistances that they are moving.

The relationship of the location of the motive and resistive forces to the axis of rotation in a third-class lever system gives the system an advantage in ROM and speed of movement for relatively light resistances. The magnitude of the motive force (when the muscle force is the motive force) that must be applied to a given resistance is greater than the magnitude of the resistive force, but the resistive load is moved a greater linear distance than the point of application of the motive force. This particular advantage in ROM is important not only in moving resistances greater distances but also when one is concerned about the speed of movement.

Figure 3.17.   Eccentric tension of muscles as an example of a second-class lever system (muscles as resistive forces).

Third-class lever systems.

Figure 3.18.

The speed advantage of the third-class lever arrangement has important implications for sport activities in which implements are involved, such as striking and throwing activities. The longer the lever, the greater the linear-speed advantage. When one needs an implement to move fairly light objects a great distance or when the amount of effort expended is not of significance, one usually selects a tool of the first or third class. The longer the implement chosen, the greater the ROM and speed advantage of the body; however, the longer the implement, the greater the force the body needs to accelerate the implement.

SECTION 2

WHEEL AND AXLELIKE ARRANGEMENTS

A second type of machine found in the musculoskeletal system is the wheel and axle. This type of machine may function to give a mechanical force advantage or an MA in ROM and speed of movement. Wheel-and-axle mechanisms are illustrated in Figure 3.19.

In each of the cases pictured, the motive force is applied to the wheel or rim segment (e.g., the handle of the volleyball net crank). The resistance is provided by the axle segment around which the net wire is turned. As is seen in this example, the wheel (handle) has a larger radius of rotation than the axle. The MA of a wheel-axle arrangement may be calculated by this equation:

Equation 3.4

$$MA = \frac{\text{radius of the wheel}}{\text{radius of the axle}}$$

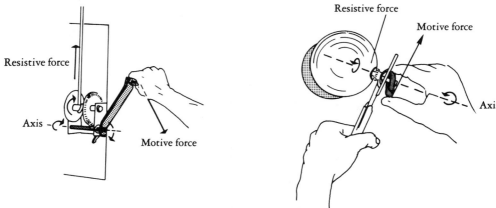

Figure 3.19.   Wheel-and-axle mechanisms.

Since the radius (force arm) for the force applied to the wheel is greater than the radius (force arm) of the force applied to the axle, the force advantage is always with the force applied to the wheel segment and is equal to the ratio of the two radii.

Another way to calculate the MA of a wheel-axle system is to compare the forces applied:

$$MA = \frac{\text{force on the axle}}{\text{force on the wheel}}$$

Equation 3.5

If the motive force is applied to the wheel rim with the larger radius and the resistive force is applied to the axle with the smaller radius, then the force advantage is with the motive force; that is, a smaller force is able to move a greater resistive force. If the motive force is applied to the axle with the smaller radius, then the motive force is at a *disadvantage* in force but is at an *advantage* in the ROM given to the resistance.

A few wheel-axle arrangements exist in the body whereby motive force is applied to a wheellike structure, but more frequent are examples in which motive force is applied to an axlelike structure. Examples of the wheel-axle are found in rotations of body segments about their longitudinal axes. The muscles that cause these rotations act on the outside surface of the bone (axle) to cause distal segments that serve as the wheel to rotate. This is illustrated in a cross section of a humerus with the elbow flexed, as shown in Figure 3.20a.

The bone serves as the axle on which the force is applied, and a second segment that articulates with the axle at some angle serves as the wheel. For instance, in medial rotation of the shoulder with the elbow flexed, the axle is the humerus, and the wheel segment is the forearm and hand. Since the motive force (muscle) is applied to the axle, the advantage of the mechanism is in the ROM and speed gained by the hand as it sweeps through the angle of rotation, as seen in Figure 3.20b.

The wheel-axle arrangement of the body structures, when using rotations around the longitudinal axes of segments, is a great advantage in producing speedy segmental movement for throwing and striking activities. Additional sport-related examples are forearm pronation in badminton and medial rotation of the shoulder joint in the tennis serve. In these examples, the implement serves to increase the radius of the distal "wheel" segment and to provide an even greater MA in ROM and speed of movement. Further movements are discussed in Chapter 14.

SECTION 3

PULLEYLIKE ARRANGEMENTS

The third type of machine that we find in the body is the single pulley. There are also arrangements of multiple pulleys, which create advantages in force and ROM or speed of movement, but these are not found in the human body. The main function

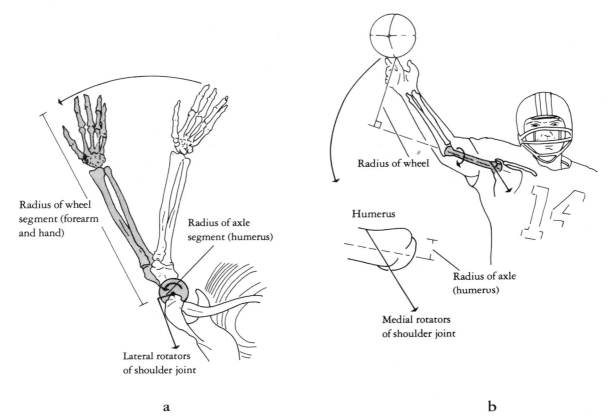

Radius of wheel
segment (forearm
and hand)

Radius of axle
segment (humerus)

Lateral rotators
of shoulder joint

Radius of wheel

Humerus

Radius of axle
(humerus)

Medial rotators
of shoulder joint

a

b

Figure 3.20.   (a) Cross section of the humerus, showing the wheel-and-axle arrangement of the lateral rotators of the shoulder joint. (b) The humerus and forearm acting like a wheel-and-axle as a player throws a football pass.

of pulley systems within the body is to change the effective direction of the applied motive force. Figure 3.21a illustrates a mechanical pulley that changes the direction of the resistive force. This application is used in the design of some weight-training machines. The most common example of a musculoskeletal pulley system is the muscular action around the malleolus on the lateral side and the medial side of the ankle. As the muscle contraction shortens the muscle toward the knee, the foot is moved downward into plantar flexion. Figure 3.21b illustrates this action.

Another example is the patella being pulled between the condyles of the femur during extension of the knee (Figure 3.21c). The quadriceps muscles pull proximally toward their bellies, and yet the knee action from flexion to extension causes the leg to move in the opposite direction. This is due to the single pulley function of the patellar tendon-patella-quadriceps arrangement.

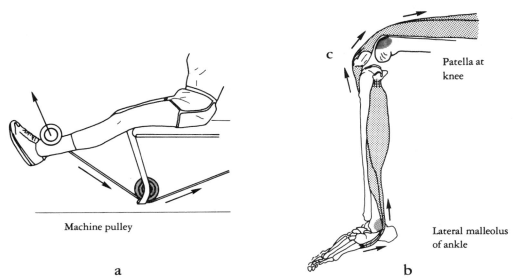

(a) A weight machine as a pulley system. (b) The malleolus of the fibula functioning as a pulley. (c) The patella at knee functioning as a pulley.

Figure 3.21.

SECTION 4

GENERAL CONSIDERATIONS OF MUSCULOSKELETAL MACHINES

As previously mentioned, most of the musculoskeletal levers in the body are of the third class, due to the close proximity of the muscle attachments and the resulting shorter force arms for the muscle forces than for the resistive forces. Consequently, the human body is built for ROM advantages and not for force advantages. In most analyses performed on the muscular system, one finds that the muscle exerts more force to move the resistance than the force of the resistance itself. The resistance moves a greater linear distance, however, and hence has a greater linear speed associated with its motion than does the motive force. This is true when the muscle functions as a motive force. Whenever the muscle is not the motive force (e.g., in eccentric contractions where gravity moves the body and the muscle functions as the resistance), then the musculoskeletal lever mechanism is of the second class. In this case, the resistance (the muscle force) is located between the axis (the joint) and the motive force (gravity). The motive force (gravity) has a greater force arm than the resistive force (muscle) and, therefore, the muscle must exert more force than the resistive force.

Those who have undertaken the identification of the types of machines in the musculoskeletal system traditionally have assumed that the muscle is the motive force acting on the lever. This is not necessarily the case, however.

If one understands the relationships between the external forces involved and the advantages that those relationships provide in a system, then one can analyze the muscular systems and body positions well enough to use the information to design and supervise movement and athletic training performances.

UNDERSTANDING MUSCULOSKELETAL MACHINES

1. Draw a diagram of a first-class lever system that allows very fast movement of a light resistance. Show the axis of rotation, the magnitude of the force, the resistance, the force arm, and the resistance arm.

2. Repeat the task in question 1, showing a machine that is able to move a heavy resistance with a light force.

3. Repeat the task in question 1, showing a machine that provides for the balancing of the two forces.

4. Examine the diagrams in Figures 4.8, 5.16, and 15.3. State whether they are the lever, the pulley, or the wheel-axle type of machine arrangement.

5. Complete the following sentences:

   a.   In concentric muscular contractions against the force of gravity, _____ is the motive force.
   b.   In concentric muscular contractions against the force of gravity, _____ is the resistive force.
   c.   In eccentric tension of the muscle, _____ is the motive force.
   d.   In eccentric tension of the muscle, _____ is the resistive force.

6. Examine Figure 3.22 to answer the following questions:

   a.   What class lever system is it?
   b.   In which position, 1, 2, or 3, will the task be the easiest?
   c.   If it takes 100 force units to move the system at position 2, what will it take to lift it at positions 1 and 3?

7. Musculoskeletal levers most generally have an advantage in what?

8. When a pulley-type mechanism is found in the human body, what is its main function?

9. It takes 50 units of force to lift 10 units of resistance.

   a.   What is the advantage of this type of arrangement?
   b.   Calculate the MA.
   c.   What class of lever probably was used?

Position 1
6"
Position 2
3"
Position 3
12"
F
Axis
R

This person is exercising his neck muscles by hyperextending his neck against the resistance provided by the machine. The headstrap can be attached to positions 1, 2, or 3 on the vertical bar.

Figure 3.22.

10. The motive force is 100 units. The balanced resistance is 50 units. The motive force arm is 0.6 m.

    a. What is the motive torque?
    b. What is the MA?
    c. What is the advantage to this type of arrangement?
    d. What is the resistive force arm?

REFERENCES
SUGGESTED READINGS

Ariel, G. B. *Computerized Biomechanical Analysis of Human Performance: An Application for Exercise Equipment Design and Athletic Performance.* Technical Report Uni-1. Fresno, Calif.: Universal Fitness Research Department, Universal Athletic Sales, 1974.

Basmajian, J. V., and MacConaill, M. A. *Muscles and Movements—A Basis for Human Kinesiology.* Huntington, N.Y.: Robert E. Krieger Publishing Co., 1977.

Coleman, J. E. "The Function of Anatomical Pulleys." In *Kinesiology*: [Proceedings of] *A National Conference on Teaching*, ed. C. Dillman and R. Sears, 63–76. Champaign-Urbana: University of Illinois, 1977.

Degutis, E. W. "A Problem Solving Approach to the Study of Muscle Action." In *Kinesiology Review*, ed. C. J. Widule, 20–31. Reston, Va.: AAHPERD, 1971.

Kume, S., and Ishii, K. "Biomechanical Analysis of Isokinetic Exercises." In *Biomechanics VII-B: Proceedings of the Seventh International Congress of Biomechanics*, ed. A. Morecki, K. Fidelus, K. Kedzior, and A. Wit, 404–10. Baltimore: University Park Press, 1981.

Piscopo, J. "Assessment of Forearm Positions Upon Upperarm and Shoulder Girdle Strength Performance." In *Kinesiology IV*, ed. J. G. Hay, 53–57. Reston, Va.: AAHPERD, 1974.

Prerequisites

Concept Modules A, B, C, D
Chapters 1, 2, 3

Chapter Contents

BIOMECHANICAL RELATIONSHIPS IN THE UPPER EXTREMITY

It is assumed that basic musculoskeletal and ligamentous structures have been studied in a previous course; therefore, emphasis is on the mechanical aspects of these structural units. The upper extremity may be divided into five functional units: the shoulder girdle, the shoulder joint, the elbow, the radioulnar joint, and the wrist and hand.

The following structures are discussed in terms of stability and mobility of an articulation: bony structures, ligamentous structures, and muscular structures. The stability provided by a muscle depends not only on the strength of the muscle but also on the muscle's angle of pull on the bone. The angles of pull determine the line of action of the resultant muscle force as well as the rotary and stabilizing or dislocating components of that resultant force. The contribution of the muscular structure to the stability of the articulation depends on the relative magnitudes of these components.

SECTION 1

THE SHOULDER GIRDLE
Structure

The shoulder girdle is made up of the clavicle and the scapula. It articulates with the trunk at the sternum and with the rest of the upper extremity at the humerus. The following bony landmarks of the scapula should be reviewed: the anterior and superior surfaces; the superior, lateral (axillary), and medial (vertebral) borders; the superior, inferior, and lateral angles; the supraspinous, infraspinous, subscapular, and glenoid fossae; the coracoid and acromion processes; and the spine. Figure 4.1 illustrates the articulations of the shoulder girdle.

The sternoclavicular joint articulates the upper extremity with the trunk at the manubrium of the sternum. An examination of the configuration of the two bones at their articulation shows that no bony prominences help hold the two bones together, and therefore the bony stability is weak. The sternoclavicular joint is the site of most of the movements of the scapula: elevation, depression, upward rotation, downward rotation, protraction (abduction), and retraction (adduction).[1]

In addition to being the location of the axis of rotation for the movements of the shoulder girdle, the sternoclavicular joint also absorbs the shock of trauma to the shoulder from sideward impact. Four main ligaments are associated with the sternoclavicular joint: the anterior sternoclavicular ligament, the posterior sternoclavicular ligament, the costoclavicular ligament, and the interclavicular ligament. These four ligaments in combination provide the ligamentous stability for the articulation of the two bones.

The acromioclavicular joint is located between the acromion process of the scapula and the distal end of the clavicle. It functions to absorb the stress of impact on the shoulder. There are no bony protrusions on any side of the articulation, and thus the bony arrangement is weak. The ligamentous arrangement is comprised of two main ligaments: the superior and the inferior acromioclavicular ligaments. Although these two ligaments provide stability to counter a pulling apart (tension) of the two bones, there is nothing to prevent the clavicle from riding up and over the top of the acromion process when the shoulder encounters a blow from the side. A dislocation in this manner is a common injury in football and wrestling.

The third articulation of the shoulder girdle is the coracoclavicular joint. Although it does not appear as an articulation (because the coracoid process of the scapula and

---

1. The terms *abduction* and *adduction,* meaning moving away from and moving toward the midline of the body, respectively, refer to movements of the scapula and are appropriate for physical therapy applications. The terms *protraction* and *retraction,* meaning to draw toward and draw back, respectively, refer to the movements of the shoulder and are more appropriate for sport activity situations. Both sets of terms refer to the same movements of the shoulder girdle as a whole, but the choice of which to use depends on the perspective of the user.

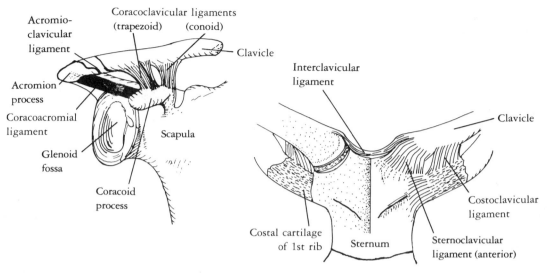

Articulations and ligaments of the shoulder girdle.   **Figure 4.1.**

the clavicle do not really come together), it is articulated by means of two main ligaments, the conoid and the trapezoid. The ligaments, which run downward obliquely from the clavicle to the coracoid process of the scapula, help to reinforce the weak acromioclavicular articulation by transferring the force applied to the acromion process of the scapula to the clavicle. In this manner, the clavicle is "pulled along" when a force is encountered by the acromion.

Muscles of the Shoulder Girdle as Stabilizers

Because the shoulder girdle is designed for mobility (i.e., for reaching and grasping types of activities), its stability is reduced. The muscular arrangements of the shoulder girdle and the shoulder joint are such that they are able to provide the stability lacking due to the weak arrangements of the bones and ligaments. The muscles must be strong enough to provide the necessary stability, however. The lack of upper body strength accounts for a great deal of injury to the shoulder region.

Figure 4.2 illustrates the muscles of the shoulder girdle that produce the six movements of the scapula. In addition to the resultant directions of muscular force indicated on each muscle, the two perpendicular components of muscular force are indicated to the side. Through the use of these diagrams, the rotary and stabilizing components for each muscle may be determined.

Since the scapula is attached by muscles to the thorax and the vertebral column, a dislocating force would be one that would tend to pull the scapula away from these attachments. A muscle that has a component directed toward the midline of the body would have a stabilizing effect. The angles with which these muscles pull

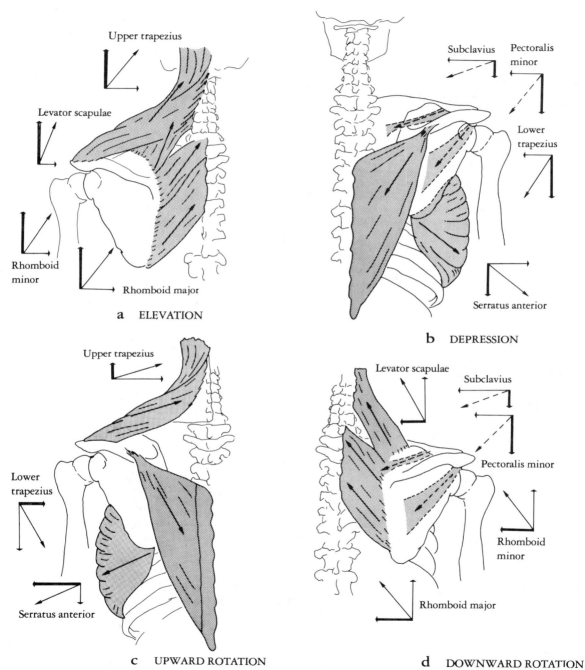

Figure 4.2.   Shoulder girdle movements and musculature, with resultant and component muscular functions indicated. Dashed arrows represent muscle forces that are located beneath the structure.

e   PROTRACTION

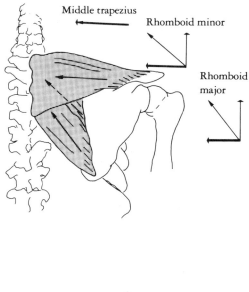

f   RETRACTION **Figure 4.2**
continued

on the scapula determine the relative amounts of moving and stabilizing that they can do. One can make this determination by observing the relative lengths of the component force vectors. (The longer arrow indicates the greater component.) All the muscles are able to function to hold the scapula in place against the antagonistic motion given to it by the muscles that attach from it to the humerus. This is particularly true when one attempts to move the trunk relative to a fixed hand, as in performing a pull-up (Figure 4.3a). If one does a straight-arm support on the parallel bars, one wishes to stabilize the scapula in depression, as shown in Figure 4.3b.

Although a throwing injury is usually thought of as occurring at the elbow or shoulder joint, injurious stress on the ligaments or the musculature of the shoulder girdle is also possible if a muscle's stabilizing components are not strong enough to hold the articulations together. In addition, since the shoulder girdle is the beginning of the upper extremity and is fairly mobile relative to the trunk, it is called upon in many instances to be a stable base on which muscles of the shoulder joint may pull.

Muscles of the Shoulder Girdle as Movers

Because the stability of the shoulder girdle is important in providing a base from which other upper extremity functions can take place, the mover function of the shoulder girdle joints is often overlooked. In most activities involving the upper extremity, the shoulder girdle provides the initiation of the movements.

Observing the movements of the shoulder girdle enables understanding of the use made of the shoulder girdle motions in performing various tasks. The elevation movement is the initiation of lifting; the depression movement, of pushing downward; the protraction movement, of reaching, throwing, or pushing forward; the retraction movement, of pulling backward; the upward rotation movement, of increasing the range of overhead reaching; and the downward rotation movement, of forceful arm adduction at the shoulder joint.

The most common example is overarm throwing. During the latter stages of forward trunk rotation, shoulder girdle protraction is initiated. The protraction initiates the forward motion of the upper extremity in the throwing pattern. A second example is performing a pull-up. Many of us have watched a person, attempting to perform a pull-up, who cannot get beyond the initial stage, which is the depression of the shoulder girdle (Figure 4.3a). To determine why the depression part of the exercise is always easier than the rest of the arm movements, consider that the direction of pull of the muscles on the scapula for depression has a large downward component. The muscles being used on the rest of the upper extremity pull at very small angles and thus have small rotary components when the shoulder joint is flexed and the elbow is extended.

SECTION 2

THE SHOULDER JOINT

Structure

The shoulder joint is made up of the articulation of the glenoid fossa of the scapula and the head of the humerus. The reader should review the following bony landmarks of the humerus: the head; the neck; the greater and lesser tuberosities; the bicipital groove; the shaft; the deltoid tubercle; the radial groove; the medial and lateral epicondyles; the trochlea; the capitulum; and the coronoid, olecranon, and radial fossae. Figure 4.4 illustrates the bony and ligamentous arrangement of the shoulder joint.

The bony arrangement of the shoulder joint consists of a shallow socket (glenoid fossa) to which is joined the one-half-spherical head of the humerus. Not more than half of the humerus is in the socket at any one time, and the bony arrangement is therefore weak. To assist in the task of stabilizing, a labrum or lip of cartilage circles around the outside of the fossa to increase the depth of the concavity and assist in holding the head in place. Because it is a ball-and-socket type of arrangement, the shoulder joint is a multiaxial joint that is able to move through the following movements: flexion, extension and hyperextension, transverse adduction and abduction, abduction and adduction, medial (inward) and lateral (outward) rotation. Two main ligaments are associated with the shoulder joint: the coracohumeral and the superior, middle, and inferior glenohumeral ligaments, named for their attachments and locations. The coracohumeral ligament serves to stabilize the humerus against upward

a   **b**

(a) The initial stage of a pull-up, showing the depression of the shoulder girdle. (b) Stabilization of the shoulder girdle in depression while a straight arm support is performed on the parallel bars.   **Figure 4.3.**

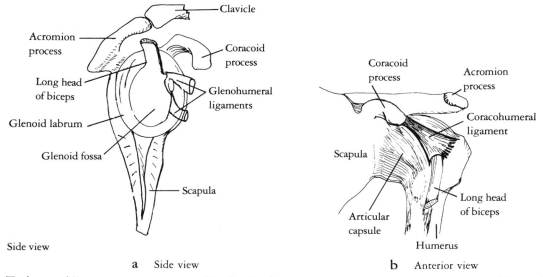

Side view

a   Side view   **b**   Anterior view

The bony and ligamentous arrangements of the shoulder joint.   **Figure 4.4.**

and lateral displacement, and the glenohumeral serves to stabilize the humerus against forward displacement. The glenoid fossa is directed slightly anteriorly. Thus, the back edge tends to prevent backward displacement of the humerus, but this leaves the forward position vulnerable to dislocations. As with the shoulder girdle, the shoulder joint is designed for mobility and therefore sacrifices bony and ligamentous stability.

Muscles of the Shoulder Joint as Stabilizers

The musculature surrounding the shoulder joint is arranged to produce large stability components of the muscle's forces. Figure 4.5 shows muscular arrangements that provide muscular stability to the shoulder joint. These muscles are called the **rotator cuff** muscles. There are four rotator cuff muscles, and all have large stabilizing components, as can be seen by the inserted component-force vectors. Three of these four muscles originate on the posterior surface of the scapula: the supraspinatus (above the spine), the infraspinatus (below the spine), and the teres minor. These three are sometimes remembered by their acronym as the SIT muscles. The fourth rotator cuff muscle is the subscapularis (below the scapula), and it originates on the anterior surface of the scapula.

All four of the rotator cuff muscles have large stabilizing components as evidenced by the large vector components directed medially. Regardless of the position of the humerus, the deltoid muscle—anterior, posterior, and middle—has a large stabilizing component due to its small angle of pull (see Figure 4.8).

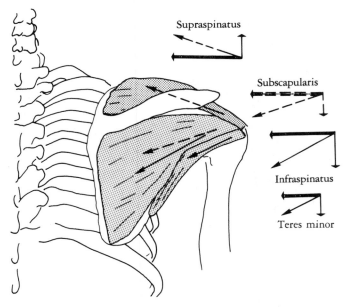

Figure 4.5. The rotator cuff muscles of the shoulder joint, which may function as stabilizers.

Further stability is provided by the long heads of the biceps brachii and the triceps, on the anterior and posterior sides, respectively. Because their tendons pass so close to the joint, each muscle's stabilizing component is large when the humerus is in the position antagonistic to the muscle's function (e.g., the stabilizing component of the biceps at the shoulder joint is great when the shoulder joint is extended).

Most of the other muscles surrounding the shoulder joint have force components that stabilize; however, their main function is to move the humerus. In addition, as the humerus moves into various degrees of abduction, flexion, and extension, these mover muscles change their angles of pull considerably; thus, they are not generally classified as stabilizers of the shoulder joint. These mover muscles are discussed in the next section.

Muscles of the Shoulder Joint as Movers

The muscles that serve as the primary movers of the humerus at the shoulder joint are shown in Figure 4.6. They are the anterior deltoid, coracobrachialis, pectoralis major, latissimus dorsi, and teres major; the long and short heads of the biceps on the anterior side; the posterior deltoid and the long head of the triceps on the posterior side; and the middle deltoid on the lateral side. Those muscles that are directed medially from their distal attachments on the anterior side function to forward flex and transverse adduct the shoulder joint. Those on the posterior side and directed medially cause extension and transverse abduction at the shoulder joint.

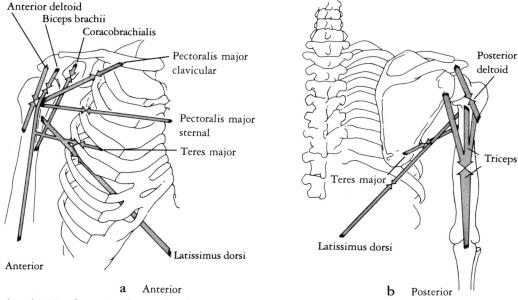

a Anterior   **b** Posterior

Anterior (a) and posterior (b) muscles of the shoulder joint that are used predominantly as movers.   **Figure 4.6.**

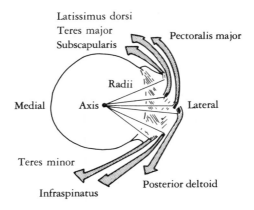

Figure 4.7.   Cross section of the humerus showing the force vectors for the medial and lateral rotators of the shoulder joint.

Figure 4.7 illustrates a cross section of the humerus showing the muscles' resultant forces that cause medial and lateral rotation at the shoulder joint.

Two of the rotator cuff muscles attach on the posterior side of the humeral head, the infraspinatus and teres minor. Each functions in a wheel-axlelike mechanism to rotate the posterior side of the humerus medially, causing lateral rotation of the humerus around the longitudinal axis of the shoulder joint. The subscapularis is attached distal to the anterior side of the humeral head and functions in a wheel-axlelike mechanism to rotate the anterior side medially, causing medial rotation of the humerus. The supraspinatus is attached distally to the top of the humeral head and above the anteroposterior axis of rotation of the shoulder joint. Thus, it functions as a first-class lever mechanism, pulling the top of the humeral head medially to move the shaft of the bone laterally into abduction.

The latissimus dorsi and teres major originate posteriorly on the trunk and insert on the anterior side of the humerus. When they shorten, they pull the anterior humerus medially in a wheel-axle arrangement to cause medial rotation of the humerus.

The humerus functions as the axle in a wheel-axle arrangement when it is medially and laterally rotated. The wheel is represented by the forearm and hand if the elbow is flexed, or by the hand if the elbow is straight and the wrist is flexed. The wheel-axle arrangement of the upper extremity is shown in Figure 3.20 (p. 181). The size of the radius of the axle (i.e., the radius of the bone) is fixed. The radius of the wheel depends on the degree to which the elbow or wrist is flexed; the greater the flexion—up to 90 degrees—the greater the radius, the more the resistance torque, and also the greater the advantage in providing range of linear motion or speed of movement of the hand (wheel) segment. The range of linear motion of the hand when the elbow is flexed to various degrees during medial rotation of the shoulder joint is an important consideration in throwing and striking activities.

As the arm is moved from anatomical position to a flexed or extended, abducted or adducted position, the resultant force vectors of the muscles surrounding the shoulder joint change as well. Because of the mobility of the shoulder joint, numerous positions of the upper extremity are possible, with each having its own resultant muscle directions.

Mechanics of Arm Abduction

This section on the nature of arm abduction is included because of the interesting and complex way in which the shoulder girdle and shoulder joint work together to accomplish this movement. The coordination of the shoulder complex (girdle and joint) not only allows the mobility necessary for the reaching, grasping, and throwing functions of the human upper extremity but also provides the structures necessary to stabilize an inherently weak, bony, and ligamentous arrangement. Figure 4.8 illustrates the important muscles that function to abduct the arm at the shoulder joint and to stabilize the humerus against the dislocating components of the mover muscles.

The supraspinatus initiates the first few degrees of shoulder joint abduction. Apparently, the first-class lever arrangement of the supraspinatus, even though it acts with a disadvantage in motive force, gives a better angle of pull than does the deltoid. The two components of force for the deltoid are always such that the stabilizing component is greater than the small rotary component throughout the entire range of abduction. At initial stages, the stabilizing component is actually a

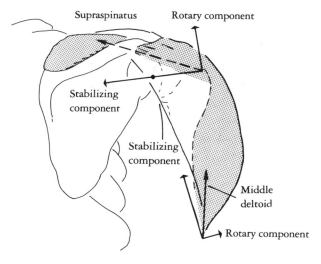

Muscles important in shoulder abduction.

Figure 4.8.

dislocating one, since it is directed in such a way that it pulls the head of the humerus upward into the inferior side of the acromion process. To overcome some of these problems, two things happen. First, as the humerus abducts, the scapula upwardly rotates at a ratio of about 1:2; that is, the glenoid fossa rotates upward one degree for every two degrees of humeral abduction. This action moves the acromion process out of the way as the greater tuberosity of the humerus approaches it. Second, the rotator cuff muscles tense to stabilize the humeral head against the glenoid fossa so that the component of the deltoid that would tend to displace the humerus upward is neutralized. Three of the rotator cuff muscles—the infraspinatus, the subscapularis, and the teres minor—have downward components to perform this stabilization (Figure 4.5).

The activities that require the shoulder joint to be abducted or forward-flexed and medially rotated cause shoulder pain in a significant number of athletes. This shoulder impingement syndrome, as it is labeled, is found in baseball pitchers, tennis players, and freestyle, butterfly, and backstroke swimmers. Since these athletes perform repetitive and forceful movements that involve shoulder abduction, flexion, and medial rotation, they are the most susceptible to the impingement syndrome. Some call this syndrome the rotator-cuff impingement syndrome, although only one rotator cuff muscle is directly involved. Moreover, the long head of the biceps, which is not part of the rotator cuff group, also becomes impinged. Most sources agree that the inflammation occurs from the squeezing of the supraspinatus tendon, which passes over the head of the humerus and under the anterior part of the acromion process and the coracoacromial ligament. The latter two structures make up what is known as the coracoacromial arch.

The compression of the head of the humerus upward and inward to the glenoid fossa and the coracoacromial arch represents motion that should be prevented by strengthening those muscles that stabilize the humerus against these motions. The muscles are those that have a downward component to them when the arm is abducted or flexed.

UNDERSTANDING THE SHOULDER GIRDLE-SHOULDER JOINT COMPLEX

1. Stand in back of a partner. Place your hand on your partner's scapula. The partner slowly abducts the arm over his or her head.

    a. What movement of the scapula occurs?
    b. When do you start to notice it (in degrees)?
    c. Why is this movement necessary?
    d. What does it do to the glenoid fossa?

2. Have your partner shrug his or her shoulders.

    a. From what articulation does this movement originate?
    b. What bones are moving because of the direct muscle pull on them?

c. What bones move because they are attached to the moving bones?

d. Observe the lines of force for the muscles that perform this function in the illustrations of the scapula and clavicle in Figure 4.2. Discuss the effectiveness of each muscle group in performing the motion (in terms of relative magnitudes of the components).

3. Move the shoulder girdle in the following ways: elevation, depression, upward rotation, downward rotation, protraction, retraction. Place your hands over your partner's scapulae during the protraction and retraction movement. What is the motion of the scapulae relative to the vertebral column?

4. What muscles should be strengthened to correct a round-shouldered condition? Which muscles should be stretched?

5. Stand facing a partner who is in anatomical position. The partner flexes the shoulder joint as far as it will go without moving the arm or forearm around any other axis besides the frontal.

a. How far will it flex?

b. What stops the movement?

c. What movement allows the partner to get the arm overhead? Why?

6. Starting from the anatomical position, measure the range of motion (ROM) for medial rotation of the shoulder joint. Starting again from the anatomical position, measure the ROM for lateral rotation. Compare the ROMs.

7. Identify the movement of the shoulder girdle and the shoulder joints in the following activities (during the execution, or force, phases): (a) a butterfly stroke in swimming, (b) a back-crawl stroke in swimming, (c) a dip on the parallel bars, (d) a pull-up, (e) a volleyball spike, and (f) drawing the arm back in archery.

8. What is an example of a wheel-and-axle arrangement in the shoulder joint? Draw a diagram that represents this arrangement. Discuss the mechanical advantage of this arrangement in terms of force requirement and ROM advantages. What is the mechanical advantage in ROM, speed of movement, or force?

SECTION 3

THE ELBOW JOINT

Structure

Technically, the elbow joint is made up of the distal end of the humerus and the proximal end of the ulna. The proximal end of the radius also articulates with the distal end of the humerus, and is therefore sometimes considered part of the elbow. The reader should review the bony landmarks of these particular areas: on the humerus, the medial and lateral epicondyles, the trochlea, the capitulum, and the coronoid, radial, and olecranon fossae; on the ulna, the olecranon and coronoid processes; and on the radius, the head and the radial tuberosity. Figure 4.9 illustrates the bony and ligamentous arrangement of the elbow joint and the radioulnar joint.

The only movements possible at the elbow joint are flexion and extension. These are accomplished by the movement of the olecranon process and coronoid of the ulna, which act as a partial cuff around the trochlea of the humerus. The bony structure makes the elbow stable and acts to prevent dislocations. The head of the radius is attached to the ulna by means of a ligament; thus, the movement of the ulna is transferred to the radius, which moves along with it. The articular surface of the radial head slides along the capitulum of the humerus. The humeral-radial bony stability is weak.

The annular ligament is a three-quarter, ring-shaped tissue. It is cup shaped, and it attaches to the proximal end of the ulna and surrounds the head of the radius. It functions to hold the head of the radius to the ulna, thereby transferring movement of the ulna to the radius and preventing distal disreplacement of the radius from the ulna. Because of its ring-shaped structure, the annular ligament allows the radius to rotate around the longitudinal axis of the ulna to provide for pronation and supination of the radioulnar joint.

Two ligaments help prevent sideward displacement of the elbow articulation: the lateral ligament (radial collateral) and the medial ligament (ulnar collateral), which prevent adduction and abduction, respectively. Because of the strong bony structure holding the elbow together, dislocation of the elbow is not as common as dislocation of the shoulder complex. Because of excessive and continual stress at the humeral-radioulnar area as a result of repeated throwing or striking activities, however, the ligaments, tendons, and even bony parts may become stressed beyond their capacity. Conditions such as tennis elbow or pitcher's elbow then result.

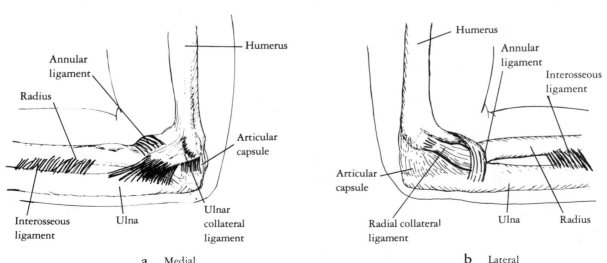

a   Medial   b   Lateral

__Figure 4.9.__   The bony and ligamentous arrangements of the elbow joint and the radioulnar joint.

Muscles of the Elbow as Stabilizers

The anterior and posterior sides of the elbow joint are stabilized by the stabilizing components of the muscle groups that cross the joint. The anterior muscles are shown in Figure 4.10a. We have already seen how the three main elbow flexors (biceps, brachialis, brachioradialis) are arranged mechanically around the elbow joint (Figure 3.9, p. 174). Other anterior muscles that pass over the elbow have their proximal attachments close to the elbow joint and their distal attachments, for the most part, below the wrist. Because the lines of force of these muscles pass so close

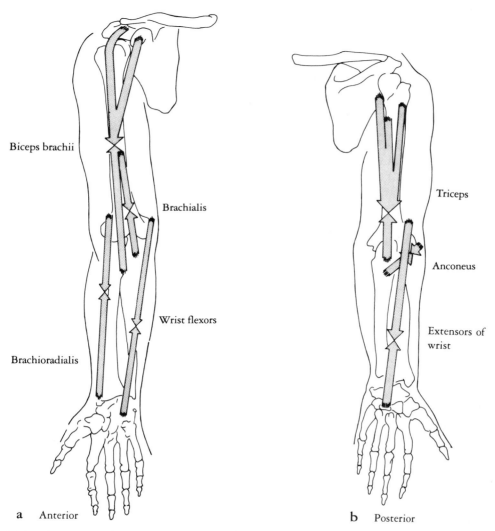

(a) Anterior muscles of the elbow joint. (b) Posterior muscles of the elbow joint.

Figure 4.10.

to the elbow joint, their torques for rotary motion at the elbow are small; thus, their function at the elbow is mainly stabilizing. The proximal attachments on the humerus, however, are able to achieve a better angle of pull than are the forearm attachments. Thus, these muscles have a greater rotary component when they act to bring the humerus to the forearm, as in a pull-up, than when they bring the forearm to the humerus, as in a forearm curl. Notice that the muscles that function mainly as stabilizers of the elbow and flexors of the wrist have their proximal attachments to the medial epicondyle of the humerus. Because of the number of muscles that act as stabilizers on the anterior side, the muscular stability of the elbow is considered strong. In positions in which the anterior muscles have dislocating components (i.e., when they achieve an angle greater than 90 degrees), the muscles are in such a shortened position that the tension is minimal owing to the length of the tension relationship.

The posterior muscles of the elbow are shown in Figure 4.10b. The main muscle on the posterior side of the elbow is the triceps. From its attachment on the olecranon process of the ulna, it proceeds up the humerus, attaching two of its heads to the posterior humerus and one long head to the scapula. Although all the heads join together to form a common belly and attach to a single distal tendon, the two shorter heads only extend the elbow, while the longer head is a two-joint muscle that extends the shoulder joint as well as the elbow. Because of the particular structure of the posterior elbow (the hooklike configuration of the olecranon and coronoid process), the triceps stabilizes the elbow whether its pull is greater or less than 90 degrees to the long axis of the ulna.

The muscles that extend the wrist also function mainly as stabilizers of the elbow and are attached to the lateral epicondyle of the humerus (Figure 4.10b). The bony arrangement of the posterior elbow is strong, and so is the muscular stability.

Muscles of the Elbow as Movers

The main elbow flexors are discussed as an example of the stabilizing and rotary functions of muscles in Chapter 3. Refer to Figure 3.9 for a review if necessary. The biceps is a three-joint muscle (shoulder, elbow, radioulnar), and therefore should be strengthened over all of its articulations. The shoulder-joint flexion exercise with the elbow extended (Figure 2.4j, p. 118) should be performed as well as the traditional forearm-curl. The elbow flexion against resistance should be performed with the shoulder joint held in extension to take advantage of the full ROM of the biceps.

The triceps as a mover of the elbow is an interesting and rare example of a first-class lever system in the body. It is shown in Figure 3.15b (p. 182). The elbow may be positioned so that the triceps pulls at a 90-degree angle to the long axis of the ulna, thus contributing 100% of its effort to the rotary function. In addition, because it is a two-joint muscle, the triceps can lengthen at its proximal end when the shoulder flexes while it shortens at its distal end to extend the ulna. Consequently, the length-tension relationship can be maintained.

To fully strengthen all three heads of the triceps one should perform resistance exercises by extending the shoulder joint with the elbow extended as shown in Figure

2.4d and by extending the elbow with the shoulder joint flexed as shown in Figure 2.4e (p. 117).

(p. 117).

SECTION 4

THE RADIOULNAR JOINT

Structure

The radioulnar joint is made up of three articulations: the proximal, middle, and distal radioulnar joints. Although their bony arrangements give virtually no stability, their ligamentous arrangements provide the necessary cohesion. The proximal radioulnar joint is supported by the annular ligament, which is described in the section on the structure of the elbow joint (page 206). It prevents downward and lateral displacement of the radius. The middle radioulnar articulation is supported by an interosseous membrane (Figure 4.9), which is located between the shafts of the radius and ulna along their entire length. Through the membrane pass blood vessels and nerves. The fibers of the membrane run obliquely from the radius distally to the ulna. This oblique direction of the fibers strengthens the articulation, helping to prevent a strong pull of the biceps and brachioradialis muscles on the radius from causing proximal displacement of the radius. Since muscles also are attached to the interosseous membrane, it functions generally to transfer stress between the radius and the ulna. The distal radioulnar joint is supported by a fibrodisc joining the two bones at the distal end and by the anterior and posterior radioulnar ligaments.

The movements of the radioulnar joints are pronation and supination around the longitudinal axis. Figure 4.11 illustrates the relative radioulnar positions in each of these movements. Notice that the proximal head of the radius rotates around the annular ligament (represented by a wire) but does not shift positions relative to the ulna. When the forearm is in pronation, the radial shaft crosses over the ulna. The distal end of the radius is then on the medial side of the ulna. The fibrodisc moves with the radius and back under the ulna when the radius supinates.

Muscular Function at the Radioulnar Articulation

The muscles of the radioulnar joint are those that stabilize the two bones and produce either pronation or supination. The four muscles that are influential to radioulnar stabilization and movement are the biceps, the supinator, the pronator teres, and the pronator quadratus. These muscles are illustrated in Figure 4.12. (The muscles that are located along the forearm and produce movements at the wrist do not play a major role in elbow or radioulnar movements, even though they cross both joints; thus they are not discussed here.)

As can be seen from the force arrows of the radioulnar muscles, three of the four muscles contribute to the stability of the radioulnar articulation. The biceps, since

a   b

Figure 4.11.   Radioulnar positions in (a) right-arm pronation and (b) left-arm supination of the radioulnar joint.

it is attached only to the radius and not to the ulna, does not have this stabilizing function. The pronator quadratus and the supinator are located so as to permit the ulna to be used as a stable base from which the muscles can pull on the radius to produce pronation and supination. The pronator teres has a stabilizing component but also pulls across the elbow to the medial epicondyle of the humerus. All three have stabilizing components because all pull on the radius toward the ulna.

The mechanics of the biceps pull as it relates to supination of the radioulnar joint deserves special attention. The attachment of the biceps on the tuberosity on the medial side of the radius allows the biceps to act in a wheel-axle configuration to produce supination when the forearm is in pronation.

When the forearm is pronated, the tendon of the biceps is wrapped around the radius by following the radial tuberosity into medial rotation. This wrapping around the radius is presented as a reason for the decrease in the effectiveness of the biceps as an elbow flexor when the radioulnar joint is pronated. Thus, a flexed arm hang or a pull-up is easier to perform when the forearm is supinated. The wrapping,

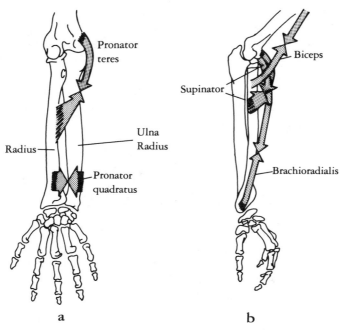

Muscles of the radioulnar joint: (a) pronators, (b) supinators.   Figure 4.12.

however, does allow the biceps to function as a strong supinator of the forearm when the forearm is pronated. Thus, elbow flexion with supination is an effective movement for using the biceps muscle at the elbow. A similar situation occurs with the brachioradialis, in that its attachments to the anterior humerus and the radius on the lateral side make it a pronator to midposition when the forearm is supinated, and a supinator to midposition when the forearm is pronated. Thus, the biceps and the brachioradialis work together effectively in producing forearm flexion with supination from the extended, pronated position. The brachialis plays no role in the radioulnar movements, since it is attached to the ulna. This particular arrangement of the elbow flexors must be taken into account when analyzing elbow-flexion exercises such as pull-ups (forearm in pronation), chin-ups (forearm in supination), and many of the gymnastics skills.

SECTION 5

THE WRIST JOINT

The wrist consists of the articulation of the distal ends of the radius and ulna to the carpal bones. The movements of the wrist joint are those of flexion and extension and radial and ulnar flexion[1] or deviation. Although the bony stability of the wrist is weak, it has fairly strong ligamentous stability, and the numerous muscle tendons that cross the wrist on all sides provide the necessary muscular stability. Since the wrist is not usually subjected to large weight-bearing forces, its ligamentous and muscular stability is sufficient to provide the necessary strength for it to withstand normal stress. Most of the time, the wrist motions of flexion and ulnar flexion are combined with forearm pronation and medial rotation of the humerus, as in throwing and overhead striking movements.

UNDERSTANDING THE ELBOW, RADIOULNAR, AND WRIST JOINTS

1. Have a partner sit with his or her elbow supported, in a slightly flexed position, and relaxed. Supinate the forearm against resistance without increasing or decreasing flexion at the elbow. Palpate the triceps. Explain why there is tension in the triceps. Which one of the three functions of muscular tension (see p. 113) is this muscle displaying?

2. Flex the forearm vigorously and stop the movement suddenly in the middle of its ROM. Palpate the triceps during this action. Why is there muscular tension felt in the triceps? What function of muscular contraction is it displaying?

3. Find a person who has a large ROM for elbow flexion and extension and a person who has a more limited ROM. Compare the ranges of elbow flexion and extension. Determine the reasons why this difference exists.

4. Starting from anatomical position for each measurement, measure the ROM for pronation and then for supination of the radioulnar joint. Have a partner combine the pronation motion of the radioulnar joint with the medial rotation of the shoulder joint and then combine the supination with the lateral rotation, keeping the elbow extended. Discuss the combined movements (shoulder and radioulnar) on the ROM of the hand in each direction.

5. Draw a diagram of the directions of force for the three elbow flexors. Discuss the change in the magnitude of force available for the flexion of the elbow (rotary component) with the elbow extended, flexed 100 degrees, and flexed 150 degrees.

6. Identify and draw an example of a wheel-and-axle arrangement in the radioulnar joint. How could one adjust the radius of the wheel segment? Discuss in terms of baseball pitching and badminton overhead shots.

---

1. Sometimes called adduction and abduction when moved from anatomical position.

7. Identify the movements of the elbow, radioulnar, and wrist joints during the force phase in these activities: (a) spiking a volleyball, (b) passing a football, (c) bowling, (d) batting a baseball (dominant arm), (e) swinging a golf club (dominant arm), and (f) the sculling motion of the arm used in treading water.

REFERENCES
SUGGESTED READINGS

Basmajian, J. V., and Latif, A. "Integrated Actions and Functions of the Chief Flexors of the Elbow: A Detailed Electromyographic Analysis." *Journal of Bone and Joint Surgery* 39 (A) (1957): 1106–18.

Basmajian, J. V., and MacConaill, M. A. *Muscles and Movements—A Basis for Human Kinesiology*. Huntington, N.Y.: Robert E. Krieger Publishing Co., 1977.

Bowers, K. D. "Treatment of Acromioclavicular Sprains in Athletes." *The Physician and Sportsmedicine* 11 (1) (1983): 79–89.

Brunet, M. E., Hoddad, R. J., and Porche, E. B. "Rotator Cuff Impingement Syndrome in Sports." *The Physician and Sportsmedicine* 10 (12) (1982): 86–94.

Dvir, Z., and Berme, N. "The Shoulder Complex in Elevation of the Arm: A Mechanist Approach." *Journal of Biomechanics* 11 (1/2) (1978): 219–25.

Fimrite, R. "Stress, Strain, and Pain." *Sports Illustrated*, 14 August 1978, 30–43.

Fowler, P. "Shoulder Problems in Overhead-Overuse Sports: Swimmer Problems." *American Journal of Sports Medicine* 7 (2) (1979): 141–42.

Gabbard, C., Gibbons, E., and Elledge, J. "Effects of Grip and Forearm Position on Flexed-Arm Hang Performance." *Research Quarterly* 54 (2) (1983): 198–99.

Gainor, B. J., Piotrowski, G., Puhl, J., Allen, W. C., and Hogen, R. "The Throw: Biomechanics and Acute Injury." *American Journal of Sports Medicine* 8 (2) (1980): 114–18.

Hang, Y. "Little League Elbow: A Clinical and Biomechanical Study." In *Biomechanics VIII-A: Proceedings of the Eighth International Congress of Biomechanics*, ed. H. Matsui and K. Kobayashi, 70–86. Champaign, Ill.: Human Kinetics Publishers, 1983.

Hawkins, J. R., and Kennedy, J. C. "Impingement Syndrome in Athletes." *American Journal of Sports Medicine* 8 (3) (1980): 151–58.

Hollinshead, W. H. *Functional Anatomy of the Limbs and Back*. Philadelphia: W. B. Saunders, 1976.

Jackson, D. W. "Problems Among the Inexperienced and Experienced Athletes." *American Journal of Sports Medicine* 7 (2) (1979): 142–44.

Jobe, F. W. "Shoulder Problems in Overhead-Overuse Sports: Thrower Problems." *American Journal of Sports Medicine* 7 (2) (1979): 139–40.

Kennedy, J. C. "Orthopaedic Manifestations." In *Swimming Medicine IV: Proceedings of the Fourth International Congress on Swimming Medicine*, ed. B. Eriksson and B. Furberg, 93–100. Baltimore: University Park Press, 1978.

Nagler, W. "Tennis Elbow." *American Family Physician* 16 (1) (1977): 95–102.

Nichols, J. "Report of the Committee on Research and Education." *American Journal of Sports Medicine* 6 (1978): 295–304.

Nirschl, R. "Good Tennis—Good Medicine." *The Physician and Sportsmedicine* 1 (6) (1973): 26–36.

Perrott, J. W. *Structural and Functional Anatomy for Students and Teachers of Physical Education*. 3d ed. Baltimore: Williams & Wilkins, 1977.

President's Council on Physical Fitness and Sports. "Endurance of Arm and Shoulder Girdle Muscles." *Physical Fitness Research Digest* 6 (3) (1976): 1–21.

Priest, J., and Nagel, D. "Tennis Shoulder." *American Journal of Sports Medicine* 4 (1) (1976): 28–42.

Richardson, A. B., Jobe, F. W., and Collins, H. R. "The Shoulder in Competitive Swimming." *American Journal of Sports Medicine* 8 (3) (1980): 159–63.

Shambes, G. M., and Campbell, S. "Inherent Movement Patterns in Man." In *Kinesiology III*, ed. C. J. Widule, 50–58. Reston, Va.: AAPHERD, 1973.

Suzuki, R. "Loose Shoulder and Suspension Mechanism of the Gleno-Humeral Joint." In *Biomechanics VIII-A: Proceedings of the Eighth International Congress of Biomechanics*, ed. H. Matsui and K. Kobayashi, 57–69. Champaign, Ill.: Human Kinetics Publishers, 1983.

Wolf, S. "The Morphological and Functional Basis of Therapeutic Exercise." In *Therapeutic Exercise*. 3d ed. Ed. J. V. Basmajian, 43–85. Baltimore: Williams & Wilkins, 1978.

Woods, G. W., Tullos, H., and King, J. "The Throwing Arm: Elbow Joint Injuries." *Journal of Sports Medicine* 1 (4) (1973): 43–47.

Prerequisites:

Concept Modules A, B, C, D
Chapters 1, 2, 3

Chapter Contents

BIOMECHANICAL RELATIONSHIPS IN THE LOWER EXTREMITY

The lower extremity may be divided into four structural units: the hip joint, the knee, the ankle, and the subtalar joint. The structure of the lower extremity is similar to that of the upper extremity; however, important differences occur because of differences in function. Whereas the upper extremity is designed for reaching, throwing, and grasping activities, the lower extremity is designed for locomotor functions and weight bearing. Thus, although the structures are similar, the lower extremity is generally heavier and more stable. The one exception to this stability is the knee joint.

SECTION 1

THE HIP JOINT

Structure

The hip joint is the articulation of the pelvis and the femur. It should not be confused structurally or functionally with the articulation of the pelvis with the vertebral column. The following bony landmarks of the pelvis and femur should be reviewed: the acetabulum, the ischial tuberosity, the pubis, and the anterior superior

217

iliac spine of the pelvis; and the head, neck, greater trochanter, and medial and lateral condyles of the femur.

The bony arrangement of the hip joint consists of a rather deep hemispherical socket, **acetabulum,** which is articulated with the hemispherical head of the femur. In itself, the bony arrangement of the hip joint is fairly strong. It is situated on the pelvis so that it is facing slightly anterior; thus, the bony arrangement is stronger in the prevention of posterior displacement of the femur than it is in prevention of anterior displacement. To assist in the task, a labrum or lip of cartilage, similar to the one found in the shoulder joint, circles around the outside of the acetabulum and the head of the femur. In addition, some strong ligaments surround the hip joint. They are shown in Figure 5.1.

Protection from anterior displacement of the femur is provided by the **iliofemoral (Y) ligament** and the **pubofemoral ligament.** The iliofemoral ligament originates on the anterior and lateral side of the ilium just above the acetabulum. As it proceeds anteriorly across the head of the femur, it splits, with one section attaching to the greater trochanter of the femur and the other running medially to the neck of the femur and the lesser trochanter. Hence, the name Y ligament. The pubofemoral ligament originates on the pubic bone and attaches to the lesser trochanter. The iliofemoral ligament is the strongest ligament in the body, and, along with the pubofemoral ligament, gives the hip the stability it needs on the anterior side due to the angulation of the acetabulum.

Protection from posterior displacement of the femur is provided by the **ischiofemoral ligament,** which originates on the ischium and attaches to the greater trochanter on the top of the femur.

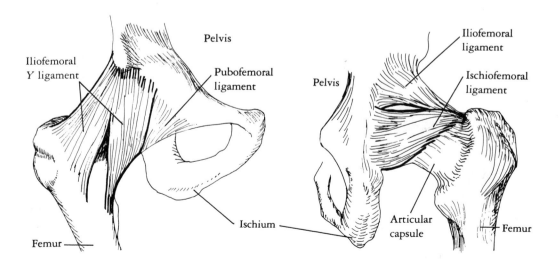

a Anterior   **b** Posterior

Figure 5.1.   The bony and ligamentous arrangements of the hip joint.

To further stabilize the joint, another ligament, the ligamentum teres, is located within the joint capsule itself. It attaches from the inside of the acetabulum to the head of the femur. This combination of ligamentous and bony arrangement provides the hip joint with exceptional stability.

Muscles of the Hip Joint as Stabilizers

The bony and ligamentous arrangements of the hip joint are strong in themselves, but the muscular arrangement provides additional stability. All the muscles that cross the hip have a stabilizing component at some part in the joint range of motion (ROM); however, the muscles emphasized here have large stabilizing components that are maintained throughout the ROMs.

The major muscles of the hip that provide stability are arranged in a similar manner to those of the shoulder. They are the six external rotators and the three gluteals on the posterior side, the adductor muscles on the medial side, and the tensor fascia lata on the lateral side. These muscles are shown with their stabilizing and rotary components in Figure 5.2.

Of particular interest in considering stability of the pelvis is the function of the muscles during one-limb weight bearing. Classically, problems of one-limb weight bearing have been the concern of physical therapists and those working with amputees. In recent years, however, the lateral positioning of the pelvis during ambulation has become increasingly important for athletes, runners, and joggers as well. Figure 5.3 illustrates the situation in one-limb weight bearing.

During the swing phases of walking and running, as in one-limb standing, the pelvis acts as a first-class lever around an anteroposterior (AP) axis that passes through the hip joint. The resistive force is considered to be the weight of the unsupported

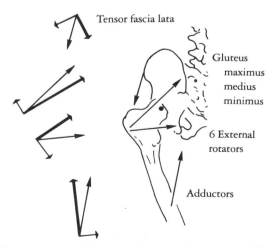

Posterior, medial, and lateral muscles of the hip, which may function as stabilizers.

Figure 5.2.

body acting through the center of gravity (CG) of the body, and the motive force is supplied by the muscles that work to hold the pelvis level (i.e., the hip abductors on the supported side). The necessity for stabilization of the pelvis by the hip abductors causes increased compression at the hip joint. Therefore, the ligaments surrounding the hip joint, and the hip joint itself, must assume an increased burden.

The weight of the body, minus the weight of the supporting leg, is represented by the force vector acting through the CG of the body. Because the line of gravity is located some distance from the axis at the hip, the resistive torque is quite great. Therefore, to lessen the resistive torque, the body is drawn over the supporting limb by the action of the hip adductor muscles, and since the foot is fixed, the body shifts.

Prevention of the unsupported side of the pelvis from dropping is achieved by the hip abductors on the supported side. They exert force at their proximal attach-

Abductors

Adductors

a   b

Figure 5.3.   Muscle forces acting in one-limb weight bearing. (a) Lateral pelvic tilt. (b) Resultant force lines of the hip abductors, which act to prevent lateral pelvic tilt during one-limb weight bearing.

ments on the superior ilium of the pelvis, thus causing the pelvis to act as a first-class lever around the hip joint and raising the unsupported side. The resultant force lines are shown for each of these muscle groups in Figure 5.3b.

The stabilizing and rotary components are indicated with arrows. The stabilizing components are relatively large, and thus the compression force on the hip joint is magnified beyond the actual weight of the unsupported body. It has been estimated to be 4.3 times the body weight (Crowninshield et al. 1978). In normal individuals and those who do not subject their bodies to continual trauma, this compression is handled easily. In the elderly and in athletes engaged in activities that involve long-term running such as marathoners or cross-country runners, the compression at the hip joint may develop into an **overuse syndrome.** This is particularly common among runners who have one limb slightly shorter than the other.

One overuse syndrome that is becoming prevalent is the **lateral knee syndrome,** or tendinitis of the iliotibial band (sometimes called iliotibial band syndrome). This may be due to the excess tension required of the tensor fascia lata to abduct the hip during one-limb weight bearing, particularly with the added impact from the foot plant during a downhill run.

Muscles of the Hip Joint as Movers

The movements occurring at the hip joint are numerous in spite of the bony and ligamentous stability. These movements include: flexion, extension, abduction, adduction, medial and lateral rotation, and transverse abduction (flexion) and adduction (extension).

Many muscles of the hip are longitudinal or unipennate in structure, which allows good ROM. Most are two-joint muscles, which ensures extra efficiency in movement of the lower extremity for locomotion. Further, several large bipennate muscles with large fleshy attachments provide the muscular strength needed to hold and move the body weight. Figure 5.4 illustrates the anterior and posterior lines of action of the muscles crossing the hip joint.

The action of the muscles should be obvious from the resultant lines of action, and the components can be identified easily. As in the shoulder joint, the medial and lateral rotations of the thigh function as a wheel-axle mechanism, with the axle being the femur and the wheel being the leg (if the knee is flexed) or the foot (if the knee is straight). The medial and lateral rotators crossing the hip joint function as the motive forces. The radius of the wheel portion varies in size depending on the degree of knee flexion or ankle flexion. Although not as prevalently used as the medial and lateral rotations of the humerus, the rotations of the hip joint can be noticed in many soccer kicks, judo kicks, or the breaststroke kick. One such situation is shown in Figure 5.5. The game of hacky-sack relies almost entirely on wheel-axlelike hip rotations to impart velocity to the footbag as seen in Figure 5.6.

Because the hip is a major weight-bearing joint, its function must be considered when the lower extremity is weight bearing and the joint is fixed, as well as when the thigh is free to move.

The action of the hamstring group presents an interesting example of a first-class lever system when it acts as a resistance to the body's bending forward (hip flexion) or as a force to raise the body from a forward bending position. With various forms of bending and stooping over, the resistive force arm for the body's weight increases, and thus the resistive torque increases. With the increase in the resistive torque, a necessary increase in the motive torque arises not only of the hamstring muscles acting about the hip but also of the deep back muscles supporting the trunk.

Figure 5.4.   The lines of action of the anterior (a) and posterior (b) muscles that cross the hip joint.

During throwing and striking activities, the movement of the pelvis at the hip joint plays an important role as the pelvis medially rotates around the supporting extremity. For example, in throwing a javelin the initial plant of the forward foot positions the forward thigh in lateral rotation. Thus, as the thrower comes forward over the foot, the pelvis is medially rotated at the hip. The muscles that produce the rotation are the same ones that produce medial rotation of the thigh when the foot is not fixed. Different motor units and parts of the muscle may be used, however.

Axle

Radius of wheel

⊦Wheel⊣

The wheel-and-axle arrangement of the lower extremity in performing a soccer pass.

Figure 5.5.

Medial and lateral rotations of the hip are used to impel the footbag in the game of hacky-sack.

Figure 5.6.

SECTION 2

THE KNEE JOINT

Structure

The knee joint is made up of the articulation of the distal end of the femur and the proximal end of the tibia. The following bony landmarks of the articulating bones should be reviewed: the lateral and medial condyles, the intracondular fossa, and the patellar surface of the femur; the medial and lateral articular surfaces, the intracondular eminence, and the tibia tubercle on the tibia; and the patella. Figure 5.7 illustrates the bony and ligamentous landmarks of the knee joint.

As can be seen, the bony articulation of the femur and the tibia consists of two shallow convex surfaces into which fit the semicircular-shaped femoral condyles. Because of these shapes, the bony stability of the knee is extremely weak. The ligamentous and cartilaginous structures are numerous. The two semicircular **menisci,** which surround the medial and lateral rims of the condular facets of the tibia, serve to increase the depth of the concavity and attempt to stabilize the movements of the femoral condyles on the tibia. The medial meniscus is the larger and more open of the two, and it allows for the slight rotary and locking mechanism of the knee joint. The cruciate ligaments cross within the knee articulation. The **anterior cruciate** is attached to the anterior tibia and crosses to the posterior femur; the **posterior cruciate** is attached to the posterior tibia and crosses to the anterior femur. The roll of the cruciates is predominantly to prevent forward displacement of the femur (posterior cruciate) on the tibia and backward displacement of the femur (anterior cruciate) on the tibia.

Stability on the medial and lateral sides is provided by the **medial and lateral collateral ligaments.** The **fibular collateral ligament** is located on the lateral side and is attached to the femur and the fibula. The **tibiocollateral ligament** is located on the medial side and is attached to the femur and the tibia. Posteriorly, the knee joint is stabilized by the **popliteal ligament,** which is an oblique ligament running from the lateral posterior femur to the medial posterior tibia. Anteriorly, the knee is stabilized by the **patellar ligament,** which attaches the distal part of the patella to the tibia at the tibia tubercle.

The functional role of the knee joint in human motion is difficult to accommodate. The knee joint must be mobile enough to allow the movements and also stable enough to absorb the forces created by the weight of the body and the counterforce of the ground reaction acting upward during locomotion and weight-bearing activities. The knee is positioned between the forceful muscles acting over the hip joint and between the stability of the hip above it and the stability of the ankle joint below it. In addition, the foot usually acts as a propulsive agent against the counterforce of friction. The counterforce stabilizes the foot and thus provides for the transfer of forces from the foot up to the knee. Much of the rotation required for turning the body while the foot is fixed must come from the muscles that surround the knee.

Bony landmarks and ligaments of the knee. (a) Anterior view. (b) Posterior view. (c) Lateral view. **Figure 5.7.**
(d) Menisci and cruciates, from the posterior view. (e) Top view.

The knee must have the stability to withstand weight-bearing forces while remaining mobile enough to maintain the ROMs required for locomotor adaptability.

Because of the dual role that the knee must play, its ligamentous stability is not constant. When the knee is extended, its task is mainly to remain stable, and the ligaments are arranged so that the articulation is surrounded by fairly taut ligaments from all sides and from within. When the knee is flexed, however, it must be mobile enough to accommodate the need to change direction during locomotion; thus, some of the ligaments loosen slightly when the knee is in flexion to allow for greater ROM in rotation.

When the knee is flexed, the anterior cruciate ligament and the collateral ligaments become less taut, allowing more mobility of the joint. Thus, the extended knee is fairly stable, but the flexed knee is unstable. When external trauma is applied, such as a blow to the thigh or leg from the side, the straight knee does not have an efficient way to absorb that force, and injury to the ligaments may result. The flexed knee is less stable and allows movement. Because of its mobility, however, it may be pushed beyond its normal ROM; this, combined with the momentum of the moving segments, may result in injury.

Muscular Stability of the Knee

Because of the dual role for which the knee is designed, the muscular arrangement is of utmost importance in maintaining the stability necessary to prevent injury. The motions that are possible in the knee joint are flexion and extension, with medial and lateral rotation possible only when the knee is flexed and with maximum rotation possible at approximately 90 degrees of knee flexion. The flexion and extension motion is used in locomotor skills. The medial and lateral rotation seems to be a mechanism for allowing the nonweight-bearing foot to turn and for allowing the body to turn at the knee joint when the foot is fixed to the ground. The basketball player in Figure 5.8 illustrates the turning of the body with the foot fixed. The knee is stabilized on the anterior side by the quadriceps, on the medial side by the sartorius and the gracilis, on the lateral side by the tensor fascia lata, and on the posterior side by the hamstring group from above and the gastrocnemius from below. These muscles are shown in Figure 5.4 (p. 222).

Because of the permanently small angle of attachment of the quadriceps group to the tibia, a large stabilizing component is always acting at the knee joint. This is particularly important when the hamstrings are contracting strongly when the knee is flexed beyond 90 degrees, because the hamstrings then have a dislocating component. The stabilizing function in this situation is shown in Figure 5.9.

In this example the stabilizing component of the quadriceps is set equal in magnitude to the dislocating component of the hamstrings.

Although the hamstrings are shortened considerably when the knee is flexed beyond 90 degrees, a flexion of the hip serves to maintain their length somewhat so that tension may be maintained. Thus, the dislocating component of the hamstrings at the knee may be influential. The popliteal ligament also may provide some stability beyond this position.

A basketball player changing direction by laterally rotating the leg at the flexed support knee.   **Figure 5.8.**

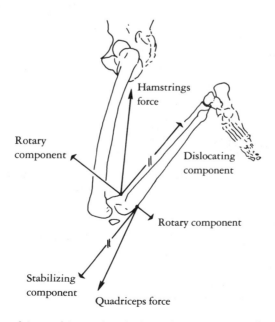

The stabilizing function of the quadriceps when the hamstrings are acting to flex the knee.   **Figure 5.9.**

The sartorius, gracilis, and gastrocnemius muscles are able to pull at an angle greater than 90 degrees to the leg; in this way, they create a slight dislocating component at the knee joint. During knee ROM from 180-degree to 90-degree flexion, most of the muscles crossing the knee provide a rotary and stabilizing effect. A greater-than-90-degree flexion of the knee, however, effects a dislocating component in some muscles, and these, along with the weak bony and ligamentous arrangements, put the knee in a weak position. Some lateral and medial stability is given by the hamstrings, and the tensor fascia lata provides additional stability on the lateral side.

Muscles of the Knee as Movers

The muscles of the knee joint are predominantly two-joint muscles acting also at the hip: the hamstrings, the rectus femoris, the gracilis, the sartorius, and the tensor fascia lata. The two-joint muscle arrangement provides efficiency of movement for locomotion; however, the common insufficiency problem of two-joint muscle arrangements also is present—that is, **passive insufficiency,** attempting to stretch the muscle over both joints simultaneously, or **active insufficiency,** contracting a two-joint muscle to move both joints fully at the same time. The two-joint muscle cannot *stretch* enough to allow full ROM at both joints at the same time, nor can it *contract* enough to produce complete movement at both joints at the same time. A common example of this is seen when one tries to flex the hip and extend the knee fully at the same time or to extend the hip and flex the knee fully at the same time. The hamstrings cannot contract enough or stretch enough to allow either of these combinations to be performed in total.

Another characteristic of the two-joint muscles of the hip and knee is that they are a balanced combination of longitudinal muscles (gracilis, sartorius, tensor, and semitendinosus) and bipennate muscles (biceps femoris, semimembranosus, and rectus femoris). This combination provides for both strength and ROM needs of the main locomotor complex of the body.

Muscular Imbalances at the Knee

Although the hamstring muscles are usually considered as a group, important differences exist among them. The biceps femoris is attached on the lateral side of the fibula, while the semimembranosus and semitendinosus insert on the medial side of the tibia. Their locations allow them to produce lateral and medial rotation of the leg at the knee when the knee is flexed. If an imbalance in strength exists between the lateral and medial muscles (e.g., if the biceps is stronger than the medial muscles), a lateral rotation at the knee occurs when the knee is flexed. This is evident in the performance of knee flexion against a resistance in a prone position on a weight-training machine, as shown in Figure 5.10. To correct this condition, a performer should attempt to work the knee flexors while keeping the legs medially rotated.

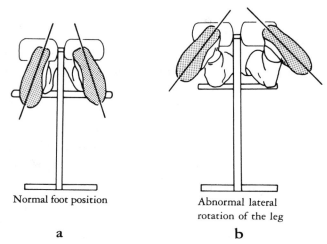

Normal foot position

Abnormal lateral
rotation of the leg

a

b

A muscular strength imbalance between the stronger biceps femoris on the lateral side of the knee and the semitendinosus and semimembranosus on the medial side of the knee causes the leg to rotate laterally during knee flexion. (a) Normal position. (b) Laterally rotated position.

Figure 5.10.

The performer will find that the resistive force probably has to be decreased for flexing in this medially rotated (toe-in) position.

When the foot is free, the stability of the knee in abduction and adduction is reflected by the relative strengths of the medially and laterally attached hamstring muscles. If the medial muscles are weaker than the lateral muscle, the leg swings forward during gait in a laterally rotated position. The tension imbalance may be transmitted to the structures even when the knee is straight and may be evident in a laterally rotated leg during weight bearing.

Similar problems develop when an imbalance occurs in the strength of the quadriceps muscles, particularly when the vastus medialis is relatively weak. Since it must stabilize the position of the patella and keep it in the patellar groove during forceful contractions of the quadriceps in knee extension, it must be strong enough to fulfill this role. If it is not, the patella becomes displaced laterally with the pull of the vastus lateralis, and it eventually wears on the inferior patellar surface, causing a parapatellar pain known as **chondromalacia.** Many of the injuries to the knee happen because of too great an abduction of the leg or because of continued lateral rotation of the leg while weight bearing. The strength of all of the quadriceps muscles is crucial to maintaining the integrity of the knee in these situations.

Instability of the Knee

Because of its inherent mobility, the knee is prone to instability and injury when subjected to continual stress or when it goes beyond the limits of its ROM because of an impact. Some of the situations that commonly occur are described in the sections that follow.

ROTATIONS WITH THE FOOT FIXED

During most sport situations, the foot is fixed on the ground during weight bearing. Exceptions to the norm are found in aquatic and aerial activities. Even during activities in which friction forces are assumed to be small, such as skiing and skating, if a performer "catches an edge," the continuing rotation of the thigh and trunk is transferred to the knee and must be counteracted by the ligamentous and muscular structures surrounding the knee. The knee is designed so that with flexion, rotation becomes possible. Its rotational capabilities make the knee a mobile adapter for turns and twists while the foot is fixed on the ground. Three common examples occur in basketball, soccer, and football, games in which turning to pass or to dodge is important. The knee has limits to its motion, and the ligamentous stability of the knee decreases with knee flexion. During normal turning and twisting motions, the knee fulfills its role quite well; however, if some external force is applied as the knee is reaching its limits of motion, causing it to move beyond its range, injury may be unpreventable, particularly when a shoe sole equipped with cleats enhances the friction force. With the hip and ankle stability as great as it is, the knee becomes the weakest link in the chain, so the structures of the knee must be strong enough to withstand the forces. For this reason, an athlete must maintain strong muscular stability and strength surrounding the knee to prevent any pushing of the knee beyond its safe limits.

LATERAL KNEE PAIN

Two muscles that help stabilize the knee are implicated as the cause of lateral knee pain in runners. The tensor fascia lata muscle fibers are located lateral and slightly anterior to the ilium and attach distally by means of a long flat band of fascia to the lateral side of the leg below the knee joint. On its way to its distal attachment, the band passes over the lateral condyle of the femur. During knee flexion, while weight bearing, the tensor fascia lata muscle contracts to help stabilize the pelvis from lateral tilt. The added tension in the band enhances the friction force over the epicondyle, which results in what is called the **iliotibial band syndrome.** The tenderness over the lateral knee is said to be diffuse, which differentiates this condition from a second source of lateral knee pain called **popliteal tendinitis.**

The popliteal muscle attaches proximally on the lateral condyle of the femur and passes medially behind the leg where it attaches on the posterior-medial side of the tibia. Its function is to medially rotate the knee and to help the posterior cruciate ligament stabilize the femur from anterior displacement on the tibia during weight bearing when the knee is flexed. It is particularly active during downhill walking or running. Since the popliteus is a medial rotator of the leg, it is subjected to tensile stress during lateral rotation of the knee. Runners whose weight-bearing posture includes a laterally rotated knee are particularly prone to tendinitis or inflammation of the popliteus tendon. This condition is enhanced especially with downhill running when the popliteus muscle actively stabilizes the femur from forward displacement. Tendinitis is distinguished from iliotibial band syndrome by its soreness being focused at the popliteal attachment on the femoral condyle rather than the more diffuse pain in the iliotibial condition.

DEEP SQUAT

A second problem with regard to knee stability is in performing a deep knee bend or squat. Much controversy exists about whether the knee is designed to withstand the stresses put on it during the full squatting motion. Whether it can or cannot withstand those forces depends on the speed with which one descends, the size of the calves and thighs, and the strength of the controlling muscles. Figure 5.11 illustrates the position of the legs during the squat.

The main danger to the knee occurs when the center of rotation for knee flexion is altered because of the pressing together of the tissues of the calf and thigh. As one descends, the center of rotation is somewhere within the knee joint, but when the tissues touch, the center of rotation moves back to the contact area. This creates a dislocating effect at the knee, as shown in the illustration in Figure 5.11b. If the

Safe position (a) and unsafe position (b) in the deep squat.

Figure 5.11.

CG of the body system is kept forward of this center of rotation by altering the lifting position or if the muscles of the thigh are strong enough to prevent the body from resting on the calves or bouncing on the calves, then danger to the knees may be prevented. The danger is enhanced, however, when squats are done by individuals who cannot control their descent properly because of weak legs; when a large external weight is held on the shoulders, which brings the performer close to the maximum lifting force; when the squats are done as a timed event for maximum number of squats per time unit; or when the position brings the line of gravity of the body behind the center of rotation. In the first two cases, the possibility exists that the performer may lose control and descend too quickly beyond the safe point; in the third case, especially near the end of the time frame when the muscles are fatigued, there is a tendency to bounce off the knees for quickening the change in direction from descent to ascent. With the gravity line being located behind the center of rotation, a first-class lever situation with a wrenching, or separating, effect at the knee is produced. In any case, the deep squat is of little danger to the knee unless these restraints are not observed.

BREASTSTROKER'S KNEE

Although in aquatic activities the foot is not fixed, the knee is still subjected to dislocation due to the muscular forces and the counterforces of the water against the leg as it contributes to the kicking motion (Figure 5.12). Particularly common is "breaststroker's knee," a syndrome characterized by tenderness on the medial side of the knee.

In the propulsive phase, the knee is extending and medially rotating with the foot in a pronated position (everted, abducted, and dorsiflexed). The medial rotation is performed by the two medial hamstring muscles. The hydrodynamic forces against the foot and medial side of the leg, as it extends and medially rotates during the propulsive phase, are directed so that they tend to abduct the leg at the knee joint.

Figure 5.12. Hydrodynamic forces on the medial side of the leg during the knee extension phase of the breaststroke kick.

The assumption is that the tender spot associated with breaststroker's knee is located at the adductor tubercle and the associated medial collateral ligament (Kennedy 1974).

Some evidence exists that breaststroker's knee syndrome is associated with the *technique* of performing the whip kick. Stulberg et al. (1980) found that painful knees occurred in breaststrokers that performed the whip kick with a greater hip joint abduction-adduction component to the kick.

Because abduction or adduction of the knee is not thought of as a natural, useful movement, swimmers often forget that the position may be forced upon the leg and that some conditioning of the muscles that stabilize it is necessary. Strong contractions of the quadriceps and hamstring groups have been shown to significantly limit forced abduction and adduction of the leg (Goldfuss, Morehouse, and LeVeau 1973). A strength-training program for these muscle groups would tend to help these swimmers.

KNEE STABILITY RELATED TO SKIING

Medial and lateral rotation at the knee is rarely used as a conditioning exercise, in spite of the fact that these motions are quite necessary to proper ski technique. Proper edging, balance, and control depend on the medial and lateral rotations not only of the hip but also of the knee, particularly when the knee is flexed, as it is in all skiing positions. The friction afforded by the edging of the skis stabilizes the foot somewhat; thus, the rotations take place as the superior segment rotates about the inferior segment.

The medial and lateral rotation of the knee is an example of a wheel-axle arrangement, with the foot or the ski being the wheel. If the ski tip is caught, a large torque is produced due to the length of the ski (radius of the wheel), and therefore stabilizing the knee against such wrenching is almost impossible. Such a situation highlights the importance of strong muscles surrounding the knee.

UNDERSTANDING THE HIP AND KNEE JOINTS

1. Measure the ROM of hip flexion with the knee extended and with the knee flexed. What is the difference? Why is there a difference?

2. Identify and draw a wheel-and-axle arrangement for the hip joint. What is the mechanical advantage of this arrangement? In what sport situations is this motion used?

3. Sit on a table with your knee flexed over the edge. Rotate the knee medially and then laterally. Be sure that the movement is from the knee and not from the hip or the foot. What is the ROM for each movement? Discuss this movement and its importance to changing directions in skiing and skating.

4. Flex your knee. Look down the longitudinal axis of your leg and draw a diagram of the cross section of the leg at the approximate points of attachment of the hamstring group. Draw force arrows to indicate the points of application of the forces of each of these muscles on the bones. Discuss the wheel-and-axle mechanism of this muscle group in nonweight-bearing situations.

5. On a weight-resistance machine, perform leg curls (lie prone and flex the knee against resistance). Does the knee tend to rotate laterally? This reaction to strong knee flexion is quite common. What is the explanation?

6. Identify the movements of the hips and knees in hurdling during takeoff flight and landing phases. What biarticulate muscles are stretched during each phase? What muscles are concentrically contracted? Are there two-joint muscles that are stretched at one articulation and concentrically contracted at the other articulation? Discuss these movements in terms of injuries.

7. Identify the hip and knee movements during the execution (force) phase of the following activities: (a) a whip kick in the breaststroke, (b) mounting a horse, swinging the right leg over, (c) a football punt, (d) a headspring, (e) a soccer-style place-kick. Are there two-joint muscles involved in the movements? Which joints do they cross? How could two-joint muscles be related to injuries?

SECTION 3

THE TIBIOFIBULAR JOINT

Although the tibiofibular joint is similar to the radioulnar joint in the forearm, no particular movements are associated with it.

The tibiofibular joint is an important force transmitter and absorber of the force-and-counterforce exchange during weight-bearing activities. The following gross structures should be reviewed: the superior, middle, and inferior tibiofibular joints; the anterior and posterior tibiofibular ligaments on the superior and inferior joints; the interosseous membrane between the two bones and the transverse ligament; and the medial and lateral malleoli. The interosseous membrane, which is located between the tibia and fibula, allows blood vessels and nerves to pass through it, and generally absorbs and transmits force between the tibia and fibula. The fibers of the membrane run in just the opposite manner to the ones in the forearm; that is, they run from high on the tibia to low on the fibula (see Figure 5.7, p. 225). One possible advantage for this arrangement may be that since the tibia is the main channel for weight-bearing forces, the counterforce of the ground is transmitted up through the tibia and tends to displace it superiorly. The membrane is structured so that this force is transmitted to the fibula. On the other hand, the fibula is the location of the origin of many of the weight-bearing, antigravity muscles that operate to plantar flex the ankle. Thus the force of those muscles on the fibula tend to pull it downward, and the fibers of the membrane, which run in a position to counteract that downward displacement of the fibula, transmit the force to the tibia.

The malleoli, located on the distal ends of the tibia and fibula, function mainly as pulleys to alter the direction of the force of the muscles' pull on the foot.

SECTION 4

THE ANKLE AND FOOT

Structure of the Ankle and Subtalar Joint Complex

Technically, the ankle joint is made up of the tibia and the talus, although the distal end of the fibula also articulates with the talus on the lateral side. Because of the bony arrangement of the ankle joint, with the distal end of the tibia being somewhat concave and the superior talus being convex, the bony stability is fairly strong. Because of the stress that the ankle must withstand, however, ligamentous stability is needed as well. The bony and ligamentous arrangements are shown in Figure 5.13. In addition to providing ankle stability, the articular capsule and the attached ligaments also extend down to the calcaneus.

The movements possible at the ankle are flexion and extension. The flexion movement is called dorsiflexion; the extension movement, plantar flexion. The axis of rotation for the ankle is not in a true frontal plane; it is oriented slightly backward from the frontal plane (13 degrees) on the lateral side and downward (7 degrees) from the medial to the lateral side (Figure 5.14a and c). The tilt creates a slight disorientation of the foot from true sagittal plane motion during plantar flexion and dorsiflexion.

The subtalar joint is located between the talus and the calcaneus. It is probably the most important articulation of the intertarsal group, since much of the inversion and eversion movements of the foot originate there. The subtalar joint is a uniaxial joint; however, its orientation is oblique, like that of the ankle joint. These two axes, ankle and subtalar, may be situated in many different combinations that vary from one individual's foot to another's. On the average, the subtalar axis is 42 degrees from the horizontal plane in the sagittal plane and 23 degrees from the midsagittal plane in the horizontal direction (Inman 1976). These orientations are shown in Figure 5.14b and c.

Because of the obliquity of the ankle and subtalar axes, the foot displays movement in an oblique plane during the motions of inversion and eversion. The actual movements of the foot simultaneously around the subtalar and ankle axes are a combination of inversion at the subtalar joint with plantar flexion at the ankle joint, and a combination of eversion at the subtalar joints with dorsiflexion at the ankle joint. The

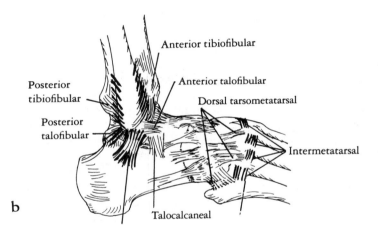

Figure 5.13. Medial (a) and lateral (b) ligamentous arrangement of the ankle.

associated movements of the ankle and subtalar joints may be seen by observing the position of the foot and leg during rising on the toes, as shown in Figure 5.15.

The subtalar joint is the main interconnection between the mobility of the foot mechanism and the stability of the ankle and leg. Thus, it allows important adaptive positioning of the foot and leg during weight bearing, particularly in running and jogging on uneven or curved paths.

The Intertarsal and Tarsal-Metatarsal Joints

Since the tarsal-metatarsal articulations are of the nonaxial, gliding type, they have no particular motions. They glide on each other to produce a combination of movements that allows the foot to become a mobile adaptor for weight bearing, particularly

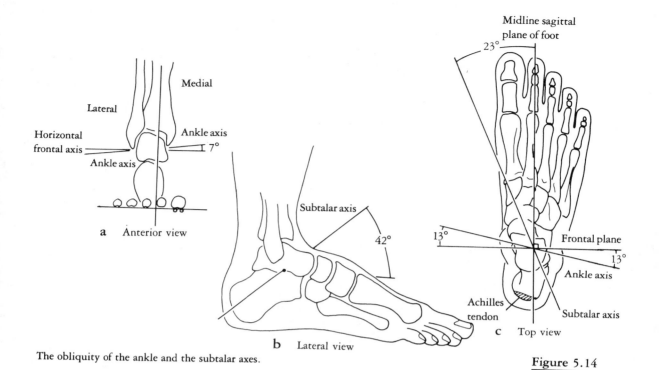

a Anterior view

Medial

Lateral

Horizontal frontal axis

Ankle axis 7°

Ankle axis

Subtalar axis

42°

b Lateral view

Midline sagittal plane of foot

23°

13°

Frontal plane

13°

Ankle axis

Achilles tendon

Subtalar axis

c Top view

The obliquity of the ankle and the subtalar axes.

Figure 5.14

The subtalar inversion associated with ankle plantar flexion as seen during rising on the toes (supination).

Figure 5.15.

on uneven surfaces, and that continually adjusts the foot and leg alignment to maintain balance during weight bearing. The bones are shown in Figure 5.14.

Muscles of the Ankle and Foot as Stabilizers

The ankle's bony and ligamentous stability is good, and therefore the tendency for the ankle to be dislocated laterally or medially is remote. The muscles that cross the ankle and foot are needed for stabilizing the subtalar joint and the intertarsal joints and for supporting the arches. The musculotendinous insertions that support the medial and lateral aspects of the ankle and foot are shown in Figure 5.16.

Numerous intrinsic and extrinsic small muscles of the foot also support the intertarsal, metatarsal, and phalangeal articulations. Maintaining strength of the muscles on all sides of the ankle and foot is important in maintaining the integrity of the structure. Any imbalances in the strength or flexibility or both of the surrounding musculature result in misalignment, putting the line of gravity of the entire body eccentric to the articulations and thus creating a torque that has to be counteracted by muscular effort or ligamentous tension.

For example, Gehlsen and Seger (1980) reported significant strength and ROM

Figure 5.16.   Medial and lateral muscular support for the ankle and foot complex.

differences between subjects who had shin splints and those who did not. The shin-splint group had significantly greater plantar flexor strength than dorsiflexor strength and a greater angular displacement of the calcaneus during the support phase of gait than the group without shin splints.

Overdevelopment of the plantar flexors tends to cause a muscular imbalance between the strength of the plantar flexor-supinator muscles and the dorsiflexor-pronator muscles, which may result in lateral ankle sprains, particularly when landing after being airborne. Even during the swing phase of gait, the foot may tend to invert excessively and not return to its straightforward position before weight bearing.

Muscles of the Ankle and Foot as Movers

Tarsal and metatarsal movements occurring in the foot primarily position the foot according to the force of propulsion and the ground reaction force. The movements of the ankle and tarsal joints that are relevant to the foot function are dorsiflexion and plantar flexion of the ankle and inversion and eversion of the subtalar joints. These movements, for the most part, are performed by multijoint muscles that cross the ankle and insert on the foot. Many of these small muscles relate to specific movements of the metatarsals and the phalanges, which are not covered in this text.

The malleoli function as pulleys to alter the direction of force of the muscles that pull on the foot. Those muscles that pass posterior to the malleoli will plantar flex, and those that pass anterior to the malleoli will dorsiflex. Similarly, those muscles that go around the medial malleolus will invert the foot, while those that go around the lateral malleolus will evert the foot.

Three compartments can be seen in a cross section of the leg: anterior, posterior, and lateral (Figure 5.17). In the **anterior compartment** are two groups of muscles;

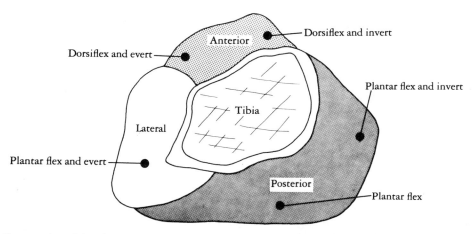

Cross section of the tibia with the anterior, lateral, and posterior muscle compartments shown.

Figure 5.17.

one group dorsiflexes and inverts the foot, while the other group dorsiflexes and everts the foot. In the **posterior compartment,** all of the muscles plantar flex; additionally, one group, which passes around the medial malleolus, inverts the foot, and the other (gastrocnemius and soleus) merely plantar flexes with no inversion or eversion function. The **lateral compartment** houses the muscles that plantar flex and evert the foot, since they pass around the lateral malleolus. The gastrocnemius and soleus, the muscles that make up the Achilles tendon, function to plantar flex the ankle, but because the gastrocnemius also crosses the knee, it secondarily serves to flex the knee joint. To stretch the Achilles tendon properly, both the gastrocnemius and the soleus must be stretched. Most of the stretching exercises advocate dorsi-flexing the ankle while the knee is straight, which seems to be a logical way to stretch the gastrocnemius. This exercise leaves the soleus in a position of little stretch, however, since the tightness of the gastrocnemius occurs before any great dorsiflexion occurs. Proper stretching of the Achilles tendon, therefore, should include dorsi-flexion with the knee straight and with the knee flexed.

Ligamentous and muscular tissues are affected by foot posture, and certain foot postures during weight bearing put excessive stress on muscle groups that are an-tagonistic to those positions. For instance, a foot that is weight bearing in a position of eversion and dorsiflexion stretches the invertor and plantar flexor groups (posterior compartment muscles). Similarly, an inverted foot stresses those muscles that evert the foot (anterior compartment). A more detailed discussion of leg and foot alignment is presented in a following section.

UNDERSTANDING THE ANKLE AND FOOT

1. Using several subjects, measure the ROMs of dorsiflexion and plantar flexion of the ankle. Do differences occur among the measurements of subjects? Why?

2. Sit on a table with the knee flexed over the edge. Gently plantar flex the ankle. What other movements occur in the foot during this plantar flexion? In what artic-ulations do these movements occur? Why are they associated with plantar flexion?

3. Sit on the edge of a table and gently dorsiflex the ankle. Do other movements of the foot tend to occur? In what articulation do these occur? Why are they associated with dorsiflexion of the ankle?

4. In general, five groups of muscles are attached to the foot and leg. Group 1 attaches to the lateral foot and lateral leg; Group 2, to the lateral foot and anterior leg; Group 3, to the medial foot and posterior leg; Group 4, to the medial foot and anterior leg; and Group 5, to the posterior foot and posterior leg. List and discuss the ankle and foot movements caused by each group's resultant muscle forces.

BIOMECHANICS OF THE LOWER EXTREMITY DURING LOCOMOTION

The walking pattern in the lower extremity primarily consists of a 35% swing phase and a 65% stance phase. During the swing phase, the leg approaches heel contact with a slight lateral rotation at the hip joint. By the time of heel strike, however, the hip normally has medially rotated so that the toe points forward. The foot is in slight inversion. Through midstance and push-off, the weight-bearing point shifts from a position that is slightly lateral to the principal longitudinal axis of the foot to a position slightly medial to the longitudinal axis. This is shown in Figure 5.18. The darkest dots indicate the greatest weight-bearing pressure. The final propulsion is given by the distal heads of the first and second metatarsals. This lateral weight transfer is accomplished by an eversion of the subtalar joint.

In running and jogging, the walking pattern is modified slightly by adding a phase of nonsupport between the stance and swing phases and by exaggerating the ROMs of the movements in the articulations to accommodate the increased force absorption

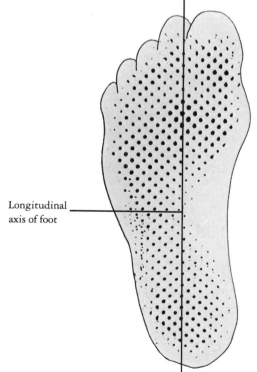

Longitudinal axis of foot

Dynamic weight bearing during the stance phase of a walking gait (from Ferrandino 1978).

Figure 5.18.

necessary during weight bearing. During running, the vertical force on the supporting foot is estimated to be at least three times the body weight.

In running, as in walking, the movements of the leg and foot generally follow a prescribed sequence. The rearfoot is positioned in a slight inversion as heel contact is made; this is followed by a slight plantar-flexion motion as the forefoot moves to the ground. The axes of rotation of the ankle and subtalar joints are positioned so that the inversion motion is associated with plantar flexion of the ankle. These motions occurring with slight adduction of the forefoot are called **supination.**

As the body weight comes forward over the foot, the subtalar joint begins to evert, the ankle dorsiflexes, and the knee and hip joints also flex. These movements help absorb the shock of the body weight coming down on the lower extremity. Because of the inclination of the ankle and subtalar axes, the movements of eversion of the subtalar joint and dorsiflexion of the ankle are associated with an abduction movement of the foot when the foot is free. This combination is called **pronation.** When the foot is fixed, however, the abduction of the foot is prevented to some extent by the friction forces acting at the foot-ground interface. Consequently, the abduction motion manifests itself by a medial rotation of the tibia. The tibial rotation is possible because of the accompanying knee flexion. These motions continue as the body weight passes over the center of the foot.

As soon as the line of gravity passes in front of the foot, the ground reaction force on the foot is able to provide an accelerating rather than a decelerating force to the body. The hip and knee joints begin to extend sequentially. The ankle continues to dorsiflex until the heel is lifted off the ground. The taut Achilles tendon may elicit the stretch reflex, which will initiate the plantar flexion of the ankle joint.

In the normally extending knee, the medially rotated tibia must laterally rotate back to a neutral position; the plantar flexion of the ankle produces the associated inversion of the subtalar joint, and, consequently, the adducted foot position. A slightly supinated position is seen at push-off, with the weight-bearing point somewhere between the first and second metatarsal heads.

SECTION 6

LOWER EXTREMITY POSTURES

The tightness or laxity of the ligaments in the lower extremity and the relative strengths and weaknesses of the antagonistic muscle groups surrounding the articulations produce lower extremity postures that are unique to each individual. For example, the relative position of the axes of the ankle and the subtalar joints varies so markedly between individuals that even an average measure cannot be used confidently in analyzing leg and foot postures and planes of foot motion. For practical purposes, however, a few simplified observations are useful in determining lower extremity postural conditions.

Ideal Alignments of Lower Extremity Segments

Normal alignment does not necessarily mean **ideal alignment,** for what is *normal* is a measure of what occurs on the average in the population, not necessarily an *ideal* measure. In fact, most people do not have ideal alignments for one reason or another.

The ideal alignment of the lower extremity segments may be likened to that of a column that supports a roof. Such a column should be as straight and as vertically aligned as possible to support the forces from above. Likewise, the midsagittal axes of the femur and tibia should be as parallel as possible with no twisting between adjacent segments. Figure 5.19 is a drawing of an ideal alignment.

In Figure 5.19 the pelvis is supported on either side by two columns made up of four structures. The structures making up the columns are the femur, the tibia, the talus, and the calcaneus. Normally, the femur is inclined slightly medial from its

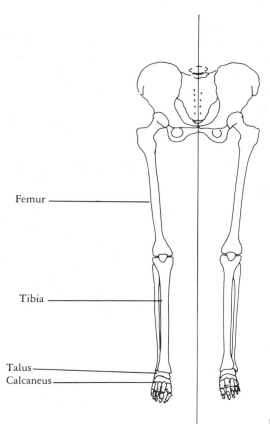

Femur

Tibia

Talus
Calcaneus

Ideal alignment of the lower extremity.   **Figure 5.19.**

proximal to distal end. The inclination is somewhat dependent on the width of the pelvis.

Figure 5.20 shows an ideal arrangement of the forefoot. The circles represent the cross-sectional ends of the metatarsals.

Ideal alignment of the feet can be determined by observing how the feet align themselves with the midsagittal body plane. These possible positions are shown in Figure 5.21. In the ideal alignment in Figure 5.21a, the longitudinal axis of the foot segment is parallel with the midsagittal body plane. A **toe-out position** is shown in Figure 5.21b and a **toe-in position,** in Figure 5.21c. In each of these positions the longitudinal axes of the feet are oblique to the midsagittal plane of the body.

Abnormal Alignments of the Lower Extremity

LATERAL ROTATION OF THE HIP JOINT

If the four column segments are aligned with one another (i.e., no angulation or twisting of one segment occurs relative to an adjacent segment), a person may still display a toe-out gait. This situation is due to a laterally rotated hip joint. Figure 5.22 illustrates this position. Notice that the subject's right toe is directed outward and that his right leg and knee are aligned with his outwardly directed toe. This means that the rotation must be occurring at the hip joint. The lateral rotators of the hip are causing the lower extremity to rotate laterally during the swing phase of the gait. This condition may be corrected by strengthening the medial rotators of the hip joint and stretching the lateral rotators. Lateral rotation of the hip joint is commonly found in ballet dancers and wrestlers. Figure 5.23 illustrates how a laterally rotated hip is beneficial in a wrestling hold.

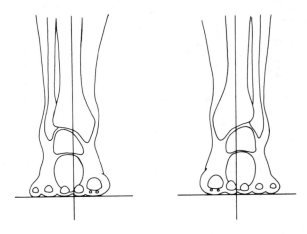

Figure 5.20.   Ideal alignment of the forefoot.

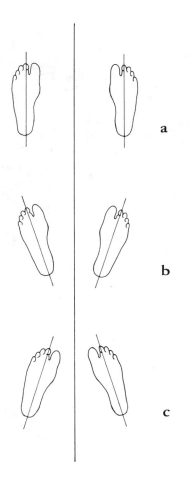

(a) Ideal, (b) toe-out, and (c) toe-in positions of the foot relative to the body's midsagittal plane.   **Figure 5.21.**

A view of the lower extremity during the swing phase of gait, showing lateral rotation at the hip joint.   **Figure 5.22.**

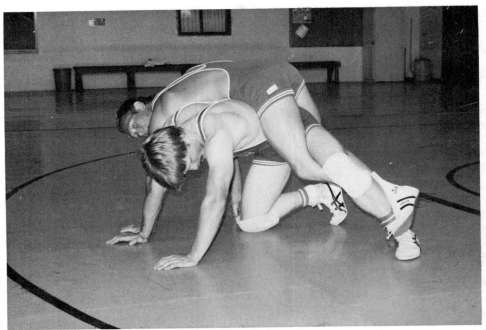

Figure 5.23.   An extremely flexible hip joint is beneficial in certain wrestling holds.

TORSIONAL CONDITIONS

Torsional conditions occur when one segment is rotated about its longitudinal axis relative to the next adjacent segment; that is, the midsagittal plane of the femur is not aligned with the midsagittal plane of the tibia.

Femoral Torsion.   Figure 5.24a shows a femoral torsion condition; that is, the femur is rotated medially relative to the tibia. Identification of femoral torsion may be made by standing with the inside borders of the feet parallel and observing the position of the patellae. The patellae should be facing forward. If they are facing medially or inward slightly, then a femoral torsion condition exists. Often this condition is referred to as "cross-eyed" or "squinting" patellae. It is seen most frequently in females and is believed to indicate an imbalance of strength in the vasti muscles of the quadriceps group. Since the vastus medialis and lateralis muscles control the patella, an imbalance of strength between these muscles may cause the patella to be pulled to one side or the other. More likely, the cause is due to misalignment. If the femur is medially rotated relative to the tibia, the patella and the femoral intracondular groove are not aligned. This misalignment manifests itself in parapatellar pain, a condition called **chondromalacia,** which is roughening of the undersurface of the patella due to its rubbing on the lateral condyle of the femur during extension of the knee. When this condition exists, strengthening the lateral rotators of the hip joint and stretching the medial rotators are advised.

a   b

(a) Femoral torsion. (b) Tibial torsion.   **Figure 5.24.**

Tibial Torsion.   The second torsional condition is called **tibial torsion** and is seen more frequently in males. As in femoral torsion, the midsagittal axes of the femur and tibial are rotated relative to each other such that the midsagittal plane of the femur is directed forward but the midsagittal plane of the tibia is rotated outward. Figure 5.24b illustrates the condition.

An imbalance in the individual hamstring muscles has been implicated as a possible cause of this condition. Recall that the lateral hamstring muscle, the biceps femoris, has a second function to laterally rotate the knee and that the medial hamstring muscles, the semimembranosus and tendinosus, medially rotate the knee. As the knee is flexed against resistance, lateral rotation of the leg at the knee commonly occurs due to the stronger biceps femoris (Figure 5.10, p. 229). If the knee is flexed against resistance without control of the medial and lateral functions, the knee laterally rotates, with knee flexion and the common occurrence of lateral rotation of the leg with knee flexion reinforced. The tibial torsion condition causes stress on the medial structures of the knee joint. It also is associated with lateral knee pain (Flood 1980) and causes a toeing-out position of the foot during weight bearing.

VARUS AND VALGUS CONDITIONS

In varus and valgus conditions of the segments of the lower extremity the longitudinal axis of the segment angles or tends outward or inward from its proximal end to its distal end.

Varus.   **Varus conditions** are alignments in which the segment angles or tends inward from its proximal end to its distal end. Figure 5.25a shows femoral varus; Figure 5.25b, tibial varus; and Figure 5.25c, rearfoot varus. For clarity, all the other segmental alignments are placed in a neutral position. Curved lines about the lateral or medial articulations represent the location of tensile (pulling-apart) stress to the surrounding structures. With a varus condition, tensile stress is placed on the lateral side of the segment's proximal articulation and on the medial side of the segment's distal articulation. The muscles located on the stressed side should be strengthened, while the muscles located on the opposite side should be stretched.

Femoral varus (Figure 5.25a) contributes to a knock-knee-like posture. It is seen predominantly in females and frequently is associated with the wider pelvis in females although this has not been substantiated. It may be more closely associated with a social milieu in which females develop a traditional "feminine" posture. Femoral valgus affects what is called the **Q-angle,** or quadriceps angle, that is, the angle formed between the longitudinal axis of the femur that represents the pull of the quadriceps muscles and a line that represents the patellar tendon. A Q-angle greater than 15 degrees is reported as being a major factor in injury (James et al. 1978). Tensile stress is placed on the lateral side of the hip joint and on the medial structures

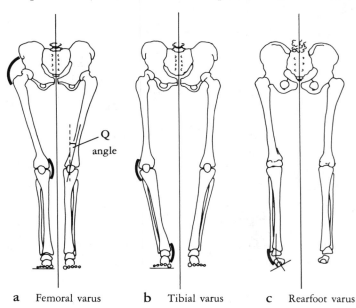

| | **a**   Femoral varus | **b**   Tibial varus | **c**   Rearfoot varus |

Figure 5.25.   Common misalignment of the lower extremity: Varus conditions.

of the knee joint. To alleviate this condition, the hip abductor muscles, which are under tensile stress, should be strengthened, and the quadriceps should be strengthened to stabilize the knee against abduction of the leg. The hip adductors also should be stretched.

The femoral varus condition may be **compensated**; that is, a second misalignment condition may arise to help correct the first. With femoral varus, a compensated tibial valgus (outward tending) is prevalent. This puts additional tensile stress on the medial knee and lateral tissues of the ankle and subtalar joints when the foot is weight bearing.

Tibial varus is shown in Figure 5.25b. It causes a tensile stress to be applied to the lateral knee joint, and it may produce the lateral knee pain called the iliotibial-band friction syndrome. If the condition is not compensated, the feet or ankles may impact one another during the swing phase of gait. This is common with tibial varus runners who wear running shoes with flared outsoles. Tibial varus often induces rearfoot valgus (tending outward), which places a tensile stress on the medial side of the ankle-subtalar joints.

Rearfoot varus (Figure 5.25c) is a positional description of inversion of the subtalar joint. It is associated with tensile stress at the lateral side of the ankle and subtalar joint. The muscles that evert the subtalar joint should be strengthened so as to pull the rearfoot into a neutral position. A rearfoot varus position leads to susceptibility of ankle sprains upon landing from being airborne.

Valgus.   **Valgus** is the condition in which the segment tends outward from its proximal end to its distal end. Valgus conditions cause tensile stress to be placed on the medial side of the segment's proximal articulation and on the lateral side of the segment's distal articulation.

Femoral valgus (Figure 5.26a) gives the impression of bowed legs. It is not a common condition, and it is usually associated with a skeletal deformity rather than a mechanically induced condition. Consequently, little can be done to correct it by strengthening or stretching surrounding tissues. Often it is seen in conjunction with tibial varus which, in this case, is also a skeletal deformity rather than mechanically induced. If the condition is compensated, rearfoot valgus is induced, and a tensile stress is placed on the medial side of the ankle-subtalar joints.

Tibial valgus (Figure 5.26b) appears as a knock-kneed alignment. Stress is placed on the medial side of the knee. To alleviate this condition, those muscles (quadriceps) that stabilize the knee from allowing abduction of the leg should be strengthened. Since stress is also placed on the lateral side of the ankle-subtalar joint complex if rearfoot varus is induced, the muscles that support the lateral side should be strengthened.

Rearfoot valgus (Figure 5.26c) is a positional description of eversion of the subtalar joint. Tensile stress is placed on the medial side of the ankle-subtalar joint complex. Strengthening exercises should be performed for the inversion muscles of the subtalar joint.

Forefoot varus and valgus conditions are best seen in a cross-sectional view of the metatarsal heads. Figure 5.27 illustrates forefoot varus and forefoot valgus. **Fore-**

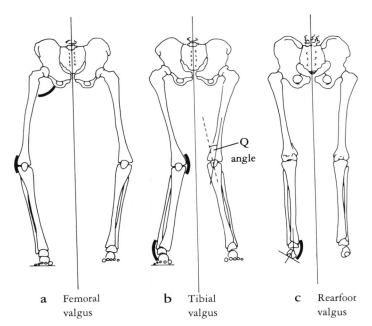

a Femoral valgus	**b** Tibial valgus	**c** Rearfoot valgus

Figure 5.26.   Common misalignment of the lower extremity: Valgus conditions.

foot varus (Figure 5.27b) is a condition in which the first metatarsals are in a more dorsiflexed position than metatarsals 3 through 5. **Forefoot valgus** (Figure 5.27c) is a condition in which the first metatarsals are in a more plantar-flexed position than metatarsals 3 through 5. Forefoot varus and valgus conditions cause important misalignments in the articulations above them during dynamic weight bearing, most noticeably in the subtalar joint. Forefoot varus results in the eversion of the subtalar joint upon weight bearing as there is little support on the medial side of the forefoot. Forefoot valgus results in the inversion of the subtalar joint as the person is weight bearing. Little can be done to correct these conditions by the use of muscle strengthening or stretching, but the use of an orthotic on the dorsiflexed side of the metatarsal heads may provide the support needed to prevent the inversion or eversion of the subtalar joint when walking or running.

PRONATION AND SUPINATION OF THE FOOT

When the ankle, the rearfoot posture, and the forefoot posture are considered, the foot may be in a neutral alignment, or it may be pronated or supinated.

Pronation.   **Pronation** of the foot is a particular combination of ankle dorsiflexion, subtalar eversion, and forefoot abduction. Forefoot abduction is a position in which the forefoot is in a toe-out position and is usually forced onto the metatarsals by misaligned weight bearing. Pronation is one of the most common misalignment conditions of the lower extremity, and causes runners and joggers many problems.

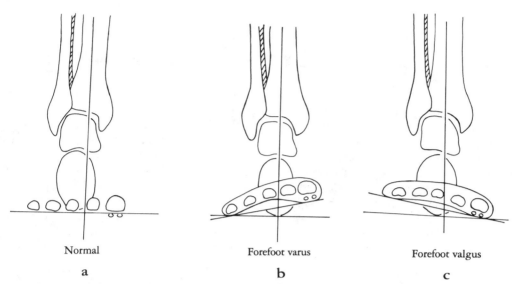

Normal   Forefoot varus   Forefoot valgus

a   **b**   **c**

Forefoot positions. (a) Normal position. (b) Varus. (c) Valgus.   **Figure 5.27.**

Exaggerated pronation is often induced by other misalignment conditions, especially when a person runs in a toe-out position. The toe-out position may be the result of lateral rotation at the hip, tibial torsion (lateral rotation of the tibia), or forefoot abduction. The toe-out position causes the line of force of the body's weight to move from the initial contact point of the foot with the ground to the medial side of the foot as a person transfers his or her weight forward. This results in the collapse of the medial side of the foot and puts undue stress on the muscles that support the arch of the foot, the tibialis anterior and posterior. The stress on the tibialis muscles is associated with a condition known as shin splints, a stressful condition along the anterior medial or lateral side of the leg or both.

Some pronation of the foot occurs naturally because of the obliquity of the ankle and subtalar axes; however, excessive pronation is harmful. Excessive pronation not associated with a toeing-out position may be caused by weakness in the structures supporting the medial arch, by an abnormally flat foot with little natural arch, or by forefoot varus. Artificial support in the form of an arch support may be used; however, one should work gradually into the use of the support so that the supporting structures can adapt.

Supination. **Supination** of the foot is the condition of plantar flexion of the ankle, inversion of the subtalar joint, and adduction of the forefoot. It is not as common as pronation nor is it associated with causing any particular problem in runners. If the inversion aspect is severe enough, lateral ankle sprains may occur upon landing from a jump or when running on uneven surfaces. The muscles on the lateral side of the ankle-subtalar joint complex should be strengthened; those on the medial side should be stretched.

ANALYZING LOWER EXTREMITY MISALIGNMENTS

Often a physical education teacher or coach is asked by students, athletes, or fitness-minded people to provide analysis and prescription. The biomechanically oriented teacher or coach should be able to analyze and diagnose simple misalignment problems. In less severe cases, exercises to correct or prevent problems may be suggested. For complex cases, consultation may be advised with a podiatrist experienced in dealing with lower extremity alignment during exercise.

The easiest way to analyze a dynamic posture is with the help of videotape or films that are developed on the spot. If these tools are not available, conditions may be recognized during the performance, although this takes practice and experience.

An observer should begin by viewing static-stance front and rear views. The following can be observed from a front view of the static stance:

1. Femoral torsion if the patella is medially aligned
2. Tibial torsion if the patella is forward looking and the leg and foot face outward
3. Lateral rotation of the hip if the patella, the leg, and the foot are rotated outward slightly but all aligned with each other
4. Forefoot abduction if the femur, patella, and tibia are forward looking and the foot points outward slightly
5. Valgus conditions if the femur or tibia tends outward from proximal to distal ends
6. Varus conditions if the femur or tibia tends inward from proximal to distal ends

The following can be observed from a rear view of the static stance:

1. Femoral and tibial varus and valgus
2. Rearfoot varus and valgus
3. A combination of rearfoot valgus and forefoot abduction in a pronated foot

Whatever is viewed from the static stance may be exaggerated during dynamic weight bearing. The observer should be alert to the conditions noted in the static-stance position and to the following:

1. The position of the sole of the foot during the swing phase provides information on where the misalignment is occurring. A neutral position is seen in Figure 5.28a. The long axis of the foot is perpendicular to the ground.
2. Evidence of a tibial torsion condition (lateral rotation of the knee) is shown in Figure 5.28b. The midsagittal plane of the femur is aligned but the midsagittal plane of the tibia is rotated outward. The long axis of the foot is in a toe-out position.
3. A supinated foot is shown in Figure 5.28c. The long axis of the foot is in a toe-in position.

4. Lateral rotation of the hip causes the leg to look like that shown in Figure 5.28d. Notice that the knee is pointed outward and that the leg and the foot cross the midsagittal plane.

5. A medial rotation of the hip (femoral torsion) causes the knee to point inward and the leg and the foot to tend outward from the midsagittal plane (Figure 5.28e).

6. From the front, the path of the foot and leg during the swing forward should be observed. A paddling motion occurs from either a medially rotated hip joint, in which case the knee rotates inward and the leg segment moves outward, or from tibial torsion, in which case the knee remains straight forward but the foot points outward.

A final factor that may cause athletes some problems is the quality and type of footwear worn. Advances are being made by shoe manufacturers in understanding the mechanics of the foot and leg during heavy use and in developing shoes to suit a variety of foot and leg postures. Some shoes may be modified to the individual user through the use of orthotic devices, which are shaped specifically for an individual's foot and placed in the shoe to counteract any misalignment or imbalance problems. For instance, excessive pronation may be prevented by using an orthotic device that provides the necessary support for the arch. An extra heel support may prevent excess dorsiflexion and restrict the subtalar joint to a more normal ROM. Sometimes a heel lift will provide the necessary adjustment to relieve Achilles tendinitis.

Orthotic devices should be individually prescribed by a podiatrist who is knowledgeable about sport injuries. The trainer or coach should be able to recognize a potential problem, however, and should bring the problem to the athlete's attention.

A way to prevent problems is to select the shoe that is best designed to give the proper support. Several factors are important: a cushioned heel to absorb shock, a firm heel counter to provide rearfoot control, a firm arch support, a sole that is wide enough to provide the lateral stability needed for running on uneven surfaces but not too wide to cause collisions with the opposite foot, enough rise in the toe box to prevent excessive rubbing on the tops of the phalanges, flexibility in the metatarsal-phalangeal area, good traction on dry and wet surfaces, permeability to control temperature and humidity and durability over long-term use of the shoe. Durability includes shock absorption durability for impact and outsole wear.

UNDERSTANDING POSTURAL ALIGNMENTS

1. Observe some joggers. From a front view, identify these positions or movements: (a) a toe-out position caused by lateral rotation of the hip joint, (b) a toe-out position caused by abduction of the foot.

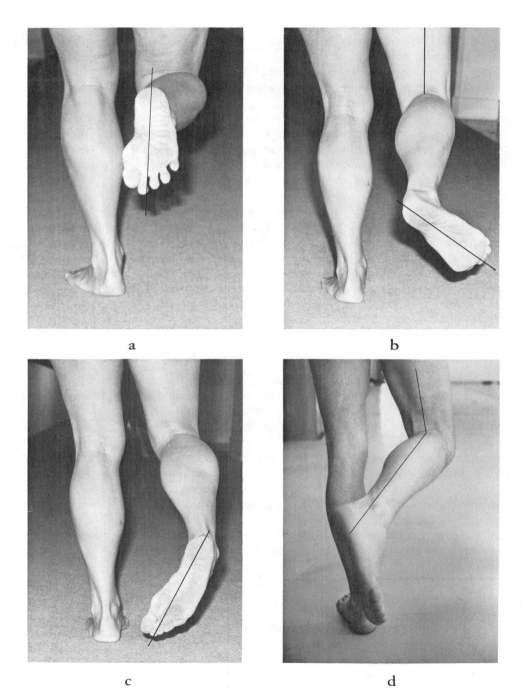

Figure 5.28.   The nonweight-bearing leg and foot. (a) Neutral position. (b) Tibial torsion position. (c) Supinated position. (d) Laterally rotated hip. (e) Femoral torsion (medially rotated hip).

e

Figure 5.28
continued

2. From a rear view of the joggers, identify these positions or movements: (a) a pronated foot, (b) a supinated foot. What combination of movements produces pronation of the foot? supination of the foot?

3. Observe three people in each of the following activities: (a) static stance, (b) walking, (c) jogging, and (d) running. Watch the hip, knee, ankle, and subtalar positions and movements. For all the gaits, observe differences in positions during the contact phase, midstance phase, and the propulsive or toe-off stage. Answer these questions:

   a. Do you notice any deviations in the static stance that were also observed in the dynamic gaits?
   b. Do changes occur when the gait is accelerated? How?
   c. Are there differences within one subject between the right and left leg and foot? What are they?
   d. What muscles need to be stretched or strengthened or both to bring the leg into neutral alignment?

4. Figure 5.29 shows two athletes about to land after being airborne. Describe for each: the misalignment, the cause of the misalignment, which muscles should be strengthened, which muscles should be stretched, and what injuries may develop from continually landing in this position.

Longitudinal axis
(left foot)

Longitudinal axis
(right foot)

a

Longitudinal axis
(right foot)

Longitudinal axis
(left foot)

Side horse vaulter

b

Figure 5.29.   (a) A long jumper about to land. (b) A gymnast approaching the Reuther board, showing impending weight bearing in nonneutral positions.

REFERENCES
SUGGESTED READINGS

American Academy of Orthopaedic Surgeons. *Symposium on the Foot and Leg in Running Sports*, ed. R. P. Mack. St. Louis: C. V. Mosby Co., 1982.

Ariel, B. G. "Biomechanical Analysis of the Knee Joint During Deep Knee Bends With a Heavy Load." In *Biomechanics IV: Proceedings of the Fourth International Seminar on*

Biomechanics, ed. R. C. Nelson and C. A. Morehouse, 44–52. Baltimore: University Park Press, 1974.

Basmajian, J. V., and MacConaill, M. A. *Muscles and Movements—A Basis for Human Kinesiology*. Huntington, N.Y.: Robert E. Krieger Publishing Co., 1977.

Bates, B., et al. "Lower Extremity Function During the Support Phase of Running." In *Biomechanics VI-B: Proceedings of the Sixth International Symposium on Biomechanics*, ed. E. Asmussen and K. Jorgensen, 30–39. Baltimore: University Park Press, 1978.

Bojsen-Moller, F. "The Human Foot—A Two Speed Construction." In *Biomechanics VI-A: Proceedings of the Sixth International Symposium on Biomechanics*, ed. E. Asmussen and K. Jorgensen, 261–66. Baltimore: University Park Press, 1978.

Brody, D. M. "Running Injuries." *Clinical Symposia* 32 (4) (1980): 2–36.

Cavanagh, P. R. *The Running Shoe Book*. Mountain View, Calif.: Anderson World, Inc., 1980.

Clancy, W. G. "Knee Ligamentous Injury in Sports." *Medicine and Science in Sports and Exercise* 15 (1) (1983): 9–14.

Clement, D. B., et al. "A Survey of Overuse Running Injuries." *The Physician and Sportsmedicine* 9 (5) (1981): 47–58.

Crowninshield, R. D., et al. "A Biomechanical Investigation of the Human Hip." *Journal of Biomechanics* 11 (1/2) (1978): 75–85.

Ferrandino, G. "Descriptive Analysis of Biomechanic and Radiographic Characteristics of the Lower Extremity of Runners With Mortor's Foot Syndrome." Unpublished master's thesis, Montana State University, 1978.

Flint, M. M. "A Differential Study of the Hip Extensor Muscles." In *Kinesiology Review*, ed. C. J. Widule, 39–48. Reston, Va.: AAHPERD, 1971.

Flood, J. E. "Selected Lower Extremity Alignment and Range of Motion Measurements and Their Relationships to Lateral Knee Pain." Unpublished master's thesis, Montana State University, 1980.

Gainor, B., et al. "The Kick: Biomechanics and Collision Injury." *American Journal of Sports Medicine* 6 (4) (1978): 185–93.

Gehlsen, G. M., and Seger, A. "Selected Measures of Angular Displacement, Strength, and Flexibility in Subjects With and Without Shin Splints." *Research Quarterly* 51 (3) (1980): 478–85.

Goldfuss, A., Morehouse, C., and LeVeau, B. "Effect of Muscular Tension on Knee Stability." *Medicine and Science in Sports* 5 (4) (1973): 267–71.

Grimes, D., Vennion, D., and Blush, K. "Functional Foot Reconditioning Exercises." *American Journal of Sports Medicine* 6 (4) (1978): 194–98.

Hollinshead, W. H. *Functional Anatomy of the Limbs and Back*. Philadelphia: W. B. Saunders, 1976.

Inman, V. T. "Functional Aspects of the Abductor Muscles of the Hip." *Journal of Bone and Joint Surgery* 29A (1947): 607–19.

———.*The Joints of the Ankle*. Baltimore: Williams & Wilkins, 1976.

James, S., Bates, B., and Osternig, L. "Injuries to Runners." *American Journal of Sports Medicine* 6 (2) (1978): 40–50.

Johnson, W. O. "This Strange and Perilous Joint." *Sports Illustrated*, 10 October 1977, 84–96.

Joseph, J., and Williams, P. L. "Electromyography of Certain Hip Muscles." *Journal of Anatomy* 91 (1957): 286–94.

Kennedy, J. C. "Orthopaedic Manifestations." In *Swimming Medicine IV: Proceedings of the Fourth International Congress on Swimming Medicine*, ed. B. Eriksson and B. Furberg, 93–100. Baltimore: University Park Press, 1978.

Kennedy, J. C., and Hawkins, R. "Breaststroker's Knee." *The Physician and Sportsmedicine* 2 (1) (1974): 33–35.

Kennedy, J. C., Hawkins, R., and Krissoff, W. B. "Orthopaedic Manifestations of Swimming." *American Journal of Sports Medicine* 6 (6) (1978): 309–22.

Keskinen, K., et al. "Breaststroke Swimmer's Knee." *American Journal of Sports Medicine* 8 (1980): 228–31.

Leach, R. E., and Corbett, A. "Anterior Tibial Compartment Syndrome in Soccer Players." *American Journal of Sports Medicine* 7 (4) (1979): 258–59.

Massey, E. W., and Pleet, A. B. "Neuropathy in Joggers." *American Journal of Sports Medicine* 6 (4) (1978): 209–11.

Mubarak, S., et al. "Acute Exertional Superficial Posterior Compartment Syndrome." *American Journal of Sports Medicine* 6 (5) (1978): 287–90.

Nichols, J. "Report of the Committee on Research and Education." *American Journal of Sports Medicine* 6 (5) (1978): 295–304.

Nigg, B. M., et al. "Gait Analysis and Sport Shoe Construction." In *Biomechanics VI-A: Proceedings of the Sixth International Symposium on Biomechanics*, ed. E. Asmussen and K. Jorgensen, 303–09. Baltimore: University Park Press, 1978.

Nobel, C. A. "Iliotibial Band Friction Syndrome in Runners." *American Journal of Sports Medicine* 8 (4) (1980): 232–35.

Osternig, L., et al. "Rotary Mechanics After Pes Anserinus Transplant: A Method for Dynamic Assessment." *American Journal of Sports Medicine* 6 (4) (1978): 173–79.

———. "Patterns of Tibial Rotary Torque in Knees of Healthy Subjects." *Medicine and Science in Sports and Exercise* 12 (3) (1980): 195–99.

Perrott, J. W. *Structural and Functional Anatomy for Students and Teachers of Physical Education.* 3d ed. Baltimore: Williams & Wilkins, 1977.

President's Council on Physical Fitness and Sports. "Exercise and the Knee Joint." *Physical Fitness Research Digest* 6 (1) (1976): 1–17.

Robertson, L. "The Effect of Two Exercise Routines on the Movement of Medial Rotation of the Leg." *Medicine and Science in Sports* 8 (4) (1976): 253–57.

Roels, J., et al. "Patellar Tendinitis (Jumper's Knee)." *American Journal of Sports Medicine* 6 (6) (1978): 362–68.

Roozbazar, A. "Biomechanics of Lifting." In *Biomechanics IV: Proceedings of the Fourth International Seminar on Biomechanics*, ed. R. C. Nelson and C. A. Morehouse, 37–43. Baltimore: University Park Press, 1974.

Shambes, G. M., and Campbell, S. "Inherent Movement Patterns in Man." In *Kinesiology III*, ed. C. J. Widule, 50–58. Reston, Va.: AAHPERD, 1973.

Sgarlato, T. E., ed. *A Compendium of Podiatric Biomechanics.* San Francisco: California College of Podiatric Medicine, 1971.

Stulberg, S. D., et al. "Breaststroker's Knee: Pathology, Etiology, and Treatment." *American Journal of Sports Medicine* 8 (3) (1980): 164–71.

Twardokens, G. "Rotations of Lower Limbs in Skiing." Unpublished paper, 1975.

Wolf, S. "The Morphological and Functional Basis of Therapeutic Exercise." In *Therapeutic Exercise.* 3d ed. Ed. J. V. Basmajian, 43–85. Baltimore: Williams & Wilkins, 1978.

Prerequisites

Chapter Contents

BIOMECHANICAL RELATIONSHIPS IN THE TRUNK

The axial skeleton includes the skull, the thorax, the vertebral column, and the pelvis. Collectively, the thorax, the vertebral column, and the pelvis are called the **trunk.**

SECTION 1

THE SKULL

The skull incorporates 29 bones into its structure. Although the specific bones of the skull are of little concern in the study of body movement, a knowledge of the skull's anatomy is valuable in understanding the effects of impact on the head. Impact injuries may occur when the head strikes a hard surface during a fall. In sports such as football, soccer, wrestling, skateboarding, and stock-car racing, the factor of fast deceleration of the head during an accelerated falling movement adds to the danger of impact.

SECTION 2

THE THORAX

The thorax includes 25 bones: the sternum, which consists of the manubrium, the body, and the xyphoid process, and 12 pairs of ribs. The biomechanical function of the thorax is to absorb the forces of impact and to serve as an attachment for many of the muscles that control various movements of the entire trunk. Of course, the thorax is of considerable importance in respiratory mechanisms and in protection of the vital organs. The latter two functions are not considered here.

SECTION 3

THE VERTEBRAL COLUMN

Structure

Probably the most significant functional unit of the body—from the biomechanist's point of view—is the vertebral column, for it is this progressive series of bones that provides the framework and foundation for most of the movements of the body and extremities. It consists of a total of 36 bones, which are categorized by function into five groups. The groups are shown in Figure A.1c. (p. 22).

All the vertebrae are similar in general structure, but two factors change when the vertebrae are viewed from the cervical through the lumbar: (1) the structures become progressively larger; (2) the direction of the articulating surfaces changes.

The spinous and transverse processes serve as handles for the attachments of the deep and superficial muscles of the back. Depending on the direction of the lines of action of these muscles, the force of pull on the processes may cause forward, backward, and lateral bendings, or small amounts of rotation of one vertebra on the next, to make possible a fairly large amount of rotation of the trunk. The increasing size of the processes down the vertebral column is an indication of the increased muscle size in the lower back and an indication of the line of action of the particular forces in bipedal movements. Comparatively, the relative sizes of the structures of the vertebrae in a dog, cat, elephant, or bison indicate the alteration in the lines of force produced in quadripedal movements. The same relationship may be observed in the relative sizes of the bodies of the vertebrae, the lower vertebrae being the ones that sustain the most vertical compression during bipedal activities.

The articulations of the vertebral column are generally of two kinds: the articulations of one vertebral body on another, separated by the intervertebral discs; and the articulations between the articular facets of successive vertebrae. The intervertebral discs allow slight movement, but function mainly for shock absorption. The articular facets between the vertebrae are freely movable joints. Although the joint between any two adjacent vertebrae does not allow a great deal of motion, a series of vertebral joints has quite a large cumulative effect in producing forward flexion, extension, hyperextension, lateral flexion to both sides, and rotation. (Action is somewhat limited in the thoracic region due to the attachments of the ribs and the longer spinous processes on the thoracic vertebrae.)

Because it lacks great bony stability, the vertebral column relies to a large extent on ligamentous and muscular structures for support. If these connective tissues become stretched or weakened, the integrity of the column is likely to be lost, and the vertebrae must absorb the forces, sometimes resulting in vertebral disc damage.

The stability of the vertebral column is maintained by six kinds of ligaments that hold the bones together. These ligaments are shown in Figure 6.1. The anterior longitudinal ligament spreads along the anterior surfaces of the vertebral bodies and discs. It serves to prevent forward displacement of either structure. The posterior longitudinal ligament serves a similar function on the posterior sides of the vertebrae and discs. The intertransverse ligament holds the transverse process of one vertebra to the transverse process of the adjacent vertebrae on each side. The ligamentum flavum joins the pedicles of successive vertebrae. The interspinous ligament joins the spinous processes of successive vertebrae, and the supraspinous ligament runs along the posterior ends of spines.

The ligaments can hold the vertebral column together, but continual reliance upon the ligaments, as a result of weak musculature or a strength imbalance between antagonistic groups of muscles, can result in a stretching of the ligaments and eventual damage to the discs, bodies, and spinous processes.

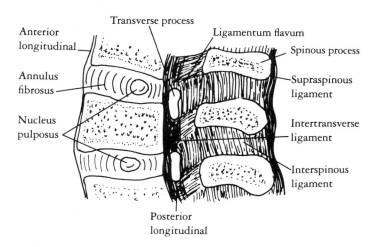

Sagittal cross section of the vertebral column.   **Figure 6.1.**

Muscular Stability of the Vertebral Column

The abdominal musculature acts to prevent the vertebral column from being continually hyperextended. The three abdominal muscles and their resulting directions of pull are shown in Figure 6.2a. The rectus abdominus acts to pull the anterior pelvis toward the sternum or to pull the thorax down toward the anterior pelvis, resulting in vertebral column flexion. In either case, the rectus abdominus has a large stabilizing component since its line of action is parallel to the vertebral column itself.

The posterior vertebral column musculature is composed of several small muscles that are repeated for each adjoining set of vertebrae. These are shown in Figure 6.2b. All of the muscles are situated so as to have large stabilizing components. For this reason, maintaining strength in the vertebral column musculature is important throughout life.

The pelvis is a segmental link connecting the trunk with the lower extremity. During weight bearing, the lower extremity is somewhat fixed, while the pelvis is able to change positions relative to the femur. Additionally, as the pelvis moves on the thigh, the vertebral column must change position since it is connected to the posterior superior section of the pelvis at the sacrum. Figure 6.3a illustrates the normal vertebral column-pelvis relationship. The muscles that function as the extensors of the vertebral column and lower extremity are called the antigravity muscles for they apply forces on the skeletal framework to counteract the pull of gravity and prevent gravity from collapsing the structure.

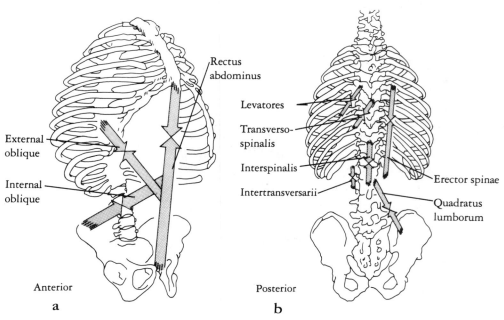

Figure 6.2.   (a) Musculature of the anterior trunk. (b) Musculature of the posterior trunk.

Postural Alignment of the Vertebral Column and Pelvis

The relative strengths and flexibilities of the antagonistic groups of muscles determine in part the alignment of the trunk and pelvis with reference to the vertebrae, the pelvis, and the thigh. Three abnormal relationships may exist: lordosis, scoliosis, and kyphosis. The basis of these abnormalities in cases in which they are correctable is the balance or imbalance in the strength and flexibility of antagonistic muscle groups.

LORDOSIS

In the anterior-tilt position, the anterior-superior iliac spines of the pelvis are located forward and downward from the normal position. If part of a person's posture, this condition is called **lordosis.** The lordotic, or anterior-tilt position, is shown in Figure 6.3b. The hip joint is slightly flexed; therefore, the muscles that produce hip flexion are shortened in the anterior-tilt position. In addition, the muscles that flex the vertebral column, the abdominals, must be lengthened or at least relaxed enough to allow the pelvis to rotate forward and downward. The

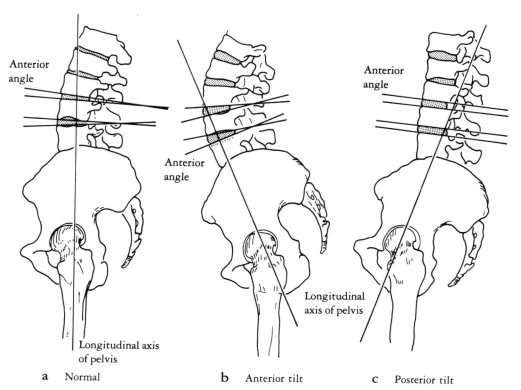

a   Normal   b   Anterior tilt   c   Posterior tilt

Pelvic inclinations. (a) Normal inclination. (b) Anterior tilt. (c) Posterior tilt.

Figure 6.3.

posterior muscles of the vertebral column and lower extremity are also affected by the anterior-tilt position. Since the hip is partially flexed, the hip extensors, the gluteals, and particularly the hamstring muscles are stretched, while the back muscles, those that extend the lumbar vertebrae, are shortened.

Generally, the anterior-tilt position is a result of weak abdominal muscles. People who have been predisposed to a lordotic posture are female gymnasts and those with weak abdominals, generally females in any age group, middle-aged men with large stomachs, and pregnant women. If the lordotic position is maintained for a period of time, the muscles adapt to the posture so that the back extensor and hip flexor muscles shorten and the hamstring and abdominal groups stretch, thus enhancing the anterior tilt. The low-back pain felt during pregnancy or in middle age is often a result of the anterior-tilt position, which causes compression of the posterior side of the intervertebral discs and a stretching of the anterior vertebral ligaments. The angle formed between the adjacent vertebral bodies is called the anterior angle.

The **posterior-tilt** position (Figure 6.3c) is brought about by or results in the opposite condition of the muscle groups involved. The hip flexor muscles and the low back muscles become stretched, while the abdominal and hamstring muscles are shortened. The posterior tilt is not as common as the anterior tilt, and is rarely brought about by lack of muscular strength. The position is seen predominantly in females and has been likened to a typical model's posture. If the hip flexor muscles become stretched enough, the person begins to "ride on" the anterior hip joint ligaments. In addition the posterior pelvic tilt puts the lumbar region in a precarious position. The backward leaning displaces the line of gravity of the trunk posteriorly, which increases the weight force arm and increases the resulting torque about the mediolateral (ML) axis. If the abdominal muscles are not strong enough to hold this position, the person tends to hang on the ligaments and spinous processes of the lumbar vertebrae, and experiences pain and discomfort.

To correct an anterior-tilt position, one should strengthen the hip extensors and stretch the lower back and hip flexors. To correct a posterior-tilt position, one should strengthen the back extensors and hip flexors, and stretch the hip extensors.

Abdominal Strengthening Exercises.   Through knowledge of the relationship between the vertebral column, pelvis, and thigh and how the movement of one segment affects the other parts, one can comprehend the important factors to consider in selecting abdominal exercises. Physical educators and coaches prescribe abdominal exercises with unceasing regularity, and yet all exercises are not proper for all groups of individuals.

Recall that the pelvis is the segmental link between the upper body and the lower body. In a general way, it acts as the fulcrum, while the upper and lower bodies act as movable levers. Also keep in mind that a muscle group may produce movement at the proximal or distal segment. Consequently, when the body is supine, the abdominals may operate to move the thorax if the pelvis is fixed, or they may operate to move the pelvis toward the thorax if the thorax is fixed. The hip flexors may act to move the thigh if the pelvis is fixed, or they may move the pelvis if the thigh is fixed. Thus, abdominal exercises may create any number of segmental positions, depending on which segments are stabilized and which are movable. Body parts may be stabilized by using external forces, such as objects or other people; in many cases, stabilization may be obtained through the use of muscle force. By observing the series of illustrations in Figure 6.4, the torques and resultant movements for several common abdominal exercises may be analyzed.

In Figure 6.4, the forces acting on the upper and lower segments are illustrated. By multiplying the weights of these segments by their respective perpendicular distances from the fulcrum (in this case, the pelvis at the coccyx), the resistance torques can be determined. The muscles involved are the hip flexors and the abdominal muscles acting to flex the vertebral column. The hands begin behind the head in all cases.

Figure 6.4a is the sit-up from the long-lying supine position. Ideally, as one sits up from this position, the abdominals work to flex the vertebral column, and the hip flexors work to prevent the pelvis from being pulled into a posterior-tilt position by the action of the abdominals. As the upper body rises, nearing the vertical position, the hip flexor muscles flex the hip joint by pulling the pelvis upward. If this sequence of events is accomplished as described, then this exercise for abdominal strength will be an effective one. Consider the requirements, however.

First, the abdominal muscles must be strong enough to flex the vertebrae to lift the trunk and strong enough to counteract the torques produced by the hip flexors in attempting to pull the pelvis into a flexed position to the thigh. If the abdominals are not strong enough to accomplish this, the pelvis initially flexes at the hip joint, which puts the lumbar vertebrae into a hyperextended position. The force line of the abdominals is changed, reducing their torque. If the hyperextension is severe enough, the line of action of the abdominals may be posterior to the lumber vertebrae and thus have an effective hyperextension torque of its own. From this position, the abdominals must act as a pulley to flex the trunk to the sit-up position. Not only does this hyperextension torque compress the posterior vertebrae, but the performer probably exercises the hip flexors more than the abdominals in this sequence.

A similar situation occurs during leg lifts, as shown in Figure 6.4b. The hip flexors initially contract to lift the lower extremity. If the abdominals are not strong enough to stabilize the pelvis on the vertebral column, the pelvis flexes and puts the low back into the same hyperextended position as in the sit-up. Thus, the performer must have quite strong abdominals in the first place to accomplish leg lifts without injury to the back.

The leg lifts are actually performed with the hip flexors; however, the abdominals must stabilize the pelvis so that it is not tilted forward by the proximal attachments of the hip flexor group, and the abdominals must, therefore, maintain a strong static (isometric) contraction. Of course, the heavier or longer the legs or both, the greater their resistive torque and the greater the motive torque necessary to lift them; therefore more stabilization is needed to hold the pelvis in line with the trunk. By putting the hands or a pillow under the pelvis, a posterior-tilt position is achieved, giving a better angle of attachment of the abdominals to the pelvis and helping them stabilize the pelvis.

In a third exercise called a curl-up (Figure 6.4c), the lower extremity is placed in a flexed position, thereby shortening the hip flexor muscles and reducing their contractile capabilities (recall the length-tension curve, pp. 124–125). In this manner,

Figure 6.4.   Abdominal exercises. (a) Sit-up. (b) Leg lifts. (c) Curl-up. (d) Snap-up. (e) Curl-up on an inclined board.

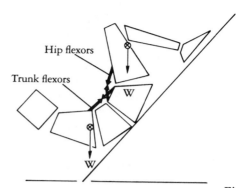

e

Figure 6.4
continued

the abdominals operate to lift the trunk, the hip flexors stabilize the pelvis somewhat, and the body curls up without the danger of hyperextension of the lumbar vertebrae occurring because of early pelvic flexion at the hip joint.

The physical condition of the performer dictates how safe and effective these exercises will be in strengthening the abdominals. No exercise should be continued if the performer experiences pain when attempting it. For a performer with weak abdominals, the hip-flexed position is the best. In addition, the performer may bring the arms down to the sides, thereby reducing the resistance torque of the upper body, and curl into the upright position by lifting only the head and neck before attempting to lift the thorax region, the lumbar region, and, finally, the pelvis.

If the abdominals are moderately strong, a sit-up in the long-sitting position may be done without fear of lumbar hyperextension injury. The performer can be taught to curl into this position as well. A word of caution: in timed events when the goal is the greatest number of repetitions, even the moderately strong may be forced into the hyperextended position toward the end of the time period, since the abdominals may become weakened by fatigue.

Two advanced methods that may be used to increase the necessary torque of the abdominals are snap-ups (Figure 6.4d) and sit-ups on an inclined board (Figure 6.4e). The inclined board places the body in such a position that the resistance torque is acting over a greater range of motion (ROM); that is, when the performer's upper body is perpendicular to the lower body in a floor sit-up, the resistance torque approaches zero because the line of action of the gravity force is through the fulcrum (coccyx). On an inclined board, however, the vertebral column must achieve a greater flexion before the resistance torque approaches zero, and thus the abdominals (and hip flexors, if the legs are straight) must be contracted over a greater ROM.

The snap-up, an exercise combining hip and knee flexion with simultaneous vertebral flexion, increases the torque that must be produced by the abdominals. The hip flexors must act with a large torque to produce the greater rotational acceleration of the lower extremity as it flexes at the hip. Hence, the abdominals, in addition to flexing the vertebrae, must also counteract that torque produced by the hip flexors to stabilize the pelvis and prevent it from rotating upward around the hip.

Electromyographic studies of the abdominal and hip flexor muscles during various abdominal exercises show that lumbar hyperextension occurs prior to the execution of all sit-ups: long-lying, hook-lying, legs-elevated, and curl-up positions (Ricci, Marchetti, and Figura 1981). The abdominals are used during the first 50 degrees of flexion, at which time the hip flexors begin to predominate for the rest of the ROM (Mutoh et al. 1983). These authors conclude that the best strengthening exercise for the abdominals while diminishing low back injury is the partial curl-up with the knees flexed and the ankles unsupported.

SCOLIOSIS

An excessive mediolateral curve of the vertebral column is called **scoliosis.** Functional scoliosis is caused by some mechanical problem (e.g., one short leg or muscle spasms on one side) and is gravity dependent. Functional scoliosis can be partially or entirely corrected by exercises or bracing. The most common and probably the most correctable scoliosis is caused by one short leg. The pelvis on the short side is dropped, and the pelvis on the long side is elevated relative to the sacrum. Thus, the lumbar vertebrae progress headward from the sacrum by being directed laterally to the short-leg side and curve back toward the midline around L1 and L2. A secondary curve then is forced to develop above the lumbar vertebrae as the column progresses headward. The secondary curve develops so that alignment can be maintained. An easy test for scoliosis is to drop a plumb line from the seventh cervical vertebra as the person is standing erect and note the deviations on either side down to the sacrum. Some leg length discrepancies may be corrected with a lift in the heel of one shoe.

If minor deviations are present, exercises that stretch the concave side and strengthen the convex side of the curve usually produce some relief. If rotation of the vertebral column is also present, the appropriate oblique abdominals must be strengthened.

Excessive scoliosis, particularly when vertebral rotation is also present, is not within the realm of treatment for the layperson or physical educator. If tests reveal major deviations, the person should be referred to a physician.

KYPHOSIS

An exaggerated anterior-posterior curvature of the vertebral column is termed **kyphosis.** Most frequently, it is an excessive forward bending of the thoracic area. Kyphosis occurs in older adults, usually women, and hence has been associated with osteoporosis and osteoarthritis. Some believe that kyphosis is possibly hereditary although this has not been substantiated. The term *flat back* is used frequently in conjunction with a kyphotic condition and is derived from the fact that with an exaggerated curvature of the thoracic vertebral column is an associated reduction of the natural lumbar curvature. To put the vertebral column and pelvis in alignment, a thoracic kyphosis that induces lumbar flattening creates a posterior-tilt condition of the pelvis so that the line of gravity passes through the middle of the base of support rather than toward the toes. As with posterior pelvic tilt, the condition creates a shortening of the hip extensors and a stretching of the hip flexors.

In gravity-induced cases of kyphosis, a strengthening of the vertebral column extensors and a stretching of the vertebral column flexors, particularly in the thoracic area, are advised. If a posterior-tilt condition co-exists, a strengthening of the hip flexors and a stretching of the hip extensors are also appropriate.

Although the term *round shoulders* is sometimes associated with kyphosis of the thoracic vertebrae, it is not the same condition. A round-shoulder condition is technically abduction or protraction of the scapula. One may have abducted scapulae as a postural misalignment without having a kyphotic condition. With kyphosis, however, the forward bending of the thoracic vertebrae produces a greater gravitational force component on the shoulder girdle such that it works to abduct (protract) the shoulder girdle over time unless the retractor muscles continually counteract the movement.

To prevent a round-shoulder condition, one would strengthen the shoulder girdle adductors (retractors) and stretch the shoulder girdle abductors (protractors).

Muscles of the Vertebral Column as Movers

In many sports, and especially during throwing and striking activities, the vertebral movements function not only to contribute force for the movement but also to position and reposition the extremities, particularly the upper extremity. The prevalent movements are lateral flexion and transverse rotations of the trunk. Some common sport examples are shown in Figure 6.5.

In upper extremity throwing and striking skills, the vertebral column transverse rotation works with pelvic medial rotation to initiate the acceleration of the dominant arm. The transverse rotation has been shown to play a major role in producing high velocity of the hand in throwing and striking skills. Training programs for any throwing or striking skill should include strength-and-power training for the transverse rotators of the vertebral column. Unfortunately, those that subscribe to common weight-training programs often totally ignore power training for the vertebral rotators. Since transverse rotation is the base upon which acceleration of the upper extremity takes place, it deserves much time in the training program of athletes performing throwing and striking skills. Lateral flexion of the vertebral column is used to position the hand in space to produce an overarm or a sidearm throw. The role of the vertebral column in this regard is discussed further in Chapter 14.

Changes in the Vertebrae With Maturation and Advancing Age

The S-shaped curves in the vertebral column of an adult (Figure A.1c, p. 22) are not present in the infant; they develop as the infant progresses through the crawling and walking stages of maturation. These positions, assumed by the child, produce changes in the directions of the weight-force lines acting on the bones. As the force lines change direction, the development of the bone structures changes slightly until,

Figure 6.5.   Sport activities in which the trunk repositions itself relative to the upper extremity.

eventually, the predominant lines of force are such that a mature structure has been created.

As one passes through middle age, certain changes take place in the bony and ligamentous structures. If strength of the musculature has not been maintained, these structural changes may develop into pathologies and cause the individual a great deal of trouble. Although the lumbar region is usually the place where these syndromes occur, the cervical region may also be implicated in degenerative conditions. Because of the secondary curves of the column, an anterior angle is created between each of the cervical and lumbar vertebrae. If the muscular stability is not maintained to support the column anteriorly, the lumbar region may increase its curvature, thereby increasing the anterior angles. If the anterior angles are greatly increased, the discs may be forced to rupture. If the anterior angles create pressure on spinal nerves, tingling or numbness may occur in the appropriate musculature.

In another condition that may arise with advancing age, the hyaline cartilage, located on the superior and inferior sides of the bodies of the vertebrae, may become worn and thin. As a result, the nucleus of the disc presses into the bodies of the vertebrae.

The upright posture, the tendency to gain weight in the abdominal region, and the tendency to neglect the strength of the abdominal muscles combine to make hyperextension of the lumbar vertebrae a common pathology. Problems may occur at the lumbosacral articulation or at the sacroiliac; however, the lumbosacral articulations are far more susceptible to pathologies. Although the term *sacroiliac* has come into common usage to describe low back pain, it is usually only with some type of impact that the integrity of this joint is lost.

UNDERSTANDING THE TRUNK

1. On a partner, identify the cervical, thoracic, lumbar, and sacral sections of the vertebral column. Demonstrate isolated flexion of the cervical vertebrae, of the thoracic vertebrae, and of the lumbar vertebrae.

2. On a skeleton, observe the changes in the sizes and shapes of the vertebrae from the cervical to the lumbar sections. Discuss the functional significance of the changes.

3. Identify the lumbosacral and the sacroiliac articulations. What movements occur in each?

4. Discuss the back trauma impending on the weight lifter shown in Figure 6.6.

5. Figure 6.7 illustrates two people performing backward stunts. Discuss the difference in the vertebral column positions. Which tends to be more injurious? Why?

6. Discuss the movements of the vertebral column and hip in a dolphin kick in swimming in terms of the movements that occur and the sequence in which they occur (see Figure 10.22, p. 457).

A weight lifter.   **Figure 6.6.**

<u>**Figure 6.7.**</u>   Body positions during (a) a back layout somersault and (b) a back handspring.

7. Observe the S-shaped curves of the vertebral column in the sagittal plane. Between which two lumbar vertebrae is the greatest anterior angle located? Which muscles act to prevent this angle from increasing? Relate the lumbar angle to back injury.

8. For the following activities, describe the contribution of the vertebral column (i.e., what movement is used): (a) a flop-style high jump, (b) a back handspring, (c) a tennis backhand stroke, (d) a golf swing.

9. Discuss the differences among the long-leg sit-up, the hook-lying sit-up, the curl-up, and leg lifts in terms of the following:
  a.   The resistive torques
  b.   The muscle forces and their lines of action for those crossing the hip and for those crossing the vertebral column
  c.   The stabilization function of the abdominal muscles
  d.   The relative effectiveness and appropriateness of each exercise for (1) people with weak abdominals, (2) people with strong abdominals
  e.   The effect of introducing the time factor in sit-up tests, in relation to potential injury of the back

REFERENCES
SUGGESTED READINGS

Anderson, G. B. L., Örtengren, R., Nachemson, A. L., and Schultz, A. B. "Biomechanical Analysis of Loads on the Lumbar Spine in Sitting and Standing Postures." In *Biomechanics VIII-A: Proceedings of the Eighth International Congress on Biomechanics*, ed. H. Matsui and K. Kobayashi, 543–52. Champaign, Ill.: Human Kinetics Publishers, 1983.

Barlow, D. A., and Neeves, R. E. "Biomechanical Assessment of Partial Iliopsoas Isolation in Women and Its Implications for Athletic Training." In *Biomechanics of Sports and Kinanthropometry: Proceedings of the International Congress of Physical Activity Sciences*, ed. F. Landry and W. A. R. Orban, 53–60. Miami: Symposia Specialists, Inc., 1978.

Basmajian, J. V., and MacConaill, M. A. *Muscles and Movements—A Basis for Human Kinesiology.* Huntington, N.Y.: Robert E. Krieger Publishing Co., 1977.

Fielding, J. W., Fietti, V. B., and Mardam-Bey, T. M. "Athletic Injuries to the Atlantoaxial Articulation." *American Journal of Sports Medicine* 6 (5) (1978): 226–31.

Flint, M. M. "An Electromyographic Comparison of the Function of the Iliacus and the Rectus Abdominis Muscles." *Journal of the American Physical Therapy Association* 45 (1965): 248–53.

Hollinshead, W. H. *Functional Anatomy of the Limbs and Back*. Philadelphia: W. B. Saunders, 1976.

Jesse, J. P. "Misuse of Strength Development Programs in Athletic Training." *The Physician and Sportsmedicine* 7 (10) (1979): 46–51.

Keegan, J. J. "The Medical Problem of Lumbar Spine Flattening in Automobile Seats." Paper published by the Society of Automotive Engineers, Inc., 1964.

Kennedy, J. C. "Orthopaedic Manifestations." In *Swimming Medicine IV: Proceedings of the Fourth International Congress on Swimming Medicine*, ed. B. Eriksson and B. Furberg, 93–100. Baltimore: University Park Press, 1978.

Klausen, K., Nielson, B., and Modsen, L. "Form and Function of the Spine in Young Males With and Without 'Back Trouble'." In *Biomechanics VII-A: Proceedings of the Seventh International Congress on Biomechanics*, ed. A. Morecki, K. Fidelus, K. Kedzior, and A. Wit, 174–80. Baltimore: University Park Press, 1981.

LeVeau, B. F. "Axes of Joint Rotation of the Lumbar Vertebrae During Abdominal Strengthening Exercises." In *Biomechanics IV: Proceedings of the Fourth International Seminar on Biomechanics*, ed. R. C. Nelson and C. A. Morehouse, 361–64. Baltimore: University Park Press, 1974.

Mutoh, Y. "Low Back Pain in Butterfliers." In *Swimming Medicine IV: Proceedings of the Fourth International Congress on Swimming Medicine*, ed. B. Eriksson and B. Furberg, 115–23. Baltimore: University Park Press, 1978.

Mutoh, Y., Mari, T., Nakamura, Y., and Mujashita, M. "The Relation Between Sit-up Exercises and the Occurrence of Low Back Pain." In *Biomechanics VIII-A: Proceedings of the Eighth International Congress on Biomechanics*, ed. M. Matsui and K. Kobayashi, 180–85. Champaign, Ill.: Human Kinetics Publishers, 1983.

Nachemson, A. "Intravital Dynamic Pressure Measurements in Lumbar Discs." *Scandinavian Journal of Rehabilitative Medicine* 2 (suppl. 1) (1970): 1–40.

Neeves, R. E., and Barlow, D. A. "Torque, Work, and Power Differences in Bent-Knee Straight-Knee Sit-ups in Women." *Medicine and Science in Sports* 7 (1) (1975): 77.

Nichols, J. "Report of the Committee on Research and Education." *American Journal of Sports Medicine* 6 (5) (1978): 295–304.

Perrott, J. W. *Structural and Functional Anatomy for Students and Teachers of Physical Education*. 3d ed. Baltimore: Williams & Wilkins, 1977.

President's Council on Physical Fitness and Sports. "Exercise and the Abdominal Muscles." *Physical Fitness Research Digest* 6 (3) (1976): 1–21.

Ricci, B., Marchetti, M., and Figura, F. "Biomechanics of Sit-up Exercises." *Medicine and Science in Sports and Exercise* 13 (1) (1981): 54–59.

Roozbazar, A. "Biomechanics of Lifting." In *Biomechanics IV: Proceedings of the Fourth International Seminar on Biomechanics*, ed. R. C. Nelson, and C. A. Morehouse, 37–43. Baltimore: University Park Press, 1974.

Shambes, G. M., and Campbell, S. "Inherent Movement Patterns in Man." In *Kinesiology III*, ed. C. J. Widule, 50–58. Reston, Va.: AAHPERD, 1973.

Vincent, W. J., and Britten, S. D. "Evaluation of the Curl-up—A Substitute for the Bent Knee Sit-up." *JOPERD* 51 (1980): 74–75.

Wolf, S. "The Morphological and Functional Basis of Therapeutic Exercise." In *Therapeutic Exercise*. 3d ed. Ed. J. V. Basmajian, 43–85. Baltimore: Williams & Wilkins, 1978.

LINEAR MOVEMENT RESPONSES TO APPLIED FORCES

Prerequisites

Concept Modules B, C

Concept Module Contents

The movement response of a system to forces and torques applied to it is determined by the magnitudes of the net force and net torque applied, the inertial characteristics of the system, and the pathway available for the system's movement.

SECTION 1

LINEAR SPEED AND VELOCITY

An identifiable change in a body's state of motion, or how it is moving, is the *movement response* of a system to the forces acting on it. The state of motion of an object can be described in terms of its being at rest (i.e., not moving relative to the ground or some other reference frame) or in terms of its being in a state of motion (i.e., moving with some given speed). **Speed** is defined as how fast a body is moving, that is, the distance covered divided by the time it takes to cover that distance.

Another factor that describes a moving object's state of motion is the direction in which it is moving at the time we are looking at it. For example, a ball is released by a pitcher at an angle of 2 degrees below the horizontal with a speed of 30 m/sec. When both speed and direction are specified for a system, it is the **velocity,** not the speed, which is defined. Velocity is a vector quantity because it has magnitude and direction; speed is a scalar quantity that designates only how fast something is moving. The speed of a cross-country runner may be 5 m/sec on the average, whereas the velocity of a sprinter in a 100-m run might be 8 m/sec in a straight line south. The equation used to find the magnitude of a body's speed or velocity is:

Equation E.1

$$v = \frac{d}{t}$$

where v is linear speed (or velocity in a given direction) of the object, d is distance (or displacement in a given direction) that the object moved, and t is time during which the distance was covered.

So far, we have two tools necessary to describe a system's state of linear motion: d, how far, and v, how fast and in what direction.

The most useful information about the state of linear motion of a system is obtained by describing the linear motion of the center of gravity (CG) of the system. Such a reference point is especially valuable when the motion of the human body, with all of its segmental motion, is examined as a single unit.

SECTION 2

LINEAR ACCELERATION

In addition to how far and how fast a system is moving, we can further describe its motion by stating whether it is speeding up (**accelerating**) or slowing down (**decelerating**) or changing direction (also a form of accelerating). When a body changes its state of motion (as in starting, stopping, changing its speed or direction), it is said to be accelerating.

To change the state of linear motion of a body, a net force must be applied to it. The greater the net force, the greater the motion change. More precisely, linear acceleration is the time rate of change in a body's velocity. That is, how fast it is changing its speed or direction or both.

Quantitatively, linear acceleration is expressed as follows:

$$a = \frac{v_2 - v_1}{t} \quad \text{or} \quad a = \frac{\Delta v}{t}$$

Equation E.2

where a is linear acceleration of the system, v_2 is final velocity of the system, v_1 is initial velocity of the system, t is time during which the velocity was changed, and Δ is "change in."

The magnitude of a body's acceleration is large if a large change in velocity occurs in a small amount of time (e.g., going from 0 to 50 km/hr in 5 sec in a sports car). The acceleration is small if the same velocity change occurs over a longer period of time (e.g., 20 sec in an old truck). Inserting these numbers in Equation E.2, the linear acceleration for the sports car is expressed as follows:

$$a = \frac{v_2 - v_1}{t} = \frac{50 \text{ km/hr} - 0 \text{ km/hr}}{5 \text{ sec}} = \frac{10 \text{ km/hr}}{\text{sec}}$$

The car is increasing its speed at the rate of 10 km/hr during each second that the driver applies the gas pedal force. For the truck, the change in speed would be at the rate of 2.5 km/hr per second (sluggish). Note that time is mentioned twice in acceleration values; this is essential for the correct understanding of the meaning of acceleration.

A body experiences acceleration only for the time during which force is being applied. When the force ceases, the body has reached its new speed and moves with that speed until another force is applied. Also, the direction of the acceleration is in the same direction as the net force applied. As would be expected, a large force is necessary to produce a large acceleration, and a small force is sufficient to produce a small acceleration. For example, a large force applied by the club is necessary to drive a golf ball off a tee so that its velocity is changed greatly in an instant. Since a smaller change in velocity is required for putting the ball on the green, less force is applied by the putter.

Qualitatively, when a body is gaining speed under the influence of an external force, it is accelerating; if it is losing speed, it is decelerating. The convention also is to designate speeding up as positive (+) acceleration and slowing down as negative (−) acceleration. Positive and negative signs must be used carefully, however, because the direction of movement also can be designated as positive or negative. For example, a body could be described as negatively accelerating when it is speeding up in the negative direction. Acceleration is discussed more qualitatively than quantitatively here, however, so that the concept may be readily applied to things we are watching. Therefore, the words acceleration and deceleration usually are used, and the direction is specified (e.g., forward, backward, to the right).

Acceleration Due to the Force of Gravity

An external force that is constantly acting on our bodies and everything else on earth is the force of gravity, or weight force. Newton's law of universal gravitation declares that the force of attraction between two masses is directly proportional to the masses of the two bodies. This means that the greater the masses of the bodies, the greater the force of attraction between them. Because the mass of the earth is so large compared to any of the masses on or near its surface, the attraction between any body and the earth appears to be manifested only by a constant force of the earth exerted on that body. This force holds us down to the ground, which exerts an upward reaction force on us so that in standing, for example, zero net force is acting on us and no acceleration occurs.

If a body is free from any contact support, however, it will be forced downward by the gravitational attraction force. As it falls, the body will continue to gain downward speed (accelerate) at the rate of 9.8 m/sec (32 ft/sec) *during each second it is falling*. Similarly, an object projected upward will decelerate at the same rate due to the downward force of gravity. For example, if a ball is tossed upward, it will decelerate at the rate of 9.8 m/sec (32 ft/sec) during each second it is rising until its vertical velocity reaches zero. The ball will then start to fall and will accelerate downward at the rate of 9.8 m/sec (32 ft/sec) during each second it is falling until it lands. The symbol **g** represents this acceleration of 9.8 m/sec/sec (m/sec^2) (32 ft/sec/sec) due to the force of gravity.

The gravitational force of attraction of two bodies is also inversely proportional to the squared distance between the two bodies, so that the farther apart the centers of mass, the smaller the force of attraction between them. This is why a body's weight (force of attraction on the body's mass) is less at high elevations (Denver) than at low elevations (Los Angeles). It also explains why an astronaut weighs less and less as she travels farther from the center of the earth, until she finally reaches a point where the earth's attraction force has no more effect, and she becomes weightless.

Zero Acceleration: Constant Velocity

A system accelerates (changes velocity) only if a net external force acts on that system. Therefore, if no net force is acting (if all opposing forces cancel out), the acceleration of the body is zero. If acceleration is zero, no change in velocity occurs. Therefore, if a body is at rest, it does not change its velocity if all the external forces acting on it cancel out to zero. Similarly, when a body is moving at some given velocity and experiences opposing forces that are equal, the result is the same: there is no change in the system's velocity. In such a situation the velocity is said to be constant, because there is no net force to cause acceleration or deceleration. This is true for a body at rest (v = 0) and for a body moving with a constant speed and not changing its direction of motion (v ≠ 0). For the body to change its direction, a net force must be applied in that direction.

A sky diver presents a suitable example for clarifying the above concept. Figure E.1 shows the forces acting on the diver at the time he jumps from the aircraft and during the descent. Gravity exerts a downward force equal to the diver's weight of 712 N (160 lb), and his body accelerates downward, gaining speed at the rate of 9.8 m/sec (32 ft/sec) during each second of descent. As speed is gained, however, the air through which he is falling flows faster and faster past his body and exerts a greater and greater upward force on his body (Figure E.1b). Air resistance increases dramatically as speed increases and as the area of the body encountering the flow

The net force acting on a falling body changes due to increasing upward air resistance as downward velocity increases. Constant velocity is reached when the air resistance is as great as body weight.

Figure E.1.

increases. The upward air resistance force increases progressively with downward speed, which is also increasing, until the diver is falling so fast that the air resistance force becomes equal to his body's weight, including his uniform and equipment (Figure E.1c). When this happens, the sum of the forces in the vertical direction is equal to zero; therefore, no acceleration or deceleration occurs, and the diver falls with a constant velocity (called **terminal velocity**). If the diver changes body position by moving the limbs, he will expose a different body surface area to the air flow and thereby alter the air resistance against it. If the air resistance increases, there will be a momentary net force upward, and the body's falling velocity will be slowed until, once again, the upward and downward forces are equal. Similarly, if he changes position so that the air resistance becomes less (assumes a streamlined position), he will accelerate downward due to the net force in that direction until the air resistance increases to a value equal to the body's weight.

The movement response of a body subjected to such force conditions was summarized by Newton and put forth in what is known as Newton's first law, the **law of inertia.** This law predicts that a body at rest will stay at rest until a net external force acts to move (accelerate) it and that a body in motion will continue to move at a constant velocity and in the same direction until a net external force acts to change that velocity. This concept may be summarized in the phrase "resistance then persistence."

Variable Velocity: Average and Instantaneous Values

Only in rare circumstances do we perform activities in a state of constant velocity. Even the sky diver in Figure E.1 experiences variable velocity due to the changing body positions and air forces acting on his body. We usually experience fluctuating net forces acting on us, and our movements are always accelerating or decelerating in response to these changing forces. Thus, an important concept concerning a system's motion is that of how its velocity changes over some period of time.

The following example will serve to illustrate velocity changes. Consider a sprinter, motionless in the starting blocks, ready to start a 100-m run. On the gun, she accelerates out of the blocks and changes her speed from zero to her top running speed. After her initial acceleration period, she runs at a steady speed, going neither faster nor slower, for a short time interval. During the time when she is running at a steady speed and does not change her direction, she is traveling at a constant velocity; that is, her acceleration (change in velocity) is equal to zero. Although the sprinter tries to maintain her top speed, some deceleration usually occurs near the final section of the distance.

From the start to the finish line of the 100-m distance, her time was 12 sec. Therefore, her velocity was 100 m/12 sec or 8.3 m/sec. The figure of 8.3 m/sec, however, represents only her **average velocity,** because she did not run that fast for the entire 100-m distance. At the start, her velocity was zero, and she had to accelerate to her top running speed. She then decelerated through the finish line and subsequently slowed to a stop. If we look at a graph of her velocity for the time she was active (Figure E.2), the variable velocity is evident. We can see that at the instant 2 sec after starting, her instantaneous velocity was approximately 5 m/sec. At the instant 6 sec after starting, her instantaneous velocity was 9 m/sec. If we take all the instantaneous values and average them, we will obtain the average velocity. Note that the average velocity of 8.3 m/sec for the whole run is below the maximum velocity and above the starting velocities. Also note that the smaller the time interval, or instant, the more precise the velocity value.

Very small time intervals in sport are often the focal point in analyzing skills. Examples of these time intervals are the instant of foot plant in a run, the instant of contact of a racket and ball, and the instant of release of a thrown discus or ball. One of the most valuable pieces of information used in the analysis of projecting objects (e.g., throwing, kicking, striking, jumping) is the **instantaneous velocity** of projection (also called release velocity, rebound velocity, takeoff velocity).

We can use an example of ball throwing for examining the instantaneous velocities of the ball as it leaves the hand and travels along its path. Note in Figure E.3 that the flight path is curvilinear. If we measure the velocity of the ball at any given instant, we can draw a vector to represent the ball's instantaneous velocity. The direction of the ball at any instant is tangent to that point on the arc formed by the ball's path.[1] The ball's direction at the instant of release is shown in Figure E.3. The vertical and horizontal components of the ball's velocity at this instant are important for evaluating the effectiveness of the throw relative to its purpose. These components are graphically determined by vector resolution.

To review this process, construct to scale a rectangle, the diagonal of which is the original velocity vector (Figure E.3). Draw in the direction lines (horizontal and vertical) from the point on the path where the tail of the original velocity vector

---

1. Tangential direction is one that is perpendicular to the radius of the circular arc at any given point on the arc.

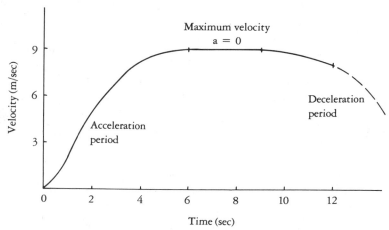

The velocity of a sprinter changes from the start to the finish. The average velocity for the total distance is less than the fastest running velocity.

Figure E.2.

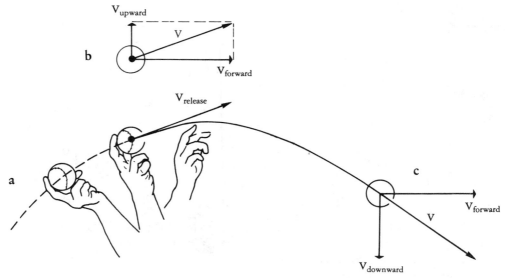

Figure E.3.   The resolution of an instantaneous velocity vector into its horizontal and vertical components. (a) The direction of instantaneous velocity of the ball is tangent to the path of the ball at that instant. (b) The instantaneous values of the vertical and horizontal components are determined by constructing a rectangle around the original vector. (c) The velocity vector and components at a point during the ball's descent.

lies. Next, starting from the head of the original vector, draw lines parallel to the horizontal and vertical lines. The points at which the vertical and horizontal lines intersect determine the lengths of the vertical and horizontal velocity components, and the arrow heads are drawn at these locations. The magnitudes of these components are then found by measuring their lengths using the same scale. Figure E.3 also shows the ball's velocity vector and its components at an instant during the descending path.

Note that as soon as the ball is released at a given speed and direction, its velocity starts to change due to two external forces: gravity (the force of the ball's weight) and air resistance. Gravity acts downward to reduce the upward speed of the ball until it reaches its peak, and then gravity acts to speed its descent. The horizontal and vertical speed of the ball is decreased by air resistance during the ball's flight. If the forces were not acting on the ball, it would travel forever in a straight line (release velocity direction) with a constant speed (release velocity speed). This does not happen because gravity is always acting downward.

UNDERSTANDING LINEAR MOTION CHANGES

1. What factor distinguishes a body's velocity from its speed?

2. Clarify the definition of linear acceleration of a body.

3. If a body is moving with a constant velocity, what is its acceleration?

4. Which runner has the greater acceleration, the one who gains a velocity of 5 m/sec in 4 sec or the one who gains a velocity of 4 m/sec in 3 sec?

5. What is the direction of the instantaneous velocity of release of a bowling ball if the straight arm is vertical when the fingers release the ball? What is the release direction when the arm is 45 degrees beyond the vertical when the ball is released?

6. What does the symbol **g** represent?

7. What is the vertical velocity component at release of a horizontally projected ball?

SECTION 3

THE RELATIONSHIP OF FORCE, MASS, AND LINEAR ACCELERATION

According to Newton's law of action-reaction, whenever two bodies or objects come into contact with each other, they exert the same amount of force on each other, but in opposite directions. If the movement of one of these bodies is to be the object of analysis, that body is the one you define as your system, or your central focus. The other object then becomes merely the source of the external force being applied to your system. The effect of this external force on the movement of the body being analyzed may easily be predicted if we are familiar with another law set forth by Newton. He observed that the movement response (acceleration) of a system depends not only on how much net external force is applied to it but also on the resistance to movement change (inertia) possessed by the system. Recall that the inertia of a body is the property that accounts for the body's tendency to remain still or continue to move at a constant speed without changing magnitude or direction. This "sluggishness" is directly related to the mass of the body for linear motion. Consequently, for linear motion, the greater the mass of a body, the greater its resistance to motion change cause by some force.

The interrelationship of the variables of external force, mass, and acceleration of the mass was set forth by Newton in his second law, the law of acceleration:

$$a = \frac{F}{m} \quad \text{or} \quad F = ma$$

Equation E.3

where a is acceleration of the body (system), F is net external force applied to the body, and m is mass of the body receiving the external force.

This relationship of factors means that the acceleration of a system is directly proportional to the net external force applied to the system and is in the same direction as that applied force. If the acceleration of the body is directly proportional to the applied force, then the greater the force applied to the body, the greater its acceleration. The law also states that the acceleration of the body is inversely proportional to the mass of the body, which means that the greater the body's mass, or inertia, the less its acceleration in response to a given applied force. A **Newton** (N) is the unit of force of such size that under its influence a body whose mass is 1 kg would experience an acceleration of 1 m/sec/sec (4.45 N = 1 lb).

In performing a motion analysis or a system, we must consider simultaneously the interdependency of all three variables. To fully appreciate the relationship between any two of the quantities, we will look at how those two vary while we assume the third quantity stays at a constant value. The process of kicking a ball will serve as an example. The ball is the body, or system, being analyzed, and the impact of the foot is the external force applied to the ball. In each of the three cases that follow, one of the three variables (m, F, or a) will be held constant:

Case I: Varying the magnitude of the kicking force applied to a ball of two mass units and observing the magnitude of the resulting acceleration is shown in Figure E.4.

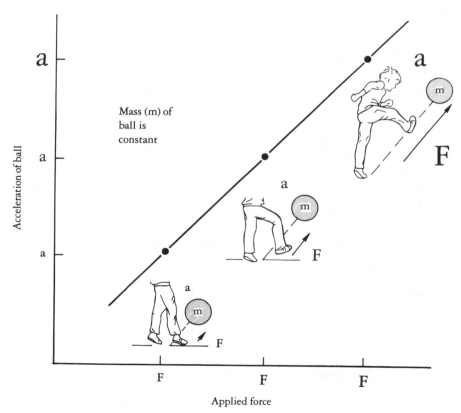

Figure E.4.   Increasing the force applied to a constant mass increases the acceleration of that mass.

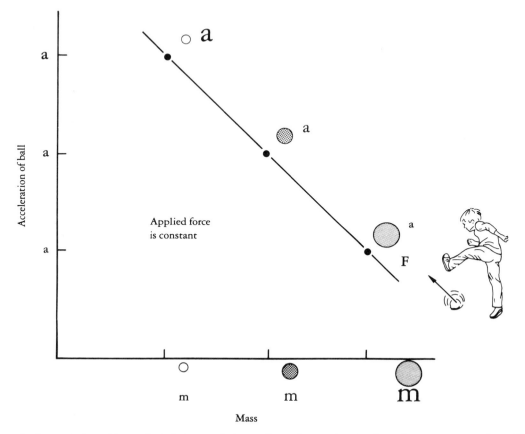

As the mass of an object or body is increased, it experiences less acceleration from the same amount of force applied to it.   **Figure E.5.**

Case II: Varying the magnitude of the mass of the ball (using different types of balls), applying the same amount of kicking force to each, and observing the resulting acceleration is shown in Figure E.5.

Case III: Varying the mass of the ball (using different types of balls), specifying that each ball be accelerated the same amount, and observing the magnitude of the applied force required to produce that acceleration is shown in Figure E.6.

The following example will serve to relate the concept of external reaction force and motion change of the body exerting the action force. A sprinter accelerates out of the blocks and by doing so increases velocity from zero to maximum running velocity. Such acceleration of the body forward is caused by an equal and opposite reaction force from the stable blocks when the legs extend to push backward against them. Recall that the leg muscles are internal forces to the system that change the shape of the system so that it exerts an action force against another mass that will

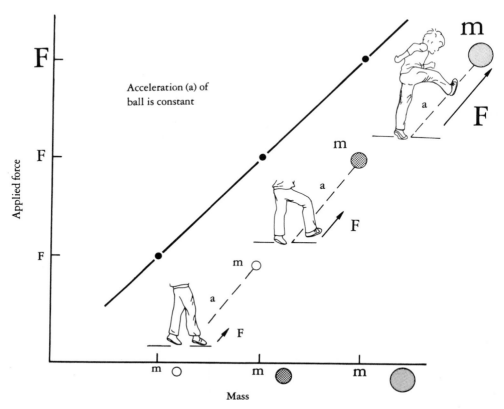

Figure E.6. As the mass of an object or body is increased, the force applied to it must be increased to produce the same acceleration.

exert an equal and opposite reaction force against the system. Figure E.7a illustrates the action force vector and the ground reaction force vector that is the external force acting to accelerate the runner during the start. The amount of acceleration that the runner will display is inversely proportional to the amount of the runner's mass.

After the initial start, the run is continued near top speed until the end of the race. After the finish, the sprinter comes to a stop. Such a decrease in speed is the system's deceleration, and this change in velocity must be caused also by an externally applied force. The external force that decelerates the body is the backward-directed ground reaction force responding to the forward-directed component of the force of the feet on the ground during the final steps (Figure E.7b). Recall that the magnitude of the runner's deceleration due to a given force depends on his mass. Such forward force and backward reaction force occurring on level ground depend on the forces of friction. The friction force depends on the roughness of the ground and the shoe soles, together with the force of the body against the ground.

To integrate the concepts of applied force, ground reaction force, net force, and acceleration, we will use a situation in which a load is lifted from a spring scale, as a   Acceleration   b   Deceleration

Figure E.7.

(a) The friction component of the ground reaction force against the foot of the runner serves to accelerate the runner forward and upward. (b) The friction component of the ground reaction force against the foot of the runner serves to decelerate the body after the race.

shown in Figure E.8. The dial reading represents the equal and opposite reaction force of the earth upward on the 80-N (20-lb) load. (Consider that if the scale platform were not there to apply an upward reaction force, the weight would move downward.) In this initial condition (Figure E.8a), the sum of the external forces is equal to zero (i.e., a negative 80-N weight force downward and a positive 80-N force upward). If a person were to apply an upward force of 60 N on the load (Figure E.8b), the scale would read 20 N. Again, no motion of the load would occur because the net force acting on the load is still zero: $(+20) + (+60) + (-80) = 0$. When the person applies an upward force of 80 N (Figure E.8c), the scale reads zero. As soon as the force applied by the lifter becomes greater than the weight force of the object, the object begins to accelerate upward in proportion to the amount of net force (lifting force minus weight force).

In this lifting example, a distinction must be made between the mass of the object and the weight of the object. The weight of the object is downward force and thus figures in calculating the net force on the system. The magnitude of the weight force downward is always subtracted from the force upward to arrive at the net force. Therefore, the greater the weight of the object, the less net force available to accelerate the object upward with a given amount of lifting force. Once the net force is determined, the amount of acceleration of the object is dependent on the subject's mass, following the relationship $a = F/m$.

Toward the end of the range of motion (ROM) of the lifter, the upward force applied on the load by the lifter decreases. Thus, the upward net force decreases

Figure E.8.   A load being lifted from a spring scale showing the changing ground (scale) reaction force to the load's changing downward force.

until it reaches a value equal to the weight of the object, and its upward motion stops.

So we see that whenever one force is greater than the force opposing it, the body will change its velocity according to the direction of the larger force. This means that (1) a body initially at rest will gain speed in the direction of the net (larger) force, (2) a body already moving in the direction of the net force will gain more speed (accelerate) in that direction, and (3) a body already moving in a direction opposite to that of the net force will lose speed (decelerate), and depending on how much force is applied or for how long it is applied or both, the body may decelerate to a stop and then begin to accelerate in the direction of the net force. An object projected upward into the air responds in this manner under the net force of gravity.

Newton's law of acceleration, $F = ma$, also can be used to relate the quantities of a body's weight, mass, and acceleration due to gravity. Since weight is a force, and g is the acceleration of 9.8 m/sec^2 (32 ft/sec^2), a body's weight can be expressed in the form of $W = mg$. Similarly, a body's mass is expressed by $m = W/g$. For example, the weight of the sky diver in Figure E.1 is 712 N, so his mass would be $712/9.8 = 72.6$ kg. In the British system his mass would be 5 slugs $= 160/32$.

SECTION 4

CENTRIPETAL FORCE AND RADIAL ACCELERATION

We have seen how a body can be accelerated by having its speed changed by an external force. Now we can apply the concept of acceleration to explain the direction change of a moving body.

Centrifugal force and centripetal force were presented qualitatively in Concept Module C. Now the relationship between force and acceleration can be presented to further clarify the concept. Consider a softball player running around first and second bases following a triple-base hit. She leans inward as she curves, exerting a centrifugal force (friction) outward on the ground. The ground friction reaction force exerted on the feet is directed toward the center of the circular arc she is traversing. This centripetal force is directed along the imaginary line that is the radius of the circular path at any given instant and is the force responsible for the runner's direction change. The centripetal force, therefore, causes a **radial acceleration** (direction change) of the runner. How fast the runner is able to travel the arc without slipping depends on the mass of the runner, the friction available, and the "tightness" (radius) of the turn.[2] The greater the shoe-ground friction available, the faster the runner can travel without slipping; however, the speed of the runner is limited by the maximum friction available. The greater the mass of the runner, the greater the centripetal friction force needs to be (using F = ma, centripetal force = mass × radial acceleration). Also, the tighter the turn (smaller radius of curvature), the greater the direction change (radial acceleration) and therefore, the greater the friction needs to be.

The same combination of variables—mass, radius of curvature, speed of travel, and the centripetal force causing the radial acceleration of the body—can be used to understand the forces operating when a gymnast swings from an apparatus. The grip taken to swing around a bar must be strong enough to prevent the centrifugal force (exerted by the body on the bar) from "uncurling" the fingers. Since the centrifugal force is the equal and opposite reaction force to centripetal, it is influenced by the same factors. Therefore, the greater the mass and the greater the speed of swinging, the stronger the grip must be. Likewise, when a ball player swings a heavy baseball bat, the grip strength is usually adequate to hold onto the bat unless the whole body is set spinning to increase the speed of the bat's turning to some hazardous level.

In the field event of the hammer throw, the centripetal force exerted by the athlete on the hammer must be great enough to *radially* accelerate the faster and faster moving hammer prior to release. The leaning position of the thrower allows the feet

---

2. The quantitative relationship of these variables is presented in Appendix II.

to push outward on the ground, thereby generating a ground friction reaction force (centripetal force) acting on the thrower and the hammer system. The importance of adequate foot-ground friction in this event is evident if one thinks of trying such a performance on ice.

UNDERSTANDING FORCE AND MOTION RELATIONSHIPS

1. If your hand applies a force of 45 N (10 lb) on a cart, how much force is the cart applying on your hand? According to Newton's third law of action-reaction, if you are receiving that force from the cart, why are you not forced to move backwards?

2. Under the same circumstances given in question 1, how would your motion response differ if you were on wheels and the cart were not? What would be the motion response of your body and the cart if you both were on wheels?

3. How is a system's acceleration related to the net force applied to it? to the amount of mass that the system has?

4. If you were to collide with another person who weighed twice as much as you, what would be the relative magnitude of acceleration of the two bodies?

5. If the force of a tennis racket causes the ball to accelerate forward, what effect does the ball's reaction force have on the racket? Which object's motion is more easily changed? Why?

6. Answer the following questions:

   a. If you apply an *upward* force of 80 N on a shot that weighs 50 N, what is the net external motive force and direction of the shot's acceleration?
   b. If you apply a *horizontal* force of 80 N on a shot that weighs 50 N, what is the net external motive force and direction of the shot's acceleration?
   c. In which situation, a or b, is the net motive force greater? Explain why.
   d. In which situation, a or b, is the shot's acceleration greater? Explain why.

7. What might be an injurious effect of your swinging an infant around you in faster and faster circles while holding its hands? Explain in terms of radial acceleration.

REFERENCES
SUGGESTED READINGS

Barham, J. *Mechanical Kinesiology.* St. Louis: C. V. Mosby Co., 1978.

Hopper, B. J. *The Mechanics of Human Movement.* New York: American Elsevier Publishing Co., 1973.

Tricker, R. A. R., and Tricker, B. J. K. *The Science of Human Movement.* New York: American Elsevier Publishing Co., 1967.

Wheeler, G. F., and Kirkpatrick, L. D. *Physics: Building a World View.* Englewood Cliffs, N.J.: Prentice-Hall, 1983.

CONCEPT MODULE F

LINEAR MOMENTUM

Prerequisites

Concept Modules B, C, E

Concept Module Contents

SECTION 1

LINEAR MOMENTUM

The way in which external forces affect the motion of a system has been described in terms of Newton's law of acceleration, $a = F/m$. The change in a system's state of motion can be examined from a different perspective, that of the momentum of the system. **Momentum** incorporates a system's resistance to change in its motion (its inertial properties) and its velocity (speed with a specified direction). The greater the resistance to change, or the greater the velocity, of a system, the greater its momentum.

In the situations described for Newton's law of acceleration, some force was applied to a mass, and that force caused the mass to change its velocity. As Newton first explained it, an object's "quantity of motion" is the product of that object's mass and velocity and can be changed by the application of an outside force. This "quantity of motion" of a system is an expression of the system's momentum, a measure of its "persistence" in its state of motion.

Equation F.1
$$M = mv$$

where M is momentum of the system (N-sec), m is mass of the system (kg), and v is velocity of the system's center of gravity (m/sec).

Momentum is a vector quantity because it has direction as well as magnitude. Whenever a system moves, it has momentum, and at any given instant it has momentum in a certain direction. Therefore, when an external force acts on a system to change its velocity, that force is acting to change the system's momentum. The greater the force applied or the longer the time the force is applied or both, the greater the change of momentum. The change in momentum of a particular system can occur very slowly or very quickly. For instance, picture the difference between the starts used for a 100-m run and the Boston Marathon. Both starts require a change in the momentum of the system (in this case, the body), but the rate of change must be much more rapid for the sprint, thus the force necessary to produce the faster rate of momentum change must be greater.

SECTION 2

LINEAR IMPULSE

The concept of the rate of change of a system's momentum and the force necessary to produce such a change leads us back to the first expression of Newton's law of acceleration, $a = F/m$, or $F = ma$. We can do some rearranging and substituting in the expression, F = ma, to show how the momentum of the system and the force on the system are related:

$$F = ma$$

where:

$$a = \frac{(v_2 - v_1)}{t}$$

substituting for a:

$$F = \frac{m(v_2 - v_1)}{t}$$

then, by multiplying the mass of the system, m, by its change in velocity:

$$F = \frac{(mv_2 - mv_1)}{t}$$

Note that the change in the system's momentum, $(mv_2 - mv_1)$, is the final momentum of the system minus the initial momentum it had before the force was applied. It can be seen from the rearrangement of these quantities that the momentum change is directly proportional to the force applied to the system. Also, it can be seen that the longer the time a given force is applied, the smaller that force need be for a given change of momentum; that is, a small force applied for a long period of time will produce the same momentum change as a large force applied for a short period of time. We can write Newton's law of acceleration, therefore, so that it expresses something about a system's momentum change:

$$F(t) = M_2 - M_1 \quad \text{or} \quad \Delta M$$

Equation F.2

where F is force, t is time during which the force is applied, M_2 is final momentum of the system, M_1 is initial momentum of the system, and Δ is "change in."

The preceding equation is known as the impulse-momentum equation, in which the quantity, $F(t)$ is the **impulse** that the system received to change its momentum. As mentioned above, the magnitude of the force can vary, and the length of time during which the force is applied can vary for any given momentum change. Frequently, and perhaps unknowingly, we manipulate these two variables as we manage equipment, implements, and our own body. Two examples in which we can apply the impulse-momentum concept are those of catching a ball (Figure F.1a) and landing from a jump (Figure F.1b). Both of these activities require reducing the velocity of the moving mass to zero: in catching, by bringing the ball to a stop in the hands,

M = mv = 10

M = mv = 0

Change in ball's
momentum = −10

M = mv = 200

M = mv = 0

Change in body's
momentum = −200

a

b

Figure F.1.   Absorbing the shock means gradually decelerating a moving mass by applying smaller forces over a longer period of time. (a) The player receives less force of impact by "giving" with the ball to stop it. (b) By flexing the joints during landing, the body's momentum is stopped by a smaller ground reaction force acting for a longer time.

and in jumping, by stopping the downward body motion as the feet strike the ground. From experience, we know that both skills involve flexion of the limbs to "absorb the shock." If no flexion took place, we would feel extremely large forces of impact as the velocity of the mass was reduced to zero in a short period of time (large force times small time equals momentum change). "Absorbing the shock" is the common phrase for receiving the moving mass gradually so that the deceleration of the moving mass is not as large as it would have been if the object had been brought to a more abrupt halt. In this way we use smaller forces for longer periods of time for the same reduction of momentum to zero. Whenever the momentum of a mass needs to be changed gradually, the time for deceleration can be increased and less force is required at any instant. Conceptually, we can picture the shock-absorption principle for a given change in momentum as:

$$\Delta \text{M} = \text{FORCE} \times \text{TIME}$$

rather than

$$\Delta \text{M} = \text{FORCE} \times \text{TIME}$$

for a very sudden stop.

Linear impulse, F(t), is also responsible for how we change direction while moving. Figure F.2 shows a runner in a manuevering situation. When the runner has motion (momentum) in one direction and wishes to change the direction of motion, a force must be applied to do it. The ground reaction friction force generated by a sudden jabbing of his foot against the ground provides the motive impulse to give a new momentum component to his existing momentum. Such a foot-jab force is applied for a short time, and accounts for the change in momentum. The resulting momentum is found by the vector composition method of completing the parallelogram of momentum vectors. Note in Figure F.2a that the impulse (and change in momentum) has a forward and leftward direction to it. The foreward part augments the existing forward momentum, and the leftward causes the sideward momentum that accounts for the direction change.

In Figure F.2b the impulse contributes nothing to the forward momentum, but is responsible for adding sideward momentum and a greater direction change.

In Figure F.2c the braking impulse causes a decrease in forward momentum due to the backward component of the impulse, and it creates momentum to the left due to the leftward component. Since the mass of the runner does not change, the impulses serve to change the momentum by changing the velocity.

Figure F.3 shows the effect of an impulse only on the direction of motion of a system, a soccer ball. By vector composition, one can see the greater change of direction of a slow-moving ball when kicked from the side as compared to the direction change of a fast-moving ball.

The foregoing applications of the impulse momentum relationship show that in human movement activities (1) the best shock absorption technique is based on receiving a small force spread over a long period of time, and (2) starting and abrupt changes of direction are based on the application of a large force applied for a short period of time.

SECTION 3

CONSERVATION OF LINEAR MOMENTUM

The first part of Newton's law of inertia, which states that a system at rest will remain at rest until forced to move, seems obvious from what we have learned from

Figure F.2.   The body's existing momentum (magnitude and direction) can be changed only by an external impulse.
(a) The impulse given by the ground reaction friction force adds momentum forward and to the left.
(b) Friction acting leftward changes the runner's existing forward momentum to diagonally leftward.
(c) Ground reaction friction force acts to slow the runner and move him diagonally to the left.

everyday experience. The second part of the law, which declares that a system will continue to move in a straight line with constant speed if no external force acts on it, is not as self-evident, because the motion of our bodies and of the objects with which we deal is governed by the external force of gravity and, much of the time,

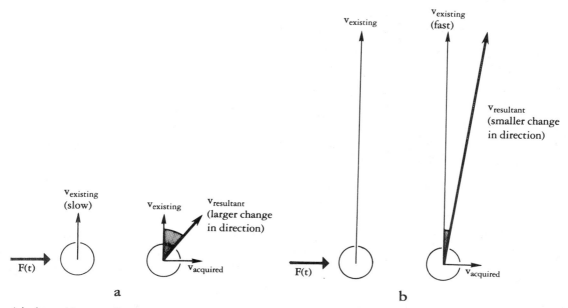

A body or object traveling with a slow velocity will experience a greater direction change when struck (a) than it will if it is traveling faster and is struck by the same force (b).

Figure F.3.

by friction. Consequently, we rarely find things moving with constant speed unless some arrangement is made to provide enough propulsive force to match the resistive forces of road friction and wind resistance. Using the concept of **linear momentum** (M = mv), another way of expressing Newton's law of inertia is to say that a system in motion will continue to move with constant momentum unless an external force acts to change it. Such a statement expresses what is known as the principle of conservation of linear momentum. For any system being considered, Newton's law of inertia declares that an external force is needed to change the system's momentum. If the system being considered includes more than one isolated body, however, the same rule would apply. For example, a 90-kg football receiver in Figure F.4 collides with the ball as he jumps vertically in the air and catches a pass.

The horizontal momentum of the football itself is changed from its initial value with a high velocity to a smaller value when its velocity is reduced as it is caught. The horizontal momentum of the receiver is changed from its initial value of zero prior to the catch to some value after the catch because of the horizontal force applied by the ball. The total momentum of the system, composed of the ball and the receiver, is not different after the catch from the total momentum of the system before the catch, however. This is because the momentum lost by the ball (when it lost most of its velocity) is gained by the receiver at impact (he gained a small amount of velocity as he caught the ball).

The conservation of linear momentum is used to predict the outcome in impact situations in which both colliding bodies are considered to be the isolated system.

$M_{system} = (.5)(20) = 10$ linear momentum units (before catch)

$M_{system} = (90.5)(.1) = 10$ linear momentum units (after catch)

a   b

Figure F.4.   The total momentum of the system (player and ball) before the catch (a) is equal to the total momentum of the system (player and ball) after the catch (b).

The total momentum (a vector quantity) of the system after collision is equal to the total momentum of the system before collision. Quantitatively this concept is expressed by

$$(m_1v_1 + m_2v_2) = (m_1v_1 + m_2v_2)$$
before collision   after collision

UNDERSTANDING LINEAR MOMENTUM

1. What is the difference between inertia and linear momentum?

2. Determine how much momentum your body has when you are running with a velocity of 4 m/sec. (Convert your weight to mass.)

3. Define linear impulse.

4. What is the magnitude of the force that would have to be applied to you to stop your motion in 2 sec? in 4 sec? (Refer to question 2.)

5. Identify several sport examples in which an object continues to move due to its momentum after the accelerating force has been removed. For each, identify the impulse that is responsible for reducing the object's momentum to zero.

6. Using the concepts of impulse and momentum, cite several examples of how body movements are used to absorb shock when a body must stop a moving object or when the moving body meets a stationary object.

7. Use the conservation of linear momentum principle to tell the direction of motion of these two players (the system) after they collide: Player A's mass is 80 kg and runs north at 5 m/sec into player B. Player B's mass is 90 kg and runs south at 2 m/sec into player A.

REFERENCES
SUGGESTED READINGS

Barham, J. *Mechanical Kinesiology*. St. Louis: C. V. Mosby Co., 1978.

Daish, C. B. *Learn Science Through Ball Games*. New York: Sterling Publishing Co., 1972.

Hopper, B. J. *The Mechanics of Human Movement*. New York: American Elsevier Publishing Co., 1973.

Resnick, R., and Halliday, D. *Physics*. Part I. New York: John Wiley & Sons, 1977.

Tricker, R. A. R., and Tricker, B. J. K. *The Science of Human Movement*. New York: American Elsevier Publishing Co., 1967.

Wheeler, G. F., and Kirkpatrick, L. D. *Physics: Building a World View*. Englewood Cliffs, N.J.: Prentice-Hall, 1983.

Chapter Contents

APPLICATION OF BIOMECHANICS TO NEUROMUSCULAR FITNESS

SECTION 1

ASPECTS OF FITNESS

Biomechanical and physiological understandings form a base for the selection and evaluation of activities used for improving or maintaining personal fitness. People engage in fitness activities for psychophysical well-being or to modify the level of caloric expenditure for weight control. Individuals who need rehabilitative movement therapy following injury or inactivity and performers who wish to increase specific aspects of fitness or to raise stress tolerances for improving skill performance also engage in various forms of fitness activities.

The nature of the movements selected for accomplishing the special purposes of each individual varies widely. Most common are exercises designed to improve flexibility of tissues for increased range of motion (ROM) of the joints, muscular strength, muscular power, muscular endurance, and cardiovascular-respiratory function. The specific movement activity chosen for a given aspect of fitness should be performed according to the best available guidelines reported by those who have investigated that fitness variable. Such guidelines are found in professional journals and books or are presented at professional meetings and workshops. Other guidelines are in the form of personal word-of-mouth testimonials, claims by equipment manufacturers and salespersons, and other commercially oriented agents of products and services. The consumer of fitness activities is exposed primarily to media advertisements for fitness businesses whose practices frequently are inconsistent with scientifically based programs for improvement. The average consumer usually is unable to distinguish the good programs or information from those that are unsound.

The content of this chapter focuses on methods and devices for improving selected aspects of fitness: muscular strength and power, muscular endurance, and flexibility. Cardiovascular fitness training, usually in the form of running, swimming, and cycling, is evaluated more in terms of physiological measures rather than biomechanical measures. Such training methods and their concomitant biochemical adaptations are more appropriately studied in exercise physiology, and the reader is referred to up-to-date sources in that area for cardiovascular fitness information.

The Specificity of Movement Fitness

Exercises performed for developing strength or some other quality in specific muscle groups should be done with appreciation of the "weakest link" concept in accordance with the *specificity principle;* that is, one should train for strength in the specific positions or movements in which that quality is needed. For example, the knee extensor muscles are used in vertical jumping, but training this muscle group in isolation, by raising and lowering a resistance while seated on a bench, does not exercise the knee extensor muscles *as they are used* while the hip is also extending, as in the vertical jump. As expressed by Vorobiev (1976) (cited by Jesse 1979), "The greatest load falls on the weakest link during execution of the entire sports movement, and an overload occurs."

Therefore, training for improving a fitness variable should replicate as closely as possible the actual total body movement for which that variable is needed. Such specificity includes not only range of joint motion but also speed. In activities that require static strength, one should train for static strength in the position demanded in performance. In activities that require moving a heavy load slowly, one should train for strength to handle the load with approximately the same speed of movement. Many activities, such as throwing, kicking, and other striking activities, require maximum speed of distal limb segments. The kinematics of the segmental movements must be understood and incorporated into the strength and flexibility training program to plan the most effective exercises. For example, to train the muscles for an overarm throw, one would want to duplicate as closely as possible the speeds and the sequence of segmental movements. To train the muscles to operate effectively for such a purpose, strength training must be performed at an accelerating rate; that is, as the resistance (the object and the body segments) starts to move, it gains momentum (mass times velocity), and the muscles must be able to shorten at a faster rate than the segment is moving at any given time; otherwise, the muscles will go "slack," or will not be pulling against any resistance. Therefore, the muscles should be used in a situation requiring an accelerating force application from the initial joint position throughout the application range.

We also know that toward the end of the joint ROM each segment begins decelerating as a result of the "braking" force provided by eccentric contraction and the elastic components of antagonist muscle groups. Concentric contraction of the initial mover muscle groups is no longer needed; eccentric contraction of the antagonists is needed, however. Strength training using decelerating eccentric contraction of the antagonistic muscle groups may serve to protect the muscles against possible strain as they must abruptly decelerate a rapidly moving segment. An exercise plan for such a situation includes identification of the movements being decelerated during a throw, kick, or striking pattern and the antagonistic muscle groups used to perform the deceleration. Strengthening those muscle groups during fast eccentric contraction is need-specific training.

SECTION 2

RESISTANCE DEVICES USED IN TRAINING

When a person uses some device for developing muscular strength, power, or endurance, the exact amounts of resistance acting or muscle torques applied are difficult to determine. Throughout the range of a segment's motion, several things are changing. The muscles' angles of pull on the bones are changing, and, due to a smaller force arm, less torque is able to be applied at the beginning and end of a segment's rotation than toward the middle. The magnitude of contractile force is also changing due to changing muscle length. The muscle force-velocity relationship is evidenced in variable muscle torques produced during variable speeds of movement. The degree of fatigue influences the muscle torques able to be produced and also the recruitment pattern of muscle fiber-type motor units (Viitasalo and Komi 1981). Another variable is whether the movement incorporates any ballistic characteristics, or motion due to momentum established at the beginning of the movement. Postural control and balance frequently affect the way a movement is performed, often to the point of compromising the effort.

To try to account for or control all of these variables during resistance training would be impractical, if not impossible. However, those variables that are significant to the *purpose of training* should be focused on when using any training device.

Devices used for muscle training come in many forms. Some merely provide more or less resistance to muscular efforts; others provide adjustable resistance that can be quantified and even recorded or stored in computer memory. The selection of a particular device should be guided by the capability of the device to allow for training of the variable needing improvement.

Simple and Handy Devices

Casual overloading of muscles can be achieved by making use of common items that may exist for purposes other than weight training.

Any item of sufficient weight and manageable size can be used as a free weight, or barbell. Plastic bottles filled with sand or water or large containers of food or drink are excellent for high-repetition weight work. A 5- or 10-lb bag of sugar in each hand is convenient and may provide more weight than books. Shock cord or rubber tubing are versatile resistance devices arranged in single or multiple bands for easy to difficult pulls. Tied to a doorknob or between the door and frame, elastic cord or tubing can provide resistance in almost any direction, and the initial tension can be increased by starting the pull with the cord at some prestretched length. Similarly, inexpensive resistance devices can be made from door or gate springs. These items can be helpful in school or club activities when funds for expensive equipment are limited.

Small equipment is also available commercially. Springs, shock absorbers, surgical tubing, and cord friction devices of many shapes and forms have been designed specifically for exercise purposes. Some have no advantage over that which can be made by the user. Others, however, have extra features (e.g., handles, hooks, pulleys) that make them more convenient to use and versatile. Some also have means for setting the resistance level, so that a quantified account of progress may be kept. No matter what the device, however, the user is the one who determines the progress made through the effort given.

Free Weights

The use of free weights or "constant" resistance such as barbells for training muscle strength and endurance is common at all levels of fitness work from rehabilitation and therapy settings to competitive weight-lifting training centers. Lifting free weights is convenient: the resistance is known and is readily modified, and the weights are portable. Usually, when one part of the body is being worked, other parts must be stabilized muscularly to balance and guide the weights. When extremely heavy weights are used to work one part of the body, however, other parts of the body could be injured if control is lost and the weights fall or if sudden great force demands are placed on weak muscles. Under these circumstances spotters should assist the weight lifter, or barbell racks should be close enough for the lifter to release the weight onto that support (Figure 7.1a).

Compared to exercising on specially designed weight machines, which come in various configurations, lifting free weights limits to some extent the segmental movements that can be used against resistance. This is because weight is gravity dependent (i.e., the only direction in which the resistive force acts is downward). Therefore, the user must often assume different body positions during the workout so that the motive muscle force moves the weight in an upward, or partially upward, direction

a   Barbell rack provides safety
     for lifter of heavy weights

b   Body orientation must be
     adjusted to control direction
     of weight's resistance

Concentric muscular tension
used when raising weight
(shoulder flexors)

Eccentric muscular tension
used when lowering weight
(shoulder flexors)

c   Same muscle group is used during
     raising and lowering weight

The use of free weights for resistance during muscular effort.   **Figure 7.1.**

(Figure 7.1b). The force exerted to accelerate any weight upward must be *greater* than the weight force (net F = ma). The greater the acceleration upward, then, the greater must be the force of the concentric contraction of muscles. At the end of the upward movement, however, the muscle force decreases to less than the weight so that the load decelerates at the top of the lift. Static contraction holds the weight prior to lowering, and eccentric contraction of the *same* muscle group controls the weight's descent (Figure 7.1c). This pattern of contraction for the same muscle group is used for up-and-down movements with weights; that is, the motive force for lifting is the same muscle group that is the resistive force during lowering. The pattern of contraction for the muscle group used is concentric, static (isometric), eccentric, static, concentric, and so on. Note that the antagonistic muscle group does not come into action when gravity (weight) does its work for it (see Chapter 2).

Moving weights horizontally overloads the motive muscle group only to the extent that the muscles accelerate the mass (F = ma). The deceleration of the mass is then accomplished by the resistive force of the *antagonist* muscle group. For example, the shoulder transverse adductors (transverse flexors) concentrically contract to accelerate the arms and the mass forward from a sideward abducted position. The shoulder transverse abductors (transverse extensors) then eccentrically contract to decelerate the arms and mass. The most effort, however, is exerted by the relatively static contraction of the shoulder abductors as they hold up the weight of the arms and mass in the horizontal position.

The body itself and its parts can be used as free weights for muscle work also. Different orientations of the body are necessary, however, so that movements are done against the force of gravity as shown in Figure 7.2a and b. Because the weight of the body and its segments remains constant, the magnitude of the weight lifted cannot be increased as when using external weights. Instead, the intensity of the exercise is increased by accelerating the weight faster during the initial lift. The eccentric (braking) contraction of the muscles at the end of a fast descent is also of greater intensity than for slow movements.

a   b

Figure 7.2.   Body segments used as free weights.

Moving body segments horizontally, as mentioned earlier, places less demand on the muscles involved than moving up and down. Faster accelerations and decelerations of the parts increase the intensity of the concentric and eccentric contractions of the active agonist-antagonist groups.

Gravity-Dependent Resistance Machines

Special devices have been designed to guide the path of weights along channels or rods so that the user need not be so concerned with balance or stabilization of other parts (Figure 7.3a). The weights to be lifted are attached to a cable that passes around one or more pulley wheels to place the handle or cuff in a convenient location for the user. The purpose of the pulleys is to change the direction the user's force may be applied to raise the weights.

Elaborate weight training stations such as the Universal Gym also allow the user to assume positions that are convenient for working on designated muscle groups

Gravity-dependent resistance machines provide for adjustable weights and the use of various body positions for exercising.

Figure 7.3.

d

Figure 7.3
continued

e

(Figure 7.3b, c, and d). The weights are stacked on a rod and can be pinned together for selection of resistance (Figure 7.3e). The user pulls or pushes on a given lever or bar that is attached to a cable running through a system of pulleys to the weights. The pulley systems make such machines convenient and versatile for working various isolated muscle groups. A disadvantage of such stations is that the balance and stabilization requirements are removed from the efforts, and in real-life muscle activity, these abilities are necessary for total movement effectiveness. Also, the ROM through which the user can move the body segments may be limited or restricted to that which a particular station permits.

As with free weights, the acceleration of the weights initially influences the muscle overload. Also, as with free weights, the return movements are controlled with eccentric contraction of the same muscle group that concentrically contracted to lift the weights.

Variable Resistance Training Devices

The torque produced on a segment by a group of muscles is dependent on the angle of muscle attachments to the bone as well as the length-tension properties of the muscle and the speed of shortening. The muscle torque required depends on the magnitude of the resistance *torque*. In lifting free weights, the weight torque to be overcome varies throughout the joint's ROM, being greatest when the weight's line of force is farthest from the joint axis (see Chapter 3). Consequently, the tension of the muscles also varies with the resistance demands. It has been proposed that the strengthening stimulus would therefore vary throughout the ROM, it being the greatest at the points where the greatest tension is required to move the load. In an attempt to overcome this apparent deficiency in free-weight, or constant-resistance, training, *variable resistance* devices have been designed to alter the amount of resistance torque within the ROM of a single repetition. Instead of simply redirecting the user's applied force via cables and pulleys to free weights, chains or cables are directed around circular gear wheels or pulleys that are kidney shaped or egg shaped (cams). In this way, the resistance force arm changes as the cable turns the cam and thus provides more or less resistance during different parts of a single movement (Figure 7.4). The proposed advantage is that the resistance can be arranged to increase at the joint position where the muscles are capable of exerting greater torque. The torque capabilities of muscles throughout a ROM vary from one segmental movement to another, however. Consequently, the cams must be shaped specifically for the segmental movement to be resisted. Although this method has not been perfected, the variable resistance device is one approach to increasing the opportunity for the muscles to develop greater tension than in constant-resistance work.

Variable resistance devices with cams, such as the Nautilus, are designed to provide differing resistance torques for differing joint positions.

Figure 7.4.

Isokinetic Devices

The term **isokinetics** was originally coined to mean a constant speed of muscle shortening as a segment worked against a device set to move at a constant speed. It has been shown, however, that a constant speed of segment rotation is not associated with a constant speed of muscle shortening (Hinson, Smith, and Funk 1979). The current use of the term applies to the muscle contraction that accompanies constant angular velocity of a limb. Isokinetic, or accommodating-resistance, machines govern the maximum *rate* of joint movement because they can be set at a predetermined speed. A large range of speeds is available for selection in most isokinetic devices, such as the Cybex or Orthotron (Figure 7.5).

The advantage proposed for such machines is that the user can generate as much force as desired throughout the whole ROM and the resistance will not accelerate as in isotonics. Therefore, the maximum muscle tension available at that *approximately* constant muscle shortening speed can be exerted throughout the repetition.

a   b

Figure 7.5. Isokinetic devices provide for relatively constant velocity of the resistance moved despite the magnitude of force applied by the user. (a) Recording Cybex Unit. (b) Orthotron.

The user *need not* apply maximum effort throughout the ROM to move at that constant speed; half the effort would move it the same way. For the motivated user, however, the *opportunity* for maximal exertion without much acceleration of the resistance is available with such devices. The resistance developed is designed to equal the force that the mover applies to it; that is, after movement is taking place at the preset speed, no matter how much muscle force is used against the machine, the machine matches it in the opposite direction (equal reaction force) but does not move faster. If maximal tension is developed in regular isotonic exercise, the resistance load is accelerated, and the muscle is then contracting against a load that has momentum and therefore does not develop maximum tension because it has to shorten at a faster rate. Isokinetic resistance devices overcome this deficiency in normal isotonic resistance exercise by allowing maximal muscle tension to be used throughout an ROM. If such a device is not available, one can work with another person who accommodates to the changing maximal muscle torques applied.

Any acceleration and deceleration phases occur only during the initiation of a movement and at the termination of the movement. If the speed on the device is set to move slowly (20 degrees/sec), the acceleration and deceleration periods are extremely brief. At the faster speeds (300 degrees/sec), however, most of the ROM contains accelerated movement because the body segment must first be moving as fast as the device (lever) to apply force to it. This means that for faster set speeds, the muscles are not exerting their maximal tension against the load until a good part, if not most, of the ROM has been used. This factor influences the accomplishment of the purpose for which the machine might be used. For example, if the leg cannot be extended (accelerated) fast enough to exert force on the lever set to rotate at 300 degrees/sec until halfway through the ROM, no resistance occurs until halfway through.

Isokinetic devices are useful not only in resistance training but also in diagnosis of muscle weakness and in evaluating progress of rehabilitation. The Cybex, for example, incorporates a recorder for a continuous printout of the range of joint angles as well as the continuously changing torque values. The peak torque angle changes, depending on the speed set for segment movement. For example, from a sitting position on an Orthotron isokinetic dynamometer, hamstring peak torque occurred at 32 degrees into knee flexion when the machine speed was set at 50 degrees/sec; the peak torque occurred at 61 degrees into flexion when the speed was 400 degrees/sec (Osternig et al. 1983). Similar results also were found for the quadriceps during knee extension: the peak torque occurrence changed from 87 degrees at a speed of 50 degrees/sec to 63 degrees at 400 degrees/sec. These results indicate that when working on isokinetic machines whose speeds can be set, the angle in the ROM where maximum torque is achieved will depend on the speed. We know also from the muscle force-velocity relationship that the faster a muscle shortens, the less force it produces. Therefore, less torque would be produced at higher speeds.

Isokinetic torque can be recorded only after the segment reaches the machine's set speed. Therefore, at fast speeds, the ROM through which the muscles can be worked truly isokinetically (at constant speed) becomes limited. Also, at high speeds, as the segment rapidly accelerates to catch the set speed and then impacts with the roller or pad, the segment is rapidly decelerated. High torque values occur at this point and the relative safety of repetitive impacts on the joints has yet to be studied (Osternig et al. 1983). Recent work has shown, however, that this impact of the segment on the lever causes an initial artifact in the peak torque printout. Such spikes should be recognized as "overshoot" artifacts rather than as representing true muscular tension development (Sapega et al. 1982).

UNDERSTANDING RESISTANCE DEVICES

1. Inspect the items in the room around you, and demonstrate how three things could be used as resistance devices with little or no modification.

2. What is the feature of variable-resistance devices that makes them different from free-weight resistance?

3. Explain the force and speed features of isokinetic devices.

SECTION 3

STRENGTH

Results of strength training studies indicate that a number of neural adaptations occur in the process of getting stronger. Among these are the ability to recruit more motor units or the ability to increase the frequency of motor unit discharges or both and the ability to increase the synchronization of motor units. Further, the possibility exists that the motor neurons involved in specific muscle activities have their level of excitability increased by strength training (Sale et al. 1983).

Heavy resistance training also leads to muscle *hypertrophy,* or enlargement of the muscle mass. The cross-sectional area of both fast-twitch and slow-twitch fibers has been shown to be increased significantly. Such increases in active tissue mass are associated with the quality we call *strength*.

Muscular strength can be defined as "the ability to develop force against an unyielding resistance in a single contraction of unrestricted duration" (Atha 1981, p. 7). This definition is suitable for describing strength in terms of muscle forces on bones or in terms of body segments applying force on devices that measure isometric (static) strength, such as tensiometers and dynamometers. The greater the force with which a muscle can pull on its connecting bones, the greater its strength. Operationally, however, the actual force of contraction of a muscle does not determine how strong an individual is; rather, the contractile force available is used to produce torque on bones, the magnitude of which depends on the muscle's angle of attachment at the time of force application, its length, and its shortening velocity. As it happens, muscle strength could be defined as the property that is measured by the device or particular test administered to measure it.

Routines for strength training have been refined from the original *progressive resistance exercise* (PRE) programs developed by DeLorme and Watkins (1951) in rehabilitation work. Since then, a multitude of weight-training routines has emerged using many possible combinations of repetitions, resistance, frequency, and weeks of training and all focused on what combination would produce the greatest strength gains.

Out of all this, three main categories of strengthening exercises have been neatly packaged for use, although, within each category, many possibilities for variation exist. These popularized categories are **isometrics, isotonics,** and **isokinetics.** Each of these types, with its variables, is described.

Isometric (Static) Strength

Isometric exercise is muscle contraction that exerts its force against an immovable resistance; that is, the length of the muscle does not change (*iso* + *metric* = *same length*). Such static tension development in muscles has been most successful for strength gain and maintenance in rehabilitation cases when movement is not possible. Gains in strength through static contractions have been most notable for relatively weak individuals, and the gains usually taper off after the first five weeks of daily isometrics.

The main variable responsible for strengthening muscle isometrically has been identified as the magnitude of the tension developed. In general, for more effectiveness of isometric strengthening the tension developed should be near maximum effort. The duration of each contraction should be long enough to fully recruit all fibers in a muscle group (about 3 to 6 sec perhaps), and the contractions should be repeated several times daily (Atha 1981). The variability allowed in the duration of each contraction for strengthening to occur stems from the differences among muscle groups in the time required to reach maximum tension. For example, Atha (1981) reported the time to reach peak isometric tension for the knee extensors was 4.42 sec, while for the elbow flexors, it was only 1.61 sec. Such variance in the speed of maximum tension development justifies the recommended longer duration of each contraction so that this "general prescription" would take care of the slower muscle groups. Atha observed that muscle damage may occur from *instantly* generating peak force against an unyielding resistance and that some kind of stiff shock absorption device used in such relatively violent *instant-maximum* efforts might provide a margin of safety.

The optimum rest interval between isometric efforts has not been firmly established, partly due to researchers' focus on the other variables in isometric training. Rest intervals ranging from less than 1 sec to 2 min and over have been used, but their relative effects are unknown. One of the most popularized features of isometric training is that it produces gains in strength at the specific joint angle held during contractions and that those strength gains are not detected at other joint angles (Clarke 1973). Although such joint-angle specificity has been demonstrated, evidence also indicates some transfer of strength gains throughout the ROM (Whitley 1967, Raitsin 1974, cited by Atha 1981). Explanations for the joint-specific strength gains so widely observed include not only the possibility of "neuromuscular learning" mechanisms but also a biomechanical reason: that synergist muscles are called into action at certain joint angles as they are needed and therefore become strengthened as members of that joint angle's "team" of muscles. At other joint angles, these same synergists may not be recruited to assist in the effort, thereby leaving the team shorthanded.

Isometric training, if undertaken for skill improvement, should be done with the recognition of its apparent joint specificity as well as its decreasing effectiveness for individuals whose state of training is more advanced than that of beginning or intermediate performers. Examples of sport situations using static strength include the iron cross on the rings or leg levers on the parallel bars. Such performances in which specific joint angles must be maintained, rather than passed through, may well be aided by isometric training in addition to other types of strengthening. The strength produced by a muscle group during a single *maximal voluntary contraction* (**MVC**) against an immovable resistance can be quantified by some type of tension-measuring device, such as a cable tensiometer or strain gauge dynamometer, which is stressed by the force exerted by a body segment in contact with it (Figure 7.6).

The *actual* strength, or force of contraction, of the muscle group can only be derived by using estimates of angles of muscle attachments to the bone, force-arm distances from the lines of action of the participating muscles to the joint axis, and the resistive force measured on the device multiplied by the distance to the joint axis from its line of force. These variables demand careful measurement during a test. The joints must be positioned at the same angles and the cuff is placed on the segment the same distance from the joint so that they can be replicated for any subsequent tests on the same performer. Careful attention also must be given to the other body parts that apparently are not involved in the task. Recall the concept of a chain being as strong as its *weakest link*. If an MVC of the elbow flexors is to be determined for the performer shown in Figure 7.5c and the vertebral extensor muscles are relatively weak, the effort to flex the elbow may be less than maximum due to the inability of the vertebral extensors to maintain (stabilize) the upright trunk position against the vertebral-flexion tendency caused by elbow flexion. (If the hand cannot be raised to the shoulder, the shoulder is pulled down toward the hand.) As the trunk flexes forward, the elbow moves into flexion, the elbow flexors shorten, and the force generated decreases with decreases in muscle length as they concentrically contract. Moreover, the angles of attachment of the flexors are changing, which produces changes in the torques produced on the bone.

Other body segments can be stabilized by strappings or by being held by an assistant. Elbow flexor strength measured in such a manner, however, has limited application for activities that demand not only elbow flexor strength but also strength of muscle groups that serve to stabilize other body parts so that the arm may have a solid base from which to move. Attempts to measure the strength of isolated muscle groups should be made with full understanding of the *weakest link concept*.

The use of a static-strength-testing device, such as a cable tensiometer, provides an indirect measure of the contractile force of a muscle group. (a) Grip strength. (b) Knee extensor strength. (c) Elbow flexor strength.

Figure 7.6.

Isotonic Strength Training

The term *isotonic* has been used to describe the presumably constant tension in muscles undergoing concentric or eccentric contraction (*iso* + *tonic* = *same tension*). Although this is not strictly true, the term remains in use, but many now prefer to use the term *dynamic contraction* or *dynamic tension.* Variations in isotonic exercise include the following: heavy resistance, progressive resistance, variable resistance, speed loading, eccentric and plyometric training, and hybrid (combination) methods (Atha 1981).

The variables that can be manipulated in isotonic training are (1) load intensity, (2) the rate or speed of repetitions, (3) number of repetitions, and (4) the rest interval between repetitions.

During the last 40 or 50 years, many combinations of these variables have been used in research in attempts to identify "recipes" appropriate for specific strength needs. Probably the most important variable is the load, or the amount of resistance moved. To standardize the load to individual capacities, the term *repetition maximum* (**RM**) has gained acceptance. It refers to the weight, or magnitude, of the load that can be moved a given number of times and no more. For instance, a 10-RM load is a weight that can be lifted only ten times and is too heavy to be lifted more than ten times. The resistance selected at the beginning of strength training must be found by trial and error. As the strength of the muscles increases, the load that represents 10 RM must be increased (usually weekly). A practice for selecting weights to be used is to determine the 1-RM load for a muscle group and then to use a given percentage of that standard load for more repetitions. For example, 80% of 1 RM could be the load selected for eight repetitions. Selecting loads in this way provides an initial frame of reference within which progress can be evaluated. Using a maximum isometric load as a reference, researchers have found a 10-RM load to be about 50% of the MVC (Clarke and Herman 1955, cited by Atha 1981).

Results from the large number of studies of strength show that the major factor for achieving strength gains is the amount of tension developed by the muscle group used. Studies on load intensity also show that 2-RM loads and 10-RM loads are not as effective as 5- to 6-RM loads for producing the most muscle tension and, therefore, the greatest strength gains.

Within these options, it is suggested that training at 6 RM for three sets, three times per week, *may* be optimal for the greatest strength gain. Guidelines drawn from research reviewed by Clarke (1973) indicate that routines between 2 RM for one set and 10 RM for each of three sets appear to produce significant gains in strength. deVries (1980) also recommends training a given muscle group three but not more than four times per week.

Research information is lacking on ideal or optimal rest intervals between repetitions and sets of repetitions. According to the promotional literature of one equipment manufacturer, a 2-min rest interval is adequate between each of four sets of five repetitions each, using 80% of 1 RM (Ward et al. 1980). Identification of an optimum rest interval, however, could alter the load intensity and number of repetitions recommended.

Increasing the speed of lifting a given load is a way to increase the load intensity, although the results of studies do not support increasing speed as being better than using greater weights slowly for improving strength (Atha 1981). The greatest load intensity and greatest tension developed by the muscles in speed lifting occurs during the initial *acceleration* of the load at the beginning of the ROM. This acceleration period does not last long because of the deceleration that must occur at the end of that ROM. Consequently, the high tension produced by the muscles (the strengthening stimulus) may not be long enough to produce the strengthening effect. If the high tension of isotonic speed loading could be prolonged through the entire ROM, the method could be more effective for building strength. Hay, Andrews, and Vaughn (1980) *tentatively* proposed on the basis of their studies that "for a given load, a fast rate of lifting is likely to yield a better rate of strength development than are slower rates of lifting" (p. 9). Note that this proposal states "for a given load" and means that the load should be lifted fast rather than slow for better strength gains.

VARIABLE RESISTANCE TRAINING

Strength gains from using free weights and variable resistance devices have been reported by Atha (1981). From his review of others' experimental findings, he notes that variable resistance devices do not produce greater strength improvements than does standard resistance training. There is some indication, however, that greater strengthening may occur at the *specific joint angle* at which *peak muscle tension* is produced by the variable resistance machine.

ECCENTRIC TRAINING

Muscle's force-velocity relationship shows that as the shortening (concentric contraction) speed becomes slower, the tension produced in the muscle increases, and the tension at zero speed is greater than during shortening. Further, greater tension can be elicited during muscle lengthening (eccentric contraction) than in the concentric or static states. Arguing that if greater tension acts to provide the strengthening stimulus, the proposal has been made that overloading (e.g., 120% 1 RM) an eccentrically contracting muscle would provide greater stimulus for strengthening and greater strength gains. A number of researchers have shown that eccentric training does cause strength gains. Eccentric training, however, has been shown to be *no more* effective in producing strength gains than concentric or isometric training. Whether eccentric training is superior to isokinetic training for producing greater strength has not been clearly established, although some investigators have reported that it is.

One aspect of eccentric training that has been noted is greater muscle soreness than that which normally results from concentric and isometric training. Such soreness, although nonpersistent, may serve to decrease effort put forth in the early sessions of training.

PLYOMETRIC TRAINING

Depth-jumping, drop-jumping, bounce-loading, and rebound jump training are other names given to plyometric, or prestretch, training. In jumping, the method of loading is by using the kinetic energy of the body landing from a jump to put the muscles on stretch and elicit an eccentric contraction followed immediately by a concentric contraction. For other muscle groups, the kinetic energy of dropped weights, caught by the lifter, serves to stretch the targeted muscle groups. The force exerted by the muscles following this storage of elastic energy (Chapter 2, pp. 122–124) has been shown to be greater than without such storage (Komi and Bosco 1978). Such observations have led to using prestretch type of loading in strength-training studies. Results so far have shown little indication that greater gains in strength occur, but the criterion measure has usually been vertical jump height, not strength (Blattner and Noble 1979, Clutch et al. 1983). Further, Atha (1981) questions the advisability of subjecting muscles to potentially injurious forces in attempts to determine whether the elastic recoil properties of the tissue are able to be improved.

Isokinetic Strength Training

Isokinetic strength training is a method in which the speed of segment rotation is limited to a constant value during ROM.

The speed factor influences the tension a muscle can develop according to the force-velocity relationship (Chapter 2, pp. 126–127). Greater strength gains, however, are reported for moderately slow isokinetic speeds than for ultra-slow isokinetic speeds that approach isometric contractions. Faster speeds are found to be less effective for building strength than slower speeds. This is not to say that fast-speed isokinetic training is not valuable for uses other than maximal strength development. Little evidence shows, however, that fast-speed isokinetic training is *more* effective than slow training for improving performance in explosive-type skills such as vertical jumps or sprint starts. Its potential continues to be studied.

Since the speed of the isokinetic device is set, there is no adjustment for the resistance, or load. The user exerts, or should try to exert, maximal tension throughout each repetition. As fatigue occurs, the force exerted decreases, but the device continues to move at the same speed, giving an equal and opposite reaction force to the user. The "load" is adjusted by the decreasing muscle tension that accompanies increasing speed. The load also may be adjusted by the user who chooses not to exert maximal effort. In such a case, the strengthening stimulus, high muscle tension, may not be produced, and gains in strength would not be realized.

The interrelated effects of contraction duration, tension level produced, speed of movement, frequency of repetitions, and rest intervals have yet to be fully explored to arrive at the best combination for maximum strength gains.

Comparison of Strength-Training Methods

For increasing strength, the consensus is that a well-designed isotonic training program is better than the isometric programs reported. No optimum combination of variables has been established, however, for either type of training. Conflicting reports exist on the superiority of isotonics and isokinetics for strength improvement.

Isokinetic strength-training programs are relatively new and their potential may not be as fully realized as that of isotonics. Evidence does favor isokinetics over isometrics, but not overwhelmingly so. Studies of hybrid training programs, which use combinations of isometrics, isotonics, and isokinetics, do not indicate that a mixture produces more strength than does isotonics or isometrics alone.

Two problems inherent in isometric programs are that motivation limitations exist during maximal attempts and that the strength gains made are joint-angle dependent. Isokinetic programs also have the motivation limitation with regard to generation of maximum effort.

The reader should bear in mind that these methods and their variations have been examined only with respect to their value in *strength* training. Variations in load, repetitions, and speed that have been shown to be less effective for strength gains may be *desirable* variations when training for other purposes.

SECTION 4

MUSCULAR POWER

Muscular *power,* the ability of a muscle group to contract forcefully with speed, is used in power-lifting events and also in less strength-demanding activities that require segmental speed. Power equals force applied times the speed that force is applied. An increase in strength (force) or an increase in the speed of muscle shortening or both produces greater power output. An attitude that seems to prevail is that great amounts of strength give the power required for any power event. Most often, however, the kind of power needed is that produced by the speed of muscle shortening.

We can think of power, then, as being *strength*-dominated or *speed*-dominated. Strength-dominated power is that exhibited by an Olympic weight lifter raising 400 lb overhead in a two-hand snatch (Jesse 1979). Speed-dominated power is that exhibited by a shot-putter, thrower, jumper, runner, or swimmer. Recall that pre-stretch and use of elastic energy help produce speed-dominated power. Strength increases are developed at very slow speeds, and the strength, or force of contraction, is not the same at higher speeds.

Strength gains made by isokinetic training at slow speeds were not demonstrated when the speed of contraction was greater than that used in training (Lesmes et al. 1978, Moffroid and Whipple 1970). Ikai (1973, cited by deVries 1980) demonstrated that force, not velocity, improved from training at 100% MVC. Training with no load and maximum velocity improved velocity but not force, whereas training at 30 to 60% MVC improved both force and velocity. Such findings are consistent with reports of Daish (1972) who noted that optimum power is produced when the load is about one-third maximum and the speed is about one-third maximum. He also noted, however, that large muscle masses tend to move toward the slow-speed ranges using more force. Large muscle-mass individuals, then, tend to be more powerful in the strength-dominated power events (e.g. weight lifting, shot put, football blocking). Smaller muscle-mass performers tend to be more powerful in speed-dominated events (e.g., jumping, running, swimming, throwing).

For speed-dominated power events in which the performer is required to maximally *accelerate* a given mass (body or implement), the performer must train at both the force and velocity specific to the event (Lesmes et al. 1978).

Power training for improving vertical jump performance takes specific and nonspecific forms. The results of two different modes of training (both fairly specific to jumping) were reported by Blattner and Noble (1979). Training on the isokinetic "Leaper" (for leg extensors) and plyometric training (depth jumps) both produced equal improvement in jumping ability. Such results are probably indicative of the improvement to be expected from training in any mode that provides for specificity of movement demands in the skill.

Greater improvement might be expected from individuals whose fiber types predispose them to either strength-dominated power events or speed-dominated power events. For example, the predisposition of individuals with a greater percentage of fast-twitch muscle fibers for fast power performance has been shown (Coyle, Costill, and Lesmes 1979). Moreover, these investigators proposed that as the velocity demand of movement increases, the fast-twitch muscle fiber composition becomes increasingly important for fast-power production. Biopsies showed that as muscle shortening velocity increased, the decrease in muscle torque (as per force-velocity relationship) was significantly less for those with more fast-twitch fibers.

The athlete, however, should not make any assumptions regarding his or her fiber type percentage; rather, the athlete should train specifically for the type of power required for a particular event or skill.

UNDERSTANDING MUSCULAR STRENGTH AND POWER

1. Select three different movement activities that depend on static muscular strength of a particular muscle group for success. Devise a skill-specific, strength-improving exercise for each.

2. Select three different activities that depend on strength or power of concentric muscular tension of specific muscle groups. Devise an exercise that would improve such muscular strength specifically for each skill in question. Do the exercises contain movements that are actually performed in the skill or are similar in terms of (a) the ranges of segmental motion, (b) the positions of other body segments, (c) the spatial orientation of the body, (d) the speed of repetitions, and (e) the acceleration and deceleration phases?

3. Repeat the steps in question 2 for three activities demanding strength during eccentric muscular tension.

4. Define muscular power.

5. For each of the exercises shown in Figures 7.1, 7.2, and 7.3, state an activity or skill for which it would be useful. Explain why.

6. Considering the same exercises as in question 5, how could you modify each exercise (spatially or temporally) to better match the exercise with the activity or skill?

7. Devise a series of exercises for strengthening the triceps. Recall its functions at both joints, its three proximal attachments, its possibility for length-tension adjustments, and its potential for active and passive insufficiency.

8. Compare the difficulty of doing straight-leg sit-ups with (a) the hands behind the neck, (b) the arms crossed over the shoulders, and (c) the arms at the sides. Explain the differences in difficulty in terms of motive and resistive torques and muscle groups being used (see Chapter 6).

9. Perform a muscular analysis of the straight-leg sit-up, the flexed-leg sit-up, and the straight-leg snap-up. What are the differences in terms of motive and resistive torques, the muscular requirements, and the stabilization function of muscle groups? (See Chapter 6.)

10. Identify three calisthenic-type exercises that can be done with less muscular effort by using stored elastic energy.

11. Identify four specific skills that require strength-dominated power for success.

12. Identify four specific skills that require speed-dominated power for success.

SECTION 5

MUSCULAR ENDURANCE

The term **endurance** usually connotes the ability to continue for a long period of time. In human movement activities, two principal, but not altogether inseparable, types of endurance are recognized: cardiorespiratory endurance (also referred to as circulorespiratory or cardiovascular endurance) and local muscular endurance.

Cardiorespiratory endurance is the degree to which the heart, vascular system, and respiratory system are able to provide the oxygen necessary to enable the mover to continue. Movements that tax the cardiovascular system are those using large muscle groups or total body movement or both at a submaximal intensity for prolonged periods (e.g., running, jogging, cycling, distance swimming). For these aerobic, or oxygen-utilizing, activities, the limiting factor is the failure of the oxygen-transport system to keep up with the demand of the muscle tissues. Training for cardiovascular endurance is one focus within exercise physiology, and the principles for improving such fitness are studied within that discipline.

Local muscular endurance is the degree to which specific muscle groups are able to continue contracting against a given load for a certain period of time or a certain number of repetitions. Such endurance is specific to the type of muscular tension exerted, the speed of contraction, the cadence of repetitions, and the magnitude of the resistance. The limiting factor is not the body's cardiorespiratory functioning, but the physiological limitations within the muscle groups being exercised and the neural control of the muscular contractions. The exact causes of muscular fatigue are not known, although several different factors have been incriminated.

Muscular fatigue can be defined as "a reduction in the capacity of the neuromuscular system to generate force or to perform work" (Bigland-Ritchie 1981, p. 85). Changes in muscle excitation, metabolism, and contractile properties all contribute to fatigue. Circulatory patterns within the muscles do not seem to be the most important determinant of muscular endurance. A number of intramuscular physiological variables play a role, including energy stores, enzyme levels, and muscle fiber type composition (Heyward 1975). In addition, fatigue during held MVC is associated with a decline in electrical activity reaching the muscle fibers from the motor neuron, indicating the source of fatigue may lie in inadequate transmission of electrical activity within the muscle cells (Bigland-Ritchie 1981).

Absolute and Relative Muscular Endurance

The degree of endurance can be expressed in *absolute* terms, such as: How long can you hold 50 N at a 90-degree position of elbow flexion? The endurance also can be expressed in *relative* terms, such as: How long can you hold a weight that equals 50% of your maximal static strength? Such relative expressions of endurance are used frequently to make meaningful comparisons among individuals' endurance levels. Absolute static muscular endurance is related to the maximum strength of the individual (Tuttle, Janney, and Thompson 1950). For example, holding a 50-N weight for 1 min is easier for a person who can exert an MVC of 500 N than for a person who can exert only 250 N MVC. The first person uses only 10% of maximum strength, whereas the second uses 20%. Static muscle endurance may be important for maintaining a particular position demanding stabilization of body parts during performance. The static strength used need not be of great magnitude, as, for example, when a certain posture is to be maintained. The important variable in a performance may be the length of time a static tension can be maintained without fatigue, rather than how much static strength is manifested. Such endurance is seen in dance performances and in activities requiring continual trunk stabilization to allow extremity movements, such as weight lifting.

Measurements of absolute and relative endurance are used also in evaluating dynamic muscular endurance. Many tests set forth procedures for evaluating dynamic muscular endurance and for comparing individuals. Concentric-tension endurance tests as well as eccentric-tension endurance tests are based on number of repetitions, which are measured in different ways. One method is to count the number of repetitions done in a specific time interval; such a procedure may be termed a "power endurance" test based on the definition of power as force times velocity of force application. Another method is to count the total number of repetitions performed at a prescribed cadence. Either of these or other approaches can be carried out with an absolute resistance, such as 40 N, or with a relative resistance, such as with a load equal to 50% of maximum static strength at midrange of the joint movement. Note that either relative or absolute endurance measures are appropriate measures of improvement for a given person pretraining and posttraining, whereas relative endurance measures are more appropriate for comparing different individuals.

No relationship between maximum isotonic strength and relative isotonic endurance seems to exist when the load for testing relative endurance is 75% of 1 RM (Shaver 1971). At lighter relative loads of 50% of 1 RM, however, maximum isotonic strength and relative endurance may be related (Berger 1970). Lighter relative loads may cause less occlusion of blood flow through the active muscles, thereby facilitating their continued ability to contract. In terms of total isotonic and isokinetic work (force times distance) output, stronger individuals seem to produce more work, due to the force variable, during a given number of contractions than weaker performers (Shaver 1972, Barnes 1980). No relationship seems to exist, however, between the isokinetic measures of strength and endurance in terms of number of repetitions performed at maximum effort (Barnes 1980). Repetitive muscular activity, therefore, should not be limited by an individual's strength level.

Training for Local Muscular Endurance

The concept of overload used for strength training applies also to improving muscular endurance. When training for strength, the strengthening stimulus is the intensity of muscle contraction, and the number of repetitions is kept small (5 or 6

RM). For muscular endurance, the repetitions are increased, but the load is less than that used for strength work. Studies show that muscular strength and endurance improve simultaneously with overload repetition work. Keeping the total number of repetitions constant, training with a greater load produced greater muscle endurance than training with light loads. Also, with the total work output held constant, training with fewer repetitions using greater loads (25 RM) produces greater muscle endurance than more repetitions at lighter loads (Hellebrandt and Houtz 1956). Moffroid and Whipple (1970) lend support to observations that high power exercise increases muscular endurance at high speeds.

For improving muscular endurance, the specificity principle should serve as a guide for designing muscle endurance training. The performer should ensure that the joint movements, resistances used, body positions, speed or cadence of repetitions, ROM used, and total number of repetitions are *specific to* and *appropriate for* the activity for which the training is being done.

UNDERSTANDING MUSCULAR ENDURANCE

1. With a heavy book in your hand, stand and abduct the shoulder to position the upper extremity horizontally. Time how long you are able to maintain that horizontal position and compare your time with the results of others.

2. Repeat the steps in question 1 with the other arm but with the elbow fully flexed. Compare the muscular endurance with your previous results. Explain the difference in terms of the magnitude of the resistance (consider mass, weight, and weight torque).

3. Using a specific muscle group, measure the maximum static force you can exert against a scale, tensiometer, or some other device for estimating force. How long can you continue to exert that maximum force?

4. Using the result obtained in question 3, determine 80% of your maximum static force. How long can you continue to exert 80% of that maximum force? Allow several minutes' rest and repeat for 50% of your original maximum force.

SECTION 6

FLEXIBILITY

The term **flexibility** is defined as the ROM available at an articulation. Flexibility is specific to each joint; that is, a person may have a large ROM at the wrist joint in all directions, but a limited ROM in one movement within the vertebral column (e.g., lumbar vertebral flexion). A lack of ROM at certain joints is a common cause for inefficient movement or skill performance. For example, swimmers who pursue more than adequate shoulder flexibility can injure the anterior capsule of the shoulder joint by stretching the muscles (and capsule) to a point at which the elbows cross behind the back. Joint laxity produced by such extreme stretching can lead to anterior dislocation, especially in the backstroke turn when the hand contacts the wall (Marino 1983). In developing flexibility at joints for a particular activity, the ROM *necessary* for performance should be the target condition, keeping in mind that the dynamic ROM may be greater than the static ROM during the actual performance.

Passive and Active Flexibility

Passive flexibility refers to the ROM available when an outside force (e.g., gravity, momentum, another part of the body, or another person) is the motive force (Figure 7.7a). **Active flexibility** is the ROM available when internal muscle forces cause the movement range (Figure 7.7b). If a segment must be moved through a ROM by the motive force of muscles during an activity, weakness in those muscles may cause the ROM to be less than what it would be passively. Holt and Smith (1982) report differences averaging 18 degrees in hip flexion ROM in favor of passive flexibility.

Both passive and active flexibility can be important variables in the performance of a skill. Passive dynamic stretching of a muscle group in the course of a movement often results in joint positions that cannot be reproduced with slow voluntary mus-

a   b

Passive and active flexibility for the hip joint (a and b) and passive flexibility of the shoulder joint (c).   **Figure 7.7.**

Inertial lag
of arm with
flexed elbow
causes extreme
lateral shoulder
rotation

Figure 7.7
continued   **c**

cular effort. For example, stretching the shoulder medial rotators in the initial execution phase of a baseball pitch allows the shoulder to be moved into extreme lateral
rotation with abduction. Figure 7.7c shows the ROM that should safely be available
to the thrower. In this case, the passive ROM is caused by the inertial lag of the
forearm and hand as the more proximal segments rotate forward.

In wrestling, passive flexibility is extremely important for injury avoidance. The
body is subjected to extreme outside forces applied by the opponent. Flexibility
enables the wrestler to "deform" enough to avoid tissue tearing as well as to slip
out of positions that would otherwise be disabling (Figure 7.8). Adequate strength
in extreme joint positions also is necessary to prevent joint structure damage by the
outside force. The greater the wrestler's active flexibility, which incorporates enough
muscular strength to cause the ROM, the better able he is to wrap his body, arms,
and legs around the opponent.

Factors Limiting Range of Motion

ROM may be limited by four factors: (1) connective tissue restrictions, (2) bone
configurations at the articulations, (3) contact of tissue masses of adjacent segments,
and (4) clothing restrictions. In addition to these factors, active flexibility is also
limited by the strength of motive force muscle groups. Physical contact of the tissue
masses of adjacent segments as well as the physical contact of the bony shapes forming
the joint itself are conditions that must be accepted and cannot be changed unless

the tissue masses that interfere with normal movement happen to be unnecessary adipose tissue. For such a restriction, a program of weight control would be in order.

A common cause of inflexibility is inactivity. When the total ROM at a particular joint is not used over a period of time, the connective tissues crossing that joint become shortened; that is, the tissues adapt to permit the ROM that is routinely performed. If a certain activity demands a large ROM at one or more articulations and that activity is performed frequently, the tissues crossing the articulation become accustomed to being lengthened and tend to remain flexible enough to impose no restriction on joint ROM. Inactivity, however, need not be total, whole-body inactivity for tissue shortening to occur. The areas of the body in which large movements of the segments are neglected because normal daily activity does not require them will exhibit the greatest movement restriction or inflexibility. Once a range is established at a particular joint and in a particular direction, that ROM will be maintained merely by frequent use.

If flexibility training is to be undertaken for greater ROM for skill improvement, the joint movements that need to be increased should be determined exactly; that is, the exercise should be specific to the need. For example, if a swimmer is unable to swing both arms above the surface of the water in the butterfly stroke, the restriction of movement may be caused by the tissues crossing the anterior side of the shoulder joints. A stretching exercise that lengthens the transverse adductors of the shoulder joint would decrease the restriction of shoulder transverse abduction. In addition, strength may be lacking in the muscles that adduct the scapula (retract the shoulder girdle) and cause transverse extension of the shoulder joints. In this case strengthening exercises would be in order. The total flexibility available to perform a given skill is as great as the flexibility of all the joints involved. This weakest link concept is applicable, therefore, in skills demanding flexibility as well as strength or endurance of various muscle groups.

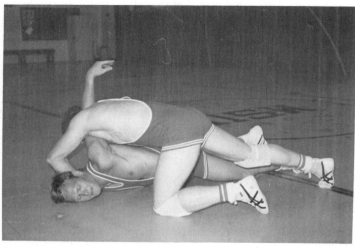

Passive flexibility of the shoulder joint subjected to extreme forces provides a margin of safety.

Figure 7.8.

Connective Tissue Properties and Implications for Stretching Methods

In most joints ROM is limited by connective tissue structures such as tendons, ligaments, muscle fascial sheaths, aponeuroses, and ligamentous joint capsules. The connective tissue network within and around muscle tissue provides most, if not all, of the resistance to stretching of the muscle (Sapega et al. 1981). Following injury, the scar tissues forming in connective tissues restrict ROM unless therapeutic stretching is done.

Because connective tissue is the target for flexibility programs, understanding the response of connective tissue to stretching, or elongation, is important. When connective tissue is elongated, its lengthening has two components: **elastic** stretching (i.e., it will recoil) and **plastic** stretching (i.e., it will not recoil). The permanence of the stretch depends on how much plastic stretch occurs; the elastic-type lengthening merely causes recoil of the tissue to its original length. The plastic elongation is directed toward the viscous (thick fluid) property of the *viscoelastic* nature of connective tissue. The proportion of the contribution of each kind to the lengthening depends on *how* the stretching is performed. The three variables concerned are (1) the magnitude of the stretching force, (2) the duration of the stretching force, and (3) the tissue temperature when the stretching is taking place (Sapega et al. 1981).

Summarizing the information provided by Sapega et al., permanent lengthening of connective tissue is produced best by lower force of longer duration applied at elevated tissue temperatures (40 °C or 104 °F and above in therapeutic settings). Cooling the tissue (by ice packs about 15 min) before releasing the tension seems to increase the permanence of the plastic elongation. In addition, under these conditions, any structural weakening of the tissues is minimized.

Elastic lengthening (elongation that will recoil) is produced by high-force, short-duration stretching at normal or colder tissue temperatures.

Methods of Stretching

Stretching methods are categorized as static or dynamic. Static stretching is also known as passive or slow, sustained stretching. Dynamic stretching is called active, ballistic, bouncing, or fast stretching. Research studies on flexibility improvement indicate that both methods are effective but that static methods are safer and result in less muscle soreness (deVries 1980, Corbin and Noble 1980, Bealieu 1981, Holt and Smith 1982).

DYNAMIC STRETCHING

Dynamic stretch of a muscle group brings into play neuromuscular mechanisms involving the muscle spindle (myotatic, or stretch reflex) and the Golgi tendon organ. In fast stretching, the momentum of the moving body segment, rather than an external force, is used to push the articulation beyond its present ROM. Common examples of this are the bouncing method of toe touching, the lateral flexion of the trunk with the arms raised over the head, and the pectoral stretch done by flinging the arms in transverse abduction.

The speed of stretch elicited by the dynamic method stimulates the muscle spindles, and the stretch reflex causes a contraction of the same muscles that are being stretched. The greater the speed of muscle stretching, the greater the stretch reflex. Therefore, even though the momentum brings the articulation beyond its normal range, the ballistic method causes a countercontraction immediately following or during the stretch and seems to reduce stretching benefits. Reports associate muscle soreness with this type of stretching; that is, before motion stops, the sudden tension put on the tissues can result in small tears in the connective tissue or muscle fibers, which lead to swelling or pain.

SLOW OR STATIC STRETCHING

To reduce the velocity of stretch that the muscles undergo and thus reduce the intensity of the stretch reflex, an external object, such as a wall or a partner, or an antagonistic muscle group is used to apply tension slowly to the muscles to be stretched and thus causes these muscles to stretch beyond the normal range. Some muscle-spindle activity results from the stretched position, but it is minimal because the spindles react more to the speed of stretch than to the stretched position.

In light of the properties of connective tissue, the static, or long duration low-force, methods seem most favorable. In addition, an easy muscle warm-up activity prior to stretching increases the plastic elongation of the tissues due to the increase in temperature. Sapega et al. (1981) propose that stretching exercises *not* be done at the beginning of a warm-up routine. Stretching prior to running or swimming, for example, should be done *following* a minimum of 5 min of light but progressive muscular activity such as walking or jogging. Stretching should be performed immediately after the main part of a workout because it is then that the tissue temperatures are the highest. Sapega et al. also point out that the clinical use of "cryostretching," or stretching combined with cold application, should be used only for limited therapeutic goals. These include cases in which adhesions are to be torn, when muscle spasticity interferes with lengthening, and when stretching is so painful that cold must be used for analgesia. Otherwise, the tissues should be warm for the best stretching.

PROPRIOCEPTIVE NEUROMUSCULAR FACILITATION STRETCHING

The proprioceptive neuromuscular facilitation (**PNF**) method of stretching in various forms is gaining acceptance (Corbin and Noble 1980, Moore and Hutton 1980, Salem 1980, Holt and Smith 1982). Reports indicate that the ROM of an articulation may be increased considerably by this method and that little soreness results. PNF is also referred to as CRAC (contract-relax with agonist contract).

The neuromuscular basis for the effectiveness of this technique is still unclear (Moore and Hutton 1980). It is based on the initial isometric contraction of the antagonist (muscle group to be stretched) while it is in its longest state; then it relaxes, and the agonist muscle group contracts to move the articulation in the direction of limited ROM. The PNF method is discussed and applied to sport activities by Holt (n.d.). The procedure is in three parts:

1. The muscle group that needs to be stretched is identified, and the performer places the articulation at the limited end of its ROM (i.e., the muscle group is placed in its longest position).
2. The performer forcefully contracts (isometrically) the muscle group to be stretched against an immovable force such as a wall, the ground, or a partner. This forceful contraction may stimulate the Golgi receptors so that relaxation may be facilitated in that muscle immediately following the contraction.
3. Immediately thereafter, a gentle external force is applied to the segment as the performer contracts the muscle group opposite to the group being stretched.

The external force exerts a force against the segment so that the previously contracted muscle group is slowly stretched. The advantages to the slow stretch are the same as those given for the static stretch method. The slowness of the stretch minimizes the suddenness of stretch on the muscle spindles so that little or no reflex contraction is elicited in the stretched muscle. The example presented in Figure 7.9 demonstrates the PNF procedure for stretching the anterior shoulder muscles to allow greater ROM for full flexion and transverse abduction.

According to Holt (n.d.), the procedure would be the following:

1. Position the shoulder joint and arms so that the "tight" muscle group is at its limited length (Figure 7.9a).
2. Gradually contract the muscle group to be stretched against the immovable resistance provided by the partner, building to maximum tension in 2 sec and then holding at maximum for 4 sec.
3. Immediately contract the agonist (motive) muscle group to cause increased ROM in the desired direction. At the same time, the partner assists with a gentle pull for 4 sec (Figure 7.9b).

Holt and Smith (1982) compared this procedure for hamstring stretch with a slow active stretch and an isometric contraction control group. Five 10-sec stretches with 10-sec rests between stretches produced greater ROM with the PNF method.

Planning a Flexibility Program

Flexibility exercises should be planned for a specific purpose—to increase a given joint's ROM. An analysis plan should include these steps:

1. Identify the articulation that has limited ROM within a movement sequence.
2. Identify the position of the joint at the point of restriction (e.g., hip flexed, shoulder abducted).
3. Note the positions of surrounding articulations that may influence the restriction of the given joint. (Look for those joints that share common muscles.)
4. Identify the general muscle group needing stretch (e.g., hip extensors, shoulder adductors).
5. Select a method of stretching, preferably static or PNF or another based on the best, most up-to-date information available.
6. Devise a plan of stretching so that the movements simulate the positions identified in steps 2 and 3; that is, stretching should be specific to the need within the activity.

The procedure used in the PNF method of stretching.

Figure 7.9.

UNDERSTANDING THE BIOMECHANICAL ASPECTS OF FLEXIBILITY

1. Differentiate between active and passive flexibility.

2. Explain the difference between the elastic and plastic elongation of connective tissue.

3. Identify three stretching exercises, each commonly used in preparing for a different sport. Evaluate the effectiveness of the exercise in relation to the movements that require a given ROM in that sport.

4. Using the same three sports as in question 3, devise a different flexibility exercise for each, using the six steps in the analysis plan on page 335.

5. Sit on the floor with your knees extended, ankles plantar flexed. Reach toward your toes and hold the position of maximum reach. While holding this reach position, dorsiflex the ankles and note the result. Flex the knees slightly and note the result. Discuss these results in terms of specificity of joint positions in an activity for which stretching exercises are given.

6. For each of the flexibility exercises shown in Figure 7.10, indicate the following: (a) the articulation being stretched, (b) the position of the articulation, (c) the muscle group being stretched, (d) the force used to push or pull the joint beyond its range, (e) the muscle group antagonistic to the group being stretched.

7. Devise an exercise using the PNF procedure for extending the ROM of the following movements: (a) shoulder girdle retraction and shoulder joint transverse extension, (b) plantar flexion of the ankle, (c) dorsiflexion of the ankle, (d) lumbar vertebral flexion, (e) medial rotation of the hip, (f) lateral rotation of the hip. For each exercise, state the following: (a) the muscle group to be stretched, (b) the passive force used to stretch, (c) the antagonist muscle group used to facilitate the stretching, (d) the procedure for the stretching.

REFERENCES
SUGGESTED READINGS

Ariel, G. B. *Computerized Biomechanical Analysis of Human Performance: An Application for Exercise Equipment Design and Athletic Performance.* Technical Report Uni-1. Fresno, Calif.: Universal Fitness Research Department, Universal Athletic Sales, 1974.

Exercises for stretching selected muscle groups.

Figure 7.10.

Asmussen, E. "Muscle Fatigue." *Medicine and Science in Sports* 11 (4) (1979): 313–21.

Astrand, P., and Rodahl, K. *Textbook of Work Physiology.* New York: McGraw-Hill, 1977.

Atha, J. "Strengthening Muscle." In *Exercise and Sports Science Reviews,* vol. 9, ed. D. I. Miller, 1–74. Philadelphia: The Franklin Press, 1981.

Barnes, W. S. "The Relationship Between Maximum Isokinetic Strength and Isokinetic Endurance." *Research Quarterly* 51 (4) (1980): 714–17.

Bartels, R., Coyle, E., Huesner, W., and McLaughlin, T. "Scientists Talk About Strength Training." *Swimming Technique* 17 (2) (1980): 14–25.

Beaulieu, E. "Developing a Stretching Program." *The Physician and Sportsmedicine* 9 (11) (1981): 59–69.

Berger, R. A. "Relationship Between Dynamic Strength and Dynamic Endurance." *Research Quarterly* 41 (1) (1970): 115–16.

Bigland-Ritchie, B. "EMG/Force Relations and Fatigue of Human Voluntary Contractions." In *Exercise and Sports Science Reviews,* vol. 9, ed. D. I. Miller, 75–117. Philadelphia: The Franklin Press, 1981.

Blattner, S. E., and Noble, L. "Relative Effects of Isokinetic and Plyometric Training on Vertical Jumping Performance." *Research Quarterly* 50 (4) (1979): 583–88.

Booth, F. W., and Gould, E. W. "Effects on Training and Disuse on Connective Tissue." In *Exercise and Sports Science Reviews,* vol. 3, ed. J. H. Wilmore and J. F. Keogh, 95–103. Santa Barbara, Calif.: Journal Publishing Affiliates, 1975.

Clarke, D. H. "Adaptations in Strength and Muscular Endurance Resulting from Exercise." In *Exercise and Sports Science Reviews,* vol. 1, ed. J. H. Wilmore, 74–102. New York: Academic Press, 1973.

Clutch, D., Wilton, M., McGown, C., and Bryce, G. R. "The Effect of Depth Jumps and Weight Training on Leg Strength and Vertical Jump." *Research Quarterly for Exercise and Sport* 54 (1) (1983): 5–10.

Corbin, C. B., and Noble, L. "Flexibility, a Major Component of Physical Fitness." *JOHPER* 51 (1) (1980): 23–24, 57–60.

Coyle, E. F., Costill, D. L., and Lesmes, G. R. "Leg Extension Power and Muscle Fiber Composition." *Medicine and Science in Sports* 11 (1) (1979): 12–15.

Daish, C. B. *Learn Science Through Ball Games.* New York: Sterling Publishing Co., 1972.

DeLateur, B. J. "Exercise for Strength and Endurance." In *Therapeutic Exercise,* 3d ed. Ed. J. V. Basmajian, 86–92. Baltimore: Williams & Wilkins, 1978.

DeLorme, T. L., and Watkins, A. L. *Progressive Resistance Exercise.* New York: Appleton-Century-Crofts, 1951.

deVries, H. A. *Physiology of Exercise.* 3d ed. Dubuque, Iowa: William C. Brown Co., 1980.

Gans, C. "Fiber Architecture and Muscle Function." In *Exercise and Sports Science Reviews,* American College of Sports Medicine Series, ed. R. L. Terjung, 160–207. Franklin Institute Press, 1982.

Garhammer, J. "Power Production by Olympic Weightlifters." *Medicine and Science in Sports and Exercise* 12 (1) (1980): 54–60.

Hay, J. G., Andrews, J. G., and Vaughn, C. L. "Effects of Lifting Rate on Elbow Torques Exerted During Arm Curl Exercises." *Medicine and Science in Sports and Exercise* 15 (1) (1983): 63–71.

Hay, J. G., Andrews, J. G., and Vaughn, C. L. "The Influence of External Load on the Joint Torques Exerted in a Squat Exercise." In *Biomechanics: Proceedings of the Biomechanics Symposium*, ed. J. M. Cooper and B. Haven, 286–93. Indiana State Board of Health, 1980.

Hay, J. G., Andrews, J. G., Vaughn, C. L., and Ueya, K. "Load, Speed, and Equipment Effects in Strength-Training Exercises." In *Biomechanics VIII-B: Proceedings of the Eighth*

International Congress of Biomechanics, ed. H. Matsui and K. Kobayashi, 940–49. Champaign, Ill.: Human Kinetics Publishers, 1983.

Hellebrandt, F. A., and Houtz, S. J. "Mechanisms of Muscle Training in Man." *Physical Therapy Review* 36 (1956): 371–83.

Heusner, W. "The Theory of Strength Development." Paper presented at the 1980 American Swimming Coaches Association Clinic, New Orleans, 1980.

Heyward, V. H. "Influence of Static Strength and Intramuscular Occlusion on Submaximal Static Muscle Endurance." *Research Quarterly* 46 (4) (1975): 393–402.

Hinson, M. N., Smith, W. C., and Funk, S. "Isokinetics: A Clarification." *Research Quarterly* 50 (1) (1979): 30–35.

Holland, G. "The Physiology of Flexibility: A Review of Literature." In *Kinesiology Review*, ed. D. H. Clarke, 49–62. Reston, Va.: AAHPERD, 1968.

Holt, L. E. *Scientific Stretching for Sport (3-S)*. Sport Research Limited, P.O. Box 7045, North Halifax, N.S. B3K 5J4, n.d.

Holt, L. E., and Smith, R. K. "The Effect of Selected Stretching Programs on Active and Passive Flexibility." In *Biomechanics in Sports: Proceedings of the International Symposium of Biomechanics in Sports*, ed. J. Terauds, 54–67. Del Mar, Calif.: Research Center for Sports, 1982.

Jesse, J. P. "Misuse of Strength Development Programs in Athletic Training." *The Physician and Sportsmedicine* 7 (10) (1979): 46–51.

Johnson, B. L., Adamczyk, J. W., Tennoe, K. D., and Stromme, S. B. "A Comparison of Concentric and Eccentric Muscle Training." *Medicine and Science in Sports* 8 (1) (1976): 35–38.

Knuttgen, H. G. "Development of Muscular Strength and Endurance." In *Neuromuscular Mechanisms for Therapeutic and Conditioning Exercise*, ed. H. G. Knuttgen, 97–118. Baltimore: University Park Press, 1976.

Komi, P. V., and Bosco, C. "Utilization of Stored Elastic Energy in Leg Extensor Muscles by Men and Women." *Medicine and Science in Sports* 10 (4) (1978): 261–65.

Kume, S., and Ishii, K. "Biomechanical Analysis of Isokinetic Exercises." In *Biomechanics VII-B: Proceedings of the Seventh International Congress on Biomechanics*, ed. A. Morecki, K. Fidelus, K. Kedzior, and A. Wit, 404–10. Baltimore: University Park Press, 1981.

Lamb, D. R. *Physiology of Exercise*. New York: Macmillan, 1978.

Lesmes, G. R., Costill, D. L., Coyle, E. F., and Fink, W. J. "Muscle Strength and Power Changes During Maximal Isokinetic Training." *Medicine and Science in Sports* 10 (4) (1978): 266–69.

"A Look at Equipment." *Swimming Technique*, August 1980, 36–38, 41–43.

Marino, M. "Sports Medicine in Action: A Look at Swimming." *Muscle and Bone* 3(3) (1983). Monograph published by Current Concepts, Inc., 850 Third Ave., New York, N.Y.

Marshall, J. L., et al. "Joint Looseness: A Function of the Person and the Joint." *Medicine and Science in Sports and Exercise* 12 (3) (1980): 189–94.

Moffroid, M., and Kusiak, E. "The Power Struggle: Definition and Evaluation of Power of Muscular Performance." *Physical Therapy* 55 (10) (1975): 1098–1104.

Moffroid, M., and Whipple, R. H. "Specificity of Speed of Exercise." Paper adapted from master's thesis, New York University, 1970.

Moore, M. A., and Hutton, R. S. "Electromyographic Investigation of Muscle Stretching Techniques." *Medicine and Science in Sports and Exercise* 12 (5) (1980): 322–29.

Osternig, L. R., Sawhill, J. A., Bates, B. T., and Hamill, J. "Function of Limb Speed on Torque Patterns of Antagonist Muscles." In *Biomechanics VIII-A: Proceedings of the Eighth International Congress on Biomechanics*, ed. H. Matsui and K. Kobayashi, 189–205. Champaign, Ill.: Human Kinetics Publishers, 1983.

Perrine, J. J., and Edgerton, V. R. "Muscle Force-Velocity and Power-Velocity Relationships Under Isokinetic Loading." *Medicine and Science in Sports* 10 (3) (1978): 159–66.

President's Council on Physical Fitness and Sports. "Endurance of Arm and Shoulder Girdle Muscles." *Physical Fitness and Research Digest* 8 (4) (1978): 1–27.

President's Council on Physical Fitness and Sports. "Joint and Body Range of Motion." *Physical Fitness and Research Digest* 5 (1975): 17.

President's Council on Physical Fitness and Sports. "Toward a Better Understanding of Muscular Strength." *Physical Fitness and Research Digest* 3 (1973): 1.

Raitsin, L. M. "The Effectiveness of Isometric and Electro-Stimulated Training on Muscle Strength at Different Joint Angles." *Theory and Practice of Physical Culture* 12 (1974): 33–35.

Sale, D. G., and MacDougall, J. D. "Specificity in Strength Training: A Review for the Coach and Athlete." *Canadian Journal of Applied Sports Sciences* 6 (2) (1981): 87–92.

Sale, D. G., MacDougall, J. D., Upton, A. R. M., and McComas, A. J. "Effect of Strength Training Upon Motoneuron Excitability in Man." *Medicine and Science in Sports and Exercise* 15 (1) (1983): 57–62.

Salem, N. "Selected Stretching Techniques Based on Mechanical and Neurophysiological Principles and Muscle Tightness." In *Biomechanics: Proceedings of the Biomechanics Symposium*, ed. J. M. Cooper and B. Haven, 352–53. Indiana State Board of Health, 1980.

Sapega, A. A., Nicholas, J. A., Sokolow, D., and Saranti, A. "The Nature of Torque 'Overshoot' in Cybex Isokinetic Dynamometry." *Medicine and Science in Sports and Exercise* 14 (5) (1982): 368–75.

Sapega, A. A., Quedenfeld, T. C., Moyer, R. A., and Butler, R. A. "Biophysical Factors in Range of Motion Exercise." *The Physician and Sportsmedicine* 9 (12) (1981): 57–65.

Shaver, L. G. "Maximum Dynamic Strength, Relative Dynamic Endurance, and Their Relationships." *Research Quarterly* 42 (4) (1971): 460–65.

———. "Relation of Maximum Isometric Strength and Relative Isotonic Endurance of the Elbow Flexors of Athletes." *Research Quarterly* 43 (1) (1972): 82–88.

Sjøgaard, G. "Force-Velocity Curve for Bicycle Work." In *Biomechanics VI-A: Proceedings of the Sixth International Congress of Biomechanics*, ed. E. Asmussen and K. Jorgensen, 93–99. Baltimore: University Park Press, 1978.

Skyne, K. "Richard H. Dominguez, MD: To Stretch or Not to Stretch?" *The Physician and Sportsmedicine* 10 (9) (1982): 137–40.

Smith, T. K. "Preadolescent Strength Training: Some Considerations." *JOPERD* 55 (1) (1984): 43–44, 80.

Stevens, R. "Isokinetic versus Isotonic Training in the Development of Lower Body Strength and Power." *Scholastic Coach* 49 (6) (1980): 74–76.

Tuttle, W. W., Janney, C. D., and Thompson, C. W. "Relation of Maximum Grip Strength to Grip Strength Endurance." *Journal of Applied Physiology* 2 (12) (1950): 663–70.

Viitasalo, J. T., and Komi, P. V. "Rate of Force Development, Muscle Structure, and Fatigue." In *Biomechanics VII-A: Proceedings of the Seventh International Congress of Biomechanics*, ed. A. Morecki, K. Fidelus, K. Kedzior, and A. Wit, 136–41. Baltimore: University Park Press, 1981.

Vorobiev, G. *Track and Field.* Moscow, USSR (7) (1976): 31–32.

Wachowski, E. "Speed and Useful Power in Strength Exercises." In *Biomechanics VII-B: Proceedings of the Seventh International Congress of Biomechanics*, ed. A. Morecki, K. Fidelus, K. Kedzior, and A. Wit, 379–85. Baltimore: University Park Press, 1981.

Ward, P., Lambert, L., Spence, D. W., and Disch, J. G. *A Manual of Weight Training for General Conditioning, Sport and Body Building.* 1980. Dynamics Health Equipment Manufacturing Co., Inc., 1538 College Ave., Houston, TX 77587.

Warren, C. G, Lehmann, J. F., and Koblanski, J. N. "Heat and Stretch Procedures: An Evaluation Using Rat Tail Tendon." *Archives of Physical Medicine and Rehabilitation* 57 (3) (1976): 122–26.

Weltman, A., and Stamford, B. "Strength Training: Free Weights Versus Machines." *The Physician and Sportsmedicine* 10 (11) (1982): 197.

Whitley, J. D. "The Influences of Static and Dynamic Training on Angular Strength Performances." *Ergonomics* 10 (3) (1967): 305–10.

Wolf, S. "The Morphological and Functional Basis of Therapeutic Exercise." In *Therapeutic Exercise*. 3d ed. Ed. J. V. Basmajian, 43–85. Baltimore: Williams & Wilkins, 1978.

Prerequisites

Concept Modules A, B, C, D, E, F
Chapters 1, 3

Chapter Contents

ANALYSIS OF PROJECTILE-RELATED ACTIVITIES

PROPERTIES OF MOTION RELATED TO PROJECTILES

To create the best possible set of circumstances in which to project objects, one must understand the factors governing the motion of projectiles and the relative importance of those factors. Four primary mechanical purposes are used in projecting: (1) to project an object or the body for maximum horizontal distance, (2) to project an object or the body for maximum vertical distance, (3) to project an object for maximum accuracy, and (4) to project an object for maximum accuracy when the speed of the projectile enhances the projectile's effectiveness.

Resolution of the Velocity Vector

Velocity is a vector quantity that possesses magnitude as well as direction. Any given velocity may be resolved into two perpendicular components. For a resultant

343

muscle force, the two components are labeled the rotary component and stabilizing component. For a velocity vector, both components are spatial; they are named according to their direction relative to some stationary frame of reference, such as the ground. At any given instant, a projectile's velocity may be resolved into a vertical velocity component and a horizontal velocity component. A projectile's motion is represented by the motion of its center of gravity (CG). When the object is traveling parallel to the level ground, its velocity has only a horizontal component; if the object is traveling straight up or down, its velocity has only a vertical component.[1] Figure 8.1a and b illustrate how two objects' projection velocities may be resolved into vertical and horizontal components at the instant of projection.

The magnitude of each component of the object's velocity depends on the angle of projection of the object. Figure 8.1c illustrates various angles of projection and how the angle changes the relative sizes of horizontal and vertical velocity components. Note that the projection velocity has equal magnitude in all of these cases. The angle of projection at which the vertical and horizontal velocity components are equal is 45 degrees from the horizontal. Any angle greater than 45 degrees produces a vertical component that is greater in magnitude than the horizontal component; conversely, an angle less than 45 degrees produces a greater magnitude

---

1. For trigonometric calculations of an object's location in space, the reader is referred to Appendix V, Section III, p. 670.

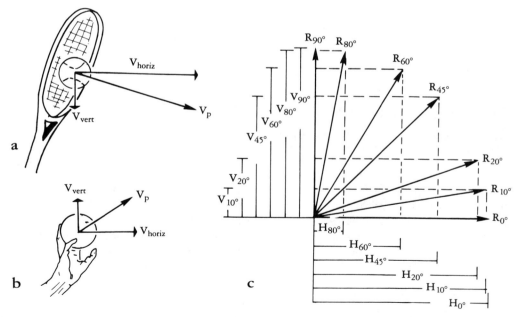

Figure 8.1.　Resultant projection velocities (V_p) of (a) a tennis serve and (b) a shot put with resolution into respective vertical (V_{vert}) and horizontal (V_{horiz}) components. (c) Relative sizes of the vertical (V) and horizontal (H) velocity components for various angles of projection.

of horizontal velocity than of vertical velocity. The arithmetic sum of the magnitudes of the two components will always be greater than the magnitude of the resultant.[2]

Forces Influencing Projectiles

Once a projectile is released from the projecting surface, only two forces can influence its motion until it reaches its destination—gravity and air force.

GRAVITY

Gravity, the force of the earth's attraction for other masses, is always directed toward the center of the earth. The force of attraction of two masses depends on the magnitude of the masses as well as the distance their CGs are from each other.

If gravity were the only external force acting on a projectile, the path the object would take would be in the shape of a parabola, which is a type of curve resembling

---

2. Since the resultant and the two components describe a right triangle, the magnitudes of the sides may be determined by the Pythagorean theorem, $a^2 + b^2 = c^2$, or they may be determined using trigonometric relationships. (See Appendix V, Section III.)

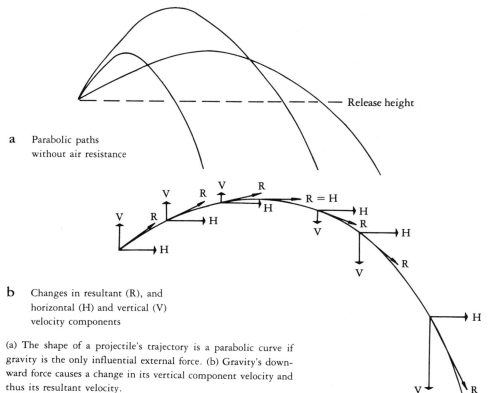

a   Parabolic paths
    without air resistance

b   Changes in resultant (R), and
    horizontal (H) and vertical (V)
    velocity components

(a) The shape of a projectile's trajectory is a parabolic curve if gravity is the only influential external force. (b) Gravity's downward force causes a change in its vertical component velocity and thus its resultant velocity.

Figure 8.2.

a hill, the steepness of which can vary (Figure 8.2a). The greater the angle of projection, the steeper the parabola.

Recall that the acceleration (g) of an object due to gravitational force is approximately 9.8 m/sec² (32 ft/sec²). The velocity of the CG of an object (i.e., a projected object's velocity) will be altered in the vertical direction by 9.8 m (32 ft) per second for every second that it is nonsupported. This acceleration due to the force of gravity on any object is constant regardless of the object's weight. Figure 8.2b illustrates the changes that gravity causes in the magnitude and direction of the projection velocity (and its horizontal and vertical components) of a projectile as it travels along its path or trajectory.

Recall that the magnitude of velocity is indicated by the length of the vector and that the shape of the path reflects only the effect of gravitational force on its vertical motion after release. Note also that the vertical component decreases during ascent and then *increases* during *descent*, reflecting gravity's decelerating and accelerating effects. In this example, the horizontal component remains the same throughout the trajectory, because the force of gravity can only alter vertical motion, and we have assumed that no other forces are acting on the object.

AERODYNAMIC FORCES

Gravity is not the only external force acting on a projectile. Forces generated by the flow of air relative to the moving projectile can play a major role in determining how a projectile will travel in its aerial path, particularly if the object is not massive. Figure 8.3 illustrates the difference in trajectory of an object traveling with and without significant influence of air forces.

In some cases, air forces are so small, as compared with other mechanical factors, that they can be ignored; for example, one can overlook air forces when jumping over a puddle. Fluid forces (air being one) are important and must be given more than superficial mention if the motion of projectiles is to be fully understood. More in-depth coverage is found in Chapter 9.

Figure 8.3.   Air resistance causes a change in the trajectory of a projected object.

PROJECTING FOR VERTICAL DISTANCE

An object may be directed in a predominantly vertical path. A vertical path may be upward, as when one attempts to throw a ball as high as possible, or it may be downward, as when one spikes a volleyball down to the opposite court. Examples of purely vertical projection do not occur frequently in sport activities. Even in jumping for height, such as high jumping, some horizontal component must be included for the jumper to move from the near side of the bar to the far side. Nevertheless, we will first consider those activities in which the purpose is to project an object as high as possible without the need for a horizontal component.

Projecting Objects for Vertical Distance

Newton's law of inertia says that an object will stay in a prescribed straight path and will move at its given speed unless some force acts to change it. Thus, an object projected vertically would continue at its given velocity (speed and direction) if it were not for the forces of gravity and air resistance. Since gravity must always act downward, it acts as a resistive force to slow an upward-directed object until it stops (at the peak of its vertical path); at that point, gravity becomes a motive force acting in a downward direction to increase the speed of the object until it encounters another force (an external object or the earth), which decelerates it to a stop. Gravity also alters the object's direction of motion when the object stops moving upward and begins moving downward.

The drag force of air is always *against* the direction of motion of the object. Thus, on the way up, air resistance is directed downward and is decelerating the object, as is gravity; on the way down, the air resistance is directed upward and opposes the force of gravity. Because with a vertically moving object, air resistance is always opposing the acceleration due to gravity, the *net* effect is a downward acceleration less than 9.8 m/sec^2. Since the air-drag force is increased with the velocity, the magnitude of the drag decreases as the object moves upward with a continuously slower velocity and increases as the object moves faster and faster downward. Remember that the direction and magnitude of the object's acceleration owing to the force of gravity are constant, while the direction and magnitude of the air resistance change according to the direction and speed of the object.

When calculating the maximum height to which a projectile will travel after release, it is readily apparent that the longer the object continues to move upward, the farther upward it travels. The object continues to move upward until the resistive forces of gravity and air decelerate it to zero vertical velocity. Thus, the more vertical velocity the object has to begin with, the longer it takes the resistive forces to slow it to a stop, and the farther the object travels upward. An object goes the highest when it is projected with the greatest vertical velocity. Remember that neither the downward acceleration due to gravity nor its upward deceleration are affected by the weight of the object. The weight, however, is a factor in calculating the net force acting on an object moving vertically through the air.

The vertical distance that a projected object will travel may be figured by dividing its squared vertical velocity component at release by 2 g.

Equation 8.1

$$D_{vert} = v^2_{vert}/2\,g$$

Note that this equation calculates the distance the object will travel vertically from its takeoff point.[3] The higher the takeoff point for a given projection, the higher the object will be *from the ground* at its peak. For example, an object that is projected from a height of 2 m from the ground and that travels 12 m upward from that point will be 14 m from the ground at its peak. The same object projected at 3 m from the ground and traveling 12 m upward will be 15 m from the ground at its peak.

For an object projected predominantly downward at a given velocity, such as a spiked volleyball, gravity will increase its initial projection vertical velocity at a rate of 9.8 m/sec for every second until the ball hits the ground. A volleyball spiked with an initial downward velocity of 7 m/sec will be traveling faster when it hits the ground because of the added acceleration due to gravity. Air resistance, however, will make the final velocity somewhat slower than the velocity calculated.

Projecting the Body for Vertical Distance

For most activities in which the human body is being projected vertically, the height of reach of the hand from the ground is the important factor.

Examples of such activities are spiking a volleyball, performing a vertical jump-reach test, or a jump ball or a rebound in basketball. Three factors determine the body's reach height: (1) the height of the CG from the ground at takeoff, (2) the vertical velocity of the CG at takeoff, and (3) the vertical distance of the fingertips relative to the CG at the peak of the jump.

HEIGHT OF THE CENTER OF GRAVITY AT TAKEOFF

The height of the CG of the body relative to the ground should be maximized prior to takeoff. Just as an object projected from a greater height will reach a higher peak, so the body's CG will reach a higher peak relative to the ground if it is higher at takeoff.

---

3. For trigonometric calculations of the vertical distance a projected object travels, see Appendix V, Section III, D.3, p. 677.

Recall from Concept Module D that the CG of the body may be moved *relative to the body* by relocating body segments. In a normal standing posture, the CG is located somewhere in the pelvic region. The CG may be raised within the body by flexing the arms overhead at the shoulder joints (both arms overhead raises it more than a single arm). Raising the CG within the body while still supported also raises the CG relative to the ground, Thus, by leaving the ground with both arms flexed overhead, one may have the CG a few centimeters higher when it peaks vertically. This technique must be employed *prior* to takeoff.

VERTICAL VELOCITY OF THE BODY'S CENTER OF GRAVITY AT TAKEOFF

The same laws govern the motion of the body's CG that govern the motion of an object's CG. As in projecting an object vertically, the vertical velocity of the body's CG at takeoff determines how high the CG will travel. Unless an external force should intervene, nothing can be done to change the determined path once the body is in the air.

Because the vertical takeoff velocity of a human body is usually relatively small and because the body is traveling through the air in a fairly streamlined position, the influence of air resistance is minimal. The air resistance force may be increased in activities in which the body is projected with the use of a spring (e.g., trampoline, diving board), because the body's vertical takeoff velocity is greater.

If horizontal displacement is unnecessary, then 100% of the resultant projection velocity should be in the vertical direction. The further the angle of projection from 90 degrees from the horizontal, the smaller the vertical component and the greater the horizontal component.

CENTER OF GRAVITY TO FINGERTIP HEIGHT

The third factor affecting the success of a vertical jump is the distance between the CG of the body at the peak of its flight and the fingertips of the reaching hand.

To maximize the CG height at takeoff, the performer should leave the supporting surface with both arms flexed overhead. If one arm is extended down to the side at the peak of the jump, the location of the CG *within the body* will be affected. The effect will be to raise the entire body upward in accordance with the fact that the CG must stay *in the same location relative to the ground*. Thus, while free of support, a performer may rearrange the body parts around the CG but may not change the location of the CG in space. Such is the case with the basketball players shown in Figure 8.4, both taking off with equal vertical velocity and CG height. One player may be able to gain a slight reach-height advantage by dropping one arm to the side just prior to the peak of his jump.

Figure 8.4.   Basketball players in a jump-ball position, with and without changing the reach height.

SECTION 3

PROJECTING FOR VERTICAL DISTANCE WITH A HORIZONTAL COMPONENT

In many sport situations, an object that is projected for height also must have some horizontal velocity. While a vertical-jump test may prohibit the use of an approach run, a high jumper would not think of using a static vertical jumping technique for the high-jump event. The high jumper, the springboard diver, or the gymnast performing an aerial floor exercise stunt uses a running approach and thus has some horizontal velocity at takeoff.

High Jumping

As the jumper's body is projected through the air, the body's CG follows the prescribed parabolic path. Gravity begins to reduce the vertical velocity after takeoff and continues to do so until it is zero. (The relatively slow takeoff velocity makes the air-drag force of little consequence as compared with the body-weight force.)

The angle of takeoff determines the relative magnitudes of the vertical and horizontal velocity components. The jumper needs just enough horizontal velocity to move from one side of the bar to the other. If, in fact, the air-resistance force is an important factor (e.g., if there is a strong head wind), the horizontal velocity will decrease significantly during flight. In such a situation, the performer needs to increase the horizontal velocity component at takeoff to move from one side of the bar to the other during flight. On the other hand, if there is a strong tail wind, the performer will have to decrease the horizontal component at takeoff, assuming that the wind will help carry the body from one side of the bar to the other.

Because we are considering air resistance negligible for a high jumper, no forces are acting in the horizontal direction to diminish or increase the magnitude of the horizontal velocity component, and therefore we assume that it remains the same.

The procedure in the high-jumping event requires that the performer jump only as high as the bar for each trial; however, the winner of the event is that jumper who can clear the highest bar during the competition. The ultimate performance of a single jumper is that in which the CG is projected as high as possible, while at the same time, the individual body parts are positioned so that each clears the bar as it passes over the bar. The highest point of the CG should be reached as it passes in vertical alignment with the bar (i.e., over, under, or through) if maximum effectiveness in the jump is to be attained. For maximum vertical height, the performer should have the vertical velocity at takeoff as large as possible. Two jumpers with the same projection speed may have different vertical velocity components because of the direction of takeoff. The one with the greater vertical component will raise the CG of the body farther during flight (see Figure 8.1c).

The intent of the performer is to attain the greatest takeoff velocity, to have the greatest vertical component of that velocity, and to maintain a large enough horizontal component to pass from one side of the bar to the other. In addition, with a given vertical velocity component, the jumper whose CG is the highest at takeoff projects the CG the highest from the ground. In this way, the taller jumper has a distinct advantage, even though the force of the jump and thus the takeoff velocity may be no greater than that of other jumpers.

Although the rules are set for this event, the truest test of vertical jumping ability would be to measure how high the jumper projects the CG from the takeoff height. A correction for the height of the CG of the jumper could be made as easily as handicaps are in golf and bowling. Classifications according to height would seem as appropriate as the weight classifications used in wrestling, boxing, and weight lifting. A second method of scoring would be to measure the jump as a percentage of the jumper's body height.

In a comparison of the paths of the CG of an elite male jumper and an elite female jumper, Atwater found that although the male jumper was reaching greater ground-to-peak height distances, both the male and female jumpers were, on the average, elevating their CG the same distances after takeoff. Furthermore, on the female's best jump, she raised her CG 5 cm higher than the male jumper raised his CG during any of his jumps (Atwater and Spray 1975).

Hay has analyzed several high-jumping techniques to determine which technique best satisfies the mechanical laws in projecting the body the greatest vertical distance and still clearing the bar (Hay 1975). The factors of importance are the height of the CG at takeoff, the vertical velocity at takeoff, and the position of the body segments relative to the CG and to the bar. The two styles of jumping that seem to be the focus of much controversy are the flop style and the straddle. As Hay points out, the straddle style has a definite advantage in that the CG at takeoff is higher, as can be seen in Figure 8.5.

Because of the high arms and high free leg of the straddle jumper at takeoff as compared with the low arms and the flexed knee of the free leg of the flopper, the straddle jump style gives the user a few centimeters or so advantage in CG height. This means that if both jumpers have the same vertical velocity at takeoff, the straddle jumper will have the CG higher from the ground at the peak of flight. As each body part passes from one side of the bar to the other, the part must be above the bar. At any given time during flight, however, the more body parts located below the

a   Straddle takeoff   **b**   Flop takeoff

Figure 8.5.   The takeoff positions of the straddle style (a) and the flop style (b) of high jumping.

bar, the higher will be the part passing over the bar. While free of support, body parts can adjust themselves about the CG point. If one part moves downward, another part moves upward. Therefore, the most effective jump is one in which only the body part passing over the bar at a given instant is above the bar; the rest of the body parts are positioned as far below the bar as possible on either side. The position in the air is similar to the position of a snake crawling over a wall. As soon as any body part passes over the bar, it is dropped to the lowest possible position on the other side. Therefore, the technique that affords the jumper the best opportunity to do this yields an advantage over other techniques. The positions of the body during the bar clearance in the flop and straddle techniques are illustrated in Figure 8.6.

When the flop technique became so successful for Dick Fosbury, one of the immediate points made was that it allowed the jumper to put all segments except the one passing over the bar in a lowered position. The success of this technique depends to a great extent on the flexibility of the back. Female jumpers find that the flop technique is successful for them because of their generally greater back flexibility. Dapena (1980b) reports that for skilled flop jumpers, the most effective bar clearance technique is one in which the jumper's CG passes through the bar (i.e., at its same level).

A straddle technique, however, enables the performer to use the flexion of the trunk and lead leg after they pass over the bar. Because one can flex the trunk to a greater extent than one can hyperextend it, there seems to be a distinct advantage to the straddle style in this respect as well.

Hay suggests that a forward dive technique using a one-foot takeoff may well be the ultimate in high-jumping techniques. In such a jump style, one is able to maximize the height of the CG at takeoff and also to curl the body over the bar, therefore keeping all body parts, except the one passing over the bar, as low as possible for the duration of the jump (Hay 1975b).

a   Flop   b   Modified straddle

The body positions while crossing the bar in a flop-style (a) and a modified straddle-style (b) high jump.   **Figure 8.6.**

Dapena (1980b) reports a horizontal velocity component of approximately 6 m/sec at touchdown and approximately 3 m/sec at takeoff for skilled flop-style jumpers. The vertical velocity component was close to 4 m/sec at takeoff. The takeoff angle was between 40 and 48 degrees. One may be led to believe that a larger takeoff angle should be used (closer to 90 degrees from the horizontal) because this would increase the vertical velocity component and therefore the height of the jump. The resultant takeoff angle may be reduced, however, by merely reducing the horizontal component, which would have no effect on the vertical component or the height of the jump.

Whether an athlete has the neuromuscular and musculoskeletal makeup to increase the vertical velocity component while decreasing or maintaining the same horizontal component is yet to be answered. What effect changing one component would have in terms of what the human body can produce is unclear/

UNDERSTANDING PROJECTIONS
FOR VERTICAL DISTANCE

1. Stand 10 m away from a partner. Throw a ball back and forth with a projection angle of approximately 45 degrees, noting the approximate amount of force used on the object during projection. Repeat the throw with a 60-degree and an 80-degree projection angle. Note the differences in the peak height and the distance that the object travels (its trajectory). In each case, explain the differences in terms of the vertical and horizontal velocities and the angles of projection.

2. Project a basketball vertically to appoximate distances of 2, 4, 6, and 8 m. With a stopwatch, time the descent from the peak height until the ball hits the ground. Discuss the change in time that occurs at the various distances in terms of the relationship to (a) the velocity of projection, (b) the mass of the object, and (c) the height of projection.

3. Perform a vertical jump and reach, and mark the height of reach. Compare the difference in height attained when both arms remain overhead at the height of the jump and when one arm is extended downward quickly after takeoff. Explain the difference. How do these findings relate to the technique used for (a) a volleyball spike, (b) a basketball jump ball, and (c) a basketball rebound? What effect does the repositioning of the body segments have on the path of the CG of the body? on the path of the hand that remains above the head? How does this relate to clearing the bar in a high jump.

SECTION 4

PROJECTING FOR HORIZONTAL DISTANCE

An object is projected for maximum horizontal distance in many more sport activities than in activities requiring projection for vertical distance. The object of all of the throwing events in track and field is to achieve maximum horizontal distance. Long jumping, triple jumping, golf drives, soccer placekicks, and punts are a few additional examples. An object or body projected for horizontal distance continues to travel horizontally until it is stopped from doing so by an external force. Usually that external force is provided by the ground. Gravity eventually halts the upward movement of the object, and the ground friction eventually halts the horizontal velocity of an object and thereby stops it from traveling any additional horizontal distance. The longer an object is in the air with a horizontal velocity component, the longer it can continue to move in the horizontal direction. Time in the air is greater if the initial upward vertical velocity component is greater. For each second that the object is in the air, however, it travels a given number of feet horizontally, depending on the magnitude of that component. An object traveling horizontally 15 m/sec for 1 sec will travel 15 m; traveling for 2 sec, it will travel 30 m.

A trade-off has to occur between maximizing the time in the air, which is determined by the vertical velocity component, and maximizing the horizontal distance traveled in that time period which is determined by the horizontal velocity component. To compare distances achieved with different projection angles, we will assume that the magnitude of the resultant projection velocity is constant. The magnitude of each component differs, however, as the angle of projection changes. These relationships are illustrated in Figure 8.7, which shows the horizontal distances covered by an object projected at five different angles.

The horizontal velocity component is maximum at a 0-degree projection angle from the horizontal plane and minimum (zero) at a 90-degree angle. The vertical velocity component is the opposite: it is maximum at 90 degrees from the horizontal plane and minimum (zero) at 0 degrees. At 45 degrees, the two components are always equal in magnitude to each other at takeoff.

Horizontal Projections for Which Takeoff and Landing Heights Are Equal

Examples of sport skills in which maximizing horizontal distance is the primary mechanical purpose and in which the takeoff and landing heights are equal include placekicks and a long football pass or baseball throw to another person catching the

Projection angle
6 = 75°
5 = 60°
4 = 45°
3 = 40°
2 = 30°
1 = 10°

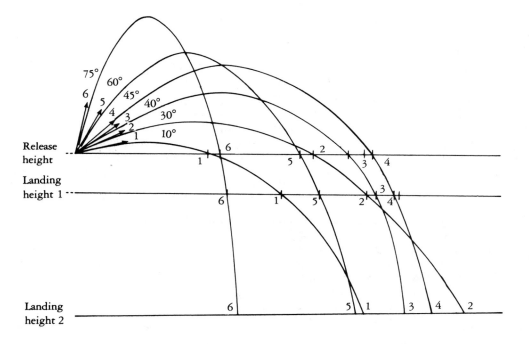

Figure 8.7.   Horizontal distances covered by an object at various angles.

ball at approximately the same height. Notice in Figure 8.7 that there are two landing heights. We will first consider landing height 1.

The greatest horizontal distance is achieved with a projection angle of 45 degrees when the takeoff and landing heights are the same. Thus, in this case, a 45-degree angle will give the greatest distance, as long as two or more projections with the same resultant velocities are compared. This angle will be optimum *regardless of the magnitude of the resultant velocity used.* This optimum angle is for activities in which how fast the object arrives at its target is inconsequential. For example, if a thrower is more concerned with how fast the baseball reaches the infield than how far it travels before it is caught, the thrower will decrease the vertical velocity component by decreasing the angle of projection to get the ball to its target quickly.

The general equation for calculating the horizontal distance of a projectile, for which the takeoff and landing heights are equal, is:

$$D_{horiz} = V_{horiz} \times t$$

Equation 8.2

The greater the projection angle, the smaller the horizontal velocity but the greater the time in the air. The smaller the projection angle, the greater the horizontal component but the less the time in the air. Thus, a 45-degree angle *optimizes* these two factors to produce the *maximum* horizontal distance.[4]

Horizontal Projections for Which Takeoff and Landing Heights Are Unequal

The sport events in which objects are projected for maximum horizontal distance may be divided into two categories: events in which objects are thrown or struck (e.g., a shot, a discus, a baseball) and events in which the body is projected for horizontal distance (e.g., long jumping, racing dives, ski jumping).

PROJECTING OBJECTS FOR HORIZONTAL DISTANCE

Throwing or striking an object for distance involves projecting the object from a height. The height of the CG of the object depends on the height of the performer and on the place where the performer releases or impacts the object relative to the body (e.g., underarm, overarm, sidearm). The landing point is usually the ground. Again referring to Figure 8.7, we will consider an object projected at various angles and reaching the ground at landing height 2. If we assume that air resistance is negligible, then the object will travel with the same horizontal velocity throughout its path.

The more time the object has to travel forward, afforded it by the extra vertical distance it can travel before landing, the farther forward it will be when it lands. Each projection has traveled farther forward at landing height 2 than at landing height 1. The greater the difference in the two heights, the greater the time the object continues to move forward. Therefore, a tall performer has an automatic advantage over a shorter performer throwing with the same projection velocity.

Notice also that in Figure 8.7, the object projected at 45 degrees no longer "wins." In fact, in this case, the 40-degree projection travels the farthest before landing. The greater the difference between takeoff and landing heights, the smaller the *optimum* angle of release, given equal projection velocities.

---

4. For trigonometric calculations of an object's projected horizontal distance, the reader is referred to Appendix II, Table II.2, p. 655.

The effect of varying the height of release on horizontal distance traveled is shown in Figure 8.8a. Given the same height and upward angle of projection, the object with the greatest velocity will go farther, as shown in Figure 8.8b. Thus, the performer able to project the object with the greatest speed will likely win. In fact, an increase in velocity provides a greater increase in horizontal distance than a similar increase in release height.

For each height and resultant speed, however, a unique *optimum* angle gives the object the greatest horizontal distance (Figure 8.8c). The greater the difference between the takeoff and landing heights, the lower the optimum angle. The greater the projection velocity, the greater the optimum angle. If the performer alters the release height or changes the speed of projection, then a different angle is optimum. Each performer, therefore, has a unique angle of projection that gives the object the greatest distance. Note that when we talk about an **optimum** or an **ideal projection angle,** we are saying that with a *given release height and speed*, there is a unique projection angle that results in the object's traveling the greatest horizontal distance compared to that achieved at *all other angles*. (This angle may not be ideal for an object projected with a different velocity or height of release.)

The horizontal distance increases with increases in the velocity and with increases in the height of release, but the *ideal angle decreases* as the *height of release increases*. Thus, the taller the thrower, the less of an angle needed to produce the greatest distance for a given speed of release. In addition, the ideal angle increases (up to 45 degrees) as the speed of release increases. Therefore, a faster thrower needs a greater angle of release. The equation showing the relationship among the variables when takeoff and landing heights are unequal is in Appendix Table II.2, p. 655.

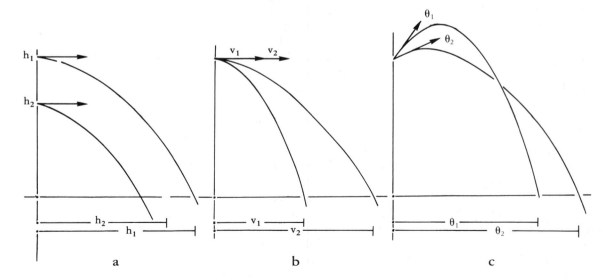

a   b   c

Figure 8.8.   The effect of varying the height of release (a), speed of release (b), and angle of release (c) on horizontal distance.

THE EFFECTS OF HEIGHT OF RELEASE (CASE A), SPEED OF PROJECTION (CASE B), AND ANGLE OF RELEASE (CASE C) ON SHOT PUT DISTANCE

Table 8.1.

Height of Release (m)	Angle of Projection With Horizontal (degrees)	Release Speed (m/sec)	Shot Put Distance (m)
C_2 2.44	45	13.41	20.60
		13.11	19.79
		12.80	18.95
C_1 2.44	40	13.41	20.73
		13.11	19.89
		12.80	19.08
2.44	35	13.41	20.29
		13.11	19.51
		12.80	18.72
2.44	30	13.41	19.43
		13.11	18.69
A_1		12.80	17.96
2.13	45	13.41	20.37
		13.11	19.53
		12.80	18.72
2.13	40	13.41	20.42
		13.11	19.61
B_3		12.80	18.80
2.13	35	13.41	19.94
B_2		13.11	19.18
B_1		12.80	18.39
2.13	30	13.41	19.08
		13.11	18.31
A_2		12.80	17.60
1.98	45	13.41	20.24
		13.11	19.41
		12.80	18.57
1.98	40	13.41	20.29
		13.11	19.46
1.98	35	13.41	19.81
		13.11	19.02
		12.80	18.24
1.98	30	13.41	18.87
		13.11	18.14
A_3		12.80	17.40

Adapted from Dyson, G., *The Mechanics of Athletics,* ed. 7 (New York: Holmes & Meier Publishers, 1978), p. 219.

The factors that determine the unique angle appropriate for various takeoff heights and speeds are important to consider when coaching athletes of various heights and muscular power. These differences are evident when working with athletes of different abilities, and they are particularly important when coaching athletes at different age levels, since heights, strengths, and muscular power change rapidly during the growing years.

Table 8.1 shows the variables of angle of projection, release heights, and speeds for a shot put and each variable's effect on the shot's horizontal distance.

In comparing three puts projected at different heights, A_1, A_2, and A_3, notice that the greater the height of release (A_1), the greater the horizontal distance. In terms of the most important factors in throwing for distance, the speed of release is the most significant. In comparing parts labeled B_1, B_2, and B_3, notice that a shot projected from a height of 2.13 m at 35 degrees and 12.80 m/sec travels 18.39 m (B_1). A gain of 0.41 m would be made by increasing the projection angle 5 degrees (B_3), but a gain of 0.79 m would be made by increasing the projection velocity 0.31 m/sec (B_2).

In comparing the parts labeled C_1 and C_2, notice that the shot projected at 40 degrees (C_1) travels farther than the same shot projected at 45 degrees (C_2).

Figure 8.9. Jump distances involved in long jumping.

Projecting the Body for Horizontal Distance

When the body is being projected for horizontal distance, as in the long jump or the triple jump, some additional factors play an important part in the total distance.

LONG JUMP

Figure 8.9 illustrates the factors that contribute to the total horizontal distance in a long jump. A horizontal distance between the takeoff board and the CG of the body at takeoff is created by the forward lean of the body. This distance is designated as d_1. The d_2 distance is designated as the horizontal distance of a projectile when the takeoff and landing heights are equal. The d_3 distance designates the horizontal distance created by the extra time of projection afforded by the differences in takeoff and landing heights. It is during this time that the body is descending beyond the takeoff height. The d_4 distance designates the horizontal distance given to the jumper between the position of the CG and the heels when heel contact is first made with the ground.

The factors that increase d_1 distance are: the height of the performer (increases the CG height), positioning the arms and legs so that the CG is even higher relative to the body at takeoff, and decreasing the angle of takeoff from the horizontal.

f

g   Position at which
     cog is equal to its
     takeoff height

h   Position at
     heel contact

i   Hip and knee
     flexion after
     contact

d_2 (continued)

d_3

F_4

Figure 8.9
continued

Factors that increase the d_2 distance are the same as for projectiles in which takeoff and landing heights are equal. The d_2 distance is increased most markedly by increasing the projection velocity; it also is increased by increasing the takeoff height or by using the proper (unique) angle for the given speed of takeoff or both. Note that the actual d_2 distance designated here disregards the compounding effects of d_1, d_3, and d_4; the d_2 distance is for equal takeoff and landing points. Thus, the specific d_2 is increased by achieving a 45-degree angle and is not affected by height of takeoff from the ground.

The factor that increases d_3 is delaying the heel contact until the last possible instant to increase the time in the air.

Finally, the d_4 distance is increased by flexing the hip to position the lower extremity as close to the horizontal as possible to place the heels as far in front of the performer's CG as possible.

In practice, not all these factors can be used. Although a coach may seek a tall athlete who can be trained as a long jumper, the athlete must possess characteristics other than height, such as neuromuscular development and interest in the event. The total distance, then, is dependent on many inherent factors, about which a coach can do little.

To maximize the d_1 distance, a coach may teach a takeoff position that increases the height of the long jumper's CG by advising the performer to keep the arms and free leg high. The performer, however, must be careful not to sacrifice takeoff speed by taking too much time to get into this position.

Second, the performer can be coached to use a smaller projection angle, thus placing the CG farther ahead of the feet. This decreases the vertical velocity component of the CG, however, and if the body lean is too great, the reduction in the vertical component of the projection velocity reduces the d_2 and d_3 distances as well. Furthermore, the lower angle may not be ideal for the performer's takeoff speed.

Typically, jumpers take off at a projection angle far below that calculated as ideal. This is explained by the fact that the human body is unable to maintain the magnitude of the resultant takeoff velocity if energy is taken to redirect the horizontally moving body in a more vertical path; that is, a reduction in the takeoff speed to achieve the ideal angle reduces the horizontal distance to a greater extent than the small increase gained by increasing the angle.

Most nationally ranked jumpers achieve a CG takeoff angle of 20 to 25 degrees. Widule (1974) calculated the theoretical projection distances of the CG for several takeoff angles of two jumpers, a female long jumper and Bob Beamon. The distances are shown in Table 8.2. Notice that the ideal angle for the given takeoff speed is calculated to be 41 and 43 degrees, respectively, although the actual angles used by the jumpers were 18 and 23 degrees, and the jump distances were 4.57 m and 8.90 m, respectively. The actual distances jumped include the d_4 distance, and the calculated CG distances are those that would have been produced if the centers of gravity had been allowed to fall to the ground. Optimum distances would have been reached had the ideal projection angles been used. Although the optimum projection angle would increase the time in the air, the human body has been incapable of achieving such a large angle without a great sacrifice in horizontal velocity. By increasing the angle of projection, one decreases the horizontal velocity component; thus, a greater projection angle requires a greater takeoff velocity to keep the horizontal component the same.

THEORETICAL RANGES OF THE CENTER OF GRAVITY FOR TWO JUMPERS			Table 8.2.
Difference Between Height of CG at Takeoff and Landing (m)	Initial Velocity (m/sec)	Initial Angle (degrees)	Distance of the CG (m)

A. Theoretical Distances of the Body's CG for the Running Long Jump of a College Woman Participant on the Intercollegiate Track Team. Based on an Initial Velocity of 7.19 m/sec.[a]

.19 (estimated)	7.19	25	5.48
		30	5.81
		35	6.03
		40	6.11
		41	6.12[b]
		42	6.11
		43	6.11
		44	6.09
		45	6.07

B. Theoretical Distances of the Body's CG for the Running Long Jump of Bob Beamon. Based on an Estimate of Bob Beamon's Takeoff Velocity of 10.06 m/sec.[c]

.19 (estimated)	10.06	25	9.52
		30	10.30
		35	10.85
		40	11.14
		41	11.17
		42	11.18
		43	11.19[b]
		44	11.17
		45	11.15

[a]Actual angle of takeoff was approximately 18 degrees. Actual distance of the jump was approximately 4.57 m.
[b]Maximum distance.
[c]World record distance was 8.90 m (takeoff to landing of feet).

Adapted from Widule 1974, pp. 168–69.

The delaying of heel contact is not difficult. Although some believe that muscular effort is required to hold the legs up toward the body, this is not the case. In free-fall situations, gravity operates equally on all segments, pulling the trunk downward toward the legs as well, and therefore the body remains in a piked position without muscular effort to hold the legs up against gravity. To increase the d_4, one can position the body segments around the CG so that the heels are farther forward of the CG point. The most convenient technique is to throw the arms backward into hyperextension prior to heel contact. Leaning slightly backward with the upper body also projects the heels forward; care must be taken, however, because one must be able to recover over the feet once contact is made. Figure 8.10 illustrates the positional change and the advantage possible with this positional change.

The system has some forward angular momentum from the takeoff, and the jumper can effectively use this momentum to carry the body over the feet. The jumper can minimize the deceleration effect of the ground-to-heel reaction force by flexing at the hips and knees as soon as the heels contact the surface. A vigorous flexion of the shoulder joints after heel contact also helps maintain the angular velocity of the rest of the body forward about the heels. Figure 8.11 illustrates this application of the motion of the arms upon landing. Further discussion of this concept is included in Chapter 13.

TRIPLE JUMP

The triple jump involves the mechanical factors of projectiles in each of three phases. During each phase—the hop, the step, and the jump—each projection is under the influence of the *same mechanical factors* as in the long jump.

Figure 8.10.   Increasing the heel distance by throwing the arms backward into hyperextension and leaning the trunk back.

Each successive phase in the triple jump is initiated at a reduced horizontal velocity. Bober (1974) states that "the competitors compensated for the drop in horizontal velocity by increasing the effectiveness of takeoff, thus resulting in comparatively high vertical velocity at the end of the takeoff and increase in the projection angle." The mean projection angles reported were 18, 16, and 20 degrees for each phase, respectively. Application of the desirable qualities of projection—increased takeoff speed, high CG position at takeoff, the closest possible angle of takeoff to the ideal angle for the speed, and delaying the heel contact for as long as possible—must be combined in such a way as to maximize each factor without a substantial reduction in the distance achieved by another factor.

Fukashiro and Miyashita (1983) studied the parameters necessary for a triple jumper to attain a distance of 18 m. They found, not surprisingly, a significant positive correlation between run-up velocity and the total distance jumped. Secondly, they estimated that the jumper needs to apply a vertical force of 3.6 to 4.4 times his body weight during support for each phase of the jump. The hop takeoff angle was calculated to be 14.72 degrees; the step takeoff angle, 13.72 degrees; and the jump takeoff angle, 20.98 degrees. These angles follow a similar pattern to Bober's findings.

The 18-m triple jump model also indicated decrease in horizontal velocity with each successive phase (9.9 to 8.6 to 7.3 m/sec) and a vertical velocity that initially decreased from the hop to the step (2.6 to 2.1 m/sec) but then increased during the jump phase to a value greater than that at initial takeoff (2.8 m/sec).

Total body angular momentum

Landing

Application of the principle of conservation of angular momentum to landing in a long jump (hitch-kick style).   **Figure 8.11.**

RACING DIVES

The racing dive used in swimming starts is classified as a skill in which the primary mechanical purpose is horizontal distance; however, this is not strictly the case due to a number of constraints placed on the dive relative to the total event. In a swimming race, the primary purpose is to move the body over a prescribed distance with the greatest speed. The dive section of that event plays a significant role in determining the total time. The following factors are considered here:

1. The human body can project itself horizontally through the air faster than it can propel itself through the water.
2. The angle of entry of the CG into the water partially determines the deceleration effect of the water on the resultant velocity of the body entering it.
3. The body configuration when entering the water has the greatest effect on how much horizontal deceleration the CG has on entering the water.

The grab start using two trajectories and two styles of entry is shown in Figure 8.12. Since the starting blocks are elevated from the water level, the difference in takeoff and landing heights suggests an optimum angle of projection less than 45 degrees. Maglischo (1982) reports that in the grab-start techniques (Figure 8.12a), the projection angle formed by a line from the hip to the toes should be 40 to 50 degrees from the top surface of the starting platform if the starting block is horizontal. Since the body's CG location is somewhat forward and upward relative to the hip joint during takeoff, the suggested angle of projection of the CG is somewhat less. Considering projectile motion parameters, Maglischo's suggested angles would produce a projection with excessive vertical velocity.

Wilson and Marino (1983) report on three types of starts: the swing technique in which the arms are swung forward to start, the grab start in which the body enters the water in a flat configuration (Figure 8.12b), and the whip start in which the

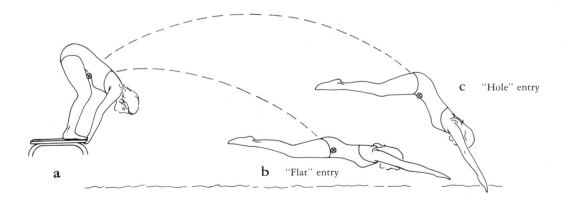

Figure 8.12.   Trajectories of the grab start (a) with the "flat" entry (b) and the "hole" entry (c) techniques illustrated.

body begins in the grab-start configuration and enters the water in a piked position (Figure 8.12c). They found no significant differences among the horizontal velocities of the styles at takeoff or entry. With respect to the angle of body lean at takeoff, a significant difference was noted between those subjects using the whip style (pike or hole entry) and those using the flat entry technique with a grab start. (The angle of body lean is defined as the angle made from a line between the shoulder and the point of contact of the feet on the block to the horizontal.) The angle of body lean in the grab with a flat-entry style was significantly smaller (19.85 degrees) than the grab with a pike-entry (whip) style (25.44 degrees). Furthermore, Stevenson and Morehouse (1979) found that varying the slope of the starting-block surface from 0 to 30 degrees had no effect on the projection angle for grab starts.

Generally speaking, the racing dive allows the swimmer to leave the starting block quickly. The resultant velocity of the swimmer's CG is therefore maximized and projected at an angle of approximately 19 to 26 degrees so that the horizontal velocity component is larger than the vertical component. The diver should increase the time in the air but not sacrifice too much horizontal velocity since the diver also should strive for the greatest horizontal distance before entering the water.

The pike entry position helps decrease the horizontal distance of the dive since the piking of the body causes the hand-entry spot to move backward slightly in space. The pike entry has the proposed advantage of allowing the hands to cut a "hole" in the water through which the rest of the body passes. This pike position also prevents the body from losing as much momentum as the flat position upon entry. Maglischo (1982) reports an entry angle of the trunk of 30 to 40 degrees relative to the surface of the water. Hyperextension of the vertebral column and hyperflexion of the shoulder joints are needed to prevent deep plunging.

UNDERSTANDING PROJECTIONS FOR HORIZONTAL DISTANCE

1. Draw a trajectory illustrating the path of a softball that is projected at 45 degrees with no air resistance (takeoff and landing heights are equal). Draw a trajectory illustrating the same object traveling with air resistance. What is the difference between the two trajectories? Why does the difference exist?

2. Draw an arbitrary trajectory for each of the following situations:

  a. Projection velocities are equal at a 35-degree projection angle from a takeoff height of 1.5 m and a takeoff height of 2 m. Both land on the ground level.
  b. Takeoff heights are equal at a 35-degree projection angle with projection speeds of 20 m/sec and 25 m/sec. Both land at the same level.
  c. Takeoff and landing heights are equal, and speeds are equal. The projection angles are 30 degrees and 40 degrees.

For each of the situations, state a general principle that applies to the effects of altering the specifications of projection on the horizontal distance.

3. From a distant side view, observe the trajectories of a javelin and a discus. What are the differences between each trajectory and a parabolic trajectory? Why do these differences occur?

4. Imagine driving a badminton shuttlecock and a tennis ball horizontally as far as possible. Draw the trajectories. What are the differences? Why do they occur?

5. Cut two pieces of heavy cardboard, 15 cm by 8 cm and 5 cm by 10 cm. As shown in Figure 8.13, pin the two pieces together so that the links are freely movable relative to each other.

   a. Hold piece A vertically and piece B horizontally, as shown in Figure 8.13a. Release piece B. What happens to it relative to A? What force is causing this motion?

   b. Place A and B perpendicular to each other, as shown in Figure 8.13b. Release both pieces at the same time, allowing them to fall to the ground. Is there

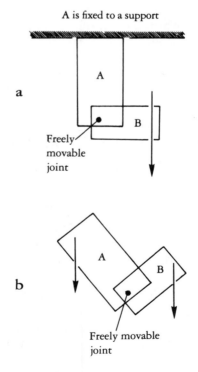

Figure 8.13.   Cardboard model with a freely movable joint, (a) with segment A fixed and (b) with segment A and B free.

any movement of B relative to A, as in the previous experiment? What force causes the movement of the system to the ground? Why does B not display the same movement relative to A as in the previous experiment?

c. Relate the findings of these experiments to the example of a gymnast doing leg levers while hanging from a horizontal bar and to the example of a long jumper descending from a long jump (see Figures 8.9 or 8.10). (A represents the trunk; B represents the lower extremity.)

d. Why must the gymnast use muscle force to hold his legs up whereas the long jumper does not?

6. Perform a standing long jump, keeping the shoulders flexed forward on landing. Perform a standing long jump, hyperextending the shoulders during flight. Is there a difference in jump distances? To what could you attribute the difference?

SECTION 5

PROJECTING FOR ACCURACY

In many sport events, projecting an object or the body to an exact location is important. Maximum distance is not the primary mechanical purpose in these events; however, optimizing the distance so that the object or body reaches the target area may be necessary. For example, in throwing a dart one does not need to throw as fast as possible, but one must project it with enough velocity to get the dart to the board. Another example is the distance given to a basketball when it is shot; the distance is *optimized* rather than *maximized*.

In sport events in which accuracy is the primary mechanical purpose, having the object travel at a high speed also may be desirable. Examples of such situations include pitching a baseball or a softball; serving a volleyball, tennis ball, or badminton shuttlecock; and most racquetball shots.

Projecting Objects for Accuracy

In several activities the primary concern is accuracy, and how fast the object is moving when it reaches the target is of little concern. These activities include slow-pitch softball pitching, horseshoe pitching, basketball shots, and approach shots in golf. The constraints under which each of these activities is performed help determine the projectile mechanics appropriate for analysis. One such constraint is where the plane of the target is located in space. There are vertical plane targets and horizontal plane targets.

VERTICAL PLANE TARGETS

Targets located in a vertical plane are found in such activities as softball pitching, dart throwing, archery, and rifle marksmanship. Accuracy is easiest when projecting to a vertical plane target if one uses a trajectory that is perpendicular to the target surface and that remains perpendicular as it coincides with the target face. Of course, the farther the projection distance, the more one has to rely on a more curved parabolic path. Consider throwing a dart at a target on the wall from distances of 2, 5, and 10 m away. For the 2-m target, one has to project the dart fairly straight-forward; for the 5-m target, one has to give the dart some vertical velocity so that the dart does not fall too much before reaching the target plane; and for the 10-m target, a considerable upward thrust has to be made.

Now consider how each of the darts tossed in the aforementioned ways arrives at the target surface. The close toss probably arrives nearly perpendicular; the angle of projection could be a few degrees on either side of the horizontal and the dart would land on target. The 5-m toss arrives at the target at some angle as it travels downward. From the peak of its flight, it continues to accelerate downward in the vertical direction until it hits an external force—the target. This vertical acceleration is difficult to judge and places a constraint on the performer tossing from a distance. The 10-m toss involves a similar but more difficult problem. The toss must be given a greater projection velocity; it peaks farther from the target and thus has a greater downward directed vertical velocity when it arrives at the target. The angle of incidence with the target also is smaller because the dart has a greater vertical velocity owing to spending more time in the air.

The smaller the angle of incidence with the target, the greater the chance of error. Generally, the more one must rely on vertical motion to get the object to a horizontal target, the greater the chance of error. The more horizontal velocity given to an object projected at a vertical plane target, the less one must rely on vertical motion to get the object to the target. For example, in archery the advent of the compound bow with its greater "weight" improved the performance of archers shooting at 50 m and greater distances.

In slow-pitch softball pitching, a peak is set on the trajectory. The pitcher not only wants the ball to pass through the target but also wants it to pass through in a particular manner. The more horizontal the trajectory as it passes through the target, the less effective it is as a pitch (i.e., a more vertically traveling ball is more difficult to contact than a more horizontally traveling ball). Thus, the less skilled pitcher probably sacrifices some effectiveness by projecting the ball more horizontally so that the accuracy is enhanced.

HORIZONTAL PLANE TARGETS

Accuracy activities in which the target is aligned in the horizontal plane are horseshoe pitching, basketball shots, clout shooting in archery, and a golf approach shot. In these activities, the object is projected upward to descend into the target area. The more vertically the object arrives at the horizontal target, the more chance of success in hitting the target as well as minimizing the possibility of sliding or rolling out of the target area.

In horseshoe pitching, additional time in the air is given to the projectile by the difference between release and landing heights. The vertical component of the velocity is important. Since the object of the game is to place the horseshoe as close to the stake as possible, a high pitch with a more vertical landing is best; however, if the objective is to bump the opponent's shoe out of the way of the stake, then a more horizontal pitch provides the horizontal momentum for the necessary impulse at landing.

The pitch shot in golf is another example. A more vertical angle of projection and landing is beneficial for the accurate placement of the ball near the target. Along with the backspin, the enhanced vertical arrival on the green prevents the ball from rolling off the green into a sand trap or another unfortunate location.

Basketball shooting trajectories are often studied. By comparing the diameter of the basket and the diameter of the ball, one finds that there is a minimum angle at which the ball can approach the basket and still go through the hoop. This angle is dependent on the height of release and vertical distance of release from the height of the basket. The closer the release height to the height of the basket, the smaller the projection angle needed and also the less the velocity of projection. One would not want to make the projection angle too shallow, however, for an opponent could easily intercede in the ball's path.

There is some consensus that the height of release is important to the success of the shot. Hudson (1983) reports that successful shots are significantly related to a height ratio that was calculated by comparing the standing height of the shooter to the height of the shooter's release. Thus, the greater the release height for any given performer, the more successful the shot. This finding was supported by Yates and Holt (1983) when they found that successful shooters have greater shoulder flexion and elbow extension at release. This position gives the shooter a higher release point, and it gave the shooters in this study a more vertical angle of ball projection.

Maugh (1981) reports that "as the height at which a shot is released increases, so do the chances of scoring. . . . If the shooter jumps two feet, the width of this scoring band . . . increases by 18%." The scoring band to which Maugh refers is an arch in space, the diameter of which increases with the height of release. It is what Maugh calls the "margin of error" (p. 107). Any shot following within this arch is successful. The most common error in shooting as described by Maugh is using an angle of projection that is too small, thus decreasing the margin of error.

Projecting the Body for Accuracy

Projecting the body for accuracy occurs mainly in activities for which the primary mechanical purpose is to move or position the body or its segments or both in a prescribed pattern with the intent of achieving an ideal or model performance. Generally, the activities are judged or evaluated on the movement quality of the performance. Part of the quality of the performance depends on how effectively one projects the body into the air. Examples of activities include aerial tumbling, diving, trampoline, apparatus dismounts, and gymnastics vaulting.

The target to which the body projects itself is an imaginary point in space and is called a **point target** in this text. This point target should be used as the target for projecting the body's CG as if one were projecting it to an ideal location in space. Placing the body's CG at this location assists in accomplishing some body maneuvers.

GYMNASTICS-RELATED ACTIVITIES

Aerial Tumbling.   Since aerial tumbling stunts progress from single turns in the air to multiple turns combined with twists, the performer must begin with a good takeoff so that multiple moves may be accomplished within the amount of available time in the air. Two principles govern this activity. First, the performance should maximize the time in the air so that the performer may have more time to turn and twist before landing. Second, the height of the CG should be maximized by lowering it within the body just prior to landing and by delaying foot contact so that additional time in the air is provided. As an example, a back layout somersault is examined, as shown in Figure 8.14. To maximize the time in the air, the performer must keep

Point target

a   Takeoff   b   Aerial phase   c   Landing   d   Landing
                                                          arms down   arms up

Figure 8.14.   Positions of the feet relative to the ground in landing from a back somersault (a and b), when the arms assume an extended position (c), and when they remained flexed overhead (d).

the angle of projection relatively large, producing a high vertical velocity. Therefore, the point target for the CG is as high as possible and peaks above the ground at a location approximately one half the performer's body length from the takeoff point. A greater vertical velocity means that the force of gravity requires more time to bring the body to a halt and more time to bring it back down again. Thus, the performer should be coached to project the body upward, rather than backward.

At takeoff, the body should be as extended as possible, with both arms fully flexed above the head, so that the performer may position the CG as high as possible. There is a tendency to flex the arms upward and bring them partially downward prior to takeoff because the performer is anxious to assume the aerial position. If full body extension and arm flexion in the single back somersault are stressed by the teacher or coach, the performer usually progresses to the double back more easily. Once the body is free of support, the arms are brought down to the sides and should remain there to place the CG location more toward the foot end. This serves to momentarily delay foot contact with the ground. This is illustrated by the two landing positions shown in Figure 8.14c and d. Recall also the foot position relative to the ground that is shown in Figure 8.4 (p. 350).

When the body precedes the aerial stunt with a run and several linear-velocity-generating stunts such as roundoffs and back handsprings, the projection of the body is less in need of horizontal velocity than vertical velocity. The projection direction in such cases is more in the vertical direction because the body already has horizontal velocity from the prior moves. In situations where a run-up precedes the aerial maneuver, the point target is close to vertical alignment from the takeoff point. The horizontal velocity combined with the vertical velocity from the vertical impulse provides the body with the proper trajectory. The point target for the performer's CG should be within 10 to 15 degrees from the vertical.

Gymnastics Vaulting. The takeoff characteristics of long-horse or side-horse vaulting are similar to those of aerial tumbling stunts in which run-ups or approach stunts precede the skill. In addition, a spring mechanism, the Reuther board, serves to enhance the vertical impulse. The approach run is usually longer in vaulting than in tumbling stunts and therefore the horizontal velocity of the performer is greater. The takeoff angle is approximately 12 degrees from the vertical for skilled side-horse vaulters performing a handspring vault (Kreighbaum 1974).

Because of the large horizontal velocity upon initiating the hurdle step, the CG location at initial contact with the vaulting board is behind the foot contact position with the board. During the short interval of board contact, the CG moves forward so that it is located slightly ahead of the vertical. The point target for the vaulter is such that the CG is at its peak just prior to horse contact so that little vertical downward motion results onto the horse. The point target for the CG for handspring-related vaults is shown in Figure 8.15.

Apparatus Dismounts. In dismounting from an apparatus, the performer must consider that the body is taking off from a position higher than the landing height. This does not result in the performer adjusting the trajectory to a lower angle;

Point target

Figure 8.15.   Point target for a long-horse vaulter.

however, it does allow the performer to do a greater number of maneuvers in the air than can be accomplished from a ground takeoff. The point target for these stunts should be no more than one half the height of the performer in the horizontal direction and high as possible in the vertical direction. A beginning performer usually senses the need to "get around" immediately and therefore errs by projecting the CG too much in the horizontal direction. Secondly, the height of takeoff seems to have a negative effect in that it convinces the performer that the body gets to the ground sooner and that therefore the somersaulting action must be done as soon as possible, which is frequently prior to the actual takeoff.

DIVING

Evaluation of diving performance includes such factors as the trajectory of the body in the air and the entry position of the body into the water. The trajectory determines the height to which the diver goes and how close the diver is to the diving platform or board.

The point target for high platform diving is not as great as that used for springboard diving because the body is already quite high, and no spring can help the diver to attain greater heights. Therefore, platform divers use a point target as high as possible but horizontally far enough from the board to clear their bodies as they rotate forward or backward while passing the board on their descent. Since platform divers do not have a great deal of vertical velocity upon takeoff, they do not move a great deal horizontally as they pass the platform on their way down. Consequently, platform divers must have greater horizontal velocity upon takeoff than springboard divers.

Springboard divers have an extra elevation to which their CG moves owing to the reaction force of the elastic recoil of the board. Therefore, the horizontal component of the velocity vector need not be great, for by the time they move vertically upward and back downward to the level of the board, their CG is farther from the board than that of divers with less vertical velocity. The point target of platform divers, therefore, is at a greater horizontal distance from the platform than that of springboard divers.

A diver should visualize the point target appropriate for the type of board or platform used. Also, the amount of vertical velocity obtained at takeoff helps determine the amount of horizontal velocity necessary to complete the dive safely.

Projecting Objects for Accuracy When Speed May Enhance the Performance

Serving the ball in volleyball is an example of a situation in which the probability of success depends on the object's speed as well as its accuracy. Widule calculated the distance for a volleyball serve when it is projected at different speeds and angles (Widule 1974). These distances are shown in Table 8.3. The impact (projection) height is 2.13 m (7 ft).

In the overarm volleyball serve, a spinning or floating serve, the movement is usually performed so that the ball travels at a high speed, passes close to the net, and is directed to land close to the back line; the server manipulates the projection variables so that these objectives are satisfied. The court is 9 m wide and 18 m long from service line to back line. The net is approximately 2.43 m high for men and 2.24 high for women.

At slower projection speeds, the angle must be increased so that the ball clears the net (note the case of the 10.67 m/sec [35 ft/sec] serve at 25 degrees). When using this slower serve, the server must increase the angle of projection to at least 30 degrees to clear the net. This results in a rather short serve (12.91 m). The ball descends at an angle greater than 30 degrees, which is undesirable because the opposing player is able to receive it with ease. Because the ball is of relatively low mass, air resistance helps decrease the resultant velocity, and thus the ball does not travel as far before it hits than would be the case with a more massive object. If the server selects a different type of serve (e.g., the sidearm or underarm), the angle of projection has to be even greater to clear the net because the projection height is lower.

Table 8.3   **DISTANCE FOR A VOLLEYBALL SERVE WHEN CONTACTED AT A HEIGHT OF 2.13 M**

Velocity (m/sec)	Angle (degrees)	Height of Ball at Net	Distance (m)
9.14	45	1.46	—[a]
10.67	25	2.01	—[b]
10.67	30	2.60	12.91
10.67	35	3.16	13.38
10.67	40	3.66	13.56
10.67	45	4.07	13.44
12.19	15	1.62	—[a]
12.19	20	2.33	13.85
12.19	25	3.04	15.11
12.19	30	3.73	16.12
12.19	15	2.24	—[a]
13.72	20	2.99	16.65
13.72	25	3.74	18.35[b]
13.72	10	1.92	—[a]
15.24	12	2.23	—[a]
15.24	13.5	2.46	16.52
15.24	15	2.69	17.28
15.24	20	3.46	19.73[b]

[a]Ball fails to clear the net.
[b]Ball lands outside of the court.

Adapted from Widule 1974.

The server can achieve success at a lower angle by increasing the projection speed. At 12.19 m/sec (40 ft/sec), a 15-degree projection does not clear the net. At the 12.19 m/sec (40 ft/sec), a 20-degree angle is the most desirable, but at this angle the ball only travels 13.85 m and falls 4.15 m short of the baseline. The angle has to increase to 30 degrees to come within 1.88 m of the baseline—still not a good mark. Of the types of serves listed in Table 8.3, the one producing the most desirable trajectory is that which is projected at 15.24 m/sec (50 ft/sec) at an angle of between 15 and 20 degrees. The ball lands 0.72 m (approximately 28 in.) inside the baseline.

When considering players of various ability levels, the laws of projectiles can be applied to determine what type of serve is best for each individual. The height of the server must be taken into consideration as well as the speed with which the player is able to serve the ball in an underarm, sidearm, and overarm pattern. Some players are not able to serve overarm well enough to impart sufficient velocity to the ball. Since such a player has to increase the angle of projection to clear the net, the player may find that serving underarm elicits a better serve with regard to velocity, projection angle, and horizontal distance.

The tennis serve has restrictions similar to those of the volleyball serve. A few differences exist between the magnitudes of some of the variables in these two serves: the tennis serve has a faster projection speed, a greater horizontal distance, and a greater projection height. The fact that the projection speed of the tennis serve is greater reduces the time that it takes the ball to get to the net. This reduces the time and, consequently, the vertical distance through which the ball drops because of the pull of gravity on it. (Note that this is because of a time reduction, not a reduction in the magnitude of gravity's force.) In addition, the tennis net is lower than the volleyball net, and the height of impact is higher so that the angle of projection is negative. In this case, the faster or taller server or both are able to decrease the angle of projection more than the slower server. Because the rear boundary of the service court is only 21 ft from the net on the far side, the smaller angle of projection provides a distinct advantage in terms of directing the ball to land within the service court.

UNDERSTANDING PROJECTIONS FOR ACCURACY AND SPEED

1. Consider the volleyball serve, given a court that is 9 m on either side of the net and a net height of 2.24 m. Using an underarm serve, identify the different trajectories that can be produced to have the ball clear the net and land within the opposite court. Specific factors that must be considered are height, velocity, angle of projection, net clearance, angle of approach to the opposing player, and horizontal distance.

2. Repeat the steps in question 1, using a sidearm serve and an overarm serve.

3. Consider three volleyball servers of various heights. What differences would there be in the ways they should be coached to serve?

4. Consider three volleyball servers, one beginning, one intermediate, and one advanced. (All are of equal height, but ability may affect velocity of impact.) What factors should be considered in coaching each?

REFERENCES SUGGESTED READINGS

Atwater, A. E., and Spray, J. A. "Kinematic Analysis of Takeoff in the Long Jump and High Jump." Research paper presented at the American College of Sports Medicine, 22nd Annual Meeting, New Orleans, May 22–24, 1975.

Ayalon, A., Van Gheluwe, B., and Kanitz, M. "A Comparison of Four Styles of Racing Start in Swimming." In *Swimming II: Proceedings of the Second International Symposium on the Biomechanics of Swimming*, ed. R. LeWillie and J. P. Clarys, 233-40. Baltimore: University Park Press, 1975.

Biesterfeldt, H. J. "A Comparison of Selected Factors Relating to Success of Running Front Somersaults." *Gymnast* 16 (1974): 32-33.

Bober, T. "Investigation of the Takeoff Technique in Triple Jump." In *Biomechanics IV: Proceedings of the Fourth International Seminar on Biomechanics*, ed. R. C. Nelson and C. A. Morehouse, 150. Baltimore: University Park Press, 1974.

Bowers, J. E., and Cavanagh, P. R. "A Biomechanical Comparison of the Conventional and Grab Starts in Competitive Swimming." In *Swimming II: Proceedings of the Second International Symposium on the Biomechanics of Swimming*, ed. R. LeWillie and J. P. Clarys, 225–32. Baltimore: University Park Press, 1975.

Dapena, J. "Searching for the Best Straddle Technique." *Track Technique* 55 (3) (1974): 1753–56.

———. "Mechanics of Rotation in the Fosbury-Flop." *Medicine and Science in Sports and Exercise* 12 (1) (1980): 45–53.

———. "Mechanics of Translation in the Fosbury-Flop." *Medicine and Science in Sports and Exercise* 12 (1) (1980): 37–44.

Dyson, G. *The Mechanics of Athletics.* 7th ed. New York: Holmes & Meier Publishers, 1978.

Ensign, P. "Projection Considerations in the Slow Pitch Softball Pitch." Unpublished paper, Montana State University, 1978.

Fukashiro, S., and Miyashita, M. "An Estimation of the Velocities of Three Takeoff Phases in 18-m Triple Jump." *Medicine and Science in Sports and Exercise* 15 (4) (1983): 309–12.

Hay, J. G. *Biomechanics of Sports Techniques.* Englewood Cliffs, N.J.: Prentice-Hall, 1978.

———. "Characteristics of the Flop." *The Athletic Journal*, January 1974, 10, 92–93.

———. "Straddle or Flop?" *The Athletic Journal*, April 1975a, 83–85.

———. "The Hay Technique: The Ultimate in High Jumping Style?" *Coaches Digest*, June 1975b, 44–47.

Heusner, W. W. "Theoretical Specifications for the Racing Dive." *Research Quarterly* 30 (1) (1959): 25–37.

Hudson, J. L. "A Biomechanical Analysis by Skill Level of Free Throw Shooting in Basketball." In *Biomechanics in Sports: Proceedings of the International Symposium*, ed. J. Terauds, 95–102. San Diego, Calif.: Academic Publishers, 1983.

Kreighbaum, E. F. "The Mechanics of the Use of the Reuther Board During Side Horse Vaulting." In *Biomechanics IV: Proceedings of the Fourth International Seminar on Biomechanics*, ed. R. C. Nelson and C. A. Morehouse, 137–43. Baltimore: University Park Press, 1974.

Lichtenberg, D. B., and Wills, J. G. "Maximizing the Range of the Shot Put." *American Journal of Physics* 46 (5) (1978): 546–49.

Maglischo, E. W. *Swimming Faster.* Palo Alto, Calif.: Mayfield, 1982.

Maugh, T. H. "Physics of Basketball: Those Golden Arches." *Science 81* 1 (3) (1981): 106–07.

Miller, D. I. "A Comparative Analysis of the Takeoff Employed in Springboard Dives from the Forward and Reverse Groups." In *Biomechanics IV: Proceedings of the Fourth International Seminar on Biomechanics*, ed. R. C. Nelson and C. A. Morehouse, 223–28. Baltimore: University Park Press, 1974.

———. "Springboard Reaction Torque Patterns During Nontwisting Dive Takeoffs." In *Biomechanics VIII-B: Proceedings of the Eighth International Congress of Biomechanics*, ed. H. Matsui and K. Kobayashi, 822–27. Champaign, Ill.: Human Kinetics Publishers, 1983.

Phinizy, C. "The Unbelievable Moment." *Sports Illustrated*, 26 December 1968, 53–61.

Stevenson, J. R. , and Morehouse, C. A. "Influence of Starting Block Angle on the Grab Start in Competitive Swimming." In *Swimming III: Proceedings of the Third International Symposium on the Biomechanics of Swimming*, ed. J. Terauds and E. W. Bedingfield, 207–14. Baltimore: University Park Press, 1979.

Toyoshima, S., Hoshikawa, T., and Ikegami, Y. "Effects of Initial Ball Velocity and Angle of Projection on Accuracy in Basketball Shooting." In *Biomechanics VII-B: Proceedings of the Seventh International Congress of Biomechanics*, ed. A. Morecki, K. Fidelus, K. Kedzior, and A. Wit, 525–30. Baltimore: University Park Press, 1981.

Widule, C. J. *Analysis of Human Motion*. Lafayette, Ind.: Balt Publishing Co., 1974, pp. 156–76.

Wilson, D. S., and Marino, C. W. "Kinematic Analysis of Three Starts." *Swimming Technique* 19 (1983): 30–34.

Yates, C., and Holt, L. E. "The Development of Multiple Linear Regression Equations to Predict Accuracy in Basketball Jump Shooting." In *Biomechanics in Sports: Proceedings of the International Symposium*, ed. J. Terauds, 103-09. San Diego, Calif.: Academic Publishers, 1983.

Prerequisites

Concept Modules B, C, D, E

Chapter Contents

CHAPTER 9

APPLICATIONS OF AERODYNAMICS IN SPORT

In many sport activities the effort used or the outcome of an event is influenced by *air resistance*. Such activities are those in which the body or a projected object is moving fast through the air and a noticeable resistance is felt. Running, cycling, skiing, skating, surfing, and long jumping are some activities subjected to appreciable resistive air forces. In many slow activities, or those of brief duration, such as walking, tumbling, climbing, wrestling, dancing, and weight lifting, air resistance can be ignored or considered negligible. Some projectiles affected by air resistance are badminton shuttlecocks, baseballs, softballs, footballs, and javelins. For example, air resistance acting on punted footballs has been estimated to reduce the achieved distance to one half what it would be if the ball were kicked in a vacuum (Cunningham and Dowell 1976).

SECTION 1

AERODYNAMIC DRAG FORCE

The term *air resistance* is commonly used to mean the type of air force that is known technically as **aerodynamic drag force.** Several variables determine how much drag force is acting on a body. To study the interaction of a body with the air through which it moves, we must focus on the motion of the air flowing past the object (realizing that the flow pattern is the same whether we look at the object moving through air or at the air moving past the object). The important condition is the *relative motion* between the object and the air. Figure 9.1a illustrates the relative velocity of air particles moving past a ball as it moves through the air. Note that the air-flow velocity relative to the ball is of the same magnitude as the ball's velocity but is opposite in direction. If a ball moves forward with a velocity of 30 m/sec through still air, the air-flow forces acting on the ball are the same as if the ball were stationary and a 30 m/sec wind were blowing backward past it. When the air particles have movement of their own, as is the case on a windy day, the movement of the air past the projectile *due to the projectile's motion* must be combined with the movement of the air particles past the projectile *due to the wind* to find the resultant velocity of the air relative to the projectile. The *flow velocity* of the air past a thrown ball in a side wind is illustrated from an overhead view in Figure 9.1b.

The ball actually experiences two air flows: air flowing backward past it as it travels forward and air flowing sideward past it due to the side wind. The ball "feels" only one resultant air-flow velocity directed diagonally backward and to the side (recall linear vector composition). Similarly, if a ball is thrown directly into a head wind (a wind blowing in the direction opposite to the direction of the ball's motion), the wind velocity is added to the velocity of the air past the ball due to the ball's

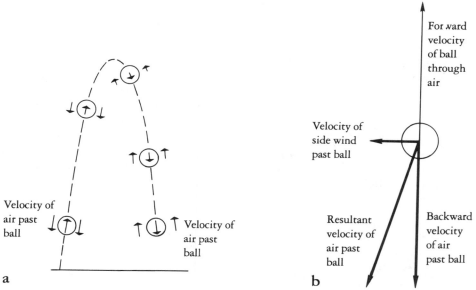

a   b

Figure 9.1.   (a) The same air-flow pattern results when a ball moves through stationary air as when the air moves past the stationary ball. (b) Vector composition of two air-flow velocity vectors relative to a thrown ball. The resultant air-flow velocity is a composite of the air flow backward past the ball (due to its forward motion through the air) and the air flow sideward past the ball (due to the side wind).

motion. For example, a ball thrown forward at a velocity of 20 m/sec into a head wind of 5 m/sec experiences an air flow past it of 25 m/sec (Figure 9.2a). On the other hand, if the same ball were thrown with a tail wind (a wind blowing in the same direction as the ball's motion), the wind velocity would be subtracted from the velocity of the air flow past the ball due to its motion (Figure 9.2b), and the relative velocity of the air past the ball would be 15 m/sec.

The foregoing examples show how the direction and speed of air flow past a moving body are determined by the velocity of the body itself and of the motion of the surrounding air; however, only velocities in the horizontal plane are used in the examples. Similar air-flow patterns relative to the projectile occur in other planes as well. Thus, a falling body experiences an upward flow of air past it, and a rising body experiences a downward flow of air past it. It is the nature of the air flow around a body as it cleaves its way through the fluid that determines the amount of drag force acting against it.

Two main types of aerodynamic drag force are of concern in sport activity: **skin friction** and **profile drag.** They act directly opposite to the body's direction of motion. Both are present and part of the total drag, but are not of equal magnitude. Both depend on the physical characteristics of the projectile and the velocity of air flow past it.

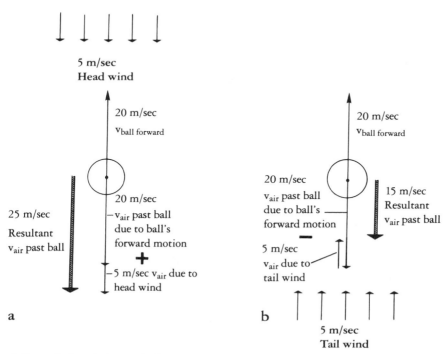

The air-flow velocity relative to a body moving through air is determined by the velocity of the body itself and the velocity of the surrounding air. A head wind causes a greater relative air-flow velocity (a), and a tail wind (following) causes a smaller relative air-flow velocity (b).

Figure 9.2.

Skin Friction

The effect of flow velocity on drag can be illustrated by the example of a ball thrown through the air. If the velocity of the air flowing around the ball is slow (i.e., the ball is barely moving), the air is caused to pass smoothly around the surface of the ball without much disturbance as the ball gently moves the air particles aside to move forward through them. Such a smooth flow pattern of air (Figure 9.3) is called *streamlined* or *laminar* flow because the layers of air around the ball's surface remain smooth and are not forced into turbulence.

With such slow, streamlined flow past an object, the most influential type of drag is **skin friction,** or surface drag. Such skin friction is generated by the object's carrying along on its surface a layer of air. This layer in turn tends to carry along the next outside layer of air, which then tugs on the next outside layer, and so on. Layer by layer, the differences in speed and in rubbing (shear) force become progressively less until there is no sliding tendency of outer layers at all. The region of relative motion between adjacent layers is called the **boundary layer.** All this layer rubbing near the surface of the object is caused by the friction among the air particles. Such friction varies from fluid to fluid and can be characterized by the fluid's resistance to deformation, or flowing; technically it is known as **viscosity.** Air has low viscosity and, therefore, little friction. Because of this low viscosity and the low friction between layers near the ball's surface, the skin-friction drag on the slowly moving ball is minimal and of no concern.[1]

Skin-friction drag will increase as the velocity of the flow increases, as the amount of surface area parallel to the flow increases (more surface to tow more air), and as the roughness of the surface increases. The larger the body and the rougher the texture of the surface, the greater the surface drag. The body and projectiles used in sport activities do not travel slowly enough through the air to sustain such a laminar, or streamlined, type of flow pattern, and therefore, profile drag is the main source of drag in sport activities.

---

1. If this same ball were to move through a more viscous fluid such as honey, the friction between the rubbing layers in the boundary layer would be appreciable and could not be ignored.

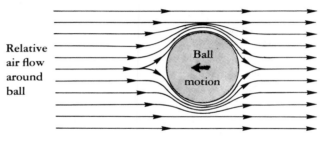

Relative air flow around ball

Figure 9.3.   A laminar or streamlined flow of air moving past a ball traveling very slowly through it. The layers of air pulled along with the ball's surface resist this pulling with internal air friction forces and constitute surface drag (skin friction) against the ball's motion.

Profile Drag

In addition to the skin-friction drag acting along the sides parallel to a body's motion, the other type of aerodynamic drag is **profile drag.** Profile drag is the main air-resistance force operating on a projectile. This type of drag also is known as *pressure drag* or *form drag,* each name being based on a factor that causes the drag. In most sports, the air particles are flowing past the body or projectile at speeds fast enough to produce a pattern of flow such that the air pressure on the leading surface of the body becomes greater than the air pressure on the trailing surface (Figure 9.4a). The velocity of the air flow past the object is too fast for the air to follow the contour of the trailing side of the object as it cleaves its way through the air particles. When this happens, a "back flow" occurs at the surface of the ball, which causes the flow to separate from the surface contour. This **boundary layer separation** causes a large, turbulent low-pressure zone to be formed behind the ball. This region of low pressure is continually being formed as the object moves through the air. Such a flow pattern is called *turbulent flow.* Although it is invisible, turbulent air flow may be likened to turbulent water flow, which can be seen easily by sweeping

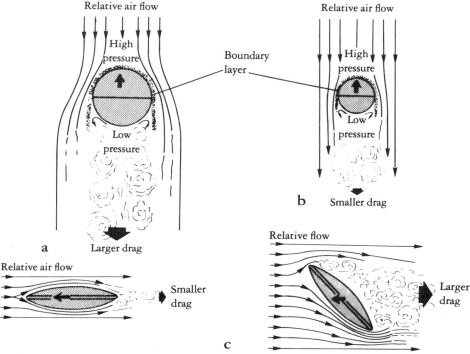

A turbulent flow of air is created by most projectiles moving through the air over a wide range of velocities. (a) An area of higher pressure exists on the leading surface, and an area of lower pressure exists on the trailing surface. (b) Profile drag is so named because the area exposed to the flow helps determine the magnitude of the drag force: a smaller ball experiences less drag than a larger one. (c) A discus in two difference orientations relative to the air flow experiences different drag forces.

Figure 9.4.

the hand rapidly along the surface of water. The motion of the air or water "down-stream" of the moving object is caused by the motion of the object relative to the surrounding fluid. The cause of the air's turbulent motion behind a projectile is the force applied by the projectile to the air as it pushes its way through. According to Newton's law of action and reaction, the air responds with an equal and opposite reaction force against the object. This counterforce is the resistive drag against the object or body.

Profile drag is the name given to such drag because the *profile*, or area exposed perpendicular to the approaching flow, partly determines the magnitude of the drag. Thus, a small ball will experience less drag than will a larger ball moving at the same speed (Figure 9.4b).

The orientation of a projectile relative to the air flow also determines the area facing the flow, such as when the air flow encounters the broad area of a discus or its edge (Figure 9.4c). This drag is also called pressure drag, because it is the *pressure difference* between the leading and trailing surfaces of the object that creates a suctionlike effect acting against the motion of the projectile. Actually, the magnitude of the low-pressure zone on the rear side of a projectile determines how much drag will act against it. The more abrupt the *change* in shape toward the rear of a body, the greater the magnitude of the suction effect.

EFFECTS OF STREAMLINING ON DRAG

Form drag is another name given to the drag caused by turbulent flow conditions, for the *form* or *shape* of the body determines how smoothly the object can cut through the air even at high speeds. Objects that are streamlined in shape are those that tend to create a streamlined flow pattern so that turbulent flow is minimized.

Figure 9.5 illustrates the effect that streamlining an object has on reducing drag. Behind the sphere in Figure 9.5a is a large low-pressure zone filling with turbulent air. But for the streamlined shape shown in Figure 9.5b, this zone is filled with the object itself, and air is able to flow gradually backward and inward toward the tapered end. The less abrupt its contours, the more smoothly a body can cut the air, without turbulent flow and an accompanying large pressure difference.

So important is the shape of a projectile in determining the drag that much attention is given to streamlining projectiles such as the discus, football, javelin, arrow, and bullet. Efforts also are directed to streamlining the body position when the body moves with such speed that air resistance is a major resistive force as in speed skating, cycling, sky diving, and slalom skiing. Such streamlining efforts are guided by streamlined examples in nature. A tapering shape is characteristic of effective stream-lining, such as the shape of a fish or the cross section of a bird's wing.

A streamlined shape is streamlined *only* if it is positioned relative to the flow so that the air can pass around it with minimal disruption. If the streamlined object or body is moving through the air in an orientation, or tilt, that causes turbulence, it is no longer considered streamlined. Figure 9.6 shows a streamlined javelin moving in a streamlined orientation and in a nonstreamlined orientation that increases the drag. Similarly, the human body may be considered streamlined with relatively low drag if it moves through a fluid from head to toe, but it is not streamlined if the

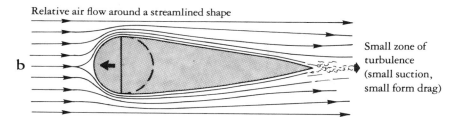

The air flow around an unstreamlined shape (a) creates much greater form drag on the body than it does around a streamlined, or tapered, shape (b). **Figure 9.5.**

flow passes front to back (e.g., a vertical dive water entry versus a belly flop). Downhill skiers and speed skaters try to perform in body shapes that are most streamlined in addition to trying to keep their frontal areas small.

EFFECTS OF A BODY'S MASS ON DRAG

Some projectiles cannot be streamlined because of the nature of the object (e.g., baseball, volleyball, tennis ball, and the badminton shuttlecock). A sphere is one shape that provides a great deal of air resistance, and in sports, the size and weight of each ball are standardized within certain limits by governing national and international organizations. We have seen how the size (profile) of a ball can influence the drag and thereby the nature of a particular game, but how is the weight of a ball important in air resistance? The weight or mass of an object moving through air (or water) is important in determining the amount of retardation, or deceleration, which is caused by whatever drag force is imposed on the object. Increasing or decreasing the mass of an object has no effect on the magnitude of the drag force acting against it. The mass of the object, however, determines, in part, how the motion of the object will be affected by the drag force. Consider, for example, a Ping-Pong ball and a golf ball (or another Ping-Pong ball filled with water). The sizes are equal, but the masses are noticeably different. If you were to drop each ball to the floor

Figure 9.6. A javelin has a streamlined shape that allows for minimum drag only if it encounters the air flow in a streamlined position (a). If it is moving at an angle to its motion direction, it is no longer in a streamlined position, and large drag force results (b).

from an elevation of 3 ft, each would take the same amount of time to hit the floor. The downward motion of the balls would serve to create an upward flow of air of a relatively low velocity because the balls would not have sufficient time to accelerate to some appreciable speed. If, however, the two balls were dropped from a higher elevation, say 10 ft, gravity would cause each to accelerate downward for a long enough time for the projectiles to gain appreciable speed. A difference in drop times would be evident: the lesser mass would be retarded more than the greater mass, even though the upward resistive drag force on each was the same. This should not be surprising, for recalling Newton's law of acceleration, a = F/m, the acceleration (or deceleration, in this case) of an object subjected to a given force is inversely proportional to that object's mass; therefore, the lesser mass would be decelerated more by the same drag force. An expression for the amount of retardation a projectile will experience is based on a similar force and mass relationship: deceleration of the projectile is equal to the force of drag on the projectile divided by the mass of the projectile. This expression means that the *slowing effect* is directly proportional to the drag force on the projectile (the greater the area facing the flow, the greater the drag force) and that the decelerating effect is inversely proportional to the mass of the projectile. When the projectiles are balls (spheres), differences in the drag force are due to differences in the area of the balls; that is, the drag force is directly proportional to the area of the ball facing the flow and to the *square* of the velocity. The difference in mass explains why a basketball travels faster when thrown than a balloon or why a whiffle golf ball travels more slowly than a regulation golf ball. The difference in area and shape explains why most people are more likely to be pushed over when facing a high wind than if they are turned sideward to it. The relationship of all the variables determining drag on a body or object follows. Note that the body's mass does not enter into it.

$$F_D = \frac{C_D \, A \, \rho \, v^2}{2}$$

Equation 9.1

where F_D is drag force, C_D is coefficient of drag (an index of "streamlinedness"), A is area facing flow, ρ (rho) is mass density of air, and v is relative flow velocity.

THE RELATIVE CONTRIBUTIONS OF THE FACTORS INFLUENCING DRAG

Coefficient of Drag.   The coefficient of drag, C_D, for the human body and odd-shaped projectiles must be found experimentally in wind tunnels because it changes for every change in orientation of the body relative to the flow. A body's C_D tells how streamlined it is. Recall that whether a body or object is considered streamlined depends not just on its shape but on how that shape is presented to the passing flow. In tables based on experimental data the C_D for a smooth-surfaced sphere is approximately 0.4. For a parachute, the C_D is approximately 1.2. The C_D for an adult male in running postures is estimated to be approximately 1.1 (Shanebrook and Jaszczak 1976). For a discus, the C_D changes with the tilt of the discus relative to the flow. If it is inclined at an 11-degree angle, $C_D = 0.10$, but when it is tilted at 35 degrees to the flow, $C_D = 0.68$ (Ganslen 1964). Similarly, as a javelin changes its inclination to the air flow, its C_D changes and is about 0.18 at a 20-degree angle (Ganslen 1967).

Usually we can assume that an object's C_D will not change for a particular shape relative to flow and for speeds that the object travels in a particular event. In a given activity, however, when the human body moves within a wide range of possible speeds, such as in running, speed skating, cycling, and skiing, the C_D may change as the speed changes (Ingen Schenau 1982; Shanebrook and Jaszczak 1974, 1976). The reason for this C_D difference is based on the changing dynamics of the air flow represented by a quantity called the Reynolds number.[2] Greater technical detail is not appropriate here, but it is important to recognize that the C_D can vary with body build and for different ranges of speed of the body.

---

2. For further technical information on flow dynamics, the reader is referred to Roberson and Crowe (1975).

Area Facing the Flow. The C_D which reflects the degree of streamlining of a body's *shape*, should not be confused with the area, A, of the body facing the flow. If the area facing the flow (frontal area) increases because of a change to an un-streamlined position, the drag is increased by the greater area *in addition to* the increased C_D. Increasing the area facing the flow increases the drag proportionately. For example, if the area is doubled, the drag is doubled.

Velocity. The C_D and the frontal area become more important at greater flow velocities because they are multiplied by the velocity *squared*. In the drag equation, the drag force increase can be seen to be proportional to the square of the velocity. To illustrate, suppose a skier goes downhill at 5 m/sec and encounters a drag force of 45 N (10 lb). If the velocity is *doubled* to 10 m/sec, the drag will be *quadrupled* to 180 N (40 lb). Such is the effect of the square of the velocity ($5^2 = 25$ and $10^2 = 100$).

Air Density. The effect of air density changes on aerodynamic drag is almost negligible. The density appears in the drag equation because it is a general equation for drag force in all fluids, including water. Therefore, if a body were moving through air as compared to water, the drag would be extremely different. The variability of air density with altitude, however, does not account for significant changes in drag when compared to the variability of the other factors.

SECTION 2

EFFECTS OF DRAG ON THE BODY AND OBJECTS IN SPORT

Activities in Which One Approaches Terminal Velocity

When an object or body is dropped through air, water, or any other fluid, the force of gravity causes it to accelerate downward. At the instant the object is dropped, it has no velocity relative to the fluid and, consequently, experiences no drag force. If air is the fluid, gravity then causes the object to accelerate at a rate of 9.8 m/sec^2 downward, because the net motive force acting on the object is the pull of gravity, that is, the weight of the object. As the object starts to fall, however, it gains velocity under the accelerating force of its weight, and as it moves through the air faster and faster, it experiences a greater and greater drag force directed upward against its downward motion. Such a situation applies to the sky diver in Figure E.1 (p. 281). This drag force increases as the square of the velocity; therefore, by the time the falling object has tripled its velocity, the drag force has increased nine times. The drag force is an external resistive force, whereas the object's weight is the external motive force. As long as the drag force against the object is less than the weight of the object, the object continues to gain downward velocity, that is, to accelerate in the direction of the net force downward. The velocity of the falling object soon becomes so great, however, that the drag force acting upward on it increases to a value equal to the weight of the object. When such a velocity is reached, the net external force acting on the falling object is equal to zero, and no further acceleration occurs. The velocity at which the upward drag force is equal to the weight of the falling object is called the **terminal velocity.** Terminal velocity is approached gradually, because as soon as the object starts to experience some upward drag force, the net force acting downward to accelerate it is decreased (its weight minus the resistive drag), and the gain in downward velocity is less than 9.8 m/sec². The greater the drag force becomes, the smaller the downward acceleration becomes, until, finally, the terminal velocity is reached, and the remaining descent is at this constant velocity.

The concept of terminal velocity is useful in understanding the differences in falling times of various projectiles, including the human body. The lighter the object, the sooner the terminal velocity is reached if the other drag-determining variables are the same (velocity, shape, area, fluid). One would expect, therefore, a feather badminton shuttlecock to reach a terminal velocity sooner than a plastic shuttle of slightly greater weight. Similarly, a light sky diver will reach a terminal velocity sooner than a heavy diver who has the same body configuration and the same surface area facing downward (facing the air flow). The terminal velocity of a sky diver also varies with the nature of the maneuvering being done. A sky diver is able to regulate the falling speed by changing the orientation of the body relative to the air flow. A horizontal spread-eagle position, for example, exposes the greatest surface area to the approaching air flow and causes the most upward drag force, whereas a vertical streamlined body position causes the least. Thus, the latter body position needs a greater downward velocity to generate enough drag force to counteract the body weight. The greater the surface area, the smaller the terminal velocity. When sky-divers work in groups, they may change the arrangement of body segments and positions to "wait" for or to overtake other members. Various arrangements of body segments also are used for maneuvers such as horizontal spins and somersaults. These maneuvers are accomplished by increasing drag on one area of the body and decreasing drag on another to create a torque on the body for rotational motion. For the final portion of descent, the diver opens the parachute to expose an extremely large surface area to the air flow so that the terminal velocity is reduced to only approximately 32 km/hr (20 mi/hr) for landing.

For some common projectiles used in sports, even if time is inadequate to reach a terminal velocity (due to insufficient height from which to fall), the reduced rate of velocity gain downward (due to the resisting drag force) will influence the object's time in the air. A badminton shuttlecock, for example, does not fall to the ground from a high clear shot as rapidly as might be expected because of its low mass and high drag characteristics. The change in horizontal shuttle velocity in a drive or smash shot is readily apparent to the observer on the sideline. The high velocity with which it leaves the racket is more suddenly reduced than its downward velocity because of the absence of any horizontal accelerating force acting on it. Such a horizontal velocity change should not be confused with the attaining of terminal velocity, which occurs when the motive force equals the resistive force. The velocity decrease in the horizontal direction will continue, due to the drag force, until the shuttle lands.

Terminal velocity can occur in any direction, not only vertically. The conditions for a body reaching a terminal velocity are merely those that specify linear equilibrium; that is, the motive forces must be equal to the resistive forces. In swimming, bicycling, boating, and other potentially high fluid-drag-force activities, therefore, a terminal velocity will be reached when the fluid-drag force and other resistive forces match the motive force being applied by the mover or machine. Note that for nonvertical terminal velocity to be reached, the moving object or body must be capable of generating continuous propulsive forces against the continuous resistive forces; otherwise, progressive deceleration due to a net resistive force will take place.

The Floater Volleyball Serve

A unique application of the effects of aerodynamic drag force on an object is illustrated by a floater serve in volleyball. The floater serve is identified by its lack of spin and its irregular pattern of deviations right and left during its flight. The large circumference of the ball with its relatively small mass makes it particularly susceptible to the influence of aerodynamic forces. A manufactured ball is never perfectly round; an air valve is located on one side of it, and the seams are arranged in a pentagonal pattern on the surface. A feasible explanation for the action of the floater serve is that since the surface texture and shape of the ball are so irregular, the presentation of a symmetrical surface on opposite sides of the ball at any one time is improbable. Because of the irregularity of the opposite surfaces as the ball travels forward, the air flow on opposite sides of the ball is irregular and turbulence is created asymmetrically on either side of the ball. The low-pressure zone created in the turbulent areas tends to shift around on the trailing surface of the ball, thus producing a drag force whose direction shifts accordingly and produces the erratic flight. For instance, if turbulence is induced earlier on the right side than on the left side due to the irregular surface on the right side, the pressure on the right side will be less than that on the left side, and the ball will be forced to the right slightly. This movement will cause a slightly different surface to be presented to the air flow. Depending on the surface irregularities on the new opposing sides, the ball will again move to the right, to the left, upward, or downward.

The Knuckleball Pitch

The aerodynamic forces on a good (erratic) knuckleball pitch are similar to those on a floater serve. A detailed experiment by Watts and Sawyer (1975) indicated that the best explanation for the midflight shifting of the baseball is that the ball spins very slowly and the location of the rough seams is changed relative to the flow. This causes a shifting of the turbulent wake from one side to the other and a consequent lateral force with each shift. Watts and Sawyer point out that too much spin would prevent these wake shifts and the resulting deflection; the most effective knuckleball rotates much less than one revolution on its way to the plate. To throw such a pitch, the ball is gripped with the first knuckles or fingernails so that little or no torque is applied to the ball at release to cause it to rotate.

The Golf Ball

The drag force on a driven golf ball would seem to be increased by the rough surface provided by the dimples. Actually, at the high speeds attained by a golf ball, the *total* drag *decreases* because of the dimples. This phenomenon is explained by the fact that dimpling, or roughening the otherwise smooth surface, causes the thin boundary layer to become turbulent earlier than it would on a smooth ball right next to the ball's surface. The result of this is a later separation of the boundary layer farther back on the rear portion of the ball. This creates a much smaller suction zone behind the ball, and the profile drag is drastically reduced. The skin friction drag is increased only slightly by the roughness. The *total* drag, profile and skin friction, is therefore less.

The Hammer Throw

Maximum distance of projection is the purpose of the hammer throw in track-and-field competitions. The diameter (and frontal area) of the metal sphere on the end of the handle and wire influences the drag force acting on it. Rule revisions effective in 1981 changed the minimum and maximum diameter of the hammer head from 102 mm and 120 mm to 110 mm and 130 mm. With the larger heads, the distances would be expected to decrease due to greater air resistance. Dapena and Teves (1982) studied the problem and found that the 110-mm-minimum-diameter head (compared to the 102 mm) could indeed reduce the distance by 0.20 m due to the increase in drag. Use of the 130-mm head could reduce world-class distances of about 80 m by 0.5 m. The minimum mass (7.260 kg) and a C_D of 0.4 for the different heads were used in Dapena and Teves's computer prediction as well as release velocities between 20 m/sec and 32 m/sec. Other factors enter into the distance achieved, but the influence of drag is a factor worth considering in selecting the implement.

The Shot Put

Air resistance is usually neglected in the shot put because of the large mass of the shot and the relatively slow release velocity. After calculating the retarding effect of drag for a world-class put, however, Lichtenberg and Wills (1978) found that with a given speed of release, a put could be reduced by over 5 cm by air resistance. The smaller the speed of release, the smaller the drag and the smaller the retardation. As in the hammer throw, the projected (frontal) area of the shot influences the drag.

Thus, in selecting a shot, the putter would want to select the smallest-diameter shot so as to reduce the area. Lichtenberg and Wills state that a world-class putter who uses the smallest permissible shot will have a "two inch advantage over a putter who uses the largest allowed shot, all other things being equal"(p. 548). Thus according to calculations, air resistance may play an important role in the shot put, just as it does in the hammer throw.

The Long Jump

Although air resistance certainly reduces the distance of a long jumper, the jumper can do little to decrease that drag and still perform the movements necessary for balance and landing position. Decreased air density, however, has been used in attempts to explain Bob Beamon's 1968 record-breaking long jump of 8.90 m (29 ft 2.5 in.) in Mexico City. Some believe the high altitude and thin air of Mexico City gave Beamon a gravitational and aerodynamic advantage, enabling him to take more than a half meter off the record. According to the analysts, the drag force was decreased due to the 24% lower density air compared with sea level air. Based on Beamon's .87-m^2 area facing the flow (A) and his C_D of 1.0, the analysts estimate that the thin air could not have allowed for an increase of more than 1% in Beamon's horizontal speed; this would have given him only 20 cm more distance. The other variable was g, the acceleration owing to gravity. (Recall that g decreases at higher altitudes.) The reduced g was estimated to have given Beamon an advantage of only one tenth of 1% over what would be expected at sea level—a negligible advantage. The conclusion of the analysts was that Beamon had simply "put it all together" for that one jump and that the aerodynamic and gravitational advantages were not totally responsible for his accomplishment (Phinizy 1968).

"Putting it all together" is one way of summarizing the conditions described by Hay (1975) as being responsible for the distance achieved: a very fast approach run (aided by a tail wind), a high angle of takeoff, and "almost perfect coordination of body segment motions at takeoff."

Running

Aerodynamic drag acting on runners has been estimated from studies on models by Shanebrook and Jaszczak (1976). Because of the constantly changing segment positions, the area and the C_D are also changing. Shanebrook and Jaszczak estimated the continuous average drag force on a world-class male sprinter traveling at 30 m/sec to be about 31 N (6–8 lb), depending on the size of the sprinter. Such a constant resistive force requires significant energy expenditure to overcome it. This total added energy requirement is not as detrimental in short duration sprints as in longer distances. In longer races the velocity is slower and the drag is less, but the time over which the drag acts is much greater. A runner at higher elevations will experience less drag, due to the lower air density factor, than a sea-level runner (given that they both have the same C_D, body area, and velocity).

The practice of "drafting" (running in the wake of leaders) by runners in groups gives the trailing runners less drag and thereby conserves their energy over a distance. Running in a tail wind decreases the relative air flow velocity past the runner and decreases the drag. A head wind increases the flow velocity and resulting drag. For a runner traveling around a track, a tail wind on one side would be a head wind on the other. The conditions would seem to cancel each other. Because of the squared effect of the relative flow velocity, however, the head wind causes much more hindrance than the tail wind provides help. For example, a runner traveling at 6 m/sec into a head wind of 2 m/sec on one side of the track experiences a relative flow of 8 m/sec. On the other side, the tail wind of 2 m/sec for the runner decreases the relative flow to 4 m/sec. The drag increases with the velocity squared, so it is four times as great in the head wind ($8^2 = 64$ and $4^2 = 16$) than in the tail wind. A side wind would be better on the straightaway. No wind is best.

Cycling

Aerodynamic drag as a factor in cycling is given much attention because the rider is able to modify it with body position changes. Because cycling speeds are much higher than running speeds, the drag is much greater. Faria and Cavanagh (1978) report some theoretical predictions that demonstrate the effect of body position on speed. Using the touring position (Figure 9.7a) as a reference for comparison, if the work effort were the same and the rider pedaled at 24.2 km/hr (15 mph), he could increase his speed by 1.13 km/hr (0.7 mph) if he assumed the low racing position (Figure 9.7b). An upright (bell and basket) position, shown in Figure 9.7c, would cause a decrease in speed of 0.97 km/hr (0.6 mph) compared to the touring position. Therefore, the speeds that could be maintained with the same work effort in the three different positions would be 23.2 km/hr (14.4 mph), upright; 24.2 km/hr (15 mph), touring; and 25.3 km/hr (15.7 mph), racing. To travel at the same speed as in the racing position, the work effort would have to be greater in the touring or upright position.

Other data presented by Faria and Cavanagh point out the differences in drag force at different speeds as well as the greatly increased work effort required for only small increases in speed. For example, cycling against a relative air velocity of 10 mph, the drag is 0.86 lb; however, at 20 mph the drag increases to 3.43 lb, and at 25 mph, the drag is 5.36 lb. The power (rate of work performed) required to pedal against 5.36 lb is 0.33 horsepower (HP), which is approximately equal to the *maximum* steady state exercise power output for average individuals working 10 min or more. For a nonexhausting 1-hr ride, 0.1 HP is realistic.

With the preceding data in mind, the importance of minimizing drag for greater speed with less effort is apparent.

In the four-person team pursuit, an Olympic cycling event, the lead rider cuts the wind, thereby forming a low pressure channel within which the other three can follow closely (Figure 9.8). The drag reduction is considerable, and members take turns at the lead to allow the former lead rider to recover.

a Touring position

b Racing position

Figure 9.7. Differences in frontal area of a cyclist riding in three different body positions.

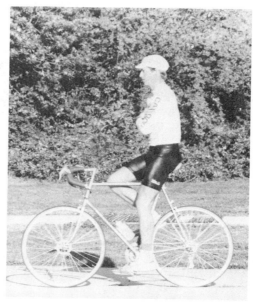

c Upright position

Figure 9.7
continued

Drag is reduced for the riders drafting in the low pressure zone formed by the lead rider. (Photo courtesy of the Bozeman Daily Chronicle, Bozeman, Montana, Cliff Willis, photographer.)

Figure 9.8.

Loose clothing also can increase the drag of a rider, and skin suits specialized for cycling are used by both competitors and recreational cyclists to minimize their drag.

In coasting downhill, differences in velocity may be observed for two riders of apparently the same frontal area and drag force. The rider with greater mass would be decelerated less than the lighter rider with the same drag force. If the two wished to remain together, however, the lighter rider could assume a racing position while the heavier rider remained upright.

Downhill Speed Skiing

In downhill ski racing, the purpose is to travel as fast as possible with control. Therefore, to try to *maximize* the terminal velocity would be to the skier's advantage. Figure 9.9 shows the resistive air drag and ski-snow friction that limit the skier's velocity increase caused by the motive force of gravity (the downhill component of the skier's weight force).

The variables that are under the control of the skier to change are:

1. **Ski-snow friction.** Reducing this friction is accomplished by proper ski surface preparation.
2. **Shape and area of the body facing the flow.** Reducing the area facing the flow and possible reduction of C_D are accomplished by crouching and by keeping the arms in close and the poles aligned parallel to the flow.

A third variable, which can be changed from one day to the next but not within a given run, is body mass. Recall that the deceleration of the body is inversely

Figure 9.9.   Aerodynamic drag force is the major source of resistance to a downhill skier's speed. Snow to ski friction is the second source of resistive force.

proportional to its mass. Gros (1979) found that a 75-kg skier with an added mass of only 1 kg could increase his terminal velocity from 30 m/sec to 30.2 m/sec. Such an increase would make a difference of about 0.5 sec over 2500 m. The greater mass effect means also that for the same body size, volume, and area, a higher density skier would have an advantage. (Recall the analogy of terminal velocity for a golf ball and a Ping-Pong ball dropped simultaneously.)

Downhill speeds of two skiers in egg-shaped and upright positions have been measured by Watanabe (1978), who found differences of over 1 m/sec even at slow speeds. Wind tunnel experiments using the same two skiers in a relative air speed of 10 m/sec showed a drag force averaging 1.6 kg for the egg-shaped position and an 8.0-kg drag for the upright posture. At an air speed of 30 m/sec, however, the body in the egg-shaped position encountered a drag of 11.8 kg (Watanabe 1981), over seven times the drag experienced at 10 m/sec for a threefold increase in speed. (The same subject may not have been used in both the 1978 and 1981 reports.)

Speed Skating

Wind tunnel experiments reported by Ingen Schenau (1982) reveal how speed skaters' C_D changes as the air velocity changes as well as how C_D changes with body build. Figure 9.10 shows a typical posture of a speed skater at one instant during a stride cycle.

Ingen Schenau found the trunk angle to be an important factor influencing speed. The smaller this angle (0 degrees = horizontal trunk), the smaller the C_D (and frontal area). As skating velocity increased from ranges below 12 m/sec to ranges above 16 to 17 m/sec, the C_D decreased. The results demonstrate that since C_D depends on flow velocity and body build and since drag force depends on the C_D, the drag encountered at different velocities is not easily predicted for all skaters as a group.

An almost horizontal trunk position is used in speed skating to reduce frontal area for minimum drag at high speeds.

Figure 9.10.

Triathlons

The triathlete should be particularly aware of the factors influencing fluid drag. In swimming, the fluid drag must be minimized to cover the distance with reasonable speed and without undue fatigue (see Chapter 10). In cycling, a body position that exposes minimal area to the approaching flow is crucial in maintaining speed without undue fatigue (see Figure 9.7b). If the cyclist were to coast on long downhill runs, a terminal velocity might be reached if the speed became great enough to generate a resistive drag force to match the motive force of gravity. In both cycling and running, the effect of "drafting" in the wake of another can save valuable energy by reducing the drag.

UNDERSTANDING AERODYNAMIC DRAG FORCE

1. Name three different skills or activities in which aerodynamic drag is significantly detrimental. If possible, how could the drag be minimized in each activity?

2. Tell which cyclist would encounter more resistive drag: (a) one riding at 20 km/hr into a head wind of 5 km/hr, or (b) one riding at 30 km/hr with a tail wind of 10 km/hr. Explain why.

3. How could the cyclists in question 2 minimize the air resistance without changing speed?

4. In what direction is air flowing past a ball at the instant it is projected at 45 degrees above the horizontal? What effect does the drag have on the ball's vertical and horizontal release velocity?

5. What is the direction of air flow past the ball in question 4 when it reaches the peak of its flight path? What is the effect of the drag force on the ball at the peak?

6. How does streamlining affect the air flow past a body so that drag is decreased?

7. Drop a racquetball and a badminton shuttle at the same time from a height of 2 ft and note which one lands first (the landings may be simultaneous). Repeat from heights of 4 ft, 6 ft, and 8 ft. Explain the results in terms of factors affecting acceleration due to gravity and aerodynamic drag force.

8. Repeat the experiment in question 7, using a tennis ball and a volleyball and then a small inflated balloon and a large inflated balloon. Explain the results.

9. Hold a piece of cardboard approximately 1 ft square, and move it quickly through a large arc so that it meets the air with its broadest surface. Repeat the movement with the edge of the cardboard meeting the air flow. Compare the difference in resistance felt. Repeat at different speeds and make comparisons of the resistance encountered.

SECTION 3

AERODYNAMIC LIFT FORCE

Whenever a body or object moves through air, it experiences an aerodynamic drag force opposing its motion. Under certain conditions a second type of force, **aerodynamic lift,** also will act on the object. Lift force, however, is always directed *perpendicular* to the oncoming flow, not parallel to the flow as is drag force.

Lift forces influence the trajectories of projectiles with particular shapes, such as the discus, javelin, and Frisbee, as well as ski jumpers and sky divers. The word *lift* suggests that all lift forces are directed upward; this is not necessarily true. *Horizontal lift* forces act to propel wind-dependent bodies such as sailboats and wind surfers. Fluid lift force is also used for propulsion by bodies whose parts move to produce lift force, such as propellers, canoe paddles, and human hands and feet in swimming.

In sport, lift force acts on bodies and objects whose *shapes* or positions influence the pattern of air flow around them. Lift force also acts on a projectile whose *spin* influences the pattern of air flow around it.

Lift Force Acting on Shapes and Surfaces

To understand how aerodynamic lift force is generated, air flow relative to the moving object must be examined. The nature of air flow past the airfoil (wing-shaped object) in Figure 9.11 demonstrates the concept of lift force. As air flows past the airfoil, it flows faster over the upper curved surface than underneath the object. Such a flow-velocity difference existing between opposite sides of an object causes a pressure difference between the two sides. The relationship between flow velocity and pressure is an inverse one, and is expressed in **Bernoulli's principle:**[3] *Where the flow velocity is fast, the pressure is low; where the flow velocity is slow, the pressure is high.* The existing pressure difference causes the wing shape to experience a force directed from the region of higher pressure (underneath) to the region of lower pressure (on top). Note that the direction of this lift force is *perpendicular to the flow direction* past the object, whereas the drag force is directed parallel to the flow direction.

---

3. Daniel Bernoulli (1700–1782) was a Swiss scientist who identified the inverse relationship between fluid flow velocity and pressure.

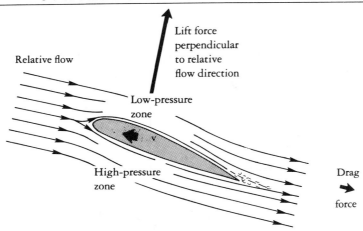

Figure 9.11. Aerodynamic lift force acting on an airfoil is not necessarily upward. Lift force is perpendicular to the relative air flow direction and is directed from the high-pressure zone toward the low-pressure zone. Drag force acts against the object's motion.

ANGLE OF ATTACK

If a body or projectile does not have the shape of a wing (curved on one side and flattened on the other), the difference in flow velocity (and pressure) may be achieved by tilting the object relative to the flow of air past it. The angle formed between the main plane (chord) of the object and the flow direction is called the **angle of attack.** Figure 9.12 shows a discus during flight, oriented so that its plane forms an angle of attack with the relative flow direction.

With no angle of attack, the flow velocity, and thus the pressure, is the same on both sides; all the air force is drag force, and no lift force is generated (Figure 9.13a). As the angle of attack increases, the difference in flow velocity and pressure on opposite sides also increases, and lift force is generated (Figure 9.13b). The increase in lift force will occur with a small angle of attack, but only up to a critical maximum angle, beyond which the lift force suddenly decreases and the drag force increases greatly due to extreme turbulence (Figure 9.13c).

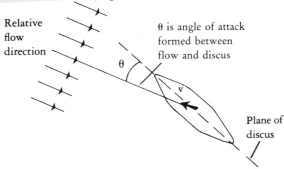

Figure 9.12. The angle of attack, θ, is formed between the main plane (chord) of the discus and the relative flow direction.

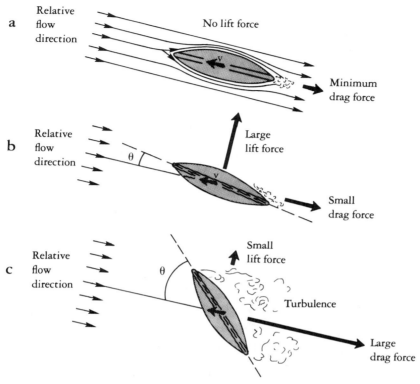

Changes in the angle of attack cause changes in the lift and drag forces acting on a discus. (a) Zero angle of attack produces minimum drag force but produces zero lift force. (b) A large lift force is produced with a small angle of attack and the drag force is increased slightly. (c) When the angle of attack increases beyond the optimum lift-producing angle, the lift force diminishes and the drag force increases greatly, leading to stall.

Figure 9.13.

This critical angle, approximately 45 degrees for the discus (Dyson 1977), is called the **stall angle.** The object stalls as a result of increasing drag force and the loss of lift force that held it up against gravity, and it falls toward the ground.

The best angle of attack for producing the greatest lift force with the least drag force depends on the shape of the object and the velocity of air flow. The angle of attack changes throughout the flight path as the relative air flow direction changes as the object ascends then descends.

ANGLE OF PROJECTION, LINE OF FLIGHT, AND ATTITUDE

The angle of attack is not the same as the angle of projection (release) of an implement. The **projection angle** is the angle of the center of gravity's (CG) in-stantaneous *velocity vector* at release, measured from the horizontal. After release, the instantaneous velocity of the CG at any instant depicts its line of flight (i.e., the instantaneous direction in which the object's CG is traveling through the air). The

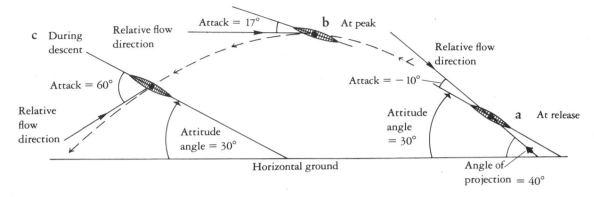

Figure 9.14. The angle of attack, angle of projection, and attitude angle of a discus at the instant of release (a), at the peak of its trajectory (b), and during its descending path (c).

attitude angle is the angle formed between the main plane of the object (chord) and the horizontal ground. It represents the orientation of the implement in space and is the angle that is most obvious to the observer. Figure 9.14 illustrates these angles for a discus at its release, at the peak of its trajectory, and during its descent. Note that the attack angle at release is slightly *negative*. This is desirable because the attack angle changes along the line of flight as the spinning discus tends to maintain its same *attitude* (spatial orientation), while the relative flow direction changes as the discus travels up and then down.

CENTER OF PRESSURE

The point at which the resultant (lift and drag) air force acts on a projectile is called the **center of pressure.** Its location on a projectile changes with the changing angle of attack. For example, the center of pressure is located approximately one third the distance back from the leading edge of a wing, and as the wing's angle of attack increases beyond the optimum angle, the center of pressure moves forward on the wing. If the center of pressure is in front of the object's CG, the projectile experiences a torque (called a *pitching* moment) that rotates the leading edge upward, resulting in stall. Figures 9.15a and b show the rotating effect on a discus and on a javelin thrown with too great an angle of attack.

The relative positions of the CG and the center of pressure are particularly important in throwing the javelin. Ideally, the javelin should be thrown at a projection angle and with an angle of attack that keep the center of pressure and the CG lined up vertically until prior to landing. The change in direction of air flow resulting from the descending flight path causes the center of pressure to move backward behind the CG. The resulting torque rotates the leading edge downward slightly and produces the desired landing position as shown in Figure 9.15c.

Just how much lift force can be produced depends on a number of factors. The

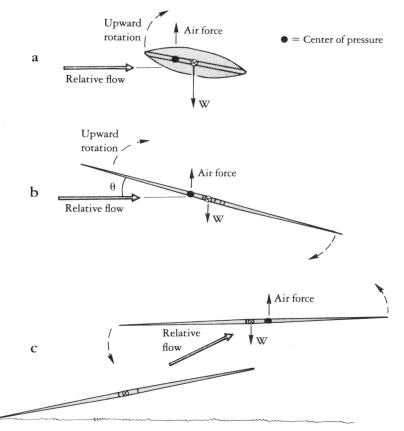

The torque produced on a discus and a javelin when the center of pressure and center of gravity do not coincide. The center of pressure is in front of the center of gravity in (a) and (b); the center of pressure is behind the center of gravity in (c), causing the tip to rotate downward prior to landing.

Figure 9.15.

variables that influence the lift force acting on a lift-producing surface are similar to those influencing drag. Their relationship is expressed by:

$$F_L = \frac{C_L \, A \, \rho \, v^2}{2}$$

Equation 9.2.

where F_L is lift force, C_L is coefficient of lift (an index of the shape's "lift producibility"), A is area of the body on which pressure acts, ρ (rho) is mass density of air, and v is relative flow velocity.

THE RELATIVE CONTRIBUTIONS OF THE FACTORS INFLUENCING LIFT

The Coefficient of Lift. The lift coefficient, C_L, is an object's index of how well it can create lift force in air flow. For example, a wing has a much greater C_L than a table. The C_L changes, however, as the angle of attack changes; the C_L of any lift-producing body or implement depends on the shape characteristics and angle of attack of that body or implement. For example, a javelin traveling at 80 ft/sec with a 20-degree attack angle has a C_L of 0.25 (Ganslen 1967). For a discus during flight, the C_L is about 1.2 at a 26-degree angle of attack; it decreases to $C_L = 0.1$ at a 2-degree attack angle, and to $C_L = 0.7$ (stall condition) at 35 degrees (Ganslen 1964). These figures for the discus demonstrate the importance of *optimizing* the angle of attack for maximum C_L throughout the line of flight.

Velocity.   As with drag force, lift force increases with the *square* of the flow velocity; that is, if the velocity is *doubled*, the lift force is *quadrupled*. For resistive drag force this relationship is a disadvantage. For lift force, which is usually desired, the squared effect is an advantage, however. Therefore, the faster a lift-producing shape moves through the air, the greater the lift force.

Area.   As with drag force, an increase in area of the body will increase the lift force. This area, however, is *not* the area facing the flow (frontal area), but is the surface area that is inclined to the flow to form the angle of attack. The dimensions of sport implements are usually specified so as to keep their areas constant; however, shapes and areas will vary among human beings seeking lift force in activities such as ski jumping.

Air Density.   With all the other factors kept the same, the more dense the fluid (air), the greater the lift force. The effects of lift force and the lower density air at high altitude, therefore, can diminish the lift force and distance achieved by the same discus or javelin throw performed at sea level (unless the *advantage* of decreased drag cancels the disadvantage of decreased lift).

LIFT/DRAG RATIO

We have seen how drag increases with the area of a body facing the flow and how the C_D changes with the object's position relative to the flow. Also, we have seen how tilting a lift-producing object gives it an angle of attack necessary for lift force. The situation that arises frequently is that such tilting for an angle of attack creates a greater frontal area for greater drag and also increases the C_D. The solution to the problem is to try to have the body or object move through the air so that the lift force is *maximized* and the drag force is *minimized*. The object will always have drag force acting against it, but not necessarily lift force. For each body, then, experimentation can determine the lift/drag ratio for different angles of attack. The value of this ratio is greatest when the angle of attack and lift force is the greatest it can be without overly increasing the drag force (i.e., when the lift force is *optimized*). As mentioned previously, the angle of attack of projected objects is constantly changing during their flight paths, and therefore, the lift/drag ratio changes also. The best attack angle at release is specific for each shape projected.

SECTION 4

EFFECTS OF LIFT ON PROJECTED OBJECTS AND THE BODY

The Discus Throw

Controlling the angle of projection of the discus's CG while at the same time controlling the release angle of attack and maximizing the release velocity requires practiced skill. The discus is relatively unstable in flight. It pitches upward throughout its flight, so the angle of attack at release must be small enough to prevent early stalling, which usually occurs when the relative flow forms an angle of attack between 26 and 29 degrees (Ganslen 1964). (When the stall occurs, the lift/drag ratio is low.) The upward pitching of the discus may be delayed if the spin imparted at release is sufficient to give it some **gyroscopic stability,** or the stability against changing its orientation in space. Measurements made from film indicate a common spin rate of about 8 revolutions per second (Ganslen 1964). Recall from Figure 9.14 that the angle of attack of a discus increases due to the line of flight, in addition to the natural pitching torque. Ganslen reports that a distance of 228 ft (69.5 m) can be achieved by releasing the discus at 80 ft/sec (24.4 m/sec) at a projection angle of 40 degrees and an angle of attack of −14 degrees. The *negative* angle of attack at release delays the increasing positive attack angle that develops through the flight, thereby delaying stall and producing more distance.

The Javelin

The angle and velocity of release and the angle of attack of a javelin greatly influence its behavior in flight and the distance achieved. The CG is located about 40% of the length from the tip, and if the center of pressure lies ahead of that point, a positive pitching moment (torque) is created. If the angle of attack is too great, it rises and then falls sharply as it stalls. According to Dyson (1977), the optimum angle of attack, therefore, should be zero with a release angle of about 30 degrees. Another option cited by Dyson is a release angle of 40 degrees with a −10-degree angle of attack. The latter is reported to be risky because of the tendency to make the angle of attack more toward zero in the difficult process of controlling the release. In general, the optimum release angle is below 35 degrees and decreases with faster release velocities. The angle of attack at release should be close to zero (Dyson 1977).

Ski Jumping

In ski jump takeoffs the relative positions of the CG and the center of pressure on the jumper's leaning body are important for success. A biomechanical analysis of ski jumping by international competitors showed that the jumper would lean far forward so that the torque produced by the reaction force at takeoff produced a forward rotation of the body around the CG. This forward rotation counteracted the lift and drag force acting on the center of pressure that otherwise would have caused a backward rotation of the jumper during flight (pitching moment). The use of these two opposing torques allowed the jumper to take advantage of the aerodynamic lift force on his trunk and he was kept in the air longer (Campbell 1980). Figure 9.16 shows how the torque can be exerted on the jumper by the lift and drag forces acting on the trunk inclined to the relative air flow.

A ski jumper who wants to increase the horizontal distance by staying in flight longer should maximize the upward lift force and minimize the backward drag force; that is, the lift/drag ratio should be maximized. As soon as the body orients itself to form an angle of attack to the flow to obtain lift force, the area facing the flow increases to increase the drag force. Experimentation, often in wind tunnels, provides information about the best angle of attack (and body position) so that the lift/drag ratio can be maximized. One such study on life-size models of ski jumpers revealed that the most effective arm position for increasing lift and decreasing drag is at the sides with the palms facing the relative flow (Watanabe 1981), as shown in Figure 9.16.

Figure 9.16.   Aerodynamic lift force acting on the ski jumper's body counters the forward rotation of the body and provides upward support for more time in the air.

Campbell reports that the top nine skiers in the 1979 pre-Olympic Games had a trunk angle of attack averaging 22 degrees at takeoff, compared to a 17.5-degree angle for U.S. ski jumpers (Campbell 1980). Greater lift force is generated at the angles of attack used by the top jumpers. These jumpers could use that lift force for upward lift and for providing a backward rotation torque that countered their greater forward rotation at takeoff.

SECTION 5

LIFT FORCE PRODUCED BY SPIN: THE MAGNUS EFFECT

Aerodynamic lift force was identified earlier in this chapter as a force acting perpendicular to the flow direction past a projectile that is inclined to the flow at some angle of attack so as to create the necessary pressure difference between two sides of the object. Aerodynamic lift force is also created on objects projected with spin. The lift force generated by a spinning object traveling through the air is responsible for the deviation in the flight path from that which is expected, such as in a curve ball. Such a lift force results from a pressure difference between opposite sides of the ball, and this pressure difference depends on the flow-velocity difference, in accordance with Bernoulli's principle. This particular mechanism by which lift force is generated on a spinning ball is called the **Magnus effect,** and the force of lift is sometimes referred to as the Magnus force.

To gain an understanding of this force, consider the motion of a ball thrown with top spin[4] in Figure 9.17. As the ball spins, it carries a thin layer of air, the boundary layer, around with it. The ball's forward linear motion creates an air flow *backward* past the ball. The boundary layer on the top surface of the ball is moving forward with the ball surface. This forward-moving top boundary layer encounters the backward flow of air past the ball. The mixing of these oppositely directed air layers results in decreased flow velocity relative to the top surface of the ball and a consequent increase in pressure. On the bottom side, the boundary layer is moving backward with the ball surface due to its spin, and the backward flow of air past the moving ball is reinforced, thus creating a lower pressure region on the bottom. The result is a net force on the ball directed downward from the region of higher pressure on the top to the lower-pressure region on the bottom. The effect of this force is to cause the ball to accelerate downward at a faster rate than it would be accelerated by gravity alone. The net force acting downward on the ball is its weight

---

4. Top spin may be defined as that spin during which the top surface of the ball moves in the same direction as the ball is traveling. In general, the types of spin are named according to the side that is moving in the same direction as the ball is traveling.

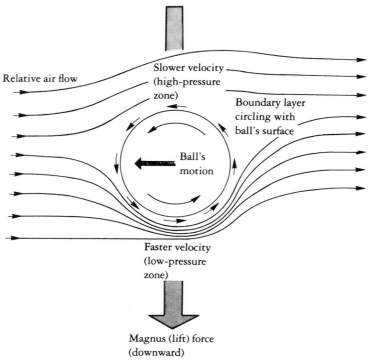

Relative air flow

Slower velocity
(high-pressure
zone)

Boundary layer
circling with
ball's surface

Ball's
motion

Faster velocity
(low-pressure
zone)

Magnus (lift) force
(downward)

Figure 9.17.   A ball thrown with top spin experiences a slower air-flow velocity, and thus higher pressure, on the top surface, and it experiences a faster air-flow velocity, and thus lower pressure, on the bottom surface. A downward-directed Magnus (lift) force is produced on the ball as a result of the pressure difference.

plus the downward force of lift. Thus, top-spinning balls are forced to the ground sooner, or faster, than balls with either no spin or other spin directions. For this reason, top spin is used for projecting balls that must fall within a court boundary, as in tennis, table tennis, and volleyball. Figure 9.18 shows a trajectory of a top-spinning tennis ball and the Magnus force acting perpendicular to the flow direction at three different points in the path.

In the initial part of the flight, the Magnus force has a downward component that supplements the force of gravity's decelerating effect. The Magnus force also has a small forward component that tends to augment the forward speed of the ball. (If the initial ascent were more vertically directed, this forward component of the Magnus force would be greater.) At the peak, where the air flow is horizontal past the ball, the Magnus force is entirely downward. During the descending portion of flight, the air flow is directed backward and upward past the ball, and the Magnus force is therefore downward and backward. This change in the direction of the air flow past the object is what causes the ball to take on a greater curve downward toward the end of its flight. The downward component continues to augment gravity's pull, accelerating the ball downward at a greater magnitude than would gravity itself. The backward component of this Magnus force resists the forward motion of

The Magnus force on a top-spinning ball has vertical and horizontal components that affect the flight of the ball differently at different points in its path. Note that the relative flow changes direction as the ball changes direction.

Figure 9.18.

the ball, causing it to fall at a steep angle of approach to the ground. It is readily apparent why top spin is an effective mechanism for restricting the horizontal distance of a ball that is traveling at a relatively high velocity: if the ball were projected with the desired horizontal velocity without top spin, it would travel too far before hitting the ground. Thus a tennis player able to impart top spin to the ball can project it with a higher velocity and still keep it in bounds. A top-spinning ball also strikes the ground at a more vertical angle than a nonspinning ball, due to the greater deviation downward near the end of its flight.

The Magnus effect is evident also on bottom-spinning balls and is illustrated in Figure 9.19a. The lift force is directed upward from the high-pressure region below the ball toward the low-pressure zone above. Bottom spin is used to project the ball for the purpose of maximizing the horizontal distance or time in the air or for accurate placement, as in golf, tennis, and soccer, because the upward Magnus force causes the ball to experience less acceleration downward due to gravity's pull than a ball with another type of spin. The net downward force experienced by a bottom-spinning ball is its weight minus the upward Magnus force. The trajectory of a bottom-spinning golf ball is shown as an example in Figure 9.19b (Daish 1972).

Note the changing direction of flow past the ball from the initial part of the trajectory to the final portion. Just as in the previous example (the top-spinning ball), the Magnus force acts perpendicular to the flow direction past the ball, but, in this case, the ball is spinning in the reverse direction. During the ascent, therefore, an upward component of force tends to elevate the ball and a backward component increases the resistance against its forward motion. Near the peak of the path, the air flow is horizontal, and the Magnus force is entirely upward. During the descent, the flow direction past the ball is such that the Magnus force is directed upward and forward. The upward component still resists the normal downward acceleration due to gravity, and the forward component acts to provide a forward propulsive force on the ball. The flight of a ball with backspin is prolonged due to the lift force. Therefore, the downward acceleration due to gravity acts over a greater period of time so that the ball strikes the ground at a more vertical angle than a ball with no spin, but not as steeply as a ball with top spin. The backspin on impact also tends to cause the ball to rebound at a steeper angle; this angle depends on the angle at

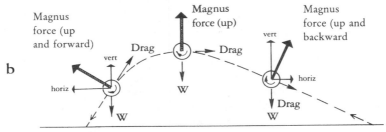

Figure 9.19. (a) An upward lift force on a ball projected with bottom spin. (b) The trajectory of a bottom-spinning golf ball experiencing a Magnus force at different points in its path. The vertical and horizontal components of the Magnus force change as the direction of the Magnus force changes.

which the ball strikes and the amount of skidding that occurs between the ball and rebound surface.

Because of the angle of the club face and the pattern of the swing, a golf ball hit for distance and hit straight usually has a backspin imparted to it. Consequently, the ball is lifted toward the tail end of its flight. Because the lift force acts to keep the ball in the air longer, there is less need to project it with a large vertical velocity component, which also serves to keep the ball in the air longer. Therefore, long shots such as drives should be projected with more horizontal velocity on club impact than shots with middle or short irons.

The Magnus effect on side-spinning, or diagonally spinning, balls accounts also for the lateral curving of the ball's path commonly seen in softball and baseball pitches. Figure 9.20a illustrates a top view of a ball thrown with right spin (i.e., the right side of the ball moves in the same direction in which the ball is traveling). A right spin causes the ball to deviate from a forward direction toward the left, that is, toward the low-pressure side of the ball.

A common observation is that a side-spinning ball "breaks" to the side late in its flight path. An explanation for this abrupt direction change is twofold. First, the direction of air flow past the ball in the latter part of its trajectory is not only backward but also backward and toward the right (Figure 9.20b), because the ball's direction has already changed to some degree to the left during the initial and middle portion of the trajectory due to the right spin. The Magnus force is therefore directed toward the left and backward. The leftward component continues to force the ball toward the left, whereas the backward component, which has developed due to the ball's changing direction, serves to delay the ball's progress and allows a greater time for the leftward component to act. Second, if the rate of ball spin is assumed not to slow appreciably during the time interval that it takes the ball to travel to the batter, the ball is being acted on by a *constant* Magnus force. The acceleration caused by a constant force applied for this length of time results in an appreciable deviation of the ball from a straight-line path. The actual distance the ball will travel toward the left increases as the *square* of the time the force is being applied (i.e., if the time of application is doubled, the ball will be moved four times the distance it moved in the previous time segment). Another way to picture this exaggerated curve is to liken the top view of the side-spinning ball's path to the second half of the parabolic flight path of a projectile seen from a side view; it is an *accelerated* change in direction. According to Daish (1972), a 5-oz baseball thrown with a side spin of 27 revolutions

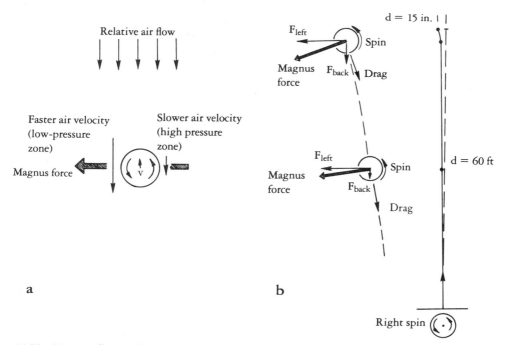

(a) The Magnus effect produces a lift force directed from right to left on a ball thrown with right spin.   **Figure 9.20.**
(b) A backward component of lift force develops as the ball continues to move toward the left and forward.

per second at 90 mph will experience a Magnus force of approximately 0.4 N. The resulting acceleration of the ball will be about one third the acceleration due to gravity (approximately 11 ft/sec^2). In the 0.5 sec it takes the ball to travel 60 ft to the plate, this Magnus force will cause a sideward movement of the ball of about 15 in.

The downward deviation from the force of gravity should not be overlooked, and the combined leftward and downward deviation results in a diagonally curving ball. In a diagonally spinning curve ball (which has side and top spin), a component of the Magnus force is directed downward, which augments the normal downward acceleration due to gravity, and it has a sideward component, which causes sideward displacement. The result of such a pitch is a "break" in the ball's path downward and to the side as it completes its path. From the point of view of the batter, who is expecting the ball to continue approaching in a straight line, the exaggerated displacement of the ball from a straight-line path seems even more exaggerated than it really is.

It is in just this way that the baseball pitcher produces various types of pitches (e.g., fastball, curve, slider). The release of the ball with a spin creates a lift force toward the side of the object with the higher-velocity air passing by it. Thus, when a ball is released with bottom spin, the velocity of the air passing on the underside of the ball is relatively slower than the velocity of air passing on the top side of the ball. The force of the lift from bottom spin on the ball prevents the ball from dropping as quickly from the downward force of gravity as it would without any spin at all.

To summarize, Magnus force is applied on any spinning ball whose axis of rotation (spin) is not in the same direction as the flow past the ball. The lift force on the ball is maximum when the spin axis is oriented at 90 degrees to the air-flow direction and decreases to zero as the axis becomes more in line with the flow direction. For example, a spiraling football, whose line of flight is parallel to its long axis, does not experience any Magnus force due to its spin. As its axis is angled to its line of flight (flow direction), however, a Magnus force is able to be generated.

Effects of the Magnus Force on Projectiles

GOLF BALL

In addition to the desirable bottom spin put on the ball for a primarily upward Magnus force, side spins may result from intentional or unintentional efforts. Just as the left lateral deflection of the baseball in Figure 9.20 was due to a right spin put on the ball, a similar but more dramatic sideward change in projection occurs in golf if the ball is hit in such a way that side spin is imparted to it. Since the golf ball is smaller, lighter in weight, travels faster and farther, and spins faster than a baseball, the hook, slice, fade, and draw are created under far more impressive conditions. These paths are shown in Figure 9.21.

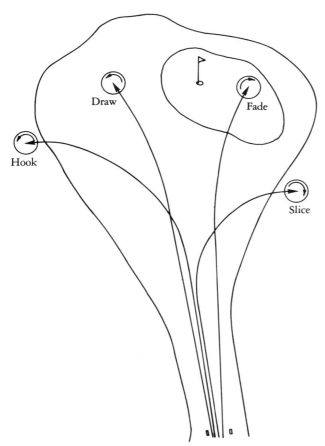

Draw

Fade

Hook

Slice

The flight paths in golf known as **Figure 9.21.** the hook, the slice, the fade, and the draw.

THE CURVEBALL

For years, the curveball in baseball has been the object of controversy as to whether it breaks suddenly before it reaches the batter. The batter perceives the top-spinning ball as approaching in a fairly straight line and then dropping quite abruptly about 10 ft from the plate. Aerodynamic analyses of actual top-spinning curveballs reveal that the illusion of the sudden break downward is caused by the same forces that are shown in Figure 9.18. Due to the constant pull of gravity, which accelerates the ball downward from the time of release, and due to the downward Magnus force acting at the same time, the descent occurs more rapidly during the latter part of the 0.4-sec flight. In addition, the backward component of the Magnus force serves to slow the forward speed during the last part of the curve, thereby allowing more time for the ball to descend before it reaches the batter. In the 0.4 sec a pitched ball is in the air, a nonspinning ball drops 0.15 m (6 in.) due to gravity alone, but a top-spinning pitch drops 0.43 m (17 in.) (Allman 1982).

The deflection of a baseball due to the Magnus force is reported to be directly proportional to the square of the ball speed up to 45 m/sec (150 ft/sec), with spins up to 1800 revolutions per minute (RPM) (Briggs 1959). Measurements made on pitched balls indicate that a baseball rotates approximately 7 to 16 turns on its way to the plate if released at 100 ft/sec. Thus, the maximum spinning rate would be about 1600 RPM. These values can be considered target conditions for throwing curveballs.

THE DISCUS

The Magnus effect has some influence on a spinning discus as well as on a spinning ball. As the discus is thrown by a right-handed athlete, it is given a clockwise spin when viewed from the top so that the left side of the discus is seen to move forward and the right side to move backward, relative to the direction the discus is traveling.

Figure 9.22 shows the underside of a discus near the middle portion of its flight path, encountering the air flow at a small angle of attack. The axis of spin is near 90 degrees to the backward flow direction. The left side of the discus carries with it a forward-moving boundary layer that reduces the flow velocity of air past the left side. The right side of the discus carries a backward-moving layer that augments the air-flow velocity on the right side. Again, according to Bernoulli's principle, the pressure will be greater *under* the discus than on top. Due to the velocity differences between the right and left undersides, however, the center of pressure is shifted toward the left side. This tends to cause a rolling of the discus so that the right side lowers and the left side rises. This rolling tendency is not observed, due to the angular momentum of the spinning discus, which gives it a certain amount of gyroscopic stability (i.e., stability against a change in the orientation of the axis of spin of the discus) (Dyson 1977).

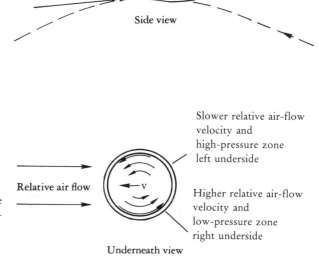

Figure 9.22. Differences in pressure between the right and left underside of the spinning discus tend to cause it to roll.

UNDERSTANDING AERODYNAMIC LIFT FORCE
AND THE MAGNUS EFFECT

1. Explain the difference between a javelin's angle of release and attitude angle.

2. Identify three different skills in which putting backspin on a ball would be desirable. Do the same for top spin.

3. For balls thrown with different types of spin, discuss the effects of spin direction (axis of rotation), spin velocity, and velocity of projection on the spatial path of the ball. Discuss different kinds of baseball pitches relative to the same factors.

4. Assemble a straw, a spool of thread, a card, and a thumbtack, as shown in Figure 9.23. (A piece of corrugated cardboard, thick enough to hold the end of the straw, can be substituted for the spool of thread.) Place the card against the spool so that the tack prevents side-slipping of the card on the spool. While holding the card to the spool, blow through the straw, and then release the card while continuing to blow. The card stays on the spool while you are blowing and drops off when you stop blowing. Explain this in terms of Bernoulli's principle.

5. Fold a piece of paper into the shape of an airplane and project it at various angles of release and at different speeds. For each, visualize the angle of attack of the wing to air flow and the center of pressure location in relation to the CG location (in

While holding card to spool, blow through straw, then release card while continuing to blow

Flow

Flow

Flow

3 × 5 Card with thumbtack only to prevent card from sliding on bottom of spool

Figure 9.23

front or behind it). Where are the relative locations of the center of pressure and CG if the plane noses upward? if the plane noses downward? if the plane glides linearly forward? Explain.

6. Throw a large whiffle ball, Nerf ball, or Trak ball as fast as you can with back spin. Visualize the air flow past it caused by its forward linear motion, and visualize also the boundary layer of air on the spinning ball's surface. Have an observer note, from a distant side view, any deviations from a parabolic trajectory. Explain in terms of Bernoulli's principle and the Magnus effect.

7. Repeat the steps in question 6, imparting top spin instead of back spin.

8. Repeat the steps in question 6 with right and left spin. The observer must take a distant front view to best note the deviations in flight-path direction.

REFERENCES
SUGGESTED READINGS

Allman, W. F. "Pitching: The Untold Physics of the Curve Ball." *Science 82* 2 (10) (1982): 32–39.

Barkla, H. M., and Auchterlonie, L. J. "The Magnus or Robins Effect on Rotating Spheres." *Journal of Fluid Mechanics* 47 (3) (1971): 437–47.

Briggs, L. "Effect of Spin and Speed on Lateral Deflection (Curve) of a Baseball, and the Magnus Effect for Smooth Spheres." *American Journal of Physics* 27 (1959): 589–96.

Campbell, K. R. "Comparative Analysis of Take-off Techniques for Olympic Ski Jumpers." In *Biomechanics: Proceedings of the Biomechanics Symposium,* ed. J. M. Cooper and B. Haven, 92–100. Indiana State Board of Health, 1980.

Chapman, S. "Catching a Baseball." *American Journal of Physics* 36 (10) (1968): 868–70.

Cunningham, J., and Dowell, L. "The Effect of Air Resistance on Three Types of Football Trajectories." *Research Quarterly* 47 (4) (1976): 852–54.

Daish, C. B. *Learn Science Through Ball Games.* New York: Sterling Publishing Co., 1972.

Dapena, J., and Teves, M. A. "Influence of the Diameter of the Hammer Head on the Distance of a Hammer Throw." *Research Quarterly for Exercise and Sport* 53 (1) (1982): 78–81.

Dillman, C. J., et al. "Biomechanical Analysis of U.S. Ski-Jumpers." In *Abstracts of the International Congress of Sports Sciences,* ed. J. Terauds and H. Gros, 95. San Diego, Calif.: Academic Publishers, 1979.

Dyson, G. *The Mechanics of Athletics.* New York: Holmes & Meier Publishers, 1977.

Faria, I. E., and Cavanagh, P. R. *The Physiology and Biomechanics of Cycling.* New York: John Wiley & Sons, 1978.

Ganslen, R. V. "Aerodynamic and Mechanical Forces in Discus Flight." *Athletic Journal,* April 1964, 50–51, 68, 88–89.

———. "Javelin Aerodynamics." *Track Technique,* December 1967, 940–42.

Gros, H. "Basic Mechanics and Aerodynamics Applied to Skiing." In *Science in Skiing, Skating, and Hockey: Proceedings of International Congress of Sport Sciences,* ed. J. Terauds and H. Gros, 9–21. San Diego, Calif.: Academic Publishers, 1979.

Gross, A. C., Kyle, C. R., and Malewicki, D. J. "The Aerodynamics of Human-Powered Land Vehicles." *Scientific American* 249 (6) (1983): 142–52.

Hay, J. G. "Biomechanical Aspects of Jumping." In *Exercise and Sports Sciences Reviews,* ed. J. H. Wilmore and J. F. Keogh, 135–61. New York: Academic Press, 1975.

Hopper, B. J. *The Mechanics of Human Movement.* New York: American Elsevier Publishing Co., Inc., 1973.

Ingen Schenau, G. J. van. "The Influence of Air Friction in Speed Skating." *Journal of Biomechanics* 6 (15) (1982): 449–58.

Kreighbaum, E. F., and Hunt, W. A. "Relative Factors Influencing Pitched Baseballs." In *Biomechanics of Sports and Kinanthropometry: Proceedings of the International Congress of Physical Activity Sciences,* ed. F. Landry and W. A. R. Orban, 227–36. Miami: Symposia Specialists, Inc., 1978.

Lichtenberg, D. B., and Wills, J. G. "Maximizing the Range of the Shot Put." *American Journal of Physics* 46 (5) (1978): 546–49.

Marino, G. W. "Selected Mechanical Factors Associated with Acceleration in Ice Skating." *Research Quarterly for Exercise and Sport* 54 (3) (1983): 234–38.

Phinizy, C. "The Unbelievable Moment." *Sports Illustrated,* 26 December 1968, 53–61.

Raine, A. E. "Aerodynamics of Skiing." *Science Journal* 6 (1970): 26–30.

Roberson, J. A., and Crowe, C. *Engineering Fluid Mechanics.* Boston: Houghton-Mifflin, 1975.

Selin, C. "An Analysis of the Aerodynamics of Pitched Baseballs." *Research Quarterly* 30 (2) (1959): 232–40.

Shanebrook, J. R., and Jaszczak, R. D. "Aerodynamic Drag Analysis of Runners." *Medicine and Science in Sports* 8 (1) (1976): 43–45.

Shanebrook, J. R. "Aerodynamics of the Human Body." In *Biomechanics IV: Proceedings of the Fourth International Seminar on Biomechanics,* ed. R. C. Nelson and C. A. Morehouse, 567–71. Baltimore: University Park Press, 1974.

Shapiro, A. *Shape and Flow: The Fluid Dynamics of Drag.* Garden City, N.Y.: Doubleday, 1961.

Soong, Tsai-Chen. "The Dynamics of Javelin Throw." *Journal of Applied Mechanics* 42E (2) (1975): 257–62.

Terauds, J. "A Comparative Analysis of the Aerodynamic and Ballistic Characteristics of Competition Javelins." In *Biomechanics IV: Proceedings of the Fourth International Seminar on Biomechanics,* ed. R. C. Nelson and C. A. Morehouse, 180–83. Baltimore: University Park Press, 1974.

Tricker, R. A. R., and Tricker, B. J. K. *The Science of Human Movement.* New York: American Elsevier Publishing Co., 1967.

Walker, J. "Boomerangs: How to Make Them and Also How They Fly." *Scientific American* 240 (5) (1979): 162–72.

Watanabe, K. "Aerodynamic Investigation of Arm Position During the Flight Phase in Ski Jumping." In *Biomechanics VIII-B: Proceedings of the Eighth International Congress of Biomechanics,* ed. H. Matsui and K. Kobayashi, 856–60. Champaign, Ill.: Human Kinetics Publishers, 1983.

———. "Running Speed of Skiing in Relation to Posture." In *Biomechanics of Sports and Kinanthropometry,* ed. F. Landry and W. A. R. Orban, 203–10. Miami: Symposia Specialists, Inc., 1978.

———. "Skiing Research in Japan." *Medicine and Science in Sports and Exercise* 13 (3) (1981): 202–09.

Watts, R., and Sawyer, E. "Aerodynamics of a Knuckleball." *American Journal of Physics* 43 (1975): 960–63.

CHAPTER 10

APPLICATION OF HYDRODYNAMICS IN SWIMMING

In aquatic activities forces must be dealt with that normally are not encountered during movement on land. In land activities, body movements are facilitated because the mover feels at home in the environment and takes a number of things for granted. We learn from infancy to expect the firm support exerted by the ground or other surface supporting the body. We learn to predict what surfaces are slippery, sticky, or rough and to know that removal of support results in a fall. In a similar manner, the more an individual is able to explore movement in the water and develop a set of expectations to depend on, the greater is the sense of feeling at home in the water. As a result, developing skills for managing the body in water becomes easier. Increasing numbers of infants and young children are exposed early in life to moving and playing in water, and they learn to expect different sensations and to predict the results of different body movements. A common practice, unfortunately, is the attempt to teach formal swimming strokes to those who have not yet developed a set of expectations that come from experience in moving the body and controlling breathing responses while in the water. The swimming teacher or coach is most qualified to expedite learning and to refine swimming skills if he or she (1) appreciates the importance of the learner developing a "feel for the water," and (2) understands how forces are generated during movements in a water environment.

The discussion in this chapter focuses on some important aspects of moving in water: (1) the nature of water as a medium and forces affecting a person's ability to float and assume different floating positions (gravity and buoyancy), (2) forces produced by the body and its parts moving in the water (drag and lift), and the roles these forces play in resisting or propelling a person in swimming and swimming-related skills, and (3) factors that determine swimming efficiency and speed.

BUOYANCY AND FLOTATION

The nature of water as a force-producing fluid must be considered for understanding how water provides support for the body as well as how it reacts to movements during aquatic activities.

Static Water Pressure

Water pressure increases with depth, and its effects on the body should be understood and appreciated by the teacher or coach of swimming or diving. *Pressure* is defined as the amount of force a mass exerts against a surface divided by the area of the surface, that is, force per unit area ($p = F/A$). Air pressure on an object is greater at sea level (10.14 N/cm^2 or 14.7 lb/in.^{2}) than at higher elevations because of the weight of the atmosphere above it. Similarly, as one descends in water, the pressure on an object increases due to the weight of the water above it. Such an increase in pressure is felt by a descending diver as the increased water pressure compresses the volume of air in the middle ear and sinus cavities. Equalizing the pressure by "popping" the ears relieves the discomfort produced at a given depth and pressure. As the diver swims deeper, the pressure continues to increase; thus, the internal and external pressures must be equalized once again. Neoprene wet suits used by scuba divers contain many tiny air cells for insulation. These are compressed as the diver descends, and the suit become more dense as it loses volume. Consequently, during descent to greater depths, some inflation (expansion) of a flotation device (vest) may be necessary to compensate for this. Figure 10.1 shows the increase in water pressure with depth. A swimmer without compressible clothing is not compressed with depth; the body volume can be changed only by lung volume changes with breathing.

Weight Density of Water

Water is attracted by the pull of earth's gravitational force and therefore has weight. As a fluid, however, water must be contained in some vessel to weigh a given amount.

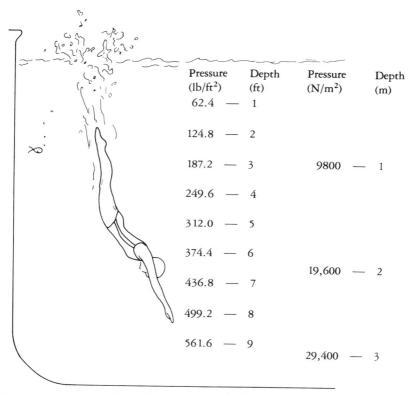

Pressure (lb/ft²)	Depth (ft)	Pressure (N/m²)	Depth (m)
62.4 —	1		
124.8 —	2		
187.2 —	3	9800 —	1
249.6 —	4		
312.0 —	5		
374.4 —	6		
		19,600 —	2
436.8 —	7		
499.2 —	8		
561.6 —	9		
		29,400 —	3

The water pressure experienced by a submerged swimmer increases with depth. The pressure at any level is exerted equally in all directions.

Figure 10.1.

Because the weight of water depends on the volume chosen, its weight is expressed in terms of a given volume such as Newtons per liter (N/l) or pounds per cubic foot (lb/ft³). When expressed in such measurement units, this quantity is called the *weight density* of water. Although *density* is the term used to express mass per unit volume, thinking in terms of water's weight per unit volume is more practical for us since weight is directly proportional to mass.

The weight density of fresh water is 9.9 N/l (62.4 lb/ft³), whereas the weight density of salt water is closer to 10.2 N/l (64 lb/ft³). The reason for the difference is that salt water due to its dissolved salt content has more mass than the equivalent measure of fresh water, and thus has more weight per unit volume. The density of water does not change with depth. Water, as a liquid fluid, is practically incompressible, so that a greater mass of water cannot be squeezed into a given volume to increase its density. The human body, being mostly water, is also incompressible. Air, however, which is a gaseous fluid, can be compressed; for instance, sea-level air is more dense than air at high elevations because it is compressed by the weight of the atmosphere above it. Air also can be mechanically compressed into tanks for

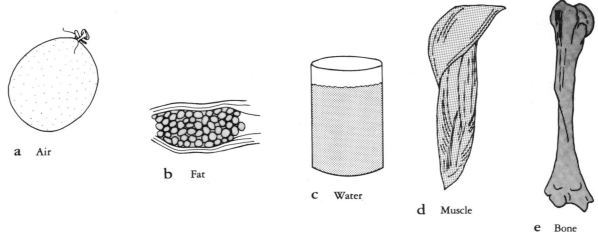

Figure 10.2.   The relative densities of air, fat, water, muscle, and bone are indicated by the degrees of shading.

use in scuba diving. The concept of density is of major importance among factors affecting floating skills. Figure 10.2 illustrates the relative densities of air, fat, water, muscle, and bone. Air is the least dense; bone is the most dense. Adipose (fat) tissue is the least dense of body tissues.

Floating Ability of the Human Body

The rule that determines whether a body will float or sink is called **Archimedes' principle,** named after the ancient Greek scholar who is credited with identifying the concept. The principle states that *a body that is partially or totally immersed in a fluid will experience an upward buoyant force that is equal to the weight of the volume of fluid displaced by that body.* Another way of expressing this concept is the following: If the weight density of an immersed body is less than or equal to the weight density of water, the body will float; if its weight density is greater, it will sink.

When we speak of a person's weight density, we are speaking of average total body density, for the different body tissues, segments, and sections throughout the body vary in density. The skeletal framework is approximately 50% more dense than water, muscular tissue is only slightly more dense than water, and fat tissue is slightly less dense than water.

The person in Figure 10.3a has the same weight density as water, meaning that her body weighs the same as water with the same volume. Therefore, when she is submerged, she displaces a volume of water that weighs the same as her body. She will float in the water with no part of her body above the surface. If she were placed 1 m under the surface and then released, she would remain suspended there because

a   Neutrally buoyant—
body density is
equal to water density

b   Positively buoyant—
body density is less
than water density

c   Negatively buoyant—
body density is
greater than
water density

Three bodies whose densities differ will experience different degrees of support from the water.   **Figure 10.3.**

her weight force downward would be equal to the buoyant force upward. She would be called *neutrally buoyant*. Since zero net force is acting on her, she will neither sink nor rise. If she were lifted partially above the surface and then released, she would displace less water and the buoyant force would decrease. Consequently, her downward weight force would be greater than the upward buoyant force (weight of the water displaced), and a net downward weight force would exist, causing her to sink. She would descend into the water until her body displaces a volume of water whose weight is equal to her weight. Her downward momentum, however, might cause her to come to rest at some level below the surface.

Figure 10.3b shows a person whose higher fat content gives her a body density less than that of water. Assume that her body volume is the same as the floater in Figure 10.3a. With the same volume but less weight in that volume, she need not be completely immersed to float; that is, she need only displace a volume of water that weighs the same as her body. She can do that and still have part of her volume above the surface. Such a floater is said to be *positively buoyant*. If she is completely submerged, the net upward force (buoyant force minus weight) causes her to rise until the buoyant force is equal to her weight.

Figure 10.3c shows a person immersed whose body composition is lean and has a higher percentage of muscle and dense bone. Her body volume is the same as each of our previous two floaters, but being made up of dense tissues, her weight density is greater than that of water. Consequently, her body volume cannot displace a volume of water great enough to obtain a buoyant force matching her weight; she will continue to sink due to the net downward force acting on her (weight minus buoyant force). She is called *negatively buoyant*.

TYPES OF FLOATERS

In the foregoing examples, we assumed that all three swimmers had equal body volumes but different weights, and therefore, different *weight densities*. Changing body density by changing the body's volume with breath control is possible, however.

Without air in the body to take up some of the body volume, the human body would have an average density greater than that of water. The thorax, however, can change its density through the breathing process. The volume of the thorax increases upon inspiration by about 4 l (0.15 ft), whereas the weight of the inspired air is negligible, only about 0.04 N (.01 lb). Control of air volume in the lungs, therefore, influences average body density and is a key factor in floating ability. A person with a body composition that allows floating when the lungs are inflated but who sinks upon exhalation is called a *conditional floater;* that is, whether the body floats or sinks depends on the expansion volume of the lungs and thorax. A conditional floater, floating with the face up, can prolong the buoyant phase by establishing a breathing pattern in which a large volume of air is in the lungs most of the time: inhale quickly and deeply, hold the breath for a few seconds, exhale quickly, and inhale again to repeat the pattern. With such a breathing pattern, the period of time during which the body's density is being increased (exhalation) is quite brief and is not a sufficient time for the face to sink below the surface before the next inhalation is made. Performance of such a maneuver demonstrates how the average body density may be manipulated, but in actual practice, slight supportive movements of the arms or legs or both are usually employed for additional upward support.

Figure 10.4a shows an 800-N (180-lb) floater with a weight density of 9.5 N/l in the jellyfish float position, which is used to test floating ability. He holds his breath after a full inspiration (the volume of his body is now 84 l), and, upon total immersion in water, he displaces 832 N of water (84 l × 9.9 N/l). His body, therefore, experiences a net upward force of 32 N (832 N upward − 800 N downward), which raises his body so that some of his body is above the surface (Figure 10.4b). As part of the body rises above the surface, less water is displaced, and the buoyant force decreases until the weight of the water displaced is equal to 800 N (180 lb). The density of this particular swimmer with an inhalation is less than water density. In Figure 10.4c when he exhales, his volume decreases by approximately 4 l and his average body density is 10 N/l. His body density is now greater than water density. The upward buoyant force exerted by the water displaced is 792 N (80 l × 9.9 N/l), thus yielding a net force downward of 8 N, which acts to sink the swimmer.

Some people float no matter whether the lungs are inflated. These people are the *true floaters*—those whose average body density remains less than that of water even after exhalation. The body composition of such individuals typically includes a greater percentage of low-density tissues, such as adipose. Girls and women have a greater percentage of body fat on the average than do boys and men. This characteristic is an average one, however, and some women do have a lower percentage of body fat than many men. Obesity is a definite advantage in floating, whereas a person with a low percentage of fat or well-developed musculature is more likely to have difficulty floating without using supportive movements.

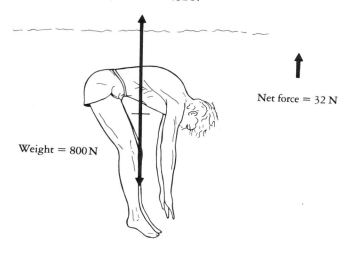

Buoyant force = 832 N

Net force = 32 N

Weight = 800 N

a Completely immersed, holding a full inspiration. Buoyant force is greater than body weight, and body will rise

Buoyant force = 800 N

Weight = 800 N

b Body stops rising when buoyant force equals body weight

Buoyant force = 792 N

Net force = 8 N

Weight force = 800 N

c On exhalation, body volume decreases, volume of water displaced decreases, and buoyant force decreases

Body density and flotation ability changes with thorax volume changes that accompany inhalation and exhalation.

Figure 10.4.

Although usually rare, the body density of an individual may be so great that even the chest expansion volume with inhalation is not sufficient to reduce the average body density enough for unassisted floating. Such a person is called a *sinker*. Blacks frequently experience greater difficulty in floating than whites because of greater average body density, which is primarily due to higher-density bone tissue. Buoyancy characteristics of any given individual, however, should not be presupposed on the basis of population norms; individual variability often accounts for the exception to the rule. Some persons who claim to be sinkers are really conditional floaters who may lack information about adjusting body density with breath control.

In a normal population, most individuals—male and female—are *conditional* floaters, some are true floaters, and few are true sinkers. The jellyfish float position (Figure 10.4) is the most convenient test for classifying an individual according to the floating type. If a person can float in this test position, then that person is able to float in other positions as well; other floating positions are discussed in the next section. For learners to understand their buoyancy characteristics is helpful, and for the teacher to identify buoyancy problems in beginning and intermediate swimmers is imperative.

Different Floating Positions of the Human Body

The average density of a person's body determines its floating *ability*. The orientation of the body, or floating *position* in the water, is determined by where the buoyant force is applied on the body (**center of buoyancy**) and where the weight force is applied on the body (**center of gravity [CG]**). Recall that the CG is that point about which all the mass of the body is balanced and is the point through which gravity exerts its resultant downward force on the body. Recall also that as body segments are repositioned, the location of the CG shifts in the direction of segment shift. The center of buoyancy of a body can be defined as the center of the volume of the body displacing the water.[1]

Look at the sealed can in Figure 10.5a, the CG of which is at the center of its volume. If the can is submerged (Figure 10.5b), it displaces a volume of water whose CG is also at its center. The center of buoyancy of the can is, therefore, in the same location as its CG. If, however, the bottom of the can is filled with cement or another dense material, the can's CG shifts to the position shown in Figure 10.5c. When this can is then submerged, it displaces the same volume of water as before, but now the CG of the can and the CG of the displaced water do not coincide (Figure 10.5d). Similarly, when the human body is submerged, its CG location is not the same as that of the displaced volume of water (Figure 10.5e and f). The CG of the displaced volume of water is the center of buoyancy of the person's body and is the point through which the water exerts its upward buoyant force on the body. The center

---

1. The center of buoyancy may be technically defined as the point that is the CG of a volume of water equal to the volume of the submerged body and having an identical shape.

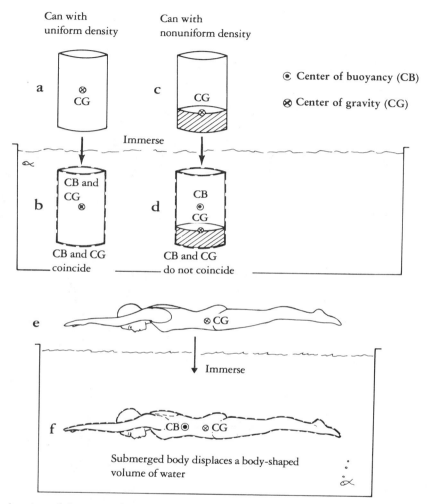

Relative locations of the center of gravity and center of buoyancy of two cans and a human body.

Figure 10.5.

of buoyancy normally is closer to the chest region (the region of greater water-displacement volume), and the CG is closer to the pelvic region. As Figure 10.6a shows, a person initially in a supine position experiences a downward force equal to the body weight acting through the body's CG.

The person also experiences an upward force equal to the weight of the displaced water acting through the center of buoyancy. The *line of action of gravity's force* and the *line of action of the buoyant force* are parallel, but the two forces act in opposite directions. If the lines of force do not coincide—that is, if the CG and center of buoyancy are not in vertical alignment—the forces cause the body to rotate. This rotation of the body occurs in a sagittal plane about a mediolateral axis located

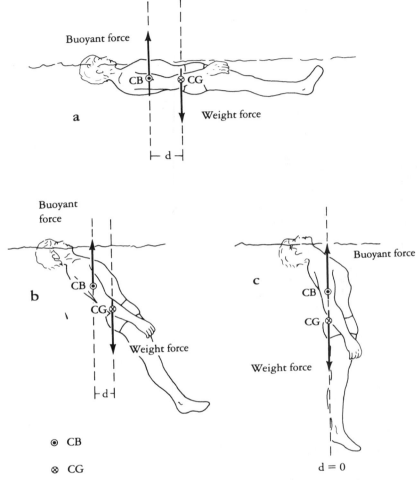

Figure 10.6. The torque exerted by forces of gravity and buoyancy (a and b) causes the body to rotate to a position of equilibrium (c).

through the center of buoyancy, thereby causing the lower body to rotate downward (Figure 10.6b). A tendency also exists for the upper body to rotate upward; however, the elevation of the upper body above the surface is precluded by the required maintenance of water displacement for upward support. The main effect, therefore, is the downward rotation of the lower body to a position in which the CG is beneath (in vertical alignment with) the center of buoyancy. When this occurs, the line of gravity and the line of buoyancy are *colinear;* no further turning action exists, and the body is in equilibrium (Figure 10.6c).

The greater the horizontal distance between the CG and the center of buoyancy, the greater the resulting torque (turning force) and the more the lower body rotates before the forces are colinear. Also, if the lower body tends to sink (rotate downward) fast, the legs' downward momentum may be enough to pull the floater's face underwater, giving the immediate impression to a conditional floater that he or she is a sinker. A nearly vertical body orientation is usually the equilibrium position for conditional floaters who are located toward the "sinker end of the buoyancy continuum." The true floater, however, tends to remain in more of a horizontal position, because the body's CG and center of buoyancy tend to be closer together. Accumulation of adipose tissue in the abdomen or pelvic region displaces more water there and shifts the center of buoyancy toward the pelvis, bringing it closer to the CG.

Floating positions can be altered by changing the positions of body segments to shift the CG closer to the body's center of buoyancy so that the torque and resulting body rotation are decreased. When body segments are repositioned, the CG has a greater change in location than does the center of buoyancy. Three common segmental adjustments are shown in Figure 10.7.

The CG does not necessarily have to be beneath the center of buoyancy for a zero torque situation; it can lie above it. This is the case for an inverted body position, but it is unstable. In this situation, all that is needed for imbalance to occur is a slight rotation in a vertical plane to create a horizontal distance between the CG and center of buoyancy, thus creating an upsetting torque. Such an inverted position is used frequently in synchronized swimming skills, and balancing movements of the hands must continually be made to maintain the vertical body position. The body is in a stable float when the CG is lower than the center of buoyancy.

The body can be caused to rotate also in its transverse plane under the action of the two vertical forces as well as in its sagittal plane. Such a "log roll" can be executed on purpose as a stunt, or it can be caused by unintentional lateral flexion of the vertebral column (as is often done by a tense beginner) or by otherwise shifting the CG location laterally. Because rearrangement of body parts caused by tension can influence body position in the water, it should not be overlooked as a possible source of position problems in swimming skills.

UNDERSTANDING BUOYANCY AND FLOTATION

1. What determines the magnitude of the buoyant force acting on a person in the water?

2. What happens to the average weight density of the body when a full inspiration is made? Why?

3. State what characterizes a conditional floater.

4. Who is more likely to float: a lean female weighing 668 N (150 lb) or an obese male weighing 801 N (180 lb)? Why?

Figure 10.7.   The repositioning of body segments causes adjustments in floating positions so that the center of gravity and center of buoyancy come to lie on the same vertical line.

5. Describe what is meant by center of buoyancy.

6. Describe the force situation that causes a person's legs to drop when attempting to float in a horizontal position on the back.

7. In the swimming pool, working with a partner or in a small group, perform the following experiments and discuss the results.

    a. Stand in chest-deep water, inhale deeply, hold the breath, and slide your hands down the front of your legs toward your feet; reverse the movement to regain the upright position.

b. Determine whether you are a floater, conditional floater, or a sinker by using the criteria discussed in the text.

c. Assume a prone float position and explain the changes in body orientation that occur as a result of (1) changing segmental positions, and (2) lateral flexion of the lumbar vertebrae.

d. Assume a prone float position with the neck fully flexed to "tuck the chin." Note the level of the body as it floats. Repeat the prone float position while hyperextending the neck; note the level of the body as it responds to this head position. Explain.

e. Attempt to use the body positions in Figure 10.6 and 10.7 to float. Explore other segmental arrangements, holding each for several seconds, and explain why your body moved to the position it did for a static float.

SECTION 2

RESISTANCE AND PROPULSION

In swimming races, the primary mechanical purpose is to move the body over a prescribed distance as fast as possible. Recreationally, the purpose may be merely to interact with the environment. For competitive synchronized swimmers, the primary mechanical purpose is to move or position the body and its segments in a prescribed pattern to achieve an ideal or model performance. For any of these purposes, hydrodynamic principles govern the performance outcome.

A body's state of motion—whether it is still, accelerating or decelerating, or traveling at a constant velocity—depends on the forces acting on that body. Identifying the forces that influence the motion of a body in water is more difficult than identifying the forces acting on a body during land activities. On land, external forces affecting body motion are more easily visualized and measured than are the forces created by the "invisible" medium of water. A swimmer uses water forces for support and for propulsion, and water forces serve also to retard the swimmer's progress. The forces of buoyancy and gravity as they affect the support of the body were discussed in the previous section. Two remaining categories of force that influence a swimmer's performance are (1) those forces that retard the swimmer's progress through the water (resistive forces) and (2) those forces produced by the swimmer's movements used for propulsion of the body (propulsive, or motive, forces). When a body moves through water, the types of force created are the same as when a body or object moves through the air, that is, the forces of **drag** and **lift.** Water is a more dense medium than air, however, and consequently generates greater drag and lift forces in response to body movements. The nature of these forces is presented here with specific application to resistance and propulsion in swimming. The similarity of hydrodynamics and aerodynamics (Chapter 9) will be readily apparent.

SECTION 3

RESISTIVE FORCES IN SWIMMING SKILLS

An understanding of the forces that resist movement of the body or segments in the water is a major factor contributing to one's ability to help others learn. Any time the body or its segments move through water the motions are resisted by the water. The direction of the resistive force is always exactly opposite to the direction of body or segment motion, and is called *hydrodynamic* drag force. The present section focuses on the kinds of drag force in swimming and discusses ways in which drag force on the body can be decreased to improve the performance.

Hydrodynamic Drag Forces

The *relative motion* between a body and a surrounding fluid determines the forces generated. This relative motion may be pictured by having the body remain still within a moving stream or by having the fluid remain still with the body moving through it. Although in swimming, the body or body part is moving through still water, we will picture the relative motion situation as one in which water is flowing past the body or part, since the nature of the flow patterns created is more easily observed.

The three types of drag force that resist the motion of a body or segment are: (1) **skin friction,** or *surface drag,* (2) **profile drag,** also known as *pressure drag* or *form drag,* and (3) **wave drag.** Surface and profile drag were considered in the discussion of a body's movement through air; wave drag was not, because the object or body was entirely surrounded by air and no surface existed on which to form waves. As we shall see, wave drag is an important source of hydrodynamic drag because it is created whenever a body is moving at or near the surface of the water, that is, at the air-water interface.

SKIN FRICTION

Skin friction, or surface drag, is a resistive force caused by the water flowing backward along the surface of a body that is moving forward through the water. When compared with the other types of drag encountered in swimming, it is the *least* significant. Skin friction is analogous to the friction of two solid objects sliding past each other. In this case, however, one of the "objects" is water, which—since it is a fluid—deforms, or flows in parallel layers at different speeds along the boundaries of the object moving through it.

If the fluid through which the body is moving were one of higher *viscosity* (thicker and more resistant to flowing), the skin friction would be much greater. Because the magnitude of skin friction increases with the viscosity of the fluid, it is also called *viscous drag.* Skin friction is less along smooth-textured surfaces and is proportional to the amount of *surface area* of the body along which the water flows (parallel and opposite to the direction of body motion). If the skin or surface conditions are extremely rough (e.g., a loose-fitting swimsuit or an inordinate amount of hair on the head or body), then alteration of these conditions may produce a significant reduction in surface drag. The smoother the skin and swimsuit and the smaller the surface area of the body oriented parallel to the flow, the smaller this source of resistance. Changes in competitive swimsuit materials have been based on the desirability of reducing this skin friction, as has the practice of shaving the body, legs, and head if the amount of hair is excessive. If the body is not exceptionally hairy, shaving may serve more of a psychological than a mechanical purpose. Swimmers who shave their bodies often report that tactile sensitivity to the water is enhanced. Also conceivable is the assertion that the swimmer's tactile sensitivity is reduced, rather than enhanced, due to the removal of hairs, which, when moved, serve to stimulate receptors beneath the skin. In either case, the sensation is different with and without hair. Whether the arms should be shaved to decrease friction is open to question, since the direction of the frictional force on the arms during most of their underwater movements would tend not to resist forward body motion but might actually contribute to the propulsive effort. The significance of this factor is probably negligible in light of the fact that skin friction is so small compared to profile and wave drag. Efforts would be better spent addressing the reduction of the significant drag forces.

PROFILE DRAG

A significant type of resistance in swimming is that created by the swimmer's body "spreading the water apart" as it moves through the water. The amount of this *profile drag* depends on the size, shape, and speed of the swimmer as well as the orientation of the body relative to the flow. The relationship of the factors determining profile drag is:

$$F_D = \frac{C_D\, A\, \rho\, v^2}{2}$$

Equation 10.1

where F_D is profile drag, A is area, ρ (rho) is water density, v is relative flow velocity, and C_D is coefficient of drag.

Profile drag is so named because the amount of drag is influenced by the profile of the body facing the approaching flow, that is, the area (A) of the body viewed as a silhouette from the front. As the body moves forward through the water, the water is "spread apart" to allow the body to pass through. The greater the area of the body and its parts that face the flow (i.e., the area you would see as a silhouette if you were the flow), the greater the drag. High-pressure zones are created on the leading surfaces of the body, and low-pressure zones are formed at the trailing surfaces where the water is moving faster and is turbulent, or full of eddies, thus creating a suction effect. The result is a net force backward against the forward-moving body and its parts. Because the drag is caused by a difference in pressure from the leading side of the body to the trailing side, it is often referred to as *pressure drag*.

Figure 10.8a illustrates the relative flow past a moving body and the pressure zones caused by the different flow characteristics. As the velocity of the body

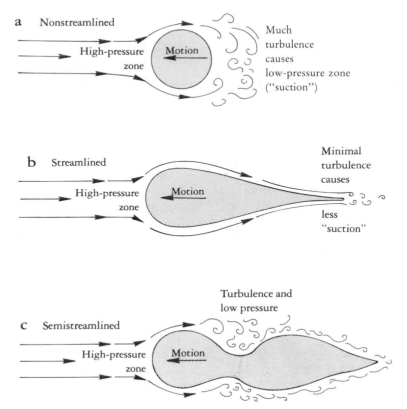

Figure 10.8.   A high-pressure zone is formed at the leading surface of a body moving through the water, and a low pressure zone is created on the trailing surfaces. The more abrupt the contour changes are, the greater the turbulence and low pressure in those areas.

increases (thereby increasing the velocity of water flow relative to the body), the pressure differential between the high- and low-pressure zones increases. The squared effect of increasing the velocity means that if the velocity of the body were tripled, the profile drag would increase by approximately nine times.

Profile drag is known also as *form drag* because the shape of the body influences the way the water flows past it. The body's shape that is facing the flow determines its coefficient of drag (C_D), an index of how nonstreamlined it is relative to the flow. The influence on drag of the actual human body shape, however, may be noticed only when the body is held in a given configuration, as in a glide from a wall push-off. Under such a condition a more streamlined body shape may be beneficial. If the shape of the body is more streamlined as shown in Figure 10.8b (i.e., if the body tapers gradually from shoulders to hips to feet), the profile (form) drag will be less than it would be for a body with irregular contours (Figure 10.8c). Contours in the body cause water to flow at varying speeds around these shapes, and turbulence is created on the downstream sides, thus producing low-pressure, or suction, zones. Note that a *streamlined* shape means that the shape encountering the water flow allows the water to flow smoothly around and past the body without much turbulence. For example, a streamlined fish body would *not* be a streamlined shape if it were exposed to the flow belly-forward in a vertical orientation.

The streamlined shape, therefore, is a function of the swimmer's body build, but the shape and area exposed directly to the flow by virtue of body position are factors that influence the drag coefficient. The influence of actual body build or shape on drag, however, seems to be limited to a moving body that is *not* changing shape (Clarys 1978). Clarys reported *no* relationship between shape and drag force measured *during* swimming. In addition, he found that the drag during swimming is twice as great as the drag on the body being towed in a prone position. Swimming movements, therefore, produce changes in the relative flow patterns that account for very large drag forces. Although we would not stop the swimming movements to decrease the drag, we can control the body position influences. If the body is maintained in a horizontal position during a swimming stroke rather than one in which the legs are lower than the upper body, the drag coefficient and thus the profile drag can be effectively reduced, and the swimmer need not work as intensely to maintain a given speed.

Figure 10.9 shows the greater drag on an *unstreamlined* body *position* during a wall push-off glide compared with the more *streamlined position*. In Figure 10.9a, the swimmer is holding his head up, facing forward rather than downward toward the pool bottom. Such a push-off glide head position is common in competitive swimming practice for two reasons: (1) to see what is approaching is safer in crowded lanes, and (2) the water pressure holds the swimmer's goggles on the face. In the more streamlined head position (Figure 10.9b), the flow of water past the face frequently wipes the goggles off the eyes. Unfortunately, swimmers in practice usually avoid the streamlined "goggle wiper-offer" head position, and the high head position used in practice carries over into competition even when goggles are not worn.

Another way in which drag can be reduced during swimming is by trying to minimize drag-producing aspects of limb recovery movements. How the limbs are brought forward under water during recovery, or preparatory, movements in swimming strokes determines the amount of resulting profile drag acting on them. Figure 10.10a and b illustrates the underwater recovery movements of a breaststroker's arms and legs. Not only do these movements expose more *area* to the backward flow, but moving the limbs forward through the water *faster* than the body (trunk) is moving increases the resistance even more. The higher relative speed between the water and limbs on recovery is the source of drag that makes the deceleration of the body so evident in the breaststroke. For example, if the body is moving forward at 1.5 m/sec and the arms are moving forward relative to the body at 1 m/sec, the water flows backward past the body at 1.5 m/sec but past the arms at 2.5 m/sec. Such an increase in flow velocity past the arms increases the drag greatly, especially if the arms are in less streamlined positions during their forward movement.

In the back crawl stroke, a common tendency among swimmers is to lift the head upright above the surface of the water to look toward the feet (Figure 10.10c). This movement leads to some body sinking (recall the effect of displacing less water for support). The arm movements are then used for the purpose of keeping the head

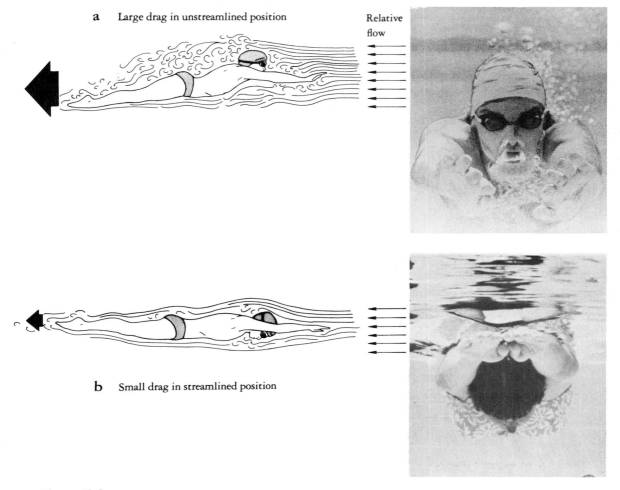

a   Large drag in unstreamlined position

Relative
flow

b   Small drag in streamlined position

Figure 10.9.   Although a person may have a streamlined body shape, the body position relative to the flow actually determines how streamlined the body is.

and upper body at the surface, that is, pushing downward toward the pool bottom. The result is usually the assumption of a slight pike, or sitting position, in the water, which increases the area exposed to the flow, undoubtedly increases the drag coefficient, and therefore increases the profile drag.

WAVE DRAG

Wave drag is the resistive force caused by any body moving along, through, or near the surface of the water and forming waves, or elevating some water in front of the leading parts. The force applied by the body or its segments to the water to form these bow waves generates an opposite reaction force applied by the waves

Profile drag on swimmers moving through the water is increased with increases in area facing the flow and in the relative velocity of limbs to water.

Figure 10.10.

against the body. The force of these waves increases with the speed of the swimmer, just as the wave against a bridge piling exerts more force as the speed of flow increases in a river. Even if a moving object or body is completely submerged but is still within several feet of the surface, wave drag is not entirely eliminated as a source of resistance. Although at low speeds wave drag is not significant, it may be the most important source of resistance at the faster swimming speeds seen in competition. As the speed of the swimmer increases, the size of the bow waves increases and the "wall" of water presses backward against the swimmer. Bow waves are formed against the leading surface of any parts of the body that move through the air-water interface. The formation of bow waves also increases with speed and with up-and-down movements of the shoulders or head found in many strokes. Consequently, more resistance is experienced by swimmers moving fast in a stroke, than swimmers moving more slowly.

Figure 10.11 shows wave drag acting against swimmers as they move forward through the air-water interface. A large bow wave can be seen in front of the face and chest of a breaststroker as the breath is taken during the arm pull. As the body is raised out of the water, exposing the surface of the shoulders to the air-water interface, more wave drag is produced to decelerate the body. This additional drag is apparently compensated for *if* greater propulsion is gained by body movements that put the trunk in this position. Up-and-down motion, even if the body is not traveling horizontally through the water, creates waves itself, and is therefore a drag-producing aspect of any stroke. Wave drag may be the factor that sets a limit on maximum swimming speed.

The bow wave formed around the head is used by skilled swimmers to facilitate breathing in the front crawl stroke. As the head is turned to the side, it need not be rotated very far for the mouth to be exposed to air, for behind the bow wave is a depression below the natural surface of the water, sometimes called a "pocket of air" (Figure 10.11d). If the swimmer is moving slowly and the bow wave by the head is small, this pocket barely exists and the head must be turned through a greater range of motion (ROM) for the mouth to be out of the water. This extra rotation may lead to a greater amount of rolling of the trunk in its transverse plane and subsequent changes in arm-stroke patterns. Many other instances of unnecessary resistance in swimming may be identified if the causes of drag are understood, for the principles may be generalized for any swimming skill.

In summary, the total body drag is the resistive force that must be matched by the propulsive forces if the swimmer is to maintain a constant speed. The sum of the three types of drag constitutes the total drag force acting on a body in water. Profile and wave drag as sources of resistance in swimming are so large when compared to skin friction drag that the latter usually may be considered negligible. If the swimmer is to increase speed, the propulsive forces must be greater than the total body drag. If this drag is greater than the propulsive forces, the body will decelerate. Although often not noticeable to an observer, a swimmer's body is changing speed continually during every stoke cycle due to the interplay of changing resistive and propulsive forces. The next section describes how propulsive forces are generated in swimming.

UNDERSTANDING RESISTANCE IN SWIMMING SKILLS

1. Name and describe each of the three types of drag force that can resist the forward body motion of a swimmer.

2. Why would a "sinker" sink faster in a vertical position than in a horizontal position?

a

c

b

d

Wave drag acts against the body parts traveling forward through the surface of the water in the breaststroke (a), backstroke (b), butterfly (c), and freestyle (d).

Figure 10.11.

3. In the swimming pool, perform these experiments and discuss the results:

   a. Lie along the edge of the pool and move your hand and forearm horizontally through the water at different speeds and with different hand shapes and positions relative to the water. Compare the forces you feel.

   b. Compare the speeds with which you can walk or run a given distance through hip-deep, waist-deep, and chest-deep water.

   c. Select a swimming stroke you can perform reasonably well. Swim a given distance with the head out of the water and count the number of strokes taken. Compare the number of strokes necessary to swim at the same speed with the head supported in the water. Explain why the numbers might be different.

   d. Force a kickboard under water to a depth of one width vertically on its edge and then in a horizontal broadside position. Compare and explain the relative difficulty of the two ways.

   e. Perform an underwater push-off glide with the same force of leg extension for a number of different arm, hand, and head positions. Explain the differences in resistance felt.

SECTION 4

PROPULSIVE FORCES IN SWIMMING SKILLS

Most explanations of swimming skills describe limb movements as they take place relative to the swimmer's body rather than how the limbs are moved through the water. The popularity of this viewpoint undoubtedly stems from the swimmer's perception of what the arms and legs *seem* to be doing in a stroke as well as what the limbs *appear* to be doing from the observer's viewpoint. As a result of such kinesthetic and visual impressions, the true nature of the propulsive hydrodynamic forces operating on the limbs usually remains obscure.

To identify these forces, we must examine the swimmer's limb movements relative to the water, not relative to the body. To do this we must focus on how the water flows past the moving part, just as we did in analyzing resistive forces, for this relative flow is responsible for the forces used for propulsion. Two types of propulsive force can be produced by the swimmer's body or limbs or both moving through water: **propulsive drag force** and **propulsive lift force**.

Propulsive Drag Force

Drag force was explained previously in terms of how it acts as resistance against the forward motion of the swimmer's body and its segments. The direction of drag force was pointed out to be always opposite to the direction of body or segment movement. Therefore, if a segment moves to the left, the drag force acts against it to the right; if the segment moves forward, drag acts backward. When drag force acts on *backward-moving* body segments, however, it is called **propulsive drag force** because it acts forward in the desired direction of body travel. Such a propulsive (forward-directed) drag force results from paddling or pushing movements of the hands back through the water, and it acts to resist the backward hand motion. As was shown for resistive drag acting on a body, a high-pressure zone is created on the leading surface (the palm) and a low-pressure zone is created on the back side of the hand. The faster the hand movement or the larger the hand area or both, the greater the forward drag force against the hand's backward movement. Using hand-arm movements that generate propulsive drag as the main source for propulsion, such as in straight-back arm pulls, is inefficient, and the reasons for this inefficiency are discussed in a following section. Figure 10.12a and b show how a drag force is produced on the hand if it moves backward through the water so that the flow is directed against the palm.

Propulsive Lift Force

In swimming activities, relative water flow past the moving body segments can provide not only drag force but also a second kind of force that plays an important propulsive function—**hydrodynamic lift force.** Although the term *lift* implies that it is an upward force, *it is not always upward.*

Horizontal lift force is used for propulsion by bodies whose blade-shaped parts move in a special way to produce horizontal lift force, just as propeller blades do.

To understand how hydrodynamic lift force can be a horizontal propulsive force in swimming, the water flow *relative to the moving body segment* must be examined. The nature of water flow past the hand (a wing-shaped object) in Figure 10.13a is responsible for the lift force that is caused by the hand's movement. The hand and forearm can be likened to a propeller blade. If the hand is positioned at an angle to the direction of flow, the water flowing past the moving hand flows faster over one side than the other. Such a flow-velocity difference existing between opposite sides of the hand causes a pressure difference between the two sides. *Bernoulli's principle*[2] expresses the relationship between flow velocity and pressure: *Across a surface where the flow velocity is faster, a low pressure zone is created, and across a surface where the flow velocity is slower, a high pressure zone is created.* The existing pressure difference causes the hand to experience a lift force directed from the region of higher pressure to the region of lower pressure (see Figure 9.11, p. 402). Note that the direction of lift force is *perpendicular* to the flow direction past the hand (and therefore perpendicular to the *path* of the hand), whereas drag force is directed parallel to the flow direction (opposite the hand motion). Therefore, lift and drag are always perpendicular to each other.

---

2. Daniel Bernoulli (1700–1782) was a Swiss scientist who identified the inverse relationship between fluid flow velocity and pressure.

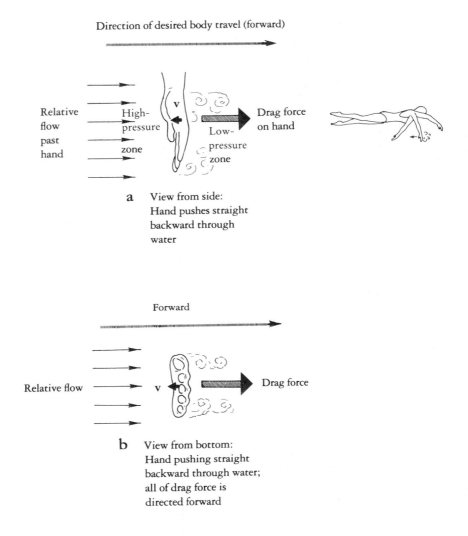

Figure 10.12.   Propulsive drag force can be generated by paddling the hand backward through the water so that the water flow past the hand and drag force is forward.

Lift force is not generated on all bodies moving through fluids; drag force is. For the flow patterns formed around the moving segment to generate lift force, the segment must have a shape and orientation to the flow that permits the formation of lift, such as an airplane wing (airfoil) or hydrofoils; the forelimbs ("wings") of a sea turtle, seal, or penguin; the pectoral fins and tails of fish, whales, and dolphins; and the human hands and feet. Lift force, directed perpendicular to the path of the "slicing" hand, is felt by the swimmer as pressure on the palm when the slightly tilted hand blades through the water, as in the sculling movements used in syn-

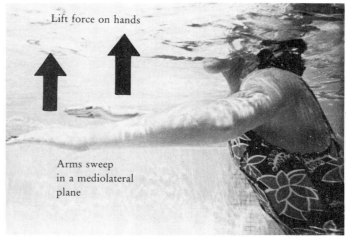

b

Slicing the hand through the water medially and laterally simulates a propeller to form a lift force from the hand. (a) A forward lift force. (b) An upward lift force.

Figure 10.13.

a

chronized swimming skills and treading water. Figure 10.14 shows the hydrofoil-shaped hand oriented at an angle relative to the flow direction so that lift force can be generated. Such tilting of the hand is described by its **angle of attack,** which is the angle formed between the direction of flow and the *chord* (main plane) of the hand.

Each hand experiences lift force due to a low-pressure zone across its knuckle side and a high-pressure zones on its palm. In this example the lift force is upward. Such lift-force producing movements of the hands are used effectively for treading water without the use of the legs. The hands are used as hydrofoils, and the arms sweep horizontally so that broad blading, or sculling, movements are made to provide what might be pictured as a "layer of force" for the hands to use for supporting the weight of the head above the surface. note that the hand's angle of attack must be small so that the palms are facing *primarily* toward the feet as they scull. Note also that the hand experiences drag force opposing its horizontal movements. This horizontal drag force contributes nothing to head support (it has no vertical component). To generate supporting lift force, the flow must encounter the palm side of the hand as it blades medially and laterally, so the lateral sweep demands more forearm pronation than does the medial sweep to produce the proper angle of attack for the

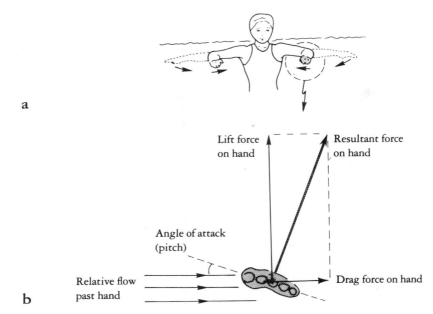

Figure 10.14.   Lift force is directed upward to support the weight of the head out of the water. (b) A close-up view of the blading hand in (a).

hand. The upward lift force geenerated on the palms serves as a "handle" as the shoulder adductor muscles contract to keep the head supported above the surface. Thus, the body and arms are kept in their same relative position.

Although our attention is focused on lift force, note that a drag force also acts on the hand. If the angle of attack becomes too large, the drag force increases, and the flow becomes so turbulent that lift force is lost. Obtaining an angle of attack that provides for maximum lift force for a given hand shape and blading speed is possible. Skilled swimmers may be able to feel for and sense the best angle as it changes throughout the stroke.

Note that the hands are not used as *pushing paddles*. They do not push downward through the water toward the feet seeking an upward *drag* force for support. Rather, the hands continue to blade inward and outward in a horizontal section, or layer, of water close to the surface. In this example, upward lift force is being used as supportive lift force; it is directed perpendicular to the path of the sideward-sweeping hands to counter the tendency of the body to sink downward. The magnitude of lift force that can be produced depends on the following factors:

Equation 10.2
$$F_L = \frac{C_L A \rho v^2}{2}$$

where F_L is hydrodynamic lift force, C_L is coefficient of lift of the hand and forearm for a given angle of attack, ρ (rho) is water density, v is flow velocity, and A is area of the palm-forearm unit.

Note that lift force, like drag, is a function of speed; the faster the hand moves through the water at an effective angle of attack, the greater the lift force. *The direction of a lift force is not necessarily upward* as it was in the treading water example. The direction of lift force is always perpendicular to the flow direction and to the drag force. Therefore, if the hand is positioned in a vertical plane with the fingers pointing downward and is then moved sideward through the water, the lift force will be directed horizontally *forward*. Visualization of the proper direction in which lift force is generated is important for understanding the role of lift force in propulsive movements in swimming. For example, if the treader in Figure 10.14 were to lie in a prone position in the water and then perform the same sculling movements ("canoe" scull), the lift force on the hands would be directed *horizontally* (Figure 10.15). This lift force would have a large forward component, since the palms would be facing primarily backward as they moved through the broad sculling motions in a vertical plane. The horizontal lift force would cause the whole body to move horizontally forward through the water rather than cause a vertically directed force to support the head weight, as was done during treading water.

The hand shape as well as its size can affect the magnitudes of both lift and drag force generated. The effects of finger separations and angles of attack were studied in a wind tunnel investigation by Remmonds and Bartlett (1981). They found that maximum lift force of about 12 N (2.7 lb) was obtained by the hand with the fingers closed and at an angle of attack of about 50 degrees. The thumb was positioned in the same plane of the hand. With some small space between the thumb and hand, such a thumb position was proposed to aid the flow conditions necessary for better lift force. Maximum drag force occurred on the hand oriented perpendicular to the flow direction. The drag force varied from 11.9 N (2.7 lb) with the fingers closed to 13.4 N (3 lb) with the fingers fully spread. Both lift and drag forces were measured at a flow velocity of 2.1 m/sec. At slower velocities, the forces were less. These values are important for determining how the hand should be used to best propel the body forward. The two methods for moving the hand-arm unit through the water are basically the *paddling* method (using drag force) and the *sculling* method (using primarily lift force). These methods are described and evaluated in the next section.

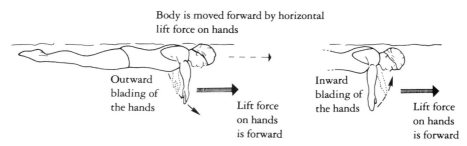

Lift force is directed forward on the hands as they scull to propel the body forward through the water. **Figure 10.15.**

Movements That Propel the Body

To understand the swimming "mechanism" responsible for effective propulsion of the body, we must recognize that the swimmer is a segmented body and that the purpose of the arm and leg movements is to move the swimmer's whole body unit forward. Because of the differences between the arms and legs in shape, joint structures, and movement capabilities, movements of these body segments are considered separately.

PROPULSIVE MOVEMENTS BY THE HANDS AND ARMS

To move the body forward most effectively we would want a situation in which the hand could grip an underwater "handle" that would not move backward as the hand pulled on it. With the hand pressing back against such a handle, the contraction of the shoulder extensor muscles would then cause the body to move forward toward and past this handle as the arm moved through its ROM. Such a hypothetical situation

a

Body travel forward

Using a hypothetically ideal "fixed" handle to move body forward

Backward hand travel through water

b

Body travel forward

Hand pushing backward through water is a "slipping handle"

Figure 10.16.　The shoulder extensors shorten to pull the body forward using an ideal "fixed" handle versus a slipping handle.

is illustrated in Figure 10.16a. If, however, this handle were not fixed solidly within a section of water, but slipped backward as the hand pressed against it, the body would not move forward through the water as far. With the arm moving through the same shoulder-extension ROM as before, the body would be moved forward a small distance as the hand holding the "slipping" handle moved backward a large distance (Figure 10.16b).

A similar analogy would be trying to climb a ladder with stable rungs to push against as opposed to trying to climb by pushing against rungs that slipped downward.

Keeping this analogy in mind, let us look at how the hand and arm can move through the water to provide a relatively *stable*, or *fixed*, "handle" rather than a *slipping* "handle." The more stable handle is created by the *sculling* method of propulsion and the slipping handle by the *paddling* method (Barthels 1979).

For some time the belief was that to move the body directly forward, the swimmer must pull or push the hands, used as paddles, directly backward through the water. If using drag force alone were the most effective means for propulsion, straight backward pushing would be desirable. Great pressure is felt on the hands and arms when they are moved backward quickly through the water, which is probably why performers have assumed erroneously that propulsive drag is the major force responsible for body propulsion. If the hand is pushed backward slowly, less force is perceived. Therefore, the tendency for the swimmer desiring to swim fast is to pull the hands backward through the water as fast as possible to feel the most force against them in the forward direction. On face value, this may appear quite valid; however, the following reasoning will show the ineffectiveness of backward pushing of the hands relative to the water. The purpose of a stroke is to move the body mass forward, and any *backward* hand movement *relative to the water* results in less forward motion of the body per arm stroke. But the hand *must* move backward through the water to create the flow that produces drag force on the hand. Therefore, if drag force on the hand is to be used for propulsion of the whole body, the imaginary handle on which the arm pulls must necessarily be a slipping handle. Moreover, if a greater drag force on the hand is desired, the hand has to move backward through the water even faster, thus yielding even *less* forward body motion by the time the arm reaches the end of its stroke. Such straight-back hand motion, however, is *not* characteristic of skilled swimmers' movements, even though it may feel as though the hands pull straight backward through the water. The ineffectiveness of using the hands solely as paddles to create a propulsive drag force by pushing straight back through the water is apparent from the ladder-climbing analogy. A more effective use of the hands for propelling the body that *is* exhibited by highly skilled swimmers involves using the hands to generate a *horizontally directed hydrodynamic lift force* with a large forward component.

When the hands are used to execute broad sculling movements within an arm-stroke pattern, the palms should form an angle of attack relative to the path of the hand so that the resulting lift force is directed forward. The function of such a horizontal lift force is to *prevent* backward hand motion relative to the water, that is, to help form a *stable* handle to be pressed against to move the body forward. Refer to Figure 10.15 in which the swimmer's body is being propelled forward by broad sculling sweeps of the hands and forearms. For faster body movement forward through the water, the body needs to be pulled forward past the sculling hand by contraction of the shoulder extensor muscles. If these muscles were to contract and shorten, as if to move the arm toward the feet, and at the same time the hand and forearm were to perform a fast, broad sculling motion within a vertical section of water, the *forward-directed* lift force on the hand would provide a fairly stable "handle." The body would be moved forward through the water with little *backward* hand motion relative to the water (Figure 10.17). Although, in such a pattern, the

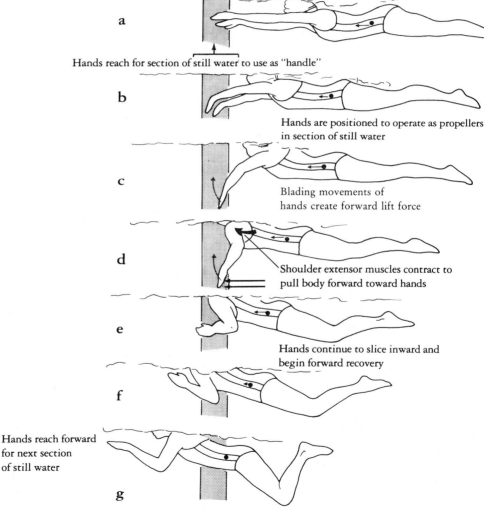

a

Hands reach for section of still water to use as "handle"

b

Hands are positioned to operate as propellers in section of still water

c

Blading movements of hands create forward lift force

d

Shoulder extensor muscles contract to pull body forward toward hands

e

Hands continue to slice inward and begin forward recovery

f

Hands reach forward for next section of still water

g

Figure 10.17.   The shoulder extensor and adductor muscles contract to pull the body past the hand. If the forward-directed lift force on the hand is great enough, very little backward hand motion through the water occurs, and more forward body motion past the hand results.

hands do not move backward through the water much at all, the swimmer has the impression that they do as the body moves forward past the sculling hand. The figure shows the swimmer blading the hand through still water along a plane that is primarily *perpendicular to the direction of body travel;* the resulting horizontal lift force on the hand provides a relatively slip-free handle, and the body can be moved over a greater distance per arm stroke by the contraction of the shoulder muscles. Such a mechanism is similar to propeller blades rotating in a vertical plane to propel a boat horizontally forward.

Observations of highly skilled swimmers confirm that these sculling motions are used in all four competitive strokes. Figure 10.18 shows a typical path of the hands of a butterfly swimmer as they move relative to the *water* (not relative to the body) from front, side, and bottom views (Barthels 1974). Recent attempts to identify the

a Front view of approaching swimmer

Hand entry Hand exit

Forward and backward hand movements are not apparent in this view

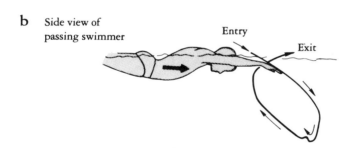

b Side view of passing swimmer

Entry Exit

Side-to-side hand movements are not apparent in this view

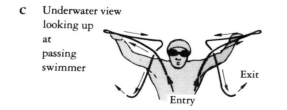

c Underwater view looking up at passing swimmer

Downward and upward hand movements are not apparent in this view

Exit Entry

The underwater paths of the hands relative to the water they interact with. The hands are seen to operate more as propellers to create forward lift force, rather than as paddles to create forward drag force.

Figure 10.18.

best angle of attack for the hand show that this best angle changes as the hand speed changes during its underwater path. Seemingly a skilled swimmer can develop a feel for the best angle for the hand as it should change throughout the stroke to produce the most useful forward force on the hand.

The hands are observed *not* to move directly backward through still water, although the swimmer may have the kinesthetic impression that they are doing so. Even though the swimmer may try to maximize the use of the sculling movements to obtain propulsive lift force, unless the hand is very large or the body is very streamlined, some backward hand motion usually occurs during the stroke. The resulting movement produces a combination of propulsive lift force and propulsive drag force acting on the hand (Figure10.19a); the forward component of the resultant force (of lift and drag) is the force that provides the "handle" for the swimmer (Figure 10.19b).

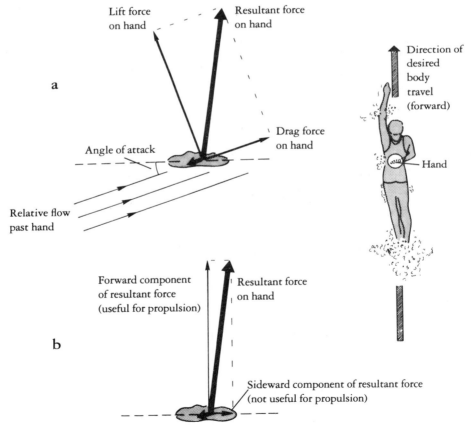

Figure 10.19.   (a) The movement of the hand through the water creates lift force and drag force. (b) The forward-directed component of the resultant force is the force used as a "handle" by which to pull the body forward.

Most of the backward hand movement occurs when the hand changes blading direction, because at this point, hand speed is lost as it stops and then reverses its direction (as it does when the elbow flexes, stops, extends, stops, flexes, and so on) (Barthels 1974). When hand speed is lost, lift force is lost. When this lift force handle is lost, the shoulder muscles pulling on the arm force the hand back through the water a greater distance than they pull the body forward through the water. Swimmers with larger hands should not suffer as much lift force loss when blading hand speed decreases because lift force is proportional to the area of the hydrofoil. Swimmers with fast stroke rates (fast turnover) seem to generate more propulsive drag force than do swimmers with slow stroke rates *traveling at the same body speed*.

Clenched-fist swimming demands an even faster stroke rate to make the body travel fast. The hands must move extremely fast backward through the water to generate sufficient forward (propulsive) drag force, since the fist shape cannot create lift force. The use of plastic hand paddles by competitive swimmers in training serves to increase the area of the hand so that a slower backward hand speed produces propulsive drag force. Consequently, the speed of the arm pull is not specific to the speed used in racing. Using hand paddles serves as a form of overload training for the shoulder muscles. Such paddles also may be effective overload devices for the shoulder muscles for the sculling arm pull since the greater area produces more lift force for a more stable handle. Swimmers using hand paddles should be closely observed so that any changes in their underwater stroking patterns may be caught and corrected.

Propulsive lift force operates in all styles of swimming. For example, the leading hand in the sidestroke can produce lift force during elbow flexion as the hand blades up toward the face (a movement traditionally accepted as the beginning of the recovery movement of the hand). In the elementary backstroke, given an adequate range of motion in the shoulder and shoulder girdle, it is possible to produce sculling arm movements similar to those in the back crawl that employ the "blading handle" mechanism.

Figure 10.20a–c shows the formation of propulsive lift force on the hand during elbow flexion in the backstroke, freestyle, and butterfly. Figure 10.20d–g is a head-on view of the propellerlike arm action of a breaststroker's underwater arm pull following her wall push-off.

PROPULSIVE MOVEMENTS OF THE LEGS AND FEET

Traditionally, the forward thrust developed by the legs with various styles of kicking has been attributed to drag force acting in a forward direction against the feet and legs. If forward-directed drag force is to be exerted on the legs and feet for forward thrust, however, the legs *must* move backward relative to the water so that the water flows past them in a forward direction, similar to the way in which propulsive drag force is generated by the arms. Such conditions producing forward-directed drag force on the legs and feet occur to some extent in the whip (breaststroke) and scissors (sidestroke) styles of kicking at the beginning of the thrust phase when the body speed is relatively slow. Backward leg movement relative to the water also occurs in the flutter kick if it is performed while the swimmer is braced against the

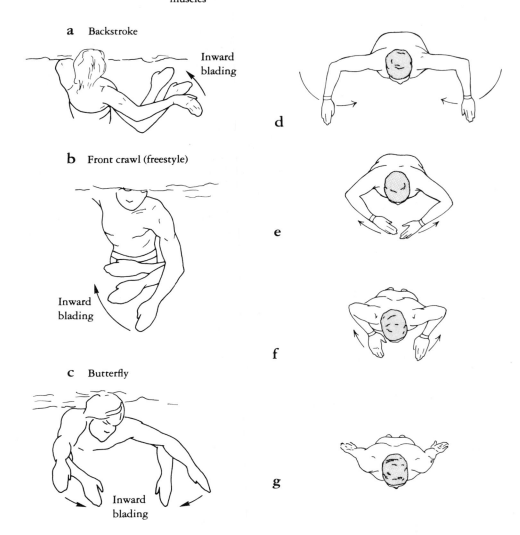

Hand and forearm scull with
elbow bending while body is
pulled forward by shoulder
muscles

a   Backstroke

Inward
blading

d

b   Front crawl (freestyle)

e

Inward
blading

f

c   Butterfly

g

Inward
blading

Figure 10.20.   Propulsive horizontal lift force is created on the hands as they blade through the water in a vertical plane. From the swimmer's point of view, and from that of an observer, the hand seems to be pressing backward through the water; however, the body is actually being pressed forward past the hand as it blades through a three-dimensional, helical path. (a) Backstroke. (b) Freestyle. (c) Butterfly. (d–g) Sequence of a breaststroker's arm movements used for the underwater arm "pull" after a wall push-off.

wall of the pool so that the body is not moving forward through the water. As the swimmer moves forward through the water using arms as well as legs, the flow past the legs becomes different, however. The legs are pulled forward along with the moving body and therefore experience a backward flow of water from that body motion. At the same time, the legs, performing a flutter or dolphin kick, move up and down to give the feet a wavy, fish-tail motion.

Figure 10.21 illustrates the nature of relative flow past the leg during the downbeat of a flutter or dolphin kick. The legs are actually snaking their way forward through the water rather than pushing backward through the water. If the resultant flow of water past the anterior surface of the moving foot and leg is examined during the downbeat, the water flow can be seen to be directed backward and upward along the shin and foot. The backward component of flow results from the leg being towed forward by the moving body, while the upward component results from the downward motion of the foot and leg. The *resultant* flow direction creates a small angle of attack with the foot surface, and the conditions for generating lift force may be present (Figure 10.21b). The forward component of the lift force (thrust) is useful

(a-b) The resultant flow direction past the foot in a flutter or dolphin kick during the downbeat of the legs of a swimmer moving forward through the water. (c) The backward-directed drag force on the leg cancels part of the propulsive thrust.

Figure 10.21.

for body propulsion, while the upward component is felt as a resistance against the downward motion of the foot. This same type of flow condition is created on the tail flukes of dolphins and other whales when the tail undulates in a vertical plane as the body moves forward. Note in Figure 10.21c that the drag force on the foot is directed upward and backward; the backward component of the drag force cancels part of the thrust created by the forward component of lift force.

The propulsive force involved in the breaststroke whip kick is somewhat different; the motion of the feet simulates the motion of a propeller rather than the undulatory motion of a fish tail. Such a propeller mechanism is similar to that involved in the formation of the lift force "handles" discussed earlier. The joint movements at the hip, knee, and ankle cause the feet to be circled in a spirallike path in a vertical plane behind the swimmer. The flow engages the sole of each foot at an angle of attack, and a lift force is generated on the foot. The forward component of this lift force provides what could be thought of as a "force wall" against which the legs can extend to push the body forward. The swimmer senses that the feet and legs are pushing backward through the water, because the legs are extending and pressure is felt on the soles. Actually the feet are blading, or sculling, and remain in a vertical section of water while the body moves forward in response to leg extension. The greater the lift force produced on the feet in a forward direction, the less the backward movement of the feet relative to the water as the legs extend. Figure 10.22 illustrates the movement of the body forward relative to the swimmer's feet, which are spiraled through a vertical section of water to obtain lift force with a forward component for thrust.

Synchronized swimmers and water polo players must use the continuous supportive lift force on their propellerlike feet and legs in the "eggbeater" kick. This kick is an alternating left-then-right breaststroke kick as illustrated in Figure 10.23.

PROPULSIVE MOVEMENTS OF THE TOTAL BODY

In most styles of swimming performed by humans, the arms and legs work as separate units to move the whole body forward through the water. Because a stable central base is necessary for arm and leg movement, the trunk is usually stabilized and most intervertebral movement is restricted, with the exception of some lateral flexion and transverse rotation that occur in response to alternating arm and leg movements or breathing to one side. The trunk, as a segment, usually is not considered a propulsive agent. In the dolphin butterfly stroke, however, the intervertebral movements of flexion and extension actually contribute to body propulsion as do the arm and leg movements. In the preceding section, the flutter kick and the dolphin kick were illustrated as being isolated from the rest of the body. In the flutter kick used in the front and back crawl strokes, each leg works as a single unit attached to a fairly stable trunk base. In the dolphin kick, however, both legs move as though they were bound together in one "tail" unit, which does not work independently of the trunk but functions more as an extension of the vertebral column to continue the waving of the body in its sagittal plane. Figure 10.24 shows the total body weaving its way through the water.

a — Section of still water to be used by feet

b — Feet are drawn forward into section of water

c — Feet are positioned to operate as propellers in section of water

d — Feet spiral around to create forward lift force

e — Hip and knee extensor muscles contract to extend joints and push body forward as feet spiral

f — Feet follow moving body

g — Feet move forward toward next section of still water

The forward component of lift force on the spiraling feet of a breaststroker forms a "force wall" against which the swimmer extends the legs to push the body forward.   **Figure 10.22.**

The dolphin kick, therefore, may be viewed as a kick that is initiated from the thoracic vertebrae rather than from the hip joints. The intervertebral flexion and extension capabilities, along with the flexion and extension capabilities of the lower extremity segments, permit an eellike movement of the total body. Such undulations result in flow patterns conducive to the generation of lift forces, with the forward-directed components useful for thrusting the body forward. The arm stroke in the dolphin (butterfly) stroke contributes intermittent additional lift force propulsion

Figure 10.23.   A synchronized swimmer performing an "eggbeater" kick to support the head and arms above the surface. The feet and legs act as propeller blades to generate an upward lift force.

Dolphin and flutter kicks
simulate propulsive
movements of dolphin

The waving movement of the legs is a continuation of the intervertebral movements and results in propulsive undulatory motion of the whole body.

Figure 10.24.

and also provides for the positioning of the head for breathing. The propulsive nature of this total body weave or wiggle is demonstrated by the progress made by the swimmer who uses only trunk and leg movements in an underwater dolphin action. Breaststrokers also use such vertebral movements, coordinated with the whip kick, so that the body contributes to propulsion, rather than remaining a rigid drag-producing unit. Figure 10.25 illustrates the weaving of the body during the kick and the beginning of the arm pull in this contemporary breaststroke technique.

In summary, propulsion of a swimmer depends on the way the water flows past the body and its parts; this flow is determined by the way in which the body and parts move through the water. Flow patterns and directions differ depending on whether the body is moving forward by means of kicking only, by arm stroking only, or by using both the arms and legs; or not moving forward at all. The teacher or coach who understands the propulsive process can best help the learner-performer, and coaching cues can be developed to focus the swimmer's attention on how the movements should feel and appear.

Figure 10.25. Intervertebral flexion and extension is incorporated into the breaststroke so that the body is not merely a rigid unit connecting the arms and legs.

UNDERSTANDING PROPULSION IN SWIMMING SKILLS

1. Explain how drag force can serve as a propulsive force in swimming.

2. Explain how lift force is produced on the hand moving through water.

3. Explain how lift force on the hand can be used to support weight above the surface of the water.

4. Explain how lift force can prevent the hand from moving backward through the water in a front crawl stroke. Is this desirable? Why?

5. In the swimming pool, working with a partner or in a small group, perform the following experiments and discuss the results.

a. Tread water (without using the legs) by using broad horizontal blading sweeps of the hands to obtain upward lift force, as shown in Figure 10.14. Repeat with the hands clenched into fists. Repeat with hand paddles. Experiment with different hand and finger shapes to determine which shape produces the greatest lift force.

b. Tread water as explained in 5a; continue the horizontal blading movements, but hyperextend the wrist about 45 degrees. What is the direction of lift force relative to the plane of your palm? Identify the two rectangular components of the lift force and the result of each directional component. Repeat with a flexed wrist position.

c. Perform the same treading movements in a prone position, as shown in Figure 10.15. Can you propel your body forward without a backward paddling motion? Note the orientation of the plane of the hand for maximum upward support (for instance, when the head is held above the surface of the water in a prone position). Repeat in a supine position, blading the hands alongside the body.

d. In a supine position, use horizontal blading movements with your palms facing the pool bottom to obtain upward lift force on the hands. Compare the sculling speeds necessary for generating enough lift force to (1) hold one knee out of the water, (2) hold one leg out, and (3) hold two legs out.

e. Using no kick for propulsion, compare the number of arm strokes necessary to swim (front crawl) one length of the pool when (1) using no flexion of the elbow during the underwater phase, and (2) maximizing the blading mechanism to obtain propulsive lift force. Repeat two or three times, maintaining the same time per length.

f. Have a partner hold your ankles as you perform front-crawl arm movements in a prone position, using (1) straight-back pushing motions with your arms and (2) blading movements with the arms as you stroke at the same stroke rate. Which movements, according to your partner, produce the greatest force for pulling the body forward? Experiment with different styles of arm pulls, hand shapes, stroke rates, and head positions to identify what factors increase the force (according to your partner) for moving the body forward. (Note that the direct force acting to pull your body forward is the shoulder muscle contraction force acting on the trunk; the movements of the hands and arms through the water serve to form the handles that stabilize the arm so that trunk movement will occur.)

g. Compare the propulsive effectiveness of the legs moving in (1) a bicycling pattern, (2) a wavy flutter pattern, (3) an "up-out-together," wedge-type breaststroke kick, and (4) a spiraling, whip-type breaststroke kick.

h. Compare the propulsive effect of the whip kick if the ankles are (1) kept in dorsiflexion throughout, (2) kept in plantar flexion throughout, and (3) moved from dorsiflexion to plantar flexion as the legs near the end of their drive phase.

SECTION 5

SWIMMING EFFICIENCY AND SPEED

Factors Influencing Swimming Efficiency

The meaning of efficiency incorporates the concepts of energy expenditure and work production. Specifically, **swimming efficiency** is the ratio of the mechanical work performed by the swimmer (propulsive force × the distance the body is moved) to the energy expended by the swimmer to do this work (determined by oxygen consumption). If the performance is examined for a given time interval, the efficiency can be expressed in terms of mechanical power (force × distance/time) divided by the rate of energy expenditure (oxygen consumption/time). Multiplying the result by 100 gives efficiency in terms of percent.

An analysis of swimming efficiency must involve consideration of biomechanical and physiological factors in the performance. Lack of research instrumentation and a number of uncontrollable variables, however, have made swimming efficiency estimates difficult to determine. Values up to only approximately 5% to 7% have been reported for moderate speed freestyle, which seems to be the most efficient of the strokes performed, followed by backstroke and then breaststroke (Karpovich and Millman 1944, Holmer 1972). No value has been reported for the efficiency of the contemporary butterfly stroke.

The economy of any given stroke performance is influenced by how the body speed fluctuates within each stroke cycle. More energy is required in variable-speed swimming than in constant-speed swimming, just as more fuel is required for driving a car that is continually accelerating and decelerating during a trip. For efficiency in swimming, therefore, a relatively constant body velocity should be sought. If sources of resistive force acting on the swimmer's body can be identified and reduced as much as possible, less propulsive force will be needed to maintain any given speed. Consider the effect of some propulsive (motive) force created by a swimmer's limb movements through the water. The body responds with a forward acceleration as long as the propulsive force applied is greater than the oppositely directed resistive forces on the body. Constant body velocity (zero acceleration) is achieved only when the propulsive forces are equal to the oppositely directed resistive forces. As the body accelerates, it gains velocity, and the resistive drag forces also increase until they become equal to the existing propulsive forces. At that time, no further acceleration occurs. As soon as it becomes physiologically or biomechanically impossible or both for the swimmer to continue applying the same amount of propulsive force to counter the resistance, the body decelerates.

Speed fluctuations are quite apparent in the sidestroke, elementary backstroke, and breaststroke because of the intermittent propulsive movements of the limbs and the large drag of the underwater recovery movements. To keep the resistive drag on the limbs to a minimum, the speed of the underwater recovery movements should be relatively slow, and the surface area of the limb facing the flow should be minimized. To take full advantage of the propulsive movements of the limbs, the rest of the body should be in as streamlined a position as possible for minimum drag. Less apparent, but still present, are speed fluctuations in the butterfly stroke. The overwater arm recovery in the butterfly eliminates the drag caused by the underwater recovery in the conventional breaststroke, and the wavelike body and leg movements in the dolphin motion provide more or less continuous propulsion. A more constant body speed is observed in the front and back crawl strokes, because the limbs operate to provide some propulsive force throughout the total stroke cycle.

A general statement that can be made is that swimming efficiency depends on swimming speed, the stroke used, and the skill of the swimmer. For each stroke and swimmer, there seems to be an *optimum* swimming speed for the highest efficiency. At very slow speeds, efficiency is low; at moderate speeds, efficiency improves; at higher speeds, efficiency decreases again.

If the mechanical purpose of swimming is merely to interact with the environment, efficiency may be of no concern. If the mechanical purpose is to cover a given distance in the fastest time possible, however, the efficiency of the swim will be compromised by the speed (pace) demanded by the distance; that is, a sprint at maximum speed would not be *efficient*, but it would be *effective*.

In competitive swimming *maximum* efficiency is not the purpose. *Optimal efficiency* for *maximum effectiveness* is the goal. The effectiveness of the swimming performance is measured by the speed with which the distance is covered.

Factors Influencing Swimming Velocity

The total time a swimmer takes to complete a race depends on swimming velocity, the time from the starting signal to when the swimming actually begins (starting time), and the time used for the turns and wall push-offs.

The most important part of the race, however, is swimming velocity. As we know, the forward velocity fluctuates within each stroke cycle; therefore, the *average* stroke velocity is the value that is analyzed.

Stroke velocity can be expressed in terms of how far the body travels per stroke cycle (stroke length) and the rate at which the stroke cycles are performed (stroke rate):

Equation 10.3

$$v = d/S \times S/min$$

where v is body velocity, d/S is distance covered per stroke cycle (stroke length), and S/min is number of stroke cycles per minute (stroke rate).

An example of the use of this relationship would be a body velocity of 1.9 m/sec obtained with a stroke length of 2.0 m per stroke and a stroke rate of 58 strokes per minute. We can see that an increase in stroke length (d/S) or an increase in stroke rate (S/sec) or an increase in both would increase the swimmer's body velocity. A large increase in stroke length obtained at the expense of reducing the stroke rate too much, however, would result in *slower* body velocity. For example, if a very long "glide" is held with each entering hand in a freestyle (front crawl) stroke, the stroke rate would be slow. Moreover, if the arms were "resting" in this fashion every stroke, there would be a large time interval of body deceleration due to the resistive force being greater than the propulsive force. Such a slow stroke rate leading to body acceleration-deceleration-acceleration would be inefficient as well.

Similarly, if the stroke rate is increased too much, the stroke length will be sacrificed. Such is the tendency among many competitive swimmers; they attempt to increase their stroke rates so much that the distance traveled per stroke is reduced greatly, resulting in slower times.

Therefore, neither the stroke length nor stroke rate should be maximized; each should be *optimized* to yield the fastest body velocity. Optimum stroke rates have been studied for swimmers in different freestyle events in the 1976 Olympic Swimming Trials (Craig, Boomer, and Gibbons 1979). The data show that stroke rates producing the fastest measured velocity vary according to the length of the event. In general, going from the longest event (1500 m) to the shortest event (100 m), faster velocity was obtained by increasing the stroke rate and decreasing the stroke length.

The next likely explanation for the decrease in distance per stroke with a stroke rate increasing beyond optimum is that the underwater stroke mechanics change to produce less propulsive force on the body; that is, the hand and arm "slips" backward through the water as the swimmer attempts to increase the stroke rate, thereby eliminating some of the sculling movements that provide the handle for pulling the body forward.

In summary, the maximum velocity attained is determined by an optimum stroke rate and optimum stroke length. Each swimmer has a unique optimum stroke rate and length, depending on the stroke and the event.

UNDERSTANDING THE FACTORS INFLUENCING SWIMMING VELOCITY

1. Identify the forces that act *directly* on the swimmer's trunk to cause it to move forward relative to the water with one arm cycle.

2. Count the number of stroke cycles performed by a swimmer for one pool length (25 yd or 50 m) and record the time for the swim. Calculate the body velocity and average distance covered per arm-stroke cycle. Calculate the stroke rate.

3. Repeat the procedure in question 2, but have the swimmer hold the hands in fists. Compare and explain the differences in body velocity, stroke length, and stroke rate.

4. Observe a 100-yd or 200-yd race. Count the number of strokes taken during the second 25-yd lap and time the lap. Do the same for the last 25-yd lap. Calculate the swimming velocity, stroke rate, and stroke length for each of these laps, and compare them. Explain the differences.

REFERENCES
SUGGESTED READINGS

Alexander, R. M. *Animal Mechanics*. Seattle: University of Washington Press, 1968.

Andersen, P. "The Use of Hand Paddles, Overload Training, and After-Effects." *Swimming Technique* 13 (2) (1976): 58–62.

Azuma, A. "Biomechanical Aspects of Animal Flying and Swimming." In *Biomechanics VIII-A: Proceedings of the Eighth International Congress of Biomechanics*, ed. H. Matsui and K. Kobayashi, 35–53. Champaign, Ill.: Human Kinetics Publishers, 1983.

Bachman, J. C. "Three Butterfly Pulls." *Swimming Technique* 20 (1) (1983): 23–25.

Barthels, K. M. "Three Dimensional Kinematic Analysis of the Hand and Hip in the Butterfly Swimming Stroke." Unpublished doctoral dissertation, Washington State University, 1974.

———. "The Mechanism for Body Propulsion in Swimming." In *Swimming III: Proceedings of the Third International Symposium on the Biomechanics of Swimming*, ed. J. Terauds and E. W. Bedingfield, 45–54. Baltimore: University Park Press, 1979.

———. "Biomechanical Research in Swimming: Past, Present, and Future." In *Biomechanics in Sports: Proceedings of the International Symposium of Biomechanics in Sports*, ed. J. Terauds, 381–90. San Diego, Calif.: Academic Publishers, 1982.

Campbell, W. A. "Relationship Between Buoyancy of the Black Male and Learning the Crawl Stroke." In *Biomechanics of Sports and Kinanthropometry: Proceedings of the International Congress of Physical Activity Sciences*, ed. F. Landry and W. A. R. Orban, 149–55. Miami: Symposia Specialists, Inc., 1978.

Clarys, J. P. "An Experimental Investigation of the Application of Fundamental Hydrodynamics to the Human Body." In *Swimming Medicine IV: Proceedings of the Fourth International Congress on Swimming Medicine*, ed. B. Eriksson and B. Furberg, 386–94. Baltimore: University Park Press, 1978.

————. "Human Morphology and Hydrodynamics." In *Swimming III: Proceedings of the Third International Symposium on the Biomechanics of Swimming*, ed. J. Terauds and E. W. Bedingfield, 3–41. Baltimore: University Park Press, 1979.

Costill, D. L., King, D. S., Holdren, A., and Hargreaves, M. "Sprint Speed Versus Swimming Power." *Swimming Technique* 19 (1) (1983): 20–22.

Craig, A. B., Jr. "The Basics of Swimming." *Swimming Technique* 20 (4) (1984): 22–27.

Craig, A. B., Boomer, W. L., and Gibbons, J. F. "The Use of Stroke Rate, Stroke Length, and Velocity Relationships in Training Competitive Swimmers." In *Swimming III: Proceedings of the Third International Symposium on the Biomechanics of Swimming*, ed. J. Terauds and E. W. Bedingfield, 265–74. Baltimore: University Park Press, 1979.

diPrampero, P. E., Pendergast, D. R., Wilson, D. W., and Rennie, D. W. "Energetics of Swimming in Man." *Journal of Applied Physiology* 37 (1974): 1–5.

Hay, J. G., and Guimaraes, A. C. S. "A Quantitative Look at Swimming Biomechanics." *Swimming Technique* 20 (2) (1983): 11–17.

Holmer, I. "Oxygen Uptake During Swimming." *Journal of Applied Physiology* 33 (1972): 502–09.

————. "Time Relations: Running, Swimming, and Skating." In *Swimming Medicine IV: Proceedings of the Fourth International Congress on Swimming Medicine*, ed. B. Eriksson and B. Furberg, 361–66. Baltimore: University Park Press, 1978.

Jensen, R. K., and Tihanyi, J. "Fundamental Studies of Tethered Swimming." In *Biomechanics of Sports and Kinanthropometry: Proceedings of the International Congress of Physical Activity Sciences*, ed. F. Landry and W. A. R. Orban, 135–42. Miami: Symposia Specialists, Inc., 1978.

Karpovich, P. V., and Millman, N. "Energy Expenditure in Swimming." *American Journal of Physiology* 142 (1944): 140–44.

Kornecki, S., and Bober, T. "Extreme Velocities of a Swimming Cycle as a Technique Criterion." In *Swimming Medicine IV: Proceedings of the Fourth International Congress on Swimming Medicine*, ed. B. Eriksson and B. Furberg, 402–07. Baltimore: University Park Press, 1978.

Maglischo, E. W. *Swimming Faster*. Palo Alto, Calif.: Mayfield, 1982.

Midtling, J. *Swimming*. Philadelphia: W. B. Saunders, 1974.

Miller, D. I. "Biomechanics of Swimming." In *Exercise and Sports Science Reviews*, vol. 3, ed. J. H. Wilmore and J. F. Keogh, 219–48. New York: Academic Press, 1975.

Miyashita, M. "Arm Action in the Crawl Stroke." In *Swimming II: Proceedings of the Second International Symposium on the Biomechanics of Swimming*, ed. R. LeWillie and J. P. Clarys, 167–73. Baltimore: University Park Press, 1975.

————. "Method of Calculating Overall Efficiency in Swimming Crawl Stroke." In *Biomechanics of Sports and Kinanthropometry: Proceedings of the International Congress of Physical Activity Sciences*, ed. F. Landry and W. A. R. Orban, 135–42. Miami: Symposia Specialists, Inc., 1978.

Nelson, R. C., and Pike, N. L. "Analysis and Comparison of Swimming Starts and Strokes." In *Swimming Medicine IV: Proceedings of the Fourth International Congress on Swimming Medicine*, ed. B. Eriksson and B. Furberg, 347–60. Baltimore: University Park Press, 1978.

Nursall, J. R. "The Caudal Fin as a Hydrofoil." *Evolution* 12 (1958): 116–20.

Page, R. L. "The Mechanics of Swimming and Diving." *The Physics Teacher*, February 1976, 72–80.

Pendergast, D. R., diPrampero, P. E., Craig, A. B., and Rennie, D. W. "The Influence of Selected Biomechanical Factors on the Energy Cost of Swimming." In *Swimming Medicine IV: Proceedings of the Fourth International Congress on Swimming Medicine*, ed. B. Eriksson and B. Furberg, 376–78. Baltimore: University Park Press, 1978.

Remmonds, P., and Bartlett, R. M. "Effects of Finger Separation." *Swimming Technique* 18 (1) (1981): 28–30.

Saito, M. "The Effect of Training on the Relationships Among Velocity, Stroke Rate and Distance Per Stroke in Untrained Subjects Swimming the Breaststroke." *Research Quarterly for Exercise and Sport* 53 (4) (1982): 323–29.

Schleihauf, R. E. "A Hydrodynamic Analysis of Swimming Propulsion." In *Swimming III: Proceedings of the Third International Symposium on the Biomechanics of Swimming*, ed. J. Terauds and E. W. Bedingfield, 70–109. Baltimore: University Park Press, 1979.

Shapiro, A. H. *Shape and Flow: The Fluid Dynamics of Drag*. Garden City, N.Y.: Doubleday Anchor Books, 1961.

Sharp, R. L., Troup, J. P., and Costill, D. L. "Relationship Between Power and Sprint Freestyle Swimming." *Medicine and Science in Sports and Exercise* 14 (1) (1982): 53–56.

Stoner, L. J., and Luedtke, D. L. "Variations in Front Crawl and Back Crawl Arm Strokes of Varsity Swimmers Using Hand Paddles." In *Swimming III: Proceedings of the Third International Symposium on the Biomechanics of Swimming*, ed. J. Terauds and E. W. Bedingfield, 281–88. Baltimore: University Park Press, 1979.

Swegan, D. B., and Thompson, H. L. "Experimental Research in Swimming." *Swimming Technique* 7 (1) (1970): 8–10, 32.

Wood, T. C. "A Fluid Dynamics Analysis of the Propulsive Potential of the Hand and Forearm in Swimming." In *Swimming III: Proceedings of the Third International Symposium on the Biomechanics of Swimming*, ed. J. Terauds and E. W. Bedingfield, 62–69. Baltimore: University Park Press, 1979.

ROTARY MOVEMENT RESPONSES TO APPLIED TORQUES

Prerequisites:

Concept Modules B, C, D

Concept Module Contents

How a system responds to forces and torques applied to it depends on the magnitude of the net force and the magnitude of the net torque. The response also depends on the inertial characteristics of the body in question, which are different for rotary motion than for linear motion. To explain how torques affect rotary movement responses, we will begin with some descriptions of rotary motion.

SECTION 1

ANGULAR SPEED AND VELOCITY

A system in rotary motion is represented by a straight line connecting the axis of rotation to a selected point in the system. The point selected might be the center of gravity (CG) of the rotating system (e.g., when describing the rotation of a gymnast swinging from a horizontal bar). The point may be some part of the body, such as a point on the head if the body is rotating about an axis through its CG, as it does when it is rotating free of support.

A body that is rotating around some axis has **angular speed,** which tells us how fast the body is changing its angular position. To determine angular speed, we measure the angular distance through which the body has rotated (in degrees or radians) and divide by the time it took to move through that arc:

Equation G.1

$$\omega = \frac{\theta}{t}$$

where ω (omega) is angular speed (or velocity) of the body (radians/second or degrees/second), θ (theta) is angular displacement of the body (radians or degrees), and t is time during which the displacement occurred (seconds).

In cycling, for example, the angular speed of the thigh rotating around the hip axis during a down stroke might be 5 rad/sec. Even though the thigh does not rotate a full 5 rad, its rate of rotation for the time it is rotating is 5 rad/sec.

If a direction is specified for the rotating body, the body is said to have **angular velocity,** a vector quantity; that is, it has speed and direction. The direction of rotation is specified by the right-hand thumb rule if we wish to draw a vector diagram, or we can specify the direction as positive (counterclockwise [ccw]) or negative (clockwise [cw]). Recall that the axis of rotation is always perpendicular to the system's plane of rotation and that direction can be specified by the spatial orientation of the axis or the plane of rotation. A phonograph record, for example, rotates with an angular velocity of 33⅓ rpm around a vertical axis and in a horizontal plane. The state of motion of the second hand on a clock is described as having an angular speed of 360 degrees per minute. The forearm may be rotating about a horizontal axis at the elbow at 100 degrees per second at some specified time during its movement. The angular velocity of the leg rotating in a vertical plane about a horizontal axis through the knee is about 700 degrees per second as a skilled runner swings the leg forward (Cooper and Glassow 1976).

LINEAR VELOCITY OF A POINT
ON A ROTATING BODY

We can describe a system's rotary motion in terms of how far (θ) and how fast (ω), and we can specify the direction of its rotation. Angular displacement (θ) and angular velocity (ω) also can be used to determine how far some point on the rotating system travels along its curved path (linear distance) and how fast it travels (linear speed). The relationship between the angular velocity of a rotating object or segment and how fast the end of it is moving linearly has direct application in understanding throwing, kicking, and striking skills.

The linear distance and speed of some point on a rotating segment depends on the distance that point is from the axis of rotation, that is, the point's **radius of rotation.** A point further from the axis moves a greater linear distance than a point closer to the axis. The greater the radius, the greater the distance the point moves as the segment rotates. The linear distance, d, that a point moves may be found by multiplying its radius of rotation, r, by the angular displacement, θ, of the segment in radians:

$$d = r\theta$$

Equation G.2

where d is linear distance of a point on a rotating segment (meters), r is radius of rotation of the point (meters), and θ is angular displacement of the point (radians).

Whenever any calculations are performed to relate angular quantities to linear quantities, radians must be used for angular measure, not degrees or revolutions. Therefore, to change degrees to radians, divide the angular displacement in degrees by 57.3 degrees (57.3 degrees = 1 radian).

We may also calculate the linear velocity of a point rotating with some given angular velocity. The linear velocity may be calculated from either the point's linear distance or its angular velocity. The relationship between the angular and linear velocities is given by:

$$v = r\omega$$

Equation G.3

where v is linear velocity of a point on a rotating segment (meters/second), r is radius of rotation of the point (meters), and ω is angular velocity of the segment (in radians/second).

The greater the angular velocity or the greater the radius of rotation or both, the greater the rotating point's linear velocity.

Figure G.1 shows the relationship between the angular displacement and linear distance of three points on a rotating segment. The figure also shows how the linear velocities of the three points are related to the angular velocity of the segment. Note in the figure that the angular displacement for all three points, no matter how far

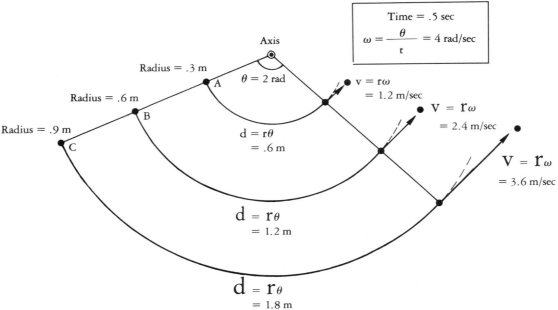

Figure G.1.   The linear distance traveled and the linear velocity of a point on a rotating segment increase with its radius of rotation.

they are located from the axis, is the same. Notice however, that the farther the point is located away from the axis, the greater the linear distance it moves for a given angular displacement. Thus, point C moves linearly farther than point B, which moves farther than point A. Recall that the distance of each point from the axis is called its radius of rotation, which is designated by a lowercase r and measured in linear units, such as meters, centimeters, feet, or inches. Thus, if the radius of rotation of point A is 0.3 m, it travels d = rθ = 0.3(2) = 0.6 m. Point B, with a radius of 0.6 m, travels 1.2 m. Point C, located even farther from the axis, travels 1.8 m.

To determine the angular velocity, ω, of the segment we must know the amount of time the segment took to rotate through the angle of 2 rad. If the time measured is 0.5 sec, the angular velocity will be ω = θ/t = 2 rad/0.5 sec = 4 rad/sec.

Just as the radius of rotation of each point determines the linear distance it travels, the radius also determines the linear velocity of each point. If we assume that the segment rotates around at the same angular velocity, ω = 4 rad/sec, then point A will have a linear velocity of v = rω = 0.3 (4) = 1.2 m/sec; point B, a linear velocity of 0.6(4) = 2.4 m/sec; and point C, with the greatest radius of rotation, has a linear velocity of 0.9(4) = 3.6 m/sec. Usually, linear velocity of any point on a rotating segment is determined for some given instant during the rotation. At the instant selected for calculating the linear velocity of the point, the direction of the linear velocity (a vector) is tangent to the arc; that is, it is perpendicular to the point's radius of rotation. Such an instantaneous linear velocity is often called the **tangential velocity,** a term that indicates its direction relative to the point's path.

The model in Figure G.1 could represent a leg swinging to kick a ball, and the linear velocity of a point on the foot would be of interest because a fast foot applies more force than a slow foot. Therefore, with a given angular velocity for two different legs, a longer leg will have a faster foot. In a following section, we will see, however, that the angular velocity of a body segment or implement could be more important in producing fast linear velocity than the radius of rotation. The influence of both factors, r and ω, on linear velocity of a point should be observed.

SECTION 3

ANGULAR ACCELERATION

How far, θ, and how fast, ω, a rotating body travels are two ways to describe its motion. Rarely, however, does a human body segment or implement rotate with the same angular velocity throughout its range of motion (ROM); it changes its state of rotary motion by speeding up or slowing down or changing direction. To effect such a change, a net torque must be applied to the system. The greater the net torque, the greater the respective motion change. Taking a body at rest and forcing it to rotate or changing the angular speed or direction of a body already rotating is defined as **angular acceleration.** More precisely, acceleration is the time rate of change in a body's velocity; that is, how fast it is changing its speed or direction or both.

We can show the relationship of velocity change and acceleration by:

$$\alpha = \frac{\omega_2 - \omega_1}{t} \quad \text{or} \quad \frac{\Delta\omega}{t}$$

Equation G.4

where α (alpha) is angular acceleration of the system, ω_2 is final angular velocity of the system, ω_1 is initial angular velocity of the system, t is time during which the angular velocity was changed, and Δ is "change in."

If a large change in angular velocity occurs in a short period of time, the angular acceleration will be large. If the arm starts to rotate downward and forward to release a fast softball pitch and it reaches an angular velocity of 20 rad/sec in 0.2 sec, its angular acceleration is $\alpha = \Delta\omega/t = 20/0.2 = 100$ rad/sec per second. In slow pitch the arm may rotate to only 5 rad/sec in 0.2 sec. Its angular acceleration then is $\alpha = \Delta\omega/t = 5/0.2 = 25$ rad/sec per second. Note that time is mentioned twice in expressing acceleration values. The change in velocity includes a time unit in its measurement and then the rate of change for acceleration adds the second time unit.

A body, segment, or implement experiences an angular acceleration (or deceleration) only during the time a net external torque is being applied. At the instant the net torque ceases, the system has reached its new velocity and maintains it until another torque is applied. The acceleration is always in the direction of the net torque acting. The greater the torque, the greater the angular acceleration.

When a body gains angular velocity, we say it is accelerating, and when it loses angular velocity, we say it is decelerating. Acceleration is also referred to as positive (+) acceleration, and deceleration, as negative (−) acceleration. Angular directions also are given + and − labels: ccw is + and cw is −. Therefore, a positive (+) acceleration value may be assigned to an angularly decelerating segment that is still rotating in the negative direction. (In essence, slowing down in the negative direction is mathematically interpreted as speeding up in the positive direction.) We will be using the more qualitative terms, acceleration and deceleration, and specify the direction when necessary (cw or ccw).

Examples of angular acceleration are readily found among segmental movements of the human body. Every time a movement of a body segment is initiated or terminated, it has been angularly accelerated or decelerated. Almost all of our movements are reciprocal, or back-and-forth movements. Rarely, if ever, do the body segments move with a constant angular speed or direction. During the course of one rotary movement, the angular velocity of the segment is variable from one instant to the next. Consider, for example, the movement of the arm in a volleyball spike (Figure G.2). The arm segment is angularly accelerated to start the backswing, or preparation phase of the spike, and then it is decelerated at the end of the ROM of the shoulder joint (Figure G.2a). Angular acceleration and deceleration of the arm occur at the shoulder joint near the ends of the ROM. The forward rotation of the arm begins, and the arm is accelerated to move the hand toward the ball rapidly forward in an arc. The ball is struck during the arm's rotation when its angular velocity is large (Figure G.2b). The arm's follow-through after ball contact is a period of angular deceleration; this deceleration must be great enough to prevent contact with the net. To some, the term *acceleration* connotes fast movement, but this is not an accurate interpretation of the concept. In fact, when velocity is at maximum value, acceleration is zero. In general, the angular velocity of a rotating segment or implement is the quantity of ultimate importance, and the magnitude of the acceleration or deceleration determines how fast that desired velocity is attained. Consider, for example, a bat accelerated from 0 degrees per second to 10 degrees per second in 0.1 sec. The final velocity is 10 degrees per second, and the acceleration is 100 degrees per second per second. Now consider a bat being accelerated from 490 degrees per second to 500 degrees per second in 0.1 sec. The bat's angular acceleration is still 100 degrees per second per second; however, the angular velocity is 500 degrees per second, and such a velocity will cause the bat to have a much greater impact force than a bat rotating at 10 degrees per second.

The magnitude of the acceleration of a body segment depends on the purpose of the movement and the constraints imposed on the performer. For example, the forward angular acceleration of the lower extremity during locomotion is considerably less in walking than it is in running.

A volleyball spiker showing the angular acceleration then deceleration of the arm in the backswing (a)   **Figure G.2.**
and in the execution of the hit (b).

Variable Angular Velocity: Average and Instantaneous Values

When segments or implements are rotated, the velocity varies during the ROM. In examining Figure G.1, we assumed that the angular velocity was constant when the linear tangential velocity of a point was determined. When we look at a rotation of varying velocity we could describe its motion by giving its **average angular velocity,** which is calculated by dividing its ROM , θ, by t (the time it took to cover that ROM). Such a gross measure, however, does not have much use in sport analysis; most rotations are performed with the purpose of angularly accelerating a segment or implement up to some angular velocity at a particular instant (e.g., swinging a bat to reach maximum angular velocity at ball contact, swinging the arm to pitch a horseshoe at an optimal angular velocity at release, and rotating the leg segments to a maximum angular velocity during a high jump takeoff). **Instantaneous angular velocity** is the velocity used for calculating the instantaneous linear velocity ($v = r\omega$).

UNDERSTANDING ROTARY MOTION

1. What distinguishes angular velocity from angular speed? Give an example for each.

2. If a body is rotating with constant angular velocity, what is its acceleration?

3. Which segment has the greatest angular acceleration: (a) an arm that gains an angular velocity of 300 degrees per second in 0.5 sec, or (b) an arm that gains an angular velocity of 200 degrees per second in 0.2 sec?

4. Perform ten different segmental movements (one at a time). For each, identify when angular acceleration and angular deceleration are taking place. Can you rotate a body segment with a constant angular velocity somewhere in its ROM?

5. What is the instantaneous release velocity of a softball released by an upper extremity, 0.5 m long, that is rotating at 573 degrees per second at the time of release? (Remember to use radians in $v = r\omega$.)

SECTION 4

THE RELATIONSHIP OF TORQUE, ROTATIONAL INERTIA, AND ANGULAR ACCELERATION

Mechanically, the magnitude of the angular acceleration of a system depends on the net torque applied and the resistance of the system to angular motion change. When external torque is applied to a system to cause its angular acceleration, the greater the torque, the greater the acceleration. In addition to this condition, however, the system's resistance to angular acceleration also plays a part in how the system responds to the torque.

Newton's second law, the law of acceleration, is expressed here specifically for rotary motion: the angular acceleration of a body is directly proportional to the net torque applied, and the acceleration is inversely proportional to the **rotational inertia**[1] of the body.

This interrelationship of three variables is expressed by the following:

$$\alpha = \frac{T}{I} \quad \text{or} \quad T = I\alpha$$

Equation G.5

where α is angular acceleration of the segment or object, T is net torque applied to the segment, and I is rotational inertia of the segment.

A detailed description of the term *rotational inertia* is necessary for understanding its significance and for appreciating its effect in all rotational movement. Recall that a body's mass is the inertial resistance to a change in that body's *linear* motion (resistance to linear acceleration). The mass of a body or segment, however, makes up only part of that body's resistance to angular acceleration. A system's resistance to a change in its state of *rotary* motion also depends on how far the mass is distributed away from the axis of rotation. The combination of these two factors, the system's *mass* and its *mass distribution* (i.e., arrangement relative to the axis of rotation), determine the system's **rotational inertia (I).** The rotational inertia is the measure of resistance to angular acceleration of a body. Since this resistance is specific to a given axis, a system's rotational inertia about one axis may be quite different from that same system's rotational inertia about another axis. The greater a system's mass or the farther from the axis of rotation the mass is distributed or both, the greater the system's rotational inertia. This mass-distribution factor is more influential than is the quantity of mass in terms of determining the magnitude of the resistance to rotary motion change. In fact, the resistance to changes in the state of rotary motion of a system is directly proportional to increases in its mass, but it increases as the square of the distance of the system's mass relative to the axis of rotation. We can express this concept by:

$$I = mr^2$$

Equation G.6

where I is rotational inertia of the segment or body, m is mass of the segment or body, and r is radius (distance) of the mass from the axis of rotation.

To appreciate better the importance of the mass-distribution factor in the determination of rotational inertia, imagine trying to swing a baseball bat while holding it at the grip end and then trying to swing that same bat while holding it at the barrel end. The relative ease with which the bat can be swung while held at the barrel end is evident, yet the mass of the bat has not changed. Examine the mass distribution relative to the axis of rotation for each swing, and a difference will be apparent. Using the wrist area as the axis in both cases, more of the bat's mass can be seen to be farther from the axis when it is held at the small end. More effort is required to

---

1. Rotational inertia is also called "moment of inertia"; however, the term *rotational inertia* will be used in this text because the name implies its meaning.

start the bat rotating in this case because the bat's rotational inertia is larger. If it were necessary to swing the bat faster in a game situation, one would not see the player gripping the barrel end of the bat to permit a faster rotation, but one would see the player choking up on the bat, or moving the axis of rotation (the wrist) closer to the barrel of the bat. Such a shift in handgrip serves the purpose of bringing the more massive part of the bat closer to the axis of rotation (wrist).

Figure G.3 illustrates the effect on a system's rotational inertia of doubling its mass, compared to the effect of doubling the distance its mass is distributed from the axis of rotation. Note that in this model, all the mass is considered to be packed into a single point. Because the mass is doubled in Figure G.3a, an increase in the rotational inertia of the system is doubled. In Figure G.3b, however, a doubling of the distance of the mass from the axis of rotation causes a fourfold increase in the rotational inertia of the same system.

In the real world of rotating systems are bodies or segments or implements whose masses are not condensed into single points as in Figure G.3; the mass is spread out along the radius and has some kind of shape. For real bodies, then, the rotational inertia is the mass times the distance that would be the radius if all the body's mass were concentrated at a single point. This distance that represents how far away from the axis of rotation a body's mass is distributed is technically called the **radius of gyration (k).** A rotating body whose mass is spread away from the axis has a large radius of gyration (e.g., a somersaulting body in a layout position). If the mass is packed in close to the axis, its radius of gyration is small, as in a tuck somersault.

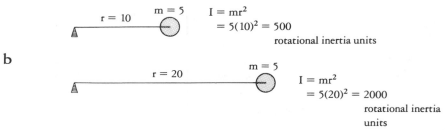

Figure G.3.   (a) Doubling the mass of a rotating object doubles its rotational inertia. (b) Doubling the distance of an object's mass from the axis quadruples its rotational inertia.

A body with a small radius of gyration has a smaller rotational inertia than that body would have with a larger radius of gyration.

The radius of gyration distance should not be confused with the distance of the CG from the axis of rotation. The radius of gyration is always a distance greater than the distance of the CG of a system from the axis of rotation.

Instead of using $I = mr^2$ for a single condensed mass, therefore, we can express the rotational inertia for real bodies as:

$$I = mk^2$$

Equation G.7

where I is rotational inertia of the system, m is mass, and k is radius of gyration.

The units are designated as "rotational inertia" units. A body's resistance to change in rotary motion, then, is the product of a body's mass and its radius of gyration squared and is specific to a given axis of rotation.

For our purposes, calculating the numerical values of a body's rotational inertia is unnecessary. What is important, however, is understanding fully the concept of rotational inertia and its influence on the angular acceleration of any body or segment that can rotate about an axis. Every time a body segment is moved (rotated), the rotational inertia of that segment determines how the segment responds to the torque applied to it. The shape of each of the segments forming our upper and lower extremities produces a relatively small rotational inertia about an axis at its *proximal* end, because the more massive part of each segment is situated close to the proximal joint, thus decreasing the amount of torque that needs to be applied to the segment to angularly accelerate the segment around the proximal joint. The rotational inertia of these segments about axes through their *distal* joints is greater because of the mass distributions of the segments. Such an arrangement of a body segment's mass relative to its axis of rotation permits rapid limb rotation.

Consider the two segments in Figure G.4, each to be rotated around the same axis. Each has the same total mass, but the distribution of the mass relative to the axis is reversed. The mass arrangement in Figure G.4a would require a much larger torque to angularly accelerate it than would the arrangement in Figure G.4b.

When the whole human body is rotated in spins and aerial twists and somersaults, the torque necessary to rotate it varies according to the body's rotational inertia around the specific axis used. The body's rotational inertia is the least when it rotates about its longitudinal axis; its radius of gyration is small because the body's mass is packed in close along the axis. The body's rotational inertia is the greatest when somersaulting in a layout position about the body's mediolateral axis because that same mass is distributed far away from the mediolateral axis.

Now that we have identified rotational inertia as the resistive property of a system to angular acceleration, we can return to the expression for Newton's second law as applied to rotary motion: $\alpha = T/I$. The interrelationship of the three variables in the expression is well worth understanding. The meaning is similar to that for linear motion. The angular acceleration of the segment is directly proportional to the applied net torque and is inversely proportional to the segment's rotational inertia. The relationship of any two of the variables can be expressed graphically while the

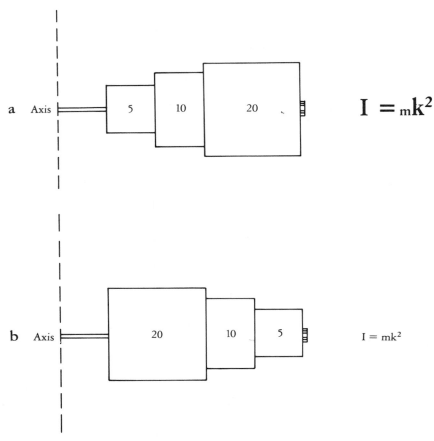

Figure G.4. Two segments with the same masses but with the masses distributed differently from the axis. Much more torque would be necessary to angularly accelerate the segment in (a) than the one in (b).

third factor is kept the same. Figures G.5, G.6, and G.7 illustrate the effect of holding one of the three variables constant to note how the other two change in relation to each other.

Case I: Varying the motive torque applied by the hip flexors to the lower extremity with its rotational inertia kept constant, and observing the magnitude of the resulting angular acceleration (Figure G.5).

Case II: Varying the rotational inertia of the lower extremity (knee fully extended to fully flexed), applying the same amount of muscle torque, and observing the resulting angular acceleration (Figure G.6).

Case III: Varying the rotational inertia of the lower extremity, specifying that the angular acceleration of the extremity is to be the same each time it is swung

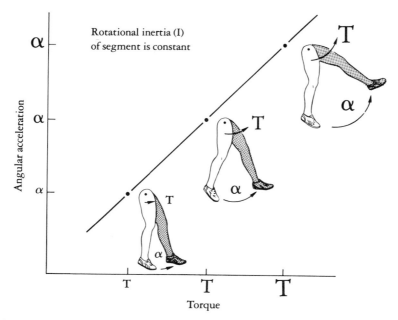

Increasing the torque applied by the hip flexor muscles increases the angular acceleration of the segment if the segment's rotational inertia is not changed.

Figure G.5.

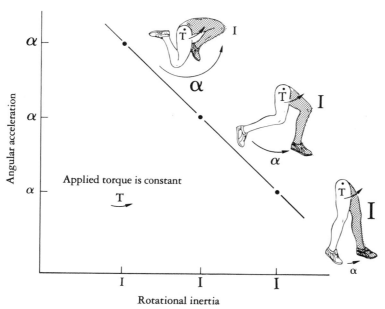

As the rotational inertia of a segment is increased, it experiences less angular acceleration from the same amount of torque applied by the hip flexor muscles.

Figure G.6.

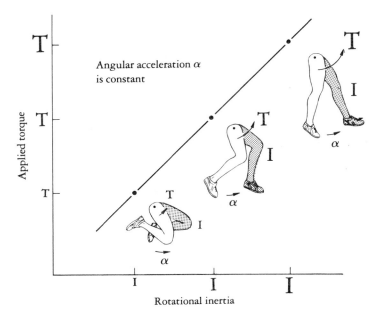

Figure G.7. As the rotational inertia of a segment is increased, the applied muscle torque must be increased to produce the same angular acceleration.

forward, and observing the magnitude of the applied muscle torque required to produce that angular acceleration (Figure G.7).

Understanding the concept of rotational inertia of individual body segments and how this property influences resulting rotary motion and necessary muscular effort is a valuable tool in exercise and skill analysis. The ability to vary the rotational inertia of the whole body and body parts relative to specific axes of rotation is a factor of primary importance in the performance of somersaults, twists, and suspension swinging skills, as will be seen in the chapters concerning rotations of the body.

We will now examine the familiar movement of swinging the leg forward in the recovery phase of running, as illustrated in Figure G.8. The system for which $\alpha = T/I$ will be represented by the total lower extremity (thigh, leg, and foot). The axis of rotation is through the hip joint. The mass of the lower extremity remains constant; however, the rotational inertia depends upon the extremity's mass distribution relative to the axis of rotation at the hip joint. The measure of mass distribution is the radius of gyration (k). In Figure G.8, this measure of the distribution from the axis of rotation is indicated by the shading. When the knee is extended, the rotational inertia is the greatest, as shown for the left leg in Figure G.8a. When the knee is fully flexed, the mass is brought as close as possible to the hip axis; therefore, the rotational inertia is the least, as shown for the right leg in Figure G.8a and b. The resistance of the extremity to angular acceleration about the hip joint in this case is the least. The external motive torque (external to the segmental system) is the contraction of the hip flexor muscles, which cross over the hip joint to pull the femur forward.

The above example explains why more knee bend is observed during fast running, when the leg must be brought forward more quickly than is seen in walking. The reduction of the rotational inertia of the lower extremity produces a greater angular acceleration of the extremity for a given muscle torque.

UNDERSTANDING TORQUE AND MOTION RELATIONSHIPS

1. Describe the difference between the mass (inertia) of your arm and its rotational inertia.

⊗ = CG of
lower extremity

a   b   c

The rotational inertia of the lower extremity around the hip joint is changed by knee flexion and extension which alters the radius of gyration, k.

Figure G.8.

2. Grip a baseball bat and rotate it back and forth horizontally. Grip it at the opposite end and rotate it as before. Compare the difficulty with which the same mass may be rotated depending on how the mass is distributed from the axis of rotation. Explain.

3. With one hand, grip each of the objects listed below at one end. Using wrist motion only, rotate each back and forth through approximately a 100-degree ROM along a horizontal plane of motion. Compare the degree of difficulty experienced with each object and rank them from greatest to least in terms of rotational inertia. The objects are: (a) a racquetball racket, (b) a fencing foil, (c) baseball bats of various weights and shapes, (d) tennis rackets of various weights and shapes (if possible), (e) a badminton racket, (f) a yardstick, and (g) a book.

4. Hold your arms horizontally out to your sides and rapidly swing them up and down in a vertical plane several times. Next, bend the elbows to place your fingers at the front of your shoulder joints. Repeat the sweeping motion of the arms in a vertical plane. Explain the difference in difficulty (you have not altered the mass of the arm).

5. Why would a front-crawl (freestyle) swimmer choose to bend the elbow as the arm is brought forward over the water to begin another stroke?

6. Why is it easier to perform jumping jacks with bent elbows?

7. Examine the masses and shapes or mass distribution of the following body segments and make a conclusion regarding the amount of muscle torque necessary to rotate these segments: (a) upper arm, (b) forearm, (c) hand, (d) fingers, (e) thigh, (f) lower leg, and (g) foot.

8. Describe an example in which a body segment is angularly accelerated by a given muscle torque. How could that segment be accelerated at a faster rate?

REFERENCES AND SUGGESTED READINGS

Barham, J. *Mechanical Kinesiology.* St. Louis: C. V. Mosby Co., 1978.

Cooper, J. M., and Glassow, R. B. *Kinesiology.* 4th ed. St. Louis: C. V. Mosby Co., 1976.

Plagenhoef, S., Evans, F. G., and Abdelnour, T. "Anatomical Data for Analyzing Human Motion." *Research Quarterly* 54 (2) (1983): 169-78.

Tichonov, V. N. "Distribution of Body Masses of a Sportsman." In *Biomechanics V-B: Proceedings of the Fifth International Symposium on Biomechanics,* ed. P. V. Komi, 103-08. Baltimore: University Park Press, 1976.

Tricker, R. A. R., and Tricker, B. J. K. *The Science of Human Movement.* New York: American Elsevier Publishing Co., 1967.

Wheeler, G. F., and Kirkpatrick, L. D. *Physics: Building a World View.* Englewood Cliffs, N.J.: Prentice-Hall, 1983.

ANGULAR MOMENTUM

Prerequisites

Concept Modules B, C, D, G

Concept Module Contents

SECTION 1

ANGULAR MOMENTUM

To understand how and why the body moves as it does in rotary motion about an axis, angular momentum must be considered. We know that a body's resistance to change in its state of angular motion is called its rotational inertia and is designated by **I.**

We have seen how the angular acceleration of a system is determined by the net external torque applied and the rotational inertia of the system. Angular acceleration of a system by a torque produces a certain amount of angular velocity, or speed of rotation in a given direction. Were it not for the application of an external torque, the system would have remained as it was, either at rest with zero angular velocity or rotating with some preexisting angular velocity.

Just as a system moving linearly possesses a certain amount of linear momentum, a rotating system has **angular momentum (L).** The magnitude of a system's angular momentum is the product of its rotational inertia (I) and its angular velocity (ω):

Equation H.1

$$L = I\omega \quad \text{or} \quad L = mk^2\omega$$

where L is angular momentum, m is mass, k is radius of gyration, I is rotational inertia, and ω is angular velocity.

Although **I** is the most frequently used symbol for rotational inertia, remember that **I** is a function of both the mass, **m,** and the *square* of the radius of gyration, **k.**

Calculations of angular momentum are not used here, but the relationship of the factors that influence angular momentum are addressed.

The significance of angular momentum of body segments and of the whole body in a multitude of movement activities cannot be overestimated. It is a primary factor involved in swinging, jumping, throwing, kicking, twisting, somersaulting, swimming, and locomotion. Angular momentum, or the quantity of angular motion, is created originally from an externally applied torque. After some angular velocity (and angular momentum) is achieved, the body continues to rotate after the removal or cessation of the motive torque, and it loses or gains angular momentum only upon receiving another external torque.

In Figure H.1a, the follow-through movements of the arm and racket after ball contact are the result of angular momentum of these segments caused by applied muscle torque. The extremity and racket continue to rotate forward and upward on their own angular momentum until resistive torque of the shoulder and arm muscles and joint ligaments causes angular deceleration of the segment. In Figure H.1b, once the gymnast executes the push-off to rotate the body in vaulting, the body continues to rotate because of its angular momentum. The body continues to rotate with this angular momentum until acted on by the external torque provided by the floor at landing.

Angular momentum of segments (a) and the whole body (b) is produced by external torque applied to the system. If the rotating system does not encounter an external torque, it will continue rotating.

Figure H.1.

SECTION 2

ANGULAR IMPULSE

To angularly accelerate a body, a net external torque must be applied. If a large angular velocity of the body is desired, the torque must be large or the torque must be applied for a longer period of time to continually accelerate the body. Whether a torque acts for a short time or a long time, the product of torque multiplied by its time of application is called the **angular impulse.** The magnitude of the angular impulse acting on the body determines the *change* in the body's angular momentum ($I\omega$ before to $I\omega$ after the impulse acts). Quantitatively, angular impulse is expressed as:

$$T\,(t) = \Delta L = I\omega_2 - I\omega_1$$

Equation H.2

where T is external torque applied, t is time during which the torque is applied, and ΔL is change in angular momentum.

Thus, a body projected into the air by a force, which acts for a period of time before takeoff and acts eccentric to the body's center of gravity (CG), will create a linear motion of that body's CG and a rotation of that body about its CG. The magnitude of the velocity of rotation will be determined in part by the magnitude of the force, the perpendicular distance of the line of force from the CG axis, and the length of time the force is applied.

The diver in Figure H.2 depresses a springboard, giving it elastic potential energy. The upward force of the board causes the diver's upward linear motion, and because the line of action of the force passes eccentric to the diver's CG ($d_\perp$), it is torque producing and causes him to rotate. The greater the force, the $d_\perp$, or the time of application of the torque, the greater the angular impulse and consequent angular momentum.

Another example of an impulse creating rotation of the body about an axis is a figure skater who wants to spin about her longitudinal axis. She initiates the spin by pushing against the ice with the toe of the skate (Figure H.3). The push is directed opposite to the spin direction, and its line of action is eccentric to the body's longitudinal axis. Figure H.3a indicates the skater's position during the force application, and Figure H.3b is a view from the top showing the perpendicular distance the force is from the longitudinal axis of rotation. The longer the time she can generate an accelerating reaction torque, the greater her angular momentum when the push ceases.

Once angular momentum is established in a body, it can be decreased by a resistive angular impulse, such as an off-center contact of the fingers receiving a top-spinning

Figure H.2.   Rotary and linear motion are caused by the eccentric force applied to the diver by the recoiling springboard.

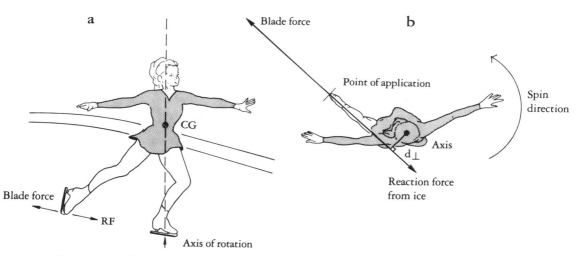

(a) A figure skater initiating a spin about the longitudinal axis. (b) A view from the top, showing the line of action of the reaction force and the force arm distance ($d_\perp$) from the axis of rotation.

Figure H.3.

volleyball. The angular momentum of an object also can be increased by a motive (accelerating) angular impulse. For example, in catching a Frisbee creatively, the glancing blows of the fingers on the rim of the spinning disc increase the spin velocity prior to its being caught. Such fast spinning of the Frisbee, like the spinning of a toy top, gives stability to the object; that is, it is resistant to changing its axis orientation, or direction. In fact, the faster the spin (angular velocity), the greater the stability of the body in its particular position or orientation. Such resistance to change in position is called **gyroscopic stability.** It accounts for the directional stability of a spiraling football pass or spinning discus, of a cyclist maintaining an upright position when the wheels of the bicycle are rotating rapidly, or of an ice skater spinning about a vertical axis. Such a phenomenon is a by-product of the body's angular momentum.

SECTION 3

CONSERVATION OF ANGULAR MOMENTUM WITHIN A SYSTEM

We have seen that once an angular impulse, T(t), has given a system some angular momentum, that angular momentum continues in the absence of external torques.

Newton's first law about the constancy of a body's angular momentum is the basis for the principle of **conservation of angular momentum.** This principle declares that the angular momentum of an isolated system will remain the same regardless of any movements or torques that are produced *internal* to the system, as long as no *external* torque is applied to the system.

The term *isolated* means that the rotating body is free from any external source that could apply a torque (e.g., a supporting surface or object, contact with another body, or air resistance or water resistance that is strong enough to create a torque). Conservation of angular momentum of the human body is evident in a number of activities in which the body is isolated, as in diving and aerial gymnastics, and also in situations in which the external resistive torque is negligible, as in spinning about on the tip of an ice skate or on a smooth shoe surface.

The diver in Figure H.4 illustrates the constancy of angular momentum during descent after leaving the board with angular momentum $(I\omega)$ about the mediolateral axis. Once the body leaves the supporting surface, the only external force acting on it is gravity. Gravity acts through the CG of the body, which serves as the location of the axis of rotation during free flight. The gravitational force, therefore, does not have any perpendicular distance from the axis of rotation and thus can produce neither torque nor angular impulse. Consequently, during free flight, gravity cannot

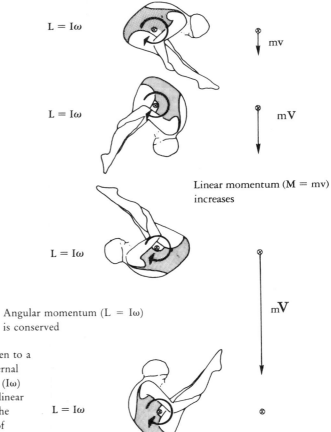

$L = I\omega$

$L = I\omega$

Linear momentum $(M = mv)$ increases

$L = I\omega$

Angular momentum $(L = I\omega)$ is conserved

mv

mV

mV

Figure H.4. Once angular momentum is given to a body that is then free from external torques, its angular momentum $(I\omega)$ will stay the same. The body's linear momentum will change under the influence of the external force of gravity.

$L = I\omega$

cause any change in the angular momentum of the body. Since there are no external torques, there will be no change in the diver's angular momentum until she lands or collides with another object. For simplicity, air resistance is considered negligible.

Note that gravity is accelerating the diver's CG linearly downward and causes her to fall faster and faster, but has no effect on her angular momentum.

Now consider the diver who initiates a forward somersault as she pushes off from the board (Figure H.5). Her initial angular velocity in a layout position is quite small, and her rotational inertia relative to the axis passing through her CG is large. Her angular momentum is the product of these two factors; once isolated in air, her

Angular momentum (L = Iω) remains constant.
As I decreases, ω increases.
As I increases, ω decreases.

The angular momentum of a diver is conserved throughout the aerial phase, during which she receives no external torque (according to Newton's first law of motion). **Figure H.5.**

angular momentum, **Iω,** will not change. If she then goes into a pike position, she brings her body mass close in toward her axis of rotation and thereby decreases her radius of gyration and thus her rotational inertia. Such a decrease in rotational inertia causes her angular velocity to increase so that the product of **I** and **ω** remains the same value as it was before she changed body position. Her angular momentum is conserved.

Before entering the water she moves out of the pike position into the layout, thereby slowing her angular velocity so that she can enter in a straight position. Once her hands enter the water, she encounters a resistive torque from the water, stopping her rotation and allowing the rest of her body to enter vertically. Such changing of segment positions while rotating changes the body's rotational inertia and leads to an opposite type of change in the angular velocity, so that the total angular momentum of the body remains unchanged. The principle of conservation of angular momentum forms the basis for controlling rotary movements of the body and its segments.

Such a situation in which an isolated rotating body is able to change its shape (and rotational inertia) with internal forces and thereby change its angular velocity can be depicted by the symbols shown in Figure H.6.

SECTION 4

VECTOR RESOLUTION OF ANGULAR MOMENTUM

The resolution of an angular momentum vector is important in understanding one method of initiating rotation in the air, a common maneuver performed in diving and gymnastics. The process set forth here is like that used for resolving a body's linear velocity, except that the angular directions must be indicated by the right-hand thumb rule that was described previously for determining torque direction. The following method demonstrates the resolution of a body's angular momentum into two perpendicular angular momentum components. For example, in Figure H.7a, a gymnast is in the process of simultaneously somersaulting and twisting around a horizontal axis in space, indicated by AB; the body's spatial angular momentum vector is directed toward B.

To resolve the body's spatial angular momentum vector into a twisting component and a somersaulting component, the graphic vector resolution method (completing the rectangle) is used. The two directions sought are along the axis for somersaulting (the mediolateral axis, which runs through the body from side to side) and along the axis for twisting (the body's longitudinal axis, which runs from toe to head). These directional lines are drawn perpendicular to each other to form two sides of the rectangle that will be completed. Figure H.7b shows the completed rectangle, the vector direction and magnitude (lengths) of the twisting momentum (OC), and the direction and magnitude of the somersaulting momentum (OD). The component

$$L = I\omega \text{ is conserved}$$

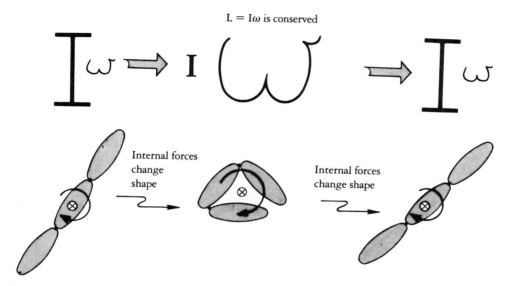

Internal forces change shape

Internal forces change shape

Internal forces can change the shape of a body to change its mass distribution (k), which changes its rotational inertia ($I = mk^2$). Angular momentum is conserved; therefore, angular velocity must change as the shape is changed.

Figure H.6.

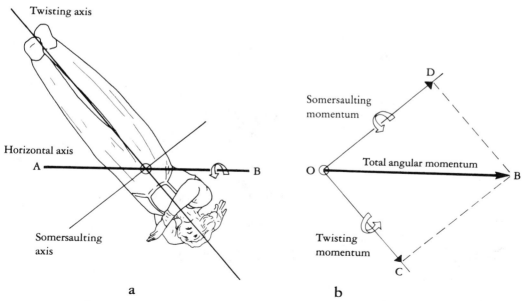

Twisting axis

Horizontal axis

A ●———————⊗————————↺——— B

Somersaulting axis

a

Somersaulting momentum

O ◉———— Total angular momentum ————▶ B

Total angular momentum

Twisting momentum

b

A somersaulting and twisting gymnast. (a) The right-hand thumb rule indicates the total angular momentum of the body around a horizontal spatial axis (A-B). (b) The body's angular momentum is resolved into its somersaulting component and its twisting component.

Figure H.7.

vector direction determines the direction of twisting and somersaulting according to the right-hand thumb rule.

UNDERSTANDING ANGULAR MOMENTUM

1. Give an example in human movement where a system has angular momentum; tell what factors comprise its angular momentum.

2. Define angular impulse.

3. Identify the angular impulse that causes a body segment to rotate and therefore gain angular momentum. Identify the angular impulse that is responsible for diminishing a segment's angular momentum to zero.

4. Hold a book in each hand with the arms held horizontally out from your sides. Turn and spin on one foot. While spinning, bring both books to your chest. Explain the body's motion response in terms of the conservation of angular momentum.

5. Repeat the steps in question 4, but return the arms out to the sides just after you bring the books to your chest. Explain the response.

6. Describe several examples in sport and dance in which the angular momentum of the body is conserved although the angular velocity changes.

7. The following experiments involve using a turntable and various pieces of external equipment. The table should be made level in the horizontal plane, have a small rotational inertia, but be sturdy enough and large enough to hold an adult. The joint between the table and the base should be as frictionless as possible. An external wheel should be available, which is weighted on the outside rim to increase its rotational inertia. It may be rotated around its axis while a person is holding onto the extended axle (Figure H.8a).

For all the experiments, the following should be noted:

    The axis of rotation of the system and of the parts

    The direction of rotation of the system and the parts

    The direction of the angular momentum vectors involved

    The relative rotational inertias (masses and radii) of the parts

    The relative speeds of rotation of parts

    The description of what happens and the reason why the experiment operates as it does

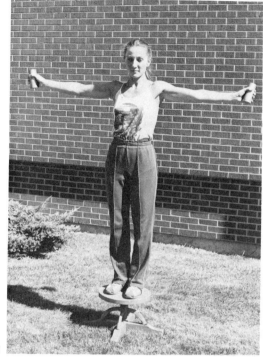

(a) Standing on a turntable isolates the body from external torques around a vertical axis. Holding a bicycle wheel by its extended axle creates changes in rotary motion of the body depending on the spin of the wheel. (b) Holding weights in the hands enables the user to easily alter the body's rotational inertia around a vertical axis.

Figure H.8.

Turntable Experiments

   a. Stand on the motionless turntable, holding a baseball bat in both hands. Swing the bat overhead in large circles.

   b. Perform the same motion as in experiment a without holding the bat in your hands. Compare.

   c. Perform the following arm actions while standing on the motionless table:

      i. Abduct the right arm to shoulder level and flex the left arm to shoulder level. Swing both arms vigorously to the left.

     ii. Perform the same experiment as in i, while holding two heavy books in the hands. Compare the results (see Figure H.8b).

    iii. Perform the same experiment as in i, with the legs spread to the side as far as they will go.

    iv. Hold both arms in abduction at shoulder level. Transversely flex them simultaneously.

     v. Perform the same experiment as in iv, holding a book in the right hand.

d. Stand on the motionless turntable and swing a baseball bat vigorously while gripping the handle. Turn the bat around so that you are now gripping the hitting end and swing it vigorously again. Compare the two reactions.

e. Hold two heavy books in the hands and abduct the arms to shoulder level. Have a partner spin the turntable. As you are spinning, pull the books in toward your chest. (Be careful, as the spin velocity may increase appreciably.) Put the arms back out again.

Wheel Experiments

The following experiments involve the turntable and the bicycle wheel:

f. Stand on the motionless turntable. Your partner spins the free wheel as fast as possible and hands it to you in a position so that the wheel is spinning horizontally; that is, the axis of the wheel is vertical. Turn the wheel to a vertical spinning position (axis horizontal).

g. Repeat experiment f, but have your partner hand you the wheel in a vertical spinning position (axis horizontal).

h. Repeat experiment f, with the person on the table spinning the wheel. Compare.

i. Stand on the motionless turntable. Your partner hands the vertically spinning wheel to you, and then spins the turntable. Turn the wheel axis to the right, return the wheel to the original position, and turn the wheel to the left.

j. Repeat experiment i, altering the turntable speeds to a slow spin, a medium spin, and a fast spin. (Be careful!)

REFERENCES
SUGGESTED READINGS

Barham, J. *Mechanical Kinesiology*. St. Louis: C. V. Mosby Co., 1978.

Dyson, G. *The Mechanics of Athletics*. 6th ed. London: Hodder & Stoughton, 1973.

Frohlich, C. "Do Springboard Divers Violate Angular Momentum Conservation?" *American Journal of Physics* 47 (7) (1979): 583–92.

Hopper, B. J. *The Mechanics of Human Movement*. New York: American Elsevier Publishing Co., 1973.

Resnick, R., and Halliday, D. *Physics*. Part I. New York: John Wiley & Sons, 1977.

Tricker, R. A. R., and Tricker, B. J. K. *The Science of Human Movement*. New York: American Elsevier Publishing Co., 1967.

Wheeler, G. F., and Kirkpatrick, L. D. *Physics: Building a World View*. Englewood Cliffs, N.J.: Prentice-Hall, 1983.

Prerequisites

Concept Modules A, B, C, D, E, F, G, H
Chapters 1, 2

Chapter Contents

CHAPTER 11

Analysis of Balance-Related Activities

Balance and *equilibrium* are often used synonymously to describe a system in a state of rest (motionless). Strictly speaking, **equilibrium** describes the state of a system that is not being accelerated (i.e., not changing its state of motion in terms of speed or direction). Such a state of equilibrium can exist for an object or body at rest, in which case it is called **static equilibrium,** or for one that is moving with a constant speed and direction, in which case it is called **dynamic equilibrium.** In human activities, however, the body is always experiencing some kind of movement change, whether it be accelerations and decelerations of individual segments or the expansion of the thorax for breathing. Appreciating this fact, we think of *balance* as a term that implies some kind of movement control, either for short or long periods of time. When we discuss the concept of **balance,** therefore, we will consider it to be a process whereby the body's state of equilibrium is controlled for a given purpose. The concept of **stability,** or the difficulty with which equilibrium can be disturbed, is encountered frequently in activities demanding static postures as well as in many skills and tasks involving the moving system. Neuromuscular mechanisms play an important role in body balance when we are apparently motionless and during movement. This chapter focuses on the mechanical determinants of equilibrium with reference to some of the neuromuscular processes associated with balance control.

SECTION 1

LINEAR AND ROTARY EQUILIBRIUM

A body can move in linear or rotary paths, and it can experience a state of equilibrium in either of these types of motion. For equilibrium to exist, no net external force can be causing a change in the system's state of linear motion and no net external torque can be causing a change in its state of rotary motion. In other words, all the forces in all directions must cancel out to zero, and all the torques in all directions must cancel out to zero.

An example of a body at rest in which no net force or torque acts upon it is provided by a student asleep in a chair in a noon class. The body weight force of 712 N (160 lb) acts downward and is opposed by the equal and opposite ground reaction force of 712 N that is transmitted by the chair. No other forces or torques are acting to upset the body's equilibrium, so no motion change occurs. The student has static equilibrium.

A moving system could be in a state of rotary equilibrium, but not linear equilibrium, and vice versa. A diver performing a pike somersault dive spins with constant angular momentum, while her center of gravity is linearly accelerated downward by gravity, gaining velocity during the time she is falling.

An example in which linear equilibrium exists while rotary equilibrium does not is provided by a dancer who spins about his body's longitudinal axis on one foot. His body's center of gravity (CG) is not moving linearly, but the floor friction provides a net resistive torque on the foot to slow his rate of turning. The most common situations encountered in human movement are those in which the body is in neither linear nor rotary equilibrium; that is, the body or its parts are changing linear and rotary speed from one moment to the next. Therefore, some net force or net torque or both are acting on the system. The body is linearly accelerated or decelerated according to the direction of the net force and angularly accelerated or decelerated according to the direction of the net torque.

A runner appears to move at a constant velocity, but if she is observed on film, small changes in the linear velocity of the CG can be detected. The relative magnitudes of the vertical forces of the body's weight and the ground reaction force on each foot as it is planted cause the CG to accelerate up and down as she travels. Variations in the backward component of the push-off force with each step cause equal changes in the forward component of the ground reaction force; these result in changes in the forward velocity of the CG. Small variations in the linear velocity are not easily observed nor perceived by the runner. Similarly, any side-to-side movements of the CG indicate accelerations resulting from net sideward ground reaction forces on the foot. Close observation of the individual body segments of a runner will reveal that they are always in a state of angular acceleration or deceleration as they rotate forward, stop, rotate backward, stop, and so forth. Note that the alternating rotary movements of the lower extremities cause the linear translation of the whole body.

LINEAR AND ROTARY STABILITY

Although the conditions for true equilibrium are practically nonexistent in human situations, they are often the target conditions of the mover who is attempting to control static balance or the static balance of another person or object. The goal may be to assume a precarious position from which equilibrium may be easily disturbed, as in a track or swimming start in which falling forward is coupled with forceful leg extension to accelerate the body.

Stability is the term that describes a body's resistance to losing its static or dynamic equilibrium, or its resistance to changing its state of motion. The body can have a certain amount of stability in terms of moving in a straight line (**linear stability**) as well as stability against tipping over (**rotary stability**). Each of these types of stability is important in most movement activities, and often one type influences the other.

Linear Stability

The situations in which the body is caused to move in a straight line are usually those involving sliding across some surface, whether the surface is horizontal, an incline, or a vertical wall or pole. The surface may be a solid floor, ice, turf, sand, dirt, water, or other kinds of material such as rock, metal, rope, rubber, fiberglass, and plastic. The body may be in direct contact with the surface, or some interface may exist between the body and the surface, such as shoe soles, gloves, and clothing, or equipment such as ice skates, skis, a skateboard, a bicycle, a canoe, a sailboat, a surfboard, a parachute, or a hang glider. Whether the body should have maximum, minimum, or optimum linear stability depends on the purpose of the activity.

A general principle concerning linear stability may be expressed as follows: *The greater the linear impulse (force times its time of application) required to upset the linear equilibrium of a body (at rest or in motion), the more stable the body.* The greater the body's inertia, or mass, the greater the linear stability, for a greater impulse is necessary to cause it to accelerate (change speed or direction). In addition, linear stability in sliding situations depends on the frictional forces generated between the contacting surfaces of the body and the environment. An ice skater is easily accelerated linearly by a small push, which is sufficient to overcome the small resistive frictional force of the ice against the skate blades. The motive force of wind on sails accelerates a boat through water, but not across the sand, because of the difference in resistive friction force on the hull. In each of these cases, the resistive friction force is an important determinant of the system's linear stability.

In situations in which the weight of the system is the force with which the two frictional surfaces are pressed together, heavier (more massive) bodies will have more friction force to enhance their stability. Thus, an increase in the body's mass increases its linear stability in two ways. Such stability is manifested by a football lineman whose mass requires a greater impulse for acceleration and whose weight gives better friction between the shoes and the ground.

Whether or not linear stability is desirable depends on the objective of the mover. Perhaps only minimal linear stability will be advantageous to performance, as in sailing or water skiing. For situations involving linear stability or instability, it is mainly the sliding tendency that should be considered as desirable or undesirable in the performance. Important here is recognizing the distinction between the desirability of linear stability and that of rotary stability, as when tipping or falling over.

Rotary Stability

When a body risks being tipped over or falling, its rotary stability is of concern. Such stability refers to a body's resistance to losing its equilibrium by being rotated about some fixed point by some motive torque. *The more stable a body, the greater the angular impulse* (torque times the time of application) *necessary to upset its rotary equilibrium.* For example, if one were to push on a block standing on edge, it would tip over or rotate about the axis formed by the bottom edge touching the supporting surface (Figure 11.1a). This push would be enough to rotate the block into a position where gravity would cause it to rotate farther away from its original balanced position. If a lesser angular impulse (push) were applied, gravity would cause the block to return to its original position.

If the block were pushed only enough to raise one edge and then held there (Figure 11.1b), the opposing torques from the push force and the weight force would cancel out and the block would remain in that position. Once the line of gravity falls to one side or the other of a body's axis of rotation, it becomes torque producing. If there is no opposing torque, as in Figure 11.1b, it causes a rotation of the body about this axis. If you were to stand rigid and someone were to push you from behind, your body would rotate about an axis formed by your toes on the ground, and you would fall forward and downward. Such a fall seldom occurs, however, because you would not remain as a single rigid unit; you would step forward automatically as you started to lose your balance, and you would be able to stop your motion as you planted your foot in front of you (Figure 11.1c). Comparing these two situations, one can see the fundamental difference in potential stability between inanimate objects and human beings. We are able to move or rearrange our segments to maintain rotary stability either by changing the location of the line of gravity relative to the base of support or by changing the base of support itself.

In weight-bearing activities, *the body will be balanced if its line of gravity passes through some part of the body's base of support.* The importance of the body's source of support warrants a careful definition. The body's **base** (area) **of support** is that region bounded by body parts in contact with some resistive surface that exerts a counterforce against the body's applied force. For example, the outline of the foot defines your base of support when you stand on one foot. If you are hanging by

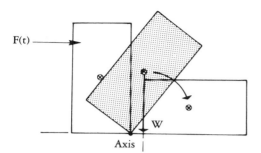

a Continued application of torque causes line of gravity to fall beyond base edge

b Lesser torque can balance weight torque to hold block in position

c Humans can quickly adapt to upsetting forces by forming new base of support

The magnitude of angular impulse created by a push determines whether an object or body will rotate and fall.

Figure 11.1.

both hands from a horizontal bar, the area enclosed between the outer limits of your fingers forms your base of support. If some object or surface exerts a counterforce against some part of your body in some direction other than the vertical, it too forms part of your base of support in that it is a force that contributes to your state of equilibrium. Figure 11.2a shows such a position of balance created by vertical and horizontal forces, similar to the block in Figure 11.1b. Other examples of support bases are illustrated in the figure as well. Note that the area of each base of support is always defined by the outermost limits of the contacting surfaces.

Figure 11.2. The base of support of a body in equilibrium is formed by the boundaries of contact with sources of support.

Stable, Unstable, and Neutral Equilibrium

The state of rotary equilibrium of a body is often classified into three categories: *stable, unstable, and neutral.* The physical characteristics and the nature of the base of support determine a body's vulnerability to upset or loss of balance. Figure 11.3a–c illustrates a model representing each of the three categories. A body in stable equilibrium requires a greater angular impulse to upset its balance than does a body in unstable equilibrium. A force applied to a spherical shape does not cause a rotary balance upset, since there is no tendency of the ball to "fall" one way or another;

its CG is said to be in neutral equilibrium and remains directly over the base of support on a level surface. If the surface were inclined, however, the ball would "fall" downhill, because the gravity line would pass beyond the base of support on the downhill side, and the net torque on the ball would cause the ball to roll (Figure 11.3d).

Various static body positions in movement activities simulate these three basic types of equilibrium. The degree of rotary stability of a body is *specific to direction* as well as being dependent on the effects of external torques acting on it. "Specific to direction" means that a body may be stable, or resistant to upset, in one direction but not necessarily in another. For example, while balancing on a narrow beam, you are relatively stable in a forward-backward direction, but not in a sideward direction, due to your narrow lateral base.

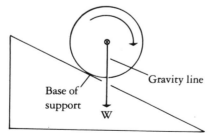

States of rotary equilibrium (a, b, c) and the loss of balance of a ball on a hill (d).   **Figure 11.3.**

For situations in which gravity and the ground reaction force are the only external forces acting on a stationary body, *balance exists if the gravity line passes vertically within the area of support.* The mechanical reason why these conditions produce balance is based on the generation of equal and opposing external torques produced by gravity and the ground reaction forces. For situations in which there is some applied external torque in addition to gravity and the ground reaction force, balance may be upset temporarily or permanently, depending on the magnitude of this angular impulse.

Rotary instability of a wide-base body can occur depending on where the gravity line passes within the base. If the angular impulse is large enough to impart sufficient angular momentum to the box in Figure 11.4a, this momentum will carry the CG up and beyond the base edge. If the gravity line passes close to the base edge, which will be the axis, a relatively small impulse will cause it to tip and fall (Figure 11.4b).

Figure 11.4c illustrates a sprinter in his set position in the starting blocks. His weight produces a clockwise (cw) torque about an axis at the hand. The ground reaction force acting on each foot forms a counterclockwise (ccw) torque about the

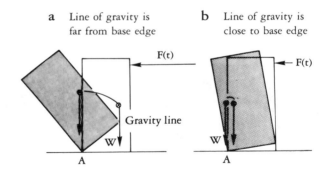

a Line of gravity is
far from base edge

b Line of gravity is
close to base edge

c Line of gravity is close to base edge

Figure 11.4. (a) When the gravity line is initially farther from the potential axis of rotation, a greater angular impulse is required to make it rotate and fall to the left. (b) If the gravity line is initially near the axis of rotation, a small angular impulse will upset it. (c) A sprinter's gravity line falls vertically through the base of support, close to the leading edge, and represents the unstable equilibrium condition.

axis. Both of these ccw torques from the blocks serve to cancel the cw weight torque, so that the net torque acting on the body is equal to zero; the body is in equilibrium. He is in *unstable* equilibrium, because he has positioned his CG forward so that his gravity line falls vertically near the forward edge of the base formed by the hands. In such a position, he is still balanced, but only a small push is necessary to upset his equilibrium and cause him to rotate (fall) in the forward direction, a move advantageous to quick starting. At the gun, the hands are withdrawn as a source of support, and the CG moves forward and upward from the accelerating forces generated by the legs against the blocks.

A frequently quoted principle for increasing stability states that the lower the body's CG, the greater its stability. This is true if other changes do not occur (Figure 11.5). It is not true if the CG is lowered and is also moved toward one edge of the

a   Less stable
    (high CG)

b   More stable
    (low CG)

CG lowered

W

W

c   Least stable
    (low CG but line
    of gravity is close
    to base edge)

W

(a-b) The lower its center of gravity, the more stable the body, but only if all other variables do not change to offset this stability advantage. (c) If the center of gravity is also moved toward the edge of the base, the body actually becomes less stable in that direction.

Figure 11.5.

base of support (Figure 11.5c); for if that base edge is the potential axis for body rotation caused by an external blow or push, the body will become less stable. Also, if the right foot of the person in Figure 11.5b were to be lifted as the CG is lowered, balance would be lost immediately because of the withdrawal of that source of support. We see, therefore, that for human movement situations in which a number of balance variables can change simultaneously, an understanding of all the mechanical factors governing stability best equips the teacher or coach for analyzing performance.

ROTARY STABILITY DURING SUSPENSION

We can evaluate the stability of a body suspended from a "base" above the body using the concepts of torque, imparted angular momentum, and position of the gravity line relative to the base of support. *A suspended body free to rotate in a vertical plane will seek a position in which the CG is at the lowest point possible within the constraints present.* If the base of support is below the body, the gravity line must pass somewhere through the area of the base for balance to exist if no other source of support is present. The gymnast in Figure 11.6a illustrates the fact

Figure 11.6.   A body free to rotate about a point of suspension comes to rest in an equilibrium position where the center of gravity is at its lowest possible point.

that the body will rotate until its CG is at the lowest point before static equilibrium is reached. If one hand is released from the bar, the body will again rotate in response to the weight torque about the axis of the single hand, and the CG will find its new lowest position (Figure 11.6b).

UNDERSTANDING BALANCE, EQUILIBRIUM, AND STABILITY

1. Stand with your heels and back against a wall. Keeping your legs straight, reach down toward your toes without moving your base and explain the results in terms of the CG, the line of gravity, and the base of support.

2. Repeat the exercise in question 1, standing away from the wall. Explain the difference in results. What is the movement that occurs at the ankle joints as you reach toward your toes?

3. Stand with your side against the wall so that your legs are parallel to your body's longitudinal axis. Slowly lift your outside foot. Describe and explain the results.

4. State a principle relating a body's line of gravity to its base of support if balance is to be maintained.

5. Perform the following movements:

a. Stand with your feet, heel to toe, along a line directed from front to back. Close your eyes, rise to your toes, and determine the direction in which you are least stable.
b. Stand with your feet spread laterally about 1 m apart, and repeat the steps in (a). Determine the direction in which you are least stable.
Using the experience gained in (a) and (b), state a principle relating the body's gravity line to its base of support for maximizing stability.

6. Assume a push-up position. What adjustment is necessary for balance if you remove one hand from the base of support? Explain why.

7. Using the concept of CG location and noting how it changes with segmental movements, explain how "pumping" in a suspended swing can initiate the swinging motion.

SECTION 3

ANALYZING BALANCE-RELATED PERFORMANCES

An understanding of the interrelationship of the mechanical factors governing the balance of a body is essential to analyze performances that depend for their success on maintenance of balance. These factors are: (1) body weight and mass, (2) the body's radius of gyration relative to the potential axis about which it will rotate or fall, (3) the height of the CG, (4) the horizontal distance of the gravity line from the potential axis of rotation (the size of the base of support), (5) friction forces, which help determine whether a source of support will "stick" to serve as an axis for rotation or will slip and no longer be a source of support, (6) the net external motive angular impulse acting to upset the body's state of rotary equilibrium, and (7) the angular momentum of the body and of the body segments.

In the following sections on static and dynamic balance, the integration of these stability determinants is illustrated for a variety of activities.

SECTION 4

MAINTAINING BALANCE IN STATIC POSITIONS

If the body is in a state of static balance, the situation is relatively simple to analyze as compared to one in which the body is in motion and the variables may be continually changing. We must realize, however, that all our static positions are achieved by movement and that the momentum of the body or its parts may carry it beyond the position to be held (e.g., pushing into a handstand). Once the body is in a static position, it is subject to upset by its own segmental movements and by external forces that may act on it. Keep in mind the condition necessary for maintaining a position of balance: *The net external torques acting on the body must be equal to zero.* This condition, one in which all opposing torques cancel, should be used as the target condition to be sought by the performer wishing to maintain a static position.

The apparently simple act of standing motionless is actually a continuing process of minute adjustments of body position to keep the CG over the base of support. The smaller the base (e.g., standing on one foot), the more accurate such adjustments must be to maintain rotary stability. Pressure of the supporting surface on the soles of the feet serves to maintain tension in the extensor muscles via the extensor thrust reflex. Because this tension prevents the lower extremities from flexing under the force of body weight, these extensor muscles are called the antigravity muscles. When relaxation occurs in these postural muscles, the joints of the vertebral column and lower extremities are forced into flexion by the body weight. When the body leans forward slightly, the gravity line moves toward the front edge of the base, increasing pressure on the balls of the feet and at the same time lengthening the ankle extensors (plantar flexors). When these muscles are so stretched, the myotatic, or stretch, reflex causes them to contract concentrically to rotate the body backward at the ankle. The gravity line is thereby shifted backward, removing the threat of a forward fall. Although the gravity line rarely shifts behind the ankle joint in normal standing, if the backward shift is too great, the ankle flexors are stretched and subsequent reflex contraction causes the body to be rotated forward at the ankle. Alternating contraction and relaxation of the ankle extensors results in what is called postural sway. The amplitude of sway is less precisely regulated if visual or auditory cues or both are not present. With increased sway, other body segments are brought into action to prevent loss of balance. The labyrinthine organs of the inner ear, which are sensitive to changes in head position and acceleration, also reflexly initiate such compensatory movements in the upright position. The head-righting reflexes must be voluntarily suppressed in inversion skills, such as headstands and handstands.

In most land activities, the body weight and ground reaction force press the body and the ground together and thus provide the normal force, which is one factor in how much friction force would be present if the body were forced to slide. This is true when the ground is horizontal, or level. If one were standing on a slope, however, the normal force would be only that component of body weight directed perpendicularly to the slope. Figure 11.7a and b illustrates the vector resolution of the force

The normal force pressing the body to the hillside (a) progressively decreases as the hill becomes steeper (b). When the normal force decreases, so does the force of friction. When the component of body weight directed along the hillside becomes greater than the force of friction of the ground on the feet, the body slides downhill.

Figure 11.7.

of body weight, showing the normal force component directed into a hillside and the component directed along the hillside surface.

In each case, as the slope becomes steeper, two changes occur: (1) the friction force is decreased, owing to a smaller normal force pressing the body into the hill, and (2) the component of the body weight that is directed along the hillside becomes greater, thereby becoming a greater and greater motive force for sliding. When the force of friction of the ground acting on the body is surpassed by the weight component parallel to the surface of the hill, the body slides downhill.

If the body's CG remains vertically above the base of support, the body slides downhill without rotating (falling over). The tendency to lean backward (toward the uphill side) on a slope often shifts the gravity line outside the base, thus producing a torque and causing rotation or falling into the uphill side of the slope. As the body mass accelerates downward into the slope, there is an unweighting of the feet, which means that the normal force pressing them to the hill decreases. Thus, the friction force is decreased, and the feet slip out from under the rotating body mass.

SECTION 5

MAINTAINING BALANCE DURING MOVEMENT

Even though human beings are influenced by the mechanical laws that govern the motion of inanimate objects, we are not rigid or single-shape bodies. We are able to move our segments independently, thereby redistributing the body mass and changing the location of the body's CG. Moreover, we can, and usually do, move our segments to change our base of support from one moment to the next to cope with impending loss of balance. Fortunately, any sudden movement or acceleration of body parts caused by external influences causes reflex movements that prevent loss of balance. Several general categories of balance-threatening situations are presented in the next section.

Maintaining Balance While Applying or Receiving a Force

When a force is applied to an object, the reaction force of the object on the body must be anticipated. If this reaction force serves as part of the body's support and is abruptly removed, loss of balance results. In one familiar case of this kind, you push against a heavy door to open it, and someone on the other side suddenly opens it, pulling it away from you; this causes you to fall forward unexpectedly with no forward base prepared. A general rule for maintaining balance in horizontal force-giving and force-receiving situations is: *The body's base of support should be enlarged horizontally in the direction of the horizontal force to be given or received.* This rule applies whenever the force given or received has a horizontal component, even if the force is not entirely horizontal. Consider how you might position your feet to prepare to push a heavy object forward. With a forward-backward stride position, you are able to step forward with the load's ensuing motion as well as able to apply the push in the desired direction. Similarly, if you are expecting a push from your right side, a wide lateral stride allows your moving gravity line to remain within your base for a longer period of time, thus allowing you more opportunity to make an adjustment to keep your balance.

When throwing a ball or other object, your leading foot must be moved in the direction of your body motion to provide a new base for the forward-moving CG. Striking objects that yield to your force often leads to the same type of weight shift, and a new base must be ready to support this weight. In catching, most objects that are caught are not of sufficient mass (or momentum) to cause body imbalance on impact. Even so, by forming a large base in the direction of the approaching object, the body position can be shifted more freely over the feet to facilitate accurate contact with the hands. If the object (e.g., a baseball) is to be caught and then immediately thrown again in a different direction, anticipation of the need to form an appropriate base for the next move contributes not only to the speed of the performance but also to better control of the segmental movements.

PUSHING OR PULLING

If a heavy object must be moved across some surface, the resistive friction is greatly reduced when the object can be rolled on wheels. When the object must be slid, however, the direction of the force applied can increase or decrease the friction force and thus influence the degree of difficulty of the task. Recall that any applied force can be resolved into its horizontal and vertical components. If the force is entirely horizontal, the vertical component is zero. Since the friction force is directly proportional to the force pressing the two surfaces together, the friction force resisting the horizontal motion of the load is neither increased nor decreased as it would be by a vertical component from the external force.

Note in Figure 11.8a that when a load is pushed forward and downward, the upward reaction force on the body causes a loss of friction between the feet and the floor. Such a situation compounds the difficulty of moving the load because the feet have less friction force applied to them and thus tend to slip; the load has more friction force applied to it and thus tends to stick. If the load is pulled, however, the downward reaction force applied by the load to the upward component of pulling force serves to increase the foot friction as the load's friction decreases (Figure 11.8b).

For certain pulling tasks, the use of a rope can change the line of force application and magnitudes of the components of the pull. Figure 11.9 shows the use of a long rope for a low-friction load and a short rope for a high-friction load. Once the load (or the foot) has started to slide, the friction force decreases, having been at its maximum just before sliding began. Therefore, decreased friction on the load during motion requires less applied force to maintain the speed of sliding than is required to start the load moving against greater static friction. In addition, recall that the force necessary to maintain the speed of an object already moving is less than that required to start it moving (to accelerate it). Advance preparation of the body's base

Figure 11.8.   (a) The upward reaction force to the downward component of a push decreases foot-ground friction. (b) The downward reaction force to the upward component of a pull increases foot-ground friction. A double advantage is gained by pulling in situations where load-ground friction is great. (F, force; RF, reaction force.)

of support in the direction of movement, therefore, is important for maintaining control of body balance, especially if the movement of the load might be sudden.

The point of application and line of action of a pulling or pushing effort can greatly affect the resulting movement of a load (Figure 11.10). If no load-floor friction exists, no fixed axis forms at one edge, and the load slides easily across the surface; only the load's inertia resists the accelerating force ($a = F/m$). Such a case is rarely seen, unless the surface is icy, oily, or covered with marbles. Often, the friction against the base of the load together with the applied push or pull serve to cause rotation instead of sliding. If the friction between the load and the supporting surface is great enough or if there is some obstruction in the path, the leading edge tends to stick and becomes an axis for the load's rotation.

If a horizontal force is applied at a low point, less torque is produced; therefore, there is less tendency for the load to rotate as it is pulled or pushed. Figure 11.10a and b show how a horizontal force applied at a low level on a high-friction load can produce sliding and how a lesser force applied at a higher level can produce rotation.

When a force is applied at a higher level, its force arm is large enough to allow a small force to cause rotation if this *applied* torque exceeds the load's *weight* torque. Such a small force often is not great enough to overcome the load-floor friction and therefore causes no sliding, only rotation. A greater force, enough to overcome the force of load-floor friction, can be applied at a lower level to cause only sliding; no rotation is produced from such a force because its force arm, and therefore its torque,

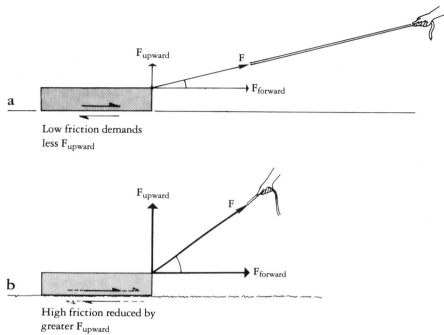

(a) Using a long rope to pull low-friction loads enables the mover to exert more force in the desired horizontal direction. (b) If the load friction is great, pulling it with a short rope produces a friction-reducing upward component, so that the horizontal component has less friction force to overcome.   **Figure 11.9.**

is so small. Both sliding and rotation are caused by the pull shown in Figure 11.10c, provided the horizontal component of the pull is greater than the load-floor friction and the pull torque is greater than the weight torque.

If the CG of the load is high and close to the edge of the base of support, a force applied at a low level, great enough to overcome the load-floor friction, can cause the base to slide out from under the CG, thus allowing the load's weight torque to cause its rotation. This situation can be demonstrated by standing a book on end and striking the side sharply at a low level. Similarly, when a football player is tackled near his support base, he is upended.

In wrestling, as well as in the martial arts, the points of application and the lines of application of the forces relative to the opponent's base and CG location are primary factors for success in upsetting his balance (Figure 11.11).

Often a load can be moved more easily by intentionally rotating it than by sliding it, especially if the support surface creates large friction forces. Figure 11.12a shows the application of torque about one leg of a heavy file to "walk" the load to its new location. A hand truck should be available for moving large or multiple loads to prevent muscle strain that could result from attempting to move one large load or from attempting to move a moderate load when the muscles are fatigued from

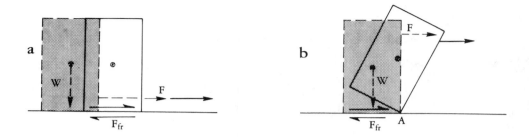

Figure 11.10.   (a) A force applied at a low level on a high-friction load produces sliding but no rotation. (b) A force applied at a high level on the load produces rotation but no sliding. (c) A force applied to produce both sliding and rotation, in accordance with the principles of net force and net torque.

Figure 11.11.   A wrestler applies force on the opponent to cause the opponent's body to rotate under the influence of his own body weight.

a Rotating heavy load to "walk" it instead of carrying it

b Second class lever on wheels is used for heavy or awkward loads

Two methods used for moving heavy loads.

Figure 11.12.

repeated light efforts. Figure 11.12b shows the torques applied to a load on a hand truck to carry out the move.

For controlling the path of a load being pushed or pulled, the effort should be applied at two points of contact, with adequate horizontal distance between these points. Compensation for any irregular friction spots that cause a change in sliding resistance can be made by adjusting the force on each point.

LIFTING AND CARRYING

When a load is lifted or carried, the mass of the load becomes part of the body mass and therefore makes a contribution to the CG location of the system (body and load). For balance to be maintained, the body's base of support must be adjusted for the new location of the gravity line if the load is sufficiently large or held far enough away from the body to cause imbalance. Alternatively, body segments can be moved in a direction away from the load to balance its effect. Figure 11.13a illustrates changing the base of support to receive the new gravity line of the body and load. In Figure 11.13b, the body must lean to the side to produce a balancing countertorque for the load. Note that leaning from near the base (the subtalar joints) eliminates the need for lateral flexion of the vertebral column and therefore results in less chance of muscle strain in the lumbar region of the vertebral column. As

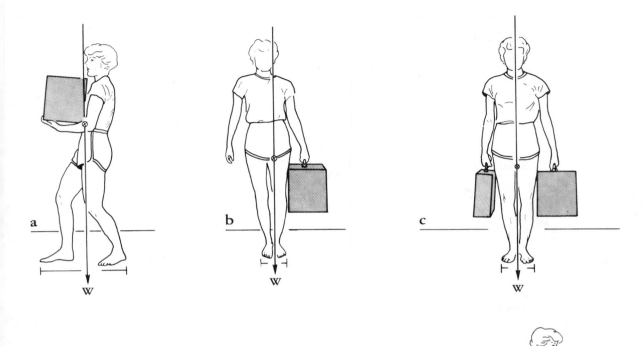

Figure 11.13.   (a-b) A base change and compensatory body movements allow
one to maintain balance while lifting a load. (c) The load is
balanced on either side. (d) Stooping to raise a load with the
strong lower extremity extensor muscles.

Figure 11.13c illustrates, carrying *two* loads (even if the total weight is greater) can
produce *less* chance of muscle strain on one side, and very few—if any—compensatory segment movements are necessary to keep the gravity line over the base
(LeVeau 1977).

Improper body mechanics employed in lifting tasks often lead to back injury. To
perform any lifting task safely, observe these steps:

1. Test the load to estimate its weight and to determine whether you are capable
   of lifting it without the help of another person or of some device.
2. Establish your support base as close as possible to the load, stabilizing the
   vertebral column in an extended position and lowering the body into position
   by flexing the hips, knees, and ankles (Figure 11.13d).

3. Raise the load, using the extensor muscles of the lower extremities concentrically without letting the extensors of the vertebral column eccentrically contract because the load is too heavy for them to hold static contractions.

Controlling Balance While Changing Speed or Direction

Skills involving starting, stopping, reversing direction, running around curves, and twirling on a narrow base are balance-important activities. An analysis of such skills must consider the desirability or undesirability of maintaining linear and rotary stability during each phase of the activity; that is , the momentary purpose of each phase must be identified, and the body mechanics used must be judged according to how effectively they serve this purpose.

STARTING AND STOPPING

If the purpose of a start is to accelerate the body mass linearly by extending the lower extremities, the body's CG should be positioned along the line of action of the support's reaction force against the feet. If rapid horizontal acceleration is desired, the CG should be positioned as low and as far forward as possible for the initial push-off (see Figure 11.4c). Balanced starting positions used in track and swimming events as well as in other situations demanding rapid horizontal acceleration are designed to put the body in a position of unstable equilibrium. In such a position, only a small angular impulse is required for rotary imbalance. For fast starting, therefore, the body's gravity line is generally positioned as close as possible to the base edge in the direction of intended motion (Figure 11.14a). The converse holds true for the body lean causing deceleration; the gravity line is taken as far away as support friction permits from the base edge in the direction of motion (Figure 11.14b).

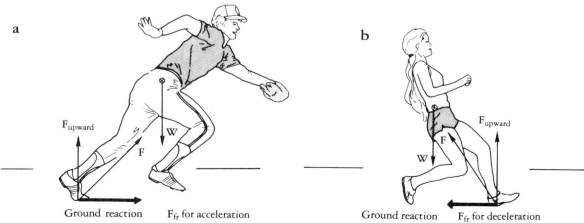

The body's gravity line is shifted toward the leading base edge for impending acceleration (a) and away from the leading base edge for deceleration (b).

Figure 11.14.

Once the body is moving in a given direction, its momentum (mass times velocity) becomes a major factor in maintaining balance if it is to change speed or direction. This is true in such activities as walking, running, surfing, skiing, skating, biking, dancing, rotating, falling, and landing. Whenever one is moving forward and wants to slow to a stop, the backward component of the ground reaction force is a deceleration force.

To decelerate, the leading foot is planted ahead of the line of gravity, causing resistive ground friction and a weight torque that tends to rotate the CG backward and downward about the foot base. The friction impulse provides some resistive force to slow the forward body momentum, which tends to carry the body forward over the foot. Several steps may be required before the friction reaction force and the backward-rotation component due to gravity stop the body's forward motion.

A similar balance situation is seen in landing from a broad jump or long jump. Because the body has forward linear and angular momentum, it continues moving forward when the heels strike the ground, and the jumper's body tends to fall forward over the feet. A longer jump distance can be achieved by using this momentum—by planting the heels farther forward, flexing the hips and knees, and allowing the body's linear and angular momentum to carry it forward over the base without danger of falling backward (Figure 11.15). As long as the body retains momentum in any direction, a base of support must be formed in that same direction until balanced is achieved.

Figure 11.15.   A jumper can delay the heel plant and gain distance without danger of losing balance backward at the landing if the forward momentum of the body is sufficient and used to rotate it forward over the base formed by the feet.

If a runner wishes to reverse directions with a pivot and a 180-degree body turn, the backward lean used to decelerate the forward-moving body becomes the forward lean necessary for acceleration in the opposite direction. If too much lean is created for deceleration or reversal, the feet become unweighted to the extent that the ground friction is insufficient to secure the foot, the base of support slides out from under the body, and the body slides linearly in the direction of existing momentum. Such a maneuver is the slide executed by a runner in baseball to drop below the opponent's tag while moving linearly forward to touch the base.

A balance principle appropriate for such linear acceleration and deceleration situations is the following: *For maximum stability in motion, the base of support must be enlarged in the direction of momentum and in the direction of intended acceleration or deceleration.* The greater the momentum, the larger the base of support should be in that direction. The greater the acceleration or deceleration, the larger the base must be in that direction.

Loss of balance (e.g., tripping and falling) can occur unexpectedly when the preplanned base of support cannot be formed in time to accommodate the weight of the forward-moving body. Such a situation exists during running when the body's CG is moving forward at a rather steady speed while each foot alternately forms a new base of support for the weight that is passing above it. If the leading foot catches a resistance, the expected base is not formed, the linear horizontal momentum of the body continues, the weight produces a torque about the lead foot, and rotary instability results. If the forward speed of the CG is not too great, the reflex-initiated movement of the trailing leg may be swift enough to form a new base below the weight. A series of recovery steps may be necessary to regain balance. Frequently, if the support surface is not hazardous, the forward angular momentum of the body mass can be used to transform an otherwise injurious or awkward landing into one less destructive, and the body is rolled to an upright position. The shoulder roll is an example of such a maneuver. It is used often in activities that demand immediate restoration of a position of readiness in the event of a fall.

The side roll, observed in volleyball, is a similar technique. The off-balance body rolls to the side and over onto the feet, rather than falling to a position that would require precious time to recover to a position of effectiveness. This technique is illustrated in Figure 11.16.

CHANGING DIRECTIONS

A change in body velocity that is more common than merely starting and stopping is one in which the body changes its direction of motion, as in running a curve, dodging other players, and maneuvering in games. To execute an abrupt linear change in direction, the body maintains some motion in the existing direction while introducing some lateral component of motion. Therefore, a change occurs in the body's momentum. Any change in linear momentum is caused by an external impulse in the direction of that change. The forward momentum of the runner in Figure 11.14b was changed by ground reaction forces that decreased her body speed to zero. To

Initial axis of
rotation

Points along body serve as
successive axes of rotation

Last
axis

Figure 11.16.   The side roll employs the sideward angular momentum of the body as it rotates about the foot as an axis upon loss of balance.

change direction without stopping requires a ground reaction force in a direction that gives the body the desired resultant motion. If a runner is moving forward and pushes to the right, the ground reaction (friction) force pushes him to the left, but does not stop his forward motion. His new path is diagonally forward and to the left. Maneuvering abruptly while in motion requires the foot-ground friction to be great enough to prevent slipping when the foot push is made. The greater the direction change desired, the greater must be the push and ground reaction force; therefore, little maneuvering can be done on slippery surfaces or with wornout shoes. The heavier the player, the greater the friction, but the greater the ground reaction force must be to accelerate a more massive player. Partially owing to this factor, larger players are not known as well for their maneuverability as are smaller, "quicker" players. The "dancing" of a tennis serve receiver in the ready position may provide more friction for forceful fast starts in a horizontal direction owing to the "over-weighting" during foot push-off (up and horizontally). The same may be said for a basketball player who jumps and lands to a stop—overweighting increases friction.

CIRCULAR TURNS

A runner can execute circular turns to change direction, as when rounding the end of a track or running bases in softball. In running around a curve, the runner must push outward on the ground to generate an inward ground reaction force to make the body turn. The turn is caused, then, by the *centripetal* ground reaction friction force on the runner's feet that are applying the *centrifugal* friction force on the ground (Figure 11.17a). The tighter the turn (the smaller the radius of the circle), the greater the centripetal friction force must be; or the faster the run, the greater the friction must be to make a given turn.

Experience tells us that if a turn is too sharp or speed is too great on horizontal ground, the support friction will be insufficient to provide the necessary centripetal

a Ground reaction centripetal
force is more friction dependent
on horizontal ground

b Ground reaction centripetal
force is less friction dependent
on banked surface

(a) The inward-directed component of the ground reaction force (friction) on the foot provides the centripetal force necessary to change the runner's direction from a straight line to a curved path. (b) Running on a banked (inclined) surface enables the runner to continue moving fast as she curves without concern for inadequate friction and slipping.

Figure 11.17.

force for the intended turn, and the feet will slip out from underneath the body as the body leans inward. Before the feet slip away, however, the runner usually slows or enlarges the turning radius or does both, thereby reducing the need for such a large centripetal friction force and body lean. Such leaning postures are assumed by track cyclists, roller skaters, and other performers who must negotiate curves, and the high speeds at which they travel require a large centripetal force. Usually the surface friction is not sufficient on a horizontal track, and therefore the curves are banked, or inclined, for circular paths (Figure 11.17b). The slope of the banked curves allows the force application and reaction force to be directed more perpendicularly to the surface, thus eliminating most—if not all—of the friction dependency for the centripetal force.

UNDERSTANDING BALANCE-RELATED SITUATIONS

1. By throwing and catching a basketball with a partner eight strides away, experiment with various foot positions and determine which position enables you to throw the ball the fastest and to catch the ball most easily without losing your balance.

2. Stand facing a partner one stride away. Placing your palms against your partner's, experiment with different foot positions and directions of force. What determines maximum stability when you attempt to push each other off balance? Explain the differences.

3. Run at a moderate speed in a circle approximately 6 m in diameter. Have an observer note the changes in inward body lean as you increase the running speed. Explain.

4. Repeat the steps in question 3 and increase the diameter of the circle without increasing the speed. Have an observer note the changes in body lean. Explain.

5. Run as fast as you can to a line 20 m away and stop on it while maintaining balance. Have an observer note the changes in body lean and foot placement as you approach and stop at the line. Explain your success or failure to stop on the line without losing your balance.

6. Explain the advantage in the baseball rule that allows a batter to overrun first base. Explain why such a wide turn is made if the hitter continues on to second base.

REFERENCES
SUGGESTED READINGS

Broer, M. R., and Zernicke, R. F. *Efficiency of Human Movement*. 4th ed. Philadelphia: W. B. Saunders, 1979.

Kobayashi, K., et al. "A Study of Stability of Standing Posture." In *Biomechanics IV: Proceedings of the Fourth International Seminar on Biomechanics*, ed. R. C. Nelson and C. A. Morehouse, 53-59. Baltimore: University Park Press, 1974.

LeVeau, B. *Williams and Lissner: Biomechanics of Human Motion*. 2d ed. Philadelphia: W. B. Saunders, 1977.

Luttgens, K., and Wells, K. F. *Kinesiology: Scientific Basis of Human Motion*. 7th ed. Philadelphia: Saunders College Publishing, 1982.

Sodeyama, H., et al. "Study of the Displacement of a Skier's Center of Gravity During a Ski Turn." In *Biomechanics V-B: Proceedings of the Fifth International Symposium on Biomechanics,* ed. P. V. Komi, 271-76. Baltimore: University Park Press, 1976.

Tricker, R. A. R., and Tricker, B. J. K. *The Science of Human Movement.* New York: American Elsevier Publishing Co., 1967.

Wheeler, G. F., and Kirkpatrick, L. D. *Physics: Building a World View.* Englewood Cliffs, N.J.: Prentice-Hall, 1983.

CHAPTER 12

ANALYSIS OF ACTIVITIES IN WHICH THE BODY ROTATES FREE OF SUPPORT

During the discussion of projectiles in Chapter 8, principles were applied to the human body as an object moving through space. The focus of attention for projectiles was the center of gravity (CG), and its motion was curvilinear and parabolic. In most projectile activities, the primary mechanical purpose is to give the greatest distance or speed or accuracy or all three to the object being projected. During activities in which the human body is projected, however, important rotational movements may occur.

The principles of rotary motion apply to the movements of the body during the air phases of long jumping, high jumping, and pole vaulting. Most of the body's rotational activities, however, are judged events in which the goal is to achieve a quality of movement rather than to attain the greatest horizontal or vertical distance. The primary mechanical purpose of most of these rotationally based activities is to move or position the body or its segments in a predetermined pattern with the intent of achieving an ideal or model performance. The quality of movement is then judged. Gymnastics, diving, dance, and trampoline activities are obvious examples.

SECTION 1

THE HUMAN BODY IN ROTARY MOTION

The Center of Gravity and Axes of Rotation

When the total body is rotating and free of support (aerial movements), body rotation takes place around one or more of the three principal axes of the body, the mediolateral (ML), anteroposterior (AP), and longitudinal axes. The three principal axes must pass through the CG of the total body whether that center is located within the body or outside the body. When any point on the total body is in contact with a supporting surface, the reaction force from that surface, elicited by a movement of any body segment against it, will cause the CG of the total body to move in the same direction as the reaction force.

When a body is free of support, however, the path in space of the total body's CG cannot be changed by segmental movements. During free flight, the body parts move relative to the CG (i.e., the body parts realign themselves around the CG).

Figure 12.1.   A vaulter performing a front somersault vault in a tuck position.

The realignment of body parts, however, does not change the path of the CG from what it would have been without segmental movement.

Figure 12.1 shows the path and position of the CG of a long-horse vaulter performing a forward somersault around the body's ML axis. Notice that the performer takes off in a layout position, moves into a tuck position, and lands in a layout position. Although the body parts realign themselves relative to the body's CG, the path is not altered; it is the same parabolic path that was established at takeoff. (The path would be the same had the performer remained in the layout position.)

Rotation of the body around any of the body's principal axes may be accomplished when the body is in a layout, pike, arch, or even a tuck position. The body may leave the ground in one of these positions and move *symmetrically* into any of the other positions without changing the principal axis of rotation.[1]

Movements of the entire body about each of the principal axes of rotation may be reviewed from Concept Module A. Rotations about the ML axis are called **turns** or **somersaulting** motions, and rotations about the longitudinal axis are called **twists.**

The aerial cartwheel is one of the few examples of a movement taking place around the body's AP axis. AP-axis motion in free flight is probably the least common of body movements, and often is the result of turning and twisting rotations being performed simultaneously.

Angular Momentum and Human Body Rotations

The angular momentum of the human body in rotational motion consists of three factors: the mass of the performer, the radius of gyration of the performer's mass relative to the axis of rotation, and the angular velocity of the performer about the axis of rotation. Since the mass of a performer does not change, it is considered a constant factor in the body's angular momentum.

Recall that the radius of gyration is a distance that represents the distribution of the mass relative to the axis of rotation. The radius of gyration of the performer's mass relative to an axis of rotation depends on which axis the body is rotating about— ML, AP, or longitudinal—and on the position of the body segments relative to that axis. As segmental movement occurs, the distribution of the mass changes, and thus its radius of gyration changes. Figure 12.2 illustrates body positions that change the distribution of the body's mass about each of the three principal axes. In Figure 12.2a, one can see that the radius of gyration about the ML axis is the largest when the performer assumes a layout position with the arms overhead and is the smallest when her body is in a tuck position. During free flight, the radius of gyration is measured from the ML axis, which passes through the CG whether the CG is located within the body (as in the layout position) or is located somewhat in front of the abdomen (as in the pike position). The body mass in this case is constant (barring

---

1. Note that the movements must be symmetrical; if not, quite a different situation occurs, as will be seen later.

any loss of clothing), no matter how the person has changed the distribution of the mass about the axis of rotation. In a tuck position, the body has a smaller radius of gyration because the mass is closer to the ML axis about which it is rotating.

In Figure 12.2b, three positions are shown relative to the body's longitudinal axis. In a large radius of gyration position, the upper and lower extremities are positioned away from the longitudinal axis, whereas in the small radius position, the extremities are packed in close to the axis. Similarly, changes in the distribution of the body's mass may be made about the AP axis by assuming the various positions in Figure 12.2c.

The two factors then that determine the body's resistance to changes in rotary motion are the body's mass and the distribution of that mass around the axis of rotation in question. When both these factors are considered, the resistance to rotation or rotational inertia (I) can be calculated. Recall that because of the particular way in which the radius of gyration is calculated for a given body position, the term is squared and multiplied by the mass (mk^2). Since we are considering the mass of the body to be constant, the *mass distribution* becomes the major focus of attention when analyzing free-rotation activities.

Applying the conservation of angular momentum to the performer, we can say

a   Mediolateral axis

Figure 12.2.   A change in the body's configuration will change the radius of gyration of the body relative to the three principal axes of rotation: the ML (a), longitudinal (b), and AP (c) axes.

b   Longitudinal axis

c   Anteroposterior axis

that the body is a single system made up of individual parts. The angular momentum that is established at takeoff is established for the system and cannot be changed unless an external torque is applied. The performer is not rigid, however, and individual body segments are free to rotate about individual axes of rotation passing through the joint centers. Any segments caused to rotate about their own axes have angular momentum produced by *internal* muscle torques; that is, they act on the segments within the system but do not act as external torques on the total system. Because the segments are part of the system, however, their angular momenta become part of the total angular momentum of the system. Because the angular momentum of the system must be conserved (cannot change), the segmental momenta cannot add or subtract from the established total momentum of the body, but the segments may "assume" or redistribute the momentum within the system. As an example, consider the performer in Figure 12.3 whose body and extremities are represented by cylinders projected into space by a force acting through the CG. Because the projection force acts through the CG, the body has linear momentum but no angular momentum at any time during the flight. If the arm segments are then circled backwards around their ML axis so that the sum of their angular momenta equals three angular momentum units, then the trunk segment must take on enough forward momentum about *its* ML axis so that the algebraic sum of all the angular momenta in the system remains zero. This can be shown by solving the equation:

$$\Sigma L = 0$$
$$L_{arms} + L_{legs} + L_{trunk} = 0$$
$$I_1 \omega_1 + I_2 \omega_2 + I_3 \omega_3 = 0$$
$$(+3.0) + 0 + L_{trunk} = 0$$
$$L_{trunk} = -3.0 \text{ angular momentum units}$$

Note that the solution to the equation indicates that the rotation of the trunk is negative, and, therefore, the trunk is rotating clockwise (cw). Knowing the mass and the radius of gyration of the trunk, we can then calculate how fast the trunk will be rotating. The mass and radius of gyration of the trunk will be much greater than the masses and radii of the arms; consequently, the trunk angular velocity will be much slower than the angular velocity of the arm rotation. Remember that the *sum* of the angular momenta of the system during flight is, and must remain, zero in this case.

The summation technique also can be used when the magnitude of the angular momentum is *not* zero at takeoff. For example, if the body has an angular momentum of +30 angular momentum units (circling counterclockwise [ccw] about the body's ML axis) at takeoff, the arms and legs then circle during flight so as to generate +2.5 angular momentum units *each* (also circling ccw) about their segmental ML axes (4 × 2.5 = 10). Thus, the trunk will be left with +20 angular momentum units. It will have its angular velocity decreased enough to let the product of $mk^2\omega$

The body represented by a cylinder having zero angular momentum. Circling the arms backward will cause the trunk and lower extremities to circle forward, thus allowing the body to maintain zero net angular momentum.   **Figure 12.3.**

of the trunk equal $+20$ angular momentum units. The calculation would be as follows:

$$L = +30 \text{ angular momentum units}$$
$$L_{arms} + L_{legs} + L_{trunk} = +30 \text{ angular momentum units}$$
$$2(+2.5) + 2(+2.5) + L_{trunk} = +30 \text{ angular momentum units}$$
$$L_{trunk} = +30 + (-5.0) + (-5.0)$$
$$L_{trunk} = +20 \text{ angular momentum units}$$

If enough angular momentum can be generated from the circling of the arms and legs, the body will cease rotating completely. Remember that the summation always must be around axes that are parallel to each other, for momentum generated around one axis in the air does not alter the momentum established around other nonparallel axes.

Application of the Right-Hand Thumb Rule for Determining Angular Momentum Vectors

To determine the magnitude and direction of the angular momentum vector for a body rotating around an axis, one may use the right-hand thumb rule, which is described in Concept Modules D and G. To determine the vector direction of the body rotating around an axis, one wraps the right hand around the axis of rotation so that the fingers are flexed in the direction of the rotation. The vector direction of that particular angular velocity (and angular momentum) is the direction in which the right thumb points. For example, if one were looking down at a gymnast performing a pirouette in the air about the longitudinal axis (Figure 12.4), she would appear to be rotating ccw, and the right hand would be wrapped around the longitudinal axis as shown. The right-hand thumb would be pointing toward the head.

The vector associated with angular motion is represented by an arrow that has magnitude and direction and may be added or resolved just like any other vector. Vector addition could be used to solve the problem of the performer circling the arms and legs in Figure 12.3. Resolution of a resultant angular momentum vector is important in understanding one method of *initiating* rotation in the air.

Vector direction

Figure 12.4.   A gymnast doing a pirouette, with the right-hand thumb rule applied to show the angular momentum vector.

UNDERSTANDING THE BODY ROTATING
FREE OF SUPPORT

1. The following figures are taken from films of sport events: Figures 6.5, G.7, 8.11, and 12.2c. In these illustrations the performer is rotating around one or more axes or the individual body segments are rotating around axes through their joint centers. For each figure, identify the axis of rotation of the body or the axis of rotation of any segments that also may be rotating.

2. How many mass units of resistance to changes in *horizontal* motion will a body weighing 400 N have?

3. How many mass units of resistance to changes in *vertical* motion will a body weighing 400 N have?

4. For the following figures, indicate about which axis or axes the mass is being redistributed, and state whether the radius of gyration increases or decreases from the initial position: Figures G.2b, 12.5, and 12.17.

5. If a body has 2 mass units and a radius of gyration of 5 cm, what is the rotational inertia? 2 mass units and a 10-cm radius?

6. What is the *change* in resistance to rotation of a body with an increase of the radius of gyration to three times what it was initially? a decrease of the radius of gyration to one fourth of what it was?

SECTION 2

CONSERVATION OF ANGULAR MOMENTUM APPLICATIONS

Altering the Velocity of Rotation

Once rotation has been initiated from the ground, the radius of gyration about the axis may be altered to slow down or speed up the existing velocity of rotation. Increasing the angular velocity of spin by decreasing the radius is probably the most common technique used in rotational moves. As with the roller skater in Figure 12.5, angular momentum is established by pushing the skate against the ground in one direction to create a torque about the vertical axis, thus initiating the spin in the opposite direction.

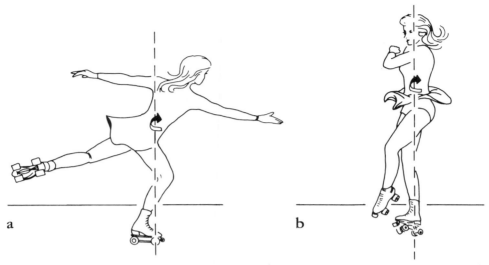

Figure 12.5.   (a) A roller skater initiating a spin about the longitudinal axis with the arms and one leg abducted. (b) The position of the arms and leg for increased rotational velocity.

    Usually, the performer has the arms abducted while applying the force. Once the spin has begun, the skater draws the arms and free leg close to the vertical axis and spins at increased speed. The reduction of the radius of gyration about the longitudinal axis causes the angular velocity to increase, but the angular momentum remains the same. Note that in the case of an ice skater performing a spin, the friction of the supporting skate on the ice retards the angular momentum slightly, but friction force is relatively insignificant in this example.

    Because every *change* in the radius of gyration is squared, the change in the angular velocity is squared also. For example, if the radius of gyration is decreased one third, the angular velocity increases 9 times; if k is decreased one half, the angular velocity increases 4 times; if one fourth, 16 times; and so forth. The same relationship exists for increasing the radius and decreasing the angular velocity. Changes in the velocities of rotation when starting from one position and then assuming another position in the air are presented as ratios in Table 12.1. The body positions used in formulating the table data are shown in Figure 12.6a–f. The data were calculated for a gymnast performing a somersault forward or backward about the ML axis. The table indicates the ratio of revolutions from the starting position, listed along the left side of the table, to the assumed position, shown along the top of the table. For instance, moving from position f in the left column, layout with arms overhead, to position a in the top row, tight tuck position, would produce a 4.67 increase in the velocity of rotation; moving from position d to position e would reduce the velocity of rotation to 0.58 of original velocity. These ratios were calculated for an average male, aged 18 to 22 years.

RATIOS OF RELATIVE SPEEDS OF ROTATIONS BETWEEN BODY   Table 12.1.
POSITIONS

Starting Position	Assumed Position					
	a. Tight Tuck	b. Medium Tuck	c. Tight Pike	d. Medium Pike	e. Layout Arms Down	f. Layout Arms Overhead
a. Tight tuck	1.00	0.69	0.69	0.47	0.28	0.21
b. Medium tuck	1.45	1.00	1.00	0.70	0.41	0.31
c. Tight pike	1.45	1.00	1.00	0.70	0.41	0.31
d. Medium pike	2.08	1.47	1.47	1.00	0.58	0.46
e. Layout arms down	3.56	2.48	2.48	1.72	1.00	0.76
f. Layout arms overhead	4.67	3.22	3.22	2.24	1.31	1.00

Modified from Biesterfeldt, H. J., "Salto Mechanics I: Moment of Inertia." *International Gymnast*, March 1975, p. 45.

Preventing or Delaying Unwanted Rotation: Error Correction

In performing some activities, a person may obtain some angular momentum from the takeoff that is not wanted or that needs to be delayed until later in the performance. Because the body works as a system of parts, the angular momentum acting on the body may be prevented or delayed by letting the extremities "assume" or take up some of that angular momentum. Mainly, these movements are used for correcting errors in the takeoff that could prove disastrous if not corrected.

SKI JUMPING

The principle of conservation of angular momentum is applied to prevent unwanted rotation in ski jumping, as shown in Figure 12.7. If the takeoff position results in an angular impulse that causes the jumper to rotate forward too fast in the air, the performer can rotate the arms forward to assume some of that forward momentum. The magnitudes of the masses and the radii of the body parts must always be compared to determine how much angular velocity must be created in the extremities to alter the angular velocity of the trunk; that is, since the arms are less massive than the entire trunk, lower extremity, and skis, the arms must rotate much faster to affect the rotation of the rest of the system.

If the ski jumper, upon takeoff, pushed slightly harder with the right foot so that a torque was set up about the performer's AP axis, the momentum established would

Figure 12.6.   Body positions with the smallest (a) to the largest (f) radius of gyration about the ML axis. (a) Tight tuck. (b) Medium tuck. (c) Tight pike. (d) Medium pike. (e) Layout with arms at the sides. (f) Layout with arms flexed overhead.

tend to rotate him to the left. The skier's angular momentum cannot change during his flight but angular velocity may be decreased. By increasing the radius of gyration about the AP axis (e.g., by abducting the arms at the shoulder joints), the angular velocity of rotation about that axis could be decreased to a point where it would not be detrimental to the jump.

A second error correction method would be to abduct only the left arm, thus creating an aerodynamic force on the left side that would result in a torque causing the skier to rotate to the right.

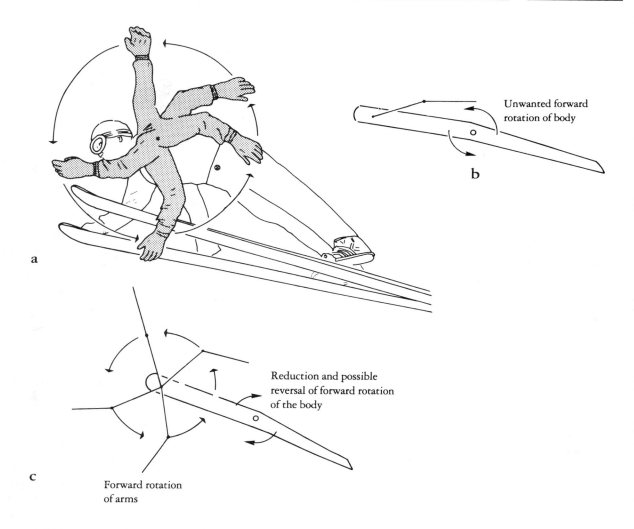

A ski jumper rotating the upper extremity around a ML axis through the shoulder joints in order to prevent unwanted forward rotation of the total body.   **Figure 12.7.**

GYMNASTICS

A gymnast who dismounts from a piece of apparatus with one side of the body coming off a little before the other side will have forced some twisting rotation in the air. If the performer does not want that twist around the body's longitudinal axis, the twist may be controlled by spreading the arms or legs to the side, thus slowing the velocity to a point where it may be unnoticed. Often gymnasts assume what is called a "cowboy" tuck position in the air to stop unwanted twisting action (Figure 12.8). In the cowboy tuck position, the knees are spread, which increases

Figure 12.8. A gymnast assuming a "cowboy" tuck position, which increases the radius of gyration about his longitudinal axis and also tends to decrease the radius of gyration about his ML axis.

the radius of gyration about the longitudinal axis and slows the undesirable twisting action. (The position also may allow performers to tuck tighter, which will decrease the radius of gyration about the ML axis and thus increase the speed of the somersaulting action.)

INCREASING ROTATIONAL INERTIA IN STRIKING SKILLS

As a volleyball spiking movement is initiated, the body is free in the air. Little, if any, angular momentum is in the system. The spiking movement consists of transverse rotation of the trunk about the vertebral column axis. Since there is no momentum about the longitudinal axis, the lower part of the body must "react" with an equal and opposite momentum to keep the angular momentum at zero. The volleyball spiker in Figure 12.9 has positioned his legs so as to increase the radius

A volleyball player increasing the radius of gyration of the lower extremity about the longitudinal axis   **Figure 12.9.**
so as to reduce the lower body's rotation, which occurs in reaction to the upper body's spiking
movement.

of gyration about the lower body's longitudinal axis. This decreases the lower body's reaction to the upper body's rotation around the longitudinal axis during the spiking movement. Thus, by abducting the hips or flexing one hip and extending the other, the radius of gyration of the lower part of the body is increased. This reduces the necessary movement response of the lower part.

Similar positional changes are made in tennis serves in which the feet are off the ground.

USING ANGULAR MOMENTUM IN THE LONG JUMP

The angular momentum generated from the takeoff in a long jump may be used to enhance the success of the jump if the rotation of the body can be delayed until landing.

In the case of a long jumper performing the hitch-kick technique (Figure 12.10), the line of force of the ground reaction force at takeoff passes slightly behind the jumper's CG and thus gives angular momentum to the system in ccw (+) direction around the jumper's ML axis. This angular momentum begins to rotate his body

Figure 12.10.   Application of the principle of conservation of angular momentum to the airborne phase of the hitch-kick long jump technique.

upon takeoff and continues to rotate it in that fashion until landing. Forward rotation is not ideal for any long jumper not wanting to do a front somersault in the air. The jumper can delay the rotation of the total body by using internal torques to rotate his arms and legs in a ccw (+) direction around their segmental ML axes through the shoulder and hip joints. As the segments rotate in the same direction as the body's angular momentum, they assume some of the ccw angular momentum of the body.

If the limbs rotate to generate enough ccw angular momentum to equal that which the body has from the takeoff, the trunk ceases rotation entirely. While the forward rotation is detrimental to the jumper during flight, such rotation is helpful when he wants to rotate forward over the heels in landing. When the arms and legs slow or stop rotating, the trunk again assumes the momentum. Likewise, if the arms and legs are rotated in the opposite direction (cw) to the body's momentum (ccw), the trunk rotates faster ccw, enough to keep the sum of the angular momenta the same. Thus, the conservation of angular momentum principle is used in this case to delay unwanted body rotation until landing.

Skill Progressions Related to the Principle of Conservation of Angular Momentum

Progressions for teaching many tumbling, trampoline, and gymnastics skills are based on altering the radius of gyration to increase or decrease the angular velocity of rotation. One of the obvious applications of the principle of conservation of angular momentum to skill progression is the use of the tuck, pike, and layout positions while airborne.

To successfully execute one or more rotations prior to landing, the performer must have a large enough vertical linear velocity component to provide the necessary height that allows greater time in the air. Secondly, the body must have enough angular velocity to complete the desired number of turns in the time available.

The greater the difference in the takeoff height compared to landing height, the less angular momentum needed to complete the desired rotations. Also, the greater the vertical velocity component, the less angular momentum needed to complete the desired number of rotations.

For the skilled performer, vertical velocity is optimized, and therefore the height and the time in the air are sufficient to complete the desired number of rotations. Beginning performers, however, usually cannot achieve the necessary height and time in the air. This may be due to several factors. The beginning performer is apprehensive about being able to complete the rotation before landing and thus becomes anxious to start rotating as soon as possible. Therefore, the beginner may start the rotation prior to takeoff.

If a front somersault is being done, the beginner may attempt to rotate the upper body forward as the push-off is being performed. This decreases the angle of takeoff and the vertical impulse, which in turn decreases the vertical velocity, the peak height, and the time in the air. The given angular momentum does not allow enough time to complete a full rotation.

Establishing angular momentum at takeoff while the body is in a layout position is particularly important so that the radius of gyration in that position will be large. Once angular momentum has been established, the body has the possibility of decreasing the radius of gyration by moving into a tuck position to complete the necessary number of rotations before landing. The tuck position in the air enables the body to make the maximum number of rotations, since moving from a layout to a tuck reduces the performer's radius of gyration the most and thus increases the angular velocity (Table 12.1).

As the performer progresses and becomes more accomplished at the skill, the linear takeoff velocity increases, which increases the time in the air. As the time in the air increases, the angular velocity needed to rotate one revolution prior to landing decreases, and the performer is able to complete a full rotation in a pike and finally in a layout position. Even in the layout position, a performer may reduce the radius by bringing the arms from a fully flexed position overhead at takeoff to an extended position at the sides during flight. (See Figure 8.14, p. 372.)

The teacher-coach is encouraged to pay particular attention to the takeoff position of a performer for that is where the stage is set for unsuccessful attempts. In tumbling activities, the takeoff time is so short that a slow-motion or stop-action film is helpful. For diving, trampoline, and apparatus dismounts, the difference in takeoff and landing heights makes the takeoff position less critical to success. The same factors influence the quality of any performance, however, and should be the focus of attention of a teacher or coach in any of these areas.

UNDERSTANDING THE PRINCIPLE
OF CONSERVATION OF ANGULAR MOMENTUM

1. If angular momentum is equal to zero at takeoff, indicate about which axis and in which direction the trunk will move with the following limb movements: (a) circumduction (circling) of the upper extremities forward, (b) circumduction of the upper extremities backward, (c) abduction of the right upper extremity and adduction of the left upper extremity.

2. If the same body has 50 angular momentum units forward at takeoff, would the trunk's rotational velocity increase, decrease, or stay the same when the movement indicated in question 1 takes place?

3. Answer question 2 for the same body having 50 angular momentum units backward around the ML axis.

SECTION 3

INITIATING ROTATIONS

Somersaults or twists may be initiated from the ground using the ground reaction force, and they also can be initiated in the air. Rotation may be begun in the the air when the body has no angular momentum about the axis of rotation or when the angular momentum that a body has from takeoff is redistributed or used for rotation around a second axis. The method of rotation may be recognized from the body positions prescribed in performing the stunt. These positions are similar for diving, trampoline, tumbling, and aerial planes of freestyle skiing and apparatus routines.

Ground Reaction Rotations

Figure 12.11 shows a performer initiating rotation around her ML and longitudinal axes by using the reaction force of the beam during a dismount.

As the gymnast leaves the beam, her CG is ahead of the line of action of the beam reaction force. Consequently, external torque is created about the ML axis through the performer's CG. The gymnast leaves the beam with angular momentum about the ML axis. In this illustration, the angular momentum is directed cw. Using the right-hand rule for determining direction, the vector would be pointing along the gymnast's ML axis and to her left.

If a person rotates some body segments in one direction around a joint axis while the feet are still in contact with the ground, the friction force of the ground on the

A gymnast initiating rotation from the supporting surface.

Figure 12.11.

feet causes a ground reaction, and the momentum of those segments is transferred to a parallel total body axis as the performer leaves the supporting surface.

In the gymnast's case, her trunk and free leg are rotated around a longitudinal axis passing through the supporting hip joint. In effect, the movement is transverse abduction of the pelvis at the right hip. After takeoff, the angular momentum created by this segmental motion during beam contact causes the body to rotate around its longitudinal axis, thus providing the twisting momentum. The vector direction using the right-hand rule is directed headward. Therefore, the ground reaction force provides an external torque that acts to give the gymnast's body angular momentum about her ML and longitudinal axes. Once the gymnast leaves the ground with her established angular momentum, she may change segmental positions and, consequently, change her body's radius of gyration about the angular momentum axes. Comparisons are then made between the size of the rotational inertia about an axis at takeoff and the size of the rotational inertia in the new position. Because of the conservation of angular momentum principle, the gymnast will increase or decrease her angular velocity about that axis.

Ground reaction torques are used in establishing momentum upon takeoff in long jumping and high jumping. In the flop-style jump, the performer leaves the ground at approximately a 40-degree angle from the horizontal. The CG of the jumper is ahead of the line of force of the ground reaction force and therefore the jumper leaves the ground with some angular momentum. Figure 8.5b (p. 352) illustrates the position of takeoff of a high jumper using the flop technique.

Two spatial axes of rotation are useful in the flop technique. The x spatial axis passes through the jumper's CG and is parallel to the bar; the z spatial axis passes through the jumper's CG and is vertical and perpendicular to the bar. A third axis, the y axis, is perpendicular to the bar, through the jumper's CG, and horizontal. The angular momentum about the y axis should be minimized. All three of these axes should be imagined to move along with the jumper's CG as she moves through the air.

The angular momentum about the x axis is produced by the jumper's CG being to the bar side of the line of action of the reaction force. This external torque causes the jumper to rotate in a backward somersaulting motion. Angular momentum is produced about the jumper's z axis when the jumper plants the takeoff foot and medially rotates her pelvis about the supporting hip and rotates her trunk in the same direction. The friction force produced between the ground and the supporting foot provides the external torque responsible for giving the jumper angular momentum about the z axis. The z axis rotation is a twisting motion.

In the straddle technique, the ground reaction force gives the body angular momentum that is produced in a similar fashion to the flop technique. The takeoff position places the CG inside the line of force of the push-off and the bar. Since the jumper is facing the bar, angular momentum is established about the x axis, which is through the jumper's CG and parallel with the bar. Since the jumper is not square to the bar, the axis is aligned from his near shoulder to his far hip joint. The jumper is in effect somersaulting forward about this diagonal axis relative to his body.

UNDERSTANDING GROUND-INITIATED MOMENTUM

A long jumper taking off from the board extends the hip, knee, and ankle joints to push off into the air. Draw a diagram of a long jumper taking off. Show the body position relative to the takeoff foot, the CG position at takeoff, and the direction and line of action of the ground reaction force. Draw arrows indicating the linear and rotational characteristics of the jumper after leaving the ground. (Using Figure 8.9 [p. 360] will be helpful.)

Initiating Rotation in the Air

Once the performer leaves the supporting surface, no increases or decreases can be made in the *magnitude* of the body's angular momentum. The performer, however, can initiate rotations about axes or can rearrange the angular momentum within the system so that rotations that were not evident at takeoff are possible.

Angular momentum, once established, may be assumed by individual body parts within the system, and the velocity of rotation can be increased or decreased by changing the radius of gyration about the axis of momentum. The following section deals with techniques that are used to initiate rotation of the total body about an axis around which it was not initially rotating or to change the velocity of existing rotation. Initiating rotation does not change the total angular *momentum* of the system while free of support; therefore, it does not contradict the conservation principle.

The advantage of air-initiated rotations, particularly in judged activities such as gymnastics and diving, is that in each of the methods the performer can easily stop any rotation that has been created by ceasing the movement that is creating it. Timing the initiation and cessation of the rotation is crucial to successful performance. Generally, rotation may be initiated by three methods while the body is free of support: reaction rotation, cat rotation, and twist from a somersault.

REACTION ROTATION

The reaction rotation technique is so named because the movement of the arms, legs, or trunk about an axis causes a reaction or movement response of the rest of the system in the opposite direction about a parallel body axis.

If the performer is free in the air while the segmental rotations are executed, the rest of the body must react in the opposite direction so that the sum of the angular momenta of the system remains constant.

For illustration, visualize a person rebounding vertically off a trampoline with the shoulder joints flexed forward to 90 degrees. The system's axis of rotation is a spatial vertical (z) axis that corresponds to the longitudinal body axis. The arms, which are moving along a transverse plane, move around their respective z axes that pass through the shoulder joints; for the total body, the axis is longitudinal and passes through the body's CG. If the performer's arms are thrown to the left (ccw as viewed from the top) during flight, the rest of the body will react by moving to the right in a cw direction so that the angular momentum generated by the arms will equal the angular momentum reaction of the rest of the body. Note that the angular momentum is equal and opposite, and therefore angular velocities may be different due to the differences between the masses and radii of gyration of the arms and the rest of the body. In this case, even with the arms having greater radii of gyration than the trunk and legs, the greater amount of mass in the trunk and legs results in the body moving only about one fourth of the distance that the arms move. The performer has now twisted only about 45 degrees.

If the performer wants to prevent a rotation of the trunk and legs back to the forward position, the arms cannot be brought back to the right (cw) for that would cause a return movement of the rest of the system and cancel out the trunk twist that was gained. To prevent that motion, the arms must be dropped down to the side, a rotation that is *not* around an axis parallel to the vertical axis. (The dropping of the arms to the side and flexing them to the front also causes reactions around other axes; however, a slower angular velocity of movement and the relative amounts of masses and radii result in a smaller reaction of the body about those axes.)

To perform a full turn around the longitudinal axis, the performer has to repeat this series of steps eight times. Clearly this technique is quite tedious and time consuming and not practical for anything but a free fall for a great distance or for playing in a gravity-free chamber! In fact, the reaction rotation method has been explored as an effective way in which astronauts may realign their bodies during periods of weightlessness without the use of cumbersome mechanical propulsion devices (Kane and Scher 1970). Mathematically, a 70-degree reaction twist is derived from a complete circle action of the legs moving in a semiconical fashion about a vertical axis, and a 30-degree reaction twist is derived from a complete circle of the arms.

Similarly, a backward somersault may be produced by circling the upper extremities forward around an ML axis that passes through the shoulder joints. Derived values for a forward or backward somersault per arm cycle were 12 degrees with the legs straight and 24 degrees with the legs tucked (Kane and Scher 1970). An adaptation of the technique may be performed while suspended by the hands from a single gymnastics ring. Beginning in a slight pike position, swing the legs in a conical fashion to describe a circle on the mat below (circumduction of the lower extremities at the hip joints). The reaction of the trunk will be in the opposite direction; it will continue to turn as long as the legs are circumducting. Biesterfeldt (1974a) notes that a male gymnast's body will react approximately 300 degrees for every leg circle; however, this depends on how far the legs are held away from the longitudinal axis during the circumduction.

Usually in gymnastics situations, the reaction rotation method is employed for error correction; that is , if a performer has too much or not enough angular velocity to land properly.

The conservation of angular momentum and the reaction rotation are useful in analyzing the motion of a high jumper during the airborne phase. Once the jumper is in the air, the angular momentum about the x axis helps the jumper rotate over the bar. Trunk hyperextension and knee flexion reduce the radius of gyration and thus increase the velocity of rotation. Two factors are important to the success of the rotation about the x axis. First, the jumper must not be too close or too far from the bar at takeoff. If she is too close, she will be unable to rotate in time for the hips to clear the bar; if she is too far at takeoff, she will rotate too much before the shoulders pass in vertical alignment with the bar and they will not clear. The second factor involves using the reaction rotation method to clear body segments as they pass down over the bar. The lowering of body parts immediately after they pass the bar will raise the next segments as they pass over the bar. For example, the head, shoulders, and lead arm should be lowered immediately after they have passed the bar so that the pelvis will be raised as it passes in vertical alignment with the bar. (See Figure 8.6a, p. 353.) The pelvis should be dropped immediately after it passes the bar (a sitting motion) so that the knees, legs, and feet will be raised. Timing is critical in this use of the conservation of angular momentum since segmental motions performed too early or too late will cause the segment to displace the bar.

The z axis rotation is used mainly for squaring the shoulders and pelvis relative to the bar. If this component were not available, the body would not be parallel to the bar as it passes over, and the right or left side probably would displace the bar as segmental movements were made.

In the straddle technique, the conservation of angular momentum is used in a fashion similar to that employed in the flop technique. Rather than hyperextending over the bar as in the flop, however, the jumper flexes his trunk and drops his lead arm over the bar after their clearance. (See Figure 8.6b, p. 353.) This serves to increase the velocity of rotation and to raise his lumbar and pelvis region as they pass the bar.

To clear the thighs, legs, and feet, the jumper must use a reaction rotation. Dapena (1974) suggests swinging the lead arm in transverse adduction across the body so that a reaction rotation in the lower part of the body allows the lead leg to clear. (If the right arm is swung to the left, the right leg swings to the right, thus allowing it to pass over the bar.) As soon as the right leg clears, the right and left arms are swung to the right and the lower body responds by rotating to the left, thus clearing the trailing left leg.

In both of these high jump techniques, angular momentum is established at takeoff and then rearranged during flight to clear the segment passing over the bar at any given time. The reaction rotation method of initiating rotations in the air is used to further reposition the body segments to enhance the success of the jump.

CAT ROTATION

The cat rotation is so called because it is the technique used by cats to land upright if dropped from an upside-down orientation. A cat falling and twisting is shown in Figure 12.12. The technique also has been called the modern twist (Biesterfeldt 1974b) and the counter-rotation twist (Hery 1975).

The cat rotation is a complicated version of the reaction rotation previously described, and it can bring about greater rotational displacement with less effort on the part of the performer. The cat rotation can be recognized by seeing a performer in a body position in which the lower part of the body is at some angle to the upper part of the body. Effective cat-rotation positions are the pike, the side arch, and the back arch. These are illustrated in Figure 12.13.

The longitudinal axis of the upper body is at some angle relative to the longitudinal axis of the lower body. The closer this angle is to 90 degrees, the more effective is this method of rotation. The twisting axis for the entire body (system) is the body's longitudinal axis through the CG, and the angular momentum about this axis is usually, but not always, zero. The cat-rotation method is commonly seen in gymnastics stunts, trampoline stunts, dives, and apparatus dismounts in which a 180-degree or 360-degree turn is required and a bending of the body is acceptable. Usually the rotation may be completed in three steps. Once the flexed or pike position is assumed, the sequence begins.

Through *internal* muscle torques, the upper body is made to rotate (twist) around its longitudinal axis to the left. In keeping with the action-and-reaction principle, a reaction must occur in the rest of the system (the lower half), and that reaction must be around the *same* axis as the action, but in the opposite direction. The radius of

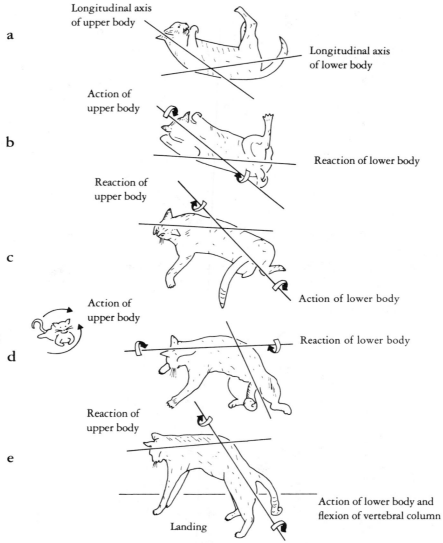

Figure 12.12.   A cat rotating to its feet when it is dropped from an upside-down position.

gyration of the lower body about the longitudinal axis of the upper body is quite large, and, therefore, the reaction is quite small. Immediately, the lower body rotates by internal muscle torques about its longitudinal axis in a similar direction as the upper body rotated. A similar response occurs in the opposite direction when the lower body twists by muscular effort about its longitudinal axis; the response of the upper body about the longitudinal axis of the lower body is quite small. If both of the twisting motions of the upper and lower halves are rotated alternately, the body moves from a pike into an arch position, facing in the opposite direction. The total system has, in effect, twisted 180 degrees.

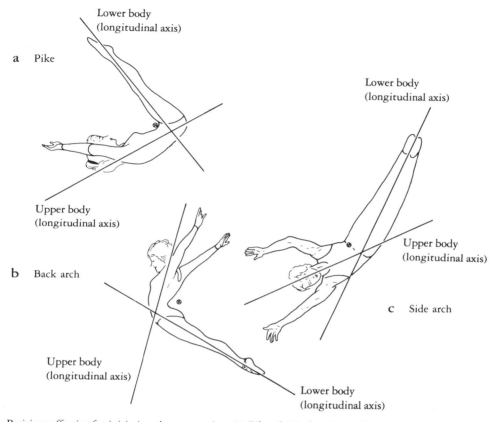

Positions effective for initiating the cat rotation. (a) Pike. (b) Back arch. (c) Side arch.   **Figure 12.13.**

Figure 12.14 shows the cat-rotation method used by a gymnast performing a vault. Notice that the performer leaves the horse without any twisting, or rotation, about the body's longitudinal axis (Figure 12.14a). By moving into a pike position (Figure 12.14b), the gymnast may use the cat-rotation method by rotating the upper and lower body portions alternately about their respective longitudinal axes. The body moves from the pike to a side-arch to a back-arch position. By flexing the hips, the gymnast can land on her feet, after a one-half twist, facing the horse.

This same technique is used for a swivel hips on the trampoline. The performer leaves the trampoline in a hip-flexed (pike) position, rotates the upper and lower halves of the body cw to a side-arch and then to a back-arch position (Figure 12.14c and d). When a one-half turn has been completed, a pike at the hips allows the performer to land in a seat drop again. The same technique can be used in performing a front drop one-half twist to a back drop, or a back drop one-half twist to a front around the longitudinal axis (Figure 12.14e).

To perform a full 360-degree twist using the cat-rotation technique, the performer must be extremely flexible in the vertebral column to maintain a large enough angle between the upper and lower sections of the body. A simplified way of testing this

Figure 12.14.   A gymnast employing the cat rotation during a vault.

technique is underwater, where the body is suspended and free of support without the dangers of falling to the ground. A second method is to have the gymnast hang by both hands from a single gymnastics ring. Beginning with a slight pike, the performer should twist the lower body to the right, around the longitudinal axis of the lower extremity, and the upper body to the right, around its longitudinal axis, so that the body ends in a back-arch (hyperextended) position facing the opposite direction. (This is not the same movement pattern described for the reaction twist, in which the legs are circled in a conical fashion [circumducted] to create an opposite reaction of the upper body.)

TWIST FROM A SOMERSAULT

Twisting from a somersault is probably the most common technique used to initiate rotation while the body is free of support because it is the most efficient of the three techniques. Unlike the other two types, it does not require a series of segmental movements, since once the twist has been initiated, the body continues to twist until the performer returns to the original position before twisting began. The body *must* have angular momentum established about some principal axis at takeoff. The axis about which the angular momentum is established at takeoff is called the **axis of momentum.** In this case, the momentum established around the performer's ML (turn) axis causes the performer to somersault either forward or backward. The ML axis is thus the axis of momentum, and the resultant angular momentum established around it does not change in magnitude or direction. The axis of momentum can be thought of as fixed in space, regardless of the change in position of the body and the body's principal axes. Factors to remember are that momentum is a vector quantity and that the resultant momentum vector may be resolved into components that are perpendicular to each other but are at some angle from the original axis of momentum. Figure 12.15 illustrates the axis of rotation of a performer doing a *backward* somersault who has taken off with angular momentum about her ML axis.

The initial position is symmetrical; that is, both arms are held above the head. During flight, the performer drops her right arm to the side, as shown in Figure 12.15b. This asymmetrical position reduces the radius of gyration of the right side of the body relative to the ML axis. The change in body position alters the body's principal axes to those shown in Figure 12.15c. In addition, by dropping the right arm cw around its AP axis (adduction), the performer causes a reaction of the body ccw around its AP axis, thus enhancing the tilt.[2]

The axis of angular momentum that was initially established does not change, but rather resolves into two perpendicular components, one about the body's principal longitudinal axis and one about the body's ML axis. Thus, the somersaulting motion around the ML axis continues even though the ML axis is now tilted from its original position, and in addition, the body begins to twist about its longitudinal axis (the other component).

The resolution of the initial angular momentum vector into two components may

2. The tilting of a body's principal axis of rotation from its original position is called **nutation** and also may be referred to as gyration or wobbling. Nutation occurs when angular momentum is established about a spatial axis that is the same as one of the body's principal axes. Changing the position of the body segments during flight causes the principal axes to move away from their original positions.

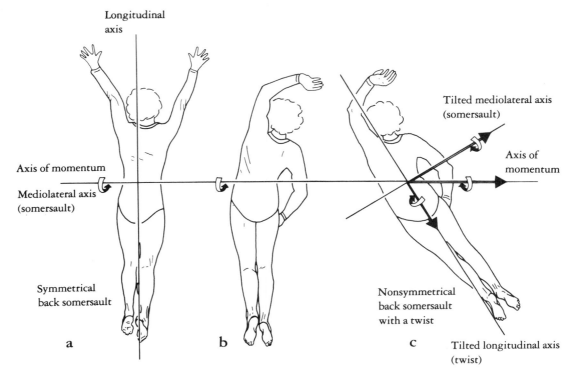

Figure 12.15.   (a and b) A tumbler somersaulting backward about the ML axis. (c) A tumbler tilting the body's principal axes in executing a nonsymmetrical back somersault with a twist.

be seen by using the right-hand rule for vectors. The arrow L_m in Figure 12.16 represents the vector direction and magnitude of the original turning momentum about the axis of momentum for the gymnast in Figure 12.15.

L_f represents the vector of the realigned principal ML axis, and L_1 represents the vector of the realigned principal longitudinal axis. Because the radius of gyration about the twisting axis (longitudinal) is small, the velocity of the twist will be large, in spite of the smaller vector magnitude as shown. Recall that for a body with a given magnitude of angular momentum, a reduction in the radius of gyration will result in an increase in angular velocity. Figure 12.17 shows a vaulter using this technique.

As soon as the performer's body assumes a symmetrical position again, the momentum vectors will compose (combine) into the original resultant vector, the axis of which will be the original axis of momentum. The angular momentum has been conserved even though it was resolved into two components. The principal ML axis of the performer and the axis of momentum will again coincide. The performer now will be somersaulting backward again.

An easier way of thinking through this technique may be employed. Recall Figure 12.15b in which the performer has dropped one arm. The radius of gyration is

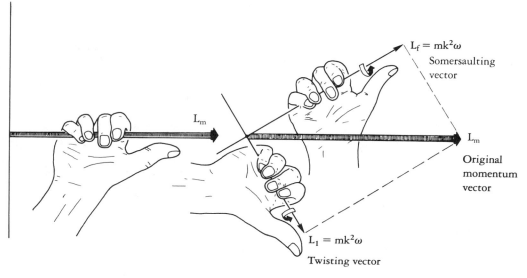

$L_f = mk^2\omega$
Somersaulting
vector

L_m

L_m
Original
momentum
vector

$L_1 = mk^2\omega$
Twisting vector

a   Original momentum vector, L_m **b**   Resolution of L_m into a somersaulting
                                                  and a twisting component

The resolution of the angular momentum vector into two components.   **Figure 12.16.**

decreased on the right side of the body, and thus its velocity backward increases about the ML axis. The velocity of the left side does not change because its radius of gyration has not changed. As the right side speeds up, it "pulls" the right shoulder backward to the left hip, thus initiating the twist to the right. If the performer were somersaulting forward, the turning speed of the right side about the ML axis would increase forward and pull the performer's right side forward. As viewed from the top, a front somersault with a right arm drop will cause the body to move into a twist represented by a headward-directed vector; a back somersault with a right arm drop will cause the body to move into a twist represented by a footward-directed vector.

Note that the body must simply resume a symmetrical position again to stop the twisting; it does not have to resume the initial position. For example, if the initial position is a layout and the performer drops the right arm to the side to initiate a twist, the body may resume a symmetrical position again and stop twisting by also dropping the left arm to the side.

Usually, the gymnastics, trampoline, and diving stunts that require a single or partial twist can be accomplished by using only one of the methods of initiating the twist in the air. The accomplishment of multiple twists, however, frequently demands the employment of more than one method. Gaining twisting momentum from the ground and enhancing this momentum with a twist initiated in the air will give the performer the greatest twisting velocity. Such a technique is used for stunts requiring double and triple twists.

Figure 12.17.   A gymnast initiating a twist from a somersault during vaulting.

Principles of Body Rotations

Angular momentum may be initiated from the ground by providing a force that acts on the body for a period of time, the line of which is eccentric to the body's CG. The greater the force, the time, or the distance from the axis, the greater the angular momentum generated.

The amount of angular momentum that a body has at takeoff cannot be changed once the body is free of support (assuming no other forces act on the body during flight). Angular momentum is not altered by the force of gravity, since gravity acts directly through the CG of the body and, consequently, has no effect on the body's turning.

The sum of the angular momenta of the body and its parts must equal the angular momentum with which the body left the ground.

Factors that constitute angular momentum may change in magnitude. In body rotation activities, the mass usually does not change throughout the execution. The body's radius of gyration may be altered in the air by moving body segments closer or farther away from the axis of rotation. The angular velocity of a rotating body increases or decreases, according to the change in the body's radius, so that the angular momentum always remains constant. The change in the angular velocity is inverse to the change in the radius and is squared in magnitude.

Body rotation about an axis may be initiated in the air without changing the body's total angular momentum. Three methods may be employed: reaction rotation, cat rotation, and the method of twisting from a somersault. In the first two methods, the body does not need any angular momentum at takeoff. In the third method, angular momentum must be established about a single axis at takeoff, and it is resolved into two perpendicular components that coincide with two of the body's principal axes.

UNDERSTANDING THE INITIATION
OF ROTATION IN THE AIR

1. For the following changes in the radius of gyration, k, state the change in the angular velocity that would be effected: (a) 1/3 k, (b) 1/5 k, (c) 6 k, (d) 12 k.

2. If a performer can do two somersaults in a layout position, how many somersaults can be done in a tight tuck? in a medium pike? Use Table 12.1 (p. 537).

3. To effect as much change as possible in the angular velocity, a performer should leave the support in what position?

4. Discuss the problems a freestyle skier would have in attempting to initiate a reaction rotation about the longitudinal axis, as compared with a gymnast attempting the same rotation.

5. Figure 12.17 shows a person initiating a twist from a somersault. Imagine that you are standing on the landing mat observing the performer coming over the horse toward you. Draw the resultant momentum vector for rotation about the axis of momentum and the two vector components. Use circles about the axes to indicate directions.

6. Figures 8.5 and 8.6 (pp. 352–353) show high jumpers using a straddle and a flop-style jump. Indicate and discuss the axis of rotation about which the jumper will be turning in the air, and discuss how the takeoff created this momentum. How could each jumper make the body position more effective while moving over the bar?

REFERENCES
SUGGESTED READINGS

Bajin, B. "Three Tsukahara Vaults." *International Gymnast*, June 1978, 58–59.

Bangerter, T. "Comparison of the Twisting Somersault in Diving and Trampoline." *Scholastic Coach* 38 (1) (1968): 68–69.

Bedi, J. F., and Cooper, J. M. "Takeoff in the Long Jump—Angular Momentum Considerations." *Journal of Biomechanics* 10 (9) (1977): 541–48.

Biesterfeldt, H. J. "Salto Mechanics I: Moment of Inertia." *Gymnast*, March 1975, 44–45.

———. "Twisting Mechanics I." *Gymnast*, April 1974a, 28–30.

———. "Twisting Mechanics II." *Gymnast*, June–July, 1974b, 46–47.

Brown, J. R. "A Comparison of Selected Factors Relating to Success of Running Forward Somersaults." *Gymnast*, December 1974, 32–33.

Brüggemann, P. "Kinematics and Kinetics of the Backward Somersault Takeoff from the Floor." In *Biomechanics VIII-A: Proceedings of the Eighth International Congress of Biomechanics,* ed. H. Matsui and K. Kobayashi, 793–800. Champaign, Ill.: Human Kinetics Publishers, 1983.

Dapena, J. "A Method to Determine the Angular Momentum of a Human Body About Three Orthogonal Axes Passing Through Its Center of Gravity." *Journal of Biomechanics* 11 (5) (1978): 251–56.

———. "Mechanics of Rotation in the Fosbury-Flop." *Medicine and Science in Sports and Exercise* 12 (1) (1980): 45–53.

———. "Searching for the Best Straddle Technique." *Track Technique* 55 (3) (1974): 1753–55.

Dyson, G. *The Mechanics of Athletics.* 7th ed. New York: Holmes & Meier Publishers, 1978.

Eaves, G. "Recent Developments in the Theory of Twist Dives." In *Biomechanics in Swimming: Proceedings of the First International Symposium,* ed. L. LeWillie and J. Clarys, 237–42. University of Brussels, Belgium, 1971.

Ecker, T. *Track and Field Technique Through Dynamics.* Los Altos, Calif.: Tafnews Press (book division of *Track and Field News*), 1976.

Frohlich, C. "Do Springboard Divers Violate Angular Momentum Conservation?" *American Journal of Physics* 47 (7) (1979): 583–92.

Goehler, J. "The Mechanical Effect of the Forward 'Leg Snap'." *International Gymnast,* October 1977, 56–59.

Hery, G. "Mechanics of Rotational Movements." Paper presented at the Southwest Gymnastics Clinic, Las Vegas, 1975.

Hopper, B. J. *The Mechanics of Human Movement.* New York: American Elsevier Publishing Co., 1973.

Igaraski, H. "The Prediction of the Quadruple Backward Somersault on the Horizontal Bar." In *Biomechanics VIII-B: Proceedings of the Eighth International Congress of Biomechanics,* ed. H. Matsui and K. Kobayashi, 787–92. Champaign, Ill.: Human Kinetics Publishers, 1983.

Kane, T. R., Headrick, M. R., and Yatteau, J. D. "Experimental Investigation of an Astronaut Maneuvering Scheme." *Journal of Biomechanics* 5 (3) (1973): 313–20.

Kane, T. R., and Scher, M. P. "Human Self Rotation by Means of Limb Movements." *Journal of Biomechanics* 3 (1) (1970): 39–49.

Kinolik, Z., Garhammer, J., and Gregor, R. J. "Biomechanical Comparison of Front Aerial

Somersaults Performed from Different Starting Positions." In *Biomechanics VII-B: Proceedings of the Seventh Congress of Biomechanics,* ed. A. Morecki, K. Fidelus, K. Kedzior and A. Wit, 531–36. Baltimore: University Park Press, 1981.

Knight, S. A., Wilson, B. D., and Hay, J. G. "Biomechanical Determinants of Success in Performing a Front Somersault." *International Gymnast,* March 1978, 54–56.

LaDue, F., and Norman, J. *Two Seconds of Freedom.* Romford, Essex, G. B.: Glover House, 1967.

Mohan, J., and Hiltner, W. *Freestyle Skiing.* New York: Winchester Press, 1976.

Page, R. L. "The Mechanics of Swimming and Diving." *The Physics Teacher,* February 1976, 72–80.

Payne, H. A., and Barker, P. "Comparison of the Takeoff Forces in the Flic Flac and the Back Somersault in Gymnastics." In *Biomechanics V-B: Proceedings of the Fifth International Congress on Biomechanics,* ed. P. V. Komi, 314–21. Baltimore: University Park Press, 1976.

Ramey, M. R. "Significance of Angular Momentum in Long Jumping." *Research Quarterly* 44 (4) (1973): 488–97.

Stroup, F., and Bushnell, D. "Rotation, Translation, and Trajectory in Diving." *Research Quarterly* 40 (4) (1969): 812–17.

Tichonov, V. N. "Improvement of Vaulting Technique." *International Gymnast,* November 1978, 56–57.

Tricker, R. A. R., and Tricker, B. J. K. *The Science of Human Movement.* New York: American Elsevier Publishing Co., 1967.

Van Gheluwe, L. "Computer Simulation of an Airborne Backward Twist Somersault." In *Biomechanics VII-A: Proceedings of the Seventh International Congress of Biomechanics,* ed. A. Morecki, K. Fidelus, K. Kedzior, and A. Wit, 200–07. Baltimore: University Park Press, 1981.

Wilson, B. D. "Toppling Techniques in Diving." *Research Quarterly* 48 (4) (1977): 806–11.

Prerequisites

Chapter Contents

ANALYSIS OF ACTIVITIES IN WHICH THE BODY ROTATES WHILE SUPPORTED

The concepts of rotary motion, which were discussed and applied to a system free of support, also may be applied to a system while it is supported or suspended. While supported, the total system appears to rotate around the point of support and possesses the same variables of mass, radius of gyration, angular velocity, and angular momentum. A net external torque is necessary to rotate the system. Although the principles remain the same, slight differences occur in their application when the body is supported.

SECTION 1

THE HUMAN BODY IN SUPPORTED ROTARY MOTION

During supported rotation, the body is subjected to two forces: the reaction force of the external support and the weight force acting at the center of gravity (CG) of the body. As long as the line of gravity falls within the base of support, the body remains in equilibrium. As soon as the line of gravity falls outside the base of support, an unopposed torque is created by the body's weight force and produces a rotation of the body. The weight force at the CG functions as a potential torque-producing force in the case of a supported body.

Figure 13.1 illustrates the lines of action of forces acting on a body when it is supported and nonsupported. W represents the weight force, and RF, the reaction force at the supporting surface. The magnitude of the weight force does not change as the performer changes positions relative to the axis of rotation, but the perpendicular distance of that line of force from the axis of rotation may be changed by altering the segmental positions. Thus, the torque produced by the weight force can increase from zero, when the weight force is in vertical alignment above or below the base of support, to its greatest magnitude, when the weight force is at its greatest horizontal distance from the base of support.

Similarly, the reaction force at the point of support also may be a torque-producing force when the axis of rotation is considered as being through the system's CG. This is particularly evident when the performer is being projected by a spring mechanism such as a diving board, Reuther board, or trampoline. With a springboard diver, the upward-directed force of the spring is easier to comprehend as a torque-producing force about the diver's CG. Also possible is the production of torques by the reaction forces of other supporting surfaces such as the horizontal bar, the parallel bars,

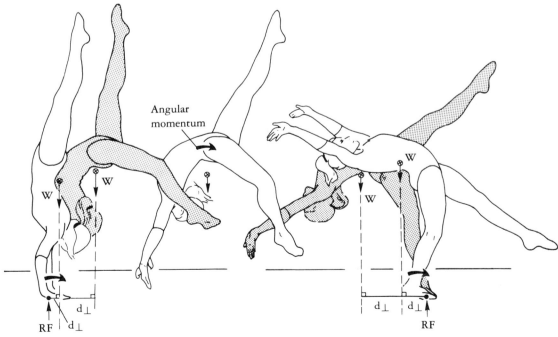

Figure 13.1.   Motive forces in a handstand walkout.

tumbling mats, and Reuther boards. Someday the rails on the uneven parallel bars may have an adjustable spring constant that can be adapted by performers of varying degrees of skill in a way similar to the spring of the diving board.

The body mass, its radius of gyration, and the resulting rotational inertia are as important in supported rotation as they are in nonsupported rotation. The axis of rotation in supported body rotation may change during the execution of a series of stunts. For instance, on the uneven bars, a gymnast may swing around the high bar as an axis until body contact is made with the low bar. A release of the high bar allows the body to begin to rotate around a new axis at the low bar.

The radius of gyration of the body varies according to which axis of rotation the body is using and the position of the body relative to that axis. Figure 13.2 shows a body rotating around a horizontal bar. In positions 1, 2, and 3, the arms are flexed at the shoulder and hip, and the knee joints are fully extended; the ankles are plantar flexed. The radius of gyration is some distance away from the axis. In positions 4, 5, and 6, the body is pulled closer to the axis by flexion of the knees, dorsiflexion of the ankles, and increased flexion of the hips. An elevation of the shoulder girdle also serves to pull the body closer to the bar. The estimated radius of gyration is indicated by the shaded portion of the illustration. Notice that the radius of gyration increases and decreases according to the body's position relative to the rail.

A gymnast moving from a swing to a pike hang on the rings provides another

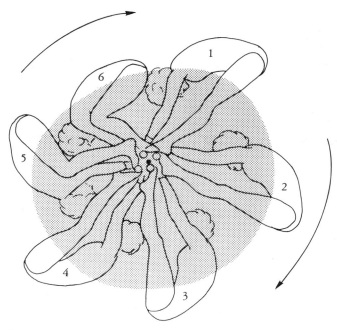

A gymnast in various positions while swinging around a horizontal bar to show changes in the body's radius of gyration while rotating.   **Figure 13.2.**

Figure 13.3.

A gymnast performing a swing on the rings (a) and moving into a pike hang (b).

example of changing the distribution of the body's mass of rotation (Figure 13.3). The gymnast begins the swing from an extended layout position (positions 1 and 2) and then changes the body position to that of a pike (position 3). As he moves from the layout position to the pike, he decreases his radius of gyration (distribution of his mass) from the axis of rotation, which in this case is the shoulder joint during the upswing. Note that as he performs the piking action, he is additionally rotating his legs about a secondary axis, the ML axis through the hips.

SECTION 2

CONSERVATION OF ANGULAR MOMENTUM IN A SUPPORTED SYSTEM

The principle of conservation of momentum applies to bodies rotating around a support; however, because support exists, additional factors must be considered. The primary axis of rotation is located at the point of support, and the force of friction acts on the point of contact between the body and the supporting surface.

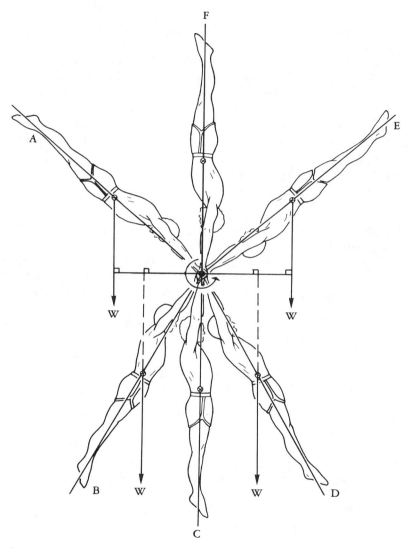

A rigid body circling a horizontal bar.

Figure 13.4.

Figure 13.4 shows a rigid body rotating about an axis. One can see that the body begins to fall as soon as its line of gravity falls beyond the base of support. The weight of the body, acting as a line of force that does not pass through the axis of rotation, continually progresses to a point that is farther and farther away from the axis of rotation. The farther the line of force of the body's weight from the axis of rotation, the greater the torque it produces. The increase in the perpendicular distance from the axis of rotation to the line of action of the force continues until the body is horizontal. The motive torque produced by the weight continues to act through 180 degrees until the body's CG is again in vertical alignment with the support; that is, the body has a motive torque acting on it from the time that its line of gravity passes outside the base until the bottom of the swing. The force of gravity is acting in the direction of body movement during the downswing and against the direction of body movement on the upswing; thus, the torque changes from a motive torque during the downswing to a resistive torque during the upswing. Certain positions of the body on the downswing may be compared with similar positions on the upswing. Similar positions are defined as two positions, one on each side of the swing where the angular momentum ideally is equal (neglecting friction and air-resistance effects).

Figure 13.4 can be used to compare various body positions during the swing. (Since this is a purely hypothetical example, friction between the hands and the bar will be neglected.) If the angular impulse acting until position A has produced a magnitude of 10 angular momentum units in the body and if the body has 30 angular momentum units by the time it reaches the bottom of the swing, then the angular impulse acting as a resistive force will cause the angular momentum of the body to be reduced to 10 angular momentum units again when it reaches position E and zero units when it reaches the top. When one considers the total swing, one can understand that a perfectly rigid body acting without friction or air resistance will come to rest at the top of the bar where it started.

Activities such as the giant swing would be simple if one could perform them without friction or air resistance, but such is not the case. The direction of the resistive forces of friction and air resistance depends on and is opposite to the direction of the moving body. Figure 13.5 indicates the directions of the forces of friction on the hands and the air resistance on the body during the downswing and the upswing phases of a giant swing.

On the downswing, both of the resistive torques are acting against the torque produced by gravity and thus are retarding the increase of the angular velocity. Similarly, on the upswing, the friction and air resistance torques are acting against the direction of movement and along with the now resistive torque of gravity to retard the angular velocity. Thus, with the directions of the motive and resistive forces as they are, a body could not possibly return to the top of the bar at the end of the swing. The angular momentum would truly not be conserved because of the external forces of friction and air resistance.

By making use of the principle of conservation of momentum, however, and remembering that, at any given time, the angular velocity of the body may be increased by decreasing the body's radius of gyration, one can compensate for the resistive torques involved. The loss of angular velocity, from what it would have been without the resistive forces at any given point during the upswing, may be compensated for by decreasing the body's radius of gyration. Because the radius of gyration is squared in the angular momentum formula, a decrease in the radius of gyration may satisfactorily compensate for a reduction in the angular momentum

a   Air resistance
    and friction
    force on downswing   Air resistance

Friction force

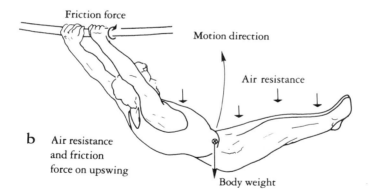

Friction force

Motion direction

Air resistance

b   Air resistance
    and friction
    force on upswing

Body weight

Directions of the resistive forces acting on a rotating body.

Figure 13.5.

due to the resistive torques by increasing the body's angular velocity. Therefore, the body in position E, Figure 13.4, has a smaller angular momentum than that in position A; however, the angular velocity of position E may be increased by a reduction of the body's radius of gyration. This increase in the body's angular velocity allows the body to return to the top of the bar.

SECTION 3

APPLICATIONS OF ANGULAR MOMENTUM PRINCIPLES TO A SUPPORTED BODY

The principle of conservation of angular momentum is applied to sport situations in which the body is supported on the basis of four general categories: (1) altering the radius of gyration to change rotational inertia, (2) altering the radius of gyration to change angular velocity, (3) altering the radius of gyration in learning progressions, and (4) dealing with angular momentum about multiple parallel axes.

Altering the Radius to Change Rotational Inertia

During the execution of some activities, the body must reduce the radius of gyration to reduce the resistance of a body segment or of the total body. The axes of rotation would be the anatomical axes through the shoulder, elbow, hip, and knee-joint centers, and the radii of gyration of the segments would be measured from those particular axes.

The change in the radius of gyration during the recovery phase in running is shown in Figure 13.6. A runner also must change the amount of flexion that occurs in the arms and legs during the recovery phase so that it matches the pace of the run. During the recovery phases of the upper and lower extremities, a sprinter must use considerably more flexion than a distance runner so that the segments recover faster and thus speed up the entire pace of the run. As the pace of the run slows, the amount of necessary flexion decreases so that a long-distance runner may be able to keep the lower extremity at a fairly large angle during the forward swing; the recovery phase of leg motion may be just enough to clear the ground with the toe.

A redistribution of the body's mass relative to an axis is experienced by the pole vaulter shown in Figure 13.7. By planting the pole in the vaulting box, the vaulter gains angular momentum from the linear momentum developed during his approach. The plant fixes the end of the pole and establishes the first axis of rotation. The system is defined as the pole and the vaulter's body as both rotate about the fixed end.

As the pole-body system rotates, the vaulter repositions his body relative to the axis. This repositioning changes the radius of gyration of the system relative to the fixed end, and since the body is internal to the system as it rotates, the repositioning causes the body and its segments to "assume" some of the angular momentum of the entire system. Since the rotations of the vaulter's body and its segments are in the opposite direction of the system's rotation, the vaulter's movements tend to reduce the system's angular velocity about the fixed end. Care must be taken so that the swing and rock back do not assume too much of the momentum and cause the pole to stall during the vaulter's ascent.

Axis (right hip)

Axis (right hip)

Axis (right hip)

Axis (left hip)

k

The changing radius of gyration
of the extremities during running.

Figure 13.6.

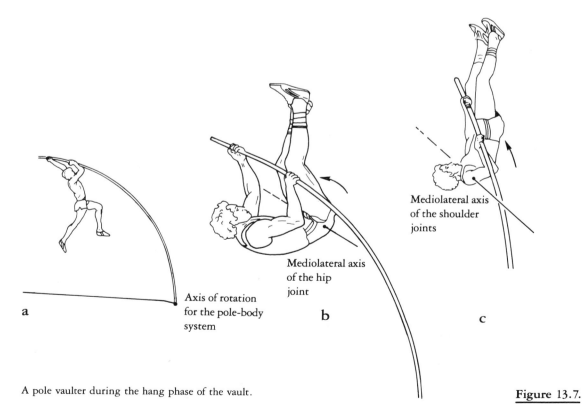

Axis of rotation
for the pole-body
system

Mediolateral axis
of the hip
joint

Mediolateral axis
of the shoulder
joints

a

b

c

A pole vaulter during the hang phase of the vault.

Figure 13.7.

The vaulter swings counterclockwise (CCW) about an axis at his hands as the pole rotates clockwise (CW) (Figure 13.7a). The rock back is initiated by extending the shoulder joints, which serves to pull the trunk ccw; by flexing the vertebral column, which serves to pull the pelvis ccw; and by flexing the hip joints, which serves to pull the lower extremities ccw (Figure 13.7b). These motions also help bend the pole. By the time the pole is ready to recoil, the vaulter should be in a vertical position, ready to receive the impulse, and the pole should have lost most of its angular velocity about its fixed end.

A third example of altering the timing of a movement is the gymnast's position during vaulting (Figure 13.8). The vaulter must gain enough velocity on the approach to carry the body from the board through the preflight, horse contact, postflight, and landing. The CG is moving linearly during the hurdle, but as soon as the feet

b Motion of center of gravity during horse contact

a Motion of center of gravity during board contact

Axis

Axis

Figure 13.8.   Two supported rotations used in vaulting (a) on the Reuther board and (b) on the horse.

contact the board, the friction force at the feet fixes the contact point and establishes an axis of rotation about the feet. The excursion of the CG during board contact is critical to the resulting body motion. The velocity of this rotation depends on the velocity of the approach run and on the position of the body during board contact. The speed of the run determines how far the CG travels during the time that the vaulter is in contact with the board. All other things being equal, a very fast runner contacting the board at the same angle as a slower runner will have the CG farther ahead of the feet than the slow runner when each leaves the board. Having the CG farther ahead of the feet during takeoff provides the gymnast with a greater torque and resulting angular momentum at takeoff. The accompanying reduction in the angle of takeoff, however, changes the linear path of the CG during preflight, the trajectory of which is a flatter arc and may not be beneficial to the vault being performed.

A body landing on the board with the arms positioned overhead rotates more slowly around the support axis than a body with the arms at waist level. Slower rotation results in a more vertical angle of takeoff. Vaulters should have the arms overhead upon takeoff, but the speed and angle of takeoff may be enhanced by the flexing of the arms during board contact. For example, the action of vigorously extending the fully flexed shoulders (throwing the arms forward and downward) while the feet are fixed by the friction reaction between the foot and board produces forward angular momentum in the system. Consequently, after the feet leave the board, the angular momentum produced by the arms is transferred to the total body and thus increases the rotational component. On the other hand, vigorously flexing the arms during contact (accelerating the arms upward) increases the depression of the board, which enhances the board reaction force and thus the linear and rotary velocity of the body at takeoff. Since either of these arm actions must occur during a time interval of no more than 0.1 to 0.2 sec, whether the vaulter can complete the arm action in that length of time is questionable.

Similar considerations are appropriate for the vaulter during horse contact. Enough angular momentum must be conserved to carry the gymnast over the point of support at the hands. If he arrives at the horse at a low angle, he has to reduce the body's radius of gyration relative to the hands so that the resulting increase in the velocity carries him over. Reducing the radius of gyration means a form break, because it is usually accomplished by flexing the hips or flexing the knees or both. A more skillful technique would be to increase the angular displacement enough during the preflight so that enough of a turn around the ML axis is executed in the air before horse contact. Thus, little excursion of the CG needs to take place during horse contact and before repulsion. In this manner, the gymnast is able to maintain a straight body position throughout the vault.

Altering the Radius to Change Angular Velocity

In the example of the performer on the high bar performing a giant swing, the torque produced by the force of gravity acted to reduce the angular momentum on the upswing. To slow the reduction of the angular momentum, the radius of gyration could be reduced.

Figure 13.9 illustrates a beginning gymnast performing a giant swing on the horizontal bar. Notice that just after passing the bottom point in the swing, the gymnast flexes in two places, the hips and the elbows, while allowing the shoulder joint to extend from a fully flexed position overhead to midposition in front of the body. These actions bring his mass closer to the bar (reduce the body's radius of gyration) and thus tend to counteract the reduction in the body's angular momentum during the upswing. By bringing the CG (not to be confused with the radius of gyration) closer to the bar on the upswing, the gymnast also decreases the force arm of the gravitational force and thus decreases the magnitude of its resistive torque. The reduction of the resistive torque produced by gravity allows his body to maintain its angular velocity for a longer period of time, and, consequently, as he approaches the top of the bar, he moves faster than he would have had he remained in the rigid position. The performer is able to help counteract the resistive forces of friction and air resistance by reducing the radius of gyration and thus increasing the velocity of rotation.

As a second example, a gymnast attempting to perform a forward stride circle on the low bar of the uneven parallel bars is shown in Figure 13.10.

The initial positions (2 and 3) are assumed to gain as much angular momentum as possible on the downswing. This is accomplished by increasing the distance

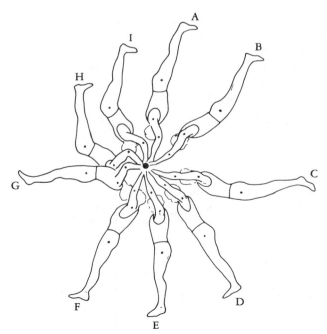

Figure 13.9.   A beginning gymnast performing a giant swing on the horizontal bar.

A gymnast performing a forward stride circle on the uneven parallel bars.   **Figure 13.10.**

between the CG of the body and the axis of rotation (the bar), thus maximizing the motive torque. A coach may cue the performer to keep the head up, and the chin, chest, and front leg out as far as possible away from the bar. Once the performer begins to fall, the extended, stretched position should be maintained for as long as possible until the bottom of the circle is reached (position 4). Upon reaching the bottom, the gymnast assumes a more flexed position; that is, she flexes the cervical and thoracic vertebrae and pulls the body into the bar with an elevation of the shoulder girdle (positions 5 and 6). The reduction of the radius of gyration in this manner increases the angular velocity on the upswing, decreases the resistive torque of gravity, and allows the performer to partially overcome the air resistance and friction on the upswing so as to come to rest on the top of the bar. Most beginners have trouble with two parts of this skill. First, a beginner frequently does not maintain the extended position for more than a split second after starting to fall forward, and therefore the motive torque on the downswing is minimized. This results in a reduction in the possible angular momentum that may be gained during the downswing. Second, in fear, the beginner usually grasps the bar tightly, which increases the friction component and also reduces the angular momentum to a magnitude that is less than that necessary to complete the circle.

As a skilled performer approaches the top of the bar (position 1), she again must extend as much as possible to reduce the angular velocity that may carry her forward into another circle. A similar analysis may be made with a forward or backward seat circle on the low bar or horizontal bar.

A final example is a gymnast performing a cast back hip circle on the uneven bars (Figure 13.11). On initiating the cast, the performer lifts her CG up to the horizontal (positions 1 and 2) and pushes it outward away from the high bar (position 3). This increases the distance of the weight force from the axis of rotation (the rail) and thus increases the motive torque. A straight and extended body on the downswing has greater angular momentum (positions 4 and 5). On contact with the low bar (position 7), the gymnast releases the high bar and initiates a rotation around a new axis at the hip. The velocity of rotation increases as the body moves to the new axis because the performer's radius of gyration relative to this new axis is smaller. The velocity shows a greater increase if the performer flexes at the hips and knees (positions 8 and 9).

Altering the Radius in Learning Progressions

In many instances, motor skills are taught in a learning progression that relies on the reduction of the body's radius of gyration to help the beginning performer through attempts at a new skill. Examples of aerial stunts were used in the previous chapter to demonstrate these progressions. Similar progressions are used when a body is rotating around an external support. Generally, the ideal performance of the most difficult stunts is that in which the body maintains a position of greatest rotational inertia, or full extension with the arms usually flexed over the head (a layout position). The intermediate level of a skill uses a pike position (flexion of the hip), and the beginning level uses a tuck position (flexion of the hips, knees, and vertebral column).

Beginning performers use obvious deviations from the ideal (layout) body position, such as flexing the hips and knees to reduce the radius of gyration to increase the angular velocity. For example, the performer depicted in Figure 13.11 would

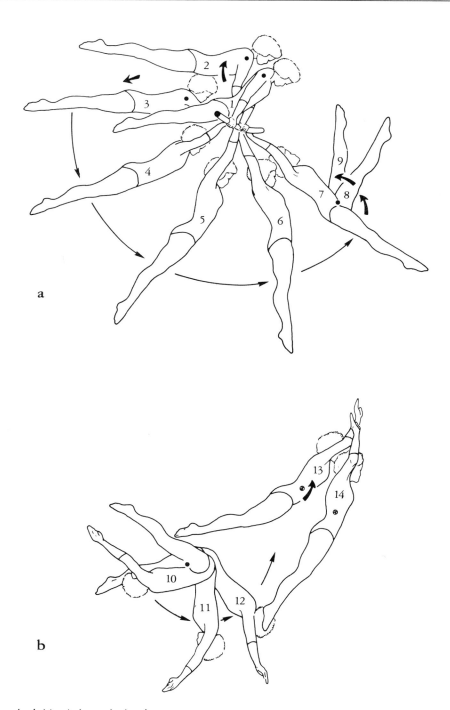

A cast back hip circle on the low bar.

Figure 13.11.

have increased her angular velocity about the low bar if she had flexed her hips and knees during the wrap. As performers become skillful in the intermediate and advanced stages, they perfect the timing of segmental movements and the positioning of the body parts and also reduce the resistive friction force in cases of hand-held support. These improvements result in greater initial angular velocity so that less reduction in the radius is necessary to complete the stunt. In fact, in judged activities, the measure of a skilled performance is that it displays as little obvious deviation as possible from the designated body position.

An example of a learning progression is a cast back hip circle (Figure 13.12). In the beginning stages of learning the stunt (Figure 13.12c), the gymnast gets a small

a Advanced

b Intermediate

c Beginning

Figure 13.12.   An advanced (a), an intermediate (b), and a beginning (c) gymnast performing a cast back hip circle on the horizontal bar.

cast; she grips the bar tightly, does not place the upper body away from the bar on the downswing as much as she should, and, therefore, must tuck as tightly as possible on the upswing to complete the circle. Her hips, knees, and vertebral column are flexed, and her ankles are dorsiflexed. In the intermediate stages of learning (Figure 13.12b), the performer increases the distance of the CG from the bar during the back drop, and decreases the tightness of her grip. Consequently, she can make it to the top by merely flexing the hips. A skilled gymnast (Figure 13.12a) performs the stunt with little deviation from the rigidly extended body position. Just before reaching the bottom, she assumes a slight flexion of the cervical and the thoracic vertebrae. During the upswing she keeps her body's CG close to the bar by not allowing her arms to flex much from their extended positions. At the top of the bar, the gymnast extends her body again to prevent the momentum from carrying her body into another circle backward.

Handspring progressions illustrate a similar change in the radius of gyration as a performer becomes skilled. These differences can be observed in a front or back handspring vault or a handspring performed on the floor. Figure 13.13 illustrates a back handspring on the floor. The progression of difficulty from least to most difficult is seen by observing a beginner (Figure 13.13c), who springs backward in a layout position and brings the body over the hands in a tuck position; an intermediate performer (Figure 13.13b), who brings the body over the hands in a pike position; and an advanced performer (Figure 13.13a), who brings the body over the hands in a near layout position. By bringing the body over the supporting hands in a tuck or pike position, the performer causes a reduction in the body's rotational inertia, making it easier to successfully complete the rotation prior to landing on the feet.

The amount of vertical and angular velocity the performer has on takeoff from the feet and the hands determines whether the body has enough time to remain in the layout position during the rotation or whether the body must reduce the radius of gyration to increase the angular velocity and carry the body over the hands and to the feet.

Angular Momentum About Multiple Parallel Axes

Few examples of supported rotational skills concern movements about only one axis. These include the giant swing on the horizontal bar or some simple rotational moves on the low bar of the uneven parallel bars, such as a forward stride circle. Understanding the movements about multiple parallel axes is desirable when one is attempting to teach coordination and timing of a stunt that involves a series of body movements, such as the kipping movements.

Figure 13.14 illustrates a glide kip mount on the low bar of the uneven parallel bars. Sequentially, the first and most obvious rotation is the body rotation about the rail; the feet are removed from the floor support and the torque produced by gravity rotates the body from positions 1 and 2. The upper body position should be kept as rigid as possible during this phase, since the angular momentum gained by the system on the downswing may be lost by allowing the shoulders to flex (i.e.,

Figure 13.13.   An advanced (a), an intermediate (b), and a beginning (c) gymnast performing a back handspring.

the body system should be rotating about only one axis at the rail until the arms are perpendicular to the floor). The second axis used is the ML axis, parallel with the rail and through the hip joints. It is used as the hips extend during the glide phase, from position 2 to 3, and as they flex during positions 4, 5, and 6. The vertebral column should be stabilized in a position of slight flexion throughout.

The next axis used is the ML axis through the shoulder joints (shoulder joint

A gymnast performing a glide kip mount on the uneven parallel bars.

Figure 13.14.

extension) as the performer brings her pelvis up to the rail from positions 7 to 8. The momentum gained on the downswing from the outside of the rail generates momentum to carry the performer up on the other side. From positions 8 to 9, the performer may have to flex the vertebral column and elevate the shoulder girdle to pull the body inward toward the axis so that the body's angular velocity increases. The proper sequence and timing of rotations about these axes are crucial to the performance, since the momentum gained or maintained within the system during one phase may be lost by improper timing of the next movement.

Initially, as the body rotates downward, it gains angular momentum from the torque produced by the force of gravity. The body's CG should be placed and carried as far as possible from the rail to increase the perpendicular distance of that line of force from the axis. As the body reaches the bottom of the swing and begins to move upward, it must not be allowed to extend too far outward from the rail. The correct position can be achieved by preventing the shoulders from fully flexing and by not allowing the lumbar vertebrae to hyperextend during the extension of the hip joints. Although the stretched (hyperextended) position is a popular one, it has little mechanical advantage since it only increases the resistive torque on the upswing, thereby enhancing the reduction of the body's angular momentum and its upward displacement. As the body reaches the midphase of the upswing on the outside of the bars, the hips are flexed. This motion takes place about a parallel axis to the rail axis and temporarily assumes some of the positive (ccw) angular momentum of the body about the rail. (The motion of the legs is in the same direction as the momentum about the rail.) As the body reaches the end of the upswing, the lumbar and hip flexion bring the legs near the rail. The body is in a position to gain negative (cw) angular momentum on the far side as the torque from the weight acts on the body to accelerate it downward again. The angular momentum gained in this phase is gained by the torque applied by the force of gravity on the CG. As the body reaches the bottom of the arc, the angular velocity may be increased by extending the shoulder joints, keeping the hips close to the rail, and further flexing the vertebral column, which brings the body's CG close to the rail and decreases the body's radius of gyration. (A retraction and elevation of the shoulder girdle also will aid in the upswing.) The body now has an increased velocity to bring it up on the near side. Important at this point is keeping the body close to the rail, for any separation of the two would increase the radius of gyration of the body, causing the body to slow to the point that it would not be able to reach the top. Beginners often have to "muscle" their way up the rail, because the angular velocity has been decreased to zero. A slight flexion of the neck and thoracic vertebrae on reaching the top of the rail also decreases the radius and aids the upward rotation.

As one teaches or coaches skills in which the concepts of angular momentum are important to the successful completion of stunts, one should watch carefully for rotation about axes other than the intended ones. Many times, unwanted rotation takes place because the body cannot stabilize its joints in the desired positions. Consequently, the body segments are allowed to rotate about joint axes while the body system rotates about an external axis. Moving about more than one axis can be undesirable if the movement about the second axis assumes some of the angular momentum needed for the successful performance of rotation about the first axis.

Figure 13.15 shows the proper (Figure 13.15b) and improper (Figure 13.15c) rotations that may take place during performance of a backward seat circle on the parallel bar. To perform this stunt correctly, the body must be stable at the shoulder joints, as in Figure 13.15a and b. The basis for completion of the circle comes from the gaining of angular momentum on the downswing by holding the body out as far away from the bar as possible to increase the motive torque (Figure 13.15a). Once the body's CG reaches its lowest position at the bottom of the swing, an elevation of the shoulders brings the body in closer to the bar, as does a flexion of the thoracic and cervical vertebrae. The decrease in the radius of gyration and resistive torque provided by the force of gravity on the upswing is enough to increase the

a Initial
   movements

b Skilled

c Unskilled

A backward seat circle.   **Figure 13.15.**

velocity and bring the body to the top (Figure 13.15b). An extension of the body with a tighter grip at the completion of the stunt stops the body from falling backward or forward again. In Figure 13.15c, however, the performer has not held the shoulder joints stable at position 4, and the angular momentum gained by the system during the downswing is assumed by the trunk and leg segments rotating about a parallel axis through the shoulder joints. Thus, the body rotation about the bar is halted. The performer ends with her feet hanging downward and with her shoulder joints in a hyperextended position. The second rotation about the axis through the shoulder joints must be prohibited. The angular momentum of the system must remain about the axis at the rail and not be assumed by the body about the shoulder joints.

UNDERSTANDING THE ROTATION
OF A BODY SUPPORTED

1. Figure 13.16 illustrates a system falling around an axis of rotation. The body's weight is equal to 450 N. If 1 cm = .1 m, what is the torque of the body's weight at points a, b, c, and d?

2. Ignoring friction and air resistance, in which positions in Figure 13.16 should the angular velocities be identical? In which positions should the angular momenta be identical? Explain why.

3. In Figure 13.16, considering friction forces at the axis of rotation, the positions on the upswing (g through l) will have an angular velocity less than, equal to, or more than the velocity of the corresponding (opposite) position on the downswing (a through f). Explain why.

4. Observe a runner jogging slowly. Note the degrees of elbow, hip, knee, and ankle flexion during recovery. Repeat for a medium-speed run and a sprint. What differences are noticed in the degree of flexion? Explain the differences in terms of the rotational inertia and muscular torques.

5. Observe gymnasts performing on the horizontal bar, the uneven parallel bars, or the parallel bars. While the body is supported by one of these pieces of apparatus, identify the axis of rotation as the gymnast performs. Can you identify when the apparatus is the axis of rotation? when the axis of rotation is located through a joint (e.g., shoulder joint, hip joint)? Observe how the axis of rotation changes from the

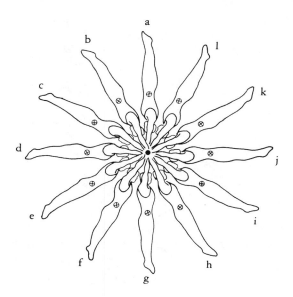

Figure 13.16

apparatus to the joint centers; at times, the body and its segments may be rotating around both.

6. Observe a beginning or intermediate gymnast. Identify three skills in which the performer had to flex the hips or knees or extend the shoulder joints to reduce the rotational inertia so that the skill could be completed, and where ideally the movements should have been prevented. Explain the relationships.

REFERENCES
SUGGESTED READINGS

Borms, J., Moers, R., and Hebbelinck, M. "Biomechanical Study of Forward and Backward Giant Swings." In *Biomechanics V-B: Proceedings of the Fifth International Congress on Biomechanics,* ed. P. V. Komi, 309–13. Baltimore: University Park Press, 1976.

Dillman, C. J., and Nelson. R. C. "The Mechanical Energy Transformations of Pole Vaulting with a Fiberglass Pole." *Journal of Biomechanics* 1 (4) (1968): 175–81.

Ganslen, R. V. "Penetration—A New Concept in Pole Vaulting Efficiency." *The Athletic Journal,* March 1974, 36–39 et seq.

Goehler, J. "The Mechanical Effect of the Forward 'Leg Snap'." *International Gymnast,* October 1977, 56–59.

Goehler, J., and Wieman, K. "Swings—Snaps—Straddles." *International Gymnast,* June 1978, 51–52.

Gowitzke, B. A. "Kinesiological and Neurophysiological Principles Applied to Gymnastics." In *Kinesiology Review,* ed. D. H. Clarke, 22–32. Reston, Va.: AAHPERD, 1968.

Hopper, B. J. *The Mechanics of Human Movement.* New York: American Elsevier Publishing Co., 1973.

Kaufman, D. A. "A Biomechanical Block Diagram of the Pole Vault." *Track Technique,* December 1973, 1732–34.

Kopp, P. M., and Reid, J. B. "Kinetic Analysis of the Giant Swing on the Horizontal Bar." In *Abstracts of the International Congress of Sport Sciences,* ed. J. Terauds, 66. San Diego, Calif.: Academic Publishers, 1979.

Nissinen, M. A. "Kinematic and Kinetic Analysis of the Giant Swing on the Rings." In *Biomechanics VIII-B: Proceedings of the Eighth International Congress of Biomechanics,* ed. H. Matsui and K. Kobayashi, 781–88. Champaign, Ill.: Human Kinetics Publishers, 1983.

Payne, H. A., and Barker, P. "Comparison of the Takeoff Forces in the Flic Flac and the Back Somersault in Gymnastics." In *Biomechanics V-B: Proceedings of the Fifth International Congress on Biomechanics,* ed. P. V. Komi, 314–21. Baltimore: University Park Press, 1976.

Stepp, R. D. "Mechanical Analysis of the Pole Vault." *Track Technique,* March 1976, 2017–18.

Tichonov, V. N. "Improvement of Vaulting Technique." *International Gymnast,* November 1978, 56–57.

Zinkovsky, A. V., Vain, A. A., and Torm, R. J. "Biomechanical Analysis of the Formation of Gymnastic Skill." In *Biomechanics V-B: Proceedings of the Fifth International Congress on Biomechanics,* ed. P. V. Komi, 322–25. Baltimore: University Park Press, 1976.

CHAPTER 14

ANALYSIS OF THROW AND PUSH PATTERNS

SECTION 1

INTRODUCTION AND TERMINOLOGY

In sport skills in which the performer is projecting an object, the primary mechanical purpose is one of the following: (1) To project the object the greatest vertical or horizontal distance, (2) to project an object for the greatest accuracy, or (3) to project an object primarily for accuracy with the speed of projection enhancing the projectile's effectiveness. The most frequently seen skills are projections for horizontal distance, such as javelin, discus, and shot put, or skills in which an object is projected primarily for accuracy with the speed enhancing its effectiveness, such as volleyball, tennis, and racquetball serves, baseball pitches, and infield throws. In the latter group, accuracy is primary, because without it, the projection is quite ineffective. In other words, speed may have to be compromised so that accuracy is not sacrificed.

Within each of these groups of skills are mechanical principles governing how the body's segmental movements best produce the desired accuracy or speed necessary to project effectively. The ability to recognize misapplications of the principles by performers, or to see errors in performance, is a key element in effective teaching and coaching. Since the mechanical principles are the same for all skills in which an object is projected for the same mechanical purpose, developing the ability to analyze performances in terms of these principles and to correct mechanical errors is relatively easy. To discuss throwing, kicking, striking, and pushing, a few terms need to be defined.

Movement Pattern

The term **movement pattern** refers to a general series of anatomical movements that have common elements of spatial configuration, such as segmental movements occurring in the same plane of motion. Within a movement pattern, the individual segmental movements may vary slightly in their ranges of motion (ROMs), velocities, and planes of motion. Throwing, kicking, striking, and pushing are all general movement patterns. These patterns may be further defined according to where the movements occur relative to the body (e.g., *overarm*, *sidearm*, or *underarm* throwing patterns of the upper extremity or a kicking pattern with the lower extremity). Atwater (1977) distinguishes an *overarm* pattern as one in which the trunk laterally flexes away from the projecting arm and a *sidearm* pattern as one in which the trunk laterally flexes toward the projecting arm.

The terms *overhand* and *underhand* technically refer to the grasping position of the hand; that is, an underhand—or undergrip—for grasping when the forearm is in a supinated position, and an overhand—or overgrip—for grasping when the forearm is in a pronated position.

Skill

When a general movement pattern is adapted within the constraints of some particular movement activity or sport, it is called a **skill.** For instance, an overarm pattern is used in reference to sport skills such as a tennis serve, a baseball pitch, a badminton smash, and a shot put. Table 14.1 offers one possibility for the classification of skills under general movement patterns.

If individual skills within a similar movement pattern are examined, the skills may be seen as slightly different in spatial and temporal terms for one or more of the following factors: the mass and shape of the projectile, or object; the mass and shape of the striking implement (if one is used); and the strength or power of the performer relative to the mass of the object to be projected or the implement to be handled. For instance, on first consideration, a tennis serve and a badminton smash are observed to be of a pattern similar enough to be identical. A critical analysis of each skill, however, shows that although the gross pattern is the same, slight variations exist between individual segmental movements in the two performances. The uniqueness of the two skills is due to the difference in the masses of the two rackets, the

SPORT SKILLS CLASSIFIED UNDER FOUR GENERAL MOVEMENT PATTERNS

Table 14.1.

Underarm Patterns	Sidearm Patterns	Overarm Patterns	Kicking Patterns
Softball pitch	Baseball throw	Baseball pitch	Football punt
Bowling ball delivery	Discus throw	Shot put	Soccer placekick
Horseshoe pitch	Hammer throw	Javelin throw	Swimming flutter
Volleyball serve	Volleyball serve	Volleyball serve	kick
Volleyball bump	Baseball batting	Volleyball spike	Walking or
Badminton underarm	Tennis drive	Basketball one-	running, swing
clear	Badminton drive	hand shot	phase
Badminton serve	Racquetball shots	Tennis serve	Dolphin kick
Field hockey drives	Squash shots	Tennis smash	
and passes	Handball shots	Badminton smash	
		and around-	
		the-head shot	
		Cricket "pitch"	

difference in the forces generated by each racket and its projectile, and the difference in the masses of the two projectiles.

A second example is the overarm throwing pattern used for projecting a basketball and a baseball for horizontal distance. The basic pattern is the same for both activities, but the positions of the upper extremity segments may be quite different. If the hand is not large enough to hold the basketball, the hand segment has to remain behind the ball so that the ball does not slip from the hand as the ball is pushed forward. The baseball can be easily grasped with the fingers. If the thrower is not strong or powerful enough to accelerate the ball when it is positioned away from the midsagittal plane of the body, then the thrower must bring the ball in closer to the shoulder.

Constraints

The variable factors of the mass of the implement, the mass of the object to be projected, the size of the target, the size of the sport environment or playing area, and the strength or ability of the performer are called **constraints**, or limiting factors, to the movement pattern. Thus, the mass of a medicine ball compared to a baseball becomes a constraint to one who wishes to use the high velocity baseball throwing pattern for projecting the medicine ball.

Throwlike Patterns

The term *throwlike*, as used in this text, is characterized by movements used to "pull" along an object that is allowed to lag back behind the proximal segments that are moving forward. The term throwlike refers to the characteristics of the general movement pattern of a throw and not to a throw per se. For example, a kick or a strike is classified as throwlike. In the case of striking activities, such as kicking or batting, the body part or the implement that will contact the object lags behind the other segments until just prior to contact, at which time it "whips" forward to catch up to its proximal segments.

Pushlike Patterns

The term *pushlike* is characterized by the body parts moving the object forward from behind the object. Examples include weight lifting in which the hand or foot is under the weight and is pushing it upward, a volleyball set in which the hands make contact below the ball and reflect it upward, a dart game in which the dart is pushed in front of the forward-moving hand, and a fencing lunge in which the foil is moved forward by the action of the hand on the grip behind the blade. The term pushlike also may be used to describe projecting the body itself as in pushing off the wall during a swimming turn or pushing the body upward in a vertical jump.

Open Kinetic Chain

In performing throwing, kicking, striking, and some pushing skills, the dominant extremity functions as a system of segmental links. In such cases, the segmental link system is classified as an *open kinetic chain*. It is an *open* system because the last, most distal, segment is not fixed but is free to move in space. (An example of a closed kinetic chain is the lower extremity acting against the ground during walking or running; the foot, which functions as the end of the chain, is fixed to the ground unless slipping occurs.) Secondly, it is a *kinetic* system because internal muscle torques act between the individual links in the system.

Review of Rotary Movement Concepts

Several previously discussed concepts are important in understanding how the body segments are used to generate maximum forces and velocities. Some of these major ideas are reviewed using Figure 14.1.

AXIS AND PLANE OF MOTION

Each body segment moves by rotating around an imaginary axis of rotation that passes through the articulation of the segment. Recall that the segment moves along a plane that is perpendicular to the axis around which it is rotating. Figure 14.1 illustrates (1) the movement of the hand in space caused by flexing the hip around its ML axis, position 1 to position 2, (2) the movement of the hand in space caused by the medial rotation of an abducted humerus around a longitudinal axis through

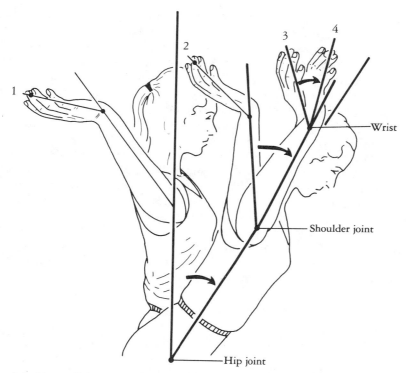

Flexion of the hip, medial rotation of the shoulder joint, and flexion of the wrist with all distal segments of the upper extremity fixed.

Figure 14.1.

the shoulder joint, position 2 to position 3, and (3) the hand movement caused by wrist flexion around its ML axis, position 3 to position 4.

ROTARY MOTION PARAMETERS

The motion of a rotating body segment can be described in terms of its angular displacement, θ, measured in degrees or radians; its angular velocity, ω, measured in degrees or radians per second; and its angular acceleration, α, measured in degrees or radians per second per second. The angular displacement for each of the motions shown in Figure 14.1 is 30 degrees or 0.524 radians.

LINEAR MOTION OF A ROTATING POINT

The *linear* velocity of any point on a *rotating* segment is directly proportional to both its angular velocity and its radius of rotation ($v = r\omega$). The **radius of rotation** for any point in a rotating system is the perpendicular distance between the contact point on the segment or implement and the axis of rotation of that segment. The radius of rotation is that to which people refer when they say that a longer implement, such as a baseball bat, gives greater leverage and hence greater velocity.

If a projectile is to be given a large linear velocity, the distal segment of the body must have a large linear velocity when the projectile is released (as in throwing) or contacted (as in striking or kicking). When the extremity is acting as an open chain, the movement of any proximal segment affects the motion of all segments distal to it. To illustrate this concept in the simplest manner, we will stabilize all segments in the chain, and allow them to move one at a time.

The radius of rotation for the fingertips extends from the fingertips to the axis where the rotation is taking place—the hip. In Figure 14.1, the linear velocity of the fingertips due to the flexion of the hip may be determined by multiplying the angular velocity due to hip flexion by the distance that the fingertips are from the ML axis of the hip joint. The greater the radius of rotation of a point or the angular velocity of a point or both, the greater its linear velocity.

To achieve an effective throw, we choose a combination of many segmental movements, with each segment moving around its own particular axis. Consequently, the throw, or any other open kinetic chain activity, is produced by the coordinated (well-timed) motion of all segments in that chain. For the throw, the velocity of the fingertips is affected by the displacement of the trunk, the displacement of the shoulder girdle, and the displacements of the arm, forearm, and hand.

ROTATIONAL INERTIA AND ANGULAR ACCELERATION

The angular acceleration (α) of the link system depends in part on the external motive torque (T) of the muscles initially producing the system's rotation and on the resistance provided by the rotational inertia (I) of the system being moved by that motive torque ($\alpha = T/I$).

The inertial resistance (its rotational inertia) of this system of linked segments to accelerations is determined by the total mass of the link system as well as by the distribution of that mass relative to the axis of rotation ($I = mk^2$).

CONSERVATION OF ANGULAR MOMENTUM

The angular momentum of a link system can be changed only by the application of an *external* torque. The conservation of angular momentum tells us that unless an external torque is applied, the total angular momentum of the system remains the same. Thus, a reduction in a system's radius of gyration, k, while it is rotating leads to an increase in its angular velocity.

UNDERSTANDING SEGMENTAL MOVEMENT CONCEPTS

1. List three general movement patterns. List three sport skills under each pattern.

2. How does one distinguish between a movement pattern and a sport skill?

3. List three sport skills displaying an overarm, an underarm, and a sidearm pattern.

4. List two sport skills in which an underhand grip is used. List two sport skills in which an overhand grip is used.

5. How does Atwater distinguish between an overarm throw and a sidearm throw?

6. List three skills that are not throws per se but which use the upper extremity in a throwlike pattern.

7. List three skills that use the upper extremity in a pushlike pattern that are not mentioned as examples in the text.

8. Define radius of gyration. Define radius of rotation. Describe the differences. In what manner does each of these concepts affect throwing, kicking, or striking movements?

SECTION 2

THROWLIKE PATTERNS: SEQUENTIAL SEGMENTAL ROTATIONS

The Kinetic Link Model

To illustrate the generation of high end-point velocity in a system of segmented links, a model is shown in Figure 14.2a. The three segments are labeled **A**, **B**, and **C**, and the three axes of rotation for these segments are labeled **a**, **b**, and **c**. The arrows on segment **A** represent muscle torques applied to segment **A** and to a fixed "ground" segment. Because the muscle torques applied to segment **A** are *external* torques (i.e., external to the system of links), they can effect changes in the system's angular motion. In the figure, the muscle torques between segments **A** and **B** and the muscle torques between segments **B** and **C** function as *internal* torques (they are internal to the system). The way such a model functions can be understood by examining the two following situations.

CASE ONE

Suppose that the muscles to the right of segment **A** apply an external torque large enough to accelerate segment **A** in a clockwise (cw) direction. The intersegmental muscle torques between segments **A** and **B** and **B** and **C** work to prevent lagging back, or counterclockwise (ccw) motion of the distal segments relative to the proximal segment as the system accelerates cw. If these internal stabilizing torques were not applied, segments **B** and **C** would "lag back" as segment **A** rotates forward. Thus, the external torques applied to segment **A** accelerate the entire system and give the entire system angular momentum.

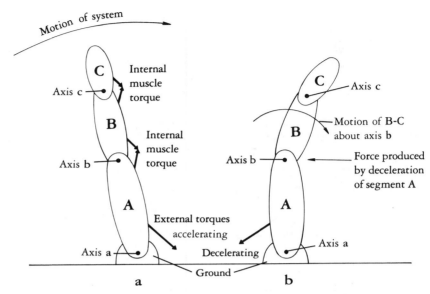

Figure 14.2. A three-segment model of the kinetic link concept with external and internal torques influencing its motion.

Now suppose that a second external torque, the torque to the left of segment **A** and axis **a**, acts to decelerate segment **A** (Figure 14.2b). The deceleration of segment **A** places a left-directed force on axis **b**, tending to "fix" that axis in space. Since segments **B** and **C** are free to move cw about axis **b**, **B** and **C** continue to rotate with the same angular *momentum* about axis **b**.

Since the axis of rotation for segments **B** and **C** has moved from axis **a** to axis **b**, the radius of gyration and thus the rotational inertia for segments **B** and **C** have decreased. Consequently, because the momentum of segments **B** and **C** is being conserved, the angular *velocity* of segments **B** and **C** increases. Note that the radius of gyration of segments **B** and **C** decreased because the axis of rotation moved closer to these two segments. Secondly, no *external* torque (force × zero distance) was applied to segments **B** and **C**, only to segment **A**. Therefore, the angular momentum of segments **B** and **C** as a system is being conserved, but the angular momentum of the original system, which included segment **A**, is not being conserved.

In this first example, external muscle torques were applied between segment **A**, or the base segment, and the "ground." In a human body application, segment **A** could be labeled as the pelvis, segment **B** as the trunk, and segment **C** as the upper extremity, all moving in a fashion similar to the action described in Figure 14.1. An external torque used to accelerate the system could be the hip flexors, and the external torque used to decelerate the pelvis could be the hip extensors. The pelvis, segment **A**, on deceleration would apply a force on axis **b**, thereby tending to cause axis **b** to be "fixed" in space. The distal segments would freely rotate around axis **b** and do so with increased angular velocity because the radius of gyration of these segments is smaller than it is relative to axis **a**.

CASE TWO

This case concerns a model of a system in which no external torque acts on any segment after the initial acceleration of the system takes place. The model is shown in Figure 14.3. The three-segment system is moving in a cw direction with some given angular velocity and therefore possesses some angular momentum. When segment **A** nears the vertical position, the muscles located between segments **A** and **B** contract, applying a torque to segment **A** in a ccw direction and to segment **B** in a cw direction (both relative to axis **b**). The muscle torque applied within the system between the segments is an *internal* torque. Since an internal torque cannot change the angular momentum of the entire system, which in this case includes segment **A**, the angular momentum of the **ABC** system is conserved. This action is similar to a body jackknifing in space.

The muscles located between segments **B** and **C** prevent segment **C** from lagging too far back relative to segment **B.** Segments **B** and **C** rotate faster as they assume the momentum lost by segment **A.**

Applying this model to a human movement, the hip flexors contract to apply an external torque to segment **A** (the pelvis) and a fixed ground (the supporting lower extremities). The external hip flexor torque accelerates the entire **ABC** system; intersegmental torques between adjacent segments prevent the distal segments from lagging back too far. After momentum has been gained, the hip flexors relax, leaving the system isolated (free from external torques). If the trunk flexor muscles contract, the effect is deceleration of the pelvis, segment **A**, about axis **a**, and acceleration of the trunk, segment **B**, about axis **b.** The trunk flexors in this example are working

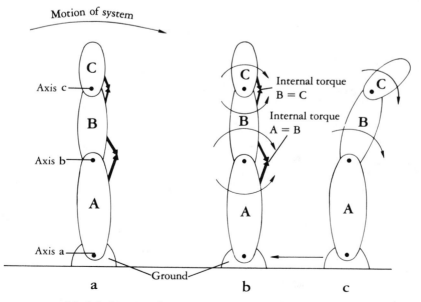

A three-segment model of the kinetic link concept with internal torques influencing its motion.

Figure 14.3.

as internal torques, and thus, the angular momentum of the system is conserved. If the intersegmental muscles between segments **B** and **C** prevent the "lagging back" of the upper extremity, segment **C** is considered part of segment **B** during its acceleration.

Likewise, as the trunk reaches a near vertical position, if the intersegmental muscles between the trunk (segment **B**) and the upper extremity (segment **C**) contract, they serve to decelerate the trunk segment about axis **b** and to accelerate the upper extremity segment about axis **c**. Because the upper extremity is less massive than the trunk segment and because the axis of rotation for the upper extremity is at axis **c**, the rotational inertia of the distal rotating segments is reduced and the upper extremity's velocity is amplified.

The model just described may be applied to any open kinetic link system with the following characteristics during the initial acceleration: (1) the system of links has a base, or fixed, end, and a free, or open, end; (2) the more massive segments are at the proximal end and the less massive segments are at the free end; and (3) an external torque is applied to the base segment to initiate the system's motion and give the entire system angular momentum. Intersegmental torques are internal to the system, and when applied, change the angular velocities of individual segments in the system but not the angular momentum of the entire system.

The previous two examples were hypothetical situations in which muscle torques were acting either within or on a system of segmental links. Due to the complexity of the human link system, predicting exactly which muscle torques might be operating at any given time is impossible. For example, the accelerating external muscle torque acting on the base segment may operate all the way through the motion, most of the way through the motion, or part of the way through the motion. The intersegmental torques may be voluntarily controlled bursts of muscular contraction, muscular contractions evoked by the stretch reflex response, torques produced by the elastic recoil of the muscles and surrounding tissues, or any combination of these. Our purpose is to understand the *possible* effects of any or all of the body's mechanisms for controlling movement.

Further consideration must be given to the effects of varying the timing of any of the responses that may occur. Timing variables are considered in the next section.

Sequencing Segmental Rotations: The Kinetic Link Principle

The sequence of segmental rotations used for throwing, kicking, or striking patterns may be likened to the motion of a whip, a fly-fishing rod, or the lashing action of a fish's tail. Figure 14.4 illustrates this motion for a fisherman casting a fly.

If segmental rotations are free to occur at each of the distal joints, the body's system of links behaves in a manner similar to a flexible chain of links, with the earth and base segment acting like the handle of a bullwhip. Just as the tip of the whip can be made to travel so fast that it has supersonic speed (hence the sonic boom heard as the crack), the small distal segments of the hand or foot can be made to

A fisherman casting a fly. The rod and line may be likened to the whiplike action of the segmental system.

Figure 14.4.

travel extremely fast by the sequential acceleration and deceleration of the body segments. The general pattern of movements is one in which the initial rotation occurs in the base segment, which is the most stable part of the system, and is followed by the forward rotation of the next distal segment. Each segment comes forward as the movement of its proximal segment reaches its greatest angular velocity (the distal end of the proximal segment has its greatest linear speed at this time). The sequencing procedure continues to occur from proximal to distal, one segment's movement overlapping the other until the most distal segment finally comes forward.

Such a pattern includes a "lagging back" of the distal segments as the more proximal segments are accelerated forward. The lagging back of the distal segments can be seen on the tip of the fly rod and line as the initial movements of the arm and hand occur. Like the action of the fly rod and line or the action of a bullwhip, the lagging back of the distal segments of the body may be due to the backward momentum developed during the original backward motion of the system (commonly known as the backswing or windup), or it may be due to the proximal segment moving out from under the distal segment, in which case it is described as *inertial lag*.

Sometime during the backswing, external muscle torque causes the proximal or base segment to begin to accelerate forward. In a system of freely rotating segments, as the proximal link angularly accelerates in one direction, the next distal link in the kinetic chain lags back in the opposite direction. The lagging back of the distal segments persists until one or more of the following occurs: (1) the acceleration of the proximal segment decreases or ceases, (2) the elastic or structural limit of a joint's ROM is reached, or (3) the stretch reflex is activated. If the stretch reflex is evoked, elastic recoil occurs, or voluntary intersegmental muscular torques are activated, the lagging segment's forward rotation will be initiated.

Ideally, as the limit of this backward motion is reached, the proximal segment begins to decelerate. This should occur sometime after the midrange of the proximal segment's motion and is the place at which the base segment has its maximum angular velocity (zero acceleration). The deceleration (reduction of the velocity) of the proximal segment is equated with its loss of a certain amount of angular momentum ($I\omega$). As was described in the previous section, this deceleration of the proximal segment and the next distal segment may be caused by either or both of the following: (1) by the muscles that are antagonists to the motion occurring in the proximal segment, in which case the muscle torques are *external* to the system of links, (2) by the intersegmental muscles between the proximal segment and the next distal segment, in which case the muscle torques are *internal* to the system of links.

If the deceleration occurs as in case one, in which an *external torque* is applied, the angular momentum of the proximal segment is lost to the ground and cannot be assumed by the distal segments in the system. The distal segments accelerate, however, because of the shifting of the axis of rotation from the *proximal* end of the *base segment* to a new axis of rotation located at the *distal* end of the *base segment*. (Recall that moving the axis of rotation out closer to the distal segment decreases the radius of gyration of the distal segment relative to the new axis and thus increases its angular velocity.)

If the deceleration of the base segment occurs because of the application of intersegmental muscle torque, which is internal to the system, then no angular momentum is lost from the system as the base segment decelerates. The distal segmental rotation (segments **B** and **C**) is faster than it was prior to the deceleration of the base segment because the distal segments are usually less massive and because the axis of rotation for the distal segmental rotation is closer to those segments, thereby reducing their radius of gyration.

Similarly, when the second segment reaches the midrange of its rotation, it too decelerates and puts a force on the next distal axis, which increases the velocity of the next adjacent distal segment in the chain. Such a sequence occurs link by link, from base to end, proximal to distal, until the end of the chain is reached.

Just as a fly rod or bullwhip is tapered, the more distal parts of the human body are composed of successively smaller and smaller masses. By virtue of the smaller mass, the rotational inertia of each successive distal segment becomes progressively less (e.g., the pelvis compared to the thigh, the thigh to the leg, the leg to the foot; the trunk compared to the arm, the arm to the forearm, the forearm to the hand, and the hand to the fingers).

The tapering of the distal masses is significant when the proximal segment is decelerated by an internal torque between it and the next distal segment, for only under the *internal* torque condition is angular momentum conserved in the system of segments. A larger mass that loses a small velocity transfers its lost momentum to a smaller mass, which necessarily gains a large velocity to conserve the total angular momentum of the system. Thus, the timed successive segmental rotations that originate from the stable base segment and terminate with the most distal segment serve to produce extremely fast linear speed on the distal end of the kinetic chain.

A Model of a Kinetic Link System

To illustrate the simplified effects of the acceleration and deceleration of the proximal segments on the distal segments, a conceptual model is shown in Figure 14.5. The presence of muscle torques acting on segments whose velocities are continuously increasing and the sequence and timing of a mechanically effective link system are shown. The model is adapted from that of Morehouse and Cooper (1950) and modified to account for the kinetic contributions of muscle torques.

Segments **A, B, C, D,** and **E** represent an arbitrary number of body segments used sequentially to perform a skill. Applying the model to a kicking motion, the segmental movements are **A**, the pelvis rotating in flexion about a lumbar inter-

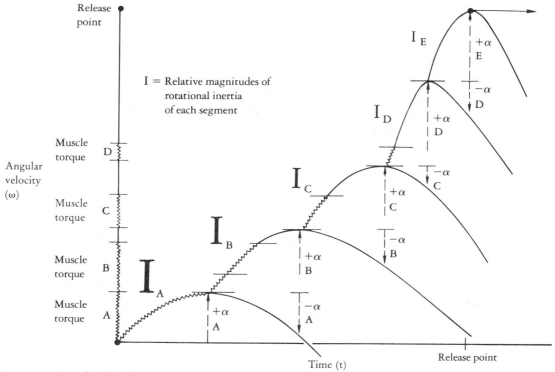

A conceptual model of the kinetic link principle.

Figure 14.5.

vertebral axis; **B**, the thigh segment rotating in flexion about the hip axis; and **C**, the leg and foot segments rotating in extension about the knee axis. In the case of kicking, three segments are used. Applying a throwing motion to the model, the segments used are (**A**), the pelvis medially rotating about the longitudinal hip axis; (**B**), the trunk rotating about the longitudinal vertebral axis; (**C**), the shoulder girdle protracting about the longitudinal sternoclavicular axis; (**D**), the arm medially rotating about the longitudinal shoulder axis; (**E**), the forearm extending about an ML elbow axis; and (**F**), the hand and ball as a single segment flexing about the ML wrist axis. In this case six segments are used. The model may be shortened or lengthened to fit the skill being analyzed.

The muscle torques are represented in Figure 14.5 by the squiggly lines. They are *external* to the system if attached to the baseline and *internal* to the system if located between adjacent segments. The angular velocity is represented by the symbol ω shown along the left side of the model. Time is represented along the baseline. The rotational inertia (I) of the remainder of the system at different times during the sequence of the skill is shown to the left of the angular velocity lines, and is sized to show differences in its magnitude.

This a conceptual model and is not to be interpreted as representing actual magnitudes. It has been developed to show the relationships of various mechanical quantities with a single *external* muscle torque applied at the base segment and *internal* muscle torques applied between segments thereafter. In actuality, external muscle torques can be applied to segments distal to the base segment, in which case all of the original momentum is not saved during segmental sequencing. Nevertheless, the model represents a theoretical, ideal pattern in which achievement of high velocity on the distal segment is desired so that an object to be thrown, kicked, or struck will travel at a high speed.

Using the kinetic link model, we will describe the skill of punting. Segment **A** represents the pelvis; segment **B**, the thigh; and segment **C**, the leg and foot. From a position of slight hyperextension of the lumbar vertebral column, the vertebral column flexors contract to flex the pelvis about an axis through the lumbar spine. Because the supporting extremity is fixed to the ground, the initial muscular contractions to initiate the forward motion of the pelvis and free extremity are *external* to the system and therefore can give momentum to the system. In this case the distal segments lag back, as would be exemplified by hip hyperextension and knee flexion. After the initial flexion of the pelvis about the lumbar axis, the hip flexors contract, causing deceleration of the pelvis relative to the vertebral axis and thigh acceleration relative to the hip axis. The hip flexors are *internal* to the system. The momentum that the pelvis loses may be assumed by the thigh segment, which is flexing about the hip joint axis. The rotational inertia of the thigh and leg-foot segments rotating about the hip is less than that of all three segments rotating about the vertebral column axis, and thus the thigh and leg-foot segments rotate faster than they were rotating previously.

Sometime during the midrange of hip flexion the knee extensors contract to accelerate the leg-foot segment about the knee axis. The knee extensors simultaneously decelerate the thigh about the hip axis. Since the leg-foot segment is less massive than the previous segments and since the radius of gyration of the leg-foot segment is less about the new knee axis, the rotational inertia of the leg-foot system is considerably less, and consequently, the angular velocity is considerably more. We are now at the end of the link system. At the maximum velocity of foot motion, the foot should contact the ball to impart the greatest velocity to the ball.

For the intersegmental torques to play a part in the more distal segments' acceleration, the muscular contractions must be fast enough not only to keep up with this fast-moving distal segment but also to apply force to it. (The angular velocity was increased by the deceleration of its proximal segment.) Consequently, the faster the distal segment is traveling, the faster the muscular contraction must be to exert a force on it. Remembering the force-velocity relationship, we know that the faster the muscle must shorten, the smaller its force on the attached segment and thus the smaller the angular impulse it can apply to the segment. After the initial contraction of the internal torque associated with the stretch reflex and the elastic recoil of the muscle, the velocity of the distal segments may be so great that the muscle contraction on the distal segments may not be able to apply a torque to accelerate them further.

In addition, considering the length-tension relationship of muscular contraction, we know that muscles can exert less tension as they become shorter. Determining the length of the muscles at any given time is difficult; however, the lagging back of the distal segments helps place the muscles in a stretched position at the time they are to provide the internal torque and thus enhances their effectiveness.

UNDERSTANDING SEQUENTIAL
SEGMENTAL ROTATIONS

1. Of the following activities, circle those to which the kinetic link principle applies: a soccer punt, a golf swing, a right jab in boxing, a back handspring takeoff, hammering a nail, a hammer throw, pushing a table across the floor, a football pass for distance, bowling.

2. Observe the masses of the arm, forearm, and hand segments. Discuss the similarities and differences in terms of the relative masses of the segments (greatest to least) and the distribution of those masses (closer to the proximal or distal end). Repeat for the thigh, lower leg, and foot segments. Refer to Appendix III to find mean values of the segmental weights and radii of gyration. List those values. Discuss the relative masses of the segments and their relationship to the kinetic link principle.

3. State three principles that relate to the use of body segments in generating velocity on the open end of the open kinetic chain.

4. Swing a no. 5 golf club using only the left arm (if you are a right-handed golfer) and note the velocities for the following conditions:

   a. Swing the club by attempting to use muscular effort to rotate the shoulder joint and wrist all the way through the swing.

   b. Swing the club by initiating the downswing by muscular effort at the shoulder joint; during the middle of the swing, relax the musculature at the shoulder joint, allowing the upper arm to decelerate. What happens at the wrist to the hand and club segments?

      i. Explain the action in terms of the kinetic link principle. What do the differences among the mass of the arm, hand, and club segment have to do with the velocities?

     ii. When using muscular effort, was it possible for the wrist muscles to keep up with the velocity of the hand segment so that the muscles could accelerate the distal segments through impact?

5. Attend a beginning class in badminton, tennis, or golf. Observe an unskilled performer and a skilled performer in the class, and compare the segments that are used and the sequencing (or lack of sequencing) of the segments in a similar skill. Does the beginning performer use the same segments and movements? Does the beginner sequence the movements, or are some of the movements used simultaneously? What differences do you notice about the speed of the object projected by each? the accuracy?

Lever Versus Wheel-Axle Rotations

Two machines used in segmental movements are associated with the kinetic link model. These mechanisms, discussed in Chapter 3, are the lever and the wheel-axle. The most common segmental motions are *lever-type* motions such as flexion-extension, abduction-adduction, and protraction-retraction. The wheel-axle motions are those motions occur around the longitudinal axis of the segment and include all of the joint movements that have the word *rotation* in the name (e.g., medial and lateral rotation, right and left rotation). Protraction and retraction of the shoulder girdle occur around the longitudinal axis of the sternum and are *lever-type* motions and are exceptions to this rule. In addition, pronation and supination of the radioulnar joint and inversion and eversion of the subtalar joint are wheel-axle movements. In wheel-axle motions, the bone that rotates due to direct application of muscle torque serves as the axle segment, and an adjoining distal segment, or segments, serves as the "wheel." (This mechanism is illustrated in Figure 3.20, p. 188.)

Lever and wheel-axle systems are both rotational systems, and therefore, when either is used for throwing, striking, or kicking skills in which a high linear velocity is desired, two aspects of that rotational motion are important: the angular velocity of that system and the radius of rotation of the contact point of the object. The point of concern in throwing, kicking, and striking skills is that point at which the projectile makes, or will make, contact with the body part or with an implement. If one wants to adjust the radius of rotation of the point of contact on a lever, one selects a shorter or longer implement or contacts the object at a different location on the lever. For example, the leg and foot in a kicking skill serve as a lever system during knee extension. To decrease the radius of rotation for that leverlike movement, one has to contact the ball on the tibia, an unlikely choice.

Unlike the lever system, the wheel-axle mechanism has an adjustable radius of rotation. By flexing or extending the distal "wheel" segment relative to the rotating axle segment, one can increase or decrease the radius of rotation for the point of contact on the wheel. Figure 14.6 illustrates how, through the use of radial or ulnar flexion of the wrist, one can change the radius of rotation for the center point on a racquetball racket relative to the axis of rotation for forearm pronation and supination. In this example, the racket serves as the wheel segment. To achieve high linear velocity at the sweet spot of the racket, one should position the racket so that the radius of rotation is as large as possible.

A second factor to consider in achieving high contact-point velocity is the angular velocity of the segment on which the contact point is located. The amount of angular velocity that a segment can achieve depends on its rotational inertia (mass × radius of gyration^2) and the torque applied.

The radius of *gyration* should not be confused with the radius of *rotation*. The radius of gyration represents the *distribution* of the rotating mass relative to the axis of rotation. Referring to Figure 14.6b, if two rackets were held at this angle, one with a piece of lead taped to its throat and one with a piece of lead taped to its tip, their masses would be equal, and their *radii of rotation would be the same* if the player hit the ball at the same spot. The location of the lead, however, would make the *radii of gyration* of the two rackets different. Accelerating the racket with the lead taped to its tip would be more difficult than accelerating the one with lead taped

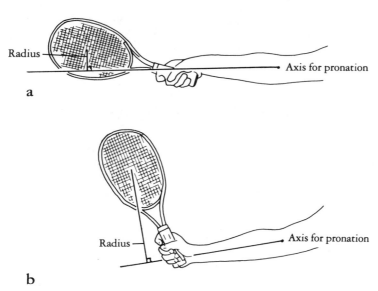

(a) Small radius "wheel" segment. (b) Large radius "wheel" segment, used in the wheel-and-axle mechanism of radioulnar pronation.

Figure 14.6.

to its throat. This would be due to the *greater radius of gyration* of the former.

Figure 14.7 shows a model of a lever arrangement of three segments and a wheel-axle arrangement of the same three segments. The lever arrangement has a greater radius of rotation (2.75 units); the wheel-axle arrangement has a smaller radius of rotation (1.72 units). Thus, if both systems were rotating with the *same angular velocity,* the end of the lever would be moving twice as fast linearly (double the radius of rotation, v = rω). In this example, however, the rotational inertia of the system used as a wheel-axle is five times smaller than the rotational inertia of the same system used as a lever.

Since the radius of gyration is squared in determining rotational inertia, it has a squared effect on the resistance of the system to acceleration by muscle torques ($I = mk^2$). Thus, for a situation in which equal muscle torques are acting for the same time period on the two systems, the smaller rotational inertia of the wheel-axle mechanism allows a five times greater angular acceleration and thus greater angular velocity. The greater acceleration in the wheel-axle system gives this system two and one half times the *linear* velocity of the lever system, although the lever system has a larger radius of rotation. Probably for this reason the wheel-axle mechanism is used prevalently in throwing-striking skills in which high end-point velocity is desired.

The torque-producing capabilities of the muscle groups involved in each of the mechanisms must be considered; that is, the relative strengths and speeds of contraction of the lever-system muscle groups compared to the wheel-axle system muscle groups.

In summary, the lever system has the potential of giving a faster linear velocity to a distal point by virtue of the contact point's greater radius of rotation, but the wheel-axle system has the potential to give considerably more linear velocity to a distal point by virtue of the wheel's smaller rotational inertia, which therefore allows a greater angular acceleration for a given muscular torque.

UNDERSTANDING THE LEVER
AND THE WHEEL-AXLE

1. With a badminton racket, assume a grip such that the radius of rotation for forearm pronation is maximized. By changing the grip and the wrist position relative to the forearm, assume four more positions that progressively decrease the radius of rotation for forearm motion. The last position should place the center of the racket's face along the axis of rotation of the radioulnar joint. Draw the five positions. Discuss these positions in terms of the forearm's potential linear velocity contribution to the swing. Which position allows the greatest potential linear velocity, and which allows the least potential linear velocity?

2. Discuss why it is impractical or impossible to position the hand through radial or ulnar flexion such that one could use forearm motions for added velocity in a baseball pitch, a tennis forehand stroke, or a basketball throw for distance.

a

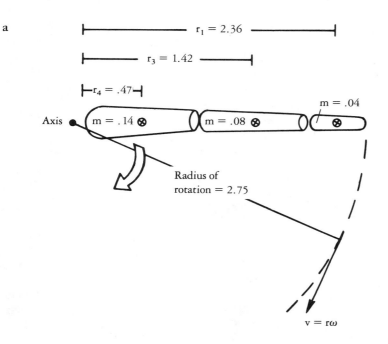

$$I_L = \Sigma mr^2 + Icg$$
$$= (.14)(.47)^2 + .02 = .05$$
$$= (.08)(1.42)^2 + .01 = .17$$
$$= (.04)(2.36)^2 + .00 = .22$$
$$I_A = .44$$
$$s-ft^2$$

b

$$I_{WA} = \Sigma mr^2 + Icg$$
$$= (.14)(.002)^2 + 0 = 0$$
$$= (.08)(.39)^2 + .01 = .02$$
$$= (.04)(1.33)^2 + .001 = .07$$
$$I_{WA} = .09$$
$$s-ft^2$$

$$\frac{\text{Lever } I_A}{W - A\ I_A} = \frac{.44}{.09} \approx \frac{5}{1}$$

$$\frac{\text{Radius of rotation lever}}{W - A\ \text{radius of rotation}} = \frac{2.75}{1.72} \approx \frac{1.6}{1} \approx \frac{2}{1}$$

$$V_L = r\omega = \frac{2}{1}\ \frac{1}{5} = \frac{2}{5}$$

$$V_{WA} = r\omega = \frac{1}{2}\ \frac{5}{1} = \frac{5}{2}$$

(a) The rotational inertia of a segment in a lever arrangement and (b) in a wheel-and-axle arrangement. **Figure 14.7.**

3. Discuss the phrase "a longer lever gives more velocity." Why is this statement misleading? In what kind of situations would a longer lever not provide more velocity?

4. List the advantages of using a wheel-axle motion rather than a lever motion when one wants to generate high end-point velocity on an implement.

SECTION 3

PUSHLIKE PATTERNS: SIMULTANEOUS SEGMENTAL ROTATIONS

The previous section described the sequence of movements that most effectively produce a throwlike motion for which the primary mechanical purpose is to generate high velocity on the end of the distal link. These movements include throwing, kicking, and striking skills.

On the other end of the continuum are those skills in which the primary mechanical purpose is maximum accuracy of projection or in which a large motive force must be applied to an object to overcome the resistive forces acting on that object. Examples of high accuracy skills are darts, horseshoe pitching, archery, the tennis volley, and the volleyball set. Examples of skills in which the primary purpose is to overcome the resistive forces are those used in weight lifting and wrestling.

Figure 14.8 illustrates the path of the hand in a throwlike motion and the path of the hand in a pushlike motion. The throwlike pattern is used for generating high linear velocity on the distal end of the series of links; therefore, the point of contact of the object on the distal link moves in a *rotary* or a *curvilinear* path. In activities involving accuracy or the overcoming of a resistive force, moving the point of contact with the object in a *rectilinear* path is important. The rectilinear path is a movement

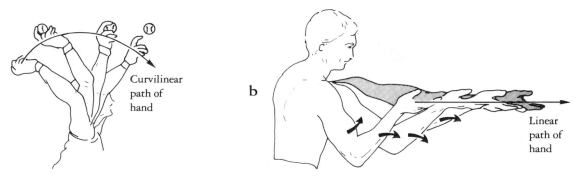

a

Curvilinear
path of
hand

b

Linear
path of
hand

Figure 14.8.   (a) An overarm throw. (b) A fencing lunge.

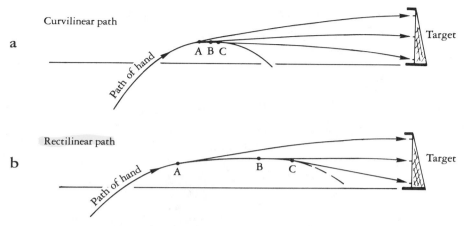

Accuracy of projection at a target when using (a) curvilinear path and (b) a rectilinear path.   **Figure 14.9.**

that may be likened to a fencing lunge. The segmental rotations are taking place simultaneously to control the hand and to cause it to move in a straight line. The importance of the rectilinear path for high accuracy is shown in Figure 14.9.

If an object is traveling in a curved path, as in Figure 14.9a, it must be released within a narrow space along the path between points A and C to hit the target. Little time would be available within the total performance for the performer to contact or release the object and be successful. In Figure 14.9b, notice that the object could be released within a wide range of space between points A and C and still hit the target. The more linear the path prior to contact or release, the more *time* the performer has to project the object accurately. A rectilinear path allows the performer more time to align the release direction with the target than does a curvilinear path. A curvilinear or rotary path requires that the performer release or strike the object along an extremely short section on the curved path so that the tangent is directed to the target.

As a practical example, picture the students in a beginning tennis class learning and practicing the serve. During the learning stages, the students may attempt to reproduce a fairly skilled sequential serving pattern. Knowing that speed as well as accuracy are important in a good serve, the students practice the skill in an attempt to develop both of these components. If the students are required to perform in a test situation, however, in which success depends to a greater extent on accuracy than on speed of serving (e.g., in counting the number of serves landing within the service area out of ten attempts), then the sequential throwlike striking pattern, designed for greater speed, usually reverts to a pushing pattern, designed for greater accuracy. A beginner's pushlike serve is shown in Figure 14.10.

The pushlike pattern of segmental movements is easily distinguished from a throwlike pattern. These four differences are noted:

1. For throwlike movements, the segment-object contact point "lags back" as the proximal segments "move out from under" the distal segment. The object

Figure 14.10.   A simultaneous serve, designed for accuracy.

is pulled along behind the advancing proximal segments. In a pushlike motion, the segments are positioned behind the object to be projected (i.e., the object is carried in front of the segments that are applying the force).

2. In throwlike movements, segmental rotations occur sequentially to produce high velocity. In pushlike movements, segmental rotations occur simultaneously to produce high accuracy or force or both.

3. In a throwing pattern, the object moves along a curvilinear path or a rotary path before contact or release; whereas in a pushing pattern, the object is kept in a rectilinear path prior to contact or release.

4. Throwlike patterns have a predominance of wheel-axle movements, and pushlike patterns have a predominance of leverlike movements. A comparison of the throwlike and pushlike patterns may be seen by observing a volleyball spike and a volleyball set pattern (Figure 14.11).

Figure 14.11a illustrates the motion of the hand as the player performs a spiking motion. The motion of the hand is curvilinear; it may be close to purely rotational, and involves the sequential rotations of segments. Figure 14.11b shows the hands moving in a rectilinear path during the setting skill. Accuracy of placement is important in this skill. The setting pattern, however, involves the *simultaneous* rotations of segments. The set is for accuracy; the spike is for high velocity.

A pushing pattern also is used in situations in which the center of gravity (CG) location of the object being moved must be kept in a precise location for balance. An example is lifting free weights in weight training. The CG of the barbell must be kept in vertical alignment with the base segments. If the barbell moves horizontally from its vertical rectilinear path, other muscle groups must be used to bring it back into alignment, or it will rotate over and fall to the floor. The use of a weight-lifting machine eliminates the necessity for the performer to maintain the vertical rectilinear direction of the resistance, and hence makes the lifting task somewhat easier and safer.

a   b

(a) Curvilinear motion and (b) rectilinear motion caused by the spatial and temporal characteristics of the segmental movements.   **Figure 14.11.**

Whether a skill ideally should be a throwlike or a pushlike motion depends primarily on the mechanical purpose of the skill; that is, whether an object must be projected at a high velocity (used in projecting for distance), projected or moved for accuracy, or manipulated as a resistance. Examples of skills in which one projects primarily for distance include throwing the javelin or discus. Skills in which one projects primarily for accuracy are the volleyball set, a horseshoe pitch, and the basketball free throw.

The choice of pattern also depends on the constraints of the activity and the performer, for the ideal pattern may have to be compromised due to the physical environment, the unique competitive situation, or the physical attributes of the performer.

SECTION 4

THE THROW-PUSH CONTINUUM

The kinetic link principle applied to the throwlike pattern may be said to govern the performance of events that demand high velocity of the object. Similarly, the pushlike pattern may be said to govern the performance of accuracy events that require precision in the direction of projection. Most sport skills, however, cannot be classified as being purely one form or the other. Therefore, we must consider a set of constraints in the activities that require *blending* of the throwlike and pushlike patterns into a combination of the two. For this purpose, skills can be placed conveniently along a **throw-push continuum,** with skills performed with entirely sequential rotations on one end of the continuum and skills performed with entirely simultaneous rotations on the opposite end of the continuum. In between are skills in which a sequential throwlike pattern occurs in the first part of the performance and a simultaneous pushlike pattern occurs in the latter part of the performance. Keep in mind that the throwlike patterns are characterized by the sequencing of the segmental rotations from most massive to least massive and from most stable to most free; pushing patterns are characterized by the simultaneity of segmental rotations (i.e., all rotating at the same time to produce a straight line motion of the distal link).

These are the constraints that influence the location of a skill on the continuum:

1. The massiveness of the object to be moved or projected (shot or basketball)
2. The size of the object to be moved or projected (balloon ball or volleyball)
3. The shape of the object (football or waterpolo ball)
4. The strength of the performer (conditioned athlete or intramural participant)
5. The skill of the performer (beginner or advanced)

To apply this concept, we will work through several examples. If high speed of the object is important for achieving distance of projection, then the most sequential pattern possible should be used. For a skilled player to throw a baseball from the outfield using sequential rotations entirely is both possible and desirable. In the shot put, however, in spite of the fact that the performer works to achieve the same mechanical purpose as the baseball thrower (i.e., distance of projection), the shot would not be thrown due to distal musculoskeletal limitations in manipulating a massive object. One should see the sequential rotations of the massive segments (the pelvis, trunk, and shoulder girdle) followed by simultaneous rotations of the less massive distal segments of the upper extremity. The shot put therefore is a combination activity that is placed in the middle of the continuum; it is partly sequential, partly simultaneous. It is an activity in which constraints on the performer demand the use of less than the ideal pattern.

An ideal pattern for projecting the shot is a throw because the mechanical purpose is that of projecting for distance that depends mainly on release velocity. The constraint in the case of the shot put is the large mass of the object to be projected. A similar adaptation is necessary if the strength of the performer is decreased. A weak performer attempting to put the shot may use all simultaneous motions without any evident sequencing. Thus, an immature or weak performer may turn an otherwise sequential movement into a more simultaneous one by ordering the initiation of the movements of the segmental links at the same or nearly the same time.

A third constraint is the size or shape or both of the object to be thrown. A javelin and a football, due to their somewhat unwieldy shapes, are thrown for distance with a small component of a push at the distal end, the javelin because of the importance of the placement of the tip and the football because of the possibility of wobble.

a   Shot put   **b**   Water polo   **c**   Baseball

Relative positions of body segments and objects for three different masses and sizes of objects being projected.   **Figure 14.12.**

One identifying characteristic of a throwing pattern that has been adapted to a partial pushing pattern owing to the previously listed constraints is that the object to be projected is brought in closer to the longitudinal body axis since the rotational inertia of the distal segment and object is too great for the torques produced by the smaller muscles to stabilize or accelerate. As the mass is brought closer to the body, the *sequential* segmental rotations become more *simultaneous* segmental rotations and combine to move the distal end of the kinetic chain in a rectilinear rather than a curvilinear path prior to release. When a less massive object is used, it can be held farther from the midline of the trunk as it is being accelerated. Figure 14.12 illustrates the patterns used for projecting three objects of varying mass and size.

UNDERSTANDING PUSHLIKE PATTERNS

1. List the primary mechanical purposes associated with pushlike patterns. For each of the mechanical purposes, list five skills that have that purpose.

2. What four factors distinguish a pushlike pattern from a throwlike pattern?

3. List five constraints of the activity, equipment, or performers that would have the effect of putting a pushlike elements into an otherwise ideal throwlike pattern.

4. For each of the three paths shown in Figure 14.13, draw an arrow to indicate the direction that an object moving along the path would travel if released at point 1, 2, or 3.

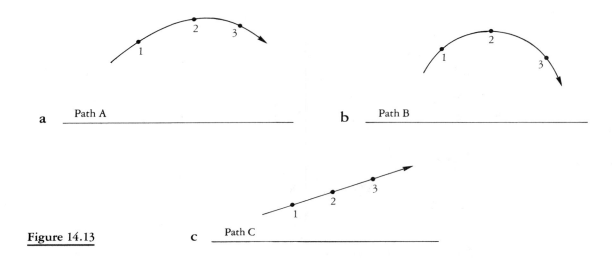

a   Path A

b   Path B

Figure 14.13   c   Path C

a. Which path is rotary?
b. In which path is the timing of release the most critical to the accuracy of the projectile?
c. In which path is the timing of release the least critical?
d. Draw these paths:
   i. The path of the head of a golf club
   ii. The path of the head of a tennis racket during a forehand drive
   iii. The path of the CG of the body just prior to and after leaving the horizontal bar during a dismount
   iv. The path of the discus prior to release
   v. The path of a basketball during a jump shot, prior to release

5. Within the following groups of activities, (a) list several examples of skills within each group, (b) list the sequence of the body segment movements used, (c) determine what influence an object's size or weight or both has on the segments used and on the sequence of the segments used, and (d) list the similarities and differences among individual skills within groups.

     Group I: Overarm striking skills in handball, volleyball, and all racket sports
     Group II: Overarm throwing or pushing skills for distance
     Group III: Kicking
     Group IV: Throwing underarm for accuracy
     Group V: Implements used in an underarm pattern to strike
     Group VI: Sidearm skills to throw or strike

6. Place all the skills listed in question 5 on a "throw-push continuum" from most throwlike to most pushlike. What effect does the object's size or mass or both have on the place at which the skill is located on the continuum?

Jumping

Whenever the body is projecting itself, as in jumping, the movement pattern resembles that of pushing the body into space by nearly simultaneous segmental rotations. The segmental rotations act to move the body's CG in a rectilinear path. A series of rotational movements producing a linear path of the body's CG is illustrated by the basketball player in Figure 14.14.

In contrast to a throwing model, the jumping model shows the most massive segment—the trunk—located at the open end of the kinetic chain, and the least massive segment—the feet—located at the fixed end. This configuration is called a closed kinetic chain. The segmental contributions are in reverse order; that is, beginning at the most free segment and ending at the most fixed segment, the feet. This is a slightly different situation from that seen for other skills on the throwing-pushing continuum. To project the body, one must have an external force; that external force is the ground reaction force that the jumper causes by pushing against it. The greater the ground reaction force, the greater the upward acceleration of the body's CG. Thus, the greater the upward acceleration of the segments, the greater

Segmental rotations producing a linear path of the center of gravity.   **Figure 14.14.**

the force downward so that the ground reaction force is increased. In the pushing pattern, the simultaneous application of segmental forces is used to produce greater force on the object to be projected. One would expect the jumping motion to be quite similar; that is, one would expect the simultaneous application of upward forces.

During the jumping motion is a simultaneous contraction of the antigravity muscles in an attempt to summate the segments' forces similar to a pushing pattern. In reality, however, a sequencing of some of the segmental rotations is done to maximize the jump.

The initial upward motion in sequencing is flexion of the arms at the shoulder joints. During their upward acceleration, the arms exert a downward reaction force on the segments below them. Sometime during the midst of their flexion, the arms begin to decelerate. This deceleration unweights the lower segments. During the deceleration of the arms is the optimum time to begin extension of the trunk about the hip joints.

The lower and less massive segments are subjected to a large downward reaction force during the upward acceleration of the large trunk segment above them. Because the lower segments are acting under such influence, they may be unable to begin their extensions simultaneously with the trunk, as would be expected in such a pushing type of movement. Even through the muscles of the lower segments may be attempting to produce the force for upward acceleration, they are so heavily loaded with the acceleration of the more massive segments above them that they may not be able to produce the force necessary to counteract the load. Thus, these lower segments may in fact be squeezed into a greater range of flexion prior to their extensions. Since the extensor muscles exert tension during their joints' flexions, they are functioning with eccentric tension. In such a case, the body segments are not functioning in a simultaneous pushing pattern to summate the forces.

The actual situation may have two important advantages, however. First, the lower segments are allowed to extend through a greater ROM. Second, and more importantly, the extensor muscles of the lower segments are stretched to a greater extent prior to their contractions. This has a twofold advantage. The stretch reflex is evoked, which enhances the muscle's contractile force, and it allows a greater use of the series elastic component of the tissues surrounding the joint. Note that merely increasing the ROM during flexion does not necessarily produce a greater extension force. The muscles must be tensed during the joint flexion phase for the recoil of the elastic component to contribute to the extension of the joints.

The acceleration and deceleration of the arms in a vertical jump or of the arms and leg during a high jump are commonly referred to as the transfer of momentum from the arms or the leg or both to the total body. The momentum of the arms or of the leg or of both (created by their upward acceleration during ground contact) is conserved within the entire system; therefore, as these segments decelerate, an increase occurs in the velocity of the body's CG upward. Consequently, the force resulting from the final extension of the supporting knee and ankle joints is used to further increase the momentum of the already upward-traveling CG. Figure 14.15

| **a** Initial foot plant position | **b** Arms and free leg accelerate upward | **c** Support leg extends, arm and free leg decelerate |

A high jump takeoff (a), showing upward acceleration of the arms and the free leg (b), and extension of the support leg (c), as the arms and free leg decelerate.   **Figure 14.15.**

illustrates the timing of the arms and of the free-leg and support-leg movements in the high jump takeoff.

Dyson (1977) calls the impulse provided by free-swinging arms and legs, as in the case of a high jumper, a *transmitted impulse*, as opposed to a *controlled impulse*, which is produced by the direct muscular effort against the supporting surface.

UNDERSTANDING PROJECTION OF THE BODY

1. Perform a vertical jump with the nonreaching arm held at the side throughout the jump and the reaching arm held above the head. Measure the jump. Repeat the jump, swinging both arms upward just prior to takeoff.

   a. Explain any difference between the two techniques in regard to the height of the projection.
   b. What is the acceleration-deceleration pattern during the ROM of the arms relative to the extension of the hips?

c. Does a sequence of segmental rotations occur during the jump, or are the rotations simultaneous?

2. Stand on a scale in anatomical position. From this position, perform the following actions while watching the weight indicator: (a) flex the elbows quickly, (b) flex the shoulder joints slowly, (c) flex the shoulder joints rapidly, (d) quickly flex the hips, knees, and ankles, (e) from a half-squat position, extend the hip, knee, and ankle joints rapidly. Explain the reactions of the scale in this experiment in terms of acceleration and deceleration of the segments. Relate this to the weighting and unweighting of the lower segments and the upward reaction force created at the feet.

3. Complete this sentence: Whenever the free end of a kinetic link system is more massive than the fixed end, the system is called a _____ kinetic chain.

REFERENCES
SUGGESTED READINGS[1]

Adrian, M., and Enberg, M. L. "Sequential Timing of Three Overhand Patterns." In *Kinesiology Review*, ed. C. J. Widule, 1–9. Reston Va.: AAHPERD, 1971.

Ae, M., Shibukawa, K., Toda, S., and Hashihara, Y. "A Biomechanical Analysis of the Segmental Contribution to the Takeoff of the One-Leg Running Jump for Height." In *Biomechanics VIII-B: Proceedings of the Eighth International Congress of Biomechanics*, ed. H. Matsui and K. Kobayashi, 737–45. Champaign, Ill.: Human Kinetics Publishers, 1983.

Atwater, A. E. "Biomechanics of Overarm Throwing Movements and of Throwing Injuries." In *Exercise and Sport Science Reviews,* ed. R. S. Hutton and D. I. Miller, vol. 7, 43–85. Franklin Institute Press, 1980.

———. "Biomechanics of Throwing: Correction of Common Misconceptions." Paper presented at the Joint Meeting of NAPECM and NAPECW, Orlands, Fla., January 1977.

———. "Overarm Throw Patterns: A Kinematographic Analysis." Paper presented at the AAHPERD Convention, Seattle, Wash., April 1970.

Biesterfeldt, H. J. "Salto Mechanics II: Energy and Height." *Gymnast*, October 1975, 54–56.

Daish, C. B. *Learn Science Through Ball Games.* New York: Sterling Publishing Co., 1972.

Dessureault, J., and LaFortune, M. A. "Biomechanical Features of Two Styles of High Jumping." In *Biomechanics VII-B: Proceedings of the Seventh International Congress on Biomechanics*, ed. A. Morecki, K. Fidelus, K. Kedzior, and A. Wit, 264–70. Baltimore: University Park Press, 1981.

Deutsch, H. "A Comparison of Women's Overarm Throwing Patterns." Paper presented at the AAHPERD Convention, Seattle, Wash., April 1970.

---

1. Additional references and suggested readings related to throwing, kicking, striking, and pushing skills are at the end of Chapter 15.

Dillman, C. J. "Effect of Leg Segmental Movements on Foot Velocity During the Recovery Phase of Running." In *Biomechanics IV: Proceedings of the Fourth International Seminar on Biomechanics*, ed. R. C. Nelson and C. A. Morehouse, 98–105. Baltimore: University Park Press, 1974.

Dyson, G. *The Mechanics of Athletics*. 7th ed. New York: Holmes & Meier Publishers, 1978.

Ellard, M., and Kerr, B. A. "A Comparative Study of Three Different Arm Actions in Developing Front Somersaults." In *Proceedings of the International Congress of Sport Sciences*, ed. J. Terauds and D. B. Daniels, 31–36. San Diego: Academic Publishers, 1979.

Hay, J. G. "Biomechanical Aspects of Jumping." In *Exercise and Sports Science Reviews*, vol. 3, ed. J. H. Wilmore and J. F. Keogh, 135–62. New York: Academic Press, 1975.

———. "Pole Vaulting: A Mechanical Analysis of Factors Influencing Pole-Bend." *Research Quarterly* 38 (1) (1967): 34–40.

Hopper, B. J. *The Mechanics of Human Movement*. New York: American Elsevier Publishing Co., 1973.

Klissouras, V., and Karpovich, P. "Electrogoniometric Study of Jumping Events." *Research Quarterly* 38 (1) (1967): 41–47.

Kreighbaum, E. "Mechanics of Side Horse Vaulting." In *Biomechanics IV: Proceedings of the Fourth International Seminar on Biomechanics*, ed. R. C. Nelson and C. A. Morehouse, 137–43. Baltimore: University Park Press, 1974.

Kulig, K., Mowacki, Z., and Bober, T. "Synchronization of Partial Impulses as a Biomechanical Principle." In *Biomechanics VIII-B: Proceedings of the Eighth International Congress on Biomechanics*, ed. H. Matsui and K. Kobayashi, 1144–51. Champaign, Ill.: Human Kinetics Publishers, 1983.

Lindner, E. "The Phenomenon of the Freedom of the Lateral Deviation in Throwing." In *Biomechanics II: Proceedings of the Second International Seminar on Biomechanics*, ed. J. Vredenbregt and J. Wartenweiler, 240–45. Baltimore: University Park Press, 1971.

McLaughlin, T., Lardner, T., and Dillman, C. "Kinetics of the Parallel Squat." *Research Quarterly* 49 (2) (1978): 175–89.

McMahon, T. A., and Greene, P. R. "Fast Running Tracks." *Scientific American*, December 1978, 148–63.

Morehouse, L. E., and Cooper, J. M. *Kinesiology*. London: Kimpton, 1950.

Ozolin, N. "The High Jump Takeoff Mechanism." *Track Technique* 52 (1973): 1668–71.

Phillips, S. J., Roberts, E. M., and Huang, T. C. "Intersegmental Relationships in Human Lower Extremity Swing Motions." Paper presented at the second annual conference of the American Society of Biomechanics, University of Michigan, Ann Arbor, October 1978.

———. "Quantification of Intersegmental Reactions During Rapid Swing Motions." *Journal of Biomechanics* 16 (6) (1983): 411–17.

Putman, C. A. "Interaction Between Segments During a Kicking Motion." In *Biomechanics VIII-B: Proceedings of the Eighth International Congress on Biomechanics*, ed. M. Matsui and K. Kobayashi, 688–94. Champaign, Ill.: Human Kinetics Publishers, 1983.

Roberts, E. M., and Phillips, S. J. "Angular Acceleration in 'Free Segment' Motion." In *Kinesiology: (Proceedings of) A National Conference on Teaching*, ed. C. Dillman and R. Sears, 328–34. Champaign-Urbana, Ill.: University of Illinois, 1977.

Roberts, E. M., Zernicke, R. F., Youm, Y., and Huang, T. C. "Kinetic Parameters of Kicking." In *Biomechanics IV: Proceedings of the Fourth International Seminar on Biomechanics*, ed. R. C. Nelson and C. A. Morehouse, 157–62. Baltimore: University Park Press, 1974.

Tarbell, T. "Some Biomechanical Aspects of the Overhead Throw." In *Biomechanics IV: Proceedings of the Fourth International Seminar on Biomechanics,* ed. R. C. Nelson and C. A. Morehouse, 180–83. Baltimore: University Park Press, 1974.

Toyoshima, S., and Miyashita, M. "Force-Velocity Relation in Throwing." *Research Quarterly* 44 (1973): 86–95.

Tricker, R. A. R., and Tricker, B. J. K. *The Science of Human Movement.* New York: American Elsevier Publishing Co., 1967.

Tsarouchas, E., and Klissouras, V. "The Force-Velocity Relation of a Kinematic Chain in Man." In *Biomechanics VII-A: Proceedings of the Seventh International Congress on Biomechanics,* ed. A. Morecki, K. Fidelus, K. Kedzior, and A. Wit, pp. 145–51. Baltimore: University Park Press, 1981.

Widule, C. J. *Analysis of Human Motion.* Lafayette, Ind.: Balt Publishing Co., 1974, pp. 80–90.

———. "Contiguous Segment Velocity, Acceleration Characteristics." Personal Communication. May 24, 1983.

Zernicke, R., and Roberts, E. "Lower Extremity Forces and Torques During Systematic Variation of Nonweight Bearing Motion." *Medicine and Science in Sports* 10 (1) (1978): 21–26.

Prerequisites

Chapter Contents

APPLYING THE KINETIC LINK PRINCIPLE IN PERFORMANCE ANALYSIS

The kinetic link principle applies to numerous skills. An understanding of the throw-push continuum and the application of the kinetic link concept may serve the following purposes for the teacher or coach:

1. To understand and analyze a particular skill
2. To help recognize performance ability levels
3. To help gain a basic understanding of the similarities and differences of skills that use the same general movement pattern
4. To gain a better understanding of the developmental patterns that are used by children as they progress through stages of learning to a mature form of a movement pattern

SECTION 1

BIOMECHANICS OF THROWLIKE PATTERNS

In previous sections, throwlike skills are defined as those in which the primary mechanical purpose is to develop high linear velocity on the end of the segmental link system. These skills may or may not include the use of an implement such as a bat or a racket. If an implement is used, it serves as an additional link in the body's link system.

The specific links used and the motions of each link in the system depend on which skill is being performed. For example, major differences occur in the segmental movements used in performing a golf swing and baseball batting or between overarm throwing and a tennis backhand drive. Slight differences occur in more similar skills, those that belong to a common pattern. Specific skills within the overarm, sidearm, or underarm patterns are slightly different. To better understand how one can begin to analyze a pattern, we can examine an overarm throwing pattern. Figure 15.1 illustrates the sequence of body positions used in this pattern.

With the first step forward, the thrower begins to initiate the end of the windup. The end of the windup is first noticed when the base segments, the pelvis and the trunk, begin to move forward. The distal segments continue to lag back until their turn to come forward. In keeping with the ordering of the segments, the movements proceed from base to free end, from proximal to distal, and from most massive to least massive.

Six segments are *in a position* to be active during the throw. They are the pelvis, trunk, shoulder girdle, arm, forearm, and hand. Each has its own movements relative to its own proximal articulation. These articulations are the hip, intervertebral,

Figure 15.1.   A baseball pitcher, showing the step and the movements of the hip, vertebral column, shoulder girdle, shoulder joint, forearm, and wrist.

sternoclavicular, shoulder, elbow, radioulnar, and wrist joints. More than one movement *could* occur in several of these articulations, and exactly which ones are used depends primarily on which specific sport skill is being performed. Since we are examining the general pattern of overarm throwlike movements, we will consider *all possibilities.*

As the leading heel approaches the ground, the pelvis begins its medial rotation about longitudinal axis of the hip joint. The next distal segment is the trunk, which moves in transverse rotation about a longitudinal axis through the vertebral column. The distal segments and their possible movements are the protraction of the shoulder girdle about the longitudial axis through the sternoclavicular joint, the transverse adduction of the arm about an AP and ML oblique axis through the shoulder joint, the medial rotation of the arm about the longitudinal axis through the shoulder joint, the extension of the forearm about an ML axis through the elbow joint, the pronation of the forearm about the longitudinal axis through the radioulnar joint, and finally, the flexion of the hand about an ML axis through the wrist joint.

Such a listing provides two types of information to the teacher or coach and performer: (1) the segments, the movements, and the muscle groups that *may be* used to produce an overarm pattern, and (2) the ordering or sequencing of the movements used in an overarm pattern. Once a general list has been made, the teacher or coach adapts this list to the specific skill that is being analyzed.

The kinematic and kinetic descriptions of the actual sport skill being analyzed depend on two other variables: the rotational inertia of the group of segments that rotates at any given time and the radius of rotation of the contact point relative to each of the axes of rotation. The rotational inertia for each combination of segments is difficult to assess; however, a general idea can be gained if the following are considered:

1. The greater the rotational inertia (mass times radius of gyration squared), the smaller the angular acceleration for a given muscle torque.

   a. The base segmental torque must accelerate the mass of all the segments distal to its axis of rotation and therefore must deal with a greater rotational inertia.

   b. The distal segmental masses are located farther from the proximal axes of rotation being used, and therefore the radius of gyration for proximal segmental rotations is larger.

2. As the sequence of movements progresses to the distal axes, the rotational inertia of the system formed by the remaining rotating segments becomes less.

   a. The axis of rotation for each successive distal motion is located farther out on the link system, hence it moves closer and closer to the end.

   b. The mass of each successive segment is progressively smaller.

   c. The radius of gyration for a segment moving in a wheel-axle fashion around a longitudinal axis is smaller than that for a leverlike movement of the same segment.

Consequently, the link system tends to move faster as the movements proceed to its distal end due to the continual reduction of its rotational inertia.

A second variable in the system is the radius of rotation (r) used in calculating the linear velocity of a point on a rotating system (v = rω). Figure 15.2 illustrates how to visualize the radius of rotation for several possible segmental rotations for an overarm pattern.

Note the larger radii of rotation for the base segments and the smaller radii of rotation for the proximal segments. Keep in mind that each axis of rotation is associated with a radius of rotation. The movements of segments distal to the axis of concern increase or decrease the radius of rotation for that axis. For example, the extension of the elbow during the overarm throwing skill increases the radius of rotation relative to the hip axis, the vertebral axis, and the sternoclavicular axis, but does not change the radius of rotation relative to the elbow axis itself.

SECTION 2

ANALYSIS OF SPORT SKILLS USING THE KINETIC LINK PRINCIPLE

Baseball Pitch

The segmental movements described by researchers who have observed high-speed films of skilled baseball pitchers are consistent with the kinetic link model. That the wheel-axlelike medial rotation of the pelvis about the hip joint axis initiates the forward action of the pitch is fairly well established. The pelvic movement continues as the trunk begins transverse rotation about the vertebral column. During this time the shoulder joint is abducted to 90 degrees, and the elbow is flexed to 90 degrees. These latter two movements serve to position the ball in space in preparation for the second part of the throwing motion rather than contribute any velocity to the ball.

The transverse rotation of the trunk is associated with extreme lateral rotation of the shoulder joint as the upper extremity and ball lag back, which is typical of the throwlike pattern. The second part of the pitching motion consists of continuing trunk transverse rotation, accelerated elbow extension, a slight amount of medial rotation of the shoulder joint, radioulnar pronation, and wrist flexion. Note that wrist flexion occurs from hyperextension of the wrist to full extension of the wrist; the wrist does not "snap forward" into flexion at any time prior to release. The sequencing of these motions follows the kinetic link principle (i.e., from proximal to distal with the exception of elbow extension occurring prior to shoulder joint medial rotation).

Researchers have experienced difficulty in trying to determine whether medial rotation of the shoulder joint contributes anything substantial to the ball velocity. The motion is difficult to measure, and the medial rotation that does occur begins

Axes of segmental rotations used in pitching a baseball.   **Figure 15.2.**

from extreme lateral rotation and is noticeable only during a brief time period prior to release. Recall also that medial rotation is a wheel-axle type of movement and thus has the advantage of a relatively small rotational inertia. Since the elbow is not *fully* extended at release, the ball has a small radius of rotation associated with the medial rotation motion of the shoulder joint.

A second segmental movement that has not been reported is shoulder girdle protraction. Whether this movement contributes anything directly to ball velocity is unclear, although it certainly is a segment located along the series of links. Isolating and measuring its motion is difficult since it is closely associated with and hard to differentiate from the transverse rotation of the trunk. Stabilization of the shoulder girdle would seem to be important during the time that high accelerations are occurring in the segments distal to it.

The third segmental movement listed in the general order of upper extremity throwlike movements is shoulder joint transverse adduction. This movement does not appear in skilled pitchers, but it has been reported as a part of the throwing movements of the unskilled. As will be discussed in a future section, placing the elbow joint ahead of a line connecting the shoulder joints prior to release is characteristic of an unskilled overarm pattern.

Since the hand and ball are closely aligned with the axis of rotation for radioulnar pronation, the radioulnar motion has no radius of rotation. Thus, the motion serves to position the hand on the ball at release and influences the amount of spin imparted to it. For producing a fastball, the palm is facing forward at release with the forearm pronated. For a slider, the forearm is not pronated quite as much as in delivering a fastball. The curveball delivery is somewhat surprising. For years the curveball was associated with supination of the forearm prior to release. High-speed films disclaimed this idea, showing that the forearm is in mid-position and that the fingers roll off the *forward* part of the ball during release (Atwater 1980). The forearm then pronates and the shoulder joint medially rotates throughout the follow-through. This sequence of motions produces a curve that has top spin and "breaks" downward. Further discussion of the deflections of a spinning ball is in Chapter 9.

The amount and location of muscle torque within the throwing motion have not been precisely determined, although muscle torque probably plays a significant role in accelerating the base segments. By the time elbow extension occurs, the link system has generated a considerable amount of angular velocity. Whether the elbow extensor muscles can shorten fast enough to keep up with or cause an increase in the angular velocity of the extending forearm is unknown. Studies have shown that the forearm extends considerably faster when preceded by proximal segmental rotations than it can extend without those rotations using only muscle extensor torque.

Javelin Throw

The segmental rotations used to project a javelin are similar to those used in pitching a baseball. Any slight differences in position are due to the angle of projection at which the javelin is thrown, which is estimated to be ideal at approximately 35 degrees above the horizontal. The body's position at release is surprisingly similar to that of throwing a baseball. The sequencing of the segmental rotations is the same; the proximal segments accelerate and then decelerate as the distal segments accelerate, resulting in maximum velocity of the forearm at release.

Since a javelin is heavier than a baseball, one would anticipate the necessity of greater muscle torque involvement in projecting a javelin than in pitching a baseball. The release velocity of the javelin is approximately two thirds that of a baseball pitch, however. The lagging back of the distal segments places the distal segmental muscles on stretch, and consequently, these muscles, through the use of the stretch reflex and their elastic properties, may apply some accelerating muscle torque to the distal segments, which may not be possible in the baseball throw.

Football Pass

A football is heavier than a baseball but lighter than a javelin. The shape of a football requires that the nose of the ball be projected forward and that as little wobble as possible be imparted. Throwing a long forward pass with a football is close to the same overarm throwing pattern as the baseball throw in terms of segmental rotations and sequencing. The elbow is not extended quite as much at release, however, and this may be due to the necessity of imparting spin to the football while holding its nose forward. The last part of the throw resembles a slight pushlike motion. The pronation of the forearm along with medial rotation of the shoulder joint imparts spin to the ball as it rolls off the fingertips. Since the hand is not able to grasp a football in the same manner as a baseball, the hand cannot easily hold a football in the lag-back position.

Badminton Smash

The general overarm throwing pattern also is used in performing overarm skills with the use of implements. The pelvic rotation initiates the forward motion while the next distal segment lags back; intervertebral transverse rotation follows. Gowitzke and Wadell (1979b) state that "it gave the impression of the body 'moving out from under the arm' with the hand staying almost motionless in space behind the head" (p. 6).

The trunk rotation is followed in sequential order by elbow extension, medial rotation of the shoulder joint, and forearm pronation. Suprisingly, elbow extension, a more distal motion, begins prior to a more proximal motion at the shoulder. This seemingly reverse order is apparent in the baseball pitch as well. In the badminton smash, the elbow extension possibly serves to position the racket head in space rather than to provide high velocity. Elbow extension and transverse rotation of the trunk *cease* prior to contact with the shuttle. Gowitzke and Waddell report that forearm pronation and shoulder joint medial rotation continue to occur through contact and follow-through. These wheel-axlelike motions provide fast racket-head velocity. Forearm pronation displays a greater range of motion (ROM) than shoulder medial rotation.

In the badminton smash performed by elite players, the wrist joint movement did not appear to contribute any velocity to the racket head since the wrist either was held in radial flexion through contact or moved from radial flexion to a neutral position prior to contact. Radial flexion was observed again after contact. Figure 15.3 illustrates an advanced pattern and a beginner's pattern for performing the overarm smash. Note the excessive wrist flexion occurring in the beginning performer. This common error is not surprising when one recalls the prevalent but misleading teaching cue, "snap the wrist." Apparently, for achieving a high endpoint velocity with a relatively light implement and object, the speedy wheel-axle movements of medial rotation and pronation are most effective. In addition, elite badminton players reposition the racket face through the use of radial flexion, which serves to increase the radius of rotation and therefore the linear velocity of the contact point for these two movements.

Golf Swing

The underarm pattern of a golf drive or long iron shot incorporates the kinetic link principle. The downswing is initiated by the base segments (rotation of the

Figure 15.3. A beginning (a) and an advanced (b) badminton player, demonstrating the forearm and wrist contributions to a smash.

pelvis about the hip joint and the trunk about the vertebral column), followed by the underarm pattern of the upper extremities across the body. An investigation into the generation of high club head velocity was conducted by Milburn (1982). The researcher concluded that the greatest acceleration of the club head occurred when a delay wrist action allowed the arm acceleration to take place as long as possible, that is, allowed the arm to reach a maximum velocity prior to the action of the wrists. The wrist motion, when it did occur, acted to decelerate the arm motion; thus, an early "uncocking" of the wrists would serve to decrease the angular motion of the entire system.

The rapid acceleration of the club head, Milburn concluded, was due to the wrist's high acceleration, which was "summed with the pushing backwards of the arm about the shoulder to bring about the greatest angular velocity of the distal segment" (p. 63).

The Kick

The kicking pattern is similar to an underarm pattern in which the proximal segments initiate the movement forward, causing a lagging back of the distal foot segment (Figure 15.4). The knee extensor muscles prevent the leg and foot from

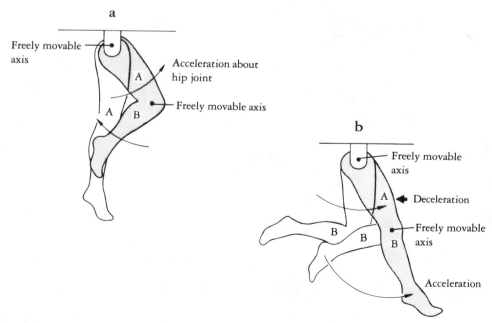

The effects of acceleration and deceleration of segments in a two-segment model. (a) Acceleration of segment A counterclockwise and acceleration of segment B clockwise. (b) Deceleration of segment A and acceleration of segment B.   **Figure 15.4.**

lagging back too far. The pattern of motion is consistent with the link principle. The acceleration of the thigh flexion about the hip joint should take place as long as possible since the acceleration of knee extension tends to decelerate the thigh segment. Thus, the longer the thigh can accelerate, the greater the angular velocity of the foot when it reaches the ball. As the internal torques provided by the knee extensors are applied, the leg and foot accelerate, and the thigh either begins to decelerate or its acceleration is reduced. The knee becomes the new axis of rotation for the leg and foot motion. Thus, the rotational inertia of those segments is effectively reduced, and their velocity is increased.

SECTION 3

COMPARISONS OF SIMILAR SKILLS WITHIN THE SAME PATTERN

Whenever a comparison is to be made of different sport skills within a similar pattern, the skills can be placed on the throwing-pushing continnum according to the purposes of the projection and the relative sizes and masses of the objects and implements used. These general principles govern the differences that occur within similar patterns:

1. The smaller and lighter the object, the greater the number of segments that may be used.

   a. Heavy-object projections rely on the larger muscle groups surrounding the hip and vertebral column to form a movement base for the remaining segments. For example, one would not try to throw an object as heavy as a medicine ball by relying solely on radioulnar, wrist, or finger movements.

   b. Some precision of movement used for projection is lost by using the larger groups. Accuracy skills tend to use the smaller muscle groups.

2. The smaller and lighter the object, the greater the radius of rotation that may be used for a given segmental movement. For example, the forward motion of the shot put is initiated with the shot carried close to the body, and the forward motion of the baseball pitch is initiated with the ball carried out to the side of the body with an abducted and laterally rotated shoulder.

   a. Heavy objects tend to be projected with a pushing motion that uses more simultaneous segmental rotations and is initiated and carried out close to the midline of the body.

   b. Lighter objects may be thrown or struck along a more curvilinear path that may be characterized by a lengthening of the radii of rotation of the links used. Increasing the radius of rotation also increases the rotational inertia of the distal links around the proximal axis. This increase in rotational inertia resists the desired acceleration and thus increases the muscle torque necessary to maintain or increase the angular velocity of the object. Thus, it may be effective only with lighter implements and objects.

3. The greater the mass of the object, the greater the contribution made by the larger segments (e.g., segments rotating about the hip, vertebral column, and sternoclavicular articulations). In the badminton smash, the medial rotation of the shoulder joint and forearm pronation are noticeable because the racket is light enough to be manipulated by the smaller muscle groups. The thrower in water polo, however, has a problem in trying to grasp the ball while throwing it. To accomplish this, the basic pattern must be adjusted. When an implement such as a tennis racket or badminton racket is used, the contact point (the face of the racket) can be positioned eccentric to the longitudinal axis of the shoulder and radioulnar joints. Thus, these movements may become effective contributors to the end-point velocity.

Badminton Smash and Tennis Serve

The uniqueness of each individual skill within a given pattern is evident if the overhand pattern of a badminton smash performed by an advanced badminton player is compared with a badminton smash performed by an advanced tennis player. Figure 15.5 shows these patterns.

The tennis racket and ball are heavier than the badminton racket and shuttlecock; thus, although the general pattern is the same, the relative importance of the segmental movements in the two skills is slightly different.

The tennis player, being used to heavier equipment, uses greater motion of the larger-muscled segments (pelvis and trunk) and lesser motion of the smaller segments (arm and forearm) than the badminton player. In a study of the volleyball overarm serve, the tennis serve, and the badminton smash, Adrian and Enberg (1971) reported that "for the subject who was very highly skilled in one sport in particular . . . , the position at contact in the other skills greatly resembled the contact position in the best sport." The reverse situation may be seen by observing a skilled badminton player attempting a shot with a tennis racket. The tendency to maintain the badminton pattern could produce injury because of the use of the smaller segments with the heavier equipment.

In executing the tennis serve, the performer uses vertebral rotation and flexion and some shoulder medial rotation at impact but less noticeable forearm pronation than in the badminton smash. In the badminton smash, however, the shoulder medial rotation and forearm pronation are maximized, while the hip and vertebral rotations are reduced or cease prior to impact. The muscle force is provided mainly by the larger muscle groups in the tennis serve. The lateral flexion of the trunk and elbow extension mainly serve to increase the radius of rotation distance between the hip, vertebral column, and the shoulder axes of rotation and the point of impact. In the badminton smash, however, 41% of the shuttle velocity is achieved from the medial

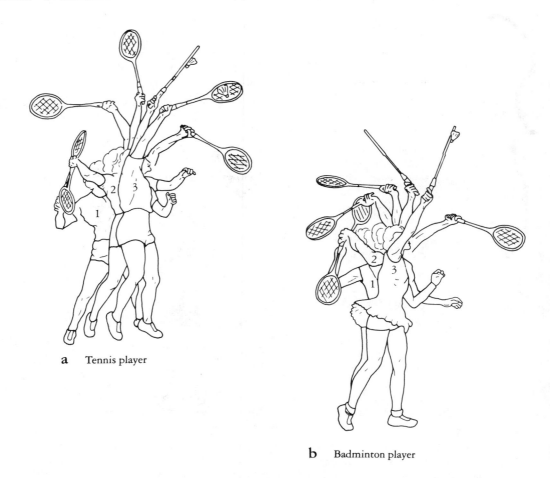

a   Tennis player

b   Badminton player

Figure 15.5.   An advanced tennis player (a) and an advanced badminton player (b) executing a badminton smash.

rotation of the shoulder joint and forearm pronation, two of the fastest movements of the body (Gowitzke 1979). Because of the smaller muscle groups associated with the arm and forearm segments, these motions are enhanced in activities in which the body is using fairly light objects and implements, such as the badminton racket and the shuttlecock.

Consider also that in spite of the fact that the hip and the vertebral movements may not occur at impact in badminton, they do move to initiate the forward "force phase" of the stroke and probably serve to accelerate the system and to increase the velocity of the upper extremity. The light weight of the racket and shuttlecock in badminton precludes the necessity of using the larger segment rotations for developing racket speed. In addition, in higher speed activities the performer has little time to employ a full-body link system during competitive situations.

SECTION 4

PERFORMANCE ERRORS: TEACHING AND COACHING APPLICATIONS

Errors displayed by performers of different ability levels may be identified and placed into one of three categories: segmental movement errors, timing and sequencing errors, and errors owing to lack of strength or power.

Segmental Movement Errors

The position of body segments during a performance often provides a clue to performance errors. Keeping in mind that one identifying characteristic of the use of the kinetic link principle is the lagging back of more distal segments, teachers and coaches should watch for segments that are positioned ahead of a more proximal segment prior to release or contact. A beginner attempting to perform a kinetic link activity often positions a more distal segment ahead of a more proximal segment. A common example is that of the location of the wrist relative to the elbow. While the wrist is noticeably ahead of the elbow, the beginner may hold the racket or the projectile back by hyperextending the wrist joint.

A second common and easily identified segmental position error that is frequently seen in the beginning performer involves the location of the elbow joint relative to a line connecting the shoulders. The elbow is positioned ahead of the shoulders prior to contact or release. Both of these errors may be seen in the illustrations of the beginning performers in Figures 14.10 and 15.3.

As was mentioned in a previous section, transverse adduction of the shoulder joint is not observed in a skilled baseball throwing pattern but is observed in a less skilled one. The transverse adduction of the shoulder joint prior to release places the elbow ahead of the shoulder line. In cases of gross errors, an entire throw or strike pattern begins and ends with elbow extension from an elbow located almost directly in front of the same shoulder joint. This error is common to most beginning or immature throwing and striking skills.

Sequencing and Timing Errors

The second area of focus for the teacher or coach is that of observing sequencing and timing errors. Segmental movements are difficult to distinguish from one another without the aid of a video or movie film. If the teacher or coach has a mental picture of the proper sequencing, however, then comparing what *is* seen with what *should be* seen is easier.

The segmental sequencing in any skill that is governed by the kinetic link concept should proceed from proximal to distal, more massive to less massive, fixed end to free end. The initial forward movement of a distal segment should occur at the point of maximum velocity of the preceding segment. Although *seeing* velocities and accelerations is impossible, the teacher or coach should come to recognize, through experience, where in a pattern a proximal segment contributes its acceleration and when the next distal segment motion should begin. As a general rule, the proximal segment uses about one half to two thirds of its ROM to reach its peak velocity.

A second comparator that may be used by the teacher or coach is a mental image of whiplike timing. One may notice that the performer gets stuck during what should be a smooth flow of segmental movements. Often the beginner moves segments in distinct *blocks* rather than overlapping each with the adjacent segments. This pattern resembles a pushing pattern in that the segments move simultaneously rather than sequentially.

At the novice level, insufficient relaxation of the muscle groups antagonistic to the desired movement can inhibit the free rotation of one segment relative to another. As the distal links are used, the internal muscular torques that act to bring those distal segments forward may be ill timed. If adequate lag back of distal segments is not noticeable, the distal segments may not be in a position to elicit the stretch reflex in the muscle tissues nor to make use of the muscles' elastic properties.

Sometimes having the performer exaggerate each segmental movement in the proper order gives the performer the idea of the proper sequencing. The exaggeration of each segmental movement is particularly helpful to beginners who are having trouble focusing their attention on individual segmental movements.

A second technique is to hold back the contact point (hand, racket, bat, or club) while the performer attempts to finish the skill. While the end point is held, the proximal segments move out from under the distal segments. The performer should feel the sequential nature of the skill.

A novice performer typically displays a more simultaneous pattern (e.g., with the contact or release point ill timed, too early or too late). Improper timing not only reduces the projection velocity but also alters the direction of the projectile. On the other hand, an intermediate performer tends to display *erratic* timing of the segments: some segmental movements may be initiated too early, some too late, and some just at the right instant.

At the intermediate level of performance the critical analysis of the teacher or coach is necessary for identifying errors. The analyst should attempt to focus on the timing of one or two segments at a time. Unfortunately, without the aid of a video or film, spotting the error or errors in one viewing is difficult, and therefore, the performer is required to repeat the skill several times.

Errors Owing to Lack of Strength or Power

The skill, strength, or power of the performer may alter the location of any skill on the continuum from that of the ideal. For instance, an immature performer may turn an otherwise sequential movement into a more simultaneous one by ordering the initiation of two or more links at the same or nearly the same time. A person who lacks the necessary power to sequentially accelerate an object with the distal links carries the object closer to the midline of the body, so that a simultaneous pushing motion is observed. The basketball throw for distance may demonstrate this concept if performers of various strengths and hand sizes are observed. Those who have hands large enough to grasp the ball and have enough upper body and arm strength demonstrate a throwlike pattern. As the sizes of hands and strengths of arms decrease in the subjects, the ball is carried closer to the body during the throw. The sequential rotation of proximal segments is maintained while the distal links either will be stabilized or will display a nearly simultaneous pushing motion. A performer who is not able to manipulate either the size or the mass of the ball demonstrates a totally simultaneous pushing pattern.

A second example of the effect of the size and weight of the equipment on throwlike patterns is observed in a tennis player who does not have the strength to hold the racket in a neutral position at the wrist. Eventually, the weight of the racket causes the wrist to fall into an ulnar-flexed position. In addition, to reduce the inertial resistance of the racket and the torque of the impact, the performer adducts the shoulder joint by pulling the elbow into the side, thus increasing elbow flexion (Ward and Groppel 1980). The increased elbow flexion is an attempt to compensate for the racket head being lowered vertically due to the ulnar-flexed position of the wrist.

The effects of the size and mass of an object or implement on the throw-strike pattern has several implications for the selection of equipment for people of differing sizes, strengths, and abilities. If the performer is to demonstrate a mature pattern with all of its segmental movement and timing requirements, then the equipment may have to be made smaller or less massive or both.

SECTION 5

DEVELOPMENTAL PATTERNS: TEACHING IMPLICATIONS

Developmental kinesiology is the subarea concerned with studying the movement patterns of children during their developmental stages of growth. Children's throwing, kicking, and striking patterns are identified in the literature.

In many ways, the developmental movement patterns are similar to the beginning, intermediate, and advanced skill levels discussed previously; that is, the developmental patterns are described by the segments being used, the positions and movements of those segments, and the sequencing and timing of the segmental movements.

Kicking

Deach (1950) identified several developmental stages in kicking patterns of two- to six-year-old children. These stages are as follows:

Stage 1.   The performer kicked the ball using a small amount of hip flexion. Little forward movement of the leg occurred after impact as well as little co-ordinated effort with the rest of the body. The knee remained relatively straight during the impact.

Stage 2.   In addition to the hip motion, a flexion of the knee produced a backswing of the leg prior to impact. The arms were used in abduction for sideward balance.

Stage 3.   The ROM of the hip extension and knee flexion was increased. The arms began to show a flexion motion as a balance mechanism for the increased forward-backward motion of the lower extremity.

Wickstrom (1977) states, "Overall the stages show gradual change from a relatively straight pendular leg action with little body movement to a sweeping, whiplike action with gross body movement" (p. 202). Further, he goes on to say that "the chil-dren . . . almost invariably tended to retract the kicking leg after the completion of the kick. They did not allow leg momentum to carry the rest of the body forward in a follow-through motion. This tendency to withdraw the kicking leg is a clearly identifiable aspect of developmental form in kicking" (p. 202).

In Deach's study, the subjects were not allowed to incorporate an approach. Bloomfield et al. (1979) found that the first three stages of kicking were similar to Deach's subjects for boys 2 to 12 years of age. They proposed three additional stages that incorporate a run-up (Stage 4), a lagging back of the leg on a forward accelerating thigh (Stage 5), and a complete run-up backswing, thigh hyperextension, and knee flexion (Stage 6).

In the early stages of kicking, little, if any, participation by the pelvis and little participation by the leg occur because of the lack of knee flexion prior to impact. Thus, the flexion of the thigh at the hip is the single link utilized by the kicker. As the kicker becomes more developed in the kicking pattern, more segments are used; that is, the leg and then the pelvis are added. In addition, an increase in the ROM of the distal links occurs because of its lagging back in compliance with the open kinetic link principle. This lag back gives the segments a greater distance over which to accelerate for the forward movements and thus allows them to generate more velocity to the free end segment, the foot. The greater knee flexion during the forward swing of the thigh provides the added advantage of reducing the rotational inertia of the lower extremity for hip flexion and therefore allows greater accleration of the thigh during the hip-flexion phase. The momentum of the lower extremity is assumed by the leg (a smaller rotational inertia segment) as the thigh decelerates.

Similar developmental progressions occur in throwing and striking, and all follow similar trends (i.e., the less mature performance generally incorporates fewer seg-ments, displays a smaller ROM for those segments used, and uses more simultaneous rather than sequential timing).

The progression of developmental patterns in kicking is similar to the beginning, intermediate, and advanced aspects of any of the throwing, kicking, and striking skills. Mechanically, a skilled pattern is characterized as a multilink system, with each link contributing its own particular movement to the production of velocity at impact with the object. Beginning from the most hyperextended position of the free hip, the links move forward in a prescribed order from the largest, most stable, and proximal link to the smallest, most freely movable, and distal link.

Throwing

Developmental stages of throwing were proposed initially by Wild (1938) as reported by Wickstrom (1983). The stages of throwing reflect an increased use of sequential segmental rotations as the mature pattern develops.

Stage 1.   The elbow is located forward of the shoulder joint. The ball is thrown primarily with elbow extension. No rotation of the trunk is visible (Figure 15.6a).

Stage 2.   A trunk rotation to the right (right-handed thrower) accompanies the backward motion of the arm. The throw is initiated by the arm swing forward accompanied by trunk rotation left. The elbow extends at variable times during the forward arm swing (Figure 15.6b).

Stage 3.   A step is taken with the ipsilateral (same side) foot. The step is followed by trunk rotation and the forward arm swing. The elbow extension occurs later than in Stage 2 (Figure 15.6c)

Stage 4.   A step is taken with the contralateral foot, the trunk rotates to the left, a transverse adduction of the arm and elbow extension ends the force phase (Figure 15.6d).

Roberton (1978) further identified segmental movement components or categories using a more kinesiological and biomechanical basis. These are (1) the action of the humerus, (2) the action of the forearm, and (3) the action of the pelvis-spine. In all categories, the pattern develops from less mature forms characterized by:

1. Block (simultaneous) rotation of adjacent segments with little or no differentiated sequencing
2. Little evidence of lag back
3. Inappropriate segmental movements (e.g., transverse adduction of the humerus and hyperextension-flexion of the trunk)

Eventually these immature forms give way to more mature forms as described previously in this chapter and in keeping with kinetic link concept.

Of interest are Anderson's findings (1977) as reported by Roberton (1978). In less-skilled throwers pectoralis major activity continued through ball release, whereas in skilled throwers the muscle activity diminished sharply prior to ball release. This

a   b   c   d

Figure 15.6.   The four developmental stages of throwing.

finding implies that muscle torque is not necessary to increase all the segmental velocities in an open kinetic chain activity.

While watching children of different developmental stages perform the same pattern, some basic differences may be observed in the sequencing and timing of the segments within the same pattern. Considering kinesiological and biomechanical as well as motor development and motor learning factors, it is questionable as to which factors are most important in helping to develop the best performance possible. If one looks to the potential mature performance, one can approach the teaching of that skill in one of two ways.

One may ask the physically immature performer, no matter what size or strength, to train using regulation equipment. In skills in which maximum distance or velocity or both are important, the ideal projection angle has to be adjusted according to the height of release and speed of projection that the individual is able to produce. (A slower speed of release dictates a higher release angle.) Alternatively, one can reduce the size and weight of the equipment in proportion to the size of the performer so that the performer may pattern his or her movements closer to the ideal mature performance.

Teachers and coaches must consider (1) whether the child-athlete gains more by training with smaller, lighter equipment and thus is enabled to closely approximate the mature movement pattern, or (2) whether training should be a continual adjustment of the movement pattern because of growth (height) and development (strength) factors.

UNDERSTANDING APPLICATIONS OF THE KINETIC LINK PRINCIPLE

1. Assemble these objects: a tennis ball, a softball, a volleyball, a soccer ball, a basketball, and a medicine ball. For two observers, perform an overarm throw for maximum distance with each of the objects in the order listed. Answer the following:

   a. Can any differences be detected among throws in terms of the simultaneous or sequential nature of the joint movements?
   b. In what order are the segments moving?
   c. Does one joint movement stop before another begins?
   d. Do two or more segments start and stop moving simultaneously?
   e. Do two or more segments start at the same time but not stop at the same time?

2. Throw and catch a softball with a partner. Identify the sequence of movements occurring when one is throwing as hard as one can. Perform the same throw with the nonpreferred arm. What differences are noted in the motion of the segments? What differences are noted in the sequencing of the segmental movements?

3. Throw and catch a softball with a partner in an overarm, underarm, and sidearm pattern. For each pattern, identify and list the sequential joint movements in the order of their occurrence and those that occur simultaneously. Compare the movements of each throw with the movements observed using the same object and the nonpreferred arm.

4. With the assistance of an unskilled partner (using the nonpreferred arm), attempt to identify the type of error that the unskilled partner is making from those listed in the section entitled Performance Errors: Teaching-Coaching Applications, pages 631–633. Attempt to correct those errors with the help of the applications given in the same section.

5. Select one of these skills: baseball batting, volleyball spike, tennis one-hand backhand, tennis two-hand backhand, badminton round-the-head shot, racquetball forehand, golf drive, cricket pitch, hurling, soccer-style place kick, water polo shot, and javelin throw.

   a. In groups of three, analyze the selected skill in terms of the following:
      i. The segments and articulations that are doing the moving

    ii. The movement that the articulation is doing

    iii. The axis of rotation used in each of the movements

  b. Draw an illustration (stick figure) of the release or contact position of a person performing the skill. Place dots or lines where appropriate to indicate the axes of rotation used by the segments as they move into the release or contact position. Draw the radius of rotation for each movement. You may need more than one view. (See Figure 15.2 [p. 623] for an example.)

  c. Discuss how the radius of gyration and the mass of the system change as each segmental movement takes place in sequence. Consider the position of all the segments distal to the segment you are considering. How do the mass and radius of gyration changes affect the angular velocity of the moving segment?

6. Attend a Little League game, go to a playground, or observe a physical education class at an elementary school. Watch the children catch, throw, and kick. Identify performance errors that are related to the developmental stages. Can you relate these performance errors to the errors listed under the section Performance Errors: Teaching and Coaching Applications, pages 631–633.

REFERENCES
SUGGESTED READINGS[1]

Adrian, M., and Enberg, M. L. "Sequential Timing of Three Overhand Patterns." In *Kinesiology Review*, ed. C. J. Widule, 1–9. Reston, Va.: AAHPERD, 1971.

Allman, W. F. "Pitching." *Science 82*, October 1982, 32–39.

Ariel, G. "Javelin Throw: Computerized Biomechanical Analysis." *Track Technique* 12 (54) (1973): 1726–28.

Atwater, A. E. "Biomechanics of Throwing: Correction of Common Misconceptions." Paper presented at the Joint Meeting of NAPECM and NAPECW, Orlando Fla., January 1977.

———. "Biomechanics of Overarm Throwing Movements and of Throwing Injuries." In *Exercise and Sports Science Reviews*, ed. R. S. Hutton and D. I. Miller, vol. 7, 43–85. Franklin Institute Press, 1980.

Bloomfield, J., Elliot, B. C., and Davies, C. M. "Development of the Soccer Kick." *Journal of Human Movement Studies* 5 (1979): 152–59.

Carlson, J. "Illustrating Kinesiological Principles: A Comparative Analysis of Two Styles of Punt Kicking." In *Kinesiology*: [Proceedings of] *A National Conference on Teaching*, ed. C. Dillman and R. Sears, 273–78. Champaign-Urbana: University of Illinios Press, 1977.

Cochran, A., and Stobbs, J. *Search for the Perfect Swing*. Philadelphia: J. B. Lippincott, 1968.

Cooper, J. M., et al. "Kinematic and Kinetic Analysis of the Golf Swing." In *Biomechanics IV: Proceedings of the Fourth International Seminar on Biomechanics*, ed. R. C. Nelson and C. A. Morehouse, 289–305. Baltimore: University Park Press, 1974.

Deach, D. "Genetic Development of Motor Skills in Children Two Through Six Years of Age." Unpublished doctoral dissertation, University of Michigan, 1950.

---

1. Additional references related to this topic are at the end of Chapter 14.

Dessureault, J. "Kinetic and Kinematic Factors Involved in Shot Putting." In *Biomechanics VI-B: Proceedings of the Sixth International Congress on Biomechanics*, ed. E. Asmussen and K. Jorgensen, 51–60. Baltimore: University Press, 1978.

Deutsch, H. "A Comparison of Women's Overarm Throwing Patterns." Paper presented at the AAHPERD Convention, Seattle, April 1970.

Dyson, G. *The Mechanics of Athletics.* New York: Holmes & Meier Publishers, 1977.

Gowitzke, B. "Biomechanical Principles Applied to Badminton Stroke Production." In *Sciences in Racquet Sports: Proceedings of the International Congress of Sports Sciences*, ed. J. Terauds, 7–16. San Diego: Academic Publishers, 1979a.

Gowitzke, B., and Waddell, D. B. "Technique of Badminton Stroke Production." In *Sciences in Racquet Sports: Proceedings of the International Congress of Sports Sciences*, ed. J. Terauds, 17–42. San Diego: Academic Publishers, 1979a.

———. "Qualitative Analysis of the Badminton Forehand Smash as Performed by International Players." *The Raquet Sports*, ed. J. Groppel, 1–15. Champaign-Urbana: University of Illinois Press, 1979b.

Groppel, J. L. "Teaching One- and Two-Handed Backhand Drives." *JOPERD* 54 (5) (1983): 23–26, 38.

Groppel, J. L., and Ward, T. "Coaching Implications of the Tennis One-Handed and Two-Handed Backhand Drives." In *Sciences in Racquet Sports: Proceedings of the International Congress of Sport Sciences*, ed. J. Terauds, 81–87. San Diego, Calif.: Academic Sports, 1979.

Ikegami, Y., Miura, M., Matsui, H., and Hashimoto, I. "Biomechanical Analysis of the Javelin Throw." In *Biomechanics VII-B: Proceedings of the Seventh International Congress on Biomechanics*, ed. A. Morecki, K. Fidelus, K. Kedzior, and A. Wit, 271–76. Baltimore: University Park Press, 1981.

Jorgensen, T. "On the Dynamics of the Swing of a Golf Club." *American Journal of Physics* 38 (5) (1970): 644–51.

Marhold, G. "Biomechanical Analysis of the Shot Put." In *Biomechanics IV: Proceedings of the Fourth International Seminar on Biomechanics*, ed. R. C. Nelson and C. A. Morehouse, 175–79. Baltimore: University Park Press, 1974.

Milburn, P. D. "Summation of Segmental Velocities in the Golf Swing." *Medicine and Science in Sports and Exercise* 14 (1) (1982): 60–64.

Miyashita, M., Tsuonda, T., Sakurai, S., Nishizono, H., and Mizuno, T. "The Tennis Serve as Compared With Overarm Throwing." In *The Racquet Sports*, ed. J. Groppel, 125–40. Champaign-Urbana: University of Illinois Press, 1979.

Murase, Y., et al. "Biomechanics in Bowling." In *Biomechanics IV: Proceedings of the Fourth International Seminar on Biomechanics*, ed. R. C. Nelson and C. A. Morehouse, 291–97. Baltimore: University Park Press, 1974.

Oka, H., Okamato, T., and Kumamoto, M. "Electromyographic and Cinematographic Study of the Volleyball Spike." In *Biomechanics V-B: Proceedings of the Fifth International Congress on Biomechanics*, ed. P. V. Komi, 326–31. Baltimore: University Park Press, 1976.

Pittuck, D. E., and Dainty, D. A. "Effects of a Modified Ball on the Mechanics of Selected Water Polo Skills in Novice Children." In *Swimming III: Proceedings of the Third International Symposium on the Biomechanics of Swimming*, ed. J. Terauds and E. W. Bedingfield, 338–45. Baltimore: University Park Press, 1979.

Roberton, M. A. "Longitudinal Evidence for the Developmental Stages in the Forceful Overarm Throw." *Journal of Human Movement Studies* 4 (1978): 167–75.

Samson, J., and Roy, B. "Biomechanical Analysis of the Volleyball Spike." In *Biomechanics V-B: Proceedings of the Fifth International Congress on Biomechanics*, ed. P. V. Komi,

332–36. Baltimore: University Park Press, 1976.

Shambes, G. M., and Campbell, S. "Inherent Movement Patterns in Man." In *Kinesiology III*, ed. C. J. Widule, 50–58. Reston, Va.: AAHPERD, 1973.

Stoner, L. J., and Ben-Sira, D. "Variation in Movement Patterns of Professional Soccer Players When Executing a Long Range and a Medium Range In-Step Soccer Kick." In *Biomechanics VII-B: Proceedings of the Seventh International Congress on Biomechanics*, ed. A. Morecki, K. Fidelus, K. Kedzior, and A. Wit, 337–42. Baltimore: University Park Press, 1981.

Ward, T., and Groppel, J. "Sport Implement Selection: Can It Be Based Upon Anthropometric Indicators?" *Motor Skills: Theory Into Practice* 4 (2) (1980): 103–10.

Wickstrom, R. *Fundamental Motor Patterns.* 2d ed. Philadelphia: Lea & Febiger, 1977.

Wild, M. "The Behavior Pattern of Throwing and Some Observations Concerning Its Course of Development in Children." *Research Quarterly* 9 (3) (1938): 20.

Yoshizawa, M., and Kumamoto, M. "'Electrical Silence in Shoulder Muscles Preceding Ball Impact in a Tennis Ground Stroke." In *Biomechanics VII-B: Proceedings of the Seventh International Congress on Biomechanics*, ed. A. Morecki, K. Fidelus, K. Kedzior, and A. Wit, 332–36. Baltimore: University Park Press, 1981.

GLOSSARY

ACCELERATION   The change in velocity (speed or direction or both) per unit of time.

ACCOMMODATING RESISTANCE EXERCISE   See ISOKINETIC EXERCISE.

AERODYNAMIC DRAG FORCE   The fluid force opposing the motion of a body moving through the air.

AERODYNAMIC LIFT FORCE   The fluid force directed perpendicular to the flow direction past an object with a lift-producing shape or past a spinning ball.

AGONIST   A muscle that causes a motion (mover).

ANATOMICAL POSITION   The upright body position in which all joints are extended and the palms are facing forward.

ANGLE OF ATTACK   The angle formed between the main plane or longitudinal axis of an object and the direction of fluid flow past it.

ANGLE OF PROJECTION   The angle at which an object or body is projected at release or takeoff; measured in relation to a stated frame of reference, usually the horizontal.

ANGULAR MOMENTUM   The product of a body's rotational inertia and angular velocity.

ANTAGONIST   A muscle that can cause the joint movement opposite to the movement being done by an agonist.

ANTHROPOMETRICS   The area of study that is concerned with the body's physical composition and quantifiable characteristics.

APPENDICULAR SKELETON   A portion of the human skeleton consisting of the upper and lower extremities.

ANTEROPOSTERIOR (AP) AXIS   An imaginary line that runs from the front to the back of the body or through an articulation.

ARCHIMEDES' PRINCIPLE   A body that is partially or totally immersed in a fluid will experience an upward buoyant force that is equal to the weight of the volume of fluid displaced by that body.

ARTICULATION   The junction of two bones.

ATTITUDE ANGLE   The angle formed between the horizontal and the main plane or longitudinal axis of an airfoil or similar lift-producing object.

AXIAL SKELETON   A portion of the human skeleton consisting of the skull, thorax, and vertebral column.

AXIS OF MOMENTUM   The spatial axis about which the resultant angular momentum of a rotating body exists.

AXIS OF ROTATION   The imaginary line or point about which a body or segment rotates.

BASE OF SUPPORT   That region bounded by body parts in contact with some resistive surface that exerts a reaction force against the body.

BERNOULLI'S PRINCIPLE   A low-pressure zone is created in a region of high fluid flow velocity, and a high-pressure zone is created in a region of low fluid flow velocity.

BIARTICULATE MUSCLE A muscle that crosses two joints.

BIOMECHANICS The area of study wherein knowledge and methods of mechanics are applied to the structure and function of the living human system.

BOUNDARY LAYER The invisible thin layer of fluid that is adjacent to the surface of an immersed body.

BUOYANT FORCE The upward force exerted on an immersed body by the water beneath it.

CARDINAL AXIS OR PLANE See PRINCIPAL AXIS or PLANE.

CENTER OF BUOYANCY The point at which the buoyant force acts on an immersed body's volume; the center of gravity of the volume of water being displaced by the body.

CENTER OF GRAVITY That point at which all the body's mass seems to be concentrated; the balance point of a body; the point around which the sum of all the torques of the segmental weights is equal to zero. The point of application of gravity's force on a mass; the center of mass.

CENTER OF PRESSURE The point of application of a fluid lift force acting on a body moving through the fluid.

CENTRIFUGAL FORCE The force directed radially outward that is exerted by a rotating body on a structure or mass that exerts a center-directed (centripetal) force on that body.

CENTRIPETAL FORCE The force directed radially toward the center of rotation that is exerted by a mass on a rotating body and that causes that body to travel in a circular path.

CLOSED SKILL A skill performed in a predictable environment so that the performer is free to move without having to make quick decisions.

COEFFICIENT OF FRICTION The ratio of the magnitude of the maximum force of friction to the magnitude of the perpendicular force pressing the two surfaces together (normal force).

COLINEAR FORCES Forces whose lines of action lie along the same line.

CONCENTRIC TENSION The contraction of a muscle during which the muscle shortens and causes movement of one or more attached segments.

CONSTRAINT A restriction to the performance of free human movement patterns; a limiting factor.

CONTINUOUS SKILL A skill in which the same movement pattern is performed repeatedly as cycles of the total act.

CRURAL INDEX A ratio of thigh length to leg length.

CURVILINEAR Refers to motion along a curved line or path.

DECELERATION The decrease in velocity per unit time.

DENSITY The mass per unit volume of an object or body (mass density); or weight per unit volume (weight density).

DISCRETE SKILL A skill in which a movement pattern is performed as a single act.

DISPLACEMENT The change in a body's location in space in a given direction.

DISTAL Refers to the end of a segment, bone, or muscle attachment that is farther from the axial skeleton.

DYNAMIC EQUILIBRIUM   The state of a body moving with constant speed and direction, that is, with zero acceleration.

DYNAMIC (ISOTONIC) TENSION   The contraction of a muscle during which the muscle changes length.

DYNAMICS   The study of mechanical factors associated with systems in motion.

ECCENTRIC TENSION   The contraction of a muscle during which the muscle lengthens and resists segmental motion.

ELASTIC   That property of a body that causes it to re-form following deformation.

ENDURANCE   The ability to continue performance of a movement activity.

EQUILIBRIUM   The state of a system whose motion is not being changed, accelerated, or decelerated.

EXTERNAL   Outside a defined system.

EXTEROCEPTORS   Sensory receptors located in or around the skin that respond to changes in the environment making direct contact with the exterior of the body.

FEMORAL TORSION   A relative position of the femur and tibia in which the femur is rotated medially around its longitudinal axis relative to the tibia (knees facing inward).

FLEXIBILITY   The range of motion permitted between two adjacent segments.

FORCE   That which causes or tends to cause a change in a body's motion or shape.

FORCE ARM (MOMENT ARM, LEVER ARM, or TORQUE ARM)   The perpendicular distance between the line of action of the force and the axis of rotation.

FORM DRAG   See PROFILE DRAG.

FRICTION   The force that resists the sliding of one surface upon another.

FRONTAL   Refers to a plane that divides a body or segment into front and back portions.

GYROSCOPIC STABILITY   The resistance of a rotating body to a change in its plane of rotation.

IMPULSE   The product of the magnitude of a force or torque and its time of application.

INERTIA   The resistance of a body to a change in its state of motion.

INFERIOR   Refers to a portion of a segment, bone, or muscle closer to the feet.

INSTANTANEOUS VELOCITY   The velocity of a body at a given instant in time.

INTERNAL   Within a defined system.

INTEROCEPTORS   Sensory receptors located within the body that respond to changes in the body's internal environment and control visceral functioning.

ISOKINETIC   Refers to a method of strength training in which the speed of segmental rotation is kept constant throughout the range of muscular contraction.

ISOKINETIC EXERCISE   Movements performed on devices designed to match the motive torque applied while maintaining a constant angular speed of joint movement (also referred to as accommodating resistance exercise).

ISOMETRIC TENSION   See STATIC TENSION.

ISOTONIC TENSION   See DYNAMIC TENSION.

KINANTHROPOMETRICS The area of study that is concerned with the body's physical measurements of size, shape, and proportion as they relate to human movement.

KINEMATICS An area of study that is concerned with the time and space factors in the motion of a system.

KINESIOLOGY The study of human movement from an anatomical or mechanical perspective or both.

KINESTHESIS The perception of segmental and body positions and movements.

KINETIC ENERGY The ability of a body to do work by virtue of its motion.

KINETIC FRICTION The friction that exists between two surfaces sliding past each other.

KINETIC LINK PRINCIPLE The generation of high end-point velocity accomplished through the use of accelerating and decelerating adjoining links, by the use of internal and external muscle torques, applied to the segments in a sequential manner from proximal to distal, from most massive to least massive, and from most fixed to most free.

KINETICS An area of study that is concerned with the forces that act on a system.

LATERAL Refers to the side away from the longitudinal midline of the body or segment.

LEVER ARM See FORCE ARM.

LEVER SYSTEM A mechanism for doing work, consisting of a body with an axis of rotation and eccentrically applied forces.

LINEAR MOMENTUM A property of a body in motion; the product of a body's mass and its velocity.

LINEAR MOTION Motion along a straight (recti-) or curved (curvi-) line.

LONGITUDINAL AXIS An imaginary line that runs along the length of a body or segment.

MASS The measure of a body's inertia; the amount of matter in a body.

MAXIMAL VOLUNTARY CONTRACTION The maximal amount of force that is exerted by a muscle during a static contraction against an immovable resistance.

MEDIAL Refers to the side closer to the longitudinal midline of the body or segment.

MEDIOLATERAL (ML) AXIS An imaginary line that runs from the medial to the lateral side of the body or through an articulation.

MOBILITY The ease with which an articulation, or a series of articulations, is allowed to move before being restricted by the surrounding structures.

MOMENT ARM See FORCE ARM.

MOMENT OF INERTIA See ROTATIONAL INERTIA.

MOMENTUM A system's resistance to change in its state of motion (inertia) multiplied by its velocity.

MOTIVE FORCE A force that causes motion or change in shape.

MOTOR UNIT A single motor nerve cell and its branches, with associated muscle fibers; the smallest functional unit of muscular contraction.

MOVEMENT PATTERN A general series of anatomical movements that have common elements of spatial configuration such as segmental movements occurring in the same plane of motion.

MULTIARTICULATE MUSCLE   Muscle that crosses more than two joints.

NEUTRAL EQUILIBRIUM   The state of a body in which, if the body is displaced, it will remain in the displaced position.

NORMAL FORCE   A force directed perpendicular to a surface.

NUTATION   Wobbling; the tilting of a body's principal axis of rotation from its original position.

OPEN SKILL   A skill performed in response to an unpredictable, changing environment.

ORTHOGONAL   Refers to the orientation of lines or planes at 90 degrees to one another.

PARABOLIC PATH   A curvilinear path (trajectory) followed by a projectile that is unaffected by air resistance.

PLANE OF MOTION   The two-dimensional space cut by a moving body; the plane along which movement occurs.

PLASTIC   Refers to the condition of connective tissue (ligaments or tendons) when it has been stretched past its limit and will no longer return to its original shape.

PONDERAL INDEX   A particular ratio of the human body's weight and height that is a measure of stature, or stoutness.

POTENTIAL ENERGY   The ability of a body to do work by virtue of its position above an object (gravitational potential energy) or by virtue of its deformation (elastic potential energy).

POWER   The product of an applied force and the speed with which it is applied; the quantity of work done per unit of time.

PRESSURE   The ratio of force to the area over which the force is applied.

PRESSURE DRAG   See PROFILE DRAG.

PRINCIPAL (CARDINAL) AXIS or **PLANE**   An axis or plane that is directed through a body's center of gravity.

PROFILE DRAG (PRESSURE DRAG or **FORM DRAG)**   A net force caused by a difference in pressure from the leading side of the body to the trailing side; the greater the differential, the greater the drag.

PROJECTION VELOCITY   The speed and direction of an object at the instant of projection.

PROPRIOCEPTORS   Sensory receptors located in and around joints and muscles that respond to changes in position, length, tension, and acceleration of the host tissues.

PROXIMAL   Refers to that end of a segment, bone, or muscle attachment that is closer to the axial skeleton.

RADIUS OF GYRATION   A measure of the distribution of a body's or segment's mass about an axis of rotation.

RADIUS OF ROTATION   The linear distance from an axis to a point on a rotating body.

RANGE OF MOTION   The total amount of angular displacement through which two adjacent segments may move.

REACTION FORCE   An equal and opposite force exerted by a second body on the first in response to a force applied by the first on the second.

RECRUITMENT   The process of increasing the number of active motor units in a muscular contraction.

RECTILINEAR   Refers to motion along a straight line or path.

REPETITION MAXIMUM   The maximum amount of resistance that can be moved a designated number of times.

RESISTIVE FORCE   A force that resists motion or change of shape.

RESULTANT VECTOR   The result of the composition (addition) of two or more vector quantities.

ROTARY MOTION   Motion that describes a circular path about an axis.

ROTATIONAL INERTIA (MOMENT OF INERTIA)   The resistance of a body to angular acceleration.

SAGITTAL   Refers to a plane that divides a body or segment into right and left portions.

SCALAR   A quantity that has magnitude only; that is, no direction is associated with it.

SENSORY UNIT   A single nerve cell, with axon, branches, and receptors; such units are located within muscle, connective, and cutaneous tissue.

SKILL   A general movement pattern that has been adapted to the constraints of a particular activity or sport.

SKIN FRICTION (SURFACE DRAG)   The fluid drag force acting on a body moving through a fluid caused by viscous friction forces.

SPATIAL   Refers to a set of planes and axes defined in relation to three-dimensional space.

SPEED   The magnitude of a body's displacement per unit of time without regard to direction.

SPRAIN   A tearing of ligamentous tissue.

STABILITY   The ability of an articulation to absorb shock and withstand motion without injury to the joint; also, the resistance to disturbance of a body's equilibrium.

STABLE EQUILIBRIUM   The state of a body in which, if the body is displaced, it tends to return to its original position.

STATIC EQUILIBRIUM   The state of a body at rest.

STATIC FRICTION   The frictional force generated between two objects tending to slide past each other when no motion is occurring.

STATIC (ISOMETRIC) TENSION   Muscular contraction during which no discernible segmental movement is taking place.

STATICS   The study of factors associated with nonmoving systems.

STRAIN   A tearing of muscular tissue.

STRENGTH   The ability of a muscle or group of muscles to exert force against a resistance.

STYLE   Individual adaptations—or modifications—to a technique, which are unique to the individual using them.

SUPERIOR   Refers to that portion of a segment, bone, or muscle closer to the head.

SURFACE DRAG   See SKIN FRICTION.

SYNERGY   The cooperative effort of two or more muscles contracting to accomplish a single movement.

SYSTEM   A body or group of bodies whose state of motion is being examined.

TANGENT   A line that meets but does not intersect a curved line or surface and that is perpendicular to the radius of curvature of the arc.

TECHNIQUE   A particular type, or variation, of the performance of the same skill.

TELECEPTORS   Sensory mechanisms receptive to smell, sounds, and visual stimuli.

TERMINAL VELOCITY   The constant velocity attained by a body moving through a fluid; this is due to the lack of a net force on the body.

TIBIAL TORSION   A relative position of the femur and the tibia in which the tibia is rotated laterally around its longitudinal axis relative to the femur (knees facing forward).

TORQUE   A turning or rotary force; the product of a force and the perpendicular distance from the line of action of the force to the axis of rotation.

TORQUE ARM   See FORCE ARM.

TRAJECTORY   The aerial path followed by a projectile.

TRANSVERSE   Refers to a plane that divides a body or segment into top and bottom portions.

UNIARTICULATE MUSCLE   A muscle that crosses only one joint.

UNSTABLE EQUILIBRIUM   The state of a body in which, if the body is displaced, it tends to increase its displacement.

VARIABLE RESISTANCE EXERCISE   Movement performed on devices designed to vary the resistance torque applied during one excursion of a joint movement.

VECTOR   A quantity having both magnitude and direction.

VECTOR COMPOSITION (ADDITION)   The process of determining the net or resultant vector from two or more component vectors.

VECTOR RESOLUTION   The process of determining component vectors from a resultant vector.

VELOCITY   The speed and direction of a body.

VOLUME   The three-dimensional space occupied by a body (length, width, and height).

WAVE DRAG   A force caused by and acting against a body moving through water, forming waves at the surface of the water.

WEIGHT   The force of earth's gravitational attraction on a body's mass.

WORK   The force applied to a body multiplied by the distance through which that force is applied.

APPENDIX I

METRIC AND BRITISH UNITS AND CONVERSIONS

The purpose of this appendix is to provide conversion factors between and within metric and British units of measurement.

METRIC PREFIXES

Table I.1.

mega	1,000,000	10^6		deci	.1	10^{-1}
kilo	1,000	10^3		centi	.01	10^{-2}
hecto	100	10^2		milli	.001	10^{-3}
deka	10	10^1		micro	.000001	10^{-6}

APPROXIMATIONS

Table I.2.

	METRIC	MULTIPLY BY	BRITISH	MULTIPLY BY	METRIC
DISTANCE	millimeters	.04	inches	25.40	millimeters
	centimeters	.39	inches	2.54	centimeters
	meters	3.28	feet	.30	meters
	meters	1.09	yards	.91	meters
	kilometers	.62	miles	1.61	kilometers
MASS	kilograms	.07	slugs	14.59	kilograms
VOLUME	cubic meters	35.31	cubic feet	.03	cubic meters
	cubic meters	1.31	cubic yards	.76	cubic meters
AREA	square centimeters	.16	square inches	6.45	square centimeters
	square meters	10.76	square feet	.09	square meters
	square meters	1.20	square yards	.84	square meters
	square kilometers	.40	square miles	2.60	square kilometers
TEMPERATURE	Celsius	9/5(°C + 32)	Fahrenheit	5/9(°F − 32)	Celsius
VELOCITY	meters/second	3.28	feet/second	.30	meters/second
	kilometers/hour	.62	miles/hour	1.61	kilometers/hour
ACCELERATION	meters/second^2	3.28	feet/second^2	.30	meters/second^2
	meters/second^2	2.24	miles/hour/ second	.45	meters/second^2

continued

Table I.2.   **APPROXIMATIONS**
continued

	METRIC	MULTIPLY BY	BRITISH	MULTIPLY BY	METRIC
FORCE	Newtons	.22	pounds	4.45	Newtons
LINEAR MOMENTUM	kilogram-meters/ second	.22	slug-feet/second	4.45	kilogram-meters/ second
IMPULSE	Newton-seconds	.22	pound-seconds	4.45	Newton-seconds
ANGULAR MOMENTUM	kilogram-meters^2/ second	.74	slug-feet^2/second	1.36	kilogram-meters^2/ second
ROTATIONAL INERTIA	kilogram-meters^2	.74	slug-feet^2	1.36	kilogram-meters^2
WORK	meter-Newtons	.74	foot-pounds	1.36	meter-Newtons
TORQUE	Newton-meters	.74	pound-feet	1.36	Newton-meters
POWER	watts	.74	foot-pounds/ second	1.36	watts
	watts	.0013	horsepower	745.7	watts
	kilocalories/second	5.88	horsepower	.17	kilocalories/second
	kilocalories/second	3234.00	foot-pounds/ second	.00031	kilocalories/second

CONVERSIONS WITHIN THE BRITISH SYSTEM

There are convenient conversions within the British system. The following are examples:

feet/second multiplied by .68 = miles/hour   5280 feet = 1 mile
miles/hour multiplied by 1.47 = feet/second   1760 yards = 1 mile

APPENDIX II

LIST OF SYMBOLS AND EQUATIONS

SYMBOLS

Table II.1.

SYMBOL	MEANING
A	Area
AP	Anteroposterior
a	Linear acceleration
C_D	Coefficient of drag
C_{fr}	Coefficient of friction
C_L	Coefficient of lift
CG	Center of gravity
D	Distance of a projectile (horizontal or vertical)
d	Linear displacement (or distance moved)
$d_\perp$	Perpendicular distance
F	Force
F_C	Centripetal and centrifugal force
F_D	Force of drag
F_L	Force of lift
F_{fr}	Friction force
g	Acceleration due to the force of gravity
h	Height
I	Rotational inertia
k	Radius of gyration
KE	Kinetic energy
L	Angular momentum
M	Linear momentum
m	Mass
ML	Mediolateral
P	Power
p	Pressure
PE	Potential energy
PI	Ponderal index
r	Radius of a point on a circle: radius of rotation
RF	Reaction force
ROM	Range of motion
T	Torque
t	Time
V	Volume
v	Speed (velocity when direction is specified)
W	Weight
w	Work
WD	Weight density

Table II.1.   **SYMBOLS**
continued

SYMBOL	MEANING
α (alpha)	Angular acceleration
θ (theta)	Angular displacement
π (pi)	Ratio of the circumference of a circle to its diameter (3.1416)
ρ (rho)	Mass density
Σ (sigma)	Sum of
ω (omega)	Angular velocity

Table II.2.   **EQUATIONS**

EQUATION NUMBER	TEXTUAL PAGE REFERENCE	EQUATION	QUANTITY
A.1	54	$PI = 10^3 \times \sqrt[3]{W}/h$	Ponderal index
B.1	68	$p = F/A$	Pressure
B.2	69	$WD = W/V$	Weight density
B.3	70	$w = Fd$	Work = force × distance the force is applied
B.4	71	$KE = 1/2\, mv^2$	Kinetic energy = 1/2 mass × velocity^2
B.5	72	$PE = Wh$	Potential energy = weight × height the weight is raised
B.6	72	$P = w/t = Fv$	Power = work/time = force × velocity at which force is applied
B.7	74	radians = $\theta/57.3°$ (θ in degrees)	Radians
C.1	85	$C_{fr} = F_{fr}/F_{\perp}$	Coefficient of friction
D.1	143	$T = F(d_{\perp})$	Torque
3.1	168	$\Sigma T = 0$	Rotary equilibrium
3.2	179	MA = resistive force/motive force	Mechanical advantage of a muscle lever system
3.3	179	MA = motive force arm/resistive force arm	Mechanical advantage of a muscle lever system
3.4	186	MA = radius of wheel/radius of axle	Mechanical advantage of a wheel-axle system
3.5	187	MA = force on axle/force on wheel	Mechanical advantage of a wheel-axle system
E.1	278	$v = d/t$	Linear velocity (speed)
E.2	279	$a = (v_2 - v_1)/t$	Linear acceleration
E.3	285	$a = F/m$	Newton's second law of motion for linear motion
F.1	296	$M = mv$	Linear momentum
F.2	297	$F(t) = M_2 - M_1$	Linear impulse

EQUATIONS

Table II.2.
continued

EQUATION NUMBER	TEXTUAL PAGE REFERENCE	EQUATION	QUANTITY
8.1	348	$D_{vert} = \dfrac{v_{vert}^2}{2g}$ or $D_{vert} = \dfrac{(v \sin \theta)^2}{2g}$	Vertical distance of a projectile with no air resistance
8.2	357	$D_{horiz} = v_{horiz} \times t$ or $D_{horiz} = \dfrac{(v^2 \sin 2\theta)}{g}$	Horizontal distance of a projectile with equal projection and landing heights and no air resistance
9.1	389	$F_D = (C_D A \rho v^2)/2$	Aerodynamic drag
9.2	405	$F_L = (C_L A \rho v^2)/2$	Aerodynamic lift
10.1	435	$F_D = (C_D A \rho v^2)/2$	Hydrodynamic drag
10.2	446	$F_L = (C_L A \rho v^2)/2$	Hydrodynamic lift
10.3	464	$v = d/S \times S/min$	Swimming velocity
G.1	470	$\omega = \theta/t$	Angular velocity (speed)
G.2	471	$d = r\theta$ (θ in radians)	Linear distance of a rotating point
G.3	471	$v = r\omega$ (ω in radians/sec)	Linear velocity of a rotating point
G.4	473	$\alpha = (\omega_2 - \omega_1)/t$	Angular acceleration
G.5	477	$\alpha = T/I$	Newton's second law of motion for angular motion
G.6	477	$I = \Sigma mr^2$	Rotational inertia of a body
G.7	479	$I = mk^2$	Rotational inertia of a body
H.1	486	$L = I\omega$	Angular momentum
H.2	487	$T(t) = \Delta L = I\omega_2 - I\omega_1$	Angular impulse

OTHER EQUATIONS

Module E	291	$F_C = mv_{tan}^2/r = mr\omega^2$	Centripetal and centrifugal force = (mass × tangential velocity)/radius (also = mass × radius × angular velocity^2)
Chapter 8	357	$X = v_0 t \cos \theta$ $Y = v_0 t \sin \theta - \dfrac{1}{2} gt^2$	X and Y are the horizontal and vertical locations of a projected object v_0 is the initial velocity θ is the projection angle
	357	$D_{horiz} = \dfrac{v^2 \sin \theta \cos \theta + v \cos \theta \sqrt{(v \sin \theta)^2 + 2gh}}{g}$	Horizontal distance of a projectile with unequal projection and landing heights and no air resistance

ANTHROPOMETRIC PARAMETERS

Table III.1. **MEAN SEGMENT WEIGHTS EXPRESSED AS PERCENTAGES OF TOTAL BODY WEIGHT**

SEGMENT	MALES (N = 35)	FEMALES (N = 100)
Head	8.26	8.20
Whole trunk	55.10	53.20
Thorax	20.10	17.02
Abdomen	13.06	12.24
Pelvis	13.66	15.96
Total arm	5.77	4.97
Upper arm	3.25	2.90
Forearm	1.87	1.57
Hand	0.65	0.50
Forearm and hand	2.52	2.07
Total leg	16.68	18.43
Thigh	10.50	11.75
Leg	4.75	5.35
Foot	1.43	1.33
Leg and foot	6.18	6.68

Adapted from Plagenhoef et al. 1983.

MEAN SEGMENT LENGTHS EXPRESSED AS PERCENTAGES OF TOTAL BODY HEIGHT

Table III.2.

SEGMENT	MALES (N = 35)	FEMALES (N = 73)
Head and neck	10.75	10.75
Trunk (hip to shoulder)	30.00	29.00
Thorax	12.70	12.70
Abdomen	8.10	8.10
Pelvis	9.30	9.30
Upper arm	17.20	17.30
Forearm	15.70	16.00
Hand	5.75	5.75
Thigh	23.20	24.90
Leg	24.70	25.70
Foot	4.25	4.25
Biacromial	24.50	20.00
Bi-iliac	11.30	12.00

Adapted from Plagenhoef et al. 1983.

SEGMENTAL CENTER OF GRAVITY LOCATIONS EXPRESSED AS PERCENTAGES OF SEGMENT LENGTHS MEASURED FROM THE PROXIMAL ENDS

Table III.3.

SEGMENT	MALES (N = 7)	FEMALES (N = 9)
Head and neck	55.0	55.0
Trunk	63.0	56.9
Upper arm	43.6	45.8
Forearm	43.0	43.4
Hand	46.8	46.8
Pelvis	5.0	5.0
Abdomen	46.0	46.0
Thorax	56.7	56.3
Thigh	43.3	42.8
Leg	43.4	41.9
Foot	50.0	50.0
Abdomen and pelvis	44.5	39.0

Adapted from Plagenhoef et al. 1983.

Table III.4. SEGMENTAL RADII OF GYRATION EXPRESSED AS PERCENTAGES OF THE SEGMENT LENGTHS MEASURED FROM THE PROXIMAL (P) AND DISTAL (D) ENDS[a]

SEGMENT	MALES (N = 36)		FEMALES (N = 100)	
	P	D	P	D
Upper arm	54.2	64.5	56.4	62.3
Forearm	52.6	54.7	53.0	64.3
Hand	54.9	54.9	54.9	54.9
Thigh	54.0	65.3	53.5	65.8
Leg	52.9	64.2	51.4	65.7
Foot	69.0	69.0	69.0	69.0
Head and trunk[a]	83.0	60.7	———	———

[a]From Dempster 1955.

Adapted from Plagenhoef et al. 1983.

Table III.5. MEAN BODY SEGMENT VOLUMES EXPRESSED AS PERCENTAGES OF TOTAL BODY VOLUME

SEGMENT	ROTUND (%)	MUSCULAR (%)	THIN (%)	MEDIAN (%)
Total upper extremity	5.28	5.60	5.20	5.65
Arm	3.32	3.35	2.99	3.46
Forearm plus hand	1.95	2.24	2.23	2.15
Forearm	1.52	1.70	1.63	1.61
Hand	0.42	0.53	0.58	0.54
Total lower extremity	20.27	18.49	19.08	19.55
Thigh	14.78	12.85	12.90	13.65
Leg plus foot	5.52	5.61	6.27	5.97
Leg	4.50	4.35	4.81	4.65
Foot	1.10	1.30	1.46	1.25

From Dempster 1955.

Table III.6. MEAN BODY SEGMENT DENSITIES

SEGMENT	DENSITY (gm/cm^3)
Head and neck	1.11
Trunk	1.03
Thigh	1.05
Leg	1.09
Foot	1.10
Upper arm	1.07
Forearm	1.13
Hand	1.16

From Dempster 1955.

MEANS AND STANDARD DEVIATIONS (SD) OF THE ROTATIONAL INERTIA OF THE BODY IN SELECTED POSTURES

Table III.7.

POSTURES	AXIS[a]	ROTATIONAL INERTIA (lb-in-sec^2)	
		Mean	*SD*
Standing	x	115.0	19.3
	y	103.0	17.9
	z	11.3	2.2
Standing arms over head (layout)	x	152.0	26.1
	y	137.0	25.3
	z	11.1	1.9
Spread eagle shoulders abducted 135° hips abducted 30°	x	151.0	27.1
	y	114.0	21.3
	z	36.6	7.9
Sitting elbows flexed 90°	x	61.1	10.3
	y	66.6	11.6
	z	33.5	5.8
Sitting elbows extended	x	62.4	9.7
	y	68.1	12.0
	z	33.8	5.9
Sitting (tuck position) hips flexed 145° knees flexed 145°	x	39.1	6.0
	y	38.0	5.8
	z	26.3	5.1
Sitting elbows flexed 80° hips flexed 80° knees flexed 168°	x	65.8	10.3
	y	75.2	14.0
	z	34.2	5.6
Relaxed (weightless)	x	92.2	13.3
	y	88.2	13.3
	z	35.9	5.4

[a]The z axis corresponds to the body's longitudinal axis; the y axis corresponds to the body's ML axis; the x axis corresponds to the body's AP axis.

From Santschi, Du Bois, and Omotu 1963.

REFERENCES
SUGGESTED READINGS

Clauser, C. E., McConville, J. T., and Young, J. W. "Weight, Volume, and Center of Mass of Segments of the Human Body." *AMRL Technical Documentary Report*, 69–70. Wright-Patterson Air Force Base, Ohio: 1969.

Dempster, W. T. "Space Requirements of the Seated Operator." *WADC Technical Documentary Report*, 55–159. Wright-Patterson Air Force Base, Ohio: 1955.

Kjeldsen, K. "Body Segment Weights, Limb Lengths, and the Location of the Center of Gravity in College Women." Unpublished master's thesis, University of Massachusetts, 1969.

Miller, D. M., and Nelson, R. C. *Biomechanics of Sport*. Philadelphia: Lea & Febiger, 1973.

Morse, R., and Kjeldsen, K. "Anthropometric Measurements." Paper presented at the AAHPERD Pre-Convention Workshop, Milwaukee, 1975.

Plagenhoef, S., Evans, F. G., and Abdelnour, T. "Anatomical Data for Analyzing Human Motion." *Research Quarterly for Exercise and Sport* 54 (2) (1983): 169–78.

Santschi, W. R., Du Bois, J., and Omotu, C. "Moments of Inertia and Centers of Gravity of the Living Human Body." *AMRL Technical Documentary Report*, 63–66. Wright-Patterson Air Force Base, Ohio: 1963.

METHODS OF CALCULATING THE CENTER OF GRAVITY

To determine the location of the center of gravity (CG) in any direction, two methods may be used. Both methods use the technique of summing torques about an axis of rotation.

BOARD-AND-SCALE METHOD

The **board-and-scale method** calls for a person to stand on a board that is supported at each end as seen in Figure IV.1. The sum of the forces downward is equal to the weight of the body plus the weight of the board, and the sum of the forces upward is equal to the sum of the reaction forces acting upward at each end of the board.

When added together, the reaction forces will equal the weight of the body plus the weight of the board. This can be confirmed easily if two scales are placed under the supports of the board. Regardless of where the person stands or lies on the board, the *sum* of the two scale readings will equal the total body weight plus the weight of the board. For convenience, the effect of the weight of the board should be ignored, and this can be accomplished easily if its weight is eliminated from the reaction by setting the readings of the scales to zero after the board has been placed on top of them. In this way only the weight of the body is considered.

To sum the torques on the system, an axis of rotation must be selected. Either end of the board may serve as an axis. If one end of the board is an axis through which one reaction force passes, only two torque-producing forces will be acting on the board about the specified axis: (1) the body weight, and (2) the reaction force acting upward at the end opposite to the axis end. The body weight line of force extends from the CG toward the center of the earth. The reaction force at the scale acts upward on the board. Because the board is not rotating, the opposing two *torques* about the axis end must be equal. The torque produced by the scale is equal to the reaction force times its perpendicular distance to the axis. This distance will equal the length of the board if the supports are placed as close as possible to the ends of the board. The opposing torque produced by the body is equal to the body weight times the perpendicular distance from the line of gravity to the axis. It is this $d_\perp$ that will be determined.

Reaction
force (RF)

Reaction force
(zero torque)

N scale

Axis

F = body weight (W)

Figure IV.1. A body standing on a board supported at each end, for calculating the front-to-back location of the CG.

This is the procedure for calculating the distance of the CG of a 667.5-N body from an axis:

$$\Sigma T = 0$$
$$W(d_\perp) + RF(1) = 0$$

where Σ is sum of, T is torque, W is weight (667.5 N), RF is reaction force (-267 N), and 1 is length of the board (243.8 cm).

$$(667.5 \text{ N} \times \text{CG distance}) + (-267 \text{ N} \times 243.8 \text{ cm}) = 0$$

$$\text{CG distance} = \frac{5094.6 \text{ N} - \text{m}}{667.5 \text{ N}}$$

$$\text{CG distance} = 97.53 \text{ cm}$$

The line of force of the body's CG is 97.53 cm from the axis. To determine where the body's line of gravity is located from front to back within the foot, the distance of the toes from the axis (86.36 cm) must be subtracted from the total (97.53 cm). Thus, the line of gravity in this case is located 11.17 cm into the supporting foot base.

To determine the location of the line of gravity of a body from head to foot and from right to left, the same method may be repeated with the body in a back lying position (Figure IV.2) and in a standing position (Figure IV.3) with one side to the axis.

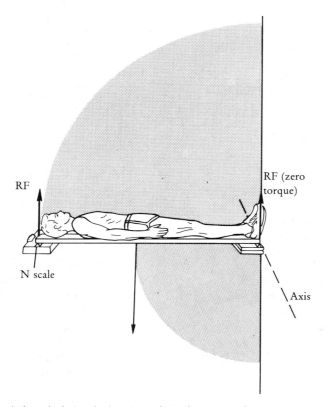

A body on a board, for calculating the locations of CG from top to bottom.

Figure IV.2.

RF (zero torque)

RF

N scale

Axis

F = body weight (W)

Figure IV.3. A body on a board for calculating the location of the CG from right to left.

If three scales are used rather than one, a similar method may be used to determine the location of the CG in two directions simultaneously; Figure IV.4 illustrates the setup. An axis is selected through scale 1 and the support (axis A). The reaction torques and the total body torque are calculated and summed, as was done previously with the board and scale, to produce the CG location from axis A. A second axis through the support and the other adjacent scale (scale 3) is selected, and the reaction force torques and body weight torques are summed to produce the CG location from the second axis, B. If a scale were positioned at the support, the sum of the reaction forces indicated on the four scales would equal the total body weight. The calculations about each axis include two torque-producing reaction forces, each with its own $d_\perp$ acting in an upward direction (out from the page), and the body weight with its $d_\perp$, the CG distance, acting downward about each axis (into the page).

The method of determining the CG location in two planes, (a) from axis A and (b) from axis B.

Figure IV.4.

$$\Sigma T = 0$$

Right-to-left location from axis A is calculated by:

$$RF_3(d_\perp) + RF_2(d_\perp) + W(d_\perp) = 0$$

Head-to-foot location from axis B is calculated by:

$$RF_2(d_\perp) + RF_1(d_\perp) + W(d_\perp) = 0$$

where RF_1, RF_2, and RF_3 are the respective reaction forces, $d_\perp$ is the respective perpendicular distances, and W is body weight.

SEGMENTAL METHOD

The second method of calculating the CG in any direction is called the **segmental method.** This method employs each segmental weight as a separate force acting at some distance from an arbitrary axis.

To use the segmental method, one needs a body outline of the performer taken from a film or photograph. Calculating from a photograph enables location of the CG for bodies in various positions during the execution of a sport skill and does not require the performer to hold a position on the gravity board while the readings and measurements are taken. Another advantage of the segmental method is that the performer is in the exact position used in performance. (A performer lying on the board has difficulty reproducing the exact position of the body during the execution of a sport skill.)

Since the actual segmental weights for every performer are not known, proportional segmental weights listed as percentages of the total body weight may be used. These data are listed for males and females in Appendix III, Table III.1 (p. 656). The proportional weight of each segment is a percentage of the total body weight. The following equation explains arithmetically why percentages may be used:

$$X_t W_t = X_1 W_1 + X_2 W_2 + X_3 W_3 \dots X_n W_n$$

where X is the distance of the CG from the arbitrary axis, W is the weight of the total body (t) or the weight of each segment (n), t is the subscript used to denote the entire body, and n is the subscript used to denote each segment, 1 to n.

If one divides both sides of the equation by W_t, one finds that the distance of the total body CG, X, from the arbitrary axis is equal to the sum of the weights of each individual segment divided by the total body weight times that segment's distance from the arbitrary axis, or the segmental percentage of total body weight times the distance of the individual segment. This relationship may be expressed by the following equation:

$$X = X_1 W_1/W_t + X_2 W_2/W_t + \dots X_n W_n/W_n$$

CG
(left arm)

CG (left
forearm)

CG (left
hand)

CG (thigh)

A hurdler with segmental CGs identified.

Figure IV.5.

For an example, calculations may be done for the hurdler shown in Figure IV.5.

One must keep in mind that since the CG is that point at which the total body weight is assumed to be concentrated, the torque produced by the total body weight from any arbitrary axis must equal the sum of all the individual segmental weights times each of their perpendicular distances from that same axis.

Therefore, to determine the location of the CG in one direction, one would repeat a procedure similar to the three scales and board method. Two arbitrary axes are drawn on the paper most conveniently outside the body figure. A $d_\perp$ for each segment's weight is drawn from the segmental CG to each of the arbitrary axes. The weight of each segment may be represented by its percentage of the total body weight, and the weight of the total body will be equal to 100%. Knowing the *actual* weight of the body or its segments is unnecessary.

A chart similar to that shown in Table IV.1 should be made for the calculation. Complete the chart in this manner:

1. List all the segments in the left-hand column.
2. From Table III.1 in Appendix III, list each segment's weight (as a percentage) in the % Segmental Weight column.
3. Measure the distance of each segmental CG from each axis and list those distances in the D_{horiz} and D_{vert} columns.
4. Multiply each distance by the segment's weight percentage and list the product in the $D_h \times (\%)$ and $D_v \times (\%)$ columns, respectively. The percent segmental weight times the distance of the segment's CG from each axis reflects the torque contribution of that segment to the torque produced by the total body's CG from that axis. Thus, the sum of all the "weighted" segmental distances is equal to the distance that the total body's CG is from that same axis.
5. Sum the head-to-foot (vertical) weighted distances, and sum the front-to-back (horizontal) weighted distances. Place the totals in the spaces provided.
6. Measure each total distance from its respective axis, and draw a line parallel to that axis through that point. The intersection of these two drawn lines represents the total body's CG location. The location of the CG from the

performer's right to left side cannot be determined from a single, two-dimensional photograph.

The segmental method is presented here only to allow the user to calculate the CG of a few subjects, enough to let one gain a feel for the contributions of the segments' weights and positions to the total body's CG location. Calculation of the exact location of the CG during the execution of a skill is usually not necessary for the teacher or coach. One should be able to estimate the location and the path of the CG, however, by knowing how the various segments contribute to and affect the CG location during movement.

A precise location and path of the CG may be determined more efficiently and precisely by using sophisticated filming and computer instrumentation.

Table IV.1.   CHART FOR CALCULATING THE CENTER OF GRAVITY USING THE SEGMENTAL METHOD

SEGMENT	% SEGMENTAL WEIGHT[a]	D_{horiz}	D_h x (%)	D_{vert}	D_v x (%)
Right thigh	_____	_____	_____	_____	_____
Left thigh	_____	_____	_____	_____	_____
Right leg	_____	_____	_____	_____	_____
Left leg	_____	_____	_____	_____	_____
Etc.					
.					
.					
.					
	100%	Total horizontal distance		Total vertical distance	

[a]From Appendix III, Table III.1, p. 656.

MATHEMATICS REVIEW AND TRIGONOMETRY

I. Decimals can be expressed as positive or negative powers of ten.

   Example: $10^0 = 1$
   $10^1 = 10$
   $10^2 = 100$
   $10^{-1} = .1$
   $10^{-2} = .01$
   $10^{-3} = .001$
   $56.24 \times 10^2 = 5624$
   $3.79 \times 10^{-2} = .0379$
   $2.1 \times 10^{-3} = .0021$

II. Proportions, Equations[1]

   A. A proportion is a relationship between two numbers or quantities. A proportion is either direct or inverse. There is a direct proportion between two quantities if an exact increase in one causes an exact increase in the other.

   Example: Given $v = d/t$, if d is tripled, v will also triple.

   There is an inverse proportion between two quantities if an exact increase in one causes an exact decrease in the other.

   Example: Given $v = d/t$, if t is doubled, v is halved (decreased by becoming two times smaller).

       (a) If two numbers are directly across from = sign or in vertical position, they are directly proportional.

       (b) If two numbers are diagonally across from = sign, they are inversely proportional.

   Example: $\dfrac{a}{b} = \dfrac{c}{d}$

       direct: a and b, c and d, a and c, b and d
       inverse: a and d, b and c

---

1. Adapted from Barham, J., *Mechanical Kinesiology* (St. Louis: C.V. Mosby Co., 1978).

III. Elementary Trigonometry

    A. Triangles, Functions

        1. In a right triangle, one angle must be 90 degrees, while the sum of the other two acute angles must be 90 degrees. The sum of the three angles of any triangle is always 180 degrees.

        2. In a right triangle, the square of the longest side, or hypotenuse, is equal to the sum of the squares of the other two sides. This yields the following equation: $a^2 + b^2 = c^2$. This is known as the Pythagorean theorem.

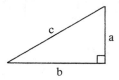

        3. In triangle XYZ, side x is opposite angle X and adjacent to angle Y; side y is opposite angle Y and adjacent to angle X; side z (hypotenuse) is opposite the right angle Z.

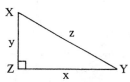

        4. Trigonometric functions are ratios between various sides of a right triangle. There are six functions. We are concerned with three of them: sine (sin), cosine (cos), tangent (tan).

    From ABC we obtain the following ratios:

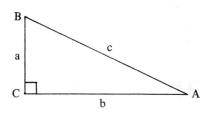

$$\sin A = \frac{opp}{hyp} = \frac{a}{c} \qquad \cos B = \frac{adj}{hyp} = \frac{a}{c}$$

$$\sin B = \frac{opp}{hyp} = \frac{b}{c} \qquad \tan A = \frac{opp}{adj} = \frac{a}{b}$$

$$\cos A = \frac{adj}{hyp} = \frac{b}{c} \qquad \tan B = \frac{opp}{adj} = \frac{b}{a}$$

    Note that sin A = cos B, and sin B = cos A.

    The value of the sine of a given angle (26 degrees) is a constant value independent of the size of the right triangle. The ratio of the side opposite the 26-degree angle to the hypotenuse will be the same whether the triangle is measured in hectometers or inches. This principle holds true for all the trigonometric functions.

5. A table of trigonometric functions appears at the end of this appendix.

   Example: sin 60° = .8660
              cos 30° = .8660
              tan 22° = .4040

6. Tables of trigonometric functions usually go up to 90 degrees.

   a. For functions of angles 91 degrees to 180 degrees, take the function of (180° − ∡). All functions are negative except the sine.

      Example: sin 120° = sin 60°
                 tan 150° = − tan 30°

   b. For functions of angles 181 degrees to 270 degrees, take the function of (270° − ∡). All functions are negative except the tangent.

      Example: cos 220° = − cos 50°
                 tan 195° = tan 75°

   c. For functions of angles 271 degrees to 360 degrees, take the function of (360° − ∡). All functions are negative except the cosine.

      Example: tan 290° = − tan 70°
                 sin 330° = − sin 30°

7. Trigonometric functions make finding all the components of a right triangle possible if the length of one side and the size of one angle *or* the lengths of two sides are given.

   Example: Given triangle LMN with angle L = 42 degrees and hypotenuse n = 20 ft. Find the length of sides 1 and m.

   $$\sin 42° = 1/20 \qquad \cos 42° = m/20$$
   $$1 = 20 \sin 42° \qquad m = 20 \cos 42°$$
   $$1 = 20 \times .6691 \qquad m = 20 \times .7431$$
   $$1 = 13.382 \text{ ft} \qquad m = 13.862 \text{ ft}$$

   Example: Given triangle QRS with sides of 8 in. and 16 in. Find the length of the hypotenuse and the size of both acute angles.

   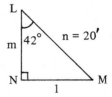

   $$\tan Q = 8/16 \qquad R = 90° − Q \qquad \sin Q = 8/s$$
   $$Q = \arctan .5 \qquad R = 90° − 27° \qquad s = 8/\sin 27°$$
   $$Q = 27° \qquad R = 63° \qquad s = 8/.4540$$
   $$s \approx 18 \text{ in.}$$

   Note: arctan x means "the angle whose tangent is x."

B. Unit Circle, Functions

1. Another way to approach trigonometric functions is by relating them to points on a unit circle (radius = 1, circumference = 2π) with its center at the origin of a Cartesian coordinate system.

    If R is a point on the circle, its coordinates are given as (cos θ, sin θ), where θ is the angle, in radians, through which R has rotated. The x coordinate is cos θ, the y coordinate is sin θ.

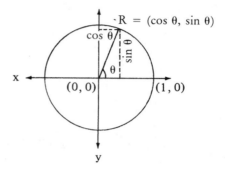

2. Determining the signs (+ or −) of the functions for angles greater than 90 degrees is easy using the coordinate system. Note that a point on the unit circle travels through 360 degrees, or a distance of 2π.

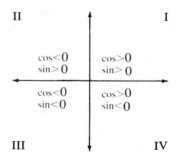

Quadrant I
Contains angles 0 degrees to 90 degrees (0π to $\pi/2$). For point (x,y), x is positive; y is positive; sin, cos, and tan are positive.

Quadrant II
Contains angles 90 degrees to 180 degrees ($\pi/2$ to π). For point (x,y), x is negative; y is positive; sin is positive, cos and tan are negative.

Quadrant III
Contains angles 180 degrees to 270 degrees (π to $3\pi/2$). For point (x,y), x is negative, y is negative, sin and cos are negative, tan is positive.

Quadrant IV
Contains angles 270 degrees to 360 degrees ($3\pi/2$ to 2π). For point (x,y), x is positive, y is negative, cos is positive, sin and tan are negative.

Example: $\sin \pi/2 = \sin 90°$
$\sin 4\pi/3 = \sin 240° = -\sin 30°$
$\tan 2\pi/3 = \tan 120° = -\tan 60°$

C. Geometry of Circles

1. The circumference of a circle is determined by the equation $C = 2\pi r$, where r is the circle's radius and π is the ratio of the circumference of a circle to its diameter. π (pi) is a constant value that is approximated to be 3.1416.

2. When a point on a circle makes one revolution, it travels through 360 degrees or 2π radians. The term radian is a geometric expression that is the ratio of the length of a circular arc, p, to the length of the circle's radius, r. When the length of the arc, p, is equal to the length of the circle's radius, r, an angular displacement of one radian has been sectioned off on the arc length. Because a radian is a ratio, one radian always equals 57.3 degrees no matter what the size of the circle's radius.

Example: Radians   Degrees

Radians	Degrees
2π or 6.28	360
π or 3.14	180
$\pi/2$ or 1.57	90

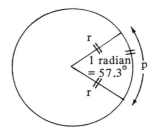

a. The magnitude of an angle θ in radians is calculated from the ratio of the arc length p to the radius r.

Example: $\theta = p/r$ radians

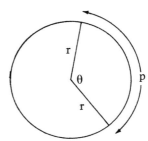

b. The angular measure of a complete circle, measured in radians, is calculated in the same manner.

Example: $\theta = 2\pi r/r$ radians
or 2π radians
or 6.28 radians

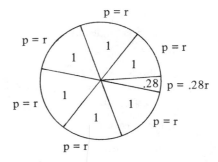

c. Since the units of measurement for r and p are the same, they can be canceled out. Consequently, a radian is a unitless quantity.

Example: number of radians = arc length/radius
= 30 mm/15 mm = 2

D. Vectors

1. A vector is defined as a line segment that has a magnitude and a direction and represents some quantity (e.g., force, velocity, momentum). The length V of the vector represents the magnitude (size). The direction of the vector is some angle θ which represents the direction. The sum of two (or more) vectors is called the resultant.

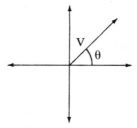

2. Finding resultants

a. A two-dimensional vector can be expressed as an ordered pair of numbers (x,y). The vector V is depicted as a directed line segment whose initial point is the origin (0,0) and whose terminal point is (x,y). The resultant of two vectors can be found by adding the ordered pairs that correspond to the vectors.

Example: Find the resultant of two vectors $V_1 = (3, -2)$ and $V_2 = (4,3)$.

Solution: $V_1 + V_2 = (3, -2) + (4,3) = |(3 + 4), (-2 + 3)| = (7,1)$

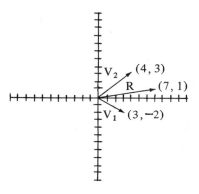

b. Resultants also may be found by simply completing the parallelogram with V_1 and V_2 as sides.

Example: Given that two forces V_1 and V_2 are applied to an object at A. Find the resultant.

Solution: Draw a vector equivalent to V_2 (same magnitude and direction) with its initial point at the terminal point of V_1. The resultant is V_3.

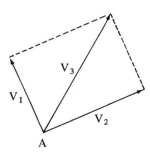

Example: Given three forces 3, 7, and 10 pounds acting on an object at 0 in the indicated directions. Find the resultant.

Solution: The resultant of V_1 and V_2 is V_a, and the resultant of V_3 and V_a is V_b. V_b is the resultant for the system.

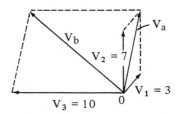

c. A resultant can be determined by placing the vectors head to tail, maintaining their magnitudes and directions. The resultant is the vector drawn from the tail of the first vector to the head of the final vector.

Example: Find the resultant of V_1 and V_2.

Example: Find the resultant of F_1, F_2, F_3, F_4.

d. To determine trigonometrically the magnitude and direction of the resultant of two vectors that form a nonright angle, the consine rule can be used.

1. Magnitude of $R^2 = A^2 + B^2 - 2AB \cos \phi$
2. Direction of $R : \theta = \arctan [(A \sin b)/(B + A \cos b)]$

b = angle between vectors A and B
θ = angle between vectors R and B
ϕ = $(180° - b)$ = angle between vectors A and B when B is repositioned at the head of A.

Example: Find the resultant magnitude and direction of two vectors, F_1 and F_2 if the angle between them is 40° and F_1 equals 20 lb and F_2 equals 60 lb.

Solution:

a. magnitude of $R^2 = F_1{}^2 + F_2{}^2 - 2F_1F_2 \cos \phi$
   $R^2 = (20)^2 + (60)^2 - 2(20)(60)(-.766)$
   $R = 76.40$ lb

b. $\theta = \arctan \dfrac{F_1 \sin 40°}{F_2 + F_1 \cos 40°}$

   $= \arctan \dfrac{20 \sin 40°}{60 + 20 \cos 40°}$

   $= \arctan .17 \qquad 9.69°$

   $= \arctan .17$

3. Finding horizontal and vertical components

   a. Often, determining the horizontal and vertical components of a resultant vector is necessary. This is accomplished by completing the rectangle (right angles) with the resultant as the diagonal.

   Example:

   b. Components also may be determined by the use of trigonometric functions.

   Example: A resultant of magnitude 80 makes a 30-degree angle with the horizontal. Find its horizontal and vertical components.

   $\dfrac{V_x}{80} = \cos 30° \qquad\qquad \dfrac{V_y}{80} = \sin 30°$

   $V_x = 80 \cos 30° \qquad\quad V_y = 80 \sin 30°$
   $V_x = 69.28 \qquad\qquad\quad V_y = 40$

Table **V.1.** **TRIGONOMETRIC FUNCTIONS**

RADIAN	DEGREE	SINE	COSINE	TANGENT	RADIAN	DEGREE	SINE	COSINE	TANGENT
.000	0	0.0000	1.0000	0.0000	.803	46	0.7193	0.6947	1.0355
.017	1	0.0175	0.9998	0.0175	.820	47	0.7314	0.6820	1.0724
.035	2	0.0349	0.9994	0.0349	.838	48	0.7431	0.6691	1.1106
.052	3	0.0523	0.9986	0.0524	.855	49	0.7547	0.6561	1.1504
.070	4	0.0698	0.9976	0.0699	.873	50	0.7660	0.6428	1.1918
.087	5	0.0872	0.9962	0.0875	.890	51	0.7771	0.6293	1.2349
.105	6	0.1045	0.9945	0.1051	.908	52	0.7880	0.6157	1.2799
.122	7	0.1219	0.9925	0.1228	.925	53	0.7986	0.6018	1.3270
.140	8	0.1392	0.9903	0.1405	.942	54	0.8090	0.5878	1.3764
.157	9	0.1564	0.9877	0.1584	.960	55	0.8192	0.5736	1.4281
.175	10	0.1736	0.9848	0.1763	.977	56	0.8290	0.5592	1.4826
.192	11	0.1908	0.9816	0.1944	.995	57	0.8387	0.5446	1.5399
.209	12	0.2079	0.9781	0.2126	1.012	58	0.8480	0.5299	1.6003
.227	13	0.2250	0.9744	0.2309	1.030	59	0.8572	0.5150	1.6643
.244	14	0.2419	0.9703	0.2493	1.047	60	0.8660	0.5000	1.7321
.262	15	0.2588	0.9659	0.2679	1.065	61	0.8746	0.4848	1.8040
.279	16	0.2756	0.9613	0.2867	1.082	62	0.8829	0.4695	1.8807
.297	17	0.2924	0.9563	0.3057	1.100	63	0.8910	0.4540	1.9626
.314	18	0.3090	0.9511	0.3249	1.117	64	0.8988	0.4384	2.0503
.332	19	0.3256	0.9455	0.3443	1.134	65	0.9063	0.4226	2.1445
.349	20	0.3420	0.9397	0.3640	1.152	66	0.9135	0.4067	2.2460
.367	21	0.3584	0.9336	0.3839	1.169	67	0.9205	0.3907	2.3559
.384	22	0.3746	0.9272	0.4040	1.187	68	0.9272	0.3746	2.4751
.401	23	0.3907	0.9205	0.4245	1.204	69	0.9336	0.3584	2.6051
.419	24	0.4067	0.9135	0.4452	1.222	70	0.9397	0.3420	2.7475
.436	25	0.4226	0.9063	0.4663	1.239	71	0.9455	0.3256	2.9042
.454	26	0.4384	0.8988	0.4877	1.257	72	0.9511	0.3090	3.0777
.471	27	0.4540	0.8910	0.5095	1.274	73	0.9563	0.2924	3.2709
.489	28	0.4695	0.8829	0.5317	1.292	74	0.9613	0.2756	3.4874
.506	29	0.4848	0.8746	0.5543	1.309	75	0.9659	0.2588	3.7321
.524	30	0.5000	0.8660	0.5774	1.326	76	0.9703	0.2419	4.0108
.541	31	0.5150	0.8572	0.6009	1.344	77	0.9744	0.2250	4.3315
.559	32	0.5299	0.8480	0.6249	1.361	78	0.9781	0.2079	4.7046
.576	33	0.5446	0.8387	0.6494	1.379	79	0.9816	0.1908	5.1446
.593	34	0.5592	0.8290	0.6745	1.396	80	0.9848	0.1736	5.6713
.611	35	0.5736	0.8192	0.7002	1.414	81	0.9877	0.1564	6.3138
.628	36	0.5878	0.8090	0.7265	1.431	82	0.9903	0.1392	7.1154
.646	37	0.6018	0.7986	0.7536	1.449	83	0.9925	0.1219	8.1443
.663	38	0.6157	0.7880	0.7813	1.466	84	0.9945	0.1045	9.5144
.681	39	0.6293	0.7771	0.8098	1.484	85	0.9962	0.0872	11.43
.698	40	0.6428	0.7660	0.8391	1.501	86	0.9976	0.0698	14.30
.716	41	0.6561	0.7547	0.8693	1.518	87	0.9986	0.0523	19.08
.733	42	0.6691	0.7431	0.9004	1.536	88	0.9994	0.0349	28.64
.751	43	0.6820	0.7314	0.9325	1.553	89	0.9998	0.0175	57.29
.768	44	0.6947	0.7193	0.9657	1.571	90	1.0000	0.0000	∞
.785	45	0.7071	0.7071	1.0000					

INDEX

Page numbers set in boldface type indicate the page on which an entry is defined.